PENGUIN BOOKS

LEAVE THE FIGHTING TO McGUIGAN

Jim Sheridan was born in Dublin in 1949. He has directed at all the major theatres in Dublin, Off-Broadway
and at the Royal Court and ICA in London. His own
plays have been performed in Ireland, England, Canada,
America and Cuba. His play *Spike* won a Fringe First
award at the Edinburgh Theatre Festival in 1983. He
has been awarded the Macaulay Fellowship in playwrit-
ing from the Arts Council in Ireland. He is currently
Artistic Director of the Irish Arts Centre in New York,
having held the same position in the Project Arts
Centre, Dublin, for many years.

D0552349

LEAVE THE FIGHTING TO
McGUIGAN

The Official Biography of
BARRY McGUIGAN

JIM SHERIDAN

PENGUIN BOOKS

For Fran, Naomi, Kirsten and Tess

Penguin Books Ltd, Harmondsworth, Middlesex, England
Viking Penguin Inc., 40 West 23rd Street, New York, New York 10010, U.S.A.
Penguin Books Australia Ltd, Ringwood, Victoria, Australia
Penguin Books Canada Limited, 2801 John Street, Markham, Ontario, Canada L3R 1B4
Penguin Books (N.Z.) Ltd, 182–190 Wairau Road, Auckland 10, New Zealand

First published by Viking 1985
Published in Penguin Books 1986

Copyright © Jim Sheridan, 1985
All rights reserved

Made and printed in Great Britain by
Richard Clay (The Chaucer Press) Ltd,
Bungay, Suffolk

Typeset in Plantin

ACKNOWLEDGEMENTS

This book would not have been possible without the help of
Roger Flaherty and John Everett. I would also like to thank
the Eastwood family, particularly B. J. and Brian; and Mrs
Cassidy, who typed the manuscript. I would particularly
like to thank the entire McGuigan family for their warmth
and encouragement.

J. S.

CONTENTS

Part One

THE BODY IN QUESTION

TERRITORIAL IMPERATIVE

Our jeep follows a small, powerfully built figure up the steep slopes that lead to the top of Carnmor. It is an uphill climb of about 2,000 feet, over $3\frac{1}{2}$ miles. Somewhere along the way the birds have given up and, once we reach the top, the panting of our jeep in first gear is replaced by a silence that is the mother of reflection. The runner, able to draw breath at last, continues on his journey and without breaking rhythm says, 'You can see most of Ulster from here. The Mountains of Mourne point right, the Sperrin Mountains left. Finn McCool's Stone is about here somewhere.'

People have lived in Ulster for six thousand years. The evidence is all around us: ancient tombs, Celtic crosses, unexplained monuments. Finn McCool's Stone is at the top of Fincairn. People believe he threw it there in a fit of temper ... it weighs four tons. Finn McCool was a giant; he left the impression of his hands on the stone. His tribe was the *Tuatha De Dannann*, a warrior tribe. From the bones of those warriors that have been excavated, it seems that the tallest of them would have been equal in height and strength to the figure now running away from us down Carnmor.

Barry McGuigan is 5 feet 6 inches tall. He weighs 125 pounds, just 9 stone. He has a chest measurement of 41 inches and a reach of 70 inches. His hands are as big as Finn McCool's, and in Ireland he is more popular and better known. He is black Irish with boyish good looks and blue eyes as deep as the ocean. His ancestry is Northern Irish and it has bequeathed him a temper that you would do well not to awaken. He keeps it under total control, walking the world a pleasant diplomatic man – until he steps through the ropes of a boxing ring. Then some ancient strength forgotten by civilized man takes hold of him and he doesn't rest until he gets the other fellow out of there and he goes home to bed. He never throws stones.

Today Barry is on a run. He will cover twelve miles around Carnmor. *Carn* is the Irish for hill and *mór* means big. It is a punishing course, especially if you are carrying pounds overweight and have a head cold. After 80 minutes the course is completed, and Barry rinses about three pints of salt-filled water from his track suit.

'That's called sweat,' he says. He drinks his customary two bottles of Lucozade and breathes deeply. 'I never thought I'd make that first hill.'

Did he ever feel like giving up? 'I never give up,' he says with absolutely no sense of defiance, just a statement of fact. 'I never give up,' he says as he takes the wheel.

Barry McGuigan knows every inch of the border roads. 'That was the smugglers' course we just completed,' he says. Those boys worked by night. The ancient Province of Ulster is split in two by the border that separates Northern Ireland from Southern Ireland. Smuggling is one of the lesser sins that this partition has brought about. 'We're in Northern Ireland now,' says Barry. 'The roads are better.'

His great-grandfather came from Pomeroy near Donaghmore. 'He was the baddest wee whore ever you met,' says Barry. 'Built like a tank. I have a photo of him holding a gun.' It's a duck gun. The gun is six inches taller than he is. He has a long white moustache curled up at the ends. He looks like a bull with the horns coming out of his nose. Every Twelfth of July, when the Protestants would be holding their Orange Parade, he would go out into the main street and scrape a line with a sword. He would score a long line across the main street and stand behind it. Then he would go back into the house to look for his scythe. He would stand behind the line swinging his scythe and say, 'Come one of you past this line.'

Barry McGuigan stands in his home imitating this longdead ancestor. You can see the scythe and hear the hum it makes. Then he takes off round his son's toys in a one-man Orange Parade. We see the lambeg drum, tin whistles, even the bowler hats. An invisible baton shoots miles up into the air above his home and comes back down through the ceiling, to be caught deftly behind his back. This pantomime ends with the lambeg drum back at the improvised borderline. With a turn of foot that sends many an opponent astray we are back face to face with his great-grandfather. Barry's right hand puts the last touch to his whiskers. The confrontation lasts, spaghetti-western Irish style, for ten seconds, then the lambeg drum turns his back and marches away. 'The funny thing was that all the Protestants loved him. They would be drinking together all year round in the pubs and then when the Twelfth came, out would come the scythe and the lambeg drum. James McShane was his name. He was a wee tank of a man.'

HANDS
ACROSS THE BORDER

Private Leslie Heron watches from his six-by-three-inch
window at what for twelve hours each day will be his world
for the next four weeks. Home is a three-foot-thick bunker
on the Fermanagh–Monaghan border. Boredom is the chief
enemy. To stay on the alert he keeps a log of the cattle in
McCabe's field. This rocky meadow straddles the border;
Private Heron divides the cattle into those under his protection and those outside his jurisdiction. Those that stay
constant on his side of the border he calls loyalists and those
that stray from the fold into the alien Republic he calls
terrorists. At 08.00 hours there were seventeen loyalists
and only three republicans, but by 13.00 hours the position
was reversed and his outpost shook with the news that
nineteen of the twenty cattle were terrorists.

Well, it was either this or the labour exchange in Balham!
Only difference is, they don't shoot you for late signing at
Balham. Suddenly a sports car roars into view and pulls to
an abrupt halt. Three men get out. One of them points out
the camouflaged bunker. 'Cheeky bastard,' says Leslie as
he reaches for his army-issue binoculars. 'Reconnoitring
right under our bloody noses,' he says to himself. He trains
the binoculars on the leader of the party. 'Seen that geezer
somewhere before,' he muses. He starts to log a description.
Small, well-built, dark hair, moustache, early twenties. His
two sidekicks start to take notes. 'Regular little Napoleon
he is,' Leslie says. Then the three figures get back into the
car and head on down the road exactly parallel to the
bunker. Leslie notes the make of car: Alfa Romeo. It's now
at an angle for him to make out the licence plate. 'That will
go into the computer,' he says to himself. The dark figure

pulls the car to the side of the road in the manner of a rally driver and is out of the door and pointing at Leslie in seconds. Two months ago the RUC station in Newry was attacked with mortars. Nine policemen died. This could be the same IRA unit.

There is some white lettering on the sleek black body of the car. Leslie focuses his binoculars and reads 'Barry McGuigan British and European Featherweight Champion'. 'Knew I seen him somewhere before,' Leslie says as he claps himself on the back for his powers of observation. He changes the age in his log-book to twenty-four. That keen eye is again focused on young Barry. 'Good-looking geezer for a boxer, got a slight twist in the nose, no cuts that I can see, no scars, not yet.'

McGuigan is on the little footbridge that the army erected in place of the road bridge that they blew up. Leslie watches him carefully put one foot on either side of the border. McGuigan is rubbing his eye. 'There's something in his eye,' says Leslie and he zooms in on them. McGuigan stares back. It's not often you come eyeball to eyeball with a world champion. Amazing concentration. He looks like an altar boy, yet when you really look into his eyes there's something else ... an attraction – a fatal attraction if you're in the ring with him. 'A cross between an altar boy and the Artful Dodger,' thinks Leslie.

Leslie's binoculars travel down the powerful torso. He picks up Barry's hands and tries to refocus. 'He never has hands that big!' he says to himself. He puts the setting back to where it was and uses young Barry's face to get the focus exactly right. Then he looks at the hands again. 'His hands are the same size as his head!' he exclaims. 'Each one is the size of a great big bloody turnip!' He looks at those hands for a long time. The knuckles are powerful, and from the scabs and abrasions on them they look like he's been hitting a wall for the past fortnight. 'Maybe he spars without gloves,' Leslie muses to himself. 'If he has feet like his hands he'd look like a duck.' Barry jumps into his Alfa Romeo and presses his small, size-seven shoes on the accelerator. 'Ah well,' says Leslie, 'I suppose it's back to the cows for the next four weeks.'

James McGuigan was a railway worker who married Mary McShane, daughter of Peter McShane of the Temper. He followed the railway line to Clones. Everybody remembers his hands. He borrowed them from a man two feet taller and ten stone heavier. He used them to couple trains. He would pick up two thirty-pound chains with a hook and double-couple them. Later he was a signalman.

In the stairs up to the home-built gym there are several blood-stained bandages. At the top of the stairs young Barry is meticulously dressing the hands that his grandfather bequeathed to him. 'I do my own bandaging,' he says. 'I spend £12 a week on bandages. I do two layers.' McGuigan prepares everything well. There are two types of tape which are hung, clothes-line style, on the banister at the top of the stairs. He never rushes his bandages. It's like an actor applying make-up, it gets him into the frame of mind to train. It's a method of concentration that takes him from the real world to that of the ring. He has no time now for anything that might disturb that concentration and he manages to get everybody round him to understand this with the minimum of fuss. As he applies the adhesive between his fingers he acts like a surgeon going into the theatre. And his training is just as clinical.

In public Barry shakes hands continually. On one recent visit to Cookstown he signed autographs for four hours and shook hundreds of hands ... An elderly lady approaches for an autograph for her niece. Barry signs. 'Can't you give us an ould smile?' she says with a face that would curdle milk. Barry looks at her for a few seconds and produces a laugh out of nowhere. A deep laugh of release. It catches the old dear unawares and she finds a smile that takes ten years off her. This she hardens into her photographic special and goes away with her niece's autograph.

After about three hours, three big burly men approach him. They look at Barry for a long time, then the first one puts out his hand . . . a proud hand . . . a hand that has done a lot of manual labour . . . a tough hand that belongs to a heavyweight. He shakes Barry's hand and shakes and shakes, waiting all the time for Barry to cringe in pain. He looks deep into Barry's eyes, waiting for the flinch that tells him that he could break the bones of the European champion if he wanted. It's only Barry's eyes that travel to his friends that make the first man release his grip. He watches as each of his friends shakes hands with Barry. Deep down none of them want to hurt Barry; they just want to show that they are men. By the time it gets to the third man he is actually friendly and shaking Barry's hand warmly. All this is conducted in silence. No need to introduce anybody, just a wink and a nod to say, 'You're not a big-headed wee get.' Barry straightens out his hand and goes back to the autographs.

Somewhere on the edge of the crowd there is a gunshot. It is actually a balloon bursting, but in Ulster that passes for a gunshot. The RUC man puts his hand to his holster and then relaxes. The last of the burly men involuntarily offers Barry his hand again. This time the handshake is different. It is non-combative. It is short. It says, 'We are survivors.'

SHOULDER TO SHOULDER

Barry McGuigan was born on 28 February 1961 at six o'clock in the evening. He was delivered without the aid of a doctor. Any mother will tell you that the pain reaches a crescendo just before the head emerges, but with McGuigan it was the shoulders. He was born with extraordinarily large shoulders.

'I remember it well,' Katie McGuigan tells me with a grin. 'They told me it was a boy and that everything was all right. They told me to try and get some sleep. I felt like a nuisance staying awake so I shut my eyes and tried to go asleep. In the back of my head I heard a child cry. At first I put it down to a dream, but even when I sat up to dispel the dream it was still there like a bad conscience. I asked the nurse and she told me he was asleep, everything was fine. But I could hear it. The little stifled cry of a child crying for help. My child. I knew it was Barry. You know your own child's cry. I brought him home and everything seemed fine. Two weeks later when I was bathing him I noticed something odd about his shoulders. One seemed different to the other. I called Pat over, I wouldn't touch it. Pat says, "I think he has a broken collarbone. It feels like a little step just here."' Katie McGuigan does not attend Barry's fights. 'I saw him get a bang on the head once, and that was enough for me.'

Perhaps the strongest part of Barry McGuigan's body is his upper torso. Maybe it was all the attention his mother gave it after the discovery of the broken collarbone, maybe it was nature doing her magic work, but, whatever the answer, McGuigan has abnormal strength in his upper body. At the top of the old wooden staircase there is a little anteroom that leads to his home-made gym. Barry has stripped down and is shadow boxing. From across the room you can hear the floor vibrate. Now you can feel, you can touch that power which sends opponents sprawling, and if you listen carefully you can hear a strange sound. It comes from McGuigan's shoulders. It's as if somebody forgot to oil them. Bone on bone . . . Book this man for assault with a deadly weapon.

The old market square in Clones is one of the biggest in Great Britain and Ireland. Its shape has given it the name of the Diamond. In the early Sixties the Urban Council replaced the old weighbridge with modern toilet conveniences. They also provided outside lighting in the shape of a thirty-foot-high lamp. People would come in to Katie serving in the shop and say nonchalantly, 'Your Barry's up the pole again.'

'I'd go out and there he'd be at the top of this thirty-foot pole surveying the Diamond like a country squire. He was only three at the time. I'd call him down and at that time they had a stay-wire attached to the pole. Well, he'd slide down the stay-wire as if he were a circus performer. He would also pull himself up the pole by his arms and hang on by one arm. I got so nervous of him that I had to ignore him. When people would say, "Barry's up the pole," I would say, "Is that half a dozen of eggs you wanted?"

'Himself and Paul Newell were out the back, and the next thing we heard this unmerciful noise. They had both jumped through the roof of Chapman's the Chemist. Poor old Newell fell right through and landed on the second floor. Luckily he wasn't too badly hurt. When Chapman went to see what had happened he found young Newell on the floor and a big hole in the roof. He didn't know for a minute that there was a second hole in which Barry was stuck. He had managed to prevent himself from falling through by holding on for dear life with his elbows. We knew after that that his collarbone was fully recovered.'

'We finally knew everything was OK the day we took him to the zoo in Dublin,' says Pat. 'We had Sharon, the two boys, Laura and the twins, Rebecca and Rachel. Barry must have been about ten at the time. We were on our way round the zoo when suddenly we noticed he was missing. We looked all over for him and there he was in the cage with the lads with the long necks. What are they called? Giraffes, aye. They're not dangerous lads but it might as well have been the elephants or the tigers. He had gone down over a moat, climbed a fence and there he was at the giraffes' ankles looking up at them.

'He was in his element. We couldn't keep him out of trouble. The only thing that held his attention was the chimpanzees' tea party. The chimps were having a rare old time. The children loved them. One of the chimps really got the kids going. We were seated round the enclosure watching them, like at the paddock at the races. There was a little rail that the children looked over. One of the chimps made it his business to scuttle along the rail and you could see all the little faces moving back like a human wave ... until he got as far as Barry who grabbed him round the neck and held him down on the ground in a headlock. Everybody, children, parents and attendants, watched for a few seconds in stunned horror. The children started cheering and one of the attendants rushed over shouting, "Get that child away from that animal, he'll take the hand off him!" He will if he ever gets out of the headlock, I thought to myself. When the attendant got to Barry he looked up at him with an innocent glee on his face. "Let him go, let him go!" said the attendant, and eventually Barry did. He said the chimp had started it!

'We didn't think it was funny at all. I pushed him on ahead of me towards the exit. He ran ahead and when we turned the next corner there he was in front of one of the cages hanging on the guard rail making faces at the poor animal. I didn't think it was funny and I stood staring at him in silence, but Dermot couldn't keep the laughter in and soon all the kids were laughing. I looked at Katie and she was laughing too, and that broke me up. That's how he got out of getting a clip on the ear at the zoo.'

MATE FOR LIFE

Of the seven roads that make Clones a crossroads, five lead into Northern Ireland. Viewed from any of the many British Army helicopters that patrol the area, the roads are littered with little white crosses painted in some form of durable paint. Time and the elements eventually wash away these man-made markings, and when they threaten to disappear entirely a crew is sent from one of the local councils in that part of the country where the letterboxes are painted red to redefine the boundaries with that part of the country where the letterboxes are painted green. These are the crosses that mark the border.

The corners of the crosses have been joined to provide some sense of order to what would otherwise be rather blunt symbolic crosses. If either of the security forces strays into the other's territory, diplomatic warnings will be dashed off to London or to Dublin. Often members of Her Majesty's security forces will walk past Barry McGuigan's home in Kilrooskey. They will be ten abreast and heavily armed for protection. Fifty yards down the road they will stop at one of the little white boxes and turn back. As they come back they will be able to take in some of the details that may have escaped them on the road to foreign territory. In front of McGuigan's bungalow, nestled against the low-lying Monaghan Hills, the beginning of a lawn is forming. It runs down to a lake that lies as contented as a saucer of milk between the hills.

Clones lies just south of the border, McGuigan's house just north of it, connected by a country road. These are the unapproved border roads. They have seen some gruesome sectarian killings, killings by paramilitaries, by members of the security forces and a lot of plain murder. Whichever way you look at it, the blood is still red and, most times, innocent. Not so long ago, a knock on the door after nightfall was an invitation to a quick end. These soldiers' eyes are peeled. They have been trained to watch for a given set of circumstances. In these conditions all scenery looks alike.

Fifty feet further on, set in a natural clearing, is a small caravan. They have observed a well-built man of about sixty years come out of this caravan every day, get on his bicycle and head towards Clones. What he does there they don't know. Beyond the white crosses it could be a wasteland, for all they care. Every evening he comes home around six. Most days he calls on the McGuigans. He doesn't carry any give-away signs as to what he works at. He seems the outdoor type with a good, healthy, ruddy complexion. He likes his bottle of stout, they know that. The man in question is Johnny McCormack, known simply by his surname.

Tonight he is not at home. It's past nine, he is probably in Clones watching the finals of the Eurovision Song Contest. Barry looks under McCormack's caravan for the rowlocks into which the oars will fit. 'Here they are,' he says, 'now we've just got to get this thing out on the lake.' Ahead of us Bandit, an impulsive German shepherd dog, is making waves before he is calmed by the lake's sudden depth. We can't push the boat to that beckoning watermark and, as if in derision at our dry efforts, Bandit drowns us with an impromptu shower. 'I'll have to go back and get the wellies,' says Barry as he heads back to the bungalow.

When he returns he has a little pup with him. 'I'll put Duran in the boat,' says Barry and he proceeds to drag the stubborn transporter out to its natural element. He gives me an effortless jockey-back out to the boat. We push out on to the lake and soon we clear the reeds that make the area in front of McCormack's caravan a natural harbour. Barry hands me one oar and, as he is fixing the other in its rowlock, the little silver horseshoe-shaped bracket tips overboard. I ask if it can be retrieved, and Barry inserts the oar in the water perpendicular, as if silently showing the water's depth.

I look at our situation with new eyes. The little dog has run to Barry's side of the boat. I assumed this was for protection but now I see that he is trying to maintain some sort of equilibrium as the rainwater in the boat finds its natural level on my side ... I am much heavier than McGuigan. The idea shocks me, not that I have not known it statistically, but I was never aware of it as lump dead weight, which is the way the lake judges us. McGuigan is, if anything, a little taller in height, and I have an idealized picture of myself as being less than nine stone. But I am actually twenty-five per cent heavier than he is. I imagine what that might do to the momentum of the boat and its direction, until Barry starts to teach me how to row.

We are out on the lake, silently and peacefully going nowhere in particular when he tells me he thinks Sandra may be pregnant again. I am contemplating this happy news when suddenly Barry's head turns to some little movement in the reeds. 'Look there,' he says, 'two ducks.' I look and it is three to four seconds before I can locate them against the camouflaging clouds. When I sight them they are flying in formation just like the immovable ducks on a thousand suburban walls. For a time these too give the impression of stillness against the expanse of sky, but then the fingers of a tree break the illusion as they fly in a north-east direction. I wonder towards what apocalyptic vision the leader is pulling his mate when suddenly the order comes to row. 'They left a nest over there,' says McGuigan.

We row three hundred yards across the lake in a straight line, only deviating when Barry has to set the boat back on course as a result of the inexperience of one of the crew. As we approach the reeds, McGuigan wants me to drive straight into them. 'We've got to get right into them,' he says. Just as our hull lunges in I can see the nest four feet into the reeds. I am sure we have crushed the nest as McGuigan puts his hand over his side of the boat.

Without taking his eyes off me he produces an egg. 'Feel that,' he says. 'Feel the warmth of that egg.'

The egg is indeed warm and I clutch it with all the protection I can muster. The egg starts to go cold in my hand. It was warmer in the nest. Gingerly, Barry puts it back. We push ourselves out into the accommodating depths again.

I am amazed at how true Barry's sense of direction was. That's eye–hand co-ordination with a vengeance. From fully three hundred yards away he heard a movement, registered its location in the splitting of a second from the birds' ascent, and then turned the boat towards the spot, all the time keeping us on a course locked to his inbuilt radar. By such stratagems our ancestors survived in the jungle. There the co-ordination of hand and eye was looked upon as a divine gift. In that twenty-foot square called a boxing ring, which is the nearest modern man gets to the jungle, eye–hand co-ordination is an asset that can't be trained. It's one of those strengths some men retain from a universal memory, when the eye was tied to the hand not by the point of a spear or a crossbow or the sights of a rifle but by some animal reaction that had been trained to the point of instinct.

'They waited as long as they could before they flew off,' says Barry. 'They always wait until the last minute.'

I ask him what kind of ducks they were.

'Mallard,' he says.

I make the familiar observation about their mating habits.

'For life,' he repeats as we row back to the bungalow and Sandra.

HOLD ON TO YOUR TOAST

Driving around with McGuigan is one of the most hair-raising experiences in the world. His reflexes are so sharp. This innate trust in his body's responses makes him drive the way he boxes: all out, all the time. He flies around the border roads overtaking just after a bend because he sees that nothing is coming from the opposite direction. Added to this is the fact that he can see anything else that moves: rabbits, partridges, hares, hawks and other assorted animals and fowl. This is his territory . . . the fields around Clones. I can't see any of the things he conjures up. By the time I have focused they are gone.

McGuigan takes the world as he sees it. His first introduction to the professional feint occurred when he went away to training camp to box for Ireland. There were four or five other boxers sitting with him at breakfast. One of them made a gesture to somebody behind McGuigan. When McGuigan looked back from the bait, his toast was gone. Blank urban eyes stared back at the country boy from Clones. I suppose it was in similar circumstances that early man trained the new initiate in the hunt in the importance of quick reflexes. It would be no good training a newcomer under the particular strain of the hunt. To be a successful hunter, you need to be relaxed – even with the threat of starvation hanging over your head. To be a good hunter, you have to train all the senses to react instinctively. The next time an important guest arrived in his vicinity at breakfast time, McGuigan held on to his toast before he looked around to verify an arrival. If you replace the toast with money, you get some idea of the nature of professional boxing.

Today we are driving towards Castle Sanderson. It is a huge mansion set in its own grounds. McGuigan has always thought it would make the ideal training camp. On the Wattlebridge Road, just after a series of bends you turn off at the gate lodge and head on through dense woodland. On the road you are in Northern Ireland. Once you pass the gate lodge you are in the South. The woods themselves are a delight, cutting the demesne off from contact with the outside world and yet not so extensive that one ever feels isolated. At the gate to the grounds proper there is a warning to trespassers. The mansion has its own church which sits lonely and abandoned at the end of a field that becomes an ordered lawn within the shadow of the house.

Suddenly Barry stops. He moves his head in that peculiar arc that is the sign language for somebody listening intently. He asks me whether I hear anything. I don't. About five or ten seconds later I hear the sound of something that could pass for a lawnmower. We hide in the bushes. Down the majestic carpet of the Finn River comes a motor boat. Barry wants to stay out of sight because of the notice. He picks up a stout branch and hands it to me, then goes to look for one for himself.

'There might be dogs about. A Dobermann pinscher could kill you. If we see one and he attacks, hit him hard with the stick,' he says.

'What about the tree,' I ask, pointing to an amenable apple tree.

Barry laughs. 'Hit him,' he says.

Later we walk round the Castle grounds, ending up in the fenced-off graveyard that hugs the little church for comfort. In its grounds lie all the captains and majors of the Sandersons and their wives. The little church is still in good repair. What sudden isolation fell upon these people when Lloyd George drew a pencil across a map in 1922! Just a quiver of his hand would have included them in Northern Ireland. What did the preacher say to them on that first Sunday when they left their homes in the Empire and ended up in the Free State? There was as much logic in dividing a cloud in two as drawing the line where they did.

The best view of the interior is from the top of an old vault. As we are looking inside, we hear a noise. McGuigan points up. I do not have the same problem with helicopters as I do with swallows. When it comes into view, it flies in our direction. I note how acute McGuigan's hearing is. 'If you hold that stick up like a gun they will swoop over here,' McGuigan says. I look up. I look at the stick. I think about the black-faced soldiers in the chopper. Maybe their vision is not as sharp as McGuigan's. Maybe their reactions are not so astute. I keep my stick in the divining position.

On the way back home Barry stops the jeep abruptly. 'There's a hawk,' he says, 'on the telegraph pole. Did you see it?' I didn't see the telegraph pole.

All of Barry's reflexes are sharp. I think about the day we went out ferreting. 'What happens is that the ferret chases the rabbits out into the net,' he tells me. All the holes are covered. The ferret goes down. There is a rumble underground. Barry's eyes are flashing in all directions. The rabbits are running into the traps. Close to Barry one of the rabbits comes flying out and jumps straight through a hole in the net. Quick as a flash Barry reaches his hand out and grabs the rabbit in mid-air. He didn't think about it. He just reached out and caught the rabbit. A totally instinctive response.

'There's a rabbit,' says Barry, bringing me back to reality. By this stage I am too tired of this game to pay much attention. I look in the general direction in which he is pointing and I see the rabbit. It's as if he appeared because I wasn't looking for him. My mind didn't say 'rabbit' and then look. I just looked and there he was. Once I stopped my active mind looking for him, there he was. I think Barry's reflexes come from the same kind of attention. Not a logical, rational response but one of a deeply relaxed nature. When Barry said after a particular fight that he must learn to be more patient, I think I know what he means. There's a hell of a difference between looking for an opening and patiently waiting for one. We don't trust our bodies enough. We don't trust our instincts, our senses. We think too much.

FIRST AID

In the autumn, children collect horse-chestnuts to play 'conkers'. The nut is attached to a string, and an opponent is challenged to see who has the strongest nut. It was commonly believed that if you put your chestnut up a chimney and left it there for a year, it would be unbeatable the following season. There were a thousand other ways to add strength to your conker.

In St Tiarnachs National School they played a similar game, only they didn't use string and they didn't use chestnuts. They used their own hands, the arms acting as a lethal human string. The game was called 'hardy knuckles'. Nobody would play McGuigan. They called his hands many names, though none as poetic as the Spanish name given to the weapons of Barry's childhood hero, Roberto Duran. *Manos de piedra* they called Duran's hands in the Spanish-speaking ghettos of Panama City. 'Hands of Stone'. It suits McGuigan.

Dermot is Barry's elder brother by a couple of years. Normally Barry played with boys of Dermot's age at school. Except at hardy knuckles. They knew better than that. One day five of them went out exploring and they found the answer to the problem of Barry's strong hands. In a house in Analore Street they found an old pair of boxing gloves. This meant that the meanest part of Barry's artillery was hidden behind a three-inch wall of what felt like cotton wool. Each of the boys tried and tested the gloves. This was a godsend. They felt happy that now they could deal with Barry. A competition was arranged. Now he had to rely on his punching power rather than his rock-hard hands. With two years' advantage the boys felt secure.

They had made a mistake. Besides strong hands he had enormous strength in his arms. He quickly won his way to the final where he faced Liam Flanagan who shall claim to his dying day that he came out with a draw against the future featherweight champion of the world.

Barry was fixated by the gloves. He couldn't get them out of his mind. During the competition, each of the boys had used only one glove. Because of his age Barry got the right hand. It was to dog him for years. It made him just a little predictable as an amateur because of his reliance on his right hand. From the day he turned professional, he had to concentrate on using his left to such an extent that ironically he almost forgot about the right.

After the competition the boys left the gloves in the abandoned house. It was as if they had stumbled upon some magical adornment that could turn a boy into a man in a matter of minutes. Biologically, boxing gloves turn the clock back a couple of millennia. One of the things that separate man from other animals is the adaptability of the thumb. Because of its flexibility it turned the hand into a clutching rather than a clawing instrument. The boxing glove, developed to combat the brutality of the bare knuckle, turns the human hand back into a paw; now survival depends again on strength. The hand loses its flexibility and becomes a piston at the end of the rod of the arm. The day he tried on the gloves McGuigan knew instinctively he had incredible strength and punching power, as well as hard hands.

If Dermot didn't really believe that his younger brother was stronger than him, when it came to a life-and-death situation he instinctively got out of Barry's way. One day, Mrs Chapman came running in from the chemist's next door. 'He's having a heart attack,' she cried. Barry and Dermot were upstairs, training in the gym. Without waiting to change they rushed down to see what all the commotion was about. Quickly they realized that Mr Chapman, the chemist, was dying in the house next to his shop. They ran out, turned right and quickly up the three concrete steps that accounted for the steep hill of the Diamond. They found the dying Mr Chapman slumped beside his bed on the first floor as if he were saying his prayers. His heart had stopped beating and he was technically dead. There was only one way to revive him. With a blow that had sent many an opponent to the canvas, Barry beat on Mr Chapman's chest. The muscles around his heart got the message. As if in response to a human power-drill, they started their life-sustaining activity again. Slowly Mr Chapman's chest rose and fell. He was breathing again. Maybe he would be a little black and blue that night, but at least he was alive.

DOWN TO EARTH

Imagine Barry McGuigan taking part in a magician's show. He's invited up on stage and sawn in half. The two halves are moved to either side of the stage. Now imagine the magician repeats this trick several times with other volunteers ... and then drops dead. The parts have to be put back together again. Somebody asks if there is a doctor in the house. The doctor comes up on stage and the first thing he sees is the top of Barry's body ... the strong chin ... the long reach ... broad shoulders; all in all a powerful torso. He crosses the stage to find the other half. There are twenty pairs of legs, all wriggling away in their separate boxes. Eventually he puts the other nineteen sets together. All that's left is a pair of boyish legs on the other side. He can't believe that such a powerful trunk is carried by such small legs. He forgets one thing! Barry McGuigan has strong legs and incredible balance.

He has just run five miles round the border roads close to his house. He is trying to lose the extra poundage he gained on holiday. This will have accumulated on the thighs and around the midsection, so Barry has wrapped himself in polythene sheeting at these crucial spots to get rid of any excess pounds. After the run he leaves out his clothes for the wash and jumps into the shower. The difference between the top and bottom halves of his body is extraordinary. For ten years he has worked to keep the weight off his legs and buttocks so that whatever strength he has will be situated in the upper body.

Biologically the big toe doesn't have any of the flexibility of the thumb. Ever since we got down out of the trees it has been used essentially as a balancing tool, an instrument to keep us upright. The strongest architectural structure, inch for inch, in support of our weight is the arch. The human foot is constructed on the basis of two self-supporting arches. One is controlled by the big toe, and the lateral one is controlled by the outside of the foot.

Most boxers rely too much on the arch controlled by the big toe. McGuigan uses both with equal facility. Going forward consists of a thousand little sideways movements that makes it very difficult to pin him down.

Most boxers, when they want to retreat, get up on their toes and back-pedal. Amateur boxers are constantly on their toes pedalling forward. McGuigan never pedals. He stalks. He stalks because he's always ready to throw a punch that way. All of McGuigan's balance and movement is designed to maximize his greatest asset: his strength. He never plods. His forward movement is not flat-footed. All his arches are working. He moves like a vacuum cleaner.

After the shower we go for a walk. 'I tried to bring the shōgun up here last week,' Barry says, 'and she nearly went over on her side.' The shōgun is Barry's jeep, with tyres that were meant to buffer the effect of the worst of terrain. The tyres are thick corrugated monsters. By contrast, Barry's feet at size seven are very small, especially in relation to the rest of his body. To carry such weight on such small pedestals, he must have extraordinary balance.

We come to a small stream, an irrigation ditch that the farmer has protected with barbed wire. On top of the barbed wire I start performing stunts that would make a tightrope walker proud. Unfortunately, most of my movements are involuntary. Eventually I have to jump and luckily I land in quite sound terrain. For a moment or two I could end up in the ditch but eventually, as they say, I find my feet. 'You have good ankles, like me,' says Barry. He crosses the fence with no problem. To maintain the balance he does on such small feet, he must have good ankles.

In the early stages of his career, McGuigan's innate sense

of balance was countered by an incorrect posture. On the walls of McGuigan's gym are pictures of all the boxers he admires: Duran, Ali, Arguello. Some have made it in the British Isles: Jim Watt, Ken Buchanan. The only other pictures are of the Kung Fu expert Bruce Lee and two pictures of gorillas. What they have in common is posture.

Posture is not necessarily something effete. In sport, posture is about finding your centre of gravity. Gravity is the strongest elemental force acting upon us. It constantly pulls us down to earth. Even when we wake up in the morning, we can be up to a half-inch taller than when we went to bed. When the astronauts circled the world in Skylab in 1974, for 84 days, they came back three inches taller than when they set out. Outside of the gravitational pull of the earth, they had grown. To get the body in alignment with this huge natural force is a very important step for all athletes. A gorilla walks with the centre of gravity in roughly the same place that Bruce Lee had his. For thousands of years now, the centre of gravity has been located for most people in or around the abdomen.

What holds the body erect is the pull of muscles in the opposite direction to gravity. When they stretch and contract, they move the bones of the body and complete the simplest of movements like walking. When a baby learns to walk, he builds up a lot of muscle memory that eventually keeps him upright and going forward. When McGuigan is boxing, he crouches like a gorilla, his knees bent, his bottom sticking out. His strong shots, his left hook and his jab, come from below.

Gravity being a field force, once you find your alignment to it, you have a powerful instrument at your bidding. The first feeling it gives you is that of well-being. Once McGuigan had adjusted to his low crouching posture, he felt and looked very good.

ICE BAG

The gypsies have a saying: 'You have to dig deep to bury your father.' Pat McGuigan has given Barry his intimidating stare, his laughing eyes and his mischievous smile. Pat is a musician, shopkeeper, storyteller, *bon vivant*, comic and the father of eight children. It's as if he spat Barry out.

He still plays in the clubs around Ireland. One night recently, just after Barry had won the European title, Pat was setting up with his friend, Eugene McElwain, when he was approached by an old lady. 'You're a good boy,' she said to him. Pat thought she was talking about Eugene, who is fifteen years his junior. After the gig, the old woman came up and said that she'd enjoyed it, then, firmly addressing Eugene, she told him to look after Barry. 'He's a good boy,' she said, 'but you want to keep a good eye on him, that boxing's a tough business.' She thought that Eugene was Pat's father and that Pat was Barry.

It's a long time since Pat was twenty-four but he still has an energy about him that gives him a Peter Pan quality. His eyes dance with the brilliance of eternal optimism. When he tells a joke, you could make a jigsaw from the laugh lines on his face. He's had that many road accidents, if he were a cat he'd be dead. He's been generous with his money, generous with his drink, generous with his humour, but the last thing you should do is cross him. All his collisions are head-on.

The most famous instance of Pat's short fuse occurred when Barry and Dermot were in their early teens. Barry was getting ready for bed when he heard Dermot answering his father back in the kitchen. You don't do that in the

McGuigan household. Pat lost his temper. Dermot saw the flashing eyes ... and away with him up the stairs to Barry. Barry hid him in his room and locked the door. Pat came to the door in a temper – and left it in a fury at his son's refusal to open. Barry was in the cleft stick between obedience and protection ... he chose protection. Pat walked down the stairs; he was gone to get a hatchet. He came back up and hacked his way through the door. By the time he had made it an entrance again, his temper had abated. From an early age McGuigan was a peacemaker.

Dermot tells a story of Barry refereeing a fight between himself and another boy. Barry was the soul of discretion, keeping them apart, even warning Dermot not to be too rough. Suddenly Dermot got hurt. Barry lost his cool. The other boy saw it happening and ran for his life. With McGuigan, you know he is keeping an incredible temper under control. The only time I saw it near the surface was when the question of his nationality was raised. 'If anybody ever called me a turncoat I'd let them ...' He pauses in mid-sentence. 'It wouldn't matter about titles or anything. I'd go for them. I don't care if I lose my title. That would be it.' As a professional sportsman Barry can't afford to lose his temper, or even show signs of it. Temper is like a runaway horse. If you don't harness it, it will do you no good. Without it, however, it's difficult to imagine a successful boxer. Deep down there has to be fire.

McGuigan has always been temperamental about his hands. One night, Barry was preparing for a fight against Richie Foster, one of his great amateur rivals, when a steward told him that the adhesive tape was too near his knuckles. Barry protested that the tape was far from his knuckles – almost at his wrist, in fact – but the official insisted on sticking to the letter of the rules. In a rare display of the McShane temper, Barry tore the dressing from his hands and went out to fight unprotected. He chipped the bone on the third left knuckle, and it was floating around inside his hand for months. It even affected his training for the Moscow Olympics ... and it could have destroyed his career.

Dermot also has the McGuigan temper. Dermot can get angry. I suppose the games they have chosen show the different qualities in temperament of the two sons. Dermot is a two-handicap golfer. If he so chose, he could be a professional. But his first sports priority is to see that Barry becomes world champion. For his part, Barry dislikes golf. He doesn't dislike the game but he dislikes playing it. I suppose out playing golf, there's maybe three, four minutes of actual action in four hours. Between shots it's all about composure, keeping cool under pressure. You keep cool and then you let everything go in one sharp action. Dermot's temper is ideal for golf. Normally he's a quiet, almost shy, deep thinker, but he's got a desperately short fuse. When it goes he will lose the head, as they say, for a couple of seconds; then he's back to normal. Barry's temper is ideal for boxing. It too is explosive, but hidden under layer upon layer of repressed will-power. When he lets it loose, it's unending.

When Ken Buchanan was brought over to spar with Barry in the very early days, the first thing he said was that Barry would have to get his temper under better control. Most people would never notice Barry's temper. It has been absorbed in most people's eyes by Barry's charisma. It's probably the secret of Barry's appeal that he has such huge reserves of strength under control. People in Ireland are angry, but they get no chance to show it; it's part of the culture not to show emotion. However, it's quite legitimate and perfectly acceptable to let it all out at a boxing match. There you can lose your head. The traditional reason for fighters grabbing the public attention is because they are fighting vicariously for the people to get out of the ghetto. The ghetto McGuigan is leading the crowd out of is an emotional one.

Temper is like a steam-engine. If you give it its head, you dilute the power. It's essential to keep a tight lid on it. It was a blessing in disguise that McGuigan had somebody who wouldn't be intimidated by him in the early stages of his career. McGuigan was immensely strong and aggressive, but Buchanan was the old dog for the long road. He sensed that Barry's temperament could be used against him. He prodded and needled him until he had Barry boiling. 'When you lose your temper, you're mine,' Buchanan told him. He gave Eastwood some advice. 'Whenever McGuigan comes to the corner, warm from frustration, put an ice bag on his head. If he is ever going over the top, shout at him in the ring, "Ice bag, ice bag." And if he doesn't cool down, let him have it when he comes back to the corner.'

Barry has managed to subdue the wild horse of his temper; but he will never bury his father in him altogether. The McGuigan temper is what gets him off his stool to answer the bell.

EVERY MOTHER'S SON

In the late Seventies, Michael Dooley was a policeman in Clones. Often he needed to perform checkpoint duty four or five miles away. If he didn't use the unapproved border roads he would have to drive twenty or thirty extra miles. Checkpoint duty often began at dawn. To avoid any inconvenience, he would dress in his policeman's uniform and then put his civilian clothes on over them in respect to the Northern State, otherwise he might be arrested. Michael has only one other image that competes with his double identity: every morning on his journey he would meet Barry McGuigan out running, followed by the prettiest girl in Clones on a bicycle.

McGuigan might get his explosive temperament from the male side of the family; he gets his discipline and determination from the female side. Katie, his mother, is the anchor of the McGuigan family. Katie is old-fashioned. She still loves her husband. Each of her children is a product of that love, and she will never let them forget that. Barry is the dark-haired 'white-haired boy'. Katie has set all her parameters within the ambit of the family. So that Pat's dream could stay alive, she worked hard behind the counter of her shop. She behaves in the same way with her children. If they have a vision, they must pursue it to the rainbow's end. Katie will stay behind in the shop making sure that the essentials of existence are looked after.

The Red Branch Knights were a group of ancient Irish warriors who served the High King of Ireland. Their training methods were legendary: they included running through the darkest part of the woods without breaking a twig or getting a splinter in one's foot. McGuigan trains towards some such mythological omnipotence with utter determination.

The times of the *Fianna* and the Red Branch Knights were dominated by some extraordinary women. Queen Maeve of Connaught ruled like a matriarch. Pat might give Barry his flashes of temper and his laughing eyes, but when you see the whites of McGuigan's eyes you are looking at his mother.

B. J. Eastwood is Barry's manager. Outside of Barry's family, Eastwood knows more about him than anyone. What he can't fathom is the depth of expression in McGuigan's eyes. He replays a video tape over and over where Barry is returning to the ring after a period of extreme self-doubt. McGuigan's head is down, he is saying, 'I'm coming back and I'm very determined.' He looks towards the camera.

'Look at the eyes,' Eastwood says as he rewinds backwards. Again the tape plays. This time the eyes communicate in silence. There is a certainty in them that is beyond words. Normally, after saying, 'I'm determined to do well,' the speaker would look up as if to seek endorsement in the listener. McGuigan looks through the camera. It's as if the sentence is incomplete without that look. The look is the full stop to the sentence.

Sandra McGuigan slept soundly on her wedding night. At the early dawn she awoke to the faint sound of a constant rhythm. The sound of deep breathing was coming from the verandah of her hotel . . . Barry was doing press-ups. There is no need to say that he has his mother's discipline in relation to training; he also has her determination.

Part Two

A PRIVATE LIFE

POOR PADDY
WORKED ON THE RAILWAY

Clones in the 1850s was the crossroads of the Northern Railway system. In the middle of the nineteenth century when the Empire was at its height the Great Northern Railway (a title apt enough for the Indian sub-continent) connected Clones to Dublin and Belfast and all points between. Oldtimers with the memory of an Empire that extended across the globe boast to this day, 'Sure you could go from Clones to anywhere in the world.'

Pat McGuigan followed his father on to the railways. He was a fireman, which meant he stoked the engine. Smoke signals from the great steam engines informed the residents of Clones that the eight o'clock from Enniskillen was on its way. In a landscape free of industrialization the railways had a mystical power that gave those who worked for them a sense of destiny denied to those who could not travel on the free day-pass to Dublin. The Great Northern Railway also allowed their employees free travel on the other railways of Britain. So to belong to a railway company was to belong to the most powerful corporation outside of State employment. Pat McGuigan remembers with childlike wonder the mechanical genius that was at the heart of the Industrial Revolution and made Britain for a time the greatest power on earth. 'The trains would come into the siding and go on to a turntable. You could push this forty-ton engine round with one hand. I remember my father taking me into the shed and telling me, "Push that train round to there." I looked at him and gave a little nervous smile. "Go on," he said, "push," and I pushed this great big engine round the turntable until it faced the necessary shed.'

With his steady job working on the railways, Pat could afford to think about marriage. He had his eye on young Katie Rooney, the daughter of John 'Papa' Rooney. Katie was a thin wisp of a girl with a figure that would make Twiggy go on a diet. She had long black hair, piercing eyes and a smile that captured the heart of the Sinatra of Clones.

In his spare time, Pat sang with a band. It was the era when big bands were in vogue. The singer may have been the centre of attention, but the band was called after the bandleader, and that's where the money went. He didn't earn much, but whatever Pat earned he put aside for his marriage to Katie. By day Pat worked at the railway depot at the bottom of Fermanagh Street, and at night he would often play in the Creighton, a railway hotel across the street.

In those days Clones was a real weekend town. People would come in from Fermanagh in the North of Ireland to an atmosphere and a licensing law more amenable to those with a thirst. The narrow, steep hill of Fermanagh Street was often impassable with pedestrians spilling out of the ten or more pubs that made the climb from the railway to the Diamond acceptable even to the arthritic and weak of heart. The cinema, halfway up the street on the left, showed the latest Gary Cooper or Cary Grant, and on nights off Pat and Katie snuggled up in the lovers' seat at the back of the cinema on the right. It was a perfectly positioned strategic point because you had total command of all incoming traffic from the entrance in the middle of the cinema and, once in, a patron would get a real crick in the neck trying to figure out who was with whom in lovers' corner. Pat and Katie got married on 27 August 1957. Katie made her own dress, and the reception was a quiet, simple, family affair.

The next time the McGuigan clan gathered for a formal occasion it spelt trouble for them, and disaster for the tiny community of Clones. James McGuigan and his son Pat assembled under their stationmaster, Michael, to watch the last train depart for Belfast and Enniskillen. The Northern authorities were unable to subsidize the loss the railways were making and although the line to Dublin and Dundalk limped along for a time, the era of the Iron Monster was at an end. The next biggest industry, the Clones Canning Factory, closed the same year . . . and the boom years were over. Amidst all the other statistics, Pat McGuigan was unemployed, with no prospect of work in a country that was hopelessly underindustrialized and in a countryside that was turning more and more to dairy farming as a means of survival.

Northerners from the time of the potato pickings had looked to Scotland in time of crisis. The journey from Larne to Stranraer seemed less of a rupture than the journey to Dublin. So Pat and Katie, only six months married, travelled to Glasgow.

They still remember Sauchiehall Street and Katie has a vivid memory of the flat they lived in in Ardgowan Street. It was one of those old Glasgow tenements with 76 steps up to the top. 'I remember because we had to clean them every other week. Everybody had a turn cleaning. We lived at the very top of the house in an attic.'

Pat got a job on the Glasgow buses. Not much time was allowed for training and within a week Pat was on his rounds. As he turned the handle at the front of the bus to Castlemilk, he imagined it to be a sleepy middle-class suburb. On Saturday night the bus was crammed with Glasgow's famed carousers. Because of the strict licensing laws, people would stock up for Sunday. The only trouble was that most of them stored it inside their own bodies or in the famous 'carry-outs' that frequently did not survive the journey home. With the zeal of the newly arrived immigrant, Pat went collecting fares. Most experienced busmen considered it an achievement not to be recognized on those late-night-Saturday runs. They loosened their ties, undid their jackets and, like the sheriff in the Westerns, hung up their meters and sat near the doors in case of trouble. Not our Pat. He went collecting fares. There were howls of protest at this late-night incursion into the milk train home. Some refused and threatened physical violence, and so Pat collected those with his sleeves rolled up, left hook, right jab, on the streets of Glasgow. Pat's sense of pride had been hurt and many of the noses alighting that night were blood-spattered.

But then word reached Glasgow that Dave Dixon was looking for a singer for his orchestra. Would Pat consider it? Pat and Katie were never happy in the big city. At heart they preferred Clones and it would be much easier for Katie to have the baby – for she was now pregnant – surrounded by family. About six months after leaving Ireland, Mr and Mrs McGuigan were on their way back. Their first child, Sharon, was born on 22 June 1958.

MOTHER COURAGE

Pat McGuigan was back in the place he loves best, doing the thing he loves most ... and getting paid for it. But it wasn't as sound as it had seemed in the first flush of enthusiasm. It was what you might call less dependable than the railway. The money was enough to keep you from starving, but it didn't come in all the year round.

For the first time, Pat discovered what Lent really meant. He knew it was a time when Catholics denied themselves the things of the flesh before Easter. Traditionally people gave things up for Lent. Pat had to give up his wages. Bands did not play during Lent; it was not done in Ireland at the time. The Church ruled all the rural Irish parishes, and dances were out of the question. If you were caught so much as thinking about dances you were 'read' from the altar. To be read from the altar meant you were a social outcast as dangerous as a leper. Pat McGuigan found himself unemployed during the six weeks of Lent.

Katie McGuigan was now a housewife with two young children and another one on the way. There was no security in the showband business. It was impossible for Katie to go out to work, so with £300 she approached Charlie Slowey who had a shop for rent in the Diamond. 'We opened the shop with very little capital. But I worked out that the kids would never go hungry if we had a grocery shop. No matter how hard things were, the kids always got the best of everything. There was no sick pay or holiday pay in the band business and often the shop saved our lives. We would never have raised eight healthy children without it.'

By the time she was thirty, Katie McGuigan had six

children and a successful business. She got up every morning at half-past six, got the children ready for school and then got the shop open by eight. She didn't close until ten at night. The shop opened seven days a week, and Katie was behind the till most of the time. There is no doubt that she did all of this work for the children's future and there is not a hint of regret from her about her life.

Painted in large letters on the walls of Barry McGuigan's home-made gym there is a proverb which several white-washings have not obliterated: 'Work hard, think fast and you will last.' Barry might almost have written it in praise of his mother. She has an unending supply of energy and a good business sense which she probably inherited from her father. 'Papa' Rooney was a bookie who laid the odds at all the little tracks around the midland. To be a successful bookie you need a quick mind and a cool head. Katie Rooney had these and determination. She has clear green eyes and the type of cheerful personality that suggests a good homemaker. All the Rooneys, it seems, are nest builders.

It was necessary to work hard. The opposition were only twenty yards across the road. They were called the Mealiffs. They were Protestants and although their shop was about the same size as the McGuigans', they had the added advantage that they could rely on their small hotel in time of a cash-flow crisis. The Mealiff hotel is in the middle of the road, halfway between the respective shops. It splits the neck of the Diamond's womb in two, separating two roads, one leading off to Newbliss and the other to Scots-house. Both shops depended on the outlying country areas for their customers. The hinterland was half Protestant and half Catholic; although the Mealiffs were Protestant, that did not mean that customers split in two on a religious basis. People shopped where prices were lowest, and for years the Mealiffs and McGuigans kept up a healthy competition with no animosity.

The most noticeable change in the countryside was the increase in the number of cars. What had been a steady trickle before the end of the railways developed into a flood in the early Sixties. The cars more than anything lessened the power of the local clergy, at least in the area of entertainment. A local curate could no longer show up at a dance and expect to scare his parishioners, because many of them came from twenty or thirty miles away and did not fear a reading from the pulpit. The Church fought its first losing battle with the car in Ireland, and in the early Sixties it was losing at the rate of fifty miles to the gallon. The local girls and boys no longer had to wait on the returned Yank to get an impression of the world outside. Instead it came over the hill in a baby Ford every Saturday night. 'The backs of cars' became the new cry from the pulpits. No Parisian brothel was ever painted as red as the upholstered seats of these new Trojan horses.

The world of the old-style orchestra was in many ways a mirror of the world that was falling apart. It was a world where authority was unquestioned. The band was called after the bandleader and not the lead singer. The leader conducted, and he contracted the other musicians, who played for a set fee. Every musician read from a score from which he did not deviate. The devil's music of the time was jazz, whose improvisatory techniques spoke of a primitive world a thousand miles away from the symphony orchestra from which the humblest dance band felt themselves descended. It was the world of radio.

Slowly this hierarchy began to break down. The dawn of the showband era was at hand. Most of these showbands got their names from America. Pat McGuigan left the Dave Dixon band to form his own little group. They were called simply the Big Four. Times were hard for the six months Pat and his three fellow-musicians rehearsed, but once they were on the road things looked up.

On 28 February 1961, Pat's second son, Finbarr Patrick McGuigan, was born in Beechill Nursery Home, Monaghan. After the initial scare about his broken collarbone, the child prospered well and things seemed to be going great guns for Katie and Pat.

The Big Four swept the countryside. Eventually they bought the ultimate status symbol of every showband, their own bus with their name emblazoned across the side. The world was young and the money was good and the *hors d'œuvres* was prawn cocktails. They lived with no thought of tomorrow – but tomorrow always comes. One of the hazards of the road stopped Pat dead in his tracks. He had a bad car accident.

Perhaps Barry McGuigan's earliest memory is of his father lying on two planks in the small room that connected the kitchen to the shop. He lay for three months on that bed, and about the only distraction he had was his youngest son who pottered around while his mother tried to keep house and home together, fifteen hours a day in the shop. At the time of his accident, Pat McGuigan was approximately five feet seven and a half inches tall. He had gone for a medical to join the railway and they had a method of sorting out those under the required five foot seven. If you tried to reach the required height by standing on your toes, a bell went off to warn the officer in charge. When Pat McGuigan had passed that part of the scrutiny a year earlier, the bell stayed dumb. Now, after three months in bed, when he stood up he was only five feet six. Crushed vertebrae accounted for the lost inch and a half. The doctor told him he would never have a normal life again and he would have to wear a brace all his life, like a horse. Katie looked to the shop in such emergencies. Pat looked at his new baby son and vowed that he would recover.

THE LONG WALK

Because of his incredible energy, Katie and Pat had to keep a constant eye on their toddler. When he was just two years of age Barry had to go into hospital for the second time in his life. Katie asked to be shown the cot they were going to use to contain him; she felt it was only fair to warn the nurses about his level of energy. A nurse showed Katie the cot. Katie felt it was too low for her son. The nurse, with a smile that acknowledged the over-concern of a mother, showed her the clamp that raised its height and made the bars of the cot into a virtual fortress. There was also a top that could be used if the child was really overreacting. It was like a turf cart, and was usually only brought in for children a couple of years older than Barry. Katie thought it would be best if it was used, as she knew that nobody really appreciated Barry's drive.

Katie herself had incredible energy. She ran the family and shop virtually single-handed. The pictures of Katie from this time, the mid-Sixties, are the pictures of a young girl who was into the latest mini-skirt fashions and full of vitality. She never looks like a shop-owner or a woman who has been beaten down by the cares of running a family and a business.

Pat himself had the same kind of continual go in him. He also had a strength that sometimes was its own worst enemy. One night he was coming home from playing at a dance and he had just passed Naas in a snowstorm when his car, in an act of self-volition, turned on its wheels and faced back towards the town as if it was a horse with a mind of its own. Pat changed down into first and put his foot on the accelerator, trying to go anywhere rather than be stuck in the snow. The back wheels spun round and round without going anywhere. Pat got out to see what he could do. Without really thinking, he decided to lift the car out of the snow. He bent down, grabbed the bumper and lifted. It inched forward. Just to make sure, Pat quickly grabbed the bumper again and gave a quick jerk. The next thing he knew, he woke up covered in a blanket of snow, looking up at what looked like an igloo. Cars passed, their headlamps like the eyes of a monster in a nightmare. This went on for some time with Pat shouting at them to stop. The shouting produced a searing pain in his lower back. Nobody stopped. He knew he was on his own.

He crawled towards the car, each movement producing a pain that almost knocked him out and sometimes did. Between consciousness and waking Pat reached the open door. When his hands touched the body of the car he knew he had to get inside fast – there was no feeling left in them. He pulled himself halfway into the car. Then he knew that it was no good: he would have to get the car started or die. He reached over in excruciating agony to grab the foot mats from under the front seat. Then he crawled back down and headed towards the back of the car again. It was this kind of determination and yet cool head that he has passed on to Barry.

He pressed the mats under the back wheels and crawled back to the car. Pulling himself up by the steering wheel, he prayed for a moment before he tried the key in the ignition. It felt like the wheezing of an old man with asthma. Pat stuck his foot full down on the throttle and got a life-saving kick. Behind him the mats were doing the business. The car took off and headed towards Naas. Pat didn't care where it went, so long as it was headed in the direction of civilization. He got to the town and sought out a doctor. He wouldn't look at him because Pat hadn't got the necessary shillings. With the kind of crazy independence that Pat still has, he headed out for home.

Most children pick up traits from their parents. McGuigan certainly picked up his energy from his mother and father, but whatever happened the night McGuigan was conceived the energy was not just the accumulation of his mother's and father's. It was as if their separate energies were multiplied together when positive hit negative that night. Anyway, the boy forming in the womb would have an uncontrollable level of energy. Katie knew that. She already had two children, but some kind of primitive intuition told her that this fellow would have abnormal resources. How do you convey that to a nurse who has seen hundreds of children?

When they visited the hospital that night, the top of Barry's cot was on the ground and he was missing. The nurse said they were looking for him ... there was nothing to worry about. Try telling that to the seven nurses in the adult wards of Monaghan Hospital asking old men in bed if they have seen a small boy. Eventually he was located at the end of a corridor behind a chair.

After that episode Katie kept a careful eye on Barry. The best thing to do was to try and distract him with toys. On his travels with the band, Pat would see various little toys that looked sturdy until they got into the hands of his son. Once in Scotland he was sold an indestructible little car; it was genuine ... there was a guarantee with it. During the next few months, Pat had it soldered three or four times until it was finally knocked out of action for good by Barry.

So long as Barry was just climbing the lamp-post in the Diamond, Katie knew where he was. If the people of Clones saw him straying out of the Diamond into Fermanagh Street or on to the Cavan Road, they would bring him back to the shop.

One day in September 1964 his mother took him on an adventure. They went all the way across the Diamond down the forbidden Fermanagh Street towards the crossroads at the Creighton Hotel. Barry almost pulled the hand off his mother as they ventured down the steep hill. This was a whole new world. Past the crossroads, they headed for Church Hill. On their left was the old railway station. They turned right along Rosslea Street, passing over the remains of the old railway lines. Overhead, like a spotted black flag, crows moved in formation as they watched the children return to school. They passed a shed in which the older boys and girls were leaving their bicycles. Past a hopeful litter bin, they entered the yard of the St Louis Convent. The first dawning moment of alarm came when the children were sucked into the building by the insistent noise of a hand-held bell.

Barry had never been introduced to anybody in his life. His mother said, 'This is Sister Camillas, Barry.' McGuigan looked at the figure in front of him. She looked a little like a woman, but she had a scarf covering her hair. Barry wanted to go home and help his mother with the shelves. The only way Katie could get some of the energy out of her three-and-a-half-year-old son was to have him stack the shelves for her. He liked doing that. He wanted to go home *now*.

The Sister brought him down to a bench. It felt like the high chair he had left behind a year and a half ago. It made him feel more vulnerable. His mother was backing off him. Barry started to yell. That worked: his mother came back a little towards him. Barry kicked the bench. His mother hung at the door with the kind of uncertainty that spells doom. For a moment Barry stopped completely. He was used to his father going off – but that happened in the house ... and he always came back to the house and he brought presents. Now his little world was falling apart. His mother was giving him away. She hung on the threshold and he could see the tears in her eyes. He stopped completely as if to blackmail her into staying by his hurt.

Katie went out of the door. She was gone. She wasn't. She stayed at the other side of the door as Barry let loose with a scream that was unearthly. She heard, in the middle of the chest-heaving sighs, Sister Camillas trying to reason with her son. Suddenly McGuigan let out a curse that shocked Katie. She was tempted to open the door and say, 'Where did you hear that?' when she heard another and another and another. Barry had gone wild. He was completely out of control. It hadn't been like this with Sharon or Dermot. They had cried, but not like this. Katie had no alternative but to go.

The nun came to the door. She looked at Katie in a fury. 'Go, go,' she said, and then as they both heard Barry's little feet running up the aisle she uttered what is almost damnation for a nun. 'Get the hell out of here,' she ordered. Katie moved away. She could hear Sister Camillas wrestling with Barry inside. She had lost that battle once or twice herself. Sister Camillas hung on with the desperation of a drowning nun. Barry's hand reached the door handle, only to be pulled back with a final desperate tug. Sister Camillas had a new, strong-willed pupil. Katie McGuigan made her way up the hill. A tear was forming in her eye. She had broken her son's heart; she would never do it again.

THE LONG WALK HOME

It was on an April evening in 1968 that Barry walked the furthest distance he had ever done out the Cavan Road. Behind him the town of Clones was ringed by a series of bonfires to announce the most important occasion in Clones in the past twenty years. A hero was coming home. Slowly a procession made its way over the little Monaghan Hills. People lining the roadside started to cheer, and behind his back the bonfires of Clones glowed in their reflected glory. Like the hero from the film *Ben Hur*, Barry's father waved at the crowd from his metal chariot. The crowd surged forward and Barry lost sight of him. Hands picked him up from behind and without turning to wonder who it was, Barry watched as his father rode in triumph into Clones. Barry wanted to reach out and touch his father to tell him to stop but the car continued on towards the town and Barry followed in the wake of his father's procession. He had his arms around Katie who waved to the crowd from the open car.

At seven years of age Barry started his long walk alone back into Clones. When Pat McGuigan came home from a tour on the road, he always made a fuss of the kids and he would bring presents. Skates were the first craze. The boys would get rid of some of their natural energy on the steep hills of Clones. The town was built especially for boys to skate on. From the Protestant church, at the top of the Diamond, steep hills ran in all directions to the low-lying land all round the town. Across the road from the McGuigans lived the only boy in town who could challenge Barry in competition. One of Sammy Mealiff's specialities was skating. He could tear round the hills and then jump a milk-crate before continuing on his journey. McGuigan was not to be bested. Sammy put down another crate and cleared it with some difficulty. McGuigan put down three crates and went right to the top of the Diamond. He came hurtling down the hill and jumped the crates with a spirit that knew no fear. That night Sammy Mealiff nursed his broken knees in his house across the Diamond.

Barry continued the walk towards Clones, wondering if his father had brought him anything this time. In the distance Barry heard the tannoy playing the song that had caused all the fuss. His father had sung it to his mother in the little kitchen at the back of the shop. He had heard his father rehearse it over and over until he got it right. A part of the song was about a light from above. Barry always thought of an angel when he heard that part. The angel had his mother's face. He always helped his mother in the shop; before he went to school he would pack the shelves, and when he came home he would carry the big sacks of potatoes from the store out the back. He loved the way his mother's eyes opened up when she saw him carrying the big heavy bags. He would race his sister Laura with bales of briquettes. She would carry one and he would carry two, and he always got to the shop first. You couldn't run in the shop, and once Barry and Laura got to the door they would have to slow down. Barry got so good at carrying the briquettes that he never even appeared out of breath when he came through it. 'That wee fellow is my wee husband,' Katie would proudly announce and then when he was gone for more briquettes she would add, 'He's the greatest wee worrier, sure he'd worry about the ducks going barefoot.' He loved helping in the shop.

The crowd that was gathered in the Diamond was bigger than the crowd that had been outside the church the day he made his communion. His mother had made the same grey flannel suits for both him and Dermot. His sister Sharon made her communion that day as well. It was a big day for the McGuigan family, but it was not as big as this. He knew all the people at his communion. In the country all the boys and girls out of the one family made their communion on the same day so that it wouldn't cost so much for the family, but it meant that you had to divide up the money you collected between three.

That day he had more money than ever before. He was annoyed when his mother wanted to change the money in his pockets for notes; the coins felt better but his mother said they would ruin his appearance. He heard people in the streets of Clones say that his father was going to be a rich man after the Song Contest. When he got to the front of the crowd he could see that there were tears in his mother's eyes.

He had seen his daddy cry once. It had shocked him a lot. It was in the graveyard, the day his grandfather died. Papa McGuigan was his daddy's daddy. He remembered the clay going in the grave and the big stones that they had forgotten to remove hitting the coffin. It was at that moment that his father started to cry. His mammy put her arms round him and carried him away. He had often heard that his father was the baby of the family. Maybe that was why he was crying that day. He didn't see any of his uncles crying. They were hard men ... everybody in the town said so. Maybe they cried on their own, the way he sometimes did. His grandfather had died last summer and he was buried on the longest day of the year. There was a big crowd at the graveyard then too, but not as big as this.

As he got to the front of the stage Barry could hear the tannoy blare out the cause of this sudden enthusiasm. The words were indistinct but Barry had heard them enough times to know what his father was singing as he put his arms round Katie in the Diamond and gave her a kiss.

> One day while I was out walking,
> I saw your face in the midst of a crowd,
> Here I thought was the chance of a lifetime.
> The chance of a lifetime with you.

Barry could remember the day his mother had almost died on the floor. The doctor had come to give her an injection. Her belly was big; the hospital said she might have two babies, and so the doctor came to help her. Something went wrong. The doctor had to ring up on the phone for another injection that would counter the effect of an earlier one. They called this an antidote. He remembers the doctor on the floor saying the rosary over his mother and his Granny Rooney crying in the chair. He thought his mother was dead, but eventually the antidote arrived and the doctor gave his mother another injection. His mother opened her eyes and the doctor started crying. Everything was all right. His mother told him that she had seen a bright white light which kept getting brighter and brighter and pulling her in, until she woke up. Ever since, Barry was afraid of injections and didn't like to let his mother out of his sight for too long. At home somebody was minding the two twins. They were called Rachel and Rebecca.

His father had originally been placed fourth in the Contest, but somebody was disqualified and his father had come third. The competition took place in London. He liked the excitement when the voting came on. A girl from Spain won and Cliff Richard was second for England. Barry wondered what the crowd tonight would have done if his father had won. He would have been the King of Europe. He was already the King of Ireland, at singing. The boys in the school looked at him differently. He was proud of his father, but he was also a little jealous of the fact that the competitions took his mother away for so long. He hadn't seen her for almost two days. He was used to his father going away, but it was different with his mother away. When he felt lonely and alone Barry's mother always put her arms round him. Not last night. He was never so close and yet so far apart from his father and mother in his life.

1 *(right).* A budding champion: Barry as a juvenile

2 *(below).* After a victory in St Joseph's Hall, Clones, just a year before he became senior champion

3 *(bottom).* August 1979, at an international tournament in Constanta, Romania, where Barry was voted best boxer in the tournament

4 *(top)*. Helping out in the family shop in Clones *(Star)*

5 *(above)*. In the kitchen in Kilrooskey *(Star)*

6 *(right)*. Dummy's Lake. Barry's house is in the background on the right *(Duncan Raban)*

7 *(right, inset)*. Who is panting most – Barry or Bandit? *(Duncan Raban)*

8 (*top*). Gold medallist at the Commonwealth Games, Edmonton. The hard work is starting to pay off. Tumat Sogolik stands on McGuigan's right

9 (*above*). Work hard, think fast and you will last

10 (*right*). Barry with son Blain, just a couple of hours old (*Daily Mirror*)

11 (*right, inset*). Blain in the ring before his Dad's fight with Juan Laporte, February 1985

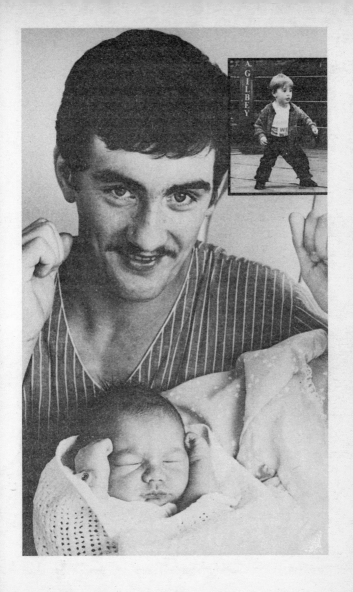

12 *(left)*. Katie and Pat in the gym *(Star)*

13 *(below)*. The record company spelt Pat's name wrong. It was easier to pronounce, so he kept it

14 *(right)*. A training run on the beach at Bangor *(Pacemaker Press International)*

15 *(right, inset)*. The guest house in Bangor where McGuigan stays while preparing for his big fights *(Star)*

16 *(above)*. Paul Huggins keeping low in the final British title eliminator, November 1982 *(Pacemaker Press Internationai)*

17 *(left)*. McGuigan's eighteenth straight inside-the-distance win, December 1984. It's Clyde Ruan who is looking up *(Pacemaker Press International)*

THE FIGHTING
McGUIGANS

In June 1967 Sister Camillas told Barry that he was going
to the big boys' school. The children were assembled in the
yard of the St Louis Convent and the boys were separated
from the girls. The girls walked in a straight line up to the
second floor of the Convent School. The boys were going
much further. They were going up to the man's world.

They marched down the steep hill from the school
to Rosslea Road where they took a right past the ever-
inquiring crows. Right again at the railway line, they headed
up Chapel Hill. They kept going on past the Catholic
church until they reached the metal gates where the boys'
school of St Tiarnachs had its name engraved in wrought
iron. Inside the front door of the one-level building they
hung up their coats. There were four classrooms with three
chimney stacks. Somewhere in one of the other four rooms
was Barry's elder brother, Dermot. Some time in the
afternoon a bell went and knowledgeable feet answered its
call to the school yard. Barry's teacher led his class out to
the little yard at the back of the school.

The boys' play was different from that of the girls. Today
the big boys were showing the initiates who owned what
territory. Running up to the church wall is a steep incline
that boyhood feet made into a mountain to be conquered.
In the fight for dominance of the hill pupils came crashing
down in an avalanche of bodies. The young boys watched,
astounded. Eventually three boys gained control. One of
them was Dermot McGuigan. To show Barry's class who
was boss they grabbed one of them, carried him gently up
the hill and then unrolled him like a wedding carpet back
to earth. They then stood at the top of the hill, their arms

raised, gladiator-style. Behind their backs on the outside of the church wall young Barry was climbing stealthily to the top. Dermot surveyed the crowd, looking for his little brother. He had been waiting for this moment all week. From behind his back he saw a pair of arms push one of his comrades down the hill. Before he could get there to help, his second companion was rolling towards oblivion. Dermot reached down to grab his attacker by the neck and the fierce eyes that were staring up at him were those of his brother, Barry. Caught in a conflict of intention, Dermot waited until his erstwhile companions regained their composure. He saw their shadows intent on young Barry. In that moment the allegiances of three years changed hands. Political pacts were forgotten as the two brothers redefined the power structure in St Tiarnachs. The school bell called a halt to a new era in school politics. The Fighting McGuigans had arrived.

Back in the classroom Dermot McGuigan made out a family tree. It was the kind they had to learn off by heart to see who should be king of where. At the top of the page on the right-hand side he put down the names of his grandparents, James and Mary McGuigan. On the left-hand side opposite he put down the names of his other granny and grandad, John and Josephine Rooney. Underneath the Rooneys he put down the names of his aunts and uncles (Leo, Paddy, Jimmy, John, Dilly, Sheila, Bridget and Angeline) and his mother, Katie. He drew a circle round his mother's name. Under the McGuigan alliance he put down the names of his uncles and aunts on the other side (Dermot, Seamus, Maureen, Peter, Dennis and Kevin) and his father, Pat. He was called after Uncle Dermot who had died when he was eighteen from meningitis. His father was the youngest of his family. He joined his father and mother together and put down the names of his five brothers and sisters: Sharon, Barry, Laura, and the twins Rachel and Rebecca.

Dermot took a red pencil out of his schoolbag and underlined the names of his four living uncles. His father had told him they would fight anybody. They would fight the devil up from hell and when they had got rid of him they would fight with their own shadows. After Dermot had underlined their names he wrote at the top of the page 'The Fighting McGuigans'. Then he added his own name and that of Barry to the list. A lineage was born.

He remembered his Grandfather McGuigan warning them before a football match not to start any trouble. 'We've seen enough trouble,' his grandfather always used to say. During the match somebody hit his Uncle Kevin an unorthodox blow. You hit one of the McGuigans, you hit them all. From the other side of the pitch his Uncle Dennis came running to sort out the offender. As he went to tackle his man, somebody jumped him from behind and started kicking him on the ground. One minute Dermot remembered his grandfather asking for peace to be restored and the next minute he was pulling a cornerpost up by its roots and heading out on to the pitch to sort everybody out. All hell broke loose. Dermot's grandfather and his sons cleared the pitch of all objectors at the cost of three black eyes and a few cuts and scratches.

Pat McGuigan, who had escaped almost unmolested, was sent home first to breach the fort. Pat pushed Dermot and Barry ahead of him as he winked at his mother in the kitchen. Behind came Dennis and Seamus and Kevin with one black eye. His mother looked at her grown sons and then said to her grandchildren: 'The next person that comes through that door with a black eye can leave this house for good.' With that her husband James came in, his eyes sunk like pearls in the middle of two black oysters.

Kevin had the worst temper and Dennis had the hardest punch. His own father usually got out of situations by joking. One day tempers were getting frayed when his father said, 'Now stop giving out about Kevin. There's nothing wrong with him. He's a well-balanced man, he's got a chip on both shoulders.' With Pat McGuigan the last line of defence was laughter.

Dermot had a lighter which he cherished. On it there was a poem:

> They were made by McGuigan a man named Dan
> In tiny little kiln of the right size and plan
> Their colour when finished was more or less white
> And far was the fame of the Broughdharag Pipe

Dan was his father's father's father. It was too complicated to add his name to the growing tree. Broughdharag was in County Derry. On the lighter was the family crest. It consisted of the Red Hand of Ulster surrounding a lion and a greyhound. The McGuigans were fighters and hunters. He was copying the family crest when he saw the teacher coming towards him. He slipped the prized lighter into his pocket. 'What's that you have there?' he inquired. 'A family tree,' said Dermot as he held up the disposable copy in mock guilt. 'The fighting McGuigans,' the teacher said, repeating the heading. 'I'll give you fighting,' he said as he clipped Dermot on the ear.

Merdie Moore was a schoolboy whom Barry mistook for a teacher. He was tall for his age and he started to shave long before he left the National School. His family were in the coal business, and besides his pocket money Merdie earned iron stomach muscles from carting coal-bags around Clones. His great treat for the new boys was to expose his stomach to blows from all-comers. Having seen young Barry on the hill he was reluctant to take him on, but he was shamed into a display of bravery by boys who knew better. He walked towards young Barry with his exposed belly-button as rigid as a tightly packed sack of wheat. The school gathered round. Barry's eye was in line with Merdie's navel. As Barry looked up at him, Merdie gave a tight smile. Barry was mystified as to why somebody should want to let him hit them undefended. 'You're to hit him there,' Dermot said, pointing below his rib-cage, 'He likes it, don't you, Merdie?' he asked. Merdie nodded assent. Barry drew back and hit Merdie a strong right hand to the solar plexus. Merdie collapsed as if punctured. Barry stood back, ready to defend himself from an onslaught. Over the whole yard silence reigned. The bell for class called the boys back to their desks. To the inquiring teacher Barry heard one of the big boys say that Merdie had stomach cramps.

THE TUNNEL OF LOVE

One day Sandra Mealiff and her brothers Sammy and David were playing in their front room. They lifted the carpet and found a huge slab. With great effort it could be moved. Underneath they found a man-made tunnel that had not been in use for almost fifty years. Slowly they ventured down into the darkness, only to re-emerge wondering where it led to and why it was begun. To answer either question it is important to know a little about how the Mealiffs came to Clones in the first place.

Clones should be a sleepy little town on the Monaghan–Fermanagh border with little or no history. Given its population of just over 2,000, there should be a murder every fifty years, three guards and a sergeant, one parish church with a parish priest and two curates, snow every third year, eight births, seven deaths and three marriages. It is not like that at all.

The Irish for Clones is *Cluain Eois* which means the 'meadow of the height'. Monaghan's nickname is 'the basket of eggs'. If you want to get a picture of Monaghan country, imagine a basket of eggs. Each egg is a little hill. Take a few of the eggs and smash them. Pour the white and the yolk over the other eggs. Where the white settles is bog water, and the yolk represents deep, clear lakes.

Clones occupied a strategic position where you could see travellers from a distance, a high meadow surrounded by water. Although it is fifty miles from the sea, east or west, it was reachable from the Atlantic through Lough Erne. This watery fact would have been unimportant to the monastic settlement that had resided at Clones from about

69

the fifth century, until the Vikings came out of the waters of the Erne carrying their longboats on their backs. The next time they came to rape, pillage and plunder, they found that the monks had unfairly ensconced themselves in a round tower, eighty feet above the ground (the tower survives to this day). So the Northmen contented themselves with the seaports, and the people of Clones remained a breed apart.

Then the Normans had a go about four hundred years later and they got round to building their own monument fort on a site even more ancient than the Round Tower. They chose the ancient fort about a hundred yards away, but they didn't last more than a couple of years; the majority of them retired to the far south of Ireland where, if the climate did not support the vine, at least it was more congenial than the cold of the North. So, apart from the occasional cattle raid, Clones went to sleep for another four hundred years. Then something happened over which it had no control.

The Protestant Reformation was born. King Henry VIII went through six wives and a few beheadings in an effort to adapt the new religion to English ways. The Catholic Church was not impressed by his method of trying to sire a son and so church land came up for grabs. Henry offered the church demesne at Clones to Sir Henry Duke. Sir Henry had problems like Henry's with the male line and the land passed to a daughter, Anne. She married Sir Frances Rushe; but again a daughter, Eleanor, inherited the estate. She married Sir Robert Loftus, and in 1641 their daughter, Anne, inherited the estate. Anne married a commoner, Richard Lennard Barrett, and between them they had a son, Dacre Lennard Barrett. He inherited the land and his family held on to it until the twentieth century. The Lennard Barretts brought in their own people, and so a family called Mealiff came from Aberdeen, and to this day they run a hotel in the Diamond in Clones. It is called the Lennard Arms after the original Lennard Barretts. And that's how Sandra Mealiff came to be born in Clones on 30 September 1960.

On Barry's mother's side, the Rooneys can trace their origins back nine generations to 1500. That's over a century before the Mealiffs arrived in Clones. Not that they would have begrudged the Mealiffs their good fortune. Still, one could not forget that the planters were newcomers, and when the Counter-Reformation reached Ireland in full spate it was only natural that the Rooneys would sympathize with the Catholic side.

For a time Clones became the centre of a European war. There were dark sectarian sides to the conflict. In 1641, fifteen Protestant men, women and children were taken from the church and slaughtered, but King William's victory at the Battle of the Boyne in 1690 settled the issue in favour of the planters. It is that victory that is celebrated every Twelfth of July. Normality returned to Clones but the lesson had been well learned and, some time in the next century or so, Protestant men began excavating the earth in Clones and they weren't looking for gold. Along with the rest of Ulster, Clones became a Protestant stronghold. The majority Catholic population had to live with that or get out. The Rooneys stayed. In 1936 Katie Rooney was born. She married Pat McGuigan in 1957 and four years later Barry McGuigan was born.

One day Barry and his brother Dermot were playing out behind their mother's shop when they noticed the ground moving. Slowly, like Lazarus emerging from the tomb, it lifted. Out climbed Sammy, David and Sandra Mealiff. Within minutes Barry and Dermot were down in these latter-day catacombs on a journey of discovery. What they found resembled a rabbit warren under the Diamond. Tunnels ran from the bank to the church and from the church to the post office. There were even tunnels that led nowhere. But what ended as child's play in Clones had been started by a fuel that has ignited Ulster sectarianism for centuries: fear.

Cut out all the blarney and look at any Irish town, and you will realize one thing immediately: all the skyscrapers are churches. Clones is no exception. The Church of Ireland, as if to signify the corporate power of the Protestants, stands like a sentry at the top of the Diamond. It is an imposing granite structure with a spire that can be seen for miles in any direction. The church was built with the supremacy of the Word in mind, and the Word was 'no surrender'. The Catholic church is equally imposing. It was built in the 1880s by the McMahons. It has a huge lawn which runs a full two hundred yards steeply up to the church door. The image is of a peasantry agitating, by sheer force of numbers, for Catholic emancipation, for repeal and for the land. These separate interests clashed throughout the nineteenth and early twentieth centuries.

Perhaps during all of this troubled history the tunnels served as a security to the threatened Protestant interest. It is said that guilty men were led from the courthouse by way of the tunnels to meet their fate. Whatever the truth, by the 1960s the tunnels' only function seemed to be as the basis for a good story. The reason that they fell out of operation is one of the paradoxes of Irish history. In 1922 the border was established. The Protestant establishment of Ulster, wishing to hold on to a permanent majority, ditched the Protestants of three counties – Monaghan, Cavan and Donegal – where the Catholic population predominated. Clones, with its Protestant hinterland in Fermanagh, became an Irish Berlin long before the Russians even contemplated the wall. As so often then in Ireland, the border was invisible and ran like a crazy pavement all around Clones. It was not meant to last. The British had set up a Border Commission whereby those towns, like Clones, whose natural commerce was with Fermanagh would get new boundaries once the politicians sat down and worked it all out. Sectarianism put an end to all that. Boundaries were created in men's hearts and it was difficult to rearrange them in reality. The border stayed. Clones for the first time in its existence was thrown into what is called

Southern Ireland and this northern town tried to adapt. At first, things went badly. The Protestant B Specials attacked Clones and the Catholic IRA retaliated. Sectarian bigotry reached its high point in the early Twenties. Then the economic reality set in. Men appeared in uniforms. They were Customs men. The invisible border became a living reality, a mundane day-to-day affair.

What happened to the Protestants after they were more or less abandoned by their northern cousins and by England? Basically nothing. Some left, of course. The rate of Catholic emigration from Clones after the Twenties was about eight per cent and the Protestant rate double that, but still in no way could it be described as a mass exodus. Slowly they realized that they had to live with each other. Blood is thicker than water, prejudice runs deep, take any cliché you like and there is one man who can topple them on their heads. He's called survival. Given the nature of the border, cross-border traffic became the means of exchange. Smuggling, poteen-making, pigs crossing over the border, all required one precondition – a close-knit community. So the divisions of the late Sixties and early Seventies never disturbed Clones too much because a spirit of co-operation on the level of survival already existed and it was difficult to shake this. By 1966 the leader of the Urban Council, a Protestant called Bob Molloy, could say, 'The tolerance meted out to me in my native town provides a striking example to other places where the people are not so tolerant.'

So it was natural, when the Mealiffs emerged from the tunnel, that the McGuigan boys did not pour scalding water on them or run into their own Round Tower. Barry McGuigan in fact had a secret, something he had found that he wanted to give to Sandra. 'I found this ring, it was a wedding ring. I invited Sandra down to the back of this meadow. There were these green leaves. Thick leaves, they were nearly as tall as us. We were lying down kissing, cuddling, making love, all the time hoping our mothers would not come down and find us. I asked Sandra to marry

73

me and she agreed. I remember it well, I was nine at the time and Sandra was older than me, almost ten. That's when I first proposed to her. Then I let things lie for a couple of years and I took up boxing.'

THE THUMB OF
KNOWLEDGE

Finn McCumhaill was one of the *Fianna*. When Kate McGuigan went to christen Barry, the priest told her there was no saint called Barry. She would have to call him Finbarr. *Finn* in Irish means fair. At school Barry learned of Finn McCumhaill's exploits. Finn had the gift of seeing into the future. He could conjure it up simply by sucking his thumb. The first person to eat the salmon of knowledge got this gift. One day Finn picked up a salmon that somebody was cooking, only to let the hot fish drop back into the fire. Sucking his thumb to ease the pain he partook of the flesh of the salmon of knowledge and he could see into the future. When Barry McGuigan sucks his thumb, he also has visions. However, his mind travels in the opposite direction to Finn. All his memories are of the past and they are painful.

In his last year in National School, Barry was slapped for some minor misdemeanour. He was hit on the thumb with a pointer and an old wound was opened. Barry has been in hospital four times with his thumb. Each time he had to have it drained of septic fluid and each time it looked as if the problem was solved ... until it swelled back up. Memories of the thumb irrigation were so painful that Barry preferred to hide his swollen thumb. The most successful way was with his boxing gloves. His father bought him these after the first time he saw him fight.

There was an open-air fête in Cootehill, which is about twelve miles from Clones. A ring was set up at the fair and a local priest matched boys of the same age against one another. Barry and Dermot volunteered. The boys they were facing were taller than either of them, as both the

McGuigans were small for their age. Barry's contest did not last long as his opponent cowered in a corner to get away from an avalanche of blows that came from every conceivable angle. Dermot had more trouble with his opponent who was a good deal bigger than he was and who had done a little boxing. To even things up, the priest gave the verdict to the other boy. Barry insisted on getting into the ring to avenge his brother. The priest smiled at the spunk of Dermot's little brother but advised his father to take him home before he got hurt. Pat was stung by this slight to Barry, so he decided to allow him into the ring for one round to see how he got on. Barry came out of the corner like a bull. The taller boy withstood him for a good two minutes until he finally succumbed to the never-ceasing volcanic eruption that rained all over his bent body. The priest separated them; there was no need to declare a winner. In the crowd was Barry's first critic. After the fight he approached Pat. 'I wouldn't let that poor boy become a fighter,' said the boxing expert,' he has no style. Once it becomes serious he will get himself hurt. You should let him be a swimmer.'

After the Cootehill Fair, Barry pestered his father to buy him a pair of gloves. Eventually Pat ordered them from Johnny McCarthy, a local trader. From the day he got the gloves Barry's hands were never out of them; it didn't look unusual to have them on all the time to protect his injury. Eventually his thumb was almost the size of its counterpart on the boxing glove. At night he kept Dermot awake, constantly turning over in his sleep. Somebody had warned him that he might lose his thumb if he didn't look after it. Reluctantly he followed his mother to Monaghan Hospital to have it looked at.

The hospital decided that it had gone too far. They would have to keep him in for observation. Katie knew Barry's moods better than anybody and she was not at all happy as she left the hospital to look after her other five children.

Barry sat on his hospital bed trying to imagine how he would pass the time. The more he thought about it the more he realized how impossible it would be to stay sane without being able to move around. He was wary of injections ever since he had seen his mother lying on the floor in the kitchen. He began to think that his boxing career might be over because of an amputated thumb.

He decided to escape. He asked the nurse in charge if he could go to the toilet before he changed into his pyjamas. She said yes. From the crack of the toilet door he watched her call the head nurse. She pointed towards the toilet. He closed the door. They were talking about him. The game was up. It was now or never. He opened the toilet door and headed straight down the corridor without looking to left or right. The head nurse made a despairing lunge at him and managed to grab hold of his pullover, but she was dragged along the corridor for twenty feet before she dropped to her hands and knees, the drops from her broken thermometer like little silver angels' tears all over the corridor floor.

Ahead, Barry was racing downstairs. The young nurse caught in the middle of flight was urged on the pursuers' path by a defiant head nurse. At the top of the stairs she called to a porter, 'Stop that boy.' The man lost his grip – and almost lost his arm in the revolving door of Monaghan Hospital.

Barry headed out along the Northern Road towards Armagh. Two male nurses started up a Morris Minor as the head nurse shouted at a gardener from the steps of the hospital. Barry knew from the curses she called out that he was in for a hiding if he was stopped there and then. The gardener dropped his rake in his orderly leaves before he moved this way and that to cut off Barry's path. McGuigan had no choice. With the one good hand left him the eleven-year-old made a fist. Whether it was the sheer power of the punch or a combination of their separate momentums nobody knows, but the result was that the gardener was left sprawled on his back with a cushion of leaves for his sore head.

The pursuit continued. It was Barry's hand that was sore

... there was nothing wrong with his legs. He continued for almost a mile until the car came too close for comfort. Then he cleared a hedge and headed into the open countryside. The pursuers had to abandon their transport and follow on foot. Barry kept going until he collapsed in a heap from utter exhaustion. The men who pursued him stood bent around him, each one asking nothing more than that he stay still until they took him back. Nothing would happen to him. That night, on an unofficial visit, Pat promised Barry that he could join a boxing club when he got out if he behaved himself.

OUT COLD

Pat McGuigan bought a Raleigh Chopper, ostensibly for Katie. It was commandeered by Dermot and Barry. It would prove increasingly difficult anyway for Katie to ride in the latter part of 1971 as she was pregnant with her youngest daughter, Catherine. Barry put the bike to good use on the slopes of the Diamond, skating up planks over milk crates in an improvised daredevil course. Soon it would carry him further afield – to his first boxing club in Laurel Hill, near Wattlebridge.

On the journey out, the ride would take McGuigan about twenty minutes as he flashed along the border roads. The road to Wattlebridge has as many digressions as *Hamlet*, jumping in and out of Northern Ireland, unable to make up its mind where it belongs. Late at night, McGuigan would travel the six miles to Wattlebridge, most nights in fading light, then go to a house close to the gym to get the key to open the old abandoned schoolhouse to train. It was a simple grey limestone building whose only excuse for being locked was that it housed the personal effects of one of Ireland's champion senior boxers, Paul Connolly.

Its windows were too high up for an eleven-year-old boy to know what was going on in the world outside. McGuigan trained on in youthful ignorance for almost a year, returning to his parents in darkness. One night he passed a couple of black plastic bags of the kind that normally contain refuse. Inside were the pitchforked bodies of two men. (Time would lay the deed at the feet of drunken soldiers.) Katie McGuigan could not get it out of her mind that her eleven-year-old son had passed this horror on his way home. Crossing the border was out of the question, even for an innocent boy. McGuigan averted the potential row with his mother by falling off a wall on his way home from school one day. He got eleven stitches in a head-wound. For well over a year boxing was out of the question.

With boxing out of the way, Barry could pursue his other love, soccer. He was a speedy outside-right, fearless in the tackle. By now Dermot had moved on to the technical school, but he and Barry often played together in the same teams. Once, in a Gaelic match, Dermot was attacked by a big full-back. Dermot could always stand his ground, safe in the knowledge 'that the old equalizer was coming up behind'. McGuigan had such prowess as a defender of his brother that opponents usually got the message quickly. At all events, the head-wound didn't worsen.

Barry's boxing inactivity was in many ways a godsend to Katie. Now she had someone to help her in the shop. The year of 1970 had been a traumatic one for her and Pat in their separate careers. The Eurovision Song Contest had brought Pat to the zenith of his career. He had worldwide exposure, and a viewing audience of 500 million. He came third, just behind Cliff Richard. Cliff was a millionaire. At the time Pat McGuigan was earning £20 a week. After the Eurovision his manager increased his wages to £22. The only way out of the contract was out of show business, and three years after his triumph Pat quit the business altogether. 'I was devastated physically and emotionally,' says Pat. 'I was playing six or seven times a week for my wages. These were the boom years of the late Sixties when you could take in thousands at the door. My share was three or four pounds out of that. I loved performing and still do, but my heart wasn't in it.' Pat McGuigan did not leave the road empty-handed. He had a lot of bills and the start of a drink problem.

Pat left the band for the quieter life of a shopkeeper in Clones. Quiet, that is, until the results of the bank strike of 1970 became evident. The McGuigans had cashed cheques left, right and centre, and a lot of them bounced very high. The shortfall was measured in several thousands of pounds.

They had trouble meeting their creditors. In desperation Pat put the shop up for sale. John 'Papa' Rooney, Katie's father, had seen more of the world and he insisted they hold on to the shop and struggle through, no matter what the cost. Over the next few years the cost was a lot of hard work.

John Rooney had at least one other instinct that was sound. He would tell Katie, 'That little boy has got something.' When he saw the McGuigan strength combined with the Rooney discipline and determination, he told Katie, 'Nobody will beat our Barry.'

In the summer of 1973, Barry wanted to take up boxing again. With the innocence of a child, he said that he could work in the shop and train in his spare time. However, his mother and father insisted that he continue his education until he got to the Inter Cert. at least. He would go to Master Duffy in St Patrick's High School, who would look after him.

There is a legendary story of Barry in his first year in the technical school. The new teacher, unused to his ways, saw young master McGuigan playing with something under the desk; his muscles were compressing and relaxing in a definite rhythm. Fearing the worst, he went to see what was up. Under his desk McGuigan was using an instrument to develop hand-muscles.

McGuigan was frustrated by the fact that there was no boxing club in Clones. Eventually, in his first year at the technical school, they found a club in Smithboro. It had only opened a couple of months beforehand. It was the same distance from Clones as Wattlebridge, but this time the road stayed defiantly within the Republic.

Time around Clones is measured first in years and then in seasons. Once these times have been pinpointed for their accuracy, the next best time anchors are birthdays and anniversaries. Deaths are measured by their distance from birthdays. The past is seen as productive and happy, not as a time of bereavement or decay. Frank Mulligan, on the other hand, remembers the time, place and hour that he first met Barry McGuigan. 'It was on 13 January 1974 he walked through the door of the Smithboro club at eight o'clock in the evening. I knew straight away he had something special.'

Frank Mulligan thirsts after some Holy Grail of the soul. He has an addictive personality. He became addicted to McGuigan. 'I couldn't say no to him. You can't say no to McGuigan. If you call that love, well, so be it.'

Mulligan and McGuigan had one thing in common: both were fanatical about fitness. Mulligan had seen the Star in the East, and he followed, no matter where it led him. Initially it just meant helping McGuigan out in the gym in Smithboro; but soon Mulligan was up at the crack of dawn and out running with McGuigan. He became McGuigan's shadow, helping to stock the shelves in the shop. At night he often slept in McGuigan's house . . . though 'slept' would be the wrong word. He was like a watchdog, one eye forever on the dawn, waiting for the first stirrings abroad that were his passport to the fields and their early morning run.

Mulligan even got in the same ring as McGuigan. He remembers being knocked out four times in the one spar. At the end of an evening's session he would have to put out the lights to stop McGuigan continuing.

One night the lights went out, but nobody had a hand on the switch. Mulligan was in the ring, weaving and ducking away from McGuigan. He was overelaborating some errors that he saw in McGuigan's make-up. To put the picture into perspective, McGuigan hit him with an unmerciful right to the jaw. Mulligan went straight down to the floor and didn't stir.

McGuigan, alone after the other boys had gone home, started to revive Mulligan. He lifted his head off the floor to try and waken him. There was no movement from Mulligan. McGuigan slapped his face playfully, certain that Mulligan was lying doggo. Slowly, he became worried. He moved backwards to the door and looked outside. There were only two lights on: one was in the local pub and the other was Father Marren's light. McGuigan mistrusted the pub. The road to Father Marren's seemed too drastic a measure to take. Besides, it was a long way away. He went back inside . . .

Mulligan lay alone and unmoved, exactly where he had left him. He went down to help him again. This time he shook him hard – to no effect. He didn't want to leave him, and at the same time he was terrified of just staying in the gym in case Mulligan might be on his way out. He rushed to the door again and stood outside, lost for action. He saw Father Marren's light again and started to pray . . . deep prayers of beseeching. Inside he heard something move. He rushed in and Mulligan was coming round, oblivious to the young boy's growing anxiety.

From the start, people followed McGuigan to his fights, even as a juvenile. He had something that is hard to define. He didn't run through his juvenile career like a child prodigy intent on glory; but nevertheless there was some attraction that made the McGuigan caravan a force to be reckoned with from his first fight; it was an indefinable charisma that was evident to his first real fan. Cathal Slowey has fought a winning battle all his life with Down's Syndrome. He is a contemporary of Pat's, the son of Charles Slowey who owned the shop in the Diamond before the McGuigans. He became McGuigan's unofficial coach, ducking and weaving and showing the people of Clones the latest punch he and young McGuigan had added to their repertory . . . He was the first disciple. In the company of Pat and Mulligan, he would take the promising young juvenile around the boxing tournaments of Ireland. When they got there, the inevitable question was: 'Smithboro? Where's Smithboro?' They were about to find out.

One day the people of Fermanagh Street in Clones noticed something unusual going on outside the local cinema. Inside, men were roping off a section of the floor. McGuigan was making a home-town debut, and what more appropriate place for the future hero of Clones than the local cinema? His supporting player was Ronan McManus from Enniskillen. McGuigan sent the home crowd out happy with a comprehensive points victory. He had one asset that was rarely seen in the juveniles, an awesome punch. If he got through to an opponent, he could knock him out, and usually he did get through. One opponent, however, dogged his early career. Conor McMahon from Ballyshannon was a tough little boxer. He got a points decision over McGuigan. For months McGuigan waited on a rematch. Again he was beaten. McGuigan dug deep into his reserves of will-power; he would get to McManus, it was only a question of time. He trained and trained, never for a second doubting his superiority. In his third contest he finally got through to the boy from Ballyshannon ...

If there was a wall in front of McGuigan he would not go round it. Eventually he was matched against Jimmy Coughlan who had been five times Irish juvenile champion. In the third round of their contest McGuigan caught up with him and Coughlan was knocked out. His reign was over.

McGuigan was different from all the other juveniles in one respect: intent. McGuigan's intention was to knock his opponent out of the ring. He had deadly intent.

One day in 1975, after a feed of brandy, Mulligan was confined to Monaghan Hospital. He was given twenty-four hours to live. His blood pressure was virtually nil and his kidneys had more or less stopped working. The priest came to anoint him. The one thing that got Mulligan out of bed and out of the hospital was the thought of training with McGuigan. 'Barry used to cry when he'd see me,' Mulligan says. 'He had that much faith in me he hated to see me drinking.'

McGuigan never liked drink. At home, Pat was having his own problems with the demon. The doctor told him he would have to go into hospital to avoid killing himself young. The amazing thing is that McGuigan and his father never had any confrontations during these years. Whenever a confrontation threatened, Barry would take himself off to his room to contemplate. It was during these long hours alone that he built up his iron will-power. True to the McGuigan spirit, one day Pat realized that he *had* to give up the drink. Instead of going into hospital, with its overtones of illness, he took himself off to the bedroom.

Pat McGuigan is not a man that habit has taken the edge off. He can't stand boring routines. He will work at three or four jobs, spreading his energy over twenty-four hours of the day; but if you confined him to Katie's job in the shop, he would lose his mind. He survived in his bedroom because the opponent he was up against had infinite powers of concentration. That opponent was himself. Twenty-one days after he locked himself up, Pat McGuigan walked out clinically independent of drink. It is not a course to be recommended to the normal person. Pat McGuigan is not a normal person.

A FULL-TIME AMATEUR

At the end of 1976, McGuigan had a disappointment. He thought he had done extra well in geography in the Inter Cert., but found out that it was the one subject that prevented him passing his exam. McGuigan is the type of individual who is not at all suited to the Irish educational system. He has amazing concentration, great discipline, an iron will-power and a unique eye for detail, but he is not able to think in the abstract easily. His is the kind of mind that would adapt itself to any given environment and develop survival tactics, but he is not at home in a rigid environment.

He pleaded with his mother and father to let him leave school. They refused and insisted that he get a sound education. A happy compromise was reached: he would stay on at school; Pat would build him a gym. They had an old mill room at the back of the shop which McGuigan's uncle, Paddy Rooney, converted into a beautiful home-made gym. He insulated the roof and built a ring made out of simple rope covered with the tape boxers use as bandages. He fastened the posts to the wall with old-fashioned stay-wires. Two reinforcing beams carried the heavy bags and speed ball. In a corner they built a plywood platform where McGuigan could concentrate on the overhead ball. They put new windows in so McGuigan had plenty of light in his retreat. It was at this time that Dermot began to work out with him.

McGuigan was the only Irish boxer who had a training schedule equal to that of the Europeans. He was doubly lucky in that he met Danny McEntee at this time. McEntee himself was a good boxer, having fought against the great

Nino Benvenuti as an amateur. He refined some of the basics McGuigan had learned in Smithboro. McEntee was as close as you could get to a professional in the amateur game. At the beginning of 1978, McGuigan was still only sixteen but he had his attention focused on the Ulster senior championships. He finally convinced his parents to let him leave school.

McGuigan looked like a boy, but he fought like a demon, to become the youngest ever winner of the Ulster senior championships. A couple of months later, he added the Irish senior title to that honour, and he was chosen to represent Northern Ireland at the Commonwealth Games in Edmonton, Alberta. The sight of the baby-faced McGuigan fighting Tumat Sogolik from Papua New Guinea in the final was astonishing. Sogolik had knocked out all his opponents up to that fight, but McGuigan went after him as if he was the one going to do the knocking out. McGuigan was forced to take two counts but he continued going after Sogolik, scoring all the time, and got the decision to become the youngest ever Commonwealth champion. It seemed that McGuigan could never be beaten in the amateur game.

One night in the summer of 1979, Sandra got her usual phone-call from Barry after a fight abroad. In the background she could hear the crowd shouting a corrupt version of Barry's name. She couldn't quite make out what Barry was saying – he was very close to tears. He had been beaten for the first time as a senior boxer. The Russian, Gladychev, had got the decision over him. There was another fight in progress in the European Juniors in Rimini, but the crowd were keeping up a violent demonstration against the decision in Barry's contest.

Sandra could not believe it; in her mind Barry was unbeatable. He had won gold medals in multi-nation tournaments in Holland and Romania against opponents with twice his experience. Sandra asked Barry whether he had fought well. Barry replied that he had fought the best fight of his life. The judges had voted two-all and then the French judge cast his vote in favour of the Russian. Gladychev went on to win the gold medal, but that was little consolation to Barry. As a sop, his contest was voted 'fight of the tournament'. All the Irish contingent felt that there had been a miscarriage of justice.

Early in 1980, McGuigan accompanied his father to London. Pat was going to see a Harley Street specialist, and Barry was going to take the opportunity to find out what it would be like sparring with the professionals. To discover why Pat wanted to see the best doctors in the world, you have to go back to a day in September, 1979.

'My mother woke me out of my sleep one night at the end of September 1979. "It's your father," she said. "There's been an accident." I asked her to tell me straight. I knew it was serious by the look on her face. I'll never forget it, it was the day the Pope came to Ireland. Eventually I said, "Is Papa dead?" "No," she said, "he's alive." He was alive barely.'

Pat McGuigan had fallen asleep on the Monaghan Road on the way to Clones. When he woke up, the car, was on the grass verge, a couple of hundred yards from Clones, and heading straight for a tree. 'I woke up for one second just before impact. The car took away a few of the posts before hitting the tree. I went straight through the window and hit the tree with my face. Then the car turned over on its back and the driver and I were unconscious. When I came to, the first thing I did was turn off the engine. I kept thinking we were going to burst into flames. I crawled over the driver and got out of the car through the window. When the police came he was still in the upturned car, held firmly in place by his safety belt. The roof where I had been was completely caved in. Had I been wearing a safety belt, I was dead.'

Pat brought McGuigan to the gym where Charlie Magri was training. Charlie Magri was a brilliant professional boxer, soon to be world champion. McGuigan sparred with him and Magri was not seen in a ring for six months afterwards. He had suffered a broken nose.

The only thing that kept McGuigan in the amateur game was the prospect of the Olympic Games for which he was chosen as Ireland's captain. As an amateur McGuigan overtrained. The Irish boxing officials took him away from his home base and kept him and the other boys in confinement at Drogheda. If McGuigan said he had done fifty rounds training the officials told him to do another fifty. McGuigan took them at their word.

After getting through the first contest against a man from Tanzania, he was beaten by Wilfred Kabunda from Zambia. Kabunda was a tall rangy boxer and McGuigan had not yet perfected the body shots that would reduce such opponents to his size. But he should still have beaten Kabunda, who was not in his league, and in his defeat Ireland lost the best prospect for a gold medal they had ever had in boxing.

Winning gold medals at the modern Olympics is a full-time occupation. It was only with time and professional experience that trainers could find out that their job would be to stop Barry training to keep him fresh. All through the Olympic preparations and the events themselves, McGuigan couldn't get one image out of his mind; that image had dark-brown eyes and black hair. Sandra Mealiff, his childhood sweetheart, had grown into a beautiful woman. McGuigan was mad about her for years but was afraid to ask her out, fearing a rejection. Sandra kept her interest under wraps for as long as she could. When McGuigan asked her out to a disco in the early part of 1979, she was delighted to go with him. Soon she would be at his side, night, noon and morning ... early morning. McGuigan got up at dawn to train and Sandra was always there, counting the number of punches he threw in a round.

While he was in Moscow for the Olympics, McGuigan saved all his expenses for the engagement ring he was going to buy Sandra when he returned home. A couple of weeks after he got back, McGuigan proposed, and Sandra agreed.

Apart from working in the shop, the only other real way Barry could think of to support a family was as a professional boxer. His mother would be against that decision ... but Barry knew if he broke the news to her gently, then she would not go against his wishes.

—— Part Three ——

THE PUBLIC LIFE

SOUTH OF THE BORDER

Bernard Joseph 'Barney' Eastwood had seen Barry McGuigan on TV. He was instantly struck by his courage and stamina, but deep down at a different level he recognized some quality in McGuigan that others couldn't see. He knew for certain that McGuigan was as territorial inside the ring as he himself was outside it. Divine instinct told him they would make a great team. He went to see McGuigan fight in the amateurs, and let it be known that he was interested. So was McGuigan. They arranged a meeting in the Ballymascanlon Hotel in Dundalk. Barry would be there with his father, Pat.

Eastwood travelled to the meeting with his old friend Davey Donnelly, 'Davey the Hat' as he was known. Donnelly and Eastwood talked for a time about McGuigan as a prospect. Eastwood was convinced that the young fighter needed more than the three rounds of amateur boxing to be at his best, but the question still remained: was McGuigan good enough to hang the revival of professional boxing in Belfast around his neck? Davey asked Eastwood why he thought so much of the young man from Clones. Eastwood pointed to his chest and then, as he made a circle that encompassed his upper body, said, 'He has a heart that big.' For a time he and Davey fell silent. As they approached the border, Eastwood's mind went back to his first encounter with boxing. It was during the Second World War.

Eastwood was a boy of seven in 1939. It was terrible ... everything was rationed. All you got were rations, and rations was what was left when you took the fun out of life. Sugar was in short supply and people started making imitation sweets that tasted awful. Barney, the little boy, thought it was the same all over. Then his mother told him about Dublin. Dublin was over the border. The people in Dublin were not at war with the Germans. Dublin in the early 1940s was like an unending bazaar to a small boy from Northern Ireland. He stayed with his mother in a hotel called Wynns and the furthest they walked was round the corner to Clearys where you could buy all sorts of stuff that had not been on sale for ages where he lived. Every day he asked his mother the same thing. Every day she refused. At the end of their week's holiday in a fit of extravagance she bought him the boxing gloves he coveted.

On the train home his mother was very nervous, he didn't know why. They were stopped at the border at a place called Gorawood. Men in uniform got on the train. They would ask people to open their bags, and then pass on. When they came to Barney's mother they asked her to get out on the platform. They were joined by more men in uniform. Their bags were emptied. The men started to take away all the things his mother had bought for the house, even some of the things she had brought with her to Dublin. They even took her watch. Barney held on to his parcel. The man in uniform asked him to open it. He refused. The man insisted. He hung on to his present for dear life. Eventually the man pulled it from him but Barney held on to one glove. The man tore the wrapping off the other glove and said that he would have to confiscate them. Barney still wouldn't let go. One of the other men in uniform said, 'Let the boy have the gloves,' and thus was born B. J. Eastwood's love for boxing.

The meeting in the Ballymascanlon Hotel was something of a formality. Each party had decided in advance that they wanted to work with the other. All that remained to be ironed out were the little nagging questions each side wanted to ask about the other. When Pat McGuigan was on the road showband managers suddenly found out that a hit record could get you three to four times your normal appearance fees. It only took a couple of thousand records sales to get you into the charts, and ten thousand would

96

make you number one. So within a few years managers' garages were full of awful records that nobody wanted. To get to the top of the international charts, these little Caesars reckoned all you needed was a garage big enough to hold all the records. So Pat was wary of little men who talked big and asked you to sign on the dotted line.

But the first signs from Eastwood were encouraging. He offered no fat contracts; all he offered were his services. So far so good. Pat and Barry had a vision. They asked Eastwood whether he shared it. Yes, Eastwood answered, Barry could be world champion. All it needed was organization.

If business structures are organized around will-power, then Eastwood's business was on a sound footing. He had started from his mother's little shoe shop in Cookstown, bought his own pub in Carrickfergus at the age of twenty, and by his mid-thirties he owned the biggest string of betting shops in Northern Ireland. By the time he reached the half-century he was becoming tired of his gambling empire and needed something to stretch his iron will-power and business brain.

He asked McGuigan what he would have to drink. Barry would have a soda water and Pat would have a watered soda. They couldn't be prevailed upon to indulge in the traditional Irish toast to the beginning of a partnership. Barry, it turned out, had rarely been in a pub in his life and had never once had an alcoholic drink. Eastwood was delighted: he had seen many a venture come a cropper under the guidance of the demon drink. Barry told Eastwood he would never drink. Eastwood was very impressed: he recognized will-power.

Before he left, Eastwood told Barry that he wanted him to think about what he was doing. He would give him as long as he wanted; he didn't want him to rush into anything. Pat asked Eastwood about strategy. Eastwood replied that no expense would be spared to get Barry to the top. He would have the best coaches and trainers. Money for Barry himself would be scarce at the beginning but, if Barry succeeded, then the rewards would be huge. It all depended on Barry being a winner.

They shook hands and walked out to the car park. Eastwood got into his Rolls-Royce. Everything about this man was impressive. The McGuigans asked themselves what he knew about boxing.

Eastwood had learned his entrepreneurial trade at about eight years of age. During the war, the American troops who were stationed in Norhtern Ireland staged boxing tournaments. They quickly developed a liking for young Eastwood as he knew the lie of the land. He had no scruples about getting the servicemen the odd small bottle of whiskey that they wanted. If any of the locals wanted tickets for the army boxing, the man to see was the boy Eastwood.

The army had a scouting policy whereby they found the best amongst the local youth and had them spar with each other. Eastwood was able to hold his own against his opponents except for one young chap called Murphy. Contests between these two brought the neighbours from far and wide. Eastwood could never understand why he couldn't beat him. One day he was explaining his dilemma to a Texan who smoked Camel cigarettes. 'It's because you both are southpaws,' said the American. Eastwood, still a boy, didn't know what a southpaw was. 'A southpaw is an unorthodox fighter,' explained the soldier. 'He stands with his right foot forward. Murphy is a southpaw, the same as you. He must have the same difficulty beating you as you do beating him.'

Thus was born Eastwood's respect for coaching and tactics. He is always willing to listen. He also knew that boxing had to be organized just like any other business. The army cards were top class, with the odd professional thrown in for good measure. People came from near and far to see the contests. It was an escape from the austerity of the war. Now Belfast was in the middle of another war. It had gone on twice as long as the Second World War and people were tired of it. They needed some outlet, and Eastwood was going to give it to them. He was a gambler.

He was staking all on one young man from Clones, a man with the heart of a lion but still with a long way to go. Eastwood would give him all the help he could.

Eastwood went home that night, convinced of a fairy-tale dream that depended in the first instance on a phone-call from Clones. He didn't have long to wait. The McGuigans had made up their minds before they arrived back in Clones. They would go with Eastwood.

In March 1981 the contract was signed.

ON THE ROAD

Two roads lead out of Clones to the world. One goes to Dublin and the other to Belfast. Pat McGuigan took the road to Dublin. It brought him eventually to the summit of his fame at the Eurovision Song Contest in London. Dublin had a more cosmopolitan atmosphere than Belfast. It had once been the second largest city in the British Isles, the capital of colonial Ireland, and it was from its environs that ambitious people went on to greater fortune. Now Belfast was in the middle of the troubles. For a time in the early Seventies most people equated playing in Belfast with playing in Beirut or Hanoi . . . a place to be avoided if at all possible. The people of Belfast, however, hungered for diversion. They needed a hero they could all get behind. In the first year of the Eighties, Belfast was beginning to come out of the doldrums, and Barry McGuigan came along that road from Clones at just the right time.

Barry hadn't been long in the city when Eddie Shaw, his new trainer, asked him home to tea. Barry had been to Belfast to train for the amateurs but he had never spent much time in it. Belfast in the mid-Seventies was not a place you loitered in, with or without intent. Barry followed Eddie to the bus that would take them up the Falls Road. Parallel with the Catholic Falls is the Protestant Shankill. Both of them run steeply towards the mountains that surround Belfast as if panting for breath. These are the mean streets of Belfast. The city itself has one of the best settings imaginable, lying between an expansive lough and the Divis Mountains.

The problem with the city is that it grew up too quickly. In the middle of the last century, people poured into it from the famine-starved countryside at a rate that saw Belfast double its population every decade. Catholic and Protestant workers were housed within the narrowest of confines. They had enough in common to join together in 1906 in a common strike. Today, as Barry journeys to the upper Falls, he will see the invisible border at Clones made manifest in the barricade that separates the embittered communities. Rocks that seem to have rolled down the mountain in a flow of lava stand at the various pubs doing mute sentry duty against car bombers. The street-names on the lower Falls have been converted to Irish, but the murals that are being painted need no decoding. Belfast is in the middle of a hunger strike and you could shave yourself against the tension in the air.

Mary, Eddie's wife, has the tea ready and Barry looks around at the collection of medals and cups that Eddie won as an amateur fighting for Ireland. In one corner is a memento of Eddie's reign as bantamweight champion of Ulster, seventeen years before McGuigan. Tonight McGuigan will stay with Eddie. Tomorrow they go to Dublin. Ever since McGuigan came to Belfast, Eastwood has tried to make the conditions as close as possible to home. Hollywood, County Down, is the kind of place where the houses as well as the people have names. McGuigan has stayed with the Eastwood family at their home on the sweet lough slopes. Frances Eastwood treated McGuigan like one of her own children. The change is not too abrupt from the townland of Clones. Every evening as he leaves Gortnagreen to train in his grandfather's boots, McGuigan can see the odd hillside lamp on the opposite shore sweep down into a riotous assembly of light around Belfast.

Tonight he's part of that illumination as Eddie Shaw takes him in a taxi to the National Forresters Club at the bottom of the Falls Road. There he will meet the beginning of his Belfast fan-club; these men know their boxing. Eddie himself is from the Immaculata Club which produced two Irish medal-winners at the Olympics. As the night goes on, the company will be swelled by men who were themselves boxers: Barney Wilson as a professional was looked after by Eastwood; Jim Jordan was an Ulster senior champion. Eddie introduces Sean Feeney who will drive him to Dublin. On 10 May they are joined by Ned McCormack and Daniel Mulleady, and they set off towards Dublin in a Renault 16 to conquer the world.

At his first fight Barry witnessed the cruel reality of professional boxing. Headlining the bill was Charlie Nash of Derry. His thirtieth birthday fell on 10 May. On that May night in Dalymount Park in the open air his professional career virtually came to an end. A year previously in a world title fight he had Jim Watt of Scotland on the floor, only to be stopped himself in the fourth round. Tonight he was defending his European title against Joey Gililisco of Spain. He took a bad beating before he was knocked out in the sixth round. Nash spent his thirtieth birthday in a Dublin hospital.

It was up to McGuigan to provide some sort of comfort to the open-air spectators. He was fighting Selvin Bell. By the end of the first round he had weighed his opponent up, and he came out in the second determined to finish the fight. Some good left hooks caught Bell in a corner before he was almost bent double with a vicious right to his body. Bell fell through the ropes and McGuigan almost followed him in his eagerness. The referee jumped in to save Bell. The fight was over in the second round.

Barry McGuigan's next fight was on a bill even higher up the ladder of professional boxing. Eastwood had managed to get him on to a world title fight bill. Jim Watt was defending his lightweight title at Wembley Pool against Alexis Arguello. The Eastwood camp wanted McGuigan to take it easy in the first few rounds of his fight with Gary Lucas. By the start of the third they could restrain him no longer, and by the fourth round Lucas was cowering under a barrage of blows. Again the referee stopped the fight.

Now Eastwood had a problem. Watt had been defeated, and there were very few prospective top-class bills to which he could attach McGuigan. Going to America was out of the question for the time being. They had to find a matchmaker closer to home. Eastwood had known Paddy Byrne since the early Sixties. Paddy was an affable Dubliner who had worked his way to a respected career in boxing after starting life as a paper-seller on the streets of Dublin. He made a match in the UK for McGuigan against a good young boxer called Peter Eubanks in the fighter's home-town of Brighton.

Eastwood and McGuigan learned more from the Eubanks fight than they did from twenty subsequent bouts. Lesson number one: never again would McGuigan fight two-minute rounds. McGuigan's biggest asset was his strength. He hadn't enough time in two minutes to get to his opponent and, when he did knock Eubanks down in the second round, there wasn't enough time to finish him off. Lesson number two: fighting in the opponent's home-town can be dangerous. The inspiration the crowd gives to the home-town fighter can just be enough to shade the decision in his favour. Eubanks won the fight by half a point. Lesson number three: to get anywhere in the fight game you have to be one hundred and one per cent fit. In the seventh and eighth rounds McGuigan slowed down. After being ahead early on, it was probably this image of a tiring McGuigan that swung the decision in Eubanks' favour. Lesson number four: Paddy Byrne was a good matchmaker. The next fight would be in Belfast. They had to take the bull by the horns. Jean Marc Renard was a world-class boxer . . . Eight three-minute rounds.

There is no such thing as a right or wrong style in boxing; there is only the most effective style. At this stage in his career McGuigan was ineffective defensively. He stood too upright so that his centre of gravity was often misplaced. He walked forward instead of stalking. Often his legs were parallel. There is nothing wrong with any of this unless you get hit. In his fight with Renard, McGuigan got hit with a good right. He was walking on to the punch and he was totally off balance. He hit the deck. He was up as quick as he went down and had the presence of mind to head straight for a neutral corner. McGuigan recovered from the knockdown to win convincingly. Once he got inside Renard's defence he caught him repeatedly with short sharp punches.

The Eubanks and Renard fights were extremely good for McGuigan psychologically: they lifted pressure off his shoulders. No longer would he have to defend an unbeaten professional record, and he had been to the canvas, and recovered to win. They proved that he had the mental resources to be a champion. After the Eubanks decision, which was considered unjust by many ringside commentators, McGuigan was in tears. Alone in the dressing room, Eastwood tried to console him.

After McGuigan had listened for a time he looked Eastwood in the eye. 'Do you think I can be world champion?' he asked.

'Yes,' said Eastwood, 'and I was never more sure than tonight.'

McGuigan stopped crying. He wouldn't do that again in public for four years.

FAMINE LACE

Sandra Mealiff had a special piece of lace she wanted worked into a dress. The only person who knew how to adapt Clones lace lived on the slopes of Carnmor. Clones lace was a craft forgotten for two or three generations around Clones.

After the famine, an English lady attached to the local Protestant church introduced the idea as a way of making some hard-earned cash from a cottage industry. What was a piece of finery to the rest of the world was a method of survival to the people around Clones. The intricacy of the work demanded daylight. The starving countryfolk worked by any light they could get until their own light faded. To be directed to the person who knew most about the delicate cloth was to be directed to a blind lady. Survival was through the eye of the needle. Eventually the industry collapsed. People were no longer literally starving and the only people making real money out of it were the middlemen. There are many stories as to why it actually collapsed. One version is that a rich aristocratic British lady saw the pain inflicted by the art and made the lace as unwelcome on the mainland as Jewish oranges in Iran. This version is mostly associated with Protestant opinion around Clones. The Catholic version would be that once the people no longer needed the art just to stay alive, it became something associated with the famine and meant that only families that were actually down and out would contemplate letting their daughters near it. Clones lace was stigmatized.

The dress that Sandra Mealiff wanted to work the lace into was her wedding dress. It says something about her attitude to the past: she doesn't live in it ... neither does Barry. He wasn't interested in attitudes to him marrying a Protestant. He was in love with Sandra and that was that. To Barry and Sandra, too many people used the past to justify the unhappy way they lived in the present. Very few had a vision of the future. Barry and Sandra saw their future together and they weren't going to let anybody stand in their way. They would be married in a Protestant church and the children would be brought up Catholic. End of story.

Only two people stood in Barry's way. One of them was from Puerto Rico. His name was Terry Pizarro. The other was Peter Eubanks. Barry had to avenge that defeat before he could get married in peace.

Eastwood decided that Ken Buchanan could teach McGuigan a lot about the fight game, and so he brought him over to Belfast to eradicate some of McGuigan's faults. From his amateur days McGuigan had a habit of turning his left hook in just before impact, as if it was a screwdriver. Buchanan asked him why; McGuigan had no answer. All it meant was that the impact of the punch was reduced and the area of the fist that actually landed was limited. Buchanan became something of a father-figure to McGuigan, teaching him to keep his temper in check and correcting mistakes in his posture and stance. Every time McGuigan threw a left hook, Buchanan hit him below the heart. McGuigan thought about that.

The Ulster Hall is a cavernous building near the centre of Belfast. With its old-style pipe organ, it's the kind of place you would expect to see a religious revivalist meeting taking place. The revival Eastwood was after was of a secular nature. Everything was done to get the crowds out. At the first contest in the hall a lot of the old-time fight fans had turned out. They liked what they saw. They would be back. Eastwood had filled the hall for the Renard fight, though not all the tickets had been sold! McGuigan's second opponent in Belfast was an unknown quantity. He soon made himself well known. 'Terrible' Terry Pizarro could talk up a storm, and he filled the hall.

Eastwood told Pizarro he would put up his picture all over his office if he knocked McGuigan out as he had boasted. As the old Jack Solomons fanfare played, Pizarro stepped into the ring. McGuigan followed, with Eastwood, the promoter, in dinner jacket. When he was introduced, Pizarro danced out backwards like a Roman gladiator. That was the best part of his performance. When McGuigan hit him a few times in the first round Pizarro put his gloves up to his head to protect himself. The only problem was that if he kept them there he couldn't hit McGuigan. The referee warned him that he would have to put up a fight. His method of doing this was to throw lefts and rights ... together ... like a demented oarsman with the water coming up over his head. McGuigan toyed with him and Pizarro was happy when the referee stopped it in the fourth round. McGuigan's body shots, he said, were 'lethal'. After the Pizarro contest there was only one fight that would fill the Ulster Hall with an expectant Belfast crowd: the return with Peter Eubanks.

It was during this contest that the Belfast roar was conceived. It wouldn't have a real life of its own until McGuigan got to the King's Hall, but even in embryonic form it was a force to be reckoned with. The battle with Eubanks was a ding-dong affair until McGuigan finally got on top in the sixth round through his superior strength. He was throwing every shot in the book at the man from Brighton when the referee heard what he thought was the bell. He separated the fighters and pointed them at their corners. When he realized his mistake it was too late. Eubanks had survived. His reprieve only lasted until the eighth round. This time McGuigan wanted to leave no doubt as to the outcome. He came forward relentlessly. The referee had no alternative but to stop the fight to prevent Eubanks taking any more punishment. The crowd went wild.

Less than a week later, McGuigan was in the Protestant church at the top of the Diamond, relatively unmarked, for his wedding to Sandra. Dermot, his brother, was the best man and the bridesmaid was a cousin of Sandra's, Gillian McMurray. After the ceremony the McGuigans, as the canon called them, headed down the steep steps of the Protestant church and around the corner into Fermanagh Street. A few hundred yards took them to the Catholic church on Church Hill where they had their own private little ceremony. A definition of ecumenical: worldwide, universal. Soon the McGuigans would be the most ecumenical couple ever to come out of Ireland.

PADDY THE IRISHMAN

After a one-sided points win against the Spaniard Luis La Sagra, McGuigan started stopping his opponents with a regularity that was frightening. Perhaps his strongest opponent in the first six months of 1982 was Angelo Licata, ranked number seven in Europe. In round two a white towel fluttered into the Ulster Hall ring. The man throwing it knew more than the crowd. McGuigan had destroyed his fighter's rib-cage, the way a power saw cuts down a tree. Every breath he took was like filling the burst balloon of his lungs with poison. Nobody could stay in the ring for more than three rounds with McGuigan without the threat of permanent damage to his health.

Before Barry and Sandra could make her a great-grand-mother, Mary McGuigan died. She had always remembered the early death of her eldest son, Dermot, but then she had the protection of youth to get her over the trauma. She had survived her husband, James, by almost fourteen years when her son Kevin died. Kevin was perhaps Barry's biggest fan. A carpenter by trade, he worked a lot with asbestos and there is no doubt that this contributed to his early death from cancer. Despite his unbounded energy and uncontrollable temper, Kevin had so often been sick in his last few years that nobody paid any particular attention when he fell ill in the early part of 1981. Within a couple of months he was dead. His mother did not survive him a year. After her funeral in 1982 Barry had only one surviving grandparent. McGuigan's dream had always been to come back to Clones to show them his world title. He was still three fights away from even a British title, and they were gone.

By now Barry had worked his way up the rankings of the British featherweight division. The only other challenger who ranked with him was Paul Huggins of Hastings. They would fight an eliminator, with the winner going on to meet Steve Sims for the title. Huggins was a non-stop action fighter, rough and ready, and a fight with him would fill the Ulster Hall to overflowing. There was just one slight problem in matching them for the eliminator: McGuigan was not a British citizen. Most of the other Irish fighters in the past qualified as British automatically because they were born in Northern Ireland or qualified as British subjects because they were born in the Republic before 1949. In that year the Irish Government withdrew the Republic from the Commonwealth, and if anybody from Southern Ireland wanted to fight for the British title he had to become a British citizen. The official communication from the British Boxing Board of Control confirmed this in their announcement of the Final Eliminator: 'This is subject to McGuigan becoming a naturalized British subject in accordance with Reg. 31, p. 4. The contest to take place in September.' Barry had four months to become a British subject. It had taken a lot of Irish people eight hundred years to go in the opposite direction. McGuigan knew his history well: his grandfather had been a member of the old Irish Republican Army.

All his life James McGuigan had been an Irishman first, a Northern Irishman second, and a British subject third. When Barry and Sandra first went out together, they would often visit Mary McShane who recounted her memories of the years in Donaghmore, Co. Tyrone. When the War of Independence broke out James McGuigan was arrested by the newly formed Black and Tans. It was the first phase of what later became known by the euphemistic term 'internment'. In essence, it was the mass jailing of a large part of the Catholic population of the largely Protestant Six Counties. James McGuigan was taken out of his house in the bottoms of his pyjamas and was led to a huge open-backed truck, the soldier in charge hitting him with the butt of a rifle to hurry his ascent; but there was no way he could do it, as his hands were tied behind his back. Mary's sister Margaret tried to intervene and the soldier put the bayonet of his rifle to her throat and told her to keep quiet or else. James McGuigan spent nine months in Ballykinlar Camp and, when he was finally released, Mary his wife hoped they could rebuild their fortunes which had declined as a result of his incarceration. Within a couple of months he was picked up again and he spent the next two and a half years in captivity on the prison ship the *Argenta* and in Magilligan Camp in Derry. Finally the RUC decided they would intern him no longer so they drove him to the border and, like Charlie Chaplin, they left him there. Penniless, with no future, James McGuigan followed the railway tracks into the nearest Southern Irish town. That town was Clones.

Although she may have felt it was an injustice, Mary McGuigan never bore any grudges that Sandra and Barry could see. Sandra Mealiff was her favourite visitor and she was delighted when Barry and Sandra announced their engagement. She never bore any grudge against Protestants. Protestants had their own crosses to bear. Sandra's cousins, the Eakins, live in Claudy, Co. Derry. In 1970 Sandra was on holiday with them. There was only a year or so in age difference between Sandra and Catherine so they were very close. On the Monday after they went home from their holiday, Catherine Eakin was dead. She was cleaning her mother's windows when a bomb went off at a garage close by. It broke her arm and cracked her skull. Mark, her brother, was standing close by at the time, but miraculously he was unhurt. He ran home past a crumpled body in the street. When he went out to look for his sister he went in the opposite direction to where Catherine lay. He didn't recognize her. She died on the way to hospital. When Sandra and Barry were married the bouquet went on her grave.

McGuigan knew enough by the age of fourteen to know that non-sectarianism would be a driving force in his life.

Every time McGuigan drives more than twenty miles from Clones in any direction, the road is littered with memories of innocent people who have died as a result of the troubles. McGuigan is a proud Irishman but he has an immense fear of sectarianism. 'I remember once at school there was a fight. It was a light-hearted affair. Suddenly one of the boys got hurt and he turned around and called the other boy a loyalist pig. Well, the temperature went up ten degrees in the next few seconds. It was frightening.' McGuigan will not be intimidated into taking sides. Every step McGuigan took retracing his grandfather's footsteps back into Northern Ireland was a courageous step of reconciliation.

When Pat McGuigan was asked, did McGuigan fight for Ireland or England, he replied that as an amateur Barry fought for his country and as a professional he fought for money. In his first year as a boxer he didn't earn very much. Sandra had opened a hairdressing salon with McGuigan's sister Sharon in May, but that wouldn't be a profitable venture for some time. The McGuigans went into debt banking on the future success of Barry as a boxer.

There was no structure for the professional game of boxing in the Republic of Ireland. Every Irish boxer who ever fought for the British title had taken out British citizenship: Spike McCormack and his sons, the gorgeous Gael Jack Doyle, Mick Leahy. McGuigan was different. He was a Catholic married to a Protestant who lived on the border. In the eyes of some people, taking out British citizenship was not just a question of bread and butter. It was a political stance. They saw it as the perfect opportunity for the British to exploit McGuigan. The only problem with this theory is that initially the British turned him down.

The application form had read like this: 'Registration of Commonwealth Citizens etc. as Citizens of the United Kingdom and Colonies'. People entitled to apply could be a citizen of any of the following countries:

Antigua and Barbuda, Australia, The Bahamas, Bangladesh, Barbados, Belize, Botswana, Canada, Cyprus, Dominica, Fiji, The Gambia, Ghana, Grenada, Guyana, India, Jamaica, Kenya, Kiribati, Lesotho, Malawi, Malaysia, Malta, Mauritius, Nauru, New Zealand, Nigeria, Papua New Guinea, St Lucia, St Vincent and the Grenadines, Seychelles, Sierra Leone, Singapore, Solomon Islands, Sri Lanka, Swaziland, Tanzania, Tonga, Trinidad and Tobago, Tuvalu, Uganda, Vanuatu, Western Samoa, Zambia or Zimbabwe.

If you colour those countries a regal red in your mind's eye you get some idea of the extent of the Empire at one time. Still, Ireland wasn't there. It existed under a different heading which said simply 'or the Republic of Ireland'. Ireland's history was different from all the other dominions. It was sadder and more painful. The necessary qualifications were a special relationship with Northern Ireland and five years' residence. McGuigan did have a special relationship with Northern Ireland. He had won a gold medal for them at the Commonwealth Games in Edmonton. He hadn't been resident the full five years, but it seemed impossible to Stephen Eastwood that they would turn down the application of someone who had driven seventy miles a day at his own expense as an amateur to fight for that country. Indeed it was part of the complexity of the relationship of Ireland and England that he should even have to apply, having fought for Northern Ireland already.

On 8 June 1982 a letter reached Eastwood House saying that as McGuigan did not fulfil the necessary requirement he could not be considered for citizenship. McGuigan as ever had to fight for everything he got. Many people who had seen Barry box and the effect it had in uniting the people of Belfast spoke up on his behalf. His greatest defender was Paddy Devlin himself, an avid boxing fan. 'Oh, I did all I could for Barry,' says Paddy. 'He doesn't allow any ill-will or hostility or triumphalism to flow from his victories. He's boxing for all of us. He's boxing for all the people of Ireland, all the people of Ulster and especially the people of Belfast. With him there's no feeling of superiority or inferiority, and everybody's behind him. We applied on the basis of his grandparents so that he could fight for the title.' The wheel had come full circle. James McGuigan was an Ulsterman, and Barry would qualify for British citizenship. On 1 August 1982 he finally got clearance. Maybe James McGuigan had not suffered for nothing after all. Everybody was happy. Only one man begrudged the action taken. His name was Paul Huggins.

THIS SPORTING LIFE

Meanwhile Barry had to go to London to fight the West African bantamweight champion Young Ali.

Close by the Grosvenor House Hotel in Park Lane there is a statue to an Irishman, Arthur Wellesley, Duke of Wellington. Achilles stands, an imposing figure, every part of his body down to his esteemed ankles cast from melted-down cannon used at various wars throughout the nineteenth century. On 6 June 1982 Barry McGuigan drove past Achilles, stopped at the door to the Grosvenor House Hotel and entered the lobby. Just inside on the left-hand-side wall is a painting commemorating one of the most auspicious occasions ever witnessed in the hotel. In it the painter is seated conveniently behind the Prince of Wales as he watches an ice-show. The skaters are dressed in motley and some are even dancing on stilts. The Prince appears to be having a good time. He and his entourage are smoking large cigars, and the rest of the company seem contented enough with the ice-show. The room in which all this is taking place is the Great Room. The Prince is seated on the lower balcony, surrounded by royalty. On the upper balcony sit the Lords, Ladies and Peers of the Realm.

The room as it stands today is almost the same as it was on that auspicious occasion in 1932 except that the lone chandelier has been replaced by no less than eight spectacular cousins that look like illuminated wedding dresses when the light is switched on. The floor in the centre of the room rises to make a natural arena.

This was not the Ulster Hall. This was fashionable London in June. The fight had been organized by the World Sporting Club. Membership of the Club was an honour. When the Club organized an event they did it well. The food matched the surroundings, which were first class. The atmosphere would be a thousand miles from that in the little Belfast hall. Displays of partisanship were frowned upon here. One did not cheer either one's champion or his opponent . . . that was not fair play. At the end of the round you clapped, depending on the level of expertise manifested by the two fighters.

It was a black-tie affair. As Barry came towards the ring he would have noticed more white coats than was normal at a fight. These were not stewards, however, they were waiters bringing drinks to the tables. Dinner had been served and now everybody was relaxing as the contests began. McGuigan got into the ring to a good round of applause. Young Ali came out. He only spoke a few words of English. He too got a round of applause. It must have spurred Ali on because that night he fought with the heart of a lion.

The bell rang for the first round. The fighters teased each other out. It is impossible to know what went through Young Ali's head that night. Here was a poor fighter from Africa in the most plush surroundings of his life, fighting a white man, watched by white men – and nobody was shouting McGuigan on. It must have had the quality of a dream. In the following rounds it would turn into a nightmare.

McGuigan for the first time in ages could actually hear what was going on in the other corner. In broken English Young Ali kept telling his corner, 'Too strong, too strong.' As if to indicate what he meant, he kept holding his gloves up to his jaw. The African's heart proved bigger and stronger than his body. In the fourth and fifth rounds McGuigan was surprised by the level of aggression Ali could mount. At the end of each round the knowledgeable crowd applauded enthusiastically. On the second balcony looking down, Alfie McLean, a life-long friend of Barney Eastwood, sat uncomfortably in his tuxedo. He felt sure he would be able to get out of it soon.

At the start of the sixth round McGuigan was amazed that Ali was still in there, considering the amount of punishment he had taken. Whether through resilience or tiredness, he had stopped protesting to his corner. McGuigan will never forget the sixth round. 'I hit him round the temples a lot. He was tired. The damage always occurs when a man is fatigued. I hit him with a punch right between the eyes. The eyes spun round in his head like the numbers on a slot machine. He fell. I stood back and he fell straight to the floor. I looked over at Mr Eastwood and he made a quick motion as if to say, "It's all over", but there was a worried look on his face. He pointed to a neutral corner and I went there, all the time looking at Young Ali.'

Up on the balcony the Belfast contingent were having a hard time behaving like gentlemen. Brian Eastwood turned to Big Alfie in euphoria. 'He'll never get up,' said Brian, not understanding the full import of what he was saying. Big Alfie was looking at the figure on the floor below him lying quiet and silent, the only motion disturbing the unnecessary count being that of the cigar smoke from a hundred private tables. Big Alfie repeated Brian's words and then added, 'That's right. He'll never get up. He's dead.'

Like McGuigan, Big Alfie underestimated the resilience of the bantamweight champion of West Africa. He rose to his feet with some assistance from his corner. McGuigan went to see how he was but was brusquely pushed away. Eastwood took him upstairs. The mood in the dressing room was sombre. Downstairs Young Ali was walking unassisted from the ring to warm applause. He fell a second time. This time he wouldn't get up. An ambulance was called. His cornermen improvised as best they knew how. They laid him out on one of the dining tables and wrapped a tablecloth around him for comfort. After about fifteen minutes he was carried from the Grosvenor House out into the night air and rushed to hospital. Sean Kilfeather was reporting another McGuigan victory back to his head office in Dublin when he heard an unusual sound. 'I heard this sound and I looked around and they were taking Young Ali out on a stretcher. He was totally inert but there was a strange noise in his throat. It was an eerie sound. I suppose it was the death rattle.' Young Ali wouldn't succumb. He hung on in a coma for dear life.

A PLAGUE
ON YOUR HOUSE

The only thing McGuigan could do was to carry on as if
everything were normal. Young Ali was in a coma for six
months. McGuigan couldn't think about the inevitable. His
father, Pat, lifted some of the burden from his shoulders,
ringing the hospital every night to see how Ali was faring.
Every night the McGuigan family prayed that he would
survive. Every detail of the fighter's personal background
became known to McGuigan. He had a wife in Nigeria who
was pregnant with his child.

McGuigan took to the hills, walking his dogs. To
stop boxing now would be to admit that Young Ali would
never recover. It was best to act as if nothing had happened.

Four months after the Ali fight, McGuigan was in the
ring against Jimmy Duncan. Duncan boxed bravely. From
deep down inside, McGuigan mustered all the aggression
he could find. In the third round he threw a right and
suddenly he was looking into the eyes of Young Ali. He
stood mesmerized for a moment. McGuigan was fighting
two opponents. One of them hit him an unmerciful punch.
McGuigan retaliated and stopped Jimmy Duncan in the
fourth round. It appeared as if he could never shake off the
other.

Young Ali was flown home to Lagos. While the African
lay in a hospital thousands of miles away, McGuigan faced
a tough new opponent, Paul Huggins, in the Ulster Hall.
The fight with Huggins was the most important so far of
McGuigan's career. The winner would go on to fight for
the British title. Huggins was a Rocky Marciano-style
fighter, willing to absorb punishment to get inside to do his

own damage. He was tough, aggressive and confident. McGuigan would need to be at the top of his form to beat him.

Huggins came forward relentlessly from the opening bell. McGuigan picked him off with every punch in the book. McGuigan wondered when the man from Hastings would learn his lesson and stop coming forward. He never did. McGuigan would have to teach him. In the fourth round McGuigan suddenly stopped still and fought Huggins inside, toe to toe. Usually that means that the boxers are just exchanging blows to see who has the greater strength. Not with McGuigan. He boxed brilliantly inside, hitting Huggins with everything and at the same time avoiding all the slugger's punches. Huggins was forced to step back. The next time he came forward McGuigan hit him with left jabs, right and left hooks. He even hit him with a punch he seldom uses, a lightning-fast uppercut. Huggins stood in the centre of the ring and shook his head as if to say, 'It doesn't hurt me.' Defiance was the only defence he had left. If boxing is a science, Huggins was being broken down into molecules of helplessness. In boxing you've got to use your head, but not the way Huggins did. It was as if he was using it as a magnet to attract McGuigan's best punches. With Huggins bleeding from the mouth, the referee stopped the fight at the end of the fifth round. McGuigan thanked God. All he could see as Huggins stood there shaking his head in defiance were the eyes of Ali.

One night after the McGuigan family had finished praying, Sandra came in to announce that she was pregnant. She and Barry would be expecting their first child in the middle of 1983. As everybody celebrated, McGuigan thought of the boy Young Ali's wife had given birth to. What would the child do if his father died? McGuigan shook the thought from his mind as he went out to look for a present for Sandra for their wedding anniversary. McGuigan would never forget his first wedding anniversary. It was the day that Young Ali died, far away.

McGuigan went into a fit of depression. He looked at his beloved Monaghan Hills with alienated eyes.

If a visitor from outer space came to Clones he might be forgiven for thinking that it was a plague town. In a deep arc about the town the small country lanes have been blocked with barriers that make passage impossible. Steel girders stick up from huge concrete slabs like metal fingers. One could be forgiven for thinking that it is the innocent-looking streams that carry the deadly virus. Like steps along a giant's pathway, bridges line the river bed. Human badgers have been at work clogging up the waterway.

McGuigan was about nine or ten when the plague started. At first it was just based in the city; slowly it spread to the countryside. Soldiers were sent to control it, but that only made things worse. Soon the atmosphere got more and more poisoned. One day it appeared on the streets of Clones. Cars seething with resentment exploded of their own volition. The drivers had been exposed to the plague and carried the deadly virus. Gradually, normality was reduced to a shambles. People resorted to desperate measures. Strangers became enemies. They pulled up the drawbridge and the traders around the town wondered what to do with their goods.

If you couldn't cure the plague, the best thing to do was to ignore it. One of the ways to do that was through sport. McGuigan boxed and he became so good that he boxed for his country. McGuigan had two countries; he boxed for both of them. Each country blamed the other for the plague. McGuigan blamed neither, he just fought. He won a gold medal for one country and then for the other. By an accident of birth and through his amazing boxing talent McGuigan had seen life from both sides of the border. People who hated each other would congratulate McGuigan after his victories. He, it seemed, was uncontaminated by the plague.

Ever since the start of the plague, McGuigan watched as his mother's business declined. The roads that are the arteries into Clones have become congealed and the town is suffering from a commercial heart attack. Shopping has become an ordeal. Whenever McGuigan meets a journalist or somebody who has never visited Ireland he will show them the border roads. He will jump into his jeep and head down towards the first army blockade. There is almost a sense of ritual about this, McGuigan has done it so often. He points out the army location, the bunkers hidden on the little hills of Fermanagh, the barricaded roads and the destroyed bridges. These crazy ruptures don't just threaten the trade of the little shop in Clones, they threaten a whole way of life. At a deep level of instinct, McGuigan is fighting to remove these barriers. Rather, he is fighting for a situation where the barriers won't be necessary. He's using his God-given strength to make a first tentative step to unblock these blood-clogged roads.

All situations reach a point where they won't be solved by logic. People need to stand back and judge the situation from a totally different perspective. With the death of Young Ali, McGuigan lost all sense of his own perspective.

In boxing, they say there is nowhere to hide in the ring. After the death of Young Ali, McGuigan had nowhere to hide, period. McGuigan felt as if a plague had been visited upon his own house. Boxing made things simple. It brought people together. Why then had God sent this tragedy to plague him personally? Every time McGuigan looked for an answer he was in a cul-de-sac. As McGuigan faced the new year he could find no reason to continue boxing. When he answered that he boxed for Sandra and the child she was pregnant with, he had to ask himself about Young Ali and the son who would never see his father. McGuigan decided to quit boxing. There was no other way out of his midwinter of the heart. Soon after New Year's Day in 1983 he journeyed to Belfast to tell Eastwood the bad news. Eastwood opened the door to him and said, 'No talking about boxing, do you hear me?' McGuigan sat there in silence and then returned home to Clones.

Two little thoughts kept McGuigan from announcing his retirement. What would it mean if he quit boxing now?

It would all have been for nothing. The training, the single-minded determination, the lost adolescence, the death of Ali, all for nothing.

And the press were fickle. Ali's memory wouldn't last beyond the next car bomb or plastic bullet. If McGuigan became world champion the people would never forget Alimi Mustapha. He would never allow them to forget. McGuigan decided that if he couldn't immortalize the African's name, then there was no point in fighting. He decided to come back and do just that. It meant he returned with an even fiercer determination than ever. Now when he got into the ring, the ghost of Ali would be standing behind him, urging him on. Every fighter lives with the presence of death. McGuigan had walked around like the old man of the sea with that demon on his back Now he had buried him deep inside. McGuigan looked through the eyes of death and he didn't blink.

AT HOME IN BELFAST

When McGuigan rang Eastwood to tell him he was coming back to fight, Eastwood immediately booked the King's Hall. The King's Hall is a huge exhibition space on the outskirts of Belfast. It holds over 7,000 people, but Eastwood was confident he could fill it with McGuigan fighting for the British title.

As McGuigan moved up the fight ladder his need for peace and quiet to help his concentration became more and more critical. Eastwood had found him the perfect training retreat in the seaside resort of Bangor. He and Buchanan could spend hours talking without interference.

One night when McGuigan was preparing for his fight for the British title, Buchanan rang Eastwood from Beresford House. 'I don't think he looks too well,' he said.

Eastwood suggested that he get to bed early, but Buchanan thought they should get him to a hospital. Soon McGuigan was in the Royal Victoria Hospital with a mysterious ailment. The events of the past few months had exerted a heavy toll. McGuigan lay limp and tired in the bed. The doctors said that he had a very severe flu and that it would be months before he could fight again. Eastwood had a dilemma: he had booked the King's Hall and McGuigan was the main attraction. McGuigan insisted he could recover.

Every night Eastwood turned up at the hospital with home-made soup, hoping that McGuigan would come round on time. Most of his problems were psychological, he reckoned. McGuigan agreed with him. One night he felt a little better. Eastwood was happy. He left the ward with McGuigan up on his feet pledging that he would get better.

That night Eastwood drove back to his new house on The Hill in Hollywood. The doctor was on the line from the hospital. McGuigan had got up out of his sick bed and started doing press-ups. He had had a relapse and he was now in a serious condition. McGuigan eventually recovered from his ordeal, but it showed the level of determination with which he was coming back to fight.

His fight for the British title eventually took place against Vernon Penprase on 12 April at the Ulster Hall. They could have sold out the smaller venue four times over. It was a fight – but no contest. McGuigan backed Penprase up with left jabs into a corner in the first round and then hit him with a lightning-fast left hook. Like a puppet whose strings have been cut Penprase fell to the floor. He had never been down in his life up to that moment but a thousand reputations couldn't have saved him from the accuracy of that punch. McGuigan came forward, saw his opportunity and let fly. Almost before the punch had landed he was facing towards a neutral corner. Penprase hauled on the ropes like a puppet whose horizontal and vertical strings have got all mixed up. He survived the round. In the second round McGuigan again pursued him and again caught him close to the ropes. A right hand sent him scuttling along the floor like a crab going sideways. He scrambled to his feet, his features lost in a cake of blood. The referee mercifully stopped the fight.

Sandra went to the hospital in Newry to get a scan on the baby. The McGuigans were amazed to see a fully formed baby appear under the conquering magic of ultrasound. The doctor could even tell the sex of the baby but the McGuigans said they didn't want to know; it would be like opening your present before Christmas. The doctor moved the sounding instruments close to the baby's heart. Sandra couldn't remember where she had heard that rhythmic beat before. The doctor moved on to other features of the baby, pointing them out to the expectant couple. Again the heartbeat came up and Sandra said, 'The Caribbean.' They had been there on their honeymoon. In the long echoing marble corridors of the hotel they were staying in, McGuigan had done his skipping religiously. The sound and tempo of the rope hitting the floor and causing the feedback of its own echo was an identical sound to the heartbeat of the baby.

After his victory in the British title fight McGuigan went on tour. His first fight took him south of the border to Navan in the Republic of Ireland. He was to meet Sammy Meck, who only a couple of months previously had fought a draw with Louis Stecca in the European championship, who went on to become Junior Flyweight Champion of the World. After the weigh-in McGuigan and Meck had a meal in the same restaurant. Eastwood remembers McGuigan's eyes lighting up at the amount of food Meck put away. 'The grub he ate you couldn't put in a five-gallon jar. He had two or three pints of stout and he ended up having ice-cream and he was smiling and laughing. Barry turned to me and said, "My God, he's going to get into the ring at least at nine stone ten." I turned to Barry and said, "He'll be ten stone nine." ' The meal didn't help Sammy. McGuigan beat him in six rounds in a very good fight. The referee stopped the fight in the sixth round after Meck took a hammering to the head and body from Barry's devastating left hook.

With the kind of foresight that sees problems before they arrive, Eastwood decided it was time to have a look at the United States. The first time most European boxers saw American opponents, they looked at them from a horizontal position. All the best trainers, coaches and managers were in the States, and most of the best fighters too.

Eastwood felt that McGuigan had gone as far as he could in Britain, and that it was time to lay the demons of the New World to rest. One of those demons, Loval McGowan, proved far less resilient than expected. He went down, and stayed there, in the first round. The real test came in the Chicago and New York gyms, where McGuigan soon became an unpopular sparring partner. Vinnie Costello's brother, Billy Costello, is a world champion, but that gave

Vinnie no right to be in the same ring as McGuigan, even in a spar. Vinnie was twenty pounds heavier than McGuigan, but he had to go on the retreat from the ferocity of McGuigan's punches. After the Costello spar, Costello's manager announced that 'McGuigan doesn't fight like a white man, he fights like a brother.'

In a corner, keeping to himself, was an old man, Bobby McQuillar. Eastwood asked him what he thought. 'Good, very good,' said McQuillar. Eastwood asked whether there was room for improvement. 'Sure,' said McQuillar. Eastwood invited McQuillar to Belfast.

When McGuigan got home from the States, Sandra was almost eight months pregnant. On 24 August she began to go cabin crazy in their home, and asked Barry to take her for a meal. After the meal her waters broke. Barry drove her to the hospital in Newry. Everything went fine until the nuns offered her St Teresa's powder. As soon as she had taken it, Sandra began to feel sorry that she had had the meal. As the Catholic nuns looked at the effect the powder had had on her, McGuigan said, 'That's the Protestant blood in you.'

Soon after midday on 25 August 1983 their son was born. McGuigan was there at the birth. If you ask him why he boxes, he won't give you any of the reasons that make good copy for the press. 'Money and fame,' he will say. Sometimes there are limits. The press wanted a picture of Sandra and the new baby. McGuigan was about to tell them to come back another day when Sandra emerged, fresh and relaxed, ready to have her photo taken. Their son, Blain, was introduced to the wider world a few hours after his birth. Neither McGuigan nor Sandra wanted to call him after his father, and they decided on Blain, which is French for 'fair'. The child lived up to his name: he had a lovely head of fair hair.

The story of McGuigan's next two fights is the story of one punch, his left hook to the body. Delivered from below in an upward arc it hits to best effect just below the rib-cage, causing the opponent to search for breath and slowing him down as effectively as lead boots. McGuigan delivers with his weight on his left-hand side. Every athlete who dominates his time has one physical attribute that sets him apart from the rest. It's his special signature. It may not necessarily be his most effective action, but it is something that sets him apart in the public eye. Pelé had an overhead bicycling kick on his back so that you were trebly confused as to what angle the ball would take. Borg had his topspin which made the ball dip over the net as if it had hit an invisible wall just before you got to it. Lester Piggott rode so high in the saddle he looked as if he was coming down from a perpetual high jump. Perhaps the most famous signature of all was the Fosbury Flop, Dick Fosbury's backward leap over the bar that looked so extraordinary when he introduced it but is now the staple leap in high jump competitions. McGuigan's left hook to the body has always been there in boxing but, because of McGuigan's strength, it is an awesome weapon for a featherweight; and because of the size of target he has to aim at, it is very difficult to neutralize. When McGuigan first used it against his early opponents, it almost doubled them in two. The only defence – apart from running – is to bend really low and bring the arms down close to the body. The result of this is that McGuigan has often been cautioned for low blows.

Ruben Herasme fought well in his first round with McGuigan, then he felt the full weight of McGuigan's left hook. The first thing Herasme registered was the pain and then the urge to get away from it as quickly as possible. In the second round another left hook to the body slowed him down. This left him open to the full McGuigan arsenal: left hook to the chin, right to the head and finally the devastating left hook to the body again. The man from the Dominican Republic went down and then spat out his gumshield in a gesture that said, 'That's it, I've had enough.'

Valerio Nati had more to fight for: the vacant European featherweight title. This was McGuigan's first fight in the

King's Hall. The Belfast crowd knew they were watching history being made. The sound they made rolled like thunder round the huge dome of the hall. To McGuigan it was worth an extra arm. Nati stumbled round the stadium like Lear in the storm. By the third round he felt as old as the Celtic patriarch. Between rounds he stood in his corner. The reason for this was that he couldn't sit down: he had suffered three broken ribs. He was a durable fighter. He stayed on his feet until the sixth round when McGuigan caught him with a couple of left hooks to the body. Nati ran for cover but couldn't find any. Most fighters go down because they have lost control of their legs. Nati's legs were still intact but his body was in ruins. He doubled up in a corner, cowering from McGuigan's body shots like a dog avoiding an irate master. It was an end that didn't do any kind of justice to the extraordinary courage he had shown.

The Belfast fight crowd are very knowledgeable. They cheered Nati in defeat. High up in the King's Hall somebody banged out a rhythm on a lambeg drum that signified the best European victory since the Battle of the Boyne. This time Catholics and Protestants were united in victory. The people of Belfast had something to cheer at last. Muhammad Ali articulated the dumb soul of black America. A voice that had been kept in thrall suddenly broke out in the words and fists of Ali. The Irish nationalist and loyalist causes had been overarticulated to the point of exhaustion. The people didn't need somebody who boasted what he was going to do, they needed a hero who did more than he said. McGuigan was one of the first of the television generation who believed more in what they saw than in what they heard. That night he saw over 7,000 people release a scream in tears of deep emotion that drowned out the frustration they had felt for years.

McGuigan has some idea of his appeal: 'In the ring, I'm their hope, their little bit of prosperity. The frustration at what Northern Ireland has become, on fight nights they let it all out. They love me. I feel so responsible for those people. I'd hate to let them down, not because I'm afraid of them. They're genuine people. They would sell their houses to go and see me. I love Belfast. Put the troubles aside, the people of Belfast are great people. That's my story. That's it in a nutshell.'

A CONTENDER

McGuigan came to Jean Anderson's guest house in Bangor just after Christmas in 1983, more determined than ever to work his way to the top. And work he did. He was like a greyhound in the gym. Eastwood and Eddie Shaw had never seen him in better condition. For his fight with Charm Chiteule of Zambia he sparred 130 immaculate rounds. Then in the King's Hall on 25 January for five rounds it looked as if he had left it all in the gym. Chiteule was a seasoned campaigner, a thorough professional. While McGuigan was warming up, Chiteule was scoring repeatedly, getting through McGuigan's defence straight to the head. By the third round one of McGuigan's eyes was swollen and by the fifth he had problems with his vision. Every time McGuigan tried to get inside, the Zambian was picking him off. McGuigan wiped his gloves on his trunks in the sixth round and brought his performance up a notch. Champions win when they are not performing well. To pull it out from where he was at the start of the sixth, McGuigan would need to be a real champion. His body punches were neutralized to the extent that he had been warned for punching low. He looked at the referee with his one good eye. It was the same man who had given the decision against him in the Peter Eubanks fight. He had to stop Chiteule. Gradually he adapted to the range that he needed for one eye. Slowly he began to get inside Chiteule and the Zambian weakened. After a barrage of punches in the tenth round the referee stopped the fight. Chiteule stood stock still in the corner into which McGuigan had driven him. It was McGuigan's toughest match to date. He would need to improve for his next fight against Jose Caba.

Jose Caba had gone fifteen rounds with the great Eusebio Pedroza in his last fight, but Eastwood reckoned that McGuigan could take him out. McGuigan fundamentally trusts Eastwood's judgement in such matters. Eastwood reckoned Caba was ripe for the taking. He had just lost the most important fight of his life against Pedroza, a big psychological blow. That fight was a real battle and Caba came out of it a wiser if sadder man.

Fighters from the United States generally regard European opposition with affection. Most of the Europeans fight a very upright fight, leaving themselves a big target for the ultra-professional Americans. Caba couldn't believe what he saw in the King's Hall. The noise the crowd let loose made his fight with Pedroza seem like an altercation in a pool hall. McGuigan fought like a man possessed. Caba could not land a blow. He had come to protect himself from McGuigan's heralded body shots but McGuigan hardly threw one all night. Instead he caught him to the head with the most flawless exhibition of boxing ever seen in Belfast. Caba's squat coming-forward style was made for McGuigan and he tore him apart. The referee stopped the fight in the seventh round.

The fight against Caba shot McGuigan up the world ratings. In some quarters he was rated as high as number four.

A few days before McGuigan's defence of his European title against Esteban Equia of Spain, Eastwood found himself in a dilemma. The fight was at the Albert Hall in London. Equia would carry the Spanish flag into the ring. Mickey Duff, the English fight promoter in association with Stephen Eastwood, wanted McGuigan to carry the Union Jack into the ring. McGuigan had walked a tightrope with the fight fans in Belfast, never alienating one side or the other. In England the Union Jack is a flag of identity. In Ulster for sixty per cent of the population it is a flag of identity and a flag of defiance. McGuigan had refused to alienate the Protestants of Belfast by carrying the Tricolour. He would alienate the Catholics by carrying the Union Jack.

Eastwood asked McGuigan what he thought. McGuigan did not want to alienate anybody. 'I'm for peace,' he told Eastwood. 'Right then,' said Eastwood, 'we'll carry a peace flag.' He and Paddy Byrne set off across London to find it. A shop-owner showed them the flags of every nationality, but he had never heard of a peace flag. 'What does it look like?' he asked Paddy Byrne. 'It's got a dove on it,' said Paddy in his best Dublin accent. The flag man looked at Paddy as if he had two heads. He had never seen a flag with a dove on it anywhere in his life. The Japanese one was a little odd with its round moon, but he had been fifty years in the flag business and he had never seen one with a dove on it. They went back to the Holiday Inn where they were staying and considered the possibility of making a flag. In the bar one man who had had a few too many started to draw what he swore was the peace flag. The manager of the hotel happened to be passing and he overheard the conversation. 'We have a peace flag,' he said, 'outside the hotel, hanging up.' They went outside and there was the only peace flag to be found in London. That decided the issue. They were fated to carry the flag of peace. They got it down off the pole and carried it to the Royal Albert Hall.

The fight itself was anything but peaceful. McGuigan had progressed to a level far beyond the usual European standard. Equia was totally outclassed. In the same hall in which his father had sung in the Eurovision Song Contest, McGuigan knocked the Spaniard out in the third round.

Now the American TV networks wanted McGuigan. He is the type of boxer the American public love: aggressive, coming forward all the time, and with a knockout punch that makes him entirely unpredictable. He also has an intense personality, good looks, and is articulate. Who could ask for more? During McGuigan's first fight on American TV, the commentators couldn't believe the atmosphere in the King's Hall. Their equipment wasn't built to cope with that level of noise. His opponent, Paul De Vorce, was rated in the top twenty in the world, but after five rounds the referee had to step between the fighters as the man from Yonkers had stopped fighting back. The Americans thought the referee had stopped it too early. They couldn't get enough of McGuigan. De Vorce had had too much.

McGuigan's next opponent, in October 1984, was a late stand-in, the six-foot-tall Filipe Orozco. McGuigan brought him down with repeated shots to the body and then a huge left hook that sent the Colombian sprawling to the canvas.

McGuigan now had to defend his British and European titles against Clyde Ruan. If Ruan could beat McGuigan, he would suddenly be catapulted into the world rankings. He tried to intimidate McGuigan with talk ... he would finish off the job his friend Chiteule had started. In the gym at the bottom of the Falls Road, McGuigan prepared in silence. Four days before the fight, just after his wedding anniversary, McGuigan was dealt a double blow. His grandfather, 'Papa' Rooney, died. McGuigan had always been close to Katie's father. He helped out in the shop and his common-sense advice was one of the bedrocks on which McGuigan had built his career. At the same time as his grandfather died, Sandra had a miscarriage. McGuigan had to reach deep down to stop this double tragedy affecting him. The man who got the brunt of his temper was Clyde Ruan. He hit McGuigan with his best shot, a left to the head. McGuigan didn't blink. After toying with Ruan for three rounds, McGuigan knocked him out with a spectacular left hook to the jaw.

By now a theory was abroad in Belfast that McGuigan was an Eastwood creation and that he would fold up against a top-class opponent. According to this theory, anybody of world stature that McGuigan had beaten was already washed up. It is true that Eastwood had looked after McGuigan spectacularly well; they prepared for each fight on its merits, getting in the best and most appropriate sparring partners and devising the best tactics. The theory would be tested once and for all by Juan Laporte of Puerto Rico. Laporte was only twenty-six and had been world champion only a year previously. He had gone the distance with the great Eusebio Pedroza. Here was real opposition at last. Most importantly, Laporte had a deadly punch.

A short right hand from Laporte in the fifth caught McGuigan flush on the jaw. McGuigan was rocked. He hung on for a second and then, for the first time in the fight, boxed on the retreat . . . but for a few seconds he had looked really vulnerable. For four more rounds, Laporte looked for a way to perfect that right he had thrown in the fifth. He had no other alternative; McGuigan was fighting like a waterfall, constantly coming forward, weaving and ducking. In the ninth round he came forward – with his guard down. Laporte saw his chance. This is what he had been loading up for all night. He caught McGuigan with a long right hand to the jaw. McGuigan's left foot left the canvas perpendicularly. It was a copybook shot. McGuigan shook his head and then came forward again. The fight was over. He had shown that he could take a sledge-hammer of a punch. Eastwood had said that McGuigan was like a classic horse who had never been off the bit. Against Laporte we saw a little of what he looked like when given a free rein. He would need to fight better than that to beat Pedroza.

Eastwood went to Panama to get the world champion to sign for the title fight, and came back empty-handed. The problem was a man called Santiago del Rio. He was Pedroza's manager and he was the toughest negotiator Eastwood had ever met. On 26 March, McGuigan was due to defend his European title against a Frenchman, Farid Gallouze, at the Wembley Arena in London. Pedroza and his manager were talked into coming over to negotiate a world title fight, but on the night of the Gallouze fight the Master of Ceremonies announced that Pedroza had a head cold and couldn't attend. The psychological battle had begun. Finally, at six o'clock on the morning after McGuigan's two-round victory, Pedroza signed a contract for the most expensive featherweight title fight ever to be staged in Britain. McGuigan packed his bags. Into a corner he put his medals and the lucky charm an Indian had given him out of the blue. McGuigan headed home to Clones to prepare for the biggest night of his life.

Part Four

DIARY OF
A WORLD TITLE FIGHT

About McGuigan there is always the feeling of forward motion. There is very little distance between the decision and the deed. There is no orange light, no flashing 'Get ready' signal. There are so many people who will say 'I won't wait' that the fun is in the amount of leeway in the statement. They'll dilly and dally and so do you, working out some comfortable relationship in the drama in which you have been cast together. McGuigan never makes statements like that, he just puts his foot on the accelerator. Today we are driving to Bangor.

There are no crowds to wish us goodbye. It's as if McGuigan wants to leave with the minimum of fuss. Today he goes off to fight the champion of the world. To make a fuss would give Pedroza a stature that McGuigan can never allow him to attain. This is what his father calls Barry's gunshot vision. He never lets the target out of his mind. For the next four weeks the target is Pedroza and Barry's vision is trained on him; but his sights are telescopic and for the moment Pedroza is in long shot. When he wants, Barry can zoom him into focus, but only when he wants to illuminate some blemish in the Panamanian's make-up. I have been with Barry day and night for months now, and I have never heard him discuss Pedroza in public. Dermot watches the videos and analyses the faults. Barry concentrates on what Barry can do. You know that nobody can really help ... that between McGuigan and Pedroza, it's a private affair. For Barry watching videos of Pedroza is like watching a home movie of a former wife where, while looking for faults to ease the pain of alimony payments, all you can see are her virtues.

McGuigan as ever drives too fast, especially on the road to Monaghan, which in the high suspension of his shōgun jeep feels as if it was built for the ass and cart. These are the kind of roads that would give you false teeth. Even blindfolded now I could tell the South from the North. And without looking I can tell when we cross the border because there are two huge bumps, camel style, to impede access to those who can separate bricks from mortar with the push of a button. I wonder, did any poor unfortunate ever cross these paths blindfolded, and then I wonder, does everybody cross these roads blindfolded?

Fifty yards inside the border at Middletown we are met by the biggest detachment of British soldiers I have seen in the past few weeks. These men could have been set down anywhere in the world and they would take up the same crouching positions. They hug the kerbside for protection, the way an old dog hugs a turf fire. With their blackened faces they look like extras from a film, but the guns are real . . . the guns are real. With a look of recognition that is too wary to be a smile, the sergeant in charge waves us on and we drive towards the city of Armagh in silence.

We have passed many McGuigan landmarks on the way and nothing has been said about them: the spot where his father crashed, his first club in Smithboro, Mulligan's house, the town where he was born, all have passed in silence. Suddenly on the motorway outside Armagh, McGuigan points out a house and says, 'The fellow that lives in there is a great guy. His wife was abducted. They just walked in, in the middle of the day, and took her away. They were after a ransom. Lucky for her she escaped.' I note that there doesn't seem to be any extra protection on the house and McGuigan answers with the resignation of one who knows, 'Sure, what can you do?'

As we skirt Belfast, McGuigan repeats the phrase that is almost a catch-cry every time the city is mentioned: 'Great city, great people.' We drive on for a few miles until we are on a steep incline and the sea in its evening silver gown makes a majestic entrance, only to disappear as quickly behind an impudence of concrete. For a couple of hundred yards it enters and exits between rows of houses with the speed of the maid in a French farce. Eventually we pull up at the back of a four-storey house. We go into the kitchen, there is nobody about. There is no mistaking the two men out front. They sit on the front porch looking out at the Irish Sea. We approach and they greet us with the only word of English they know: 'McGuigan.' Barry nods. Eventually Jean Anderson appears and lays out a meal. It's not known if the Panamanians are hungry and eventually it is established that they are in fact starving. What do they want to eat? Now everybody is in on the pantomime. 'What is it? Fish? Eggs? Do they want pineapples or something?' Jose resolves the dilemma by squatting down, spreading his elbows out from the sides and squawking. 'Chicken,' says Barry as he erupts in laughter.

We take a walk down to the sea. On our walk we see a sign which tells us that the French National Circus are performing at the Castle Grounds until the 18th. The harbour is well laid out. Bangor is a seaside resort. The sea is faintly hinting at its elemental power. I walk a narrow strip that serves as a landing for small craft. 'I don't like the sea,' says Barry. I look surprised. 'I'm afraid of it,' he says. Fear is not a word I associate with McGuigan.

TUESDAY
14th May

First day in the gym. The Panamanians turn out to be Jose Marmalejo and Ezekiel Muskera. The cool one is Ezekiel: he watches the road into Belfast with an amused indifference. Jose holds on to his piece of Panama with the blaring Latin sounds from his Walkman. We pass a barbed-wire army encampment and a helicopter shoots out from the trees like a surprised iron bird. The words 'First Border Regiment' flash by and if you are going slowly enough to catch anything else you're on a bicycle. We pass a football stadium, well decorated in graffiti. On the side of the stand a gin bottle pours a perpetual liquid that turns into a silver cordial in strong sunlight. It possesses an other-world charm. When first erected it must have had the brashness of neon.

On our right ahead loom two fifty-foot iron goalposts emblazoned with the initials of their owners. HW. This is Harland and Wolff. This is the yard that built the *Titanic*. From here a largely Protestant workforce marched like an army all through the hungry Thirties and Forties to their homes. These were the hard men of the North. At school I learned that the reason the *Titanic* sank was because they had given it the number, NO. 909E. When you hold that up to a mirror it says NO POPE. In Catholic retribution God turned a portion of the North Atlantic into iced water and the demonic intentions of the Protestants were sunk with all hands on deck. We pass other monuments to the Protestant work ethic. Short Bros, the Sirocco Works. Within a half-mile we are crossing Bridge End and heading for Eastwood House.

It's only much later that I realize our journey to Chapel Lane performs bypass surgery around the heart of Belfast. The centre of the city is City Hall and on any map issued after 1975 the streets within a quarter-mile semicircle due north of it are coloured a deep red. The legend will tell you 'limited access'. This is the bleeding heart of Belfast.

At the outer perimeter of this half-circle where the red arteries turn white, Chapel Lane meets Castle Street. A casual passer-by might be forgiven for thinking that this is the Grand Central Station of Belfast. Taxis leave this junction at the rate of five a minute. This is the Belfast black taxi service that feeds the Catholic Falls. A hundred yards away another feeds the Protestant Shankill. They replaced the normal buses that were discontinued at the height of the troubles and are the tip of the iceberg of an alternative economy that grew up around the troubles. The Eastwood gym is at the bottom of the Falls Road, but it doesn't matter which taxi you take, you'll get into the workshop without being asked your religion. All you'll be asked is, 'Can you defend yourself within the Marquess of Queensberry rules?'

The posters in Bangor gave the wrong location for the Circus. It's here in Chapel Lane. There are three or four television crews, a dozen cameramen, a reporter for every cameraman and a friend for every reporter. The only shade from the hot glare of the television lamps is the fog of smoke that ascends from the mouths of all the non-sportsmen in the room. The man who is responsible for these overcast conditions enters the gym with his usual walk that says 'I'm going somewhere'. This time it's straight to the changing room at the bottom of the room. There he sits for a moment and considers the interest he has created and the hope he has awakened. There are some familiar faces around who can help get the work in perspective. Eddie Shaw is there. Eddie is a rock. He just gets on with the business. This won't faze Eddie. McGuigan strips and gets ready. He will spar with Jose and Ezekiel. When Jose gets into his gear his name is emblazoned all over it: 'Marmalejo' on the back and 'Jose' on the pants. No mistaking this man in a crowd. It's only then that I realize that McGuigan has no personalized items apart from the gown he steps through the ring in.

Eddie has assembled his bits and pieces on a trolley at the far end of the ring nearest the changing room. The adhesive tape hangs from the top deck where a large basin holds a few floating gumshields. On the lower deck there is olive oil and vaseline. Eddie applies the vaseline to Barry and Ezekiel with a deftness that belongs more to the theatre than the boxing ring. It gives McGuigan's face an odd sheen, almost as if Eddie were moulding him for a bust. The purifying fire will come in the ring. McGuigan warms up. Most boxers do this by throwing shapes. It's a kind of performance before the main event, like a prima donna clearing her vocal cords, but with McGuigan you never get the feeling that it is a performance. He is not throwing blows at an imaginary opponent. It's as if he's throwing punches at himself and listening for the response his body makes.

For the first time since I met him, Barry is wearing a protective helmet. Ezekiel is about 21 pounds heavier than McGuigan and he never loses his cool. Because he never loses his cool he keeps on the move from McGuigan's blows, hugging the ropes with the speed and tenacity of a car on the Wall of Death. And when he moves inside he has the uppercut that Pedroza has perfected. It's not just the result of a conscious style, this is the method that best suits the fluidity of the Panamanians' make-up, physically and emotionally. It was something of a scoop for Eastwood to get these two Panamanians and there is a glint in those genial eyes when he is asked what effect it will have on Pedroza when he hears that two of his fellow countrymen are helping McGuigan out. Round one to Eastwood. After two rounds with Ezekiel, Jose jumps through the ropes. His style is a variation on a common denominator whose name is Muhammad Ali. The same rapid flow movement, stop, attack, retreat and flamboyance. Suddenly McGuigan hits him with a weapon from the arsenal. Jose lets out a piercing wail that is a coded war-whoop and stands toe to toe with McGuigan, centre ring, blows landing from every angle, the long wail punctuated with the thud of padded gloves. Eastwood and Eddie are delighted at McGuigan's condition. They are delighted that he is not too sharp, there is something to work on. He has been telling the truth. He has not been sparring at home. The press love Jose's performance and when he quits the ring after two rounds he keeps up the act on the overhead ball, only he hits the bag with his elbows. The press turn their arc-lamps on Jose and all eyes turn to the little platform underneath the speedball. Cameras flash. Alone in the ring, fighting his own particular shadow, McGuigan takes all this in. The media's eyes are as quicksilver and fickle as those of the magpie.

Today is election day in Belfast. It is not the elections to the mother parliament in the United Kingdom, but the elections that control all the little local and urban councils, the ones that control sanitation and water rates rather than defence and the umbilical link across the Irish Sea. In the gym it's work as usual. Since coming to Belfast, Barry has been constantly in demand by the media, and the cracks are beginning to show. He tells a journalist from a Southern Irish paper that the dressing room is private which, given the evenness of Barry's temperament, is a major gaffe. Eastwood is busy keeping everybody happy. He has promised Barry that all the press will stop on Monday the 20th. It's different from when Eastwood started the boxing in Belfast. Then he had to go looking for stories to try and fill the Ulster Hall.

George Ace is the journalist closest to Eastwood. 'When Eastwood rang me to tell me he had got McGuigan, I said we need boxing here in Belfast like we need a hole in the head. Belfast was a dead city at night. The city centre was deserted.'

After training, Eastwood is in the Hercules bar across the road from the gym. The local journalists who have followed Barry since his first professional fight are feeling that their territory is being invaded by the Fleet Street hordes, not to mention 'women' journalists from *Newsweek* and *The New York Times* who have not a clue about boxing. McGuigan is becoming before their very eyes that most

149

hated of journalistic clichés, 'a human interest story'. Their fears and paranoias are focused on where they will actually sit at the fight and whether in fact they have been allotted seats at the ringside. Eastwood leans forward with his elbow on the bar and his upper body bent at the most obtuse angle to the company. He has a talent for making public utterances sound like boudoir stories. 'There will be tickets for all you lads. See, if the Queen of England and King Kong were sitting there, it's get them out of here and let these boys in. That's the story. There will be tickets for everybody.' Eastwood might flirt with the international press, but he knows he has to live with these boys. 'Do you remember the first time I had a press conference to announce McGuigan?' Eastwood asks philosophically. 'People said, "You're wasting your time. Boxing is dead here. Why don't you let it sleep? You're living twenty years ago. You won't fill half the hall. McGuigan is not even a local boy." I went down that road that night talking to myself.'

THURSDAY
16th May

By now Barry has settled into some sort of a routine. Most mornings he gets up around half-past eight and goes for a five-mile run. Then it's back to the Beresford for breakfast, which usually consists of All-Bran, some prunes, orange juice and coffee. Then it's back to bed in room seven. Barry chose this room because seven is a lucky number for him, and the fact that it doesn't look out on the seafront is a decided advantage. There are no distractions, not even the Irish Sea and Bangor Harbour. I reckon Barry spends twelve to fourteen hours a day in this room in total isolation. He doesn't sleep all the time. Some of the time he just lies there and thinks. The only thing he can think about clearly is the upcoming fight with Pedroza. He spends from eleven until one or two o'clock in his little bedroom. Then he packs for the gym and heads off. He arrives at the gym usually about three o'clock, spends about thirty to forty-five minutes getting ready. Between sparring and other workouts he usually does the equivalent of eighteen rounds until five o'clock, when he heads back to Bangor for dinner at seven. After dinner he walks between two and four miles and then it's back to bed and up again at half-past eight the next morning for more of the same. That he can keep an even temperament while doing this mind-boggling routine is extraordinary. This week he has the added pressure of the media. The only break from the routine is the nightly phone-call to Sandra. He will discuss how things went and what's happening in Clones. I knew that he trained every day in Clones, but there he would train at different times and in different ways. Here the punishment is constantly the same. It seems that he has reduced the outside world to a point where it has little or no effect on him. He concentrates like a Buddhist on the task ahead. It's as if he is storing energy, but it takes an immense inner calm to be able to store that energy without demanding release in any form. The evening walks seem to be designed to wear off the effects of dinner. He never stops and chats or lets his attention wander for longer than a few seconds. Then it's back to the room and Mr Wall. Some nights I know he doesn't sleep till three or four in the morning, and all the time he is thinking about the contest ahead. The contest he seems to be having now is with himself. He seems to be gaining total control of his environment and himself and forcing all his concentration towards one explosive hour in London in three and a half weeks.

By Thursday Ezekiel and Jose, in a joint effort to counteract McGuigan's strength, are urging each other on. Ezekiel is shouting. The word he uses means 'toes' in English and it doesn't need elaboration. Jose renders Barry immobile by standing on them. Inside he pulls him to the floor and both he and Ezekiel constantly use the uppercut . . . what Pedroza's camp call his bolo punch. Boxing depends a lot on hand–eye co-ordination. A boxer's reflexes are like a wireless that shifts its setting until it picks up the particular wavelength of the opponent. The wavelength Barry is picking up this week is as foreign as the Spanish the Panamanians speak. It needs constant fine tuning to adjust and then a complete shift from one wavelength to another as something new crops up. Once the opponent's technique becomes familiar it loses a lot of its terror.

Each night and early morning, McGuigan plays over in his mind the sparring of the previous day. In one simple move to block Pedroza's bolo and left hook there were twelve separate moves before he could get in his own left hook to the body. Twelve different physical actions in two seconds, and then if the combination changes you must be ready to adapt. That would blow a fuse in a computer. McGuigan is training to adapt and paying dearly for the privilege. He shows me the underpart of his chin where the Panamanians have repeatedly caught him with uppercuts over the past three days. There are many small scars and welts, but the day he shows it to me is the day he has the problem licked. From that day on, I could count on one hand the number of times he's caught by the uppercut. That's the way McGuigan works.

On Thursday Eddie is happier. With the kind of triumphant sarcasm that is peculiar to boxing he tells Barry that Jose is '. . . eating that left. He's eating it.' Eastwood is leaning over the ropes whispering encouragement. 'One up, two down. You see, this Pedroza if you catch him with one of a combination you'll not catch him with two. If you hit him once to the head switch to the body.' Eastwood has the eyes of a child. He sees things simply. He has the tongue of a hundred-year-old yogi. He rarely speaks above a whisper so that you lean forward to hear what he has to say and if he raises his voice he's in a temper. I noticed, all the time we were in Clones, McGuigan looking to the mirror to get confirmation or inspiration. Outside of Clones, Eastwood is his mirror. Today, Eastwood is happy enough. 'No sparring tomorrow, that's enough for the time being, we'll just work out tomorrow, give the boys a day off.'

FRIDAY
17th May

Today the election results start to come in. The Unionist Party have regained the lead as the majority Protestant party, relegating the Reverend Ian Paisley's Democratic Unionist Party to second place. On the Catholic side the vote is split almost fifty-fifty between the moderate S D L P and Sinn Fein who are the political wing of the Provisional I R A. Nobody in the gym or around it has mentioned elections or politics since the day we arrived. Today Barry is not sparring and while he and Eddie walk round the ring like Mowgli and Baloo in *The Jungle Book*, it's time to look round the gym. It's a complete contrast to the one in Clones. Everything is custom-built and, unlike most gyms throughout the world, it is spotlessly clean. It is about fifty feet in length with a large window stretching across its twenty-foot width at the Castle Street end. There are three heavy bags at this end and a speedball. From the windows all the way down to the ring are photos and mementoes. It's an indication of how long Eddie Shaw has been around that there is a framed picture programme from the time he was on the same bill as Sonny Liston in the early Sixties.

Elsewhere there is a picture of the last time big-time boxing hit Belfast. In it Freddie Gilroy and Johnny Caldwell stride through Belfast with a gait that tells us that these boys owned the city. Their fight at the King's Hall in October 1962 is part of Belfast folklore. Although they were from different sides of the religious divide, the bout was unmarked by any form of sectarianism. Boxing's history in this regard is a proud one.

The ring itself is the one that the last undisputed Irish world flyweight champion, Rinty Monaghan, used for training. Barry was one of the last people who visited Rinty in hospital just before he died of cancer in 1984.

Over the next few weeks I will watch the pictures on the wall come alive. That night in the Hercules I see a face at the end of the bar. 'That's Johnny Caldwell,' says George Ace. Eventually we are introduced and Johnny almost pulls the hand off me with a handshake that still carries some of the power he took with him into the ring. Asked who he thinks will win, Johnny says he doesn't know, he has never seen Pedroza box, but he says, 'That McGuigan is a bad quilt,' which is Belfast slang for destroyer. Perhaps behind Johnny's reticence on Pedroza is the fact that when he boxed for the undisputed bantamweight title of the world, he came up against Eder Jofre, one of the great fighters of all time. Maybe at the back of his mind is the fact that Pedroza might be in that league. That would put paid to speculation as to whether Pedroza is over the hill because of his age. It is unimportant whether Pedroza is twenty-nine or thirty-two when one considers that Jofre won the title back at the age of thirty-seven.

On the way back to Bangor we have to go round Belfast because of a bomb scare. Although there is an army presence everywhere, the city is much improved from the nightmare of the early Seventies. Even at the barricade outside the door of the gym in Castle Street, people are rarely stopped. Spot searches are conducted, but the reality of the situation is that there hasn't been a bomb in the centre of Belfast in two years.

We are sitting in the Beresford, waiting on Ray the driver to take us to the gym, when in the distance we hear the sound of a marching band. It's a beautiful Saturday and the seafront at Bangor is lined with weekend tourists. As the crowd look up Grays Hill we can hear the approaching thunder of lambegs. Not since the old Corpus Christi processions have I seen such spectacle and colour. As flamboyant as a Spanish feast-day in Guatemala, the banners march down the steep hill towards the sea. Bibles, crowns and keys are the chief emblems on the banners which are carried fluttering along Queens Parade at the seafront. Most enigmatic of all is what looks like a musketeer on a horse. This is the legendary King William of Orange, defender of the Protestant faith. These are the insignia of true-blue northern Protestantism. The crown spells loyalty, although the man on the horse was a Dutchman who overthrew the Catholic King of England. The melody is carried in delicate high notes by an abundance of tin whistles and flutes and the rhythm is banged out on side drums and the huge lambegs. This is a parade of young schools, so the lambegs are carried by the older, stronger pupils. The parade itself is marshalled by the elders who are dressed in the main in suits and bowler hats with the orange sash draped over their shoulders. Most carry umbrellas which sometimes double as stewarding instruments. The parade takes us on a tour of Bangor.

In most northern towns the Catholic and Protestant steeples battle to dominate the skyline like actors trying to upstage one another. In Bangor both the steeples are of the Protestant denomination. The parade mounts Main Street. At the top of the street it turns abruptly away from the first Presbyterian church, one of the oldest in Bangor, and continues down Dufferin Street past St Comghalls Parish

Church and past the Masonic Hall. The parade comes to a halt outside Dufferin Hall and the boys in an orderly fashion divest themselves of their instruments and lodge them in the hall. The True Blues of Portadown are still holding the fort outside as boys in cockaded hats re-emerge into the sunlight. The boys head down to the seafront to get hamburgers and chips and the ones carrying the lambegs head to watering holes to relieve their thirsts. One chap has his lambeg belt undone and his name inscribed on the inside: 'Dutch'.

The RUC have nothing to fear from this parade. In their armoured cars at the seafront they sit eating pink ice-cream cones as they wait for their pizza to cook. At home in Beresford House, McGuigan sits in his room, unmoved by the spectacle. The parade could have come through the house itself and I don't think McGuigan would have noticed.

SATURDAY NIGHT

The little walkabout has stimulated some interest in Bangor. Like most Irish towns it had a religious beginning. It was in Bangor that St Comghall built his monastery. The offices of the order are recorded in the Antiphonary of Bangor. The regime of the enclosed monastic order was one of the toughest in the British Isles; it would have suited McGuigan down to a 't'. It's only in the dedication of those early Christians that I can think of a parallel with the man in room seven staring at the wall. This man has been fighting since he was eleven, and for the last ten years he has had his mind bent on becoming champion of the world. His dedication has been frighteningly inhuman. His discipline is of an order that is religious in its fanaticism, and his determination is such that soon he will start having ice-cold baths so that he can start the day fresh. Jumping into those baths filled with cubes of ice, he looks like a seal on holiday. The difference between him and the monks is that theirs is a life-long vocation. I wonder how Barry will react to normal life.

The Orange Parade is Protestant voodoo. More than anything, it is meant to keep the world view of popery at bay. The drums were banged long into the night to keep at bay a lifestyle that led millions of Irish people into the starving ditches. The message the drums beat out is hard work, thrift and independence, qualities that the man in room number seven has in abundance. Maybe that's why the Protestant people of Ulster have taken him to their hearts.

SUNDAY
19th May

Sunday is a day of rest. Sandra has come to visit Barry and Blain has come to see his daddy. As McGuigan trains in the old Rocky Marciano style, Sandra stays with Blain at the other side of the house. The contact is of the daytime variety. It suddenly strikes me that while I have been admiring Barry's dedication and discipline, I have forgotten Sandra's. For the next few weekends she will drive to Bangor from Clones, talk to Barry for the whole day and then go off to her own little bedroom with Blain. When in Clones she has to keep the house going and work in the hairdressing salon.

On Sunday night Gerald Hayes arrives. He is to coach Barry for the next few weeks. He has been over once before as a sparring partner, but now he is semi-retired from the game, which means that he will fight only if the money is right. Gerald has fought six world champions, including Pedroza. He has fought the best in the business, Chacon, Arguello, Lockridge, Pintor and Laporte. Gerald Hayes was what they call 'the opposition' in boxing. Too dangerous ever to get a title shot, he was willing to go anywhere. His story of his fight with Pedroza is astonishing. They fought one weight up from feather in the super-featherweight division. Pedroza looks well overweight in the fight clips. 'It was a quick weigh-in,' says Gerald with the tired knowledge of an old pro. He flew to Las Vegas, only to be told that the fight had been rerouted to Panama. So, like a true professional, he flew on to Panama. He was twenty-four hours non-stop in transit before he stepped into the ring. Then, astonishingly, he caught Pedroza with a right in the third round and landed him on his seat. In the tenth Pedroza hit him with a few but, as Gerald says, he never took a step back. The referee intervened to award a technical KO to Pedroza. The Panamanian was ahead on points at the time but they were taking no chances before a home crowd.

Gerald is a non-stop talker. He has seen videos of the Laporte fight with McGuigan and he says Barry was doing a lot wrong. In America, where managers know how to name themselves, Johnny Boss recommended Gerald as the best to Eastwood. Gerald Hayes didn't make much money from the fight game. He had two things going against him: one, he was just another black fighter in a division where the purses are normally small, and two, he didn't have a manager like Eastwood.

From today Barry starts to keep a diary ... what he eats and how much he spars. There's not much else to record. There is precious little else he does except conserve energy. The first entry of note he makes is 'Please God the interviews will end tomorrow'. Gerald Hayes is almost the extreme opposite to Barry as a personality. He is highly voluble and is not afraid of expressing his opinions to all and sundry. For the past eight days Barry has been getting constant attention from the press. The only time they can get to talk to him in peace is when he is eating, so interviews are conducted over breakfast, dinner and lunch. The most wearying part of the interviews is the constant repetition of detail. That's what a public figure expects and Barry handles the media perfectly. He has the ability to be himself most of the time. Given the fact that the peace issue has assumed such an important dimension, especially for the American press, he has to be constantly on his guard as to what he says. Asked his political opinions, Barry asks the interviewer, 'Do you want this interview to end here and now?' Irish history is so complex, it's like being asked to walk across Niagara Falls on stepping stones. Some of the stones appear solid, well-embedded and have names like Peace, Charity, Hope and Love, but anybody who has tried to cross will tell you that the rocks are as slippery as eels.

Over dinner he is asked how the death of Young Ali affected him. He tries to give as precise an answer as possible without becoming oversentimental, and at the same time not to dismiss the most traumatic event of his life with a shrug. It's not good psychologically for him to be thinking about death in the ring so close to the most important fight of his life, but there is the danger that constant repetition of the same story will leave a dangerous gap between his real emotions and the ones he must constantly repeat for the newsreel.

Today Barry parks his shōgun in the car park in Chapel Lane and goes across the road into St Mary's Church. He blesses himself as he goes through the door and turns to the statue of St Anthony. He holds the left foot of the saint and says his own private prayer. Then he picks up his bags and heads for the gym. This is the last day for the press, and again the gym is crowded. The television lights have turned the gym into a hot-house. Gerald Hayes stands at the side of the ring and keeps up a Joycean stream of consciousness throughout the sparring. 'Feint and throw the right. Feint and throw the right. Keep the right foot back. Walk him off the ropes, walk him off the ropes. Keep low. He's taller than you, his jab is going to be in your face if you don't keep low. You're too square-on. Turn your body, don't present such a big target. Keep your left shoulder up, chin well down in it. Get the weight on your right-hand side.' The press love the voluble Gerald. Ezekiel gets into the ring and the television lights go on full blast. The electronic bell rings and Barry and Ezekiel touch gloves in a friendly gesture. Ezekiel is moving with his usual cool confidence when suddenly, with his back to the camera, Barry catches him with a left hook. He takes four or five quick steps away and ends up dazed on the ropes. Barry slows down and asks, 'Are you OK?' It is the first indication I have had of Barry's extraordinary power. Ezekiel is twenty-one pounds heavier than McGuigan, but to watch them in the ring is to imagine you are watching two men of equal strength – until the cameras are turned on and McGuigan goes to work. It is the only glimmer we have seen in a week of McGuigan's punching power.

David Irvine and Peppy Muir start sparring. These are what's called the bottom end of the bill. Down there the punishment's just the same, sometimes worse. Last year Peppy broke his jaw and is only now recovering. Dave looks like a boxer fashioned in the public imagination. He has an attractive quality, but his face is well marked . . . his nose flattened. 'I used to work for a car salesman,' says Dave as he skips. 'It was a job. There wasn't much else going. I had

to give it up. He didn't like me coming in with dark glasses.'
Dark glasses is boxing for the way boxers try to camouflage
their injuries. 'He didn't like the black eyes. It wasn't good
for his image. Now I just do a little bit of work for Mr
Eastwood and box.' Dave is on the London bill, trying to
avenge a defeat at the hands of the Scot, Dave Haggerty.
Eddie Shaw pays the same attention to the lads in the ring
as he did to the star of the gym. Peppy's arms and shoulders
are covered with tattooed characters and at the end of the
spar all of them are sweating profusely.

THURSDAY
23rd May

With the TV cameras departed, Monday slips into Tuesday, and Tuesday slips into Wednesday, which turns into
an undistinguished Thursday. The only common denominator for these days is hard work. In Barry's diary he will
record every day that he is getting caught too often and that
he is taking some really bad shots. He is desperately trying
to adapt to what Gerald Hayes is saying. By Thursday he
is confused. On the seafront he tries to work out what
is wrong. He knows that what Gerald Hayes is saying is
correct, only it seems to be for a different fighter. He is
desperately afraid of changing his style so close to the big
fight. 'What he is trying to tell me is OK for him,' Barry
says. 'Those blacks are more fluid than us. They move
easier. It must be the temperature they live in.' Barry has
his own unique style, with his centre of gravity low down,
working from a crouching position. Most of the time the
weight is on his left foot to accommodate his famous left
hook. Gerald wants him to switch to his right-hand side,
but McGuigan is terrified of losing the strongest weapon
in his arsenal.

About the only mental diversion Barry will have these days is the decision as to what number plate he should get for his new Lotus sports car. This is the closest he gets to a projection of ego. There are three or four choices, and the numbers begin to assume importance far above what they would in normal situations. They are like worry beads for Barry over the next few days. Significantly, he chooses 'BAX 1T' because that's the way they pronounce it in Belfast. 'BAX IT,' says Barry in his best Sandy Row accent. It's as if he needs something close to home.

With the clothes pulled up to his chin in bed, Barry suddenly looks like the teenager that won the Commonwealth championship in Edmonton. There is the look of the waif about him, lost, abandoned. He could have stepped out of the film *Oliver*. But this fragile-looking character has decided for himself that he must do at least ten rounds of sparring on Saturday to see how his fitness is shaping up. He's a glutton for punishment.

Late that night Eastwood and Gerald Hayes are discussing tactics up on The Hill. Eastwood is beginning to worry about Barry's training form. He is beginning to seriously worry, as they say in Belfast. We are watching a poor-quality video of Hayes versus Pedroza. At the start of the third round Hayes catches Pedroza with a right and the champion hits the deck. 'He's a sucker for a feint with the left and then a right cross,' says Gerald. Eastwood is listening intently. He knows that Gerald is a brilliant technician, but he is also aware that he is beginning to undermine Barry's confidence. Physically McGuigan is perfect, it's the tactical approach that is worrying Eastwood.

We watch a video of McGuigan versus Charm Chiteule, probably the hardest fight Barry ever had. 'They say McGuigan left it all behind him in the gym before this fight, but I don't know. Chiteule was a good boxer, maybe Barry just couldn't get to him.' For Eastwood even to intimate a negative comment about McGuigan, things must be at a low ebb. As we watch the video, Gerald is constantly enunciating what must be done in a nightmare litany. 'Feint with the left. Right foot back. He is setting up the shots but he's not throwing them,' says Gerald.

The amazing thing about Eastwood is that you can't see him thinking. Most people would show the wear and tear of the situation. There is the feeling with Eastwood that he listens to everything and then does what is necessary. Not what's right or wrong but what's necessary. He gets a phone-call from the manager of the Harris brothers. They have an appointment somewhere in the Welsh valleys, making it difficult for them to get to the airport. Eastwood wants them here on Friday. He needs familiar faces to counteract the Panamanians and Hayes. 'I will send a plane to pick them up,' says Eastwood. 'The plane will be there at ten in the morning; have your boys ready to go.' Eastwood's own private plane will leave Newtownards Airport next morning at eight o'clock. Before it does, Eastwood will make two phone-calls. First, he calls Joe Colgan, Barry's masseur from the amateur days, and then he calls the manager of Dwight Pratchett, the new North American lightweight champion. He too is packing his bags. One side of his luggage tag says Dwight Pratchett, Gary, Indiana, the other c/o Beresford House, Queens Parade, Bangor, Co. Down.

FRIDAY
24th May

By Friday night the Harris brothers have arrived. They quickly strike up a friendship with the Panamanians and Gerald Hayes. That night there is a disco in Bangor and all the boys go off together in the best of form.

While they are away McGuigan is in the little room that connects the dining room to the kitchen. He is pouring water into a pair of gloves. 'Loosen them up,' he says to the question that doesn't need to be asked. McGuigan uses every opportunity to focus his concentration. What for others would be a chore he turns into a ritual to loosen some valve that will allow his mental approach to be fine-tuned. It is not simply that a little water will make the gloves more flexible, more importantly it allows McGuigan to get to know them. He applies the same meticulous approach to every item of clothing and protective gear. By the time he steps through the ropes, even in a spar, he likes to feel that he has reduced the variants in the situation to a position where he can control them. Then he lets everything go. Which is why it is ultra-important that he can trust Eastwood and those in his corner. They become extensions of his own internal dialogue. When you are talking to McGuigan about the fight it's not a question of opinions and response. What he needs to feel is that whoever he is talking to is on his wavelength and that his own thoughts are finding vindication in the outside world. His will-power is so strong that he will just phase out negative opinion, however well intentioned. That strength can only come from some deep inner resource where he feels utterly secure. The word most often used by Eastwood about Barry is 'love'. It's not a word you normally hear in boxing.

To get through to him, one has to proceed on instinct and not try to rationalize his strengths and weaknesses into a shopping list. What he does is not rational. Boxing is not a rational sport ... cricket and soccer are rational sports. They are sports in which the violent side has been civilized and on the surface they appear a gentleman's game, but they frazzle with untapped violent energy. They are games for sophisticates. Boxing is raw and uncivilized with all its violent energy on display, and so it is the most international of all sports. They say that in some ancient societies the strongest men of the tribes fought to see which tribe would carry off the victory. In that situation the warriors fought for everybody in the tribe and their future. It still carries memories of that elemental social battle. In no sport are there more gangsters ringside and more saints in the ring. A boxing match seems to bring out the most violent side of human nature. I hesitate to say the worst of human nature because it seems self-evident that human nature is violent. Sometimes boxing, having brought out these ancient emotions, purges them. Rarely at a fight is there crowd trouble. Not to the same extent that there is at other sports.

McGuigan leads with will-power. He is not the kind of boxer who can be broken down like a machine into assemblable parts: a good right hook, strong chin, etc. The fighter Gerald is trying to fine-tune is an ideal fighter who presents the smallest target in the world and waits tactically until the opponent is open. There is a faint suspicion that that fighter might be of a dark complexion with the kind of supple body movements that make the limbo dance a national pastime. All of what he is telling McGuigan is correct, but it can only be grafted on to a very different style gradually. McGuigan's greatest asset outside of his will-power is his strength. His method is to get to his opponent and wear him down with superior strength. Pedroza is a master technician and will exploit all Barry's forward movement mercilessly. What seems to be difficult for Barry this week is to break down Jose and Ezekiel's style to individual parts and then exploit this in sparring. He seems to be taking the whole of their similar styles as given, and taking some punishment to learn about it. Barry's world view is consistent, open and whole; Gerald's is cagey, airy and experienced. There is a clash of world views going on here.

Today is the day Barry is going to do as many rounds as he is allowed. His diary reads: 'Got up 11.45, All-Bran, cup of coffee, one glass of orange juice. Gym 2 o'clock. 11 rounds spar.' At the end of two rounds' sparring with Barry, Peter Harris's nose is as black as a pint of Guinness. Peter looks upon it with the kind of friendly contempt one reserves for relatives who visit too often. With a shrug he passes off its appearance. You feel that he has had more condolences about it than a double widower. After three rounds with Ezekiel, Barry fights two with Jose. It's difficult to remember that all his sparring partners get into the ring fresh after he has gone through maybe three or more rounds. It's difficult because McGuigan never shows any signs of wear and tear. He always looks as fresh as his opponent. Now after ten rounds he is in the ring with Roy Webb, a boxer who is a division lighter than Barry. Roy won a silver medal at the Commonwealth Games, and as an amateur he was Irish champion. He is a good boxer, but he doesn't seem to be moving any quicker than Barry, and this after McGuigan has gone ten rounds with four different opponents. Barry has proved what we already knew: he is a superbly fit athlete with unlimited stamina. Apart from that, he has not fought spectacularly well for his high standard.

18 *(above)*. Trainer Eddie Shaw keeps a watchful eye on what's happening *(Pacemaker Press International)*

19 *(above, inset)*. Barry and brother Dermot facing up to each other *(Duncan Raban)*

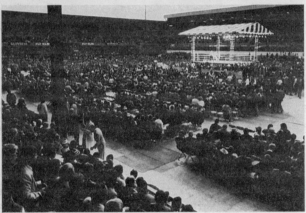

20 *(top)*. Eastwood lays down the law to Ramos Yordan, the W.B.A. supervisor. Stephen Eastwood is in the background, Paddy Byrne to the right *(Pacemaker Press International)*

21 *(above)*. The scene at Loftus Road, Saturday, 8 June 1985 *(Pacemaker Press International)*

22 *(right)*. Everyone is backing Barry at the Pedroza fight *(Star)*

23 *(above).* The knock-down in the seventh round which turned the title fight McGuigan's way *(Pacemaker Press International)*

24 *(left).* Christodoulous shows obvious concern for a great champion in the thirteenth round *(Star)*

25 *(right, above).* The nobility of the champion as he concedes defeat *(Star)*

26 *(right, below).* Celebrating victory with Barney Eastwood *(Pacemaker Press International)*

27 The morning after the night before – Barry and family at the
Holiday Inn *(Star)*

28 *(right)* and 29 *(below)*. Coming back in triumph to the biggest crowd in Belfast since V.E. Day *(Pacemaker Press International,* right, and *Star)*

30. Clones prepares to greet its most famous son *(Star)*

Today Jose and Ezekiel spar Peppy Muir and Dave Irvine.
There is a big gap in class and experience. Jose is really
performing. When McGuigan spars you never get the
feeling that the other fellow is out of his depth. It's not that
Barry comes down to their level, it's simply that he brings
his performances up only a fraction beyond theirs. There
is very little for the hare to learn in a race with the tortoise
if he runs off miles ahead. There is also a feeling that
McGuigan is aware of the potential humiliation involved.
When others box there is a feeling of triumphalism when
they are on top. With them it becomes a glorifying performance. Never with McGuigan; with him, it's almost an
exorcism, some dark monster he has to overcome. Self-
aggrandizement would amount to blasphemy. There are
days when dark thoughts cross his mind. He has been
caught by an elbow during sparring. 'This is the toughest
game in the world,' he tells me. 'Some days after a really
hard spar my memory goes for a moment. Like I'll be
talking to you and suddenly I'll forget what I'm saying
completely. It just goes out of my mind.' McGuigan pauses
for a moment. 'What did I just say?' he adds with a smile.

The Cliftonville Road runs off the Antrim Road on the
outskirts of Belfast city centre. It is a mixed area which
means it is neither wholly Catholic nor Protestant. It is a
dangerous place to be when sectarian murder raises its ugly
head. Dangerous for either denomination. The crime then

is to be alive. For a time it was known as murder mile, and when they say that in Belfast they mean it. It's not the kind of place you'd pick up a lift late at night from passing strangers. About halfway up the road on the left-hand side there is a residence sheltered from the outside world by a high wall. In contrast to most other communities in Northern Ireland, it is not protected by barbed wire. This is the home of the Poor Clares.

When McGuigan looks for psychological succour he goes to a community whose lifestyle is more reclusive (and possibly more demanding) than his own. The Poor Clares live an austere life, as can be gathered from their name, but they do not cut themselves off completely from the outside world. They are painfully aware of it. Of all the people in Belfast, the Poor Clares are the closest mentally to the psychological consequences of the troubles. They try to mend invisible scar-tissue. Sister Pasquele will tell you that those who have suffered bereavement are amazingly charitable in their response. Loss seems to appease the lust for revenge. Their thoughts are constantly for the other poor mothers, fathers, brothers and sisters who will have to go through what they have already suffered. The Poor Clares are the unpaid psychologists of Belfast troubles. To them McGuigan is not an answer to the problems, or even the beginnings of a solution; but talking to him has helped to relieve some of the profound sadness they bear as witnesses to such suffering. Yet they know that hope begins with the smallest turn of the wheel. They will talk to Sandra, Barry's wife, too. They know that pain is non-denominational.

On Wednesday, 29 May, Sister Pasquele is waiting for Barry. He parks his shogun outside the gates and goes past the Sisters' private chapel into their house. In one room Barry gets a key which will open the door into another. A hand draws back the green curtain. Sister Pasquele and Barry exchange greetings. Barry can be certain that for the first time in weeks it won't be a heavy in-depth talk about boxing. He will leave with a simple assurance that the community will pray for him. Barry believes that prayer that issues from such deep knowledge and such silence is powerful. The visit will do him a world of good. Barry is the community's favourite visitor. That night at dinner in the refectory Sister Pasquele will casually mention that Barry was in to visit. No need for second names. Thirteen nuns will crowd around to see how he is doing and to hear how training is going, how Sandra is doing and what Blain is saying. Penance prayers and obligations will fly out the window for a moment. Sister Pasquele has one further ace up her sleeve. Normally the Sisters can only watch religious programmes on television but she has obtained a special dispensation for the community to watch the world title fight. The sight of thirteen nuns cheering McGuigan on has convinced me that Pedroza has no chance.

On Wednesday, 29 May, one of the reconnaissance helicopters from the Palace Barracks sent back a message that a large platform was in the process of construction just a mile down the road in the shelter of a bungalow. The bungalow itself was being renovated, but that might just be a cover for paramilitary activities. The barracks was well within the range of the IRA's rocket-launchers. The pilot of the helicopter radioed back that the work was being supervised by a middle-aged white-haired man. They worked long past twilight and the last cars' headlamps left the driveway just before midnight. Whatever work they were up to it was of an urgent nature. First dawn would see the reconnaissance helicopter leave the headquarters of the First Border Regiment.

When they flew over the residence that the computer called 'Broome Cottage' the white-haired man was already there, issuing orders. The instruments on this sophisticated flying bird told them that the platform was about twenty feet square. (They were two feet out.) A young soldier watched. Within minutes they would radio back to base that the mystery platform was in fact a boxing ring. Home base confirmed the computer's accuracy with one word: 'McGuigan'. The Eastwood on the computer was McGuigan's manager. One mystery was solved.

All day long the sun shone on the bleached white hair of Ned McCormack. He gave his last instructions in the early afternoon and prayed that the weather wouldn't change. Eastwood himself came down to congratulate Ned on the work. Then Ned was dismayed to hear Eastwood say that they wouldn't use it until late that night. Pressed for his reasons, all Eastwood would say was that it was 'psychological'. He wanted McGuigan to be getting into the ring at about the same time as he would in London.

The only people outside the camp who knew about it were those in the intelligence room at Palace Barracks – and they were likely to keep it a secret. They returned at three and then at four because they knew that the McGuigan party drove to the gym every day at about half-past two. They missed out. McGuigan didn't turn up for training until half-past seven. The only people there were those close to the camp: Trevor McClintock, Joy Williams and George Ace, along with the training team. Today Eastwood left Jose and his distractions in Bangor. Dwight Pratchett had proved to be an ideal sparring partner for Barry, and into the bargain he was a quiet easy-going mid-Westerner.

The ring looks huge in the back garden at Broome Cottage. It's a big ring, twenty-two by twenty-two. On a diagonal, it takes eight to nine paces to cross, but there is nowhere to run if you are in trouble. This is the size of the ring they will use in London. Eastwood is hovering around all the time talking to Barry. It's too late now to change much physically. Now all he can do is build on the patterns that have been developed over four years and refined a little in the past two weeks.

Barry boxes like the sun, brightly, brilliantly, without a stop. It's as if he has left all his problems behind in the gym. Eastwood is like a two-year-old, beaming like a child who has been promised candy-floss. Behind the childlike appearance however, the old yogi is thinking. He stops at seven rounds, almost annoyed that McGuigan wants to go on. They have reached some sort of psychological plateau, it can be only downhill from here. Amazingly, Eastwood won't allow McGuigan to train outdoors any more. It's as if he wants to preserve the memory of the outdoor boxing at Broome Cottage as some sort of little epiphany . . . a small oasis on the Stations of the Cross. A blue sky, white ring and the best sparring so far is what will remain in McGuigan's mind. But after the fresh air it's back to the prison of room seven.

FRIDAY
31st May

The most important thing about Joe Colgan (apart from the fact that he is an excellent masseur) is that he knows Barry from the amateur days. With anybody else, some of Barry's energy would have to be displaced in formal introductions and the process of getting to know each other. Although Joe is one of the most prolific talkers in the game, this will not faze Barry. He can listen to Joe and faze him out whenever he wants, without any hurt taken or given on either side. Sometimes Joe will ask you a question and then answer it himself. Joe uses language like a message. You do not have to interpret everything he says or answer him.

I have noticed in the last few weeks that language is not as important to the boxers as the physical signals they receive. Their trade pre-dates language in the tribe. A week ago a video arrived from Teddy Atlas in the US. In it he was giving some instructions to Barry on how to fight Pedroza. Something was wrong with either the equipment or the cassette, because it was very difficult to hear the soundtrack. I was trying desperately first to correct it, and then, when it was fifty per cent right, to make out what was being said. After a few minutes I looked at McGuigan. He knew exactly what was going on. He didn't need to hear the words; he was watching a universal language.

Ireland is a country where language has run riot. At one time it was the only thing we could spend freely, and so it was dispensed with all the liberated wealth of the slave turned master. A lot of us Irish are caught in thought-patterns that are language- and not action-based. Emmet's speech from the dock is seen as a victory rather than the last hurrah of an ill-planned uprising. We are trapped by the faculty of speech, but the horror is that as Irishmen we can't communicate the bare essentials of humanity to each other. Like myself with the video, too many people listen and do not see.

FRIDAY NIGHT

After his big evening meal and his usual walk, it's time for Barry's battered body to get some relief. He lies face down on the improvised massage table just off the kitchen. Joe applies some oil.

'The only place I can see Barry improving is in the ring,' says Joe. 'For his height, his size, his whole body is in proportion. It can't get any better. You'll see guys with a great pair of shoulders and a little pea head. Barry's not like that, he's not freaky. He's got a great structure. He's a little Adonis.' Joe begins on Barry's back. 'Over the years Barry's got to know a lot about his body, the different muscles. He has developed each part of his body to perfection. He's got great stomach muscles. Great back muscles. Look, if you poured water on there it would just flow off. It's the muscles in the arms and shoulders for punch power. They are all connected like a girl's plaits. Twisted round and round and interconnected. The punch gains power not just from the biceps but from the muscles here in the chest and round the back, the pectorals and the deltoids.'

Barry by now is falling asleep. He has heard Joe's description hundreds of times and he is aware that Joe thinks Barry is the best amateur Ireland ever had.

'It's in the arms and shoulders for giving and in the legs and neck for taking. The legs are most important to any boxer. It's his foundation. You'll see boxers in the ring, they might have a powerful upper body but they get hit with a good shot and you'll see the legs going like what?' Joe answers his own question with one word, 'Jelly.' For a guy receiving a punch the most important thing is a good neck and strong legs. 'Am I right, Barry?' Joe asks, not expecting an answer. Barry growls in the affirmative. 'Am I right or wrong,' Joe asks as part of a tennis match he and Barry have played before.

'Exactly,' Barry drawls in almost as many tired syllables as there are letters. Barry moves on the table and starts to explain. 'The worst thing,' he says, 'is the jarring sensation. The more powerful your neck is, the more you can take it.' What's jarring is the brain. It's sitting there nicely protected by its own little crate, the cranium, when suddenly it is jarred by a blow out of nowhere. Barry has taught his body to react instantly to such an eventuality. He will ride with the punch. This has the effect of stopping the brain rebounding forcibly off the wall of the skull. The brain has its own particular suspension which can only withstand so much pressure before it passes on the impact. At that stage some of the motorized functions of the brain are impaired and, because of their position and length, the impact is most obvious in the legs. When the springs and supports that assist the brain are battered too much then they lose their elasticity and it's not long before the motorized functions spread their damage to every part of the body. Then it's not the legs that wobble but the speech.

Every day Dave McAuley kisses his wife Wendy goodbye
and heads from his home in Larne towards Belfast. Today
he will pack all the clothes he needs to keep him in London
for a week, along with his training gear. Dave is slightly
smaller than Barry, fighting in the flyweight division. He
is the next-best prospect in the gym. He appears relatively
unmarked from his boxing career, which prompts the
thought that the most ruthless boxers are those who don't
look like boxers. If Dave wins his fight on the London bill,
he will get a shot at the British title – which would mean
that he wouldn't need to be on the same bill as McGuigan
to fill the Ulster Hall; he would be a draw in his own right.
The contest means a lot to him. That is one of the reasons
he will not overextend himself in training today. It's too
near the fight for heroics. Besides, being in the same boxing
stable, as they so ignominiously call it, Dave and Barry are
good friends, on the look-out for each other's welfare. It's
in such conditions that Barry receives the worst injury of
his sparring. Reaching out a long lazy left jab he pulls a
muscle somewhere near his left elbow. Eastwood looks
round the room. There are only five or six people about.
All of them are sworn to secrecy. Time will tell how
bad the injury is, but the psychological damage could be
devastating if it plays on McGuigan's mind.

Time to leave Beresford House. Outside, Eastwood pulls up in his Rolls-Royce. Everybody else has left for the airport; McGuigan is on his own. For the last time he goes back into room seven to say a silent prayer and to pull into his physical being the psychic energy he has displaced all over the walls and ceiling of this hidden little room. His fears, dreams and hopes hang in the air. He gathers as much of the energy as possible and heads out to Eastwood in the car.

The atmosphere on the plane is jovial, just like any group going on a high adventure anywhere in the world, the only difference being that there are very few drinks sold. The man who sits across the aisle from me I have seen in the gym, but I am not particularly sure of his position on the team. He carries a long canvas container, the kind that would hold a fishing rod, except it is much too broad. It's about the length of a shotgun, but I can't see any need for such an instrument on our trip. Eventually curiosity overcomes me. 'That's the peace flag,' says a small dapper man who looks as if he might be a civil servant in a neatly tailored suit. He carries the flag solidly between his legs. 'I will carry it into the ring.' Billy remembers the time he carried another flag. 'I remember the day I went to Dublin. I was to meet Harry Taylor on the station at Victoria Street in Belfast. He didn't turn up. It was for the European championships. It was a Sunday, I remember, 1946 or thereabouts. It is probably the greatest memory of my life getting off the train at Amiens Street in Dublin. There was Father McGloughlin in his clerical uniform and President Carroll. When he saw me, Father McGloughlin threw his cap into the air and came running down the platform, and lifted me off the ground, just because an Ulsterman was there to represent Ireland at the European Games.'

It's part of the cancer of partition in Ireland to classify

people according to their religion when they are from Ulster. There is no sense of triumphalism about any of this man's stories, so my lazy classification of him as a Catholic is now in doubt.

'Then when I was asked to box for Ireland at the Olympic Games, T. D. Morrison, head of Northern boxing, called me into his office. I had carried the flag at the European Games and he asked me, if I had to fight for Ireland, at least not to carry the Tricolour round Wembley. In my absolute innocence I said to him I didn't know if I would have the honour. I was as proud to carry that flag for Ireland as I am today carrying the peace flag for Barry.' He says he's a Shankill Road man, born and bred. That seems to be my answer: he is a Protestant. I ask him, is he? Without any belligerence he tells me religion has nothing to do with it. 'McGuigan has no relation to the troubles. People just can't help loving him. Especially the womenfolk of today. He's such a nice fellow, it's my delight in life to have helped him in whatever sense I might have done it.'

I ask him what he thinks of him as a boxer.

'I try to liken him to Sugar Ray Robinson. He can build himself up to the degree required and that degree is a winning degree. I think McGuigan will win inside the distance.' A sign tells us to put on our seat belts. 'Here we go, here we go, here we go.'

Barry and Eastwood sit together on the coach into London. From now until after the fight they will be inseparable. Dermot, Barry's brother, is on the bus as well. We drive towards the Holiday Inn. Our route takes us past the Grosvenor House Hotel in Park Lane. This is where Young Ali met his death in the ring with Barry. I wonder what he must be thinking as we drive past. In the past three months this tragic event has appeared on the perimeter of my attention six or seven times. I wonder how many times in little ways it affects Barry. We head on down to Marble Arch and on to the Edgware Road. There are about twenty in the party and our luggage is blocking the little London side-streets. Outside the Holiday Inn there are four flags, the Union Jack, the Canadian flag, the Holiday Inn flag, and what must be the peace flag. It flies limply in the cool June air.

Barry McGuigan wakes up on Tuesday after a fretful night to a throbbing pain in his left elbow. He needs treatment immediately. This is a multi-million-pound problem. When Eastwood hears the news, he has two reactions: the first is regret and the second is terror. What he is afraid of is that the news will leak and the papers will carry scare stories and McGuigan will be subjected to constant talk about his injury. He has to keep this injury quiet. Most people in this situation would pull down the blinds and pretend nothing has happened. Instead, Eastwood gradually lets the word slip through the camp over two or three days so that by Thursday there are nine or ten people going around keeping a secret that only they, Eastwood and Barry are aware of. Amazingly, it works. Nobody in the press suspects anything until after the fight. The odds stay the same, so even Eastwood's compatriots in the bookmaking fraternity live in blissful ignorance – and these guys can usually tell whether the eggs were scrambled or easy over. The whole episode tells me something about Eastwood and McGuigan. Neither of them ever complains.

Apart from the fact that it has a peace flag conveniently outside the door, another reason the Holiday Inn was chosen is that it is close to one of the biggest parks in London. Hyde Park runs away from Marble Arch for a couple of miles. The corner of the park that is nearest the hotel is Speakers' Corner. This is where you can speak

177

sedition and get a clap for it. It works on the old British tradition that if you put a man on a soapbox, you render him harmless. Barry will go for a run in the park for the next few days. On his first day running he sees a party of four or five black men. It's Pedroza's team. Barry takes an alternative route. It's too early yet to meet. He's not going looking for Pedroza yet.

Back at the hotel, Barry is feeling tired after his run and there's a press conference at the Portman Hotel at noon. To steel himself, he has an ice-cold bath. He will train later. He is expected at the Thomas A'Becket gym in the afternoon. On the podium at the press conference there is a new face. It is that of Mickey Duff. And what a face ... it's the kind of face with a thousand stories to tell, depending on the occasion. Above a boxer's nose, eyes ever in flight survey the assembly as if to say, 'Who's out to get me today?' He waits for the moment when he can claim his part in the drama.

McGuigan as ever has the press at his fingertips. By now any statement that he makes of a positive nature almost has the stature of fact so that when he says simply, 'I will win,' everybody nods in the kind of unconscious agreement that was last seen at Stalin's fourth Party Congress. Eventually Barry, having kept the press happy and his elbow under wraps for half an hour, departs for the Holiday Inn. At the press conference *The New York Times'* journalist confesses that she has never covered boxing before, but that the editor wants a story on McGuigan, and while pardoning herself she asks Gerald Hayes to spell his name. This is Mickey Duff's chance. He begins with a big G, follows with a big E, then an R straight out of *Sesame Street*, and A from the start of the alphabet, an L that in his cockney accent feels like a warm place to be, and he closes his introduction with a D that is as pronounced as the D in 'how de'. Gerald Hayes mops his brow, as much as to say, 'Thank God somebody got me out of that, us blacks can't spell.' Hearing the laugh that emanates from the assembled reporters, Mickey Duff looks at the little piece of mime Hayes is engaged in and smiles a big broad grin that says, 'It's all show business, we're funny guys up here, me and Gerald.'

Somebody asks, will there be drink on sale; Stephen Eastwood hedges his bets. This is a delicate subject with the Eastwood camp. They hate the image of the drunken Irish. But Stephen is annoyed that the British Boxing Board of Control have announced there will be no drink on sale; in the first place it's not their business, and in the second place it issues those who do want to see the fight through rose-tinted glasses with a forewarning to turn up legless.

Somebody asks if it is the biggest fight ever in Europe. Mickey sees another chance: 'It's the biggest fight since Henry Cooper fought Cassius Clay at Wembley Arena in 1962.' As I am thinking that is the first time I have heard the name 'Cassius Clay' in public in years, somebody corrects Mickey from the floor. Mickey listens and then again begins in a regal tone: 'I apologize, my friends, it was at Wembley Arena in June 1965. I ought to remember, because it was the week my son was bar-mitzvahed.'

'But you forgot, Mickey, that the man's name at that time was Muhammad Ali.'

Mickey smiles up and down the podium at his gaffe, as much as to say, 'Sure they don't believe a word I say anyway.'

Back at the hotel, Eddie Shaw and Barry train in the quiet of the penthouse. Barry does two or three rounds' skipping ... two on the pads and two rounds shadow-boxing. All through the routine Barry feels tired. From now on he begins to dry out. More than anything else, it's the physical manifestation of the upcoming battle. With the thirst come the nerves, which make the thirst worse. Without the nerves things would not be natural. So for the time being Barry is feeling thirsty and nervous and normal. At the Thomas A'Becket gym the caretaker will tell the assembled press, 'McGuigan won't be here today but certainly tomorrow.'

Early Wednesday morning, Barry goes for his last run before the fight. Back at the hotel, Danny lets Barry in for breakfast. Danny has been Barry's minder since the early days. Danny is as big as his personality. I've noticed the bigger the man is, the more he admires Barry. Danny's admiration shines out of his eyes at all hours of the day and night. This job minding Barry is different from Danny's usual police activities, but his disciplined, quiet presence is exactly the kind of company Barry needs in these last few days. Danny is always apparently relaxed but as alert as an actor on first nights. If all the men in the vicinity were asked to give their left arm for McGuigan, there would be a lot of one-armed men in the penthouse.

Barry's elbow has responded to the treatment, and there is less swelling. At two-thirty, Barry starts to train again in the penthouse. He does about thirty minutes altogether between shadow-boxing, skipping and the pads. The reporters at the Thomas A'Becket are again disappointed. McGuigan is getting the reputation of Howard Hughes. He has spent ninety per cent of his time since arriving in the penthouse. All he has for company is Eastwood and Danny and occasional visitors. If the truth were known, it's worse than that: most of the time in the penthouse McGuigan spends in his own room. He makes occasional sorties to the fridge for ice to have a cold bath. Eastwood and Danny only talk to him after he addresses them. Tomorrow at last Barry must leave the room. According to the WBA regulations there has to be a trial weigh-in two days at least before the fight.

The weigh-in is to take place in the gym in which Pedroza works out. According to the arrangements, the two fighters are to be weighed in separately, the first meeting to take place at the official weigh-in on Saturday. This unofficial version is a medical precaution to prevent the fighters losing too much weight close to the contest. They have to weigh in within five per cent of 9 stone, which would make 9 stone 6 pounds safe enough.

The gym is in Carnaby Street. I go down a dark flight of stairs to a basement. In a brightly lit gym two men are sparring. One of them I don't know, but the other is the longest reigning champion in any division. This is the legendary Eusebio Pedroza who has had more defences than any man since the great Joe Louis. This is what McGuigan has been hearing about since he was seventeen. From the day he won the Commonwealth gold medal at Edmonton, the name of Pedroza has stood at the top of the world's featherweights, as immovable as the Ten Commandments. This is the word made flesh, *El Campeon Mundial de Peso Pluma*. The action in the ring is unreal after the level of aggression at McGuigan's workouts. The boxers glide round the ring, bent double like two grannies exchanging notes about crochet. They throw light punches at each other, then show one another the punch that could do the damage without landing. The immediate feeling with Pedroza is of a king at the end of a game protecting his territory with masterful, simple moves. McGuigan on the other hand is as exciting and unpredictable as a knight errant, but if this fight is to be dictated by a preconceived tactical pattern, then the champion looks a past master.

On the T-shirt of one of Pedroza's cornermen are the words PARTIDO REVOLUCIONIRA DE LOS TRABAJAD-DORES. What that means translated into English is that Pedroza is a legislator in the Panamanian assembly for the

Revolutionary Democratic Party. Only six of Pedroza's defences have been in Panama; it is not the richest country in the world, and Pedroza has had to go wherever the money was best. He will get more for the fight with McGuigan than for his first eight defences put together. For a poor boy whose family lived in the broken-down shacks that housed the canal workers, one of the only ways upwards was through fighting. In the last couple of decades there have been seventeen Panamanian world champions. Each one of them receives a stipend from the government of £400 a month as a token of appreciation. Pedroza's hero and mentor was the General, Omar Torrijos Herrera. He was the kind of man Graham Greene went to Panama to vilify and remained to praise. He negotiated a treaty with the US that gave Panama control of the Panama Canal. Four years later he died in a mysterious plane crash. For Pedroza, the politician trying to better the lot of his people, possession of the world title is almost as strategically important for him as control of the canal is for the people of Panama. In that country most things revolve around the canal. His two trainers, who glory in the names of Henry Douglas and Lyonel Hoyte, are descendants of Jamaican immigrants who came to build it. Pedroza knows the power of a man fighting for a whole nation. He can detect somewhere on the perimeter of his radar that McGuigan means as much to the Irish people as all the seventeen world champions rolled into one. He doesn't fully understand why, but he has heard of Belfast and he will not go there to fight . . . and Pedroza will go anywhere in the world.

The rest of Pedroza's workout is a revelation. He attacks the heavy bag with a maniacal fury, landing punches from all angles. He skips in front of the mirror, urging himself on in inspirational Spanish, all the time letting out strange war-whoops which are translatable in any language as 'Kill'. Another cry is translated by a sparring partner from New York City as 'McGuigan is bullshit'. Pedroza understands that word. He confirms with a look and then adds in derogatory English, 'Bullsheet.' All the time Pedroza is urged on by Hoyte and Douglas, whose combined age is somewhere around one hundred and fifty years. Their bodies are twisted into the shape of men who might have picked cotton for seventy years. It's not just a world title that McGuigan threatens to take away from these men, he threatens to take away their world. What they don't know about the fight game you couldn't sell for fifty cents in Caledonia, Panama City's Harlem, the place where they were born and bred.

One figure stands out from the rest in the Pedroza camp. He has a name as impressive as his pleated white shirt. Mr Santiago del Rio feels like a man who, having just signed the best contract of his life, fears that it might be his life contract, and that the terms are not really as impressive as he had first thought. The Mephistopheles who got him into this situation is Mr Barney Eastwood. He has bought out all the options so that their whole future depends on defending the title successfully, in front of a slightly partisan crowd of 25,000 halfway round the world and, yes, I suppose you could say that Santiago is on edge. It's the kind of edge that knows all the ropes. He knows every trick in the book. When McGuigan doesn't show up at the appointed hour, he starts telling the press that it is a calculated insult to them. Trying to turn the press against McGuigan is like King Canute trying to turn back the tide. Santiago himself hasn't the gift of tongues and each voice he hears is speaking an unidentifiable language. In these situations, persistence gains more in stature than communication, and one man is very persistent. To add to his stature he has the initials ILHGA on the pocket of his blazer. He has been promised an audience with the champion. Santiago del Rio is pointing to the watch and asking the man with the initials, 'Where is McGuigan?' A messenger arrives. 'Eastwood understood that Pedroza did not want to meet him so why is he an hour and a half behind his schedule?' Santiago listens to the translation and then says, 'OK, if they are afraid to meet us, we go ahead with our weigh-in, McGuigan can come in when the champion is finished.' He promises that Pedroza will stay in his dressing room until McGuigan is gone. Pedroza has now been at full tilt for over an hour . . . He must be having weight problems. He moves towards the scales. Santiago del Rio stands to his right. They weigh him. The crowd hear 8 stone and the rest is lost in a gasp. The champion is underweight already. This will have a psychological effect on McGuigan. Pedroza does not need to work hard any more to lose weight. He holds his index finger up in the air. 'Numero Uno,' he says in international language.

The man from the I L H G A is talking to Pedroza. The press is waiting for McGuigan. Somebody from the Pedroza camp says McGuigan is scared. Pedroza moves away from the man with the initials. 'Where is he going?' asks somebody from the press. 'To the dressing room,' says the man with the initials. 'Where is McGuigan?' somebody asks. Nobody knows. 'Who is in charge?' asks a press man. Somebody asks the man from I L H G A what the initials stand for. 'Oh that,' says our man, 'that's the Irish Left Hand Golfers Association.' The mad hatter has taken control.

Another crowd moves from the door towards the weighing scales. The empty space in the middle is occupied by McGuigan. There is no more telling difference between their heights than the fact that McGuigan is not visible until he steps on to the scales. He strips close by and then the pale small frame ascends the scales. 8 stone 13 pounds and some ounces. There is an ounce or two in it. It's unbelievable that the two men weigh the same, given the difference in frame. McGuigan makes no gestures.

Pedroza's animal energy is different from that of McGuigan. Pedroza can summon huge reserves at will. With McGuigan it is ever present. It's as if that animal force uses Pedroza's body as a diving instrument through which it passes so that in the gym you will know where he is because of the waves he makes through the crowd. McGuigan simply does not displace that amount of energy.

Pedroza emerges from the dressing room. In the boxing

lexicon the word they use to describe him is dour. It's a word that short-changes the man. It's just that his smile is detached from his eyes. The bottom half of his face has learned to be a politician, but his eyes are those of the ghetto in the land of plenty. He watches McGuigan for a time.

Carefully Pedroza puts on a cap that would do a lumberjack proud, the kind of cap they issue in the baseball little leagues in Panama ... the kind that adds three or four inches to your height. He adjusts it to get the maximum benefit. As McGuigan heads towards the exit, he comes forward and holds his hand out. McGuigan reciprocates the gesture. They shake hands. They freeze. Pedroza's face is smiling, but his eyes are not. McGuigan pulls his hand away and heads for the exit. Later, Pedroza will claim that McGuigan was scared. On the way out Barry meets Ove Ovesen, the Danish judge. 'Ah, Ove,' says Barry, 'I remember you from when you were refereeing the ...' If he has such presence of mind when he's scared, what's he like when he's fearless?

THURSDAY NIGHT

Besides the weigh-in there are other obligations on this Thursday. It is the feast of Corpus Christi and Barry goes to eight o'clock mass around the corner from the Holiday Inn. I try to remember which Station of the Cross we are sitting behind; it's only later that I realize it was Christ meeting His stricken mother. Barry is praying intently. At home, Sandra has journeyed from Clones to Belfast to speak with the Poor Clares before she goes on to London. She will stay at a guest house in Kilburn, well out of Barry's way, until the fight is over.

Back at the hotel, Eastwood is pacing up and down his

room. McGuigan is in the room beyond. Between the rooms are two doors. Eastwood's is open all the time. When McGuigan opens his, Eastwood knows he wants to talk. Until then, he keeps an almost silent vigil. The press have been looking for Barry all week, but they have been kept at bay. McGuigan has spent most of the time in his own room, opening the door occasionally to talk about old stories, small talk, nothing important.

Suddenly Eastwood stops. 'I was standing here,' he says, 'and he was standing there. I said to him, "This bigotry is terrible. If you come from the country it's not too bad though it's bad enough there, but if you come from the Shankill or Falls Road, it's bred into you." He looks at me with the eyes. "Something will have to be done about it, Mr Eastwood," he says. "What's your idea, Barry?" I says. He says, "All the grandparents and great-grandparents, shag the lot of them. If we started off now, all the young people. It's our country, let us all live in peace. No more of this ******** bigotry. Bring your children up and say, 'So you're a Protestant, you're a Catholic.' Live with them, mix with them. Marry them. Get involved with them and vice versa. You see; in ten years the improvement would be terrific."' Eastwood pauses for a moment. 'In the House of Commons he would have got a standing ovation.' We tiptoe back into the room with the ice in it.

Eastwood tells me of the time he went to Haiti to see the Laporte–Gomez fight. Out of Gomez's corner came this voodoo woman. Everybody laughed, but Eastwood remembers the look in Laporte's eyes. 'When Pedroza gets into the ring, I'm going to produce this midget from under the ring. I'll have him stored there from early on, and then at the appropriate moment we'll produce him. I'm going to get him to go over to Pedroza and shake his fist. An Irish leprechaun. What'll he think?' Eastwood asks the question, knowing full well what he'll think.

Friday is one of those days that you can never anchor. The ship sails on over incalculable depths which nobody can sound.

At a meeting in the Imperial Hotel there are seven men. Six of them are men made flesh, the seventh is the ghost of Brussels. It's only a couple of weeks since the Liverpool–Juventus Cup Final at which nearly forty people died. 'How will the crowd react if a man is counted out after the bell at the end of the round,' asks the referee, Stanley Christodoulous. The importance of the crowd is stressed again and again. Santiago del Rio is not here, so Eastwood can relax. He leans forward and whispers. All the heads lean in and consider what he is saying. When they lean back they look as if they have been taken into the confidence of a man who will go as far as possible to accommodate anything they want.

Eastwood continues to confide in them: 'Santiago del Rio wanted American gloves, then he wanted English gloves, then he wanted gloves from anywhere in the world. I told him he could have American, English, South American, Italian, anything he wanted.' The grin with which Eastwood says it could mean any number of things. Now Eastwood is in his stride. 'Look at the tape situation. He wanted unlimited tape, then he wanted ten feet of tape, then he wanted something else. I told him we'd fight any way he liked, no tape at all if that's what he wanted.' Everybody laughs a little. Everybody knows that the rule says ten feet of tape, but the bravura with which Eastwood announces things endears him to everybody. Eastwood epitomizes the difference between the con man and the artist. With the artist you know you are being conned and you love it.

The public rules meeting will take place at the Portman Hotel. All over West London the lights are out. In the foyer of the hotel a lone harpist, undisturbed by the enveloping gloom, plays a melancholy air. As we begin our ascent up the dark stairs, the harpist resolves the cascading strings into the Beatles' 'Michelle'. We turn up a second flight, to be met by a generous window that allows the meeting to be held in some kind of twilight.

Santiago del Rio is there, as accommodating as a well-fed cat in the absence of Eastwood. Everything is resolved quickly.

Back at the Holiday Inn, Eastwood is exploding. 'I don't care what ABC says, that's not the way it's being done. I don't care about their money. They can take the money and go back to the States. I have the cheque downstairs. I haven't cashed it yet. I don't care about prime time or half time or any other kind of time, Pat McGuigan is singing "Danny Boy" and he's singing it for 1 minute 45 seconds. I got Phil Coulter to arrange it, 25,000 people will join in. When Pedroza hears it, it will send shivers up his spine. You can come up here to the penthouse now but I won't change my mind.'

Eastwood storms around his side of the penthouse. Over on the other side Father Salvian Maguire is saying mass for Barry. The grey-haired Father Maguire is a Passionist father who bears the marks of having listened to a hundred thousand confessions all over Ireland. Today he heard morning confessions then drove to Belfast to take the plane to London to say mass for Barry, as has been his custom ever since they became friends. Everybody has that look about them that says, 'Let's stay calm,' but the atmosphere is electric.

The phone rings again and Eastwood picks it up. 'Hello, Mickey,' he says. 'Sure the boy is calm. He can stand up to the pressure. I never saw him so calm. There's been an awful lot of money for Pedroza. There was one bet of 50,000 and another of 60,000 and several of 25,000. They rang Adrian at the head office and asked, could they lay some off. Adrian said he could lay 25,000 without thinking but if it was any more he'd have to call me. I told them they could have 100,000 and when I say 100,000, maybe they could have a bit more. Do you think maybe they are trying to check us out? Would they have heard about McGuigan's elbow, do you think? The only person I can think of with that sort of money in cash is Pedroza. Is he backing himself? Yes, check the odds in Las Vegas and ring me back.' Eastwood hangs up the phone. He asks the air, 'Who is backing Pedroza for that sort of money?'

Arrangements are made to get Father Maguire a room to stay in. McGuigan is in his room on his own, but his unseen presence haunts the sociable side of the penthouse, the way the ghost of Parnell haunted Irish politics for decades. McGuigan has used up all the ice on the eleventh and twelfth floors. We have to get Ross Mealiff, Sandra's brother, to go two floors below.

Eastwood starts to talk. He talks the way McGuigan boxes. In public he is reserved, quiet, aware that the talk is for general consumption, but in private his talk is like a succession of hammer blows. When he talks about the McGuigan–Pedroza fight, it's as if his words have some magic quality capable of influencing the event ahead. He looks into his glass as if he can divine the future in there. 'Look, here's what it's all about, boys. There's nobody knows as much about Pedroza as I do. There's certainly nobody on this side of the Atlantic. I could tell you the colour of his wife's eyes, I know so much about the man. He's a legendary fighter. He's the fighter for the connoisseur. He mightn't suit the Falls Road man or the Shankill Road man, who want to see two guys battering each other, but the cuteness of him, the way he can block and move! He can do it all. The wee short ones he can hit you with, and he can stamp on your toes. He's got the cunning, he's got the craft, he's great at all the naughty stuff but, look, I've said to Barry, he's an old man. He could be your dad. You've got the strength, you're twice as strong.' Eastwood pauses. 'He's real hungry to win.' Then he adds ominously, 'He's got to win for all of us.'

When Eastwood says all of us, he doesn't mean the people in the room or Barry's mother and father or the people at the fight or the Catholics and Protestants watching in their separate pubs and homes in Belfast, or the Irish throughout the world. He means everybody. It's as if mankind itself would benefit from McGuigan winning. That's the kind of way he believes in the Cyclone. This mystical faith in McGuigan is both frightening and compelling.

Eastwood continues: 'There's a wee signal that he's been saying to me all week without saying anything at all. He's saying, "I'm ready," without saying anything at all.' Eastwood pauses in imitation of McGuigan's silent communication. Their strength comes from silence. 'You see the eyes. It's the eyes. You see he'd be doing something there and we're just footering about and he'd look up like that ... Sssush,' Eastwood makes a noise that primitive man might have made to describe a charging bull. 'Just like bullets coming out of his eyes. You couldn't describe it.' He just has. He holds everybody spellbound, describing an energy most of us have not felt since our childhood. A passionate anger beyond logic. 'If I'm any judge of a fighter, this guy is going to produce everything tomorrow night.' With that the beginnings of 8 June start. We go to bed at dawn. The weigh-in is at ten o'clock.

SATURDAY MORNING
8th June

On Saturday morning, Barry is still in great form. Eastwood is up early, trying to protect this mood. The Friday night papers have been talking about Barry's sombre mood of resignation. He has been totally isolated at the top of the Holiday Inn for almost a week and he is gaining a reputation Howard Hughes would have envied.

At seven o'clock that morning, Pedroza has weighed in privately at the Leicester Square Odeon. Stephen Eastwood is there with Trevor McClintock. They are not allowed within twenty feet of the weighing scales. Pedroza steps up and Santiago del Rio adjusts the scales. He says, the entourage translate, 'Nine stone,' and they clap each other on the back.

With McGuigan there is no problem making the weight – although there *is* a problem making the scales, as there are more people at the weigh-in than were at his first half-dozen fights. Barry and Eastwood push their way towards the stage. It's ten o'clock and they should be weighing-in by now. Santiago del Rio, thorough professional that he is, points to his watch, saying in effect that McGuigan is late, his man is going to get up on the scales first. By this stage, Eastwood and Barry, with Danny and Vince McCormack protecting them, are halfway down the aisle. Pedroza steps on the scales and gets off quicker than the three-card-trick man. The scales nod for a moment and then come back to rest. Stephen Eastwood says he didn't see what happened, and then his attention is caught as he sees McGuigan climb on to the stage.

Things are about to die down when McGuigan says to Eastwood, 'Stephen is not happy, Mr Eastwood.' Eastwood catches McGuigan's words and fully understands his drift. He explodes. The dam of protection that he has been building round Barry has been burst.

With the same kind of hand–body movements that Michael Jackson and Mick Jagger use to whip a crowd into frenzy, Eastwood is all over the stage. Everybody is culpable. To look at it objectively you would say that he has gone over the top. His eyes have the same kind of maniacal fury that Ali had before his first fight with Sonny Liston. Everybody is astonished at the performance, but what nobody knows is that McGuigan caused it. One little word of doubt from him is enough to send Eastwood down to hell, to bring back the fire of self-belief. This is what McGuigan needs to retain that calm that has descended like a gown of snow around self-doubt. He knows that Eastwood will let nothing pass.

For his part, Eastwood believes in his soul that, given a fifty-fifty chance, McGuigan can take the title. He is pointing to Pedroza and then pointing to the scales. You don't need a translator to know what Santiago del Rio is saying: 'He crazy – he loco.' They are staying where they are. Their trial is over. Nothing can calm Eastwood; he stalks about the place. He asks Ray Clarke of the British Boxing Board of Control, 'Is this the way we are going to be treated?' It looks like the fight is off now, because Eastwood won't let McGuigan go ahead until Pedroza is put on the scales again. Santiago del Rio sees his chance and Pedroza is out through the door.

Quietly McGuigan goes over to Eastwood and says, 'Let's go ahead.' Immediately Eastwood goes to the scales. Mickey Duff wants to make an announcement, but Eastwood grabs the microphone. 'The way we have been treated is a disgrace. I hope we are not treated as bad tonight. They have won all the rounds so far, we are going to start winning from the first bell tonight.'

The British press are aghast. No stiff upper lip here. Suddenly the weight of what McGuigan is fighting for has shown in Eastwood's reaction. From now to fight time, he will be as calm as McGuigan. The thunder has spoken.

SATURDAY EVENING

The rest of Saturday passes quickly. Barry spends the day eating, filling himself up with carbohydrates. Dermot is there most of the day. He and Barry exchange jokes. At seven o'clock the bags are packed. It's time to go.

'Make sure you have everything now,' Eastwood says.

'Can we get out of here quietly?' We press the lift button that only has one direction on the twelfth floor. It seems to take forever.

'Anything but boxing now, do you hear me, lads?' Barry says, and then adds, 'please.' Still the lift is not here. Barry again:

> 'One fine day in the middle of the night,
> Two blind men got up to fight,
> Back to back they faced each other ...'

No need to guess at Barry's dreams now. Somebody moves impatiently at the lift's tardiness.

Eastwood responds:

> 'For a man he is fool
> For when it's hot he wants it cool
> And when it's cool he wants it hot
> And always wanting what is not.'

Here are two of the bravest men I have ever met talking nonsense rhymes before perhaps the most important night of their lives. But the rhymes have that ability to hold reality together as if they answered some deep, simple need: the subconscious nightmare of McGuigan and the wish fulfilment of Eastwood.

Eventually the lift arrives. We get in ... seven of us. We have an uninterrupted ride to the fourth floor where the lift opens to reveal a couple of tourists. Their way is barred with the magic word, 'Security.' Down in the bowels of the hotel feet echo in the car park. Ray jumps into the van. He has driven the route to Loftus Road many times, but still his nerves are on edge.

On the way McGuigan is telling most of the jokes. They are the kind of jokes that would be best appreciated in Clones. Mostly they are about local characters and their mannerisms. It's as if Barry is trying to remember who he is and where his roots are, like the Beatles and their early, overexaggerated Liverpool accents. The one that could apply to Pedroza gets the biggest reaction: 'He's so thin the one eye would maybe do him.'

A car has been following us for some time and Danny asks who it is. It turns out to be the Harris brothers, as carefree as if they were going to a carnival. We pull round Shepherd's Bush, and the traffic gets thicker. People going to the fight start to recognize McGuigan. Their faces light up in instant pandemonium. 'Go Barry, get him!' they scream. They roll down the windows of taxis at the same time as they open the door, their co-ordination lost in the tumult of their well-wishing. We drive on past the overflowing pubs. At five minutes to eight we pull up at the players' entrance at Loftus Road and are quickly lost in the narrow tunnels that lead to the dressing rooms.

The scene in the dressing room is in marked contrast to the world of the Holiday Inn and the good-natured press conferences. This is where the blow lands. It's stunningly easy to tell which fighters are getting ready and which fighters are getting repaired. Roy Webb's eye looks like something out of *Star Wars*: it has grown to monstrous proportions and along its hard-boiled circumference there is a gash an inch long from which I recoil, expecting every second a human eye to emerge and survey the passing caravan that troops into McGuigan's dressing room. Webb has won – I dread to think what his opponent looks like in the other dressing room. Paddy Byrne berates the texture of Webb's skin for its lack of resistance. 'That Webb fellow, he cuts too bloody easy,' he says with a child's sense of bafflement. 'I know he bloody well won,' says Paddy, 'but he cuts too easy.' Paddy's anger is with the epidermis of mankind, its tissue-like softness under attack. This mild outburst out of the way for the rest of the evening, Paddy will be the coolest man in Loftus Road. This outburst just serves notice that his adrenalin is flowing. He's on his toes.

The room has been picked for its defensibility. Only one door gains admittance and with his back to it, as immovable as Samson, stands Danny. McGuigan sits on the bed, cut off from the outside world by a field force that keeps his eyes focused on the floor. Looking at his eyes, I expect him every minute to turn into the Incredible Hulk. It's impossible to tell that there are other fights going on at this moment. To make sure that reality hasn't gone amiss I go out into the stadium grounds. Far away I see the illuminated square. One figure is on the canvas. I look at the TV monitor in the dug-out. The little beetle on all fours turns into the familiar figure of Dave McAuley. It's the fifth round. The referee is beginning to count. He beats the count and I go back to the dressing rooms.

Back in the dressing room McGuigan is under attack. Santiago del Rio has just burst through the door demanding to see McGuigan's bandages. The man doing McGuigan's hands, George Francis, is the best in the business. He has managed many world champions and, as they say euphemistically in boxing circles, 'he can take care of himself'. Santiago del Rio pushes George aside and suddenly it looks like the tension is going to explode prematurely here in the dressing room. He wants McGuigan's hands re-done. Suddenly the room is full of officials, translators, peace-makers and peace-breakers. Santiago is pulling at McGuigan's hands. It is an obvious attempt to break McGuigan's composure, and that is the only reason Eastwood keeps his cool. 'Get this man out of here before any damage is done,' he keeps repeating. It is decided to re-do Barry's hands. Again Santiago is not happy: 'The bandage cannot go near the knuckle,' he is translated as saying. Again, Vesuvius rumbles and McGuigan's eyes cloud over with a mist that is either anger on the boil or the tears of frustration. Dermot appears at the door and the protection that was tribal turns animal. This is the leader of the pack protecting the cub. This is a blood-brother on the rampage. He stares at Santiago del Rio. All need for translation goes out of the door. This is no play-acting. Another false move and all hell will break loose. The hands are shown to the officials. The referee comes in through the door. 'Of course the hands are OK.' Santiago del Rio moves towards the door. A half-smile plays across his lips at a job well done. It's the last time he will smile tonight.

I walk out to the tunnel again where Wendy McAuley, Dave's wife, is crying her eyes out. I am about to console her when she turns her eyes away. The St John's Brigade are carrying a stretcher into the dressing-room area. I look in horror at the figure, and then to my utter relief I see that he is fair-haired. It's the Scottish opponent, Bobby McDermot. Wendy's tears turn to relief and then to joy; Dave has won.

In the dressing room they are taking off his gloves. He broke his left hand in the third round. He had to keep throwing out the left jab for several more rounds so that his opponent wouldn't know that he was as predictable as a one-armed bandit. Dave's face looks like a boiled lobster. No sculptor would ever stretch the skin so far on such a small frame. Congratulations pour in from all sides. His fellow professionals say nothing. They know that victory smiles bring pain. Eddie Shaw takes the glove off with his ruthless delicacy. His hand has been inside that glove, too. In the tenth round Dave knocked his man out.

Davey Irvine is getting ready to go out. He seems calm and relaxed, but once you put on those gloves you know there's going to be pain. Like a pregnant woman, no matter what happens, there's going to be pain. Back in Barry's dressing room, Dermot is whispering to him. The next hour flies past and suddenly everybody is saying it's time to go.

Somebody asks, 'Have you got the iron, Paddy?' You can't forget things out there. Paddy is a true professional and so he has made a list of all the things he needs. What he needs most is calm. He needs the presence of mind of an airline pilot who never reacts in a hurry, no matter what the situation. 'Cut men' in the fight game are rogue surgeons. They need the cool of a surgeon and the touch of a faith-healer. Razor blades and ice are the alpha and omega of their trade and they strike while the iron is cold. The fighter depends on them for his vision. With a swift application of the iron they can add a second dimension when a boxer is fighting from one eye. Tonight, Paddy Byrne is one of the 'I've seen it all before' school, but deep down he knows it's never the same twice.

'Let's go,' McGuigan says with all the cool of a commando. He's ready. In that moment a burden is lifted. It's too late to stop now. We are sucked down the long corridor by a tremendous noise. Desire made manifest in the shape of one long inexhaustible howl that would be a continuous scream except for the fact that it breaks like waves, each succeeding one crashing into the slipstream of its predecessor. What depth of passion created this roar?

The long corridor to the ring has a life of its own, opening and closing like a demented accordion. Ahead, the peace flag mast-head of this crazy caravan dances on the edge of a whirlpool that constantly threatens to pull us down. Eddie Shaw is a boxer, he fights his way through the crowd. There is no etiquette in hell. Tonight the roar is McGuigan's theme song and the score from *Rocky* plays a muted second fiddle, like a crazy violinist reading from the wrong stand. For 25,000 people at a football stadium in London, McGuigan is not the Great White Hope, he's the only hope.

The swell ends at the no-man's-land where the paying public meet the ringside commentators. Viewed from outer space, McGuigan is the centre of a sparkling necklace as a hundred photographers try to pull reality down to earth in a flash. Reality tonight is a dream come true. McGuigan is getting into the ring to fight for the world title. Ireland is good news for once, and 25,000 people erupt as He Who Never Steps Backwards comes through the ropes. He dances forward. 'Buy land,' said W. C. Fields, 'they don't make any more of it.' McGuigan dances across the ring, each hook and jab a down-payment on this piece of real estate. For fifteen rounds tonight this space is up for grabs. A boo stifled at birth warns us that the other bidder is on the way, and then the boo turns into the sustained applause worthy of this world champion.

Now all the forces are assembled and it's time for the

national anthems. The British national anthem doesn't sit easy on the shoulders of 25,000 Irishmen, but eventually everybody behaves with the decorum invented in the heart of that other great empire ... for a couple of minutes we are all in Rome. Suddenly from nowhere comes a sound as remote as the theme from *Rocky* was. It's impossible to make it out in the din. Pat McGuigan, microphone in hand, answers this musical quiz with the deadly ear of the born crooner.

> But come you back when Summer's in the meadow
> and when the Valley's hushed and white with snow

Now everybody knows what it is and Pedroza looks around in belligerent defiance as the whole crowd join the chorus:

> 'Tis I'll be there in sunshine or in sorrow
> Oh Danny Boy, oh Danny Boy, I love you so.

These are 'the men that God made mad, For all their wars are merry and all their songs are sad'. If Pedroza is pulled in by the deceptively beautiful air then he's lost a psychological round. 'Danny Boy' is a recruiting song for war. It's a brilliant ploy from the Eastwood camp, uniting the crowd in a lull before the storm.

Now each corner has one last trick to play from its psychological armoury. True to form and with a little nod to Carl Jung, Eastwood produces his from a subterranean level. Paddy Byrne lifts the skirts of the ring and the dwarf emerges. They wait till Pedroza turns away and then the little man jumps into the ring. The crowd shouts. Pedroza turns and the look in his eyes is astonishing. It's as if for a moment he allowed his subconscious to think that this was McGuigan. If only it were so ... Reality returns and the cheekiness of the gesture demands a smile which Pedroza gives with a cool mastery. The MC's announcement of 'My Lords, Ladies and Gentlemen' is drowned out, presumably by the gentlemen. It's time for the seconds to get out of the ring. Eastwood feels something tugging at his sleeve. McGuigan looks around. '£5,000, my man at even money,' says Lyonel Hoyte. Eastwood looks into his eyes. '£5,000, my man will take him out,' repeats Hoyte. Eastwood looks for the green which is nowhere in sight and so he pulls away. Money talks, bullshit walks. There are no more ploys to play.

The opening round is marked by a combination of speed and phenomenal concentration. Pedroza's concentration is remarkable, given the fact that he is fighting on foreign territory – but then he has already performed in front of the grass-skirted warriors of Papua New Guinea. He has an amazing mind. He goes on his bicycle, shooting out long left jabs and keeping well out of McGuigan's way. The first solid blows are landed in the neutral corner where Dermot McGuigan has parked himself. They came from Barry. Dermot claps. McGuigan pursues the champion for the whole three minutes, but Pedroza wins the round with the effectiveness of his counter-punching.

Round two is much the same as round one, with one small exception. McGuigan, instead of following Pedroza around the ring, starts to cut off his territory. It's like the snake and mongoose, but Pedroza is not hypnotized. He leans down in the middle of the round, staring into McGuigan's headlamps. Fighting inside, Pedroza can use his famed bolo punch which comes from below like an upwardly mobile piston. In this round he also lets loose a strong left hook, but the inescapable fact is that he is not overwhelmingly superior inside. McGuigan has neutralized the Panamanian's greatest asset.

From his commentary position Harry Carpenter is shouting, 'This can never go fifteen at this pace.' The third is the start of thirteen rounds that will make a liar of him. At the opening of the third round Pedroza fights brilliantly, whipping in a punch that is a combination of an uppercut and a bolo. Pedroza is such a craftsman he invents punches. This one lands under the heart. It should have slowed McGuigan down. It didn't. McGuigan keeps coming forward, and now he begins to slip Pedroza's jabs and counters with his own hooks to the body. The champion is acting as if these are having no effect on him. McGuigan's cheeks are rouged from Pedroza's left jab, but he never looks in trouble. This is not just a physical contest, this is going to be a battle of minds. That both men are in perfect physical condition is obvious from the first nine minutes. At the end of three rounds, nobody is ahead in either the psychological or the physical battle.

At the start of round four, Pedroza hesitates. The bell goes to call them to the centre of the ring and the champion turns back to get his gumshield. It is the first lull in the action. It lasts only five seconds but it's like a blemish on perfection. Is it a conscious ploy of Pedroza's or his unconscious asking for respite? Pedroza has trained himself to go fifteen rounds. He has trained to go three minutes a round – but not like this, this is inhuman. Not since the legendary Henry Armstrong has a fighter thrown as many punches per round as relentlessly as McGuigan. Each one of them is intended to take Pedroza's head off. He knows he is in with somebody desperate to win, fearless and strong. Pedroza is the master tactician looking for time to work out his strategy. He isn't getting any.

Immediately the round opens, McGuigan catches him with a hard right. Pedroza shoots back a left hook and right uppercut. Most people at the ring think they see Barry smile as if the punches had no effect on him. He was in fact grabbing his gumshield in his mouth. McGuigan has two reactions when he has been stung: he grabs his gumshield tighter and he wipes off the gloves on his trunks as if to obliterate all that's gone before.

After that it's as if he's moving the contest on to a higher, more demanding level. It's this ability constantly to bring his performance up to the required level that reminds people of Sugar Ray Robinson. During the fourth and fifth rounds he wipes off his gloves on his trunks several times. Pedroza has only one answer: he must stand his ground. Somehow he has to stop this Niagara pouring over him. In the middle of the fifth, he tries to move Barry back. They stand toe to toe, exchanging orthodox and unorthodox blows. The kid is brilliant inside. And strong. Too strong. Pedroza decides to get on his bike again. This time he has a slow puncture.

Boxers are so alert physically in the ring that they sense what will later be revealed only by slow motion. At the end of the fifth round McGuigan sensed that Pedroza was slowing: he moved against the ropes in McGuigan's corner, looking for a breather. McGuigan didn't give him an inch. He loaded up to land the big one. When he threw out his long left jab he felt a tear at the elbow. The psychological advantage had been countered by a physical problem. McGuigan told his corner that his arm was acting up. Eastwood said he could beat Pedroza with one arm. He didn't get a chance to throw that arm until the seventh round.

Towards the end of the sixth round, a strong right to the body catches Pedroza. His knees buckle momentarily. Pedroza is hit with a strong overhand right. He stumbles and then looks to the ground as if he missed his footing and slipped. This man never gives out hurt signals. This is the technique Ali used against George Foreman until the champion ran out of heart. McGuigan's heart is as big as Loftus Road.

There's no faking the reaction to the right McGuigan hits Pedroza with at the end of round seven. His legs give out from under him and, before he can bring up his instinctive right arm in defence, McGuigan's left glances off it and sends him to the canvas. The champion has been humiliated. He recovers as best he can, getting up at three and acting as if an unruly banana-skin had just entered his life. McGuigan comes scything his way across the ring, a figure of Death. Pedroza escapes the harvest. He is the coolest man in Loftus Road.

In McGuigan's corner Gerald Hayes is banging the canvas, screaming, 'Feint and throw the right hand.' McGuigan's feint at the end of the seventh was worthy of catching a world champion. He feinted with his head as if he was going to throw a left to the body and then followed up with the big overhand right. Before Pedroza hit the canvas the crowd was on its feet.

The eighth round is Pedroza's best of the fight. He keeps McGuigan at bay with long left jabs and extraordinary counterpunching. Towards the end of the round he exchanges short sharp punches with McGuigan. This man is not going out without a fight.

At the start of the ninth round Pedroza catches McGuigan with a good right. He punches and boxes the same cool round as he did in the eighth, but then lightning strikes again. In almost the identical spot in the ring, McGuigan hits him with another right. McGuigan follows this up with a right to the temple and suddenly Pedroza looks like a Rip Van Winkle who has just woken up with his legs full of pins and needles. He stumbles across the ring. He lurches and tosses, miraculously avoiding the raging torrent that is McGuigan. Somewhere in his head, bells are ringing and blows are falling from all angles. At the end of the round Santiago del Rio is in the ring protesting to Mr Christodoulous that Pedroza has been hit after the bell. He holds up three fingers. Pedroza stands in the centre of the ring and then arches his back like one of the Scots Guards outside Buckingham Palace and heads back to his corner. This proud man is still featherweight champion of the world.

Pedroza slips at the start of the tenth round. He looks at the floor where the dwarf had sprinkled his gold dust as if to say, 'So that's why I've been falling in the same spot.' He has his mind trained so that it is impossible to lose, but his body will not obey. The tenth to thirteenth rounds are purgatorial. In each of them the champion boxes with the fervour of redemption, only to have his potential salvation snatched away at the end.

Pedroza tries his best shots in the thirteenth, hitting McGuigan with a long left and then a strong right hand. McGuigan hits him with another powerful right. By now Pedroza knows the reaction to that particular weapon: grab tight and hold on for dear life. He reaches out and grabs McGuigan with both hands. With pure animal strength McGuigan shrugs him off like a sack of potatoes and hits him with left hooks for his trouble. The referee raises his hands to stop the fight and puts them down as quickly again. Hope is deferred and Pedroza survives the round. At the end of the round Pedroza's corner gives him something that looks like ammonia to revive him.

At the start of the fourteenth Pedroza blesses himself as though it is the last, and then spends most of the round hanging on, determined to go out on his feet. Late in the round Pedroza is crouched low, trying to avoid McGuigan, when suddenly he sees his chance. He shoots a long straight right through McGuigan's guard to the chin. It is the hardest punch he has thrown all night. It is too late.

When Pedroza goes back to his corner at the end of the fourteenth round he sees Eastwood raise three fingers. He is three minutes away from losing his world title. In his corner, McGuigan is asking Eastwood, 'Are you sure I'm ahead?' Eastwood answers, 'You're as far ahead as from here to Belfast.'

Both men touch gloves at the beginning of the fifteenth round. Pedroza behaves with decorum and nobility. He is making his final exit with style. McGuigan ducks and weaves in close to Pedroza. This is what a normal fight looks like in round one.

The three minutes go by on a wave of euphoria. McGuigan is on his way to the world title, but somewhere deep down in him is the fear the verdict might be given against him. Close to the end of the fight he lunges at Pedroza with a Saturday-night special. The distance he misses by is a measure of Pedroza's class as world champion. The bell goes and Pedroza hugs McGuigan. The Eastwood camp are in the ring. Daniel McGuigan watches as Sean McGivern and Ross Mealiff in the company of the whole Eastwood entourage lift McGuigan shoulder high. Pedroza is acknowledging McGuigan as champion, but when his team get into the ring they quickly raise his hand in a last, empty, professional gesture.

Like the Ali–Frazier epics, this fight defies mere professionalism. It's as if the divorce proceedings are over and McGuigan and Pedroza can become friends. There is no doubt that the old champion respects the pretender to his title. The announcement that officially confirms McGuigan as world champion is lost in a huge roar. Possessed young men hurl themselves at the ring as if they could levitate over the hunched journalists. They rise on the substantial backs of the penmen and engulf the ring, searching for McGuigan in an entranced fit.

As McGuigan realizes that the title is officially his, he looks to his brother Dermot as if seeking proof that he won't wake up from this dream. Dermot rubs his head, and for the first time in months I see the fact that Dermot is the elder brother manifest itself.

The TV announcers are trying to get to McGuigan. He thanks everybody, starting off with Mr Eastwood. This man is champion of the world and all the McGuigan charisma starts to come out. He begins to say something about Young Ali: 'One thing I've been thinking about all week. I want to dedicate the fight to the young lad who fought me in 1982.' Suddenly McGuigan starts to falter. It's as if the words 'young lad' have opened up a well that lies too deep for mere words. 'I want to dedicate it to him,' he continues bravely, and then before the eye of the camera he runs ahead of the tears, 'I would not like it to be an ordinary fighter who beat him ...' he says before the tears take centre stage, 'but the world champ.' He has ended in a flood of emotion with the humblest possible affirmation.

Back home in Clones, Irish Television are asking Katie McGuigan if she is proud of her son. 'I'm happy,' she says. 'Pride is not a word I like. Just say I'm happy.'

Amidst the milling crowds McGuigan is led back to his dressing room. Davey Irvine congratulates him. All the rest of the boxers on the bill congratulate him. When he has gone into his own dressing room I ask Davey Irvine how it went. 'Beaten,' he says, 'in the third round.' He pauses. 'Or was it the fourth? That will just tell you how it went. That's it. That's me finished. I'm retired. I'm not tough enough. I hurt too easy.' The amazing thing about Davey Irvine is that there is not an ounce of self-pity or jealousy in his words. He appears as happy as a man can be who has finally resolved some inner truth about himself.

Paddy Byrne comes in and goes straight to Peppy Muir. 'There's your money,' says Paddy. 'I don't know if there's any point in fighting out there, but there's your money anyway. It's bedlam.'

Peppy Muir looks at Paddy and then says, 'I want to fight. I want to be able to say that I fought on the McGuigan bill.' As McGuigan goes upstairs to meet the world's press, Peppy Muir goes out to fight a lonely fight with Simon Eubanks.

I have been with these boxers for two months now and the amazing thing is I have never felt any aggression from any of them. I don't mean aggression towards me, I mean aggression as part of their personality. It's as if they leave all their aggression in the ring. The world of the boxers themselves is a closed silent order where they can communicate with each other with a simple nod of the head.

Upstairs, at the heel of an enormous press throng, one of Gerry Cooney's people keeps asking rhetorically, 'Who trains this guy? I want to meet the man that gets this kid into that condition.'

Brian Eastwood tells him, 'You'll never meet him. We only stop McGuigan getting fit. That's our job – to stop him training too much.'

Cooney's man keeps shaking his head and saying, 'I wish I had fighters like that.'

Ferdie Pacheco, Muhammad Ali's fight doctor, is there. Long ago he recognized the special qualities in McGuigan. He presented McGuigan with his paintings of all the world champions. Ferdie knows talent when he sees it.

McGuigan can never redefine boxing in the way Muhammad Ali did, but he could redefine the definition of sport in this bloody business. He has the talent to be one of the major sportsmen of the second half of the twentieth century. In the midst of all the congratulations McGuigan has one priority: to get Sandra and Blain back to the hotel safely. In the confusion of the night, Sandra forgot to get nappies. The taxi-driver takes her all over London. All the chemists are closed. When he discovers who she is, he insists on taking her home to get a couple of nappies from his own kids.

There is a huge crowd outside the hotel. Eventually McGuigan arrives. He will not join the party. He goes straight up to his room to have a meal. Pat arrives at the celebration, accompanied by Frank Mulligan, Barry's first trainer. Dermot is there, as hoarse as a man suffering from laryngitis. All McGuigan's sisters are there except Rachel, who is keeping her mother company at home.

With all the hype and media attention, somebody somewhere was bound to have a nervous breakdown. The part of the McGuigan household in which it happened and the time at which it occurred almost led to a tragedy of Greek dimensions. Phil Coulter had just finished singing 'The town that I love so well', in the Holiday Inn in London when Katie McGuigan and her sister, Bridget Rooney, went to bed in Clones. As Phil sang, Katie switched off the lights one by one. The video-cassette of the fight was still in the machine, stopped where the MC says, 'By a unanimous decision,' and the crowd lets out a deafening roar. At the touch of a tired button, that roar had been stilled. The electrical wiring in the house was making its own silent protest at all the demands being made on it. All night it smouldered with resentment and, as if to time its explosion with the maximum damage, it erupted at five-thirty in the morning after the night before.

What by daytime would have been an inconvenience by night turned into a roaring inferno. Upstairs, Bridget turned over in her sleep. With that sense of alertness that comes from sleeping in strange surroundings, she smelt something amiss. She walked casually down the stairs, to be met by flames in the kitchen. It was too late for do-it-yourself fire-drill. The only thing to do was to try and wake Katie and Rachel, and get them the hell out to safety. By the time Katie had rubbed the sleep from her eyes all of her movable memories had gone up in smoke. Besides what the world knew of Barry, there were all the other little possessions that made her other children as important to her as her most famous son: gone were the pictures of her wedding day; gone were Rebecca's drawings; gone were marriage certificates, birth certificates, everything that proved you existed; and on its way out was the door to Barry's gym, the fire eating its way unconsciously into the heart of a legend. Now the steps were ablaze. Katie backed off.

The fire brigade were on their way. They hadn't far to come but, by the time they arrived, the private part of the McGuigan world was gone. The fire almost split their world in two. The public shop was still there, putting up a brave front as ever. It would be open in a few hours. With a crash the roof caved in on the kitchen. Katie listened to her world collapse. Two dozen handless gloves gave up the fight without any resistance. Muhammad Ali, Alexis Arguello, Jim Watt, all watched their paper worlds ignite and pass away. When the water had washed out what the fire spared, the gym stood lonely and abandoned, perched like a treehouse at the bottom of the yard.

Katie did not want to tell Barry. It would ruin his first day as world champion, but a fire brings hasty news, and Barry found out. Dermot flew home as Barry held the fort at a press conference in the Holiday Inn. He stood out from the rest of the Eastwood camp as he was the only one who could speak without the deep rasp that comes from prolonged abuse of the vocal cords. Hoarse throats were carried round the Holiday Inn like a badge of honour. The English press, with the hyperbole that is an integral part of boxing, told Barry that he had done more than any man to unite Ireland in seven hundred years. No matter which way

you calculate it, they were out by a couple of hundred years
... but then they were only speaking metaphorically. When
Barry mentioned that Blain had asked for champ, the pun
was lost on the English. The Irish contingent, anxious to
hold on to Barry as one of their own, urged him not to
explain that 'champ' is a mixture of potatoes and onions.
Everybody wanted to claim him.

Barry had meant to stay an extra couple of days, but
he decides over dinner to go home to have a look at the
damage. In Belfast and Clones, people will try frantically
to cope with a schedule whose pace has been set by
fire.

At another table Barry Cluskey is telling tales. He is an
old family friend. 'I think they even called Barry after me.
I was there the day he was born. After the fight people went
mad. One fellow was jumping up and down with a towel in
his hands. "I got the towel," he says. "I got the towel.
Look," says he, and he holds the towel up in my face.
"Look," says he, "it's the towel. The blood and all." Don't
be showing me that, says I. I've got his fucking nappy.'
Cluskey, in the company of about 25,000 others, had a few
jars after the fight ... This had the effect of dislodging his
memory somewhat and he ended up in the Grosvenor
House Hotel, insisting that he was staying there. He turned
round and saw the former champion come through the
door. 'I turned round and there was the head and his
entourage. I got a surprise, so kind of spontaneously I
started to clap and all the people in the lobby started
clapping too. Pedroza just froze on the spot and then tears
started to come out of his eyes. Down his cheeks. He saw
the cross around me neck and he came over and bent down
to kiss it. With that his hat fell off. I stood back in surprise
like and there was a momentary pause and I didn't know
what to do. I got the feeling like that it might be an insult
to him to pick it up for him. He bent down to pick it up
and he couldn't make it. He couldn't bend down.' Barry's
eyes start to mist over. 'What a champ. One of his people
came over and picked it up for him. He couldn't bend

down with his ribs. That's how much punishment he had taken. Then he put the baseball hat on and just walked away.'

By nine o'clock we are in the VIP lounge at Heathrow. Sandra is doing her best to keep Blain's attention away from the fact that he is exhausted. Behind his dark glasses McGuigan is talking about the fight: 'I couldn't hit him a solid blow. He was slippery. Even the right in the seventh round. It was a good punch but it didn't travel far enough. Then when I swung in the left hook he already had his right hand up so I caught the top of his glove and he fell over with the impact. He said to me that I'd be a great champion. I learned a lot from this fight. I was better than him inside. That's his best aspect, and I was better than him at it. I couldn't throw long lefts with the pain in my elbow. He was hurt. Normally he would grab me inside like a vice.' With two upraised arms Barry imitates the carpenter's tool. 'Then he'd go whap. Grab. See, in the ninth round he didn't grab me, I went whap whap and I could see his legs begin to buckle. Feel that,' McGuigan says. On his chin there is a lump the size of a bull's eye. Barry explains its origin. 'Do you know what round I got that? The fourteenth. I thought I had him going, I could see Christodoulous from the corner of my eye. He made a move as if he was going to stop it and I dropped my guard for a second. Whap. He hit me a straight left.' Barry says it in obvious admiration. 'It was his best shot of the night.' It was the left of a drowning man delivered with all the venom of one fighting for the people of Panama whom he represents. From the silent nodding of heads one gains the impression that the former champion's stock is rising all the time. They begin to realize what Barry has actually accomplished.

On the plane there are two TV crews trying to record Barry's every move. An unsuspecting passenger stops in awed silence for a second before he realizes that his reaction is the centre of attention. Happiness overcomes embarrassment and he rescues himself with one word: 'Barry.' This time it's said not in awe but with a simplicity that means 'I was there'. Saturday, 8 June, is assuming legendary status already. Participation confers a brotherhood on strangers whose nodding silence speaks a religious fervour. What will Belfast be like?

As the plane comes down, people are singing 'Danny Boy', but the melody dies in the expectation of the Belfast welcome. Out on the tarmac nobody is working. Men in overalls stand on top of the Customs Hall waiting for their hero. The press are kept back a respectable distance. Everybody wants a shot of the hero returning home. The walk from the plane to the airport lounge is civilized enough but, once inside the building proper, mayhem becomes the order of the day. People crowd in, trying to touch Barry. There is no point trying to thank his supporters, it's too dangerous. There are certain situations where you must keep going. Danny tries in vain to offer Barry some form of minimal protection. Eventually he arrives at the half-decent sanctuary of a press room. One of the photographers being pushed and jostled moves with a familiar expertise. Hughie Russell is in the front row of men snapping away. It's not quite as dangerous as when he was in the ring with McGuigan, but it's a good workout.

The questions fly at Barry. Yes, he's glad to be home in Belfast. He wants to thank the supporters. He doesn't want to be a flash in the pan. Some question about boxing in general. Barry grabs the opportunity. He thanks all his supporters who have welcomed him home. He points to Russell. 'Especially wee Hughie Russell, my old pal.' Some word in there breaks through the public occasion to the private heart of a man. Hughie turns away. You can't take good photographs with watery eyes. Hughie regains his composure and snaps away.

Outside, Barry's new Lotus waits in the car park. Some question as to whether it's safe to drive it into Belfast. Where is the reception? Outside the offices of the *Belfast Telegraph* and then on to City Hall. Now it's every man for himself.

Outside the *Belfast Telegraph* it's as if the crowd had been reassembled after the fight. The emotion is identical to that at Loftus Road. It's impossible to believe that two nights have passed since McGuigan was crowned world champion. Here it's as if the crowd have been in suspended animation, only to be released from this twilight world by the appearance of their hero. McGuigan jumps on the float and the crowd surge forward with that familiar life of its own. Only this time it's grannies, teenagers, and babes in arms. It seems like all of Belfast has taken the day off. 'Barry, Barry, Barry, Barry,' they keep chanting.

McGuigan is in great form, reaching out to as many as he can touch. One young girl follows the float, hammering all the time at the boards of the makeshift ring. From her deep trance-like depths some demon is being exorcized.

The float has been designed to pass through the gate that blocks the way to that target of targets, City Hall. It only just passes through, forcing those at its sides to a temporary halt. Belfast has been caught unawares but there hasn't been any better improvisation since Van Morrison led a band called Them in the early Sixties. Coloured toilet rolls stand for bunting that defy any political overtones in a city where colour is often a badge of hatred. The political ranting of religious bigots has been shredded from the morning papers into a ticker-tape of snow.

Usually when the TV cameras are on Belfast, the smoke signals in the distance inform an incredulous audience that another car bomb has just exploded in this city of ancient hatred. Today it's different. Today the Romeo and Juliet on the back of the float are not poisoned by family hatred, they are the one speck of hope that the cancer of sectarianism may respond to treatment. When Barry and Sandra hold Blain aloft, the crowd goes wild. At last they have something to cheer about. Still the crowd keeps coming. The ropes and cornerposts of the ring have come asunder, all protection is gone as we gain the sanctuary of City Hall. This is the biggest crowd since Victory in Europe Day, 1945.

Once inside City Hall, Barry insists on speaking to the crowd outside. Barry crawls through a window that has not seen a similar exit since the masons laid the first stone. He picks up the microphone, it fails. No matter, a picture tells a thousand words. Eastwood holds Barry's hand on high and the crowd gives one last united cheer before they journey home to their separate realities.

MONDAY NIGHT

Barry and Sandra get into the Lotus with Blain. They wave goodbye to the City Fathers. A Councillor from the Shankill Road ventures the opinion that Barry could be the first Catholic councillor if he ran against him in the local elections. Barry drives away from that prospect. Eastwood rings his pilot, and within half an hour his son Adrian is driving us to the airstrip at Newtownards. As we sit on the runway ready for take-off, Eastwood whistles a tune, one of those melodies you have heard somewhere before but that you can't quite put your finger on.

We take off and in a couple of minutes we have left the industrialized heartland of Ireland behind. Three minutes' flight time puts paid to the length and breadth of industrialized Ireland. The smokestacks are only a minute behind us when the largest stretch of inland water in Ireland looms up ahead. It's about twenty miles long and ten wide, but our iron bird treats it with disdain. Past Lough Neagh we travel between Cookstown and Donaghmore, respectively Eastwood and McGuigan strongholds.

Somehow the shouting of voices over the roar of the engine brings back memories of Loftus Road. The hoarseness of Brian, Trevor McClintock and Eastwood is in harmony with the mechanical tattoo of the engines. McGuigan's great feat is made greater by a realization of the supporting role played by Pedroza. 'The calibre of the guy he was fighting,' Eastwood suddenly announces, with an emphasis on the word 'calibre' that makes it seem odd in conjunction with a human being. It's as if he wants to compare Pedroza's accuracy with that of a gun and his nerves with its steel. 'Look, I must confess,' he continues, 'after all the trouble the manager put me through, I couldn't help feeling sorry for the fighter. Barry says with the exception of Hagler and Curry, Pedroza is the best pound-for-pound fighter in any division. I say he's better than those two. He's foxier. Only a genius could have stayed up there in the last five rounds. He was kidding to McGuigan the last five rounds. He was gone, but he braved it out.'

The talk centres on the merits of Pedroza for a minute, but Eastwood wants to take the conversation higher. 'There is something different about this, about the whole McGuigan phenomenon. I've seen some great sporting occasions. I won an All-Ireland medal myself, but this is different. The emotion of it, it's an emotional thing. I don't cry, I never cry, but I saw people today at the City Hall and they couldn't stop crying. Girls, ladies, all crying. It wasn't just the women. I saw three or four lads from the Shankill. I know two of them, just got out of Long Kesh, and they were crying. Big baby tears rolling down their face. It's bigger than any of us. It must be this peace thing. Barry's supporters are not boxing people. It's the people who live up in Lesson Street want a bit of peace.'

Eastwood is whistling the same melody again. I know I have heard it somewhere before but I just can't remember where. Somewhere to our right as we begin our descent is

Boa Island. On it is a carved statue which pre-dates Christian Ireland. One of its heads looks north and the other looks south. It's stuck there on an island in the middle of Lough Erne for no particular reason. A two-headed idol with eyes in the back of both his heads.

As we drive into Clones the roads for miles around are lined with parked cars. People are coming from all over. It's like a scene from the Bible, thousands of people converging on this tiny little Irish town. The town itself is a mass of bunting and flags. Each trade and shop has contributed its own sign. The butcher's shop in Fermanagh Street has 'We steak the lot on you Barry' emblazoned across its front. Up the street the Italian fish and chip shop has 'It's a pizza cake', one of the drapers has 'Sock it to him Barry'.

The Diamond has never seen such a crowd in its history. The whole square is full. From an open-ended truck, officials are addressing the crowd. When Barry comes on stage he starts to thank everybody, even the Monaghan team who won the league a couple of months before and whom he hadn't had a chance to congratulate. It's almost become a joke, this congratulating of Barry's. Somebody told him he might be going overboard once. He listened for a long time and then said, 'If you're telling me to stop congratulating the people I want to, then I will just start by saying somebody told me I sound foolish congratulating everybody and maybe I do but still these are the people I want to congratulate.' McGuigan does not really mind if his genuine emotions upset people. The way he sees it, they have the problem and not him. For a time the crowd seems to be getting out of control, the people coming in from the outlying countryside continually pushing those at the front nearer the stage. McGuigan makes an appeal for everybody to take two steps back and they do, almost in unison: about thirty or forty rows of people step back calmly and in order.

After the orations we slip into the local library, which will lead us by another entrance to the back of the McGuigan shop. We go into the yard to see the fire damage.

It's much worse than we expected. Where the kitchen used to be is a black heap of ashes. It's as if some cruel fate in the midst of triumph has raped and pillaged his past.

Sandra starts to cry. Pat McGuigan is leading us through the debris as if our visitation could somehow bring back the past. 'Everything I worked for,' he says simply.

At twelve forty-five we are again on the runway in Enniskillen. In absolute darkness we take off. There is a sadness about this leg of the journey; leaving McGuigan is like leaving the Land of Youth. For a couple of weeks leading up to the fight and for a time after it, nothing mattered. Time stood still . . . a land of eternal youth where we could all play out our childhood fantasies through this extraordinary young man called McGuigan, the last of the cool clean heroes. A boyhood hero stepped from the comics of our childhood, fearless, strong and full of insane life. No comic-strip writer would have the audacity to pen McGuigan's story as it happened. Even they have respect for the boundaries of soap opera. The man who is sitting beside me is bursting at the seams with fulfilment. The tune he is whistling is the Panamanian national anthem. For ever and a day they will remember McGuigan. Whenever boxing is spoken of, somebody will eventually say, 'But do you remember Barry McGuigan?' Everybody will. Some old wag in the corner will lean forward and say, 'Who was the man behind him? What was his manager's name?' He will pause with all the confidence of one who knows and say: 'McGuigan and Eastwood, sure there was never another team like them.'

Eastwood says little on the flight. He's thinking of the future. 'How many of us depend on McGuigan? Look at the team of us. There must be thirty people close to him – and when he goes, we go. There's no need for Ned doing the ring, no need for Harry O'Neill, no need for wee Billy Barnes, no need for a sponsor, no need for a manager. When he loses his title everybody's shagged, and we're back to porridge again.'

Suddenly, in the immense blackness we are flying

through, an oasis of light appears below us. 'What's that?' I inquire.

The pilot, Tom Tuke, looks out. 'Oh, that's Long Kesh,' he says.

Until there are one million Barry McGuigans Ulster will never sleep.

APPENDIX:
BARRY McGUIGAN'S
PROFESSIONAL RECORD

10 May 1981   Beat Selvin Bell; referee stopped
                         fight, round 2
                         Venue: Dalymount Park, Dublin

20 June 1981   Beat Gary Lucas; referee stopped
                         fight, round 4
                         Venue: Wembley Pool, London

3 August 1981   Lost to Peter Eubanks; points,
                         round 8
                         Venue: Brighton

22 September 1981   Beat Jean-Marc Renard (Belgium);
                         points, round 8
                         Venue: Ulster Hall, Belfast

27 October 1981   Beat Terry Pizarro (Puerto Rico);
                         referee stopped fight, round 4
                         Venue: Ulster Hall, Belfast

8 December 1981   Beat Peter Eubanks; referee
                         stopped fight, round 8
                         Venue: Ulster Hall, Belfast

8 February 1981   Beat Ian Murray; referee stopped
                         fight, round 3
                         Venue: World Sporting Club,
                         London

23 February 1981	Beat Angel Oliver (Spain); referee stopped fight, round 3
	Venue: Ulster Hall, Belfast
23 March 1982	Beat Angelo Licata (Italy); retired (towel), round 2
	Venue: Ulster Hall, Belfast
22 April 1982	Beat Gary Lucas; knockout, round 1
	Venue: Enniskillen, Northern Ireland
14 June 1982	Beat Alimi (Ali) Mustafa (Nigeria); knockout, round 6
	Venue: World Sporting Club, London
5 October 1982	Beat Jimmy Duncan; retired, round 4
	Venue: Ulster Hall, Belfast
9 November 1982	Final eliminator for British title
	Beat Paul Huggins; referee stopped fight, round 5
	Venue: Ulster Hall, Belfast
12 April 1983	For vacant British featherweight title
	Beat Vernon Penprase; referee stopped fight, round 2
	Venue: Ulster Hall, Belfast
22 May 1983	Beat Sammy Meck (France); referee stopped fight, round 6
	Venue: Navan, Eire

9 July 1983	Beat Loval McGowan (U.S.A.); knockout, round 1 Venue: Chicago
5 October 1983	Beat Ruben Herasme (Dominican Republic); knockout, round 2 Venue: Ulster Hall, Belfast
16 November 1983	For vacant European featherweight title Beat Valerio Nati (Italy); knockout, round 6 Venue: King's Hall, Belfast
25 January 1984	Final eliminator for Commonwealth title Beat Charm Chiteule (Zambia); referee stopped fight, round 10 Venue: King's Hall, Belfast
4 April 1984	Eliminator for W.B.C. world featherweight Beat Jose Caba (Dominican Republic); referee stopped fight, round 7 Venue: King's Hall, Belfast
5 June 1984	In defence of European championship Beat Esteban Equia (Spain); knockout, round 3 Venue: Royal Albert Hall, London
30 June 1984	Beat Paul De Vorce (U.S.A.); referee stopped fight, round 5 Venue: King's Hall, Belfast

13 October 1984	Beat Filipe Orozco (Colombia); knockout, round 2 Venue: King's Hall, Belfast
19 December 1984	Defence of European and British titles
	Beat Clyde Ruan; knockout, round 4 Venue: Ulster Hall, Belfast
23 February 1985	Beat Juan Laporte (Puerto Rico); points, round 10 Venue: King's Hall, Belfast
26 March 1985	Third defence of European title Beat Farid Gallouze (France); retired (towel), round 2 Venue: Wembley Pool, London
8 June 1985	World title Beat Eusebio Pedroza (Panama); points, round 15 Venue: Loftus Road, London
28 September 1985	Defence of world title Beat Bernard Taylor (U.S.A.); retired, round 7 Venue: King's Hall, Belfast
15 February 1986	Defence of world title Beat Danilo Cabrera (Dominican Republic); referee stopped fight, round 14 Venue: Royal Dublin Society's Hall, Dublin

EPILOGUE

McGuigan's title defence against Bernard Taylor on 28 September 1985 was the first world title fight in Belfast since September 1949, when Rinty Monaghan successfully defended his title against Terry Allen. In training McGuigan looked even sharper than he had before the Pedroza fight. His opponent had an impressive record. In thirty-four professional fights Taylor had never been beaten, and he had fought a draw with Pedroza. Known as the 'B.T. Express', he had a very quick defensive style, fighting mostly on the retreat.

At the weigh-in before the fight Taylor was found to be twelve ounces over the featherweight limit and had to do an extensive work-out to get down to the nine-stone mark. That was only the start of his problems. The capacity crowd in the King's Hall were partisan, to say the least, and Taylor must have been intimidated by the roar that greeted McGuigan when he appeared in the aisle of the cavernous arena. The fight went as predicted, with Taylor constantly on the run. He made full use of the ring, and McGuigan pursued him doggedly, waiting for Taylor to stand still long enough to land a solid blow. It didn't happen in the first round. Taylor managed the occasional ineffective flurry as he sped around the ring as if repelled from McGuigan by a magnet. This was the pattern for the next four rounds.

Taylor was slow to answer the bell in the second round, perhaps because in Europe no buzzer warning is given to the boxers. He needed all the respite he could get because McGuigan was constantly cutting down the ring, waiting for his opponent to slow down. In the fifth round, as McGuigan landed a glancing left, there were indications that Taylor was slowing a little. He knew from the Pedroza fight that McGuigan could keep up the pursuit for fifteen rounds. Finally in round six the pursuit ended as Taylor, too tired to keep out of range, had to come inside. In this department he was completely out of his depth. McGuigan switched his attack to the body. By the seventh round Taylor was winded, and by the eighth he was almost defenceless. He lay on the ropes, his hands held high to avoid a knockout blow. McGuigan stood back and measured him, and then delivered a strong right to the body that seemed to go almost through Taylor. Between the eighth and ninth rounds the white towel came fluttering into the ring to announce the end of McGuigan's first defence of his title, against the number-one contender. Belfast was happy.

After the Taylor fight McGuigan had a prolonged absence from the ring. Sandra was expecting their second child in January, and Barry insisted he couldn't fight until after that event. During his absence from the ring a formidable opponent appeared on the scene. Azumah Nelson put the heart across Barry's supporters with a stunning one-round knockout of former British idol Pat Cowdell. The precision and the fury with which the man from Ghana eliminated a respected opponent made a confrontation with McGuigan inevitable at some time in the future.

Meanwhile every boxer within range of McGuigan's weight was clamouring to take him on. In the featherweight division McGuigan is big box-office. Eventually it was decided that Fernando Sosa would be his next opponent. The aggressive style of the well-respected Argentinian appealed to the US TV networks.

On 4 January 1986 Sandra gave birth to a baby girl, Danika Catherine. Almost immediately McGuigan had to go into training for his meeting with Sosa, scheduled for 15 February. Two weeks before the fight Sosa injured his right hand and withdrew from the bill. An opponent had to be found and fast. The problem was to find one in training at that time. Eastwood scouted around the world until finally he came up with Danilo Cabrera, who had been due to defend his Dominican title but was prepared to reroute to Dublin to fight McGuigan if the terms were right. Cabrera was looked upon as the sacrificial lamb by the press: by general consensus the fight would end early with Cabrera looking up at McGuigan. From McGuigan's point of view he had everything to lose and nothing to gain. He had no videos of Cabrera to allow him to study the Dominican's style and to prepare a game plan, whereas Cabrera had plenty on McGuigan.

From the opening bell it was obvious that this fight was going to be different from the Taylor fight. Cabrera had come to take his chance. During the first three rounds he often stood toe to toe with McGuigan, trading punches. By the end of the third round it was obvious why he was rated number six by the WBA. McGuigan was getting through with some good left hooks and the occasional right, but they were not having the same devastating effect that they had had on Taylor and Pedroza.

Cabrera himself had not landed any big punches, but by the end of the third round Paddy Byrne and Eastwood were working overtime on a swelling under McGuigan's right eye. (McGuigan would later claim that Cabrera was constantly using the thumb.) By the fifth round McGuigan was beginning to assert his authority, getting in some strong left hooks to the body. After one of these exchanges Cabrera suddenly turned away and indicated to the referee that McGuigan had hit low. It was an extraordinary thing to do because technically the fight was still in progress and McGuigan could have followed up with more blows to a man who had left himself virtually defenceless. Luckily for Cabrera, the referee came to his assistance and, after checking with a judge, seemed to instruct them to deduct a point from McGuigan's score. McGuigan had won all the rounds up to this moment, but he had not stamped his authority on the fight in the way that the crowd had expected.

By the seventh round McGuigan was slowing Cabrera down with some whiplash shots to the body, but in the eighth round Cabrera suddenly struck back and McGuigan emerged from the exchange with a gash under his right eye. This seemed to spur him into action and he came forward like a bull. A strong overhand right connected with Cabrera; before he could steady himself, McGuigan shrugged him off with a powerful left hook. Cabrera hung on for dear life, and by the end of the round he was holding on to McGuigan and tangoing round the ring like a drunken dancer. McGuigan pushed him away, and Cabrera stumbled round the ring.

The referee called halt, and Barry's brother Dermot led the entourage into the ring. Meanwhile Cabrera's people were protesting furiously that the bell had gone before the referee had stopped the fight and so, technically, it could not be over. The ringside judges confirmed this opinion, and the ring was cleared to restart the fight. The ninth round was totally McGuigan's, but he could not put Cabrera away. The Dominican had enough time in between rounds to recover and gain a second wind. While he didn't ever lose control of the fight, rounds ten to twelve were worrying ones for McGuigan, and Cabrera even managed the unthinkable in backing McGuigan up towards the end of the tenth and twelfth rounds.

By this stage McGuigan was way ahead on points and there didn't seem the least likelihood that Cabrera could knock him out, but it didn't appear to be McGuigan the destroyer that we were watching that night. At the end of the thirteenth round, when the bell called a respite, Cabrera stumbled to his corner as if he had suddenly let his guard down. By now the fight had gone on far longer than anybody had expected.

Early in the fourteenth round McGuigan hit Cabrera with three strong left hooks and a right to the body, and Cabrera hung on, defenceless. He staggered round the ring and eventually almost fell through the ropes. The referee waved the fight on, but as McGuigan came in to finish Cabrera, he was presented with the sad sight of the brave Dominican trying to pick up his gumshield like a drunk trying to pick an ice cube off the floor. McGuigan waved his hands at the referee and Ed Eckert called a halt to that hard day's night: McGuigan was still featherweight champion of the world.

constant, all-consuming. It torments you. It strengthens you. It drives you to feed – and gives you the power to do so.' In his voice was promise, commiseration, a dark seduction that went beyond mere recitation of demonic qualities. How much of his own nature was he drawing on in order to establish this rapport? As he reached down to touch Ciani, to lay one slender hand over her heart, it struck Senzei for the first time just how like their enemy he was. The Hunter and Ciani's tormentor might feed on different emotions, but they both served the same dark Pattern.

When Tarrant touched her, Ciani cried out – and then was suddenly still, so much so that Senzei feared for her. For a moment she lay like one dead, so utterly unmoving that Senzei found himself searching in vain for any sign of breathing, any tremor of a heart-beat. There was none. Then she trembled, and her eyes shot open. Black, utterly black, with no sign of iris or white. Pits of emptiness, which anything might fill.

'Who are you?' the Hunter demanded.

In a voice that was Ciani's but not Ciani's, she answered, 'Essistat sa-Lema. Tehirra sa-Steyat. Ciani sa-Faraday. Others.' A ghastly sound escaped her lips, that might have been intended as laughter. 'I don't remember all the names.'

Tarrant looked up at Hesseth, who nodded shortly. *Rakh names*, the gesture indicated. For once, the *khrast*-woman seemed as tense as the human company.

The Hunter turned his attention back to Ciani. '*Where* are you?' he asked.

Again the ghostly laugh – then, in a cryptic tone, 'Night's turf. Hunter's den. The basement of storms.'

'Where?' Tarrant pressed.

The thing that was Ciani shut her eyes. 'In darkness,' she whispered at last. 'Beneath the House of Storms.'

'In the earth?'

'No. Yes.'

'In caverns? Tunnels? Man-made structures?'

Her eyes shot open, fixed on him. '*Rakh*-made,' she corrected fiercely. 'Where the Lost Ones dwelled until we drove them out. We fed on their memories, too – but those were narrow things, all tunnels and hunger and brainless mating. Not like the memories of the other rakh.' She closed her eyes, and a shudder passed through her frame; strangely sexual, like the first shiver of orgasm. 'Not like with the humans,' she whispered. 'Nothing like that.'

Again Tarrant glanced at Hesseth, and this time he mouthed the words. *Lost Ones?* Her brief nod sufficed to indicate that she knew the reference, would be willing to explain it later. Or so Senzei hoped.

Tarrant returned his attention to Ciani. The black depths of her eyes gleamed like obsidian as she watched him.

'Do you fear?' he asked her.

'Fear?'

'As the rakh do. As humans do.'

'Fear? As in "for my life"? No. Why should I?'

'You feel safe.'

'I *am* safe.'

'Protected,' the Hunter probed.

'Yes.'

'Efficiently.'

The empty eyes opened; a hint of violet light stirred in their depths. 'Without question.'

'How?'

She seemed to hesitate. 'Lema protects. The Keeper shields.'

'Against what?' When there was no answer, he pressed, 'Against the rakh?'

'The humans,' she whispered. 'They're coming for us. That's what Lema said. They're coming, with a Fire that can burn away the night. Can burn *us*.'

'But you're not afraid.'

'No.' The voice was a hiss. 'Lema protects. The Keeper is thorough. Even now—'

She hesitated. Gasped suddenly, as if in pain. Tarrant said quickly, 'It took a lot of planning.'

'Not much,' she answered. Her body seem to sag into the ground, as if in relief, and her voice was strong once more. Senzei sensed that some barrier had been not overcome, nor destroyed, but somehow sidestepped. 'Only a misKnowing. The rest is up to us.'

Senzei saw something flicker in Tarrant's eyes, too subtle and too quick for him to identify. Fear? Surprise?

'A misKnowing?' he whispered.

'Yes. The demon said that would be best. To turn their own Workings against them. To let them feel confident in their knowledge, while all the while they were walking into a trap. That's the only way to take an adept, Calesta says. Trick them, using their own vision.'

For a moment, there was silence. Shadows of forms began to shiver into existence about the Hunter's body, bits of misgivings seeping out from his soul, given shape by the night. A death-mask. A spear. A drop of fire. In another time and place such images might have gained real substance, but his hungry nature swallowed them up again as quickly as they were formed. Only a brief after-image remained, black against black in the night.

'Tell me,' he whispered tightly. 'The misKnowing. What is it?'

Ciani seemed about to speak, then hesitated.

'Tell me.'

She gasped soundlessly, like a fish out of water. Seemed incapable of making the words come.

He reached forwards and grasped her by the upper arms; his power flowed into her like a torrent, purple fae marked with his hunger, his purpose. 'Tell me!' he demanded. She tried to resist, tried to pull away – and then cried out, as the cold power wrapped itself around her soul. Senzei saw Damien start forwards, then force himself back. Because she might die if he interfered. Only because of that. But there was murder in his eyes.

'Tell me,' the Hunter commanded – and Senzei could feel him using the dark fae to squeeze the information out of her, like juice from a pulped fruit.

'Sansha Crater!' she gasped. There were tears running down her face, and she was shaking violently in his grip. Information began to pour out as if it had a life of its own, words and concepts struggling to get free. 'The humans' Knowings will lead them there in search of us. They'll believe that our stronghold is there, beneath the House of Storms. Most important, *he* will believe it – their adept – because Calesta took the image from his mind. When he looked at his maps and said *this is where the enemy will be*, the Hungry One noted it. And the Keeper will let them think that he was right, warp his Knowings to serve that end . . . and the adept's own Workings will lead them into ambush.'

For a moment Tarrant was still, and utterly silent. The look in his eyes was terrible – shame and fury and blind, raw hatred, intermingled with even less pleasant emotions that Senzei didn't dare identify – but Ciani, or whatever manner of creature now inhabited her body, seemed oblivious to it. Had his own word not bound him to protect her, Senzei was pretty sure the Hunter would have struck out at the body before him, Working the dark fae so that it would transmit the damage to Ciani's possessor; but he *was* bound, and by his own will, and so his rage went unexpressed.

'Where is the House of Storms?' he hissed. Dark purple tendrils swirled about his rage, dissolved into the night. 'Where is your people's stronghold?' When she didn't answer him his eyes narrowed coldly, and she gasped; Senzei could see the last of her resistance crumble.

'On the point of power,' she whispered. 'Where the earth-fae flows in torrents, hungry for taming. Where the plates sing in pain as they crush the power out. Where the Keeper—'

Ciani's body went rigid. She mouthed a few words, soundlessly – and then a spasm of pain racked her body, traveling from head to foot like a wave. 'No!' she cried out – Ciani's voice, Ciani's pain. She pulled against her bonds with a force that almost dragged the tent pegs from the earth. 'Gerald!' But the adept did nothing to help her.

'Stop it!' Damien hissed. He started forwards – and then forced himself to halt, though his fists were clenched in fury. *To interrupt this Working is to give her soul to the enemy.* 'Stop it, damn you! She can't take any more!' As if in answer to him, blood trickled from Ciani's mouth. And Tarrant did move, at last. He put his hands to the sides of her face – and she tried to bite him, wild as a wounded animal – but he grasped her firmly and held her head back against the earth, while her body struggled against its bonds. Fixing his eyes on hers, pinioning her to the ground by the power of his gaze. A power that Senzei could see, a vivid purple that vibrated with the force of his hatred.

'Let go,' he whispered fiercely. 'This is not your flesh, not your place. Obey me!' She struggled in his grasp – helplessly, like an infant. Blood poured down her cheek and smeared on his hand, deep purple in the fae-light. It dripped to the ground. He took no notice of it. *'Obey me,'* he whispered. And the power that flowed from him was so bright, so blinding, that Senzei had to turn away.

For a brief moment, the whole of Ciani's body went rigid; her bonds creaked as she strained against them. Then, suddenly, all the strength went out of her. She lay on the bloodied earth like a shattered doll, her intermittent gasping for breath the only sign of her survival. After a moment, Tarrant released her. Her eyes – now human, heavily bloodshot – shut. She shivered, as if from cold.

'Take out the Fire,' the Hunter said quietly to Damien.

'You're sure—'

'Take it out!'

He stood as the priest complied with his command, and put a few hurried steps between himself and the rest of the party. Nevertheless, he was clearly loath to go too far from Ciani; he remained close enough that when the Fire was uncovered its light burned a swathe across his face that blistered an angry red as he watched her.

For a moment, Senzei could see nothing: the Fire's light was brilliant, blinding. He felt his Seeing fade, knew that it would be long minutes before he could conjure such vision again. But there was no need for it. The dark fae was gone, consumed in an instant by the force of that Church-spawned blaze. And with it, whatever remnants of the night's power that had clung to Ciani. She whimpered softly as Damien went to her, clung to him as he severed her bonds and gathered her up in his arms, the light of the Fire pressed into her back.

'She'll be all right,' the Hunter promised. 'Keep the Fire out until Casca rises. No. Until the sun comes up. She'll be safe, once she's exposed to true sunlight; neither his power nor mine can cling to her then.'

'But if you—' Damien began.

'You'll have to function without me,' he said sharply. 'There are several things that want looking into, and I can handle them best alone.'

'Not to mention the Fire,' Damien said quietly.

Tarrant turned towards him, slowly, and let him watch as the sanctified light spread across his features. The skin of his face and hands reddened, tightened, began to peel – but his cold eyes gazed steadily at Damien, and there was no hint in his manner of any pain or hesitancy.

'Don't underestimate me,' he warned. Blood pooled in the corner of one eye, and he blinked it free; it travelled down the side of his face like a tear. Still he did not turn away, nor shield himself from the Fire's light. 'Don't ever underestimate me.'

'I'm sorry,' Damien said at last.

'You should be,' he agreed. And he bowed to Ciani – a minimal gesture, hurried but graceful. 'It's vital that you don't discuss what happened here tonight – any of it – until the sun rises. Otherwise your attacker might learn . . . too much. Lady?'

She whispered it. 'I understand.'

He stepped – and was gone, more quickly than the eye could follow. Reddened flesh fading into blackness, burnt skin swallowed up by darkness. Salved, by the true night's special power.

'The Fire didn't hurt him,' Senzei whispered, 'Not like it should have.'

'Of *course* it hurt him,' Damien said sharply. 'And it would have killed him if he'd stayed here long enough.'

'But he didn't seem—'

'No, he didn't, did he? And what gets to me is that he would have stayed there, endured the pain – till the Fire fried him to a crisp, if that's what it took. Just to prove a point.'

He drew in a ragged breath, and closed his arms tightly about Ciani.

'That's what makes him so vulking dangerous,' he muttered.

Rain fell. Not the gentle rain of days before, a chill but tolerable mist that wet the land without truly soaking it, but a downpour that swept in from the East, borne on winds that had coursed over thousands of miles of open sea, scooping up foam and spray and converting them into thick, black storm clouds. If Casca rose, they never saw it. Water fell in sheets, interspersed with bits of hail and clumps of crystal, as if it couldn't decide what form it wanted to take – but it was all cold, and dark, and drenching.

They huddled inside the rakhene tent, thick hides stretched across hollow poles to form a cone-shaped shelter. The women, that was. Senzei and Damien stayed outside long enough to fashion a primitive shelter for their animals. Already the real horses were straining at their tethers, and the xandu, unbound, milled nervously about the campsite as if they were beginning to regret their faebound allegiance to the rakh-woman and her companions. But the two men managed to find a granite overhang near the camp, and jam enough branches into a crevice above it that when soaking leaves were stuffed in between them they stayed in place. The downpour became a trickle within the shelter, a turbulent sheet at its edge. Good enough, Damien indicated. They led the drenched animals inside, the light of the Fire casting harsh shadows across jagged granite walls, and saw that they were safely settled there before returning to the camp.

Tarrant, perhaps predictably, did not return. Damien muttered something about him not wanting to get his hair wet, which Senzei assumed was facetious. The men wrung out their clothing as well as they could, exchanging their soaked cloth for cold but dryer garments. In the tent's narrow interior comfort was difficult, privacy impossible – but four warm living bodies in that narrow space slowly warmed it until the air was tolerable, and by the time dawn came at last Senzei discovered that he had fallen asleep sometime in that interminable darkness.

Dawn. They assumed it came, because the sky grew slowly lighter. But the sun was hidden by deep grey storm clouds, and its light was filtered through sheets of rain. Several times Senzei saw Damien hunch over towards the tent's small opening, studying the sky with narrowed eyes. Waiting for sunlight to break through the cloudcover. Because until Ciani was exposed to the sun's cleansing power, none of them dared talk about what they had seen, or heard, or feared in the night. Nor could they make plans.

It was the longest day they had ever spent together.

Towards sunset, a break came at last. A glimmer of light in the distance, that broke up the downpour into a thousand glittering jewels. A break in the clouds that showed first the sun, then the Core. White light commingled with gold warmed the frozen land slowly, and broke up the rain into a fine silver mist. Soon a patch of clear sky passed overhead, and then another; nevertheless, it was many long hours before Ciani could stand in the full light of day, shivering in pain as the solar fae burned the last vestiges of true night's Working from her flesh.

Gerald Tarrant returned at sunset. By then they had reclaimed their mounts — the animals were skittish and hungry, but otherwise unharmed by the downpour — and found enough dry twigs beneath the tent, and in other places, to kindle a feeble fire. The four of them sat about it, silent, while Tarrant reestablished his wards. Guarding against eavesdroppers, Senzei guessed. At last he seemed satisfied, and lowered himself to a place by the fire. His hair, Senzei noted, was not only dry but perfectly groomed.

'I had hoped for several more nights of travel before certain decisions were necessary,' he told the group. 'We need more information than we have, and I'd hoped to find it in Lema. But I think it's clear we've run out of time. Our enemy has anticipated us, and the result is that we nearly walked right into his hands. So we have to decide a few things here and now — what we're doing, and how we mean to do it — so that we can set everything in motion now, before our enemy realizes that we're on to him.'

'Without knowing the land we're traveling to?' Senzei asked.

'One doesn't win a war by letting one's enemy write the rules. And he's trying to do just that. We need to plan — quickly, and thoroughly. Otherwise we may as well march into Sansha Crater and deliver the lady to him ourselves.'

'What are the chances he's aware of what you did last night?' Damien asked.

Tarrant hesitated. 'In a general sense, that's unavoidable. No sorceror could miss it. In a specific sense . . . I was very, very careful. And the dark fae is my element, remember; its manipulation is as natural to me as breathing is to you. If he investigates the matter, he'll discover that we tried to use the link between Ciani and himself to facilitate a direct assault. And failed. Not that information flowed in the opposite direction, towards us.' He turned to the rakh-woman. 'There are some facts we need, before we make any decisions. He mentioned some names that were unfamiliar to me. They may be crucial. And you seemed to recognize them.'

'The Lost Ones.'

'And Calesta.'

She shook her head. 'That name is unfamiliar to me. But the Lost Ones . . . that's a rakhene term for a tribe of our people that disappeared back in the years of the Changing. You understand, we had no language then, and our form was still unstable; each generation differed from the last, making social continuity nearly impossible. We have only oral records from those times, and even those are uncertain. Bear that in mind as I speak.

'The rakh who came here – the ones who survived the Worldsend crossing – spread out across the land, each group establishing its own territory. They weren't even tribes then, more like . . . extended families. Many settled in the plains because that land was so hospitable. Others went south, into the swamplands. Or east. Our ancestors were territorial creatures, who needed their own space as much as your people need food and water; it was humanity's intrusion into our lands in the first place that caused—' She drew herself up sharply, inhaled through gritted teeth. 'That's dead and gone, now. Our people spread out. They changed. We gained language. Sophistication. *Civilization*. Eventually the plains rakh began to travel, to see what our world had become, and learn more of yours – thus the *khrast* tradition – and slowly, warily, the scattered tribes made contact once again. We discovered two things: that even though man's Impression still dictated our general evolution, we had adapted to our chosen lands. The rakh who hunt for sustenance in the southern swamplands bear little resemblance to my people, or any other tribe; in some cases the differences are so great as to preclude intermating, implying – according to your science – that we have become several species.

'Second, we discovered that during the time of our dispersal a large number of rakh were lost. They had chosen to settle in the mountains – these mountains – and had lived there during the early stages of their development. We found artifacts of their civilization – tools, trash heaps, broken ornaments – but never any hint of where they had gone. Legend says,' – and here she breathed in deeply – 'that they went underground. That there was a time of terrible cold, when debris from an upland volcano cut us off from the sun's warmth, and the mountains were covered in ice. Certainly, most rakh would rather seek shelter under their territory than abandon it utterly. If so, they never came out again. Only legends remain.'

'And now this testimony,' Damien said. *'Where the Lost Ones dwelled, until we drove them out.* If we knew how long ago that was—'

'Three centuries,' Tarrant said coolly. 'give or take a decade or two.'

Damien stared at him in astonishment. 'How do you know that?'

'The rakh-girl from Lema. Remember? I . . . interrogated her.'

For a moment, Damien was speechless. Then he hissed, 'You *bastard.*'

Tarrant shrugged. 'We needed information. She had it.' His eyes glittered darkly. 'I assure you, any interest in her emotional state was strictly . . . secondary.'

Damien made as if to rise, but Ciani put a hand on his shoulder. Firmly. 'It's over,' she said. 'You can't help her now. *We have to work together.'*

He forced himself to sit back; it clearly took effort.

'Go on,' he growled.

'Three centuries ago,' Tarrant repeated. 'The Lost Ones were alive and thriving then, and they built their tunnels. Or adapted them from existing caves – our informant seemed to indicate both. Then came this foreign sorceror. Lema's human Master, who built his citadel above their warren. And the demons who served him took refuge in the caves beneath, driving out their former inhabitants. So that they might be protected from sunlight.'

'Three centuries,' Ciani mused. 'The lost rakh might still be alive.'

'Adapted to the darkness – and thus very photosensitive. I doubt that they care much for sunlight themselves – in fact, it stands to reason that their underground domiciles would be interlinked. So that they might go from one to the other without ever coming above-ground.'

'Including—' Senzei began.

Tarrant nodded. 'That one.'

'Underground access,' Damien whispered.

'If their tunnels were rakh-made, no. The new tenants would have sealed those off, for defensive purposes. Or they'd have them guarded. But if we're talking about natural caverns, with all their infinite variety . . . there's a real possibility of finding some way in that our enemies don't know about. Or creating one, through adjoining chambers.'

'Coming in through the back door,' Senzei mused.

'Just so.'

Damien turned to the *khrast*-woman. 'What's the chance of finding these underground rakh? Of communicating with them, if we do?'

'Who can say where they are – or even if they still exist? No one's seen them for centuries. As for communication . . . they wouldn't speak English, I'm sure; that was a later development. They might still speak fragments of the rakhene tongue . . . or they might not. Too much time has passed to be certain.'

'But the tunnels will be there, regardless,' Tarrant said.

Damien turned to him. 'You think you can find them?'

He chuckled. 'Just what do you think I do every morning, when it comes time to find shelter? Locating caves is child's play for anyone who can See the currents. It's much the same skill that Senzei used, bringing us to shore. But locating the *right* caverns . . .' He nodded thoughtfully. 'That will take some effort.'

'All right, then,' Damien said. 'Let's say that we may have a way to sneak up on them. And we have an effective weapon, if they're sun-sensitive.' He patted the pouch at his hip. 'There's time enough ahead to decide how best to use it. As for our enemy's ambush . . . now that we know what game he's playing, we should be able to counter it. Which leaves us with only one question left—'

'Where the hell we're going,' Senzei supplied.

Tarrant withdrew a sheet of vellum from his pocket; it had been folded so many times that it was barely as wide as two fingers, yet it opened up to display a sizable map of the area. 'I sketched this from memory, soon after losing the original. I can't guarantee its accuracy, but I believe that the general form is right.' He spread it out before them. It was a map of the rakhlands and its surrounding regions, superimposed over a webwork of jagged ink lines.

'Fault lines,' Damien whispered.

Tarrant nodded. 'Missing a few minor ones, no doubt, but I believe the major plate boundaries are all in place.' This map, unlike the first, was labeled. *Greater Novatlantic plate. Eastern Serpentine. Lesser Continental.* He pointed to where those three plates met. 'Here's the single point of power for this region,' he mused. 'I assumed he would have settled somewhat near it. According to our informant, however, he's sitting right on top of it.'

'I thought you said—' Damien began.

'That only a fool would do that? I did. And I'll stand by it. Don't ask me how he's kept his citadel standing, in a region this seismically active. Wards alone won't do it. He must be counting on something else. Maybe luck. The girl said there hadn't been a quake in this area for a long time. Years.'

'That's impossible,' Damien muttered.

He nodded. 'Certainly odd, to say the least. The small ones sometimes go unnoticed, of course . . . but even so, we're talking about a considerable seismic gap in this region. I just hope it holds long enough for us to get where we're going.'

'Speaking of which,' Damien said, 'is there any way to keep the Master of Lema from tracking us? He seemed to read through your Obscuring—'

'You can't blind a man to the obvious,' Tarrant said sharply. 'But you can divert his focus. Last night I prepared a Working that should do that. It will take effect . . . here.' He indicated a point on the map some two days' journey east of them. 'We have to stay with the pass this far to get to Lema; he knows that. But once the five of us reach this point, I've arranged for simulacra to take our place. They will continue along this path,' – his finger traced a line through the mountains, into Lema, towards the place where the three plates met – 'to here.' He indicated a point some twenty miles to the east of that place of power, and looked at the rakhene woman for confirmation.

She reached out and moved his hand a few inches southward. And nodded. 'The crater is there.' She looked up at him. 'And the ambush.'

'While they travel towards it, his Workings will be drawn to them. We will be all but invisible.'

Damien stared at him. Something in his expression made Senzei's skin crawl.

'You used people,' he said quietly. 'Rakh.'

'A good simulacrum can't be created out of thin air. Such an illusion wouldn't fool an adept for an instant. There has to be enough substance that when one probes beneath the surface—'

'*Innocent* rakh.'

The Hunter's expression darkened. 'This is a war, priest – and in a war, there are casualties. The innocent are sometimes among them.'

'You have no right!'

'*But I have the power.* And that's all there is to it. I won't argue this point. Not when my own survival is at stake. I have far too much already invested in that, and one hell of a reception awaiting me if I die. The Working exists. I've already warded it. When you reach this point,' and he tapped the map aggressively, 'five simulacra will leave for Sansha Crater. And because my Working was bound to living flesh they will be convincing, and our enemy will watch them, *not* us, until they die.' He shook his head slowly. 'I don't intend to perish here, priest. Certainly not for your morals. You'd better come to terms with that.'

Speechless, Damien turned to Ciani. 'Cee—'

'Please. Damien. He's right.' She put a hand on his arm; he seemed to flinch at the contact. 'We have no choice, don't you see? We need this Working, or something like it. Otherwise, we might as well just give up now. And I can't do that, Damien. Can't give up. Can you?'

Wordlessly, he pulled away from her. His expression was unreadable – but there was a coldness in it that made Senzei shiver.

'You have me,' he muttered at last. 'I won't interfere. I can't. But you'll pay for those lives – in blood. I swear it.'

The Hunter laughed softly; it was an ominous sound.

'Those and a thousand others,' he agreed.

Morning. Next day. She came to Senzei while he was gathering wood. And startled him so badly that he nearly dropped his bundle.

'Ciani?'

Sunlight poured down through the half-stripped branches above them, illuminating her pallor. Her weakness. The possession of two nights before had taken more out of her than any of them wanted to admit.

'I thought you might like company,' she offered.

The words were out of him before he could stop them. 'You shouldn't have left camp.'

She shrugged; the gesture, like all her gestures, was a mere shadow of her former state. Even her gaze seemed weakened. 'You worry as much as he does.' She looked about for something to sit down on, settled on a broken stump. 'Which is a little too much, sometimes.' She lowered herself onto it with a sigh. 'Sometimes you have to get away . . . from fears, from people.' She met his eyes, held them. 'You know what I mean?'

He could feel the colour come to his face; he fought the impulse to turn away from her. 'It's too dangerous, Cee. You shouldn't be alone, not even for a few minutes.'

'I know,' she told him. 'And yet . . . it's as if too much risk numbs the mind to danger. Is that possible? Sometimes I have to consciously remind myself how close we are to our enemy, how much power he has . . . but even then it's distant, somehow. Unreal. As if I have to work to be afraid.'

She looked down at her hands, as if studying them for answers. And at last said, quietly, 'I never had a chance to tell you. About the memories. Just bits and pieces . . . but I had them again, for a time. During Gerald's Working. As if, while that creature used my body, I could sense something of his. My memories, stored in his flesh.' She looked up at him; her brown eyes glistened in the sunlight. 'I relived . . . when you came to me. Do you remember, Zen?'

It had been so long ago – and was so much a part of a different world, to which he no longer belonged – that it took him a minute to recall it. To recall himself, at that age.

'Yes,' he said softly. And he winced, remembering.

'You were young. So young. Do you remember? That was the image I got when we made contact. Your face – what I saw in it – what I Knew of you. But what I remembered most of all was your youth. Gods, you were so young . . .'

'I'm only thirty-four now,' he said defensively.

'Yes. Still young. Body not ageing yet – not irrevocably, anyway. Still at an age where the fae can regenerate flesh . . .' She let the thought trail off into silence. Let him finish it for himself. 'Do you remember why you came to me? What you wanted?'

The colour was hot in his face now, and he did turn away. 'Cee, please . . .'

'It's nothing to be ashamed of.'

He shook his head slowly, and bit his lower lip; it alarmed him that the memory could still awaken such pain. 'It's not shame, Cee. It's . . . I didn't understand. That's all. I wanted the world to be something that it wasn't.'

'You came to me seeking vision,' she said softly. 'Not power, not wealth, not even immortality . . . not any of the things that other men seek. Just the Sight.'

He kept his voice even, but it took all his self-control; beneath that surface he could feel himself trembling, his whole soul shivering with humiliation. 'And you explained the truth. That I couldn't ever have it.'

'Yes. I had to. Dedication like yours deserved honesty, no matter how much the truth might hurt. And maybe, if the knowledge hurt that much, it was in part because so many people had lied to you – had led you to believe that there was some kind of hope, when there wasn't—'

'They weren't adepts,' he said quickly. 'They couldn't know.'

'It's just – I'm sorry,' she whispered.

He shut his eyes; his soul ached with regret, with the pain of shattered dreams. 'You did what you had to.'

'It was what I believed. What we all believed. That adeptitude was an inborn trait; one either had it or one didn't. That no act of man, no manner of Working, might cause the Sight to exist in one who hadn't been born with it.'

He heard her draw in a deep breath. Gathering her courage? 'I was wrong, Zen.'

He turned to her. Not quite absorbing her words, or what they might mean. The shock was too great.

'I *believed* what I told you,' she assured him. 'And any adept would have said the same – any honest one. But that's only because none of us had lived long enough to understand—'

She stopped herself suddenly, as if her own confession distressed her. He could feel his hands shaking, with need and fear combined, and he felt as if he stood on the edge of a precipice. Balanced at the edge of a great yawning Pit, about to topple into it.

'Long enough for what?' He could barely manage the words. 'What are you saying, Cee?'

She whispered it – furtively, as if afraid that some other might hear. 'No *act of man* could do it, I told you. No act of man could wield enough power to break down the soul's own barriers . . . no act of a *single* man,' she stressed. 'But what if hundreds of sorcerors were to combine their skills – what if *thousands* were to pour all their vital energy, all their hopes and dreams, into one all-powerful Working – wouldn't that be enough? Couldn't the laws of Erna be altered with such a force as that?'

He stared at her in disbelief, could find no words to say.

'Gerald made me aware of the pattern. Showed me what to look for. He was around when that kind of power was first conjured, saw with his own eyes what it could do . . . but I don't think even he thought of this. Or would have told you, if he did.' She leaned forwards, hands on her knees. Her voice was couched low, but there was fever in her tone. 'The *Fire*, Zen. That's what it is. The power of thousands, concentrated in that one tiny flask. Tamed, to serve man's will.' She paused, giving the words time to sink in. Their meaning burned like flame. 'I believe it could free you. I believe it could give you what you want.'

She rose from where she sat and came to him; not close enough to touch, but nearly. 'I don't have all my old knowledge,' she told him. 'I can't know for sure that it'll work. But the more Gerald tells me about the kind of power that was wielded in the days of the Holy Wars, the more I think . . .' She drew in a deep breath. 'It could *change* you, Senzei. Give you what you dreamed of, in those days. You still want it, don't you?'

'Gods, yes . . .' Was it really possible? He had worked so hard to bury that hope, so that he might not destroy his life with it. Now, to consider it again, after all those years . . . For a moment he could hardly speak in answer. He was afraid that in the place of words might come something less dignified, like tears, or gasping, or simply speechless trembling. The emotion was almost too much to bear.

'Does he know?' he managed. 'Damien. Did you tell him?'

'How could I?' she said gently. 'He'd never let you have it. Such a use would be . . . blasphemy, to him.'

'Then isn't this – your being here – isn't that a kind of betrayal?'

'I don't share his faith,' she reminded him.

'But doesn't that mean – I mean, Damien—'

'Don't mistake me. I care for him, deeply. But philosophically . . .' She seemed to hesitate. 'We're from different worlds, it seems sometimes. The faith he serves . . .' She shook her head. 'It's not that I don't respect it, or him. But gods! They're living in a dream-world, filled with misty hopes and misguided passions . . . and I'm simply a pragmatist. A realist. This is my world. I accept it. I *live* in it. And if you give me a source of power, I'll use it – as the gods intended.'

She touched a hand to his cheek, gently; the storm of emotion inside him made the contact seem an almost alien thing, oddly distant from him. 'Romance between man and woman is such a fleeting thing,' she said softly. 'You of all people should know that. But the devotion of a true friend . . . *that* endures forever. My loyalties are just what they should be, Zen. And I'll stand by them to my grave.'

He should have had so many misgivings, so many fears – but the pounding of his heart drowned them all out, until it was hard to focus on any one thought. Feebly – mechanically – he protested, 'It's his weapon. *Our* weapon.'

'And do you think this will lessen it? Would the whole pint of Fire be so diminished by a few drops? He spared that much to Work his weapons, back in Mordreth. And again in the rakhene camp.' Her voice was a whisper, barely audible above the sound of the breeze stirring the leaves — but he heard every word as though it were a shout, felt her meaning etched in fire upon his soul. 'One drop, maybe two,' she whispered. 'That's all it would take. I *know* it. And think, Zen, if it worked . . . then *you'd* be our weapon. You'd be able to use everything that's inside you, instead of keeping it all pent up in your brain. Take the hunger of all those years and turn it into power . . . and he'd still have nearly a pint left. He'd never even know it was gone! And Zen . . . you'd be able to help us, like you never could before. Wouldn't that be a fair trade? If you could only manage that, then we wouldn't have to rely so much on—'

She stopped suddenly, and wrapped her arms around herself as if her own words had chilled her.

'The Hunter?'

She whispered it. 'Yes.'

He chose his words carefully, tried to keep his voice steady. 'Damien wouldn't give it to me.'

'No. Not willingly.'

'Is there any other way?'

She hesitated. He felt mixed emotions — elation, terror, need — flood his soul. 'Please, Cee.'

'I can Distract him,' she said softly. 'Gerald taught me how. He didn't mean it for this purpose . . . but he wouldn't have to know, will he? I can give Damien dreams while he's sleeping. Keep his attention fixed on them, so that he doesn't wake up. You'd only need minutes. Later . . .' She breathed in deeply. 'Later you could Work him yourself. Like an adept, Zen. *You'd be an adept.*'

He shut his eyes, felt a violent trembling course through his body. The dream, the need . . . it was almost too much to bear. The hope itself was too powerful, too overwhelming; like an ocean tide, it threatened to drag him under.

'Dangerous . . .' he whispered.

'The sun-power? The church's fae? How could it be? That's

a force born of pure benevolence, bound together for cleansing purposes. What could be possibly be safer? You saw him use it last night – saw him hold it against me, to protect me from the dark fae. Did it burn me? *Could* it burn me?' When he said nothing, she pressed, 'What's the only Working that his church will tolerate, even now? Healing. Because that's what his faith is all about, Zen – that's where their power lies. *That's what the Fire is.*'

He had lost his voice, and with it his resistance. The dream had hold of him again, and the hunger that had burned in him for so long had become something else – a lover, a seduction – no longer fever-hot but cool, blissfully cool, like the touch of a woman whose skin had been chilled by the night, all fluid ice and liquid passion and burning need at once . . .

Then she touched a finger to his lips and whispered – so low that he could hardly hear her – 'We can't discuss this again, you understand that? There's a link between Damien and me, strong enough that he might read your intentions through it. And as for Gerald . . .' She turned away from him; a shiver seemed to pass through her flesh. 'There's nothing I can keep from him now. Nothing. Not after I submitted my soul to him.' She shook her head. 'It would be too dangerous, you understand that? He depends on his adept's skills to control the party. And me. If he thought for a moment that there was a way you could challenge his dominance—'

He shivered in fear – but the fear was enticing. Challenge Gerald Tarrant? 'I understand,' he whispered.

'I think I can keep him from knowing, for a time. Despite . . . what's between us. But I can only manage that if I can pretend that nothing's happening. Pretend I don't know myself what you're planning. So we can't discuss it again, ever.'

'But if you do that – I mean, how can you—'

'Help you?' She turned back to face him. Her eyes were bright. 'I can Work Damien's dreaming ahead of time. Gerald taught me how. If I do that, and then you go to his side when he's sleeping, nothing short of a quake would wake him up. I promise it. You don't even have to tell me your decision. It would be safer if you didn't – for both of us. Only . . .' she hesitated. 'If you do it, it has to be soon. We don't have many more days before . . . before . . . gods.' She lowered her head, and he thought he saw her tremble. 'We'll be in their territory,' she breathed. Her voice so soft that he could hardly hear it. 'Soon.'

'Cee. You'll be all right. I promise you.' He put his arm around her – her flesh was cold, her skin so pale – and she cupped his nearer hand in hers and squeezed it. So much love in that simple gesture. So much support. He ached to know how to return such emotion. If he only had the skills of an adept, with which to Work a suitable response . . . he ached with longing, just thinking of it. The old dreams were taking hold of him again. The old reckless-ness. *Soon*, he promised himself. *Soon*. If the Fire freed him, then all the rules could change. For the better.

'Be careful, Senzei,' she whispered.

In a party of four, only so many duty combinations were possible. With two of the company sleeping and two sharing watch at any given time – and at least three days' travel left before they reached Lema's western border – the odds were good that chance would favour Senzei, and give him the opportunity he required.

Or so he told himself. Because *waiting and hoping* was easier – and safer – than *doing*.

I don't want the power just for myself, he told himself, as the cold sweat of guilt kept him from sleeping. *I want to be able to help Ciani. I want to be able to do my share, like she said. And I could, if the Fire would free me*.

He wanted it so desperately. And feared it, with equal fervor. Most of all he wanted the decision to be out of his hands; wanted the dreadful balance of *need* versus *betrayal* to swing one way or the other without him, so that he might be spared such an awesome responsibility.

It's not betrayal. Not if I take what the Fire gives me and use it to help others. Is it?

Ciani, I need your counsel! But her warning had been a sound one: to speak of anything, in this company, was to risk being heard by all. And he couldn't afford that. Not if he meant to do it. Any of them would stop him. Any one of them . . .

Damien, I wish I could confide in you. I wish your faith would allow it.

On the second day, during the late afternoon shift, his chance came at last. Hesseth and Ciani took the watch together, removing themselves to a nearby promontory from which they might view the surrounding area. Damien and Senzei were left to get what rest they could . . . but there was no question of Senzei sleeping. Long after Damien had wrapped himself in blankets against the chill of the afternoon, long after his husky snoring indicated that he, at least, had found some respite, Senzei's pounding heart kept him awake, and the rush of adrenaline through his body made him tremble with need.

Now. Do it now.

Carefully, he pushed back his own blankets. Quietly, he dressed himself. Thick shirt and jacket, worn leather boots. The weeks of traveling had taken their toll on his wardrobe; nearly every layer was patched or repaired in some place.

When he was done, he crept to where Damien lay and settled there, watching him. The priest slept clothed, as always, and his sword was laid out by his side. Ready for battle, even in slumber. Ready to respond to the slightest disturbance with a lunge for that sharpened steel, and—

Stop it!

A cold sweat filmed his forehead as he studied the sleeping form. Would Ciani's Working take? Would it hold? How would he know when – or if – it was happening? But even as he watched, a change in the priest's demeanor became apparent. His eyes flickered rapidly beneath closed lids, as if scanning some dreambound horizon. A soft hiss escaped his lips, and his brow furrowed tightly. His hands began to flex, like a sleeping animal's, and the muscles across his shoulders tightened as if in preparation for combat. Whatever dream had him in its thrall, he was wholly its creature.

Now. Do it.

Gently he folded the priest's blanket down to his waist, then crouched back nervously to see if there was any response. None.

With trembling hands, then, he reached out to where the small leather pouch was bound to the man's belt and somehow managed to slide open its clasp. Damien groaned once, noisily, but the sound was clearly in response to some dreamworld menace, not Senzei. Carefully, gently, he slid the silver flask from its housing. Golden light warmed his hand, made his skin tingle with anticipation. Even the few drops of moisture still trapped in the crystal vial had that much power; how much more was in his hands, in that precious pint of fluid?

Shaking, he managed to get the pouch closed again. It was important to leave things just as they should be, so that if Damien awoke too soon he wouldn't suspect what had happened. Would Ciani's Distracting work again so that Senzei could return the Fire to its housing? He didn't know; he should have asked. But that was the least of his concerns. By that time – gods willing – he would be an adept himself, capable of protecting his own secrets.

For a moment he simply sat there and cradled the silver flask in his hands; its warmth soothed his nerves, drove out the chill that had been part of him for longer than he cared to remember. If he had feared that the Fire might harm him, the touch of its light was utter reassurance. Like the sunlight that it mimicked, it had no power to harm an ordinary man; the force of its venom was directed at the nightborn, the demonic, creatures that shied away from the source of life even as they fed upon its bounty.

With care he crept from the camp. Gods alone knew what would happen to him when he took in the Fire, what form such a transformation of the soul might take; he didn't want to risk waking Damien and facing both his rage and the Fire at once. Hand closed tightly about the precious flask, he found his way through an insulating thicket of trees, and did not stop until he was safely out of sight of his companions' camp. Only then, safe in a tiny clearing, did he dare to unfold his fingers and regard the smooth polished metal, and the light that seemed to radiate even through its substance.

'Gods of Erna protect me,' he whispered. And with shaking hands, he unstoppered the small container.

Light spilled out from it, a cloud of purest gold. Even in the bril-

liant sunlight it was visible, driving back the afternoon shadows
that filled the tiny clearing and suffusing the air with clear, molten
luminescence. For a moment he just stared at it, at its effect, drinking in the promise of its power. And fearing it. The hunger was so
strong in him that he could barely hold his hand steady, and it was
several minutes before he dared to pour out a few drops of the
precious elixir. With utmost care, he gentled them into his palm.
And raised his hand to his lips, that his body might drink and absorb
that cleansing power.

*I willingly accept change, in whatever form it comes. I willingly
accept the destruction of everything I have been, in order to create what
I must become.*

He touched his tongue to the precious drops and shivered in fear
and need as his flesh drew the moisture in. Heat surged through
him, not the essence of the Fire yet, but something from a far more
human source: a heat in his loins that made him stiffen with need,
the hunger of his soul made manifest in his flesh. His heart pounded
wildly as he swallowed the church-Worked water, its beat so loud
in his ears that he couldn't have heard his companions if they'd
called to him. For a moment, sheer anticipation surged through his
veins – and with it a giddy ecstacy a thousand times more intense
than sexual excitement, more intoxicating than a gramme of pure
cerebus. He nearly cried out from the force of it. Pure hunger, pure
need, coursing through his veins like blood; he shook from the
onslaught, embraced the pain of it, felt tears come to his eyes as the
desperate need of an entire lifetime was coalesced in one burning
instant.

Do whatever you want to me, he thought – to his gods, to the Fire,
to whatever would listen. He felt tears coursing down his cheeks –
and they were hot, like flame. *Whatever it takes. Whatever will change
me.*

Please . . .

The Fire was inside him now, and its sorcerous heat took root
in his flesh. His muscles contracted in sudden pain as the burning
lanced outward, heat stabbing into his flesh like white-hot knives.
The pain pulsed hotter and hotter with each new heartbeat: the
agony of sorcerous assault, of transformation. With effort he gritted

his teeth and endured it, though his whole body shook with the effort. Tears burned his face like acid as they coursed from his eyes to his cheeks, and then dropped to the ground; he thought he heard them sizzling as they struck the grass, and the thick smell of dry leaves smoking filled his nostrils, crowding out all oxygen. Inside him, he could feel his heart laboring desperately to keep pace with the transformation, and its beat was a fevered drum-roll inside his ears.

He had shut his eyes in the first onslaught of pain; now, somehow, he managed to open them. The trees about him had been stripped bare as if by fire, and he could see between their blackened trunks to the sun beyond, a thousand times more bright and more terrible than any mere sun should be. With one part of his mind he acknowledged how deadly it was to gaze upon that blazing sphere for more than an instant – but then he knew with utter certainty that it had changed, that *he* had changed, and that no mere light could harm him. And so he stared at it defiantly even as new pain racked his flesh; kept his vision fixed on it as his muscles spasmed erratically, pain overwhelming him in spurts of fire. The very woods about him seemed to be burning now, with a flame as pure and as white as that of the sun itself; he heard its roaring eclipse the sound of his racing pulse, felt the song of its burning invade the very marrow of his bones. The clearing he was in was surrounded by fire, and white flames licked at him, smoking his clothing, scalding his flesh. He fought the urge to flee, to scream, to try to unmake the bond that was transforming him. *Whatever it takes!* he repeated, as fresh pain speared through his flesh. Blood sizzled in his ears, his fingers, its red substance boiling within his flesh. *Whatever is required!* The whole sky was ablaze with light, the whole forest filled with fire – and he was a part of it, his flesh peeling back in blackened strips as he embraced the flames, his blood steaming thickly in the superheated air. A sudden pain burst in his eyes and his vision was suddenly gone; thick fluid, hot as acid, poured down his cheeks.

It was then that he began to fear. Not as he had before, but with a new and terrible clarity. What if he didn't consume the Fire, but rather, *it* consumed *him*? What if its power was simply too vast, too untempered, for mere human flesh to contain it? He tried to move his body, but the roasted meat that his flesh had become would not respond. *Daylight can't hurt you*, Ciani had said – but it could, he realized suddenly, in enough quantity. It could burn, and dehydrate, and inspire killing cancers . . . he struggled to move again, to gain any sense of control over his flesh, but the precious nerves that connected thought to purpose had sizzled into impotence, and his body would not respond. Uncontrolled, his body spasmed helplessly on the dry, cracked earth. Flame roared skyward with a sound like an earthquake – and then was suddenly silenced, as the mechanism that allowed him to hear split open and curled back in blackened tatters, releasing one last bit of moisture into the conflagration.

And somewhere, amidst his last fevered thoughts – somewhere in that storm of pain, that endless burning – the knowledge came to him. Not a knowing of his own devising, but one placed there: a last sharp bit of suffering to make the dying that much more painful, so that the creature who fed on it might be wholly sated. Knowledge: sharp, hot, and terrifying. Despair burned like acid inside him as he saw her approach – as he submitted to the vision that was placed in his brain, in the absence of true eyes to see it with.

Ciani. Cold, and dark against the fire. She came to his side and knelt there. Not concerned, not upset . . . only hungry. And he could feel the hot tongue of her hunger lapping at his suffering, as he slid down into the fevered blackness of utter despair.

The last thing he saw was her eyes. Backlit by fire.

Gleaming, faceted eyes. Insect eyes.

Ciani!

Damien scanned the sky anxiously. In the west the sun had already set, and the bloodstained bellies of the farthest clouds were the last vestige of a short but dramatic sunset. Soon the last of the stars would follow, leaving Domina's crescent alone in the heavens. Dark, it was nearly dark. So where the hell was he?

'There.' Ciani pointed. 'See?'

In the distance: white wings, gleaming like silver against the evening sky. Not for the first time, Damien wondered at the

Hunter's choice of colour; black seemed much more his style, both for its ominous overtones and its very real value as camouflage. Of course, it was always possible that he did it just to irritate the priest. That would be very much his style.

While the three of them waited anxiously, Tarrant circled twice above the camp, checking out the surrounding terrain before he landed. Damien wondered what he would find. Would his bird's-eye view give him some insight into what had happened, and make explanations unnecessary? Or would he come to ground as ignorant as they were, and thus dispel the last of their fevered hopes? Something in Damien's chest tightened as he watched. *He doesn't know what happened*, he told himself. *So if he doesn't see anything special in the currents, it might be because he doesn't know what to look for*.

The Hunter came to ground before them, wings curling so fluidly to brake his flight that the action seemed a ballet, a dance of triumph of one man's will over mere avian flesh. Then coldfire blossomed, consumed him; white features melted into flesh with practiced efficiency, a display that never ceased to awe. But this time Damien had other more important things on his mind, and the few minutes that it took for the Hunter's flesh to readopt its human form seemed a small eternity. At last, when the coldfire finally faded, he searched the Hunter's face anxiously, looking for some hint of what the man might have discovered. But the adept's expression was the same as always: cool, collected, a smooth stone mask meant to frustrate prying eyes. If he had seen anything useful, it couldn't be told from his face.

So he said the words, and made it official – the act, and the fact of their ignorance. 'Senzei's gone.'

The Hunter drew in a breath, sharply; he didn't like it any more than they did, though probably for other reasons. 'Dead?'

Damien felt that bitter sense of helplessness rising in him again, which he had been fighting all afternoon. The frustration of total ignorance. The shame of forced inaction. 'Missing. Sometime in the afternoon. He was in the camp with me, sleeping . . . and when I awoke he was gone.' He shook his head tightly. 'No sign of why or where.'

'Did you track him with the fae?'

Damien's face darkened in irritation. 'Of course. And we found a trail leading to the edge of the forest. That ended there. Abruptly. As if—' He hesitated.

'Something had erased it,' the Hunter supplied.

Damien felt something cold stir inside him, that was half fear and half anger. 'Possibly.'

'Did you search for him? Bodily?'

It was Ciani who spoke. 'As much as we dared.' Hearing the tremor in her voice, Damien took her hand and squeezed it. Her flesh was nearly as cold as his own. He explained, 'It meant dividing the party so that one of us would be alone. Or leaving the camp unguarded. We didn't dare—'

'No,' the Hunter said shortly. 'Because if something had waylaid Mer Reese for the express purpose of rendering you vulnerable, you would be playing right into its hands.' He glanced at the party's mounts – packed and dressed and ready to go – and at the campsite, already scrubbed clean of any sign of human habitation. 'Did you find—'

'Nothing,' Ciani whispered. She lowered her head. 'No sign of him beyond that which led to the edge of the camp. No trail.'

'We could hardly scour the woods at random,' Damien said.

'You did exactly what you should have done, and – more important – you avoided doing those things which might have gotten you killed.' The silver eyes fixed on Damien and seemed to bore into him. 'To feel any guilt over the matter—'

'That's my business,' the priest said harshly. 'And if I want to feel lousy because a friend of mine might have been in danger – dying, possibly – while I had to sit here and twiddle my thumbs until night fell . . . you just stay out of it, all right? That's part of being human.'

The breeze had shifted direction, bringing a gust of cold towards them from the east. Tarrant blinked a few times, as if something in the chill air had caught in his eyes. 'As you wish,' he said quietly. 'As for the trail, or lack thereof . . .' He turned to the rakh-woman. 'Did you search with them?'

Her lips parted slightly, displaying sharpened teeth. 'I packed the camp,' she told him.

'She hasn't tracked in the woods before,' Damien said. 'I asked. She wouldn't know the kind of sign—'

'Maybe not. But there are senses which atrophied in humankind that may still function among the rakh. And if our enemy doesn't yet know that a nonhuman travels with us, he might not have allowed for them.'

'You mean, that a trail might still exist for her.'

'Precisely. His attempts to obscure—'

He coughed suddenly, and brought his hand up to his mouth in unconscious reflex, to mask the rasping sound. Such behaviour was so uncharacteristic for him that no one said anything, merely watched as he breathed once, heavily, as though testing the air. And then coughed again. When at last it seemed that the spasm had ended, he lowered his hand from his mouth and seemed about to speak. And then he looked down at his hand, and all speech left him. What little colour he had faded into white – the hue of fragile vellum, of corpses. It made Damien's blood run cold.

'Gerald?' It was Ciani. 'What is it?'

Silently he opened his hand, and turned it so they could see. Moonlight illuminated a smear of deep carmine. Blood. His.

'Something's very wrong,' he whispered. He looked up, and out into the night. His manner reminded Damien of a hunting dog, testing the air for a scent of its prey. Or perhaps of a deer, seeking the smell of predators.

At last he turned to the priest. His eyes were bloodshot, their pupils shrunk to mere pinpoints. His face was flushed, as if from fever. Or sunburn?

In a voice that was tense, he asked, 'Where's the Fire?'

It took Damien a moment to realize what he was asking, and why. When he did so, he reached to the pouch at his side and hefted it slightly in answer. But the weight that should have been in it wasn't. He fumbled with the catch, finally got the small pouch open. The crystal vial was still intact, and it glowed with reassuring light – but the silver flask, its companion, was gone.

Gone.

He looked up at the Hunter. The man had one hand raised, while the other was shielding his eyes. It was clear that he was

Working – or trying to. His breathing was labored, and obviously painful. After a moment, the wind shifted direction. After several moments, it held.

The Hunter lowered his hand from before his eyes – they were red, a terrible red, like balls of congealed blood – and asked, in a hoarse whisper, 'Is it possible that Mer Reese would betray you?'

'Never!' Ciani cried, and Damien muttered, 'No. Not that.'

'Are you sure?' He looked at each of them in turn, fixing them with his bloodshot gaze. 'So very sure? What if our enemy offered him what he wanted most of all – an adept's vision, in return for one simple betrayal of trust? Wouldn't that tempt him?'

Damien shook his head – but something in him tightened, something cold and uncertain. 'Tempt him, maybe. Seduce him, no. Not Senzei.' His voice was firm, as if he was trying to convince not only Tarrant but himself. Was he? 'Not like that.'

Ciani offered, 'He might have gone off alone if he thought there was something he could do that way, to help—'

'He didn't have that kind of courage,' the Hunter said harshly.

'He had courage enough to put his life on the line for a friend,' Damien said sharply. 'That counts in my book.'

'Can you find him?' Ciani asked. 'Can you use the Fire?'

He turned his eyes on her; already the redness was receding, but he was still a terrible sight. 'I can't, in any form, shape, or manner, *use the Fire*. But we do have a direction in which to search, now.' He looked eastward, towards the source of the Fire-laden breeze. 'With that, and Hesseth's senses, we may succeed in picking up his trail.' He looked at the rakh-woman; she nodded. 'Only one thing worries me—'

'That the wind was no accident,' Damien supplied.

He looked at him sharply. 'You felt that?'

Damien shook his head. 'Call it good guesswork.'

'There's the touch of a foreign hand on the weather patterns. Fleeting, evasive . . . and the Fire burns too brightly. I can't read its origin. But it's a good bet that someone – or something – wants us to go after him.'

The priest walked to where his horse was tethered and patted it once on the neck. He removed the springbolt from its pack, and pulled back on it hard, to load. 'Then we go armed,' he said. 'And we go damned carefully. Right?'

For once, they all agreed.

They found him in a small clearing perhaps a mile from the camp. Hesseth had picked out the smell of death and led them towards it, so they already knew what they might find. Nevertheless it was a shock to see him lying there – lifeless, so utterly, obviously lifeless – that for a moment no one could say anything, only stare at the corpse of their companion in terrible, mute silence, as the magnitude of the loss only slowly hit home.

Senzei was dead. And he had not died easily; that much was clear from the condition of his corpse. His mouth was open, as if in a scream. The eyes were wide, and rolled up into his head so that the pupils – mere pin-points, hardly visible – lay at their upper edge, against the lid. Every muscle of his body was rigid, as if death had merely frozen him in his suffering; his muscles stood out like gnarled ropes along his neck, wrists, and face, giving his skin the striated texture of a mummy. His body was arched back in the manner of corpses left in the sun to dry, and his fingers were splayed apart in a grotesque mockery of a Working-sign.

'He died in terror,' the Hunter told them. 'Or perhaps, *of* terror.'

Damien approached. Behind him, he heard the soft scrunch of grass as Ciani did the same. She went to the body. He went to the place some feet distant from it, where a single glint of silver in the moonlight hinted at an even more terrible loss.

It was there, lying on a bed of browning leaves. The silver flask, unstoppered. Open. Empty. There was still a faint shimmer about the ground where it had fallen, but the light was so dim compared to the Fire itself that it was clear the thirsty earth had drawn the water down, deep down, where no simple act of man might retrieve it. What little had remained for the air to claim had been carried to them on the wind, and was now dissipated. The Fire was gone.

He picked up the emptied container, and its metal was cold to the touch. Almost as cold as his flesh. Inside him was a bleak and terrible emptiness, as if all the accustomed warmth of his soul had deserted him. Sorrow took its place. And in its wake, shame.

He turned back to the body. Ciani was kneeling by its side, clasping Senzei's hand in hers as though somehow the contact could bring him back to life. But the emptiness in her eyes told a different storey.

'He's gone,' she whispered. Her voice, shaking, was barely audible. Her hands tightened about Senzei's. 'I did . . . I can't . . .' She looked up at him; her eyes were wet with tears. 'For me,' she whispered. 'He died because of *me*.'

'He did what he felt he had to.' The words of comfort came automatically, dredged up from some distant storehouse of priestly wisdom. 'That's all any of us can do, Cee. You can't blame yourself.'

'The Fire's gone?' It was the Hunter.

He shut his eyes, felt the shame rising again. *Damn you, Tarrant. Damn you.* 'Yes,' he said quietly. 'The Fire's gone.' He looked at Ciani, felt a wetness on his cheeks to match her own. 'We'll bury him,' he said softly.

It was the Hunter who responded. 'There's no soul here to do honour to – surely we all know that. To waste time administering to empty flesh—'

'Burial isn't for the dead.' He looked up at Tarrant, found the man's eyes and skin already healing. He wondered if the wounds in his own soul would heal as fast. 'It's for the living,' he whispered. 'Part of the healing.'

'Even so, we can't—'

'*Hunter!*' He could feel the coldness come into his own gaze, like ice, could hear it in his voice. 'You don't understand. You *can't* understand. That part of you's been dead for so long you couldn't remember it if you tried. And you don't want it back,' he whispered hoarsely. 'You willed it to die. All right. You succeeded. The living have their needs. You have yours. So just go, and leave us alone. Stand guard if you want – or go kill something if it makes you happy. Anything. Just *leave*. You have no place here.'

Tarrant's expression was unreadable – and for once, Damien had no desire for insight. Then he turned, and with a swirl of his cloak disappeared into the deepening shadows. The depths of the forest hid him from sight.

A soft noise from Hesseth caused him to look in her direction. The rakh-woman had taken out a small shovel from among their camping supplies, and was offering it to him. Wordlessly, he took it. And began to dig.

And he prayed: *Forgive me, God. Forgive me, for my human weaknesses. Forgive me, for my failure to rise above the distractions of day-to-day life, and keep my spirit fixed on Your higher ideals. Forgive me, that in that moment of shock I forgot Your most important lesson: that a lost object might be replaced, a lost work recreated, a lost battle rejoined . . . but a human life, once lost, can never be restored. Forgive me, that I forgot that primal truth. Forgive me that when I came here my first thought was for the Fire – a mere object! – and not for the loss of a human life, or the sorrow of the living.*

He dug his blade deep into the chill earth, pressed onto it with a booted foot to drive it even deeper.

And help me to forgive myself, he pleaded.

35

Gerald Tarrant thought: *It has to be here. Somewhere.*

Beneath his wings the vast expanse of the eastern divide rippled with the currents of fae pouring over rocks: brilliant blue earth-power, the rainbow flicker of tidal forces, strands of vibrant purple that licked forth from the deepest shadows as if testing the air for sunlight. To the east of him the sky was already lightening, midnight black and navy blue giving way to a sullen grey, first harbinger of the dawn. He should be in hiding by now. He should have found some place deep beneath the earth and already be settling himself into it. So that the powers that hid from sunlight might wrap him in their soothing chill, and renew his failing strength.

But not yet. Another few minutes, another few miles. It must be here, somewhere . . .

In the east, slowly, deep grey gave way to a sickly green; he winced as the light burned his feathers but kept on flying. He had chosen a white form, and that should protect him for a while; nothing short of direct sunlight would make it past that reflective coat. Nevertheless, his eyes felt hot and tender, and his talons throbbed painfully in time with each wingbeat. Time to land, soon. Time to take shelter. How many minutes left till sunrise? He was cutting it damned close, that was certain.

Taking chances, Hunter? Not like you.

Hell. This whole damned trip isn't like you.

With careful eyes he scanned the ground beneath him, searching for . . . what? What shape would the Lost Ones' caverns take, that would be reflected in the currents above? What kind of sign would there be, and would he know how to read it? Most important of all – would he find such a sign before the sun's hateful light drove him underground once more, so that he might return to his companions with some measure of hope?

Damn them all, he thought darkly. And: *Damn the fate that brought me to this place*.

He would be hard put to say exactly what drove him to continue, as dawn's increasing light made each wingstroke harder to manage, each rational thought that much harder to muster. He had already found two caverns that would have been more than adequate shelter for the coming day, but had entered neither of them. Instead he had turned towards the north and begun to search for some sign of the Lost Ones, some gesture of hope that he might bring back to his grieving party. And even while he searched, it irritated him that he cared enough to bother. Cared enough to risk the pain of sunlight in service to their cause. That was dangerous. That was *human*. But the feeling was there, too strong to ignore. Not born of sympathy, however, but of anger.

My failure, he thought grimly, recalling Senzei's body. It wasn't the man's death that bothered him so much; that life was as valueless as any other, and in another place and time he might have snuffed it out himself, with no more passing thought than one gave to the squashing of an insect. No – what bothered him was simply the fact that he, Gerald Tarrant, had been *bested*. Tricked. His own Working had been turned against him, without him even sensing it. *That* burned him, more than Domina's light and the coming dawn combined.

You're going to die, my enemy, and not pleasantly. I promise you that.

He searched the land with an adept's eye, reading the currents that coursed beneath him. It was no hard task to locate mere caverns; the eddies that formed above them made them as visible as rocks in running water, and he easily assigned to each a location, size, and probable shape. But he was looking for something different this time. A smoother flow, perhaps, or staccato burst of turbulence; something that would indicate a cave-but-not-cave, an underground structure that rakh, not nature, had created.

And then, just as the sky turned a forbidding gold at its lower edge – just as he knew that he must take shelter immediately, with or without reaching his goal – he saw it. His attention fixed wholly on the ground ahead of him, he banked to a lower altitude. And studied the area closely. Yes. There.

A unique pattern of earth-fae marked the western slope of the mountain beneath him, a succession of whorls and eddies too uniform to be wholly natural. The ground above tunnels might look like that, if the tunnels were uniform enough. He looked about, saw other slopes with the same pattern; the whole area must be riddled with tunnels. He fought the urge to explore further and dropped down to the earth, seeking shelter. His muscles burned from the light of dawn; overhead, the stars of the Rim were already fading from sight. He searched the ground about him quickly, looking for some sign of the enemy's presence; there was none. At last, satisfied that he was safe – for the moment – he let the current take him. Let his flesh dissolve, so that no more than his faith remained to maintain the spark of his life. It was terrifying, never ceased to be terrifying, not in all the years he had practiced it. And it was made no easier by the rakhland's currents, which were barely strong enough to support a simple Working, much less one of such vital complexity. But one did what one had to, in the name of survival. There was no other option.

The changing drained him of the last of his strength, and because the humans weren't present he allowed himself to *be* drained, to take a precious second and indulge in the sheer exhaustion of it. He had been growing weaker nightly, forced to rely upon primitive rakh and sometimes even more primitive animals for his sustenance. If the fae had to come from within him instead of being garnered from without, he would have been forced to stop Working long ago. The humans had no idea how much this trip was draining him – and they damned well weren't going to find out, either. It wasn't that he was afraid, exactly. Certainly not of that brash, swaggering fool of a priest. It was more a question of . . . pride. Stubbornness. And of course, self-defence.

Fat lot of good that'll do you if you stay outside past dawn.

He searched for the patterns of earth-fae that would indicate some sort of entrance. This was where the tunnels began, so didn't it stand to reason that there was some kind of opening here? He searched for long minutes, using all his skill and all his strength, and at last he found it. Barely in time. Already the rising sun had cast its first blazing spears across the sky, to light up the western peaks in warning. Even that much reflected light was enough to burn him, and he felt his exposed skin redden and peel as he tore away the tangled brush that hid the entrance to the rakhene tunnels. Barely in time, he crept inside. And worked his way to where a large protruding rock cast shadows of true darkness beyond. There he rested, while dawn slowly claimed the valley he had just left, and the mouth of the tunnel behind him.

Playing it close, Hunter. He put a hand up to his face, felt a blister split beneath his fingertip. *Too damned close.* Ahead of him, cool darkness beckoned. Utter blackness, soothing and sweet; the healing power of total lightlessness. For the first time since he had overseen Ciani's possession, he felt something akin to optimism. And when some of his strength had returned to him – not all of it, by any means, but enough – he pushed himself away from the rock at his back and began to make his way into the lightless labyrinth.

Soon dark fae began to gather around his feet, humming with the power of the underearth. The song of it was a subtle symphony compared to the blazing cacophony of day, and he drank in the delicate harmonies with relish. Behind him the last notes of dawn crashed their way through fissures and passages, but the light – and the sound – could not penetrate this far. He breathed a sigh of relief, knowing himself safe at last. And penetrated further, into the Lost Ones' ancient lair.

The underground rakh had settled themselves in a system of interlinked caverns, altering the natural pattern only when necessary. The larger rooms were thus exactly as nature had carved them, vaulted cathedrals filled with the limestone residue of a million years of erosion. The tunnels connecting them, on the other hand, had clearly been enlarged, and chisel marks scoured the rock where ceiling and walls had been altered to allow for easy passage. There was no sign, anywhere, of recent occupancy. On the contrary, the one relic Tarrant found – a slender knife blade chipped from obsidian – was affixed to the floor by a thin film of limestone, that told of centuries passing since its deposition.

A good enough place to rest, at least. And I do need that. Sleeping in this secure a place would give him a chance to renew himself, and he needed that desperately. Time enough later to explore, when the darkness had healed his wounds.

Suddenly, there was a sound behind him. A faint whisper only, like the breath of silk against flesh. But it was enough. He had Seen that there was nothing alive in these caverns, would never have taken shelter here otherwise. So whatever might greet him here was not alive, neither human nor rakh – and therefore, it was likely to be dangerous. He braced himself to Work, took a precious second to bind the wild power to his will, then turned—

And froze. Only for an instant – but that was enough. His concentration shattered. The fae he had bound broke free of his will, and dispersed into the pool of its making. In that instant, that terrible instant, he knew just how much danger he was in, and he drew his sword in a last attempt to save himself; coldfire blazed forth from the Worked steel, filling the cavern with icy light.

And *she* stepped forwards. Flawless in beauty, as she had been the day he'd killed her. Red-gold hair gathered about her shoulders like an aurora of light, warm skin and delicate blush defying the harsh illumination of the fae. Almea . . . It couldn't be. It wasn't. The dead never returned once Death had claimed them; at best this was a Sending, mindless and soulless, that had taken on her face in order to gain access to him. Or a demon, with some even darker intent. He forced himself to move, to strike – but it was too late already, he saw that in her eyes. Even as he unfroze, she moved. Delicate hands turning, canting forwards an object whose surface flashed purple and blue as it moved. A mirror. Even as he raised his sword it fell into position, caught hold of a slender beam that had filtered down somehow through a crack in the earth—

Sunlight. It struck him full in the face, hard enough to send him reeling back against the rock. He shut his eyes against the terrible pain of it, felt his hands spasm helplessly as they burned, his sword dropping noisily to the rock beneath his feet. The dark fae sizzled and smoked about him, the reek of its dying thick in his nostrils. He tried to move, to find some kind of shelter – anything! – but the beam of light followed him. He tried to Work, gritting his teeth against the pain of it – but the earth-fae was too weak here, or else he was simply incapable, the pain of it was making concentration impossible . . . He reached back with numbed hands to the rock beneath him, and closed his shaking fingers about the thick folds of his cloak. And raised it, so that the cloth might cover his eyes. At least he might have that much darkness. But even as he did so, the light was diverted upward. A prism hidden deep in a fissure caught the beam, and divided it. Mirrors set in the rock reflected it once – again – a thousand times – until the whole of the cavern was filled with it: a vast cacaphony of light, a symphony of burning. It wrapped about him like a web and speared through his skin at every unguarded point – pierced through the cloth itself and seared his flesh within, so that his muscles refused to obey him and he fell helplessly to the wet stone floor, unable to protect himself.

The lines of light connected, bent, became a terrible prison of pain that surrounded him on all sides. Gleaming mirrors reflecting the killing light of the sun down onto him, prisms dividing it into a thousand beams, a thousand colours, each one a separate note of agony, a separate flame in his flesh. Slowly, his struggles subsided. His body, incapacitated by the light, refused to respond to him; only his will remained, trapped within it like a caged animal. But even that was being drained of strength. The light was like a massive jewel, and he was in its centre; there was no escape. Slowly darkness came to him – hot darkness, desolate of comfort – and the brimstone scent that lurked behind it was almost enough to start him struggling again. Almost. But the sun had burned him dry of life, and nothing remained but fear. Pain. And the absolute certainty of what awaited him, on the other side of death.

The last thing he heard was his dead wife's laughter.

36

'He's not coming back.'

For a moment, silence. Only the words, hanging in the air between them like a knife. Sharp and chill. Even in his absence the Hunter had that kind of power.

Ciani wrapped her arms around herself and shivered. 'Or he'd be here by now,' she whispered. She stared out into the night as if daring it to contradict her. Her voice was shaking. 'He's not coming back, Damien.'

The priest bit back at least a dozen reponses – sharp answers, empty optimisms, they were unworthy of her. Something cold was uncoiling inside him. Dread? Fear? He fought it back with effort, tried to keep the sound of it out of his voice. 'Something must have happened,' he agreed. He forced his tone to remain even, unimpassioned. Now, most of all, they needed his strength. Now, most of all, *she* needed him.

Dusk. Twilight. Nightfall. They had waited through it all, the various stages of evening, and had received no word or sign from the Hunter that might explain his absence. How long did one wait, before finally giving up hope? Before admitting that the enemy's *divide and conquer* policy seemed perfectly capable of taking on a single man and destroying him? Even such a man as Tarrant was. Preternaturally fae-fluent. Utterly cautious. If the enemy could take on someone like that, what hope did that leave for the rest of them?

He was trying not to think about that. And failing, miserably.

'What now?' Ciani whispered. 'What do we do now, Damien?'

He forced his voice to be calm, though the rest of him was anything but. 'We go on,' he said quietly. He reached out to touch her, gently – and then took her into his arms. He felt her soften, as if her flesh was a hard clay warmed by the heat of human contact. Slowly the stiffness of her fear gave way to the weakness of utter desolation, and finally exhaustion. Her face buried in the thick wool of his jacket, she wept. Gave way to the pressure of the last few weeks at last and let it all pour out, all the terror and the hope and the striving and the loss. *Too much*, he thought, as he tightened his arms around her. *Too much for anyone*. He could feel the tears building inside himself, tears of frustration and rage, but fought them back; she needed him now, too much for him to let go. First Senzei's death. Then the loss of the Fire. Now ... this. His thoughts were a jumble, fear and mourning and hatred and dread all tangled up so thoroughly that it was impossible for him to isolate any one emotion, to analyse its source. Which was just as well. Some things didn't stand close inspection.

'We go on,' he repeated.

'Can we?' She drew her head back and looked at him. Her eyes were bloodshot, red-rimmed from lack of sleep. It struck him suddenly how very fragile she looked – not like Ciani at all. When had her strength given way to this? Or was that only a trick of his mind, that insisted on seeing her vulnerability plastered across her face? 'If they could get to Gerald—' she began.

'That means nothing,' he said firmly. Keeping the doubt carefully out of his voice. He had to sound confident for her sake. 'Tarrant was vulnerable,' he told her. 'Powerful, yes, and manipulative, ruthless ... but fatally flawed, in the Working that sustained his flesh. Remember what the Fire did to him, even from a distance? All our enemy would have had to do was keep him from finding shelter before daylight and he would be finished. That simple. It wouldn't even require a direct confrontation.' He drew in a breath, sharply. '*If* he knew how to do that.' How did one entrap the Hunter? It frightened him more than anything that their enemy had figured out how.

'He should have stayed with us. We could have protected him.'

'Yes. Well.' He drew in a slow breath, tried to calm his own shaking nerves. 'There wasn't much likelihood of that, was there? He trusted me only slightly less than I trusted him. And now we're both paying the price for it.'

Him more than me. A thousand times more. What kind of hell awaits a man like that? He tried to imagine it, and shivered. *I wouldn't wish that on any man. Not even him.*

'What now?' the rakh-woman asked. 'What plans, without the killer?'

He turned to face her. In the light of Prima's crescent she looked particularly fierce, blue-white light glinting off her teeth like sparks of coldfire. His stomach tightened, to think of that power lost. That deadly potential.

'We wait out the night,' he told her. 'Let him have that much time before we give up on him for good. If by morning he hasn't come . . . then we make other plans.' *Plans that don't include him or the Fire. Or Senzei.* He tried not to let his face betray his misgivings. *Too much. Too quickly. How does one compensate for something like this?*

He pulled his sword from its sheath, felt its leather grip warm to the touch of his hand. Already there were shadows gathering about the edges of their camp that were more than mere darkness: bits of the night given independent will – and hunger – by the party's misgivings. How solid would such things become in the rakhlands' inferior currents? How many such creatures would come to hover about the camp, thirsting for a taste of the human minds that had helped birth them? Ever since Tarrant had joined the company in Kale his presence had driven off such threats, in a manner they had come to take for granted. Now, how many of their own fears would Damien have to kill – or at least frustrate – before the light of dawn scoured the landscape clean of such monstrosities?

Damn you, Tarrant, he thought grimly, as he hefted his sword. *You picked a lousy time to die.*

Maps. Spread out in the sunlight, dappled leaf-shadows mottling their surface like lichen. The breeze stirred and their edges lifted, struggling against stone paperweights.

'These are all we have left,' Damien said grimly.

'Not the survey map.'

'No. He must have had that on him when . . . whatever.' It was safest not to speak of what had happened. Speaking led to questioning, which led to wanting to Know. And Knowing was dangerous. Whatever force had bested Tarrant might be waiting for them to establish just such a channel, in order to take them all. They dared not risk it. Not even to lessen the sting of ignorance.

'I've copied the important information, so we can each have a copy. In case we get separated.' He saw the fear coalescing in Ciani's eyes, reached out to squeeze her hand in reassurance. Her flesh was cold, her eyes red. Her face was dry with exhaustion; had she slept at all since Senzei's death? It bothered him that he didn't know.

'We have to plan for it,' he told her, gently. 'We have to plan for everything. I don't like that any more than you do, but it's suicide to do otherwise. The enemy's strategy is clear: pick us off one by one, before we can get to his stronghold.' *Leaving only the one he wants,* he thought. *You.* But he didn't say that. 'God alone knows how he got to Tarrant, but with Senzei we can venture a guess. And when you've got an enemy that can play on your weaknesses like that . . . we've got to be prepared, Cee. For anything.'

'Do you still think there's hope?' Her voice was a whisper, utterly desolate. 'Even after all this?'

He met her eyes, and held them. Tried to will strength into his gaze, that she might draw on it for courage. 'Very little,' he admitted. He wished he had the heart to lie to her. 'But that's as much as there ever was, on this trip. As for our chances now . . . remember, we planned this journey before we even met Tarrant. We'll manage without him.'

'And Zen?' she asked softly. 'And the Fire?'

He looked away. Forced his voice to be steady. 'Yes. Well. We'll have to, won't we?'

He pulled the nearest map towards him and studied it, hoping she would do the same. Hesseth was silent, but her alien eyes followed his every movement. Carefully, he circled a few vital landmarks. Sansha Crater. Northern Lema's focus of power. The trigger-point that Tarrant had Worked, so that when they reached it their duplicates – their simulacra – would begin the hazardous journey into ambush. The taste of that plan was bitter, but there was no stopping it now. And part of him was grateful. God knows, they needed a good Obscuring now. More than ever. He hated himself for feeling such gratitude.

Damn you, Hunter. Even in your death you haunt me.

'According to this, we've reached the point Tarrant meant us to.' He looked eastward – as though somehow mere vision could pierce through rock and span the miles, so that he might see that doomed quintet of doppelgangers. Quartet? Trio? How many? 'Which means that even now the simulacra are setting out, to take our place.'

'So the enemy will focus his attention on them.'

'We can only hope so.'

He said it would be automatic. Said that when we reached this point, five rakh would depart for the Crater, wearing our forms. But we're no longer five ourselves. Did he allow for that possibility? He was a thorough man, who anticipated so much . . . but would he ever make allowance for his own death?

He couldn't imagine Tarrant doing that. And if not, then the whole scheme was wasted: five innocent rakh were marching towards death for no purpose. Because the minute their enemy saw that the numbers didn't match, he would know that something was wrong. The thought of it made Damien sick inside – and he tried not to think about whether it was the death of five innocents that bothered him most of all, or the failure of Tarrant's deception.

Carefully, he folded the maps. 'We go north,' he said. 'Towards the House of Storms. And we try to make contact with the Lost Ones. If we're lucky – and Tarrant's Working is a good one – we won't be watched on the way.'

'And if not?' the rakh-woman asked.

He looked at her. And cursed the alien nature of her face, which made it impossible to read. 'You tell me.'

'Can you back it up?' Ciani asked. 'Do an Obscuring independent of Tarrant's, in case the simulacra . . .' She hesitated.

'Don't work?' he said gently.

She nodded.

'That would be very dangerous,' he said. Not meeting her eyes. 'There was a . . . a channel, between the Hunter and myself.' *Don't ask me about it*, he begged silently. *Don't ask me to explain.* 'If I were to attempt such a Working, while the fragments of his own still clung to the party . . . I could very well open up a clear channel between ourselves and the force that killed him.' *And anything that could take on the Hunter could probably destroy us without pausing for breath.*

'So all we have is what he did,' she said quietly. Eyes downcast; voice trembling slightly.

'Maybe.'

She looked up at him.

'*I* can't do it. And neither can you. But that leaves one other person.' He looked at Hesseth meaningfully. 'And I think she might have exactly the skill we need.'

The *khrast*-woman's lips parted slightly; a soft hiss escaped between the sharp teeth. 'I don't do human sorcery.'

'But it wouldn't be human sorcery, would it? And it wouldn't involve the kind of fae that humans could manipulate. Would it?'

'The rakh don't Work,' she said coldly.

'Don't they?' He turned back to Ciani. 'Let me tell you something I discovered about the rakh. I was going through Zen's notes last night, you see, and I found a bit of early text he'd dredged up somewhere and copied. About the rakh's ancestors. They were true carnivores, it seems. Unlike our own omnivorous ancestors, they were utterly dependent upon hunting for their foodstuffs. No agriculture for them, or the complex social interaction that farming inspires.' He glanced at the rakh-woman. 'They were pack animals. As we were. But with a markedly different social structure. The males spent their lives in competition with each other, expending most of their energy in sexual display and combat. When they hunted they did so in large groups, and only went after dangerous game. The risk seemed to be much more important than the food, and their social hierarchy was reshuffled – or reinforced – with each hunt. What they killed they ate on the spot, or left to rot.'

'Sounds like some men I know,' Ciani said, and Damien thought he saw something that might be a smile flit across Hesseth's face. Briefly. Then it was gone again, replaced by guarded hostility.

'The females hunted for the rest of the pack,' he explained. 'And fed them, in accordance with the local hierarchy. Dominant males first, then children, then themselves. With scraps for the lesser males, if any remained. Mammalian social order at its finest.'

He leaned forwards tensely. 'Do you see it? *The females did the hunting*. Not for show, but for sustenance. Not to display their animal machismo, but to feed their young. And the fae would have responded to their need, as it does with all native species. And what two skills does that kind of hunter need the most? Location and obscuring. The ability to find one's prey, and the capacity to sneak up on it unobserved.' He looked to the rakh-woman, met her eyes. There was challenge in his tone. 'If a rakh female were to Work the fae, wouldn't those be the two areas in which her skills would be strongest? The two very skills we need so desperately right now.'

The *khrast*-woman's voice was quiet but tense. 'The rakh don't *Work*.'

'Not like we do. Not with keys, pictures and phrases and all the other hardware of the imagination. They don't need that, any more than a human adept does.' He paused, watching her. 'But it isn't wholly unconscious anymore. Is it? Somewhere along the line your people ceased to take the fae for granted and began to manipulate it. Improved intellect demands improved control. Maybe on a day-to-day basis the old ways were enough . . . but I know what I saw in Morgot,' he told her. 'And that was deliberate, precise, and damned powerful. A true Working, in every sense of the word.' When she said nothing he pressed, 'Do you deny it?'

'No,' she said quietly. 'As you define your terms . . . no.'

'Hesseth.' It was Ciani. 'If you could work an Obscuring—'

Her eyes narrowed. 'That's a sorcerer's concept, I can't—'

'Call it whatever you like,' Damien interrupted. 'We'll find a rakhene word for it, if that makes you happy. Or make one up. Damn it, can't you see how much is riding on this?' *Careful, Damien. Calm down. Don't alienate her.* He forced himself to draw in a deep breath, slowly. 'Tarrant's gone,' he said quietly. 'So's Senzei. Even if I could Work this myself, my skills in this area are limited; sneaking up on enemies isn't a regular part of Church service. Whatever cover the Hunter Worked for us is going to fade away now that he's dead – if our enemy doesn't Banish it outright.'

'*Could* you help us?' Ciani asked her. 'If you wanted to? Could you keep the enemy from finding us?'

She looked them over, one after the other. Reviewing her natural hostility to their kind, perhaps, and seeing how far it would give.

She picked her words carefully. 'If you were my kin,' she told them. 'My blood-kin. Then I could protect you.'

'Not otherwise?'

She shook her head. 'No.'

'Would you, if you could?' Damien challenged her.

She looked at him. *Into* him: past the surface, past his social conscience, into the heart of his soul. The animal part of him, primitive and pure. Something unfamiliar licked at his consciousness, warm and curious. Tidal fae?

'Yes,' she said at last. 'If that comforts you. But you're not my blood-kin. You're not even rakh. The fae that answers to me wouldn't even acknowledge your existence.'

'Then force it to,' Damien told her.

She shook her head. 'Not possible.'

'Why?'

'The tidal fae never has—'

'—and never will? I don't buy that kind of reasoning.' He leaned forwards, hands tense on his knees. 'Listen to me. I know what the rakh were, when humans first came here. I understand that those animal roots are still a part of you. *Have* to be a part of you. But you're also an intelligent, self-aware being. You can override those instincts.'

'Like the humans do?'

'Yes. Like the humans do. How else do you think we got here, ten thousand light-years from our native planet? Of all the species of Earth, we alone learned to override our animal instinct. Oh, it wasn't easy, and it isn't always reliable. I don't have to tell you what a jerry-rigged mess the human brain is, as a result. But if there's any one definition of humanity, that's it: the triumph of intelligence over an animal heritage. And you inherited our intellect! Your people could be everything to this planet that we were to ours. All you have to do is learn to cast off the limitations of a more primitive time—'

'And look where that got you!' she said scornfully. 'Is this supposed to be our goal? To have our souls divided, with each part pulling in a different direction? Like yours? Vampires don't haunt *us* in the night; ghosts don't disturb *our* sleep. Those things are humanity's creation – the echoes of that part of you which you've buried. Denied. The "animal instinct" which screams for freedom, locked in the lightless depths of your unconscious mind.' She shook her head; there was pity in her eyes. 'We live at peace with this world and with ourselves. You don't. That's *our* definition of humanity.'

She stood. The motion was smooth and unhuman, silken as a cat's. 'I'll do what I can – on my own terms. *Rakh* terms. And if the fae will respond to me . . . then I guarantee you, no human sorceror will read through it.'

'And if it doesn't?' he asked quietly.

She looked northward, towards the point of power still far in the distance. Observing the currents? Or imagining the House of Storms, and its human master?

'Then your own Workings had better be good,' she said. 'Damned good. Or we'll be walking right into his hands.'

37

Power. Hot power, rising up from the foundations of the earth. Sweet power, filtered through the terror of an adept's soul. Raw power, that reverberated with pain and fear and priceless agony of utter helplessness. The taste of it was ecstacy. Almost beyond bearing.

The demon asked: 'It pleases?'

'Oh, yes,' A whisper of delight, borne on the winds of pain. That delicious pain. 'Will it last, Calesta? Can you make it last?'

The faceted eyes blinked slowly; in the dim lamplight they looked like blood. 'A thousand times longer than any other.' His voice was the screech of metal on glass, the slow scraping of a rust-edged knife against a window. 'His fear and the pain are perfectly balanced. The earth itself supplies the fuel. It could last . . . indefinitely.'

'And he'll cling to life.'

'He's terrified of death.'

'Ah.' A deep breath, drawn in slowly and savoured. 'How marvelous. You do know how to please, Calesta.'

'The pleasure is mine,' the demon hissed.

'Yes. I'm sure it is.' A low chuckle, half humour and half lust, sounded from the Master's lips. As raw power lapped against the smooth stone walls, staining them with blood-coloured fae. The colour of pain. The colour of delight.

'See that you have something equally suitable arranged for when *she* gets here.'

38

Snow. It wasn't unexpected – Hesseth had smelled it coming, and even Damien had made note of the ominous colour of the sky that morning – but that was little consolation. The last thing they needed now was for winter to begin in earnest. Damien cursed himself for failing to anticipate such weather, even as he beat the powdery white stuff from his jacket. He should have checked for it regularly. Weather was hard to predict, but not impossible – general trends betrayed themselves some days in advance – and he could have turned this choice bit of misery into something else, if only he had

Seen it coming. A little push to the wind pattern there, perhaps a little shove to the jet stream . . . there were a dozen and one ways in which the weather might be Worked, but all of them involved advance planning. And Damien had been too wrapped up in other things to remember that a good winter storm might lay ruin to all their plans.

The snow deepened to ankle height, gusted in billowy dunes to the level of their mounts' knees, caught in their collars and their boot-cuffs and trickled down inside their clothing as ice-cold water. Still they pressed onward, making what progress they could. They couldn't afford to slow down, not now. Once or twice the snow turned to hail, or hail mixed with freezing rain, and they were forced to stop. Battered, disheartened, they took what shelter they could find and waited for the downpour to abate. And began moving again as soon as they could, anxious to make up for lost time.

He wondered, in those cold times of waiting, if their enemy might not have sent the storm. Certainly it seemed the perfect tool for his purposes, in that it struck at both their strength and their spirit. And there was damned little Damien could do about it, either way. Oh, he tried. But weather-Working had never been his forte, and trying to alter a storm once it had actually begun was a task that would have given an adept nightmares. The best he could do was to Know it carefully, which allowed him to reassure his party that the worst of it had in fact passed them by; the flatlands east of the mountains had received a tempest ten times worse. But as cold, dark days gave way to icy nights, that was little consolation.

Tarrant could have shifted it away from us, he thought. *Tarrant would have seen it coming, and known what to do.* Bitterly he tried to drive such thoughts from his head, but they kept returning. It bothered him that he had any positive feelings about the Hunter, even so vague a one as that. Whatever worth the man had once possessed had become buried beneath so many centuries of corruption and cruelty that the resulting creature was more demon than man, and hardly a suitable subject for admiration. Especially for one of Damien's calling.

But he was of my calling, too. A founder of my faith. How do you reconcile those two identities?

They travelled in sombre silence, their passage soundless but for the crunching of fresh snow and ice beneath their animals' hooves. The xandu were growing restless, in a way that made Damien uneasy. Apparently it bothered Hesseth, too, for when they finally made camp she tethered the animals as though they were horses, so that they might not wander off. Over dinner she explained that the mountain snows of the Worldsend often triggered a migration instinct in the beasts, driving them to lower ground. Perhaps they were responding to that ingrained mandate. All night Damien could hear the xandu struggling against the pull of the leather leashes, snorting in indignation at their bondage. When it came his turn to sleep, he tried to shut out both the noise and the cold with a thick cocoon of blankets, but he was unsuccessful. The best he could manage was a restless half-slumber that refreshed his body but did little for his nerves.

Through calf-deep snow they resumed their travels in the morning. The clouds parted just long enough to confirm that the sun had risen, then closed overhead and plunged them into a timeless dusk of cold, white flurries alternating with sleet. Once Damien's horse slipped and nearly fell, while precariously close to the edge of a sheer drop – but it managed to stay on its feet somehow and edged past the dangerous spot.

I feel like a jinxer, the priest thought. *Like some poor fool who Works the earth-fae without even knowing it – only it does the exact opposite of what he wants. Isn't this how it works with that kind? You just manage to figure how bad things really are, and just then another disaster crops up.*

Would it be possible to use that as a Cursing? To take a mind that affected the currents naturally, and warp it so that its affect was negative? After several hours' contemplation – and a cold lunch, eaten hurriedly beneath the half-shelter of a rocky overhang – he decided that it would be impossible. There were too many variables to account for; too much was still unknown about the relationship of brain and fae. If you tried to Work a system like that, the whole thing would come crashing down around your ears. Only nature could alter biology on that scale and get it right.

But then he remembered the trees of the Forest – a whole ecosystem, redesigned to suit its human master – and he shivered, thinking of the kind of man it took to Work that. And what manner of sacrifice he had made, to conjure that kind of power.

A man who could Work the Forest could do it. A man like that could do anything, Then: *Anything except save himself,* he added grimly. And he tightened his knees about his horse's cold flanks, and tried not to think about how much this weather – cold and lightless – would have pleased the Hunter.

He's dead. And you wanted him dead. So forget him. But the memory of the man hung about him like a ghost. Was that because of the channel that had been established between them? Or simply the force of the man's personality? It was impossible to say. But sometimes when he looked at Ciani he saw the ghost there, too – a fleeting image, in the back of her eyes. What had gone on between the two of them, in the Hunter's last days? Damien hungered to know – and didn't dare ask. It was dangerous to pose questions, when you weren't sure you could handle the answers.

All day, the snow continued to fall. They rode. And somewhere in the distance, an unknown number of unknown rakh hiked northward, snow blinding them to the sight of their destination. Five of them, or perhaps three. Wearing alien faces, marching to an alien purpose. Struggling their way through this very storm. To their deaths.

Or – Damien thought suddenly – had that Working dispersed when its maker died? That was a frightening thought. What if the simulacra had never started out in the first place? What if, now that Tarrant was dead, the party had no cover at all?

Then we must depend on Hesseth's skill, he thought. And he looked at the rakh-woman, and wondered just how strong her power was. And how willing she would be to harness it to their need if all other defences failed them.

Fire. Brilliant, like sunlight: white-hot, molten, filling the air with a blazing heat. Senzei's face, like wax: melting, sizzling, running down into the grass like Fire, sucked down into the soil. Flesh running free like water, blood and bones dissolving into liquid fire, essence burning, dissolving . . . transforming. Until the hair is Core-golden, soft strands tangling in the thermal gusts. Until the eyes are silver-white, hot as metal freshly poured into a wound. Until the mouth is solid enough to voice a scream – and it screams, and the screams resound along with the roar of the flames, across the burning heavens, and as far beneath as the gates of hell and beyond.

The Hunter's face.

The Hunter's eyes.

The Hunter's screams . . .

He awoke. Suddenly. Not because of the dream. He was too exhausted for a mere nightmare to awaken him, too in need of the sleep that had been shattered. Besides, he'd seen those images before. Never in that form, never with such terrible clarity . . . but ever since Tarrant's disappearance he had been envisioning fire, both waking and sleeping. Had dreamed of Tarrant, in fire. Ciani had also. He'd had to reassure her that such dreams were only natural, given their recent experiences. Her dreaming brain was combining the elements of Senzei's and Tarrant's deaths, fusing the two disasters into a single, gut-wrenching nightmare. It was frightening, but only that. Not meaningful, he assured her. It couldn't possibly be meaningful.

Could it?

Carefully, he freed himself from his blankets. More than anything else he hated this weather because of the vulnerability it fostered. The tight cocoon of blankets which he needed to combat the cold was the last thing he wanted to be trapped inside if danger came calling. Even fully clothed it was bad enough – and he knew damned well that if he *really* wanted to be warm he should be naked inside that cocoon, his body heat warming the blankets and the air inside it rather than lost to his clothing. But that was where he drew the line. He'd once had to fight off a pack of ghouls in below-zero weather with nothing on but a pair of socks, and it wasn't an experience he was anxious to repeat.

He looked about the campsite, quickly took in details: Ciani, curled tight in uneasy slumber; Hesseth crouching by the campfire, springbolt in claw; the mounts half-asleep, restless. Nothing else amiss – or at least, nothing that was immediately obvious. Thank God, the snow had stopped at last.

He came to where Hesseth was and crouched down beside her. But the position which came so naturally to her rakhene form was painful for his cold-stiffened limbs, and after a moment he simply sat.

'How goes it?' he asked quietly.

She nodded towards where their mounts were tethered. 'The horses are starting to get edgy now.'

'And the xandu?'

She shook her head. 'Increasingly restless. There's obviously something here they're responding to . . . but damned if I know what it is.'

'Scent of a predator, perhaps? If something were following us—'

'I'd smell that,' she reminded him.

He drew in a sharp breath. 'Of course. That was . . . human of me.' He managed a halfhearted grin. 'Sorry.'

She shrugged.

He looked out into the night, wondered what unseen dangers the darkness was obscuring. As he had done each night since Tarrant's death – and each day, and morning and evening besides – he Worked his sight and studied the currents. They were harder than ever to see now, faint blue veins of shadowy light barely bright enough to shine through the blanket of snow that covered them. But after a few minutes he was able to focus on them and discern their current state. Which was just what it had been yesterday, and the day before, and probably countless days before that as well. Weaker than earth-fae should be here. Weaker than earth-fae should be in any mountain range.

It's as if there was no seismic activity here, he thought. *None at all*. But that simply wasn't possible. Even on Earth the mountains weren't *that* quiescent. Or so logic dictated. Certainly the colonists had been familiar enough with the nature of seismic disruptions to scan for such activity when they arrived – which said that they understood the nature of that particular danger, because they had experience in dealing with it.

Weak currents. Inexplicably stable terrain. A nest of demons. And a human adept who had settled himself right at the juncture of three crustal plates, heedless of the risk which that entailed. How did those elements fit together? It seemed to Damien that if he could only determine how they were interlinked, he could find the answers they so desperately needed. But the more he studied the puzzle, the more it seemed as if there was a vital piece missing. One single fact, which might make the whole pattern fall into place.

If we knew how they trapped Tarrant we might understand them better. We might understand them enough.

With effort he forced himself away from that train of thought and turned his attention back to his companion. Animal-alert, she was scanning the brush around their camp for any sign of movement.

'How's your Working?' he asked her.

She shrugged. 'As humans would say, I *Called*. Last night, when the moons passed overhead and the tidal power was strong. If the Lost Ones are anywhere within hearing, they'll come to us – or we'll go to them. Either way, we'll meet.' She shook her head slowly, as her eyes scanned the white-shrouded land encircling their camp. 'There's no saying how, of course. Or when.'

'Or if?'

Again she shrugged.

'Is that how Zen called you to us?'

'Very similar. In my case I read his message directly, and decided to respond to it. But the result is much the same. If this attempt succeeds, my call will fix on a Lost One whose path might cross our own – if such is available – and the currents will shift in response, to maximize the odds of our meeting. If the Lost One is conscious of the currents she may be aware of that process. I was. If not . . .' She raised her hands, palms open, suggestively.

'You say *she*.'

The corner of her mouth twisted upward in a slight smile. 'They are rakh,' she pointed out. 'If they have anything similar to a Worker, it will be a female. Our men generally lack the . . . time for such pursuits.'

'And the interest?'

'Their interests are quite limited,' she agreed. She looked him over, top to bottom; it was an appraising glance, clearly meant to assess the features of his manhood. 'But they do have their uses,' she told him finally.

'It's nice to be good for something,' he said dryly.

'I meant *rakh* men,' she corrected. 'Who knows what humans are good for?'

She stood, in one fluid movement that belied the discomfort of her previous posture. And threw the springbolt to him so that he caught it in his lap.

'Your turn to stand guard,' she told him. 'I'm going to try to get some sleep.'

Then she looked over to where their mounts were tethered, and her whole body suddenly tensed. Eyes narrowed, her attention focused on . . . what? What special signs were visible to her rakhene senses, that went unnoticed by his human sight?

'Watch the xandu,' she said quietly. 'If anything happens . . . it seems to be focusing on them. Watch them carefully.'

'What is it?'

'I don't know,' she whispered. 'But I don't like the feel of it.' She shook her head slowly. 'I don't like the feel of it at all.'

Nightmares. Of Tarrant and conflagration, and the two combined. Of pain, bright and molten, that shot through the brain like burning spears. And fear – so primal, so intense, that they shook from the force of it long after their bodies had awakened, their minds still vibrating with otherworld terror.

Nightmares. Identical. Every time he and Ciani shut their eyes, every time they tried to rest. The same dreams for both of them. But *only* for both of them. Neither their rakhene guide nor the animals were bothered. It seemed that only humans could dream such dreams . . . or perhaps, only those who had established a blood-link with the Hunter.

And it was Ciani who first voiced the fear. Or was it a hope?

'I don't think he's dead,' she whispered.

*   *   *

Riding. Endless miles of snow-shrouded earth. And questions that needed to be asked, no matter how painful the answers might be.

'What happened between you two?' he asked Ciani. He spoke softly, but even he could hear the strain in his voice. How could he keep his tone light when his spirit was anything but?

The ice underfoot crunched beneath the horses' hooves, broke beneath the xandu's toenails. It made for a complex rhythm, not unpleasing.

'You really want to know?' she asked him.

'I think I should.'

White ground, snow-shrouded trees. The creaking, tinkling sound of limbs overburdened with ice. Periodically a bough would crack loose and fall to the path before them, scattering snow in its wake. The worst of the storm had passed to the east of the mountains, but it would be long before the destruction truly ended.

'He apprenticed me,' she said quietly.

He felt something tight and cold coiling inside him, forced it to loosen its death-grip on his heart. *She was desperate for sorcery, in any form. It would have been worth the price . . .*

'Anything else?' he asked stiffly.

And she answered gently: 'Isn't that enough?'

There was no more intimate link in the world than that. A true apprenticeship would colour one's development for the rest of one's life – long after the training period itself ended. Even if her memory was returned to her now, all her Workings would bear the Hunter's mark. His taint.

The woman I loved will never come back now. Even if her memories are restored to her, she'll be . . . different. Darker. That taint will always be there.

And the part that hurt most was not that it had happened. It was knowing that she didn't care – knowing that the very aspects of the Hunter which made him so abhorrent to Damien were little more than items of curiosity to her. Never before had the gap between them seemed so wide, so utterly impassable. Never before had he so clearly understood its nature.

'And you?' she asked him. 'What was there between the two of you?'

He shut his eyes and told her, 'I bled for him.'
Even now, I bleed.

It was Hesseth's warning cry that woke him up. He came to with the reflexes born of a decade of living with danger – fully awake, fully armed, and half free of the blankets that bound him before he even paused to take in his surroundings. Domina's light filled the camp, which meant it was near midnight; the full orb of Erna's largest moon made it easy to locate the source of the disturbance, to see—

The xandu. They seemed to have gone mad, were striking out at everything in their vicinity. Pale manes flying, sharp horn tips stained with blood. He could see where one of the horses had gone down, and the other was straining at its tethers, trying to get as far away from the maddened animals as possible. The fallen horse was lying still, and blood pooled thickly about its chest; nevertheless the nearer xandu impaled it once – twice – again with its horns, as if maddened by its refusal to fight back.

Hesseth was drawing near the creatures, as if intending to calm them. 'Stay back!' he ordered. The maddened squealing of the animals made it hard for him to make himself heard. 'Back!' She glared at him but at last gave ground, springbolt braced against her shoulder. As he approached the horses, she scanned the surrounding woods quickly for danger. A good move. The screams of the animals were deafening; anything that hadn't known they were in this part of the mountains sure as hell knew it now.

His practiced eye picked out details of the fight, and he struggled to make some sense of it. The horses seemed terrified, but no more than was reasonable under the circumstances; any attempt on their part to break free seemed to be survival-motivated. And it seemed that one of the xandu – the louder one – was fighting to defend its flesh, rather than struggling for freedom. That left only one out of four to be causing the trouble, and with only three riders to be carried—

He swung his sword in a powerful moulinet, stepping in quickly on the downstroke. Gleaming horns passed within inches of his chest even as the steel blade struck leather and parted it, and he jumped back quickly. The xandu reared back in rage, as if intending to crush him – but when it realized that it was free it turned about and bolted from the camp, almost toppling itself in its mad rush for freedom.

Hesseth looked at the other animals, then at him. 'Follow?' she asked.

He glanced at the remaining animals – somewhat calmer, but still agitated – and nodded curtly. 'But we don't separate, under any circumstances. And we don't leave without our gear. For all we know this is some new gambit to split us up . . . or to separate us from our possessions. We've got good light; there'll be a visible trail. Let's pack it fast and move.'

'It could be a trap,' Ciani said. Her voice trembling, ever so slightly.

'It could be,' he agreed. 'And we're going to be damned careful because of that.' He nodded in the direction the xandu had fled mere seconds before. 'But if we don't find out what the hell happened here – and why – it may happen again, later. And that would leave us with too few mounts. Not to mention no answers.'

They broke camp quickly. Within minutes their possessions were bundled onto the three remaining animals, pack straps carefully tightened. It took longer to affix the saddles, as the animals were still highly nervous; Damien had to spare a precious moment to do a Calming, in order that they might be mounted.

Then he knelt by the side of the fallen animal and took its measure. A large, ragged hole had gouged it through one side; the froth that formed on its lips as it struggled to breathe was stained deep red. He put down his sword long enough to draw a knife from his belt, and with one quick motion sliced across the animal's neck. Quickly, and deeply. There was no struggle, no cry, only a gush of blood that stained his blade and the surrounding snow crimson as the animal died.

He caught Ciani's eyes on him as grabbed the reins of Tarrant's horse – the only true horse remaining – and mounted. 'Carotid artery,' he muttered. 'Kills almost instantly.'

He gestured to his two companions, assigning them positions

behind him. 'You in the middle,' he told Ciani, 'and stay there. Because if you get picked off . . .' *Then there's no point in any of this*, he finished silently. Her grim nod said she understood, and she pulled in behind him. Followed by Hesseth, and then—

Into the woods. Ice-laden branches creaking as they passed, miniature avalanches spilling to the ground before and after them. Damien had his springbolt out, braced against his shoulder in a one-handed grip. He could fire it that way if he had to, with his other hand tight on the reins. Not for the first time he wished for his own mount, that had drowned in the river. That animal could have been guided by his knees alone, leaving both his hands free for battle . . . but it was dead and gone now, and wishing for it was no use to anyone. This was what he had to work with, and at least it was a proper horse. – And probably a damned good one, given that Gerald Tarrant had raised it.

The trail was easy to see but hard to follow, a furrow gouged into the snow that wheeled erratically between the rocks and trees as if the xandu itself had no idea where it was going. And maybe it didn't. Maybe some Working had stung it on the ass – so to speak – and it was fleeing blindly, with no particular destination in mind. Which was marginally reassuring. If the xandu was supposed to lead them into ambush it would probably be following a more direct course, one designed to bring them in at the right angle, at the right time, and in the right frame of mind.

He shouldered his springbolt and aimed at the treetops ahead, watching for motion. But unlike the trees of the Forbidden Forest these had been stripped of their mass by the coming of winter; moonlight clearly illuminated a canopy bereft of life, that offered neither threat nor cover.

And then they came upon it. In a clearing, spacious and well-lit by moonlight. Damien heard his horse's hooves break through ice as he approached, felt the cold spray of water about his ankles. A stream, frozen over by winter's chill. He warned the others with a wave of his hand, heard them fording it carefully. The xandu was before him, and it snorted as if in rage – but its eyes were fixed on nothingness, its hot gaze utterly empty. It seemed to be struggling – but with what, Damien couldn't say. It was almost as if some unseen rope was pulling it backwards, while all its brute instinct urged it to flee; animal flesh versus some unseen power, with the latter slowly winning. There was foam on its lip, speckled with red, and when it struck the ground with its front feet Damien could see that it had sprained an ankle, or worse. He glanced back worriedly at the other xandu . . . but whatever madness had claimed this one, it did not extend to the others. It was almost as if whatever power had focussed in on it was content to claim one animal and leave them the rest. A truly chilling concept.

Then the xandu staggered backwards, and the ground gave way beneath its feet. First the area directly beneath it, then the ground surrounding – as if the earth itself had lost all support and was falling in on itself. It screamed and struck out blindly – but there was no solid footing, not within reach, and as the ground opened up it fell, limbs flailing, into the lightless hole beneath.

And then a scream pierced the night. One scream, utterly horrible. It was pain and fear and confusion combined, the dying scream of a soul drowning in terror. Damien's skin crawled to hear it, and he had to pull back on his reins to hold his mount steady. Beside him he could hear the others doing likewise, and he glanced at them briefly to see how they were doing. Hesseth's eyes were scanning the clearing with fevered urgency, her hand tight on the springbolt's stock. Ciani's face was white, but her sword was drawn; fear hadn't immobilized her. Good.

And then: silence. Utter silence, unbroken by anything save the ragged breathing of their three mounts.

After a moment Damien slid from his saddle; his boots sank deeply into the snow as his horse snorted anxiously, concerned. Ciani's eyes met his, and she seemed about to say something – and then simply nodded and took his reins from his hand.

He walked forwards slowly, utterly cautious. Long sword probing the ground ahead, testing for weakness. The snow was deep here, which made for uncertain footing, but he made certain of each step before he committed himself to the next one; he couldn't afford to be off-balance, not for a moment.

He could hear sound now, from the place where the xandu had fallen. A soft scraping sound, like that of cloth against snow. Or flesh? Something about it made his skin crawl. Inch by inch, he worked his way to the place where the earth had given way.

—And stared down into a massive pit, splattered with blood. There were wooden stakes set in the bottom, a good six feet long, perhaps two feet apart from each other. Easily as thick as a man's arm, but narrowing to a slender point. The sharpened tips pointed upward, as neatly arrayed as soldiers in formation; waiting for some animal to fall through the earth and impale itself, with such utter finality that struggle was meaningless.

And in the centre of the pit, their xandu. Or rather, the collection of meat and hide that had once been a xandu. Now, blood-splattered, it was barely the shell of its former self, a mere parody of life; its rainbow horns, coated with blood, were stripped not only of beauty but purpose, and its flesh was so ruptured by its brutal impalement that it was hard to imagine its owner running free on the ground above only moments before.

A hunting call, Damien thought. *That's what got it. Something needed food, and its hunger Worked the fae*. He stared down at the trap and corrected himself. *Not something – someone*.

'Damien?' It was Ciani.

'Come look,' he murmured. 'Carefully.'

Something was moving in the depths of the pit, between those sharpened stakes. Something that dipped in and out of shadow, its form utterly elusive. And then another one. They were clearly mammalian, though something about their skin reminded Damien of a slug. Then one of them looked up at him. He was dimly aware of details: a long tail, hairless, like a rat's. Immense pale eyes, filmed with a thick mucus. Hands shaped like the human extremity, but with fingers that seemed stretched to twice their accustomed length, that twined like nervous serpents as their owner looked up at him.

Not skin, no. Fur, short and close-lying. Ears flattened down against the skull, but a small tuft was still visible at their tips. And in those eyes . . . a hint of amber?

He looked up as Ciani and Hesseth came up beside him, their horses tethered to trees far behind them. 'What is it?' Ciani asked, as she came to the edge of the pit. But his eyes were on the *khrast*-woman. She came to where the earth had caved in, and gazed at the tableau below – and then drew back, hissing, her claws unsheathing as she braced herself for conflict. Her ears had flattened, in self-defence, and there was no mistaking the shape. Or the resemblance.

'It's the rakh,' he told her. 'The Lost Ones.'

There were five of the creatures in all. The sight of their dead-white eyes and altered limbs made Damien's skin crawl, but he managed to bury his revulsion deep inside him. Jelly eyes, tentacle fingers . . . he looked at Hesseth, saw her body go taut with hostility. A reaction to the scent of the strangers, no doubt – an instinctive response to the right-but-not-right odour of their presence.

'Hesseth.' He hissed the name softly, and as a result it sounded truly rakhene. He waited until she looked at him before he spoke again. 'You can't follow your instinct here. You *can't*. It's fine for territorial conflict, but it won't get us where we're going.' The eyes were gleaming with feral hostility. 'Hesseth. You understand me?'

After a moment, she nodded. Stiffly. A shudder seemed to pass through her flesh, as though pain had suddenly racked it. Her lips drew back from her teeth and she hissed: a warning. But then her ears seem to relax somewhat, and they lifted slightly. The fire in her eyes became a mere smoulder. Her claws sheathed – halfway.

'Human tricks,' she hissed.

He nodded grimly. 'It's the name of the game right now.'

Beneath them, four of the five misshapen rakh crouched tensely, waiting for them to make a move. The fifth had gone forwards to the xandu carcass, and was beginning to carve it up into manageable chunks with a crude obsidian blade; but even she was wary, and she cast frequent glances at the travellers standing above her to make sure that they were keeping their distance.

She. Four of them were female. The fifth was male, but nearly as slight of build as his companions. A lesser male, Damien guessed, who had adopted a female role in order to get access to food. He hoped for all their sakes that the male was firmly ensconced in his new role; that way, they might get through this meeting with no need for macho heroics.

'Talk to them,' he urged Hesseth. 'See if they understand you.'

For a moment, she seemed incapable of speaking. Then, quickly, she barked out a few sharp phonemes. It was obviously taking great effort for her to speak at all, much less in a civil manner. The lone male looked up at her, his alien face utterly unreadable. After a moment he stepped back to where his companions stood, his tentacular fingers wrapped tightly about the base of his blade.

'Try *hello*,' Damien prompted.

She shot him a searing glance, then turned back to the Lost Ones. And rasped out some other sounds, that sounded like a cross between a command and an invective.

This time they reacted. The male glanced at his companions, then handed his knife to one of them. And dropped back into the shadows that veiled the back of the pit, and from there into darkness.

'Not good,' Damien muttered. 'Gone back for reinforcements?'

'How bad can it be?' Ciani asked. 'We're armed, and it would take them time to climb from the pit—'

'No need to. You saw what they did to the xandu.' His expression was grim. 'Their enemies come to them.'

Ciani turned to Hesseth. 'What did you say to them?'

'What had to be said,' she answered sharply. 'With words, since they lack all the other signs.'

Damien looked down at the agitated foursome and realized, suddenly, just how much of a barrier there was to communication. Their alien physique would certainly alter their body language, and it was clear that they lacked the right scents . . . that left only words, and words were a poor second in rakhene communication. No wonder Hesseth was edgy.

That, and her instinct. God give her strength to override it . . . and the desire.

They waited. In silence, the nervous pawing and snorting of their mounts the only sound within hearing. Damien shifted his weight cautiously, as the wet snow began to invade one boot; otherwise, there was no movement.

And then the shadows in the back of the pit stirred to life, and several figures emerged from it. The lesser male. Two others, like him. And a figure nearly twice their height, a male who was clearly decades past his prime. His fur hung in patches on wrinkled skin, folds of loose flesh hanging from his bones like an oversized tunic. His skin was pierced: not merely in one place, or a dozen, but all over the surface of his body. Thorns, sharpened twigs, thin blades whittled from bone, pins carved from precious stone, all those had been thrust through the soft folds of skin to serve as a gruesome adornment. A thin shaft of shell, clearly precious, had been thrust through one cheek, and tiny beads dangled from its larger end; delicate needles of carved jet had been passed through the skin of his penis. It made Damien's skin itch just to look at him.

The pierced male addressed them — and there was no mistaking his authority, even without a common tongue between them. It surrounded him like an aura; it seeped forth from him, like blood from his manifold wounds.

Without consulting the humans, Hesseth answered. She had no time to translate before the next question came, or the one after that; the ghastly figure voiced his challenges too quickly, and she dared not hesitate in answering. But though he understood none of the words and even less of the kinesthetics, Damien grasped what was happening. *Who are you?* the pierced rakh was asking. *What are you? Why are you here?* He wondered what Hesseth considered suitable answers to be — and wished that it were possible for her to confer with him before she answered.

Watch it, he told himself. *She's smarter than you give her credit for, and she knows her people better than you ever will.* He studied the pierced rakh as he spoke, and he shivered in sympathy. What was his position in the social hierarchy, and why was he . . . like that? Damien had seen no equivalent among the plains rakh that he might compare it to. He envied his ancestors, whose knowledge-base had encompassed an entire planet with thousands of diverse cultures; how much easier this would have been for them, with so many different examples of primitive behaviour to draw on!

At last the pierced one gestured shortly. There was a scurrying sound behind him, in the shadows. Then footsteps. Then the slow scraping of metal on rock as something was dragged out of the shadows. And into the open, where they might see it.

Tarrant's sword.

It was every bit as brilliant as he remembered it, and every bit as malevolent. Its vivid unlight filled the pit's interior with disarming colour, turning human skin a pasty white and the Lost One's skin an even less wholesome colour – and yet it did nothing to dispel the shadows that ranged close behind it, or to otherwise illuminate the scene. The darkness that had gathered beneath the lip of the pit seemed to draw fresh life from the sword's presence and became even blacker. The shadows became sharper-edged, unyielding. A cold wind swept upward from where the Lost Ones stood, and Damien shivered as it touched him – not wholly because of the temperature.

The pierced one spoke to them. It was a short question, harshly voiced. Hesseth turned to them to translate.

'He asks, is this yours?'

Damien drew in a deep breath, glanced towards Ciani. But her eyes – and her attention – were fixed on the sword. On what it meant, that the sword was here.

'Tell him . . . that it belongs to one of my people. One of my blood-kin,' he chanced.

He thought he saw her nod slightly in approval as she translated. It was clear that the Lost Ones' dialect differed greatly from her own – which was only to be expected, given their isolation – but there seemed to be enough common ground that the pierced one understood her.

'Ask him where he found it,' Damien said quietly.

She did.

'He says, far south of here. Many one-walks. His people . . . *sensed* that it was there and went to investigate.' She hesitated. 'The language is very different, I'm not sure of that one. Perhaps, *heard* it?'

'Ask if there was a body nearby when they found it.'

It all centred on that. He wished he knew what answer it was that he wanted to hear.

'He says, no.'

Beside him, he felt Ciani stiffen. He forced himself to speak again, to keep his voice even.

'Or anywhere near it?'

She asked, and the pierced one answered. 'No.'

'Did you find any part of a body? Or . . . personal equipment?'

She conversed at length with the pierced rakh; it seemed they were defining terms. At last she turned back to Damien, and told him, 'Nothing. Only the sword. No a sign of how it had gotten there.'

'That means he's alive,' Ciani whispered.

'Or was, when they took him,' Damien corrected.

Hesseth looked at them sharply. 'Can you be sure?'

He shook his head. 'No. But it's only logical. If their only concern was to kill him, they would have left the body where it fell. Or whatever remained of it. If they wanted the kind of power you can conjure from a corpse – or needed his flesh for some symbolic purpose – can you think of anything more powerful, or more personal to him, that *that*?' He indicated the sword. 'Even if they killed him and then got rid of the body, they would have included the sword in their plans. Would have had to, to keep his spirit from wielding further influence. But if all they wanted was him, alive . . . what would it matter that his weapon of choice was left behind? It only meant that much less danger for them.'

Hesseth's tongue tip touched the edges of her teeth as she considered that. Ran over them, lightly. It was a ferocious expression.

The pierced one spoke again; clearly some sort of command. Hesseth stiffened, and barked back a sharp response.

The pierced one snarled. The rakh in the pit tensed, as though readying themselves for battle.

'What was that?' Damien demanded.

'He says that if this is a thing of your blood-kin, then it's now yours. You must come and take it.'

He looked at the glowing blade, felt something inside his gut go ice-cold at the thought of touching it. 'Okay,' he said quietly. 'That's fair enough.'

'He means . . .' She floundered for the proper English words to describe it. 'That is . . . he *challenges* you to come get it.'

And suddenly he understood. Understood all the levels of status that were involved, all the crucial posturing. And the risk.

Their females hunt for food. Their males hunt for status. —And the more dangerous the prey, the better.

'All right,' he said at last. He began to move towards the edge of the pit, looking for a way down. And hoped he was guessing right about their customs.

'Unarmed,' Hesseth added.

He looked up at her and said sharply, 'What?'

'Unarmed,' she repeated. 'He said that. Actually, *naked of threat* is what he said.'

He looked at the pierced one. And something in him darkened – some part that had had its fill of tact and diplomacy and was very near the breaking point.

'Tell him I'll be happy to disarm,' he said coldly. 'Provided he removes his teeth and claws.'

'They have no claws.'

'Then translate the rest.'

She looked at him somewhat oddly, then did so. The pierced one snarled but otherwise said nothing.

'I'll take that as a yes,' the priest told her.

'Damien—' Ciani began. She hesitated, then whispered, 'Be careful.'

From somewhere he dredged up a hint of a smile; it cracked ice crystals from his beard, that had set in a harder line. 'I think we're past that point.'

He found a place where the nearest stake was several feet distant from the wall of the pit, and lowered himself down. But the seemingly firm earth crumbled to bits beneath his fingertips and he was forced to drop the last few feet, landing unceremoniously on his side as the icy ground refused him purchase.

The Lost Ones watched.

He gained his feet quickly, noting for future reference that the ground down here offered little traction. Undoubtedly the snow drained into this area when it melted, only to freeze again come nightfall. He made his way carefully between the sharpened stakes, noting that their bases were set deep into the ice; a permanent hunting site, then, or at least semipermanent. Coarse wood caught at the wool of his coat as he passed; sometimes he had to press the stakes aside in order to squeeze his bulk between them.

Couldn't draw a sword in here even if I wanted to. He passed by the carcass of the xandu, felt a momentary pang of loss at seeing such an elegant creature reduced to formless carrion. And then he was clear of the deep-rooted spears and opposite the Lost Ones. They seemed larger from up close than they had from the ground above, and their smell was rank and musty, the reek of enclosed spaces. He could see now that their fur was edged with green, as if some species of mould had adopted them as its habitat; rosettes of pale grey marked the shoulder of one and muddy brown the haunches of another. Those growths added their own smell to that of their hosts, the odour of mildew and decay. In addition it seemed that some of the pierced one's ornaments were olfactory in nature; the sharp smell of pine needles and the pungence of musk drifted about his person like fog, a miasma of adornment.

He came as close as he could to his challenger and postured himself opposite the creature. Though the Lost One was taller he was also considerably thinner, and he lacked Damien's layers of insulating wool and fur. Though he tried to provide an imposing presence, he was no match for the priest's hefty bulk – and his ritual hostility was nothing compared to the potential for violence that lurked beneath the priest's carefully controlled facade, waiting for its first excuse to surface.

'You make one wrong move,' Damien growled, 'and I'll cut your vulking head off. —Don't translate that,' he warned.

'No chance of it,' Hesseth assured him.

The pierced one hissed angrily, but made no move to harm the priest. Instead he stepped aside, so that the sword behind him was visible. The malevolent power of it blasted Damien in the face like an arctic wind; it took everything he had not to react visibly, so that the Lost Ones wouldn't know his weakness. With a cold, tight clenching in the pit of his stomach he went to where the sword lay. And regarded it. He glanced over his shoulder to make sure the Lost Ones were keeping their distance from him – they were – and then reached down to where it lay, and closed his hand about the grip

—and pain exploded in his hand, like spears of ice thrust suddenly into his flesh. He could feel all the warmth in his arm coursing down towards his hand, through it, drawn out to feed that hungry steel. He gritted his teeth and raised the weapon up, his

fingers numb from the searing cold of it – but he held on, despite
the pain, despite the panic that was rising up inside him. *The Hunter
feeds on fear*, he told himself. *His weapons would be Worked to inspire
it*. He fought the panic down, forced his fingers to stay wrapped
about the leather-bound grip even as the killing power flowed into
his flesh – his lungs – his heart. He had submitted to Tarrant's coldfire once, and this felt much the same – a hundred times more
powerful, a thousand times more terrifying, but its nature was
clearly similar. He closed his eyes and remembered that ordeal, used
it to fortify himself as the power filled him, remade him – *tested*
him, against some dark and terrible template – and then withdrew,
until the pain became bearable. Somewhat. Until the cold, though
still piercing, was no longer a direct threat to his survival.

He turned to the Lost Ones, fingers still wrapped tightly about
the sword's grip. His hand was still numb from the cold of it, but
the blade seemed to have a life of its own; he had no doubt that if
he had to wield it, he could.

*And it will drink in life, like its owner does. It will drink in the terror
of the wounded . . .*

The pierced one spoke. His tone was challenging.

'He says, that thing has killed many.'

Yes, Damien thought. He noted the rope still wrapped about its
quillons, which they had used to drag it here. *And the only reason
it didn't kill me just now is my link to Tarrant. The sword knows its
own.*

'It belongs to my blood-kin,' he repeated. The weight of it was
like ice in his hand, but he refused the temptation to put it down.

The pierced one spoke again.

'He says, it eats souls.'

Damien drew in a deep breath, forced himself to think before
answering. 'Tell him . . . that we came to kill an eater of souls. An
eater of *rakhene* souls. Tell him . . . sometimes it takes power of the
same sort to kill one like that.'

He could see them react as Hesseth translated. He waited. Dark
power flowed up his arm, wrapped itself around the circuitry of his
brain. *Kill*, it whispered. *Kill, and be done with them*.

He shifted his grip on it and tried to block out its message.

Tendrils of malevolence continued to seep into his brain, but he refused to acknowledge them.

'There is only one eater of souls here,' Hesseth translated for them. 'In the . . .' she hesitated. 'I think he means, the House of Storms.'

'What did he say, exactly?'

'I'm not sure. Their speech is so different . . .'

'Then don't try to translate the concept – just give me the words.'

Her brow furrowed tightly as she considered. 'The place of . . . blue lightning?'

'Blue lightning?'

'I'm not sure. I—'

'*Blue* lightning?'

'I *think* that's the word. Why?' she demanded. 'Is it so significant?'

He was remembering the sky over Jaggonath, when the earthquake struck. The blinding spears that had shot up from the earth, filling the heavens with light. So much like nature's lightning, only a hundred times more intense. And, of course, silver-blue – earthfae blue – as opposed to nature's white.

He tried to recall what it was that Hesseth had described, back at her people's encampment. *Lightning*, she'd said, *that filled the sky for months on end. Thunder so loud it made speaking impossible.*

That's what it was. That's what the storms were. Not real lightning at all. Power; *bound* power.

My God, the implications . . .

'Tell him what we need,' he ordered. He could hear his voice shaking as he spoke, tried to steady it. So much seemed to depend upon a display of strength, with these people. 'Ask him if he'll help us.'

An overload, firing heavenward. But an overload of what? There are no earthquakes in this region. And the currents here are so weak . . . It was hard to think clearly with the power of the Hunter's sword chilling his brain. Even so, he sensed that he had glimpsed the last piece of the puzzle. Finally. He had only to see where it fit into the whole picture, and then they would know where to strike . . .

Tarrant would have understood it. Then he corrected himself, grimly: *Tarrant still may.*

'He'll lead us,' Hesseth told them. 'As far as the . . . *region of no*, is the phrase.'

'Forbidden zone?' Ciani offered.

'I don't know. What he says . . . it's not a concept I'm familiar with.'

'Can we get from there to the House of Storms?' Damien asked. 'To the tunnels underneath them? That's all that matters.'

'He says . . . that region is a place of dying. The tunnels beneath the House of Storms are filled with dying. Those are the . . . the *places of no.*' She shook her head. 'I'm sorry.'

'Taboo,' Damien guessed. 'As any dwelling place would be, once demons moved in.' He looked at the pierced one. 'Tell him yes. Tell him that's what we want. What we *need*.'

He looked to the dirt wall behind the Lost Ones, to the tunnel mouth that waited there. Somewhere at the far end was their human enemy. Ciani's assailant. And — just possibly — Gerald Tarrant.

'That's our entrance,' he whispered.

39

The winter wind howled across the eastern flatlands, flinging snow across everyone and everything in its path. It was a bitter wind, fresh from the arctic regions, and the moisture it had picked up while crossing the Tri-Lakes area and the Serpent made it doubly vicious. There was nothing to do but find shelter from the storm and stay there, and the various inhabitants of eastern Lema had done just that. The local rakh huddled in their tents, gathered tightly about their fires, and waited for the storm to pass. Flatland browsers were packed tightly in their caves and their tunnels, yawning as the first waves of hibernation dulled their minds with drowsiness. Even winter's predators had taken shelter, and they paced restlessly in their cramped hiding places as they waited for the worst of the storm to pass, so that they could follow the trails made by their prey in the smooth, white snow.

It was no time for animals or rakh to be abroad, and all the inhabitants of Lema seemed to know this.

All but three.

They walked like humans, though their anatomy was clearly rakhene. It was a mismatch of body and purpose, as though somehow a human persona had been welded to native flesh. They were furred, like most rakh, and heavily clothed, but the wind that whipped across the open plains was more than a single coat could ward against. Beneath the thin fur, warm flesh was already turning white with death. Extremities first: the fingers and toes, then nose, lips, cheeks . . . in the frigid cold of winter's first storm they labored for breath, and the moisture of their lungs gathered like frost on their lips as they exhaled, gasping, into the wind.

Mindlessly they staggered forwards, their legs knee-deep in snow. *Driven* to stagger forwards, by a force they could neither comprehend nor fight. It had taken their memories, this alien force, and replaced them with others. Foreign pictures; alien recall. Names and places and hungers and needs, feelings so intense that their own memories were mere shadows beside them. Shadows that faded as day turned into night turned into day again, as the hours of travel became endless and the goal ahead – if there was one – seemed forever beyond their reach.

The wind gusted suddenly. And one of them fell. It was the youngest of the three, a female barely old enough to mate. Exhaustion had robbed her limbs of strength and she lay in the snow, her face cracked and bleeding from the cold. Panting lightly, as if she lacked even the strength to breathe.

The other two looked at her. They were her father and sister, blood-kin to her flesh . . . and they looked at her now, and were unaware of any kinship. Were unaware of anything save the force that drove them north-ward, and its demands.

For a moment was silence. Within them, and without; a precious moment of non-being in which the alien memories ceased their

clamour, and the flesh was emptied of all thought. A single instant
of peace, in the midst of their nightmare journey.

And then it came, as a whisper. Invading their flesh, their souls.
Two is enough, it said. *Move on. Leave the dying one here.*

The female hesitated, then turned away. The male looked down
at his daughter. Some memory stirred in the back of his mind that
might have involved warmth and paternal devotion . . . but then it
was gone, crowded out by alien images. *Human* images. He fought
them for a moment, but the force that had implanted them was
stronger than he was – and at last he gave way, and the old memories died within him.

Slowly, he, too, turned away. Slowly they began to move again,
breaking a trail through the knee-deep snow. Two of them, now.
But two was enough. The force that had bound their wills made
that clear.

In the snow behind them, in a shallow grave of crystal and ice,
the simulacrum who had once been their blood-kin breathed her
last.

40

They let the horse and the xandu go free. They could hardly take
them underground, and had no way to lodge them safely until they
returned. *If* they returned. So they let them go. The xandu were
born to the wild, and could easily return to it. As for the Forest
steed . . . Damien debated killing it, to spare it a slower death by
freezing or starvation. But the horse had ridden beside the xandu
for so long that when they were freed to go it tried to go off with
them, like one of their number. Well enough, Damien decided. It
was the Hunter's stock, after all; doubtless it could manage to fend
for itself.

The sword was another matter. That had to come with them,
there was no question about it. But even wrapped in multiple blan-

kets it radiated power, and its aura of malevolence was so intense that Damien wondered how long he would be able to carry it. The mere thought of contact with the Worked steel made his blood run cold with dread, and revived echoes of a voice – and a person – he would rather forget.

Just like him, too. Even in death his evil affects us.

Or in imprisonment, he corrected grimly.

Carrying their most vital possessions on them – the rest had been buried, or given to the Lost Ones – they entered the narrow tunnel that led from the back of the hunting pit. Dark earth closed in about them, walls too close and ceiling too low and the whole of it damp, rank with the smell of that mildewed species. Damien could see Hesseth shiver in revulsion as they descended, deep into the reeking earth, and he prayed that she could hold out. Her sense of smell was stronger than all the humans' put together, and the odour seemed to awaken some primal fight-or-flight instinct within her. He hoped she had the strength – and the desire – to overcome that response. For all their sakes.

As the moonlight faded far behind them, no light took its place that unaltered humans might see by. The pierced one seemed to wend his way by the light of the earth-fae, his pale eyes split wide to reveal a glistening pupil, as broad as Damien's palm. If the tunnels descended deep enough, Damien thought, only the dark fae would be available for illumination. He debated using the Fire to facilitate his own sight, or even kindling a small lamp. But in the end he simply Worked his own vision and saw as the natives did. He turned to check on Ciani, to offer her a similar service – and found to his surprise that it wasn't necessary. She had Worked her own vision, using the techniques that Tarrant had taught her.

Good for her, he thought. But his soul was sick as he contemplated the cost of that Working, the darkness that would slowly be taking root inside her.

She'll never be what she was, he thought grimly. And what bothered him most of all was not that it was happening, or that he didn't know how to stop it. It was that she didn't care. Didn't even recognize the problem.

It's all the same power to her. He's just another adept. More interesting than most, perhaps – but that only makes him more desirable. The cost of it means . . . nothing.

By the light of the dark fae alone they descended, so deep into the earth that only a few wisps of earth-fae coursed about them; Damien felt strangely naked, in a world without that omnipresent power. He cast about with a cautious Working, anxious to catch wind of any threat to his party before it manifested. But he found himself incapable of Working on that level, and the truth of what Tarrant had said to them earlier finally hit home: *The power does not come from within us, but from without.* Which meant that in a place where the earth-fae was scarce, there was no Working. Period. It was all he could do to maintain his altered vision, and who knew how long he could keep that up? If their Workings should fail them they would be trapped here in true darkness, hundreds of feet beneath the earth. Totally helpless. He reached back instinctively to feel the haft of his sword, to comfort himself that even facing such adversity he could hold his own. But his fingers closed about the grip of Tarrant's sword instead – he had strapped it to the same harness, as a means of carrying it without having to look at it – and its chill power shot up his arm with stunning force. He tried to release it immediately, but his hand was slow to respond. Ice-cold power slammed into him, and the tunnel erupted in violet iridescence. Twisting threads of light filled the air about him, too bright to look at directly. They tangled about his feet, clung to his clothes as though seeking the flesh beneath. And burned, with a purple brilliance that was blinding. He forced himself to release the sword, and after a moment – a very long moment – the power subsided. And with it, the vision. He forced himself to breathe steadily, slowly.

The dark fae, he thought. Awed by the vision, so unlike anything he had ever seen. *Is that how it looks to him?* It was an incredible concept, that the man who seemingly thrived on darkness lived in a world of such brilliant light. Never lacking illumination, because his vision was always Worked.

Ciani was like that. That's what she lost. And his hands clenched at his sides, remembering what the loss had done to her. *That's what we're getting back for her.*

The pierced rakh led them onward without a word, through an underground labyrinth of dizzying complexity. Natural tunnels met and merged in combination with rakh-carved corridors, that twisted back on themselves and merged again and opened out into natural chambers, with a thousand nooks and crannies in which the dark fae lurked . . . Damien tried to memorize the pattern of their progress, but it was impossible. Which meant they had no hope of finding their way back, or of locating any other exit, without the pierced one's help. It was a kind of helplessness he despised – and it was all the more frustrating because there was nothing he could do about it.

After a time the rakh-made caverns altered in nature. The ceiling became more even, the cave floor more regular. And the walls . . . they had been reinforced with the bones of the Lost Ones' prey – long, sweeping femurs and radia cemented into place beneath fragile stone formations, like the armature of some ghastly sculpture. These increased in number as they progressed, their sheer profusion giving the tunnels the aspect of a behemoth's rib cage seen from within. Those gave way in turn to larger spaces, in which Nature had seen to the decorating: huge vaulted chambers whose ceilings dripped limestone formations like icicles, waterfalls of crystalline calcite that gleamed like fresh snow in the dark fae's light, underground lakes that were no more than an inch or two deep, but that seemed fathoms in depth – and always there were the veils of memory that the dark fae conjured, that parted like silk curtains at their approach and fluttered slowly into misty darkness behind them. Evidently their fears had no power to manifest in the pierced one's presence, which was fortunate for all of them.

Damien was exhausted – from walking, from Working. When they at last stopped to rest, he kindled a small tin lamp and let his eyes take a break. Ciani dropped down by his side, equally exhausted, and he saw her rub her eyes as if they hurt her. He put his arm around her, tenderly, but there was little comfort he could offer. Except to whisper that he would keep the lamp out from now on, that its light was inferior but they would have to make do with it. They couldn't keep Working forever.

'But we tried, yes?' she whispered. And despite their redness her eyes gleamed with pride, because she had Worked as long and as well as he had.

It was hard for them to get moving again. Even Hesseth seemed to bend beneath the weight of her pack, as though it had doubled in weight since she had last borne it. The pierced one watched them in silence, and seemed to need no rest; his own body was clearly more accustomed than theirs to the rigors of underground hiking. And in the end it was his searching gaze that got them moving again, the sight of his mucus-filmed eyes searching for weakness in them. Any weakness.

And then – hours later, miles later, who could say how far they'd come, or how long they'd been traveling? – there was life. At last. First the smell of it: musty and close, like the Lost Ones themselves. Then a faint whiff of smoke, that drifted tantalizingly past them and then, just when they had noticed it, disappeared. Followed by the pungent aroma of the rakh's fur-mould, which they could now see clinging to the damp cave walls, as well as to the pelt of their host. And the scent of warmth – of fire – of blessed heat, that drove the last of winter's chill from their weary limbs and promised at least a brief respite from their exertions.

The corridor turned, and widened. And opened into a vast chamber filled with the wide-eyed Lost Ones. They were gathered in small groupings – families? – whose members huddled close together as they stoked their small fires, scraped and polished bones, carved ornaments, picked at each other for parasites. The nearer heads shot up as the party entered the vast common chamber, and Damien caught the glint of firelight on ornaments, thin needles of stone and shell thrust through cheeks, nostrils, even eyelids. Mostly on the men, he noted. And the stronger ones wore more of them and courted more painful placement. What manner of rakh did that make their guide? Damien glanced at the pierced one, saw him studying the inhabitants of the chamber with clear authority. Some sort of leader, then. Or priest. Did the cave-rakh have priests?

The walls were ornate, albeit primitive in design, and had been painted with charcoal and bits of lichen in crude but intricate patterns. Once more, the Lost Ones had used the bones of their food-animals to reinforce the walls, but here the effect seemed more decorative than structural. Polished to a gleaming white, the bones glittered like candleflames in the relative brilliance of the rakhene cookfires. Toe bones and hand bones and slender fingers, worked like mosaic tiles into some sort of native cement—

And then he looked closely at those gleaming bits and hissed softly, rakhlike, as he recognized some of them. He felt his arm muscles tensing as if for battle, had to forcibly keep himself from reaching for his sword.

Not here. Not yet. Find your way out of this warren first.

He took care to position himself so that the women had no chance to see the wall behind him; he could only hope there were no similar displays elsewhere. He felt despair growing inside him, the impotence that came of feeling totally powerless. And he was, indeed, made powerless: by the darkness, by the labyrinth, by the lack of Workable fae in this place – but most of all by their enemy's all-Seeing power, which was probably even now scouring the rakhlands in search of them. There was some small comfort in that, at least – as long as they were this far underground, not even he would be able to find them.

The cave-rakh began to gather around them, half-crawling, half-walking, coming as close as they dared and then sniffing noisily, white nostrils distended as they tried to catch the strangers' scents. Tails whipped urgently behind them, twining about each other like serpents in the darkness. How they could smell anything over the mouldy reek of their own bodies was beyond Damien; this close, their odour was nigh on overwhelming. He gathered Ciani close to him, a protective arm about her shoulder; Hesseth he kept behind him, lest the like-but-unlike quality of her scent should trigger some violence among these creatures.

The pierced male spoke to them. After a moment of waiting, he snapped another few phrases in the rakhene tongue, hurling them at Hesseth like knives. With effort she composed herself, barely enough to translate, 'He says these are the fringe-folk, who live on the borders of the . . . the no-place. He says . . .' She drew in a deep breath, shaking; it was hard for her to translate calmly when all her animal senses were screaming at her to flee. 'He is the dream-one, the seeing-one, and they'll respect his wishes. Because he asks it, they'll keep us here, so that we may sleep in – in – I'm sorry,' she said, flustered. 'I just don't know that one.'

The pierced one continued. 'From here they can show us the House of – the place of blue light,' she corrected herself. Damien could hear the strain in her voice, echo of a self-control that was alien to her and her kind. *That's it*, he thought approvingly. *Keep it up.* 'He says that the tunnels we want are under this place, but they are not easy tunnels. The small ways are too narrow, and the walls are . . . *falling-threat*, he says. Which is why the tunnels were abandoned.' He saw her nostrils flare in terror, innate response to some half-sensed threat. Once more she drew in a deep, slow breath, as if struggling for air. 'Very dangerous,' she gasped. Was she translating the dream-one's words, now, or referring to their general situation? 'In past times there was much death, in the no-place. No rakh ever goes there, now. No rakh *will* ever go there.' The pierced one grinned, displaying crooked teeth. 'But I will go there,' she translated, as he slapped his breast proudly. A thin drop of blood welled forth from the base of a pectoral ornament he had struck. 'I, the seeing-one, the dream-one, who dares the places of no, I will take you there.' The filmy eyes fixed on Damien with clear hostility. 'I think this is some kind of male statement—'

'I understand it,' he told her. Oh, yes: the social pattern was very familiar. Primitive, even bestial . . . and not without its congruent among human males. He remembered one young boy braving the true night alone, in order to achieve the status that only foolhardy courage could earn. Because of a dare, he remembered. It was always because of a dare.

'Tell him yes,' he said brusquely. 'Tell him I want to see if he can lead us there, to the place where no rakh go. I want to see if his . . . if his *seeing* is stronger than his fear. —Say it that way,' he urged her.

He watched the pierced one's face as his challenge was voiced. And therefore did not see the faces surrounding them, as several rakh gasped in response to his audicity.

But the pierced one merely nodded, once, tightly, as he accepted the challenge. 'After sleep, then,' he told them through the *khrast*-woman. 'After you have seen the lightning-place. We go then.' He waved to one of the local females, who scurried off ratlike into the darkness. 'The fringe-folk give you shelter, for resting in. You will not be sleeping together, so—'

'*We stay together*,' Damien said sharply. And he sensed, rather than saw, relief in Hesseth's eyes. 'At all times.'

The pierced one fixed wide black eyes on him, as if trying to stare him down. *Fat chance*, Damien thought. He stared back with equal vigour. At last the rakh nodded, somewhat stiffly. 'All three together,' he pronounced. The myriad impalements of his face made his expression particularly grotesque. 'You come, then, and the fringe-folk will bring food—'

'No food,' Damien said sharply. He said it again, when the pierced one hesitated. '*No food.*'

It seemed to him that several of the smaller rakh giggled – or some gurgly equivalent – and for a brief moment nausea washed over him, as he recognized the source of their mirth. But he kept his expression stern, puffing himself up in his best rakhene-male manner. And after a moment of silent confrontation, the pierced one nodded stiffly.

'There will be no food,' he agreed. 'Come,' He waved back the mildewed crowd, giving them room to move. Just in time, Damien reflected; the air had become nearly unbreathable. He kept a protective arm about Ciani as they fell in behind him, and a close eye on Hesseth.

'I gather you got the upper hand,' Ciani murmured to him, as they were led from the common chamber. 'I don't suppose you'd care to explain what that last little bit was about?'

He glanced back towards the vast cavern, towards its ornamented walls, and shivered. 'Don't ask,' he muttered. 'Not till we're out of here, at least.' *Don't ever ask*, he pleaded silently.

And he remembered the polished bones that he had seen on the cavern wall, remnants of the Lost Ones' meat-animals applied to decoration. Much as a man might make a rug from the hide of his kill, he thought, or hang its head on the wall. There had been hundreds of bones in that place, all of them smooth and gleaming, some of them carved in intricate patterns . . . and among them at least one hand, nearly human-sized, that was not from a beast. He remembered the fingers of that one – remembered them very clearly

– slender bones with rakhene claws at the tip. The retractable talons of the plains-rakh, without doubt. Glued to the wall like some grisly trophy, a momento of past feasts relished.

He hoped with all his heart that Hesseth hadn't seen it. He wished with all his heart that he hadn't, either.

'I didn't think their food would agree with us,' he muttered.

Darkness. Closeness. The chill of stone, close about them. Packed earth, at their backs. In a sleeping-crevice so narrow that the three of them were forced to huddle together, like a family of Lost Ones might have done. It was not uncomforting, under the circumstances. But it was a bad position to be in, should they be attacked.

Damien cradled the clear vial of Fire against his chest, and let its light drive back the dark fae that even now was trying to reach them. As soon as the cave-rakh had left them, that dark force had begun to manifest their fears, with the result that several amorphous shapes were now lying in sliced-up bits around the party. But that was before. The golden light of the Fire was enough to keep it at bay, and Damien meant to keep it out until the Lost Ones returned to them. After one-sleep, they had said. Whatever the hell that meant.

Beside him, cradled against his chest, Ciani moaned softly, trapped in the grip of some nightmare. He nudged her gently, hoping to urge her out of the dream state without quite awakening her. On his other side Hesseth slept fitfully, deep growls and animal hisses punctuating the soft, whistling snore that counterpointed her slumber. And he . . . he needed sleep desperately, but didn't dare succumb to it. There was too much here that was unknown – too much that was dangerous. If the Lost Ones considered their cousins to be food-animals, what would they make of the humans, who were even more unlike them? He was acutely aware of the stone shelf close overhead, of his inability to swing a sword without first climbing down from the sleeping-crevice. But to take up guard elsewhere meant that either he or his companions must be without the Firelight, and that was simply unacceptable; the dark fae was too responsive, their fearful imaginations too fertile. They would be overwhelmed in moments. So the best he could do for them was to remain where he was and doze as he had in the Dividers: mere moments of sleep, quickly claimed and quickly abandoned. Mere moments of darkness, punctuating long hours of alertness.

Too many hours. Too long a vigil. But who could say how long the night took to pass, in a place where the whole world was darkness?

'There it is.'

They stood upon a ridge of naked granite which the wind had scrubbed clean of snow, and tried to adjust to the harsh morning light. In the distance, barely visible to the naked eye, the House of Storms rose from the ground like some sharp, malignant growth. All about it the land had been flattened, a no-man's waste of barren ground that made their enemy's tower all the more visible by contrast. Whatever defences their enemy might value, invisibility was clearly not one of them.

'Don't Work,' Damien warned Ciani. 'Whatever you do, don't Work to see it. Or for any other reason.' Not knowing how much she remembered – or, more accurately, how little – he explained, 'Any channel we establish can be used against us, no matter what its purpose. We're too close now to chance that.'

'And it would let him know we've arrived?'

'If he doesn't already know,' he said grimly.

'What's the chance of that?' Hesseth asked.

'Hard to say. We've had nothing happen since Tarrant's death, to further thin the ranks of our party . . . but that could just mean that he considers us sufficiently weakened already.'

'Or that his attention's fixed on the simulacra instead.'

He hesitated. All his gut instinct warned him not to bank his hopes on that one deception – *never count on anything you can't See yourself*, his master had cautioned him – but to deny Ciani such a small hope now was little less than cruelty. 'Let's hope so,' he muttered. And he raised the small farseer to his eye.

The fortress seemed to leap towards him: slowly he coaxed it into focus. And drew in his breath sharply as its bizarre design gradually became clear.

'Damien?'

'No windows,' he muttered. 'No windows at all.' But even those words couldn't capture the oddity of it. The utterly alien quality of its design. 'He's a paranoid bastard, that's for sure.'

What rose up from the distant ground was a polished obelisk of native stone, whose slick surface betrayed no hint of doorway, viewport, or any structural joining. It was as if it had not been raised up from the earth, but rather carved from the mountainside itself. A massive sculpture of cold, unliving stone that required no petty adornments – such as entrances or windows – to proclaim its purpose. He studied its surface for many long minutes, and had to bite back on his urge to Work his sight further. That would be too dangerous. He sought mortar lines, the thin shadows of juncture, any hint that mere mortals might have erected that eerie sculpture, but there were none. Not a single crack in the polished surface, that might serve as handhold to an invader. Not even a tiny viewport, through which weapons or gas might enter. *Or an agile invader*, he thought. Fear of attack was written across every inch of the structure.

'Utterly defensive,' he muttered. 'To say the least.' He handed the farseer to Ciani, heard her gasp as she brought the strange edifice into focus. For a moment he looked at her, concerned; was it possible that old memories were surfacing, this close to her tormentor's fortress? Her hands shook slightly as she held the farseer, and she drew in a long, ragged breath as she stared through it. But no, that was impossible. Her memories weren't buried, but wholly absent. Taken from her. And if he made the same mistake Senzei had – of confusing *absence* with *suppression* – he might well be courting a similar fate.

'Cee?'

'I'm all right. It's just that it's so . . .' She fumbled for an adjective, shivering. 'That's it, isn't it? Where we're going.'

'That, or somewhere beneath it.' He took the farseer back from her and handed it to Hesseth. Who looked it over with catlike curiosity before finally raising it to her eye to look through it.

Naked stone, polished to an ice-slick surface. A six-sided tower that rose up from the earth like a basalt column, as though Erna herself had vomited it up from the volcanic depths of her core. A structure that widened as it rose so that the walls were forced outward, doubly discouraging anyone who might try to scale it.

It was structurally impossible, plain and simple. Earthquakes might not strike here, but the sun still shone and the seasons still progressed, as in any normal place. And any mass that huge, that solid, was bound to develop flaws as Nature went through her paces. Uneven expansion and contractions, the erosion of wind and ice, the deforming pressure of its own top-heavy mass ... such a monument could not exist and therefore it did not, simple as that. Not even a Warding would hold it together, against such complex forces. Which meant that something else was involved.

'Illusion?' he mused aloud.

The women looked at him. 'You think?' Ciani asked.

'"When one is in the presence of the seemingly impossible, that which is merely unlikely becomes more plausible by contrast." That's a quote, you know, from—' He stopped suddenly, even as the words came to his lips. And forced himself to voice them. 'The Prophet,' he told them. 'His writings.'

'Gerald,' Ciani whispered.

He said nothing.

'He's in there, isn't he?' Her voice was low and even, but in it was such yearning, such hurting, that it made his soul ache to hear it. 'Trapped in there.'

'That's likely,' he agreed. Knowing, even as he spoke, that it was more than likely. It was certain. He could feel that in his bones, as if his link to the Hunter had allowed knowledge to take root there, without his even knowing it. 'Whatever's left of him,' he said quietly. 'Remember the dreams of fire.'

She nodded, remembering. More than mere dreams, but less than true Knowings. How much could they trust such visions?

She stared at the distant citadel, and whispered, 'He's in pain.'

'Yeah.' He forced himself to look away, towards the citadel in the distance. 'So are a lot of other people, whose lives he destroyed. Not to mention the hundreds he's killed.'

'Damien—'

'Ciani. Please.' He knew what was coming, and dreaded it. 'He took his chances. If he's—'

'We have to help him,' she whispered.

He could feel his chest tighten – in anguish, in fury. But before he could speak she added quickly, 'It's not just because he needs help. That wouldn't be enough for you, I understand that. It's because we *need* him.' With slender hands she turned him to face her, so that his eyes were forced to meet hers. 'In that citadel – or beneath it – are three things. A human sorceror, who's already proven himself capable of killing our best. A high-order demon who may be defended by dozens – if not hundreds – of his kind. And a single man who can wield more power than you and I could ever dream of – and *will* wield it, in our defence, if he's free to do so. Don't you see?' She shook her head tensely, her bright eyes fixed on him. There was wetness gathering in the outer corner of one of them. 'It's not a matter of sentiment, Damien, or even ethical judgement. It's the odds against us, plain and simple. Gods, I want to come out of this alive. I want to come out of this *whole*. And now, with your Fire gone, Senzei murdered . . . don't we stand a better chance of success, with Tarrant's power on our side?'

'I would sooner walk through the gates of hell,' he told her, 'than loose that man on the world again. Do you realize what he is? Do you realize what he *does*? The hundreds of people who will suffer because of him – the thousands! – because we set him free?'

'You had an agreement with him. You said that for as long as we were traveling together—'

'And I damned well stood by that agreement, though every minute I encouraged him rather than cutting him down will count against me at my day of judgement. No, I wouldn't have made a move against him while we were traveling together – but God in heaven, Cee, am I supposed to go in after him now that someone else has? Risk my life to save him?'

'He's trapped in there because of *me*—'

'He's in there because he values his own vulking life more than fifty of yours – and mine – combined! Because some little footnote in his survival contract dictated that he come here in order to safeguard his own existence. Nothing more than that – nothing, Cee!

The man's a monster – even worse than that, a monster who once was human. That's far more dangerous than your average demonkind. Do you think he really cares for you? Do you think he cares for anything, other than his own continued existence? He'd sacrifice you in a minute if you stood in his way.' The words were pouring from him like a flood tide, and with it poured all his anger. All his hatred for the man and what he represented. Everything he had been suppressing for weeks. 'Do you know what he did to his wife, his family? Do you imagine you'd rate any better, if he thought that it would profit him to kill you? Do you think he values you more than he valued those of his own blood? He would kill you without a second thought – and worse, if he stood to gain from it.'

'Don't get me wrong,' she said quietly. 'I have no illusions about his nature. I think maybe I even understand him a little better than you can' – and her eyes narrowed – 'seeing as I'm not half-blinded by theological prejudice. Let me tell *you* what he is. Strip away the sword and the collar, and all the accoutrements of his evil . . . and what you come up with is an adept, plain and simple. *What I was.*' She just stared at him for a moment, giving the words time to sink in. 'We're the same,' she whispered, 'he and I.'

'Cee, you're not—'

'*Listen to me.* Try to understand. It's not what you want to hear, I know that. Why do you think I never said it before? For all our closeness, there's a part of me you never really knew. A part you didn't *want* to know. A part no nonadept could ever understand . . . except maybe Zen. I think, sometimes, that he did.'

She put a hand on his arm – but the contact felt cold, and strangely distant. Uncomforting. 'We were born the same way, Gerald Tarrant and I. Not like your kind, in the midst of a comprehensible world, born to parents who could foresee your troubles and prepare for them. Most born adepts don't make it past infancy. Or if they grow up, they grow up insane. The infant brain just can't handle that kind of input – it's too much, too chaotic, they can't sort it out. We spend our lives trying to adapt, fighting to impose some kind of order on the universe. He did it. So did I. Different paths, but the end goal was the same: stability. Of ourselves, and of our world.'

'And now, suddenly, you remember all this?' he asked sharply. He hated himself the minute the words left his mouth, for how they might hurt her. But it was as if the hatred had opened a floodgate; he could do nothing to stop the words from coming.

'I Shared his memories. He offered,' she said quickly. 'And why not? It's a means of learning, isn't it? They weren't memories from the . . . not from the time after he changed. Not that, oh no. But from his human years. And gods, the richness of them, the depth . . .'

He closed his eyes, understanding at last. The darkness within her. The taint he had sensed, without knowing how to define it. Tarrant had poured his soul into her, to fill the empty places in hers. And in the short term it had probably assuaged her pain, somewhat. It had certainly given her a knowledge base to replace what she had lost, something to draw on. But in the long run . . . he had to turn away from her, lest she see the rage in his eyes. The hate. And the mourning . . .

She would be unable to leave him behind. Physically unable, due to his influence. Period. No matter what he said or did, it could be no other way.

'As for what he is, that's just his adaptation,' she said. 'Don't you see? To you it means something else, it's all tied up with questions of faith and honour – but to me it's just that. A terrible adaptation, it's true – I don't deny that – but does that make it any less of an accomplishment? He's *alive*. He's *sane*. Not many of our kind can lay claim to that much.'

'I wonder about the sanity,' he muttered, bitterly.

'Damien.' She said it softly, her tone so gentle that it awakened memories of other places, better times. She touched the side of his face with a soft hand, chilled by the morning breezes. 'Don't you want him on our side? Don't you want that kind of *power* on our side?'

And live with that, all the rest of my life? He shuddered at the thought. *The knowledge that I was the one who made it possible for the Hunter to feed again. All the hundreds he would torment, feast upon, kill . . . their deaths would be on my head, all of them. A multitude of innocents who would have been alive, but for me.*

'I can't,' he whispered. 'I can't do it.'

For a moment there was silence. Then a hand touched his arm. Strong, and with sharp nails that pierced through his sleeve. Not Ciani.

He opened his eyes, and saw Hesseth standing before him.

'Listen to me,' she said softly. Her voice a half-whisper, half-hissing. 'It's not just your species at risk here, remember? I was sent with you because rakh are dying, in every part of this region. People every bit as real and as "innocent" as the humans you ache so to protect. Suffering, no less than the victims of your Hunter. Are all those lives worth nothing to you?' She glanced back at Ciani. 'I despise your killer companion. I sympathize with your hatred of him. But I also tell you this: Our chances of success in this are next to nothing without him.' She bared her teeth, an expression of warning. 'You tell me to bury my primitive instincts, act with my head. Now it's time for you to do that. Because if we fail here, we doom my people to more and more attacks like the ones that take place in Lema now. Maybe even outside the Canopy, later, among your own people. Is that what you want? To waste all our effort?' She growled softly. 'I say we go to this place and see what our options are. If we have a clear shot at our enemy, we use it. But if not, and we think we can liberate this Hunter of yours . . . then we'd be fools not to, priest, and that's the simple truth. And I have no tolerance for foolishness when it threatens my life.'

For a moment he couldn't answer. For a moment the words were all bottled up inside him, like a wine under pressure. Waiting to explode. And then he exhaled slowly, slowly; an exercise in self-control. Two breaths. Another. At last he spoke, in the low monotone of one who has choked back so hard on his feelings that nothing, not even normal emotions, can surface in his speech.

'All right,' he said. 'As you say. We'll see what the situation is, first, and then decide. The three of us.' He felt somehow polluted, shamed by his betrayal of . . . what? His people? The rakh? The matter was too complex for simple answers, and he knew it. But he felt as though he had betrayed his faith – himself – and the shame of that burned like fire. He turned away from them both, lest they see the hot reddening of his cheeks. Lest they guess at his shame. Lest they realize that beneath his bitter hatred of Tarrant there ran an undercurrent of something else. A sharp sense of relief, that when they finally went into battle they might have Tarrant's power backing them. And that shamed him more than anything.

Damn you, Tarrant. Damn you to hell.

'All right,' he whispered. Hoarsely, as though the words hurt his throat. 'Let's do it.'

You'd better be worth it, you bastard.

41

Caverns. Not like the tunnels of the Lost Ones, which had been carved and plastered and buttressed and adorned for rakhene convenience; these were empty spaces, utterly lifeless, whose silence was broken only by the slow drip of water as it wended its way down from the surface, chamber by chamber. Tunnels that were comfortably six feet in height would shrink to a mere crawlspace yards later. Room-sized chambers that accommodated four people would be reduced to mere crevices at their further end, requiring a painstaking divestment of all supply packs before the party could pass through. Steep inclines dead-ended against blank walls and pits dropped down into seeming nothingness, while shallow lakes, mirror-surfaced, made it all but impossible to guess at the hazards that lay underneath.

Under the best of circumstances, progress would have been slow. With what they had to deal with – inadequate lighting, lack of proper tools, and an enemy who might turn their own Workings against them – it was maddeningly frustrating. Though they knew that they were only a short distance from their objective, it was impossible to travel a straight line in the torturous underground system. Sometimes the most promising route would double back on itself, returning them to a point they had passed by hours ago. The pierced one was doing what he could to guide them, but even his rakhene sense of direction could do them little good in such a place. They could only fight their way forwards step by step, chamber by chamber, and hope that *ground gained* exceeded *ground lost in the long run.*

What kept them going was the knowledge that there was, for them, no other way. Unless they were ready to break into the citadel itself, this was the only known entrance to the labyrinth beneath it. And so they fought on, and kept their weapons tightly in hand as they wended their way through the underearth – ever aware that if the demons attacked them, it would be without light, without warning, and without mercy.

At last, wary of the weakness that exhaustion would conjure, they found themselves a chamber more defensible than most and slept. Briefly. Having no knowledge of how many hours had passed since they had first entered the random tunnels, or whether sunlight or darkness reigned in the world above. They stood guard in teams, as they had above ground, but silently Damien questioned the efficacy of such an arrangement. If the demons they sought could shed their human form, then there was no truly defensible place; the earth was too full of mysterious cracks and crevices, and dark pits that extended to other levels of the labyrinth. So he made sure that his sword was close at hand and napped in a sitting position, spring-bolt braced against his knees.

How much time did they have to search? He wished he knew. Even if Tarrant's Working had succeeded in buying them cover it would only work for as long as the party's doppelgangers were alive. The minute those poor doomed souls reached Sansha Crater and the ambush took them, the deception was ended forever. And in that moment their enemy, who very likely knew the party's purpose – or at least guessed at it – would begin to search his domain with a fine-toothed comb, searching for them.

He hoped that the simulacra would take longer than expected to reach their goal. And hated himself for doing so. He hated himself for wanting the deception to work at all; for being grateful that five innocents had been doomed to a grisly death, instead of his own party. But worst of all were those rare instants when he was honest enough to admit that he was grateful to Tarrant for making that move without asking him. Without giving him the chance to stop it. That gratitude was like a cancer on his soul, a growing uncleanliness which he lacked the knowledge – or perhaps the will – to eradicate.

It's what he said he would do to me, he thought darkly. *Exactly what he described.* The thought of going in to rescue the man was doubly abhorrent because of it. But the longer they travelled, the closer their destination loomed in his mind, the more Damien was forced to admit that they needed him. Plain and simple. As for the ramifications of that . . . he would deal with them later.

When he slept he dreamed of fire, and it burned in his brain with such an intensity that his skin was actually flushed with fever when he awakened, as though the fire burned within him. From the place where Ciani lay curled up, asleep, he heard soft moans of anguish, and he knew without needing to ask that the same dream had her in thrall. Neither Hesseth nor the pierced one seemed troubled by such visions, but who could say whether the mechanism of their sleep bore any similarity to a human standard? There was no way to judge whether something was in the currents that only humans might respond to, or – a far more alarming possibility – whether Tarrant himself was the source of those visions, using his links with Damien and Ciani to communicate in symbols what he lacked the ability to send in words. But fire? From the Hunter? He considered many possible causes for that, in the hours they travelled, and all of them were chilling.

It wasn't until long after their sleep break – when they were taking a brief rest in a large, dry chamber – that he thought to mention it to his rakhene companions. To his surprise the pierced one responded immediately.

'It is the *fire of the earth*,' Hesseth translated. Suggesting by her hesitation a far more complex phrase, with connotations that had no parallel in her own dialect. 'It lives in this place.'

Damien heard Ciani's sudden indrawn breath, felt excitement stir within him. 'Fire of the earth? What is that? Ask him?'

She did so. And listened to the answer at length, and questioned him about it, before turning again to her human listeners. 'I'm not sure of this,' she warned them. 'His language is very unclear. Highly symbolic. But what I make of it is that here, somewhere in these caverns, is a fire which the earth itself supplies with fuel. He says it burned when his people first came here, and kept burning in all the time they occupied this region. Before the falling-threat finally drove them away. It has some kind of . . . spiritual significance, I think.'

'The word is *religious*,' Damien said quietly. 'Go on.'

'That's all he knows. They don't have the kind of oral tradition we do; all he remembers are snatches of stories, that were retold because of their dramatic value.' She smiled slightly. 'I gather the young of his kind are threatened with being thrown into this fire if they misbehave too often.'

'A fire of the earth,' Ciani whispered.

And he nodded. Not in response to what she said, but to what she was thinking. Because there was no question about it: the fire of the earth was Tarrant's fire, the same yellow flame that haunted their dreams and their thoughts, which seemed to guard the secret of their dark companion's disappearance. As soon as he even considered that connection he knew it for the truth. It was as though some some vital circuit in his brain had finally closed – or as though the channel between Tarrant and himself allowed that much knowledge to flow, before distance and distaste could occlude it. And he knew, without asking Ciani, that her experience was the same.

'Tarrant's fire,' he muttered. 'Fed by the earth? I'd guess fossil fuel, in some form. Probably solid, or a shifting of the earth would have cut the supply channel at some point.'

'Except that the earth hasn't moved here,' Ciani reminded him.

'It's moved some. Maybe not enough to shake the ground hard – maybe so little that no one's ever aware of it – but it moves. It *has* to.' He turned to Hesseth. 'Ask him if he knows where it is. Ask him if he can tell us anything of how to find it.'

She talked to the pierced one again, and this time it was clear he was the one having difficulty. After a time he answered her, haltingly, and she told the humans, 'Deep down. Very deep down. I'm not sure whether he means the lowest caverns in this system, or the lowest caverns not underwater. Or even the lowest caverns not rakh-made; there might be tunnels that were dug below that level, later.'

'Good enough,' Damien muttered.

'Damien?' Ciani put a hand on his arm; he noted that she was trembling slightly. 'What are you thinking?'

'That it may be a safe way in,' he told her. He put his own hand over hers, and squeezed it tightly in reassurance. 'We can't Know the caverns, because then our enemy would See exactly where we are. We can't Locate Tarrant, because the minute we tried we'd be opening up a channel that our enemy could use to strike at us. But a fire? A simple fire? A straightforwards Working, fixed on that . . . it would be doubly safe, because he'd never anticipate it. How could he know that we'd even heard of the *fire of the earth*? How could he anticipate that we would understand its significance? It just might work, Cee. *Safely*. We just might get away with it.'

In a voice very still, very fragile, she asked, 'You'll go after him?'

For a moment there was only the darkness around them, and the chill silence of the underworld. Then, choosing his words very carefully, he told her, 'I said I'd take the best way in, didn't I? I said if it turned out the best thing to do, I'd go with it.' *You have no idea what it's going to cost me to save that man*, he thought grimly. *Or of what it will cost our world, to have him free in it. But Hesseth was right. If his strength and his knowledge can help end this plague, then I have no real choice, do I? We use the tools we must.* 'If nothing else, it gives us a clear road in. And God knows, we need that.'

Then he took her hand in both of his, warmed it between his palm. 'The relationship you had with him means that you know him better than I can,' he said softly. Trying to keep his voice utterly neutral, trying not to let his tone and manner betray how appalling he found that fact. 'He knows how abhorrent I found him. He knows how much I despised him, for everything he represented. Tell me this, if you can . . . if he were in trouble – captured, let's say, and in pain, incapable of helping himself – does he think that I would come after him?' When she hesitated, he added, 'Or that I would let our party come to help him? Or does he think I would leave him to die — perhaps even be grateful to our enemy for arranging it?'

For a long time she stared at him, as if by doing so she could read what was in his mind. But he was careful to keep his expression neutral, and at last she answered, 'There's not any real question about that, is there?'

'*He* believes it.'

She hesitated, then nodded.

'He believes it *utterly*.'

This time the nod came faster.

'What is it?' Hesseth asked. 'What does that mean?'

'If our enemy were rakhene, nothing. But it has to do with the way human sorcery works — with the way that our enemy would naturally use Gerald Tarrant as a focus for any Working that concerned us.'

'He would take the knowledge of our plans from his mind?'

'Either that, or use it as a . . . say, a filter of sorts, for a more general Knowing. But either way . . .' His hands tightened about Ciani's. A familiar excitement was beginning to course through his veins, driving out all memory of fatigue and frustration. This was the approach they needed, at last; it felt *right*, in a way that years of experience had taught him to trust. 'He wouldn't see us coming,' he whispered fiercely. 'If Tarrant thinks what you say he does, if he's that certain of it . . . why would the enemy assume him wrong? It means that way would would be only lightly guarded, if at all. And probably not Worked against us. But most important . . . it means we have a way to find our way through this damned labyrinth without being caught at it. Praise God,' he breathed. 'Now, let's just hope that when we get that bastard back . . .'

He released Ciani and lifted his springbolt. And tested the draw, to make sure it was tightly cocked.

'Let's just say he'd better earn his keep,' he warned her.

Caverns. So deep within the earth that the earth-fae itself faded to a whisper: a mere hint of power with no sense of motion about it. A shallow pool of unWorked potential, utterly unlike the swift-

flowing currents that coursed on the planet's surface. But for what
Damien intended, it was enough. He cast his will out upon the
mirror stillness of its surface and shaped it slowly, carefully, to serve
his intentions. After a moment, there was a ripple – more felt than
seen, like a shadow of thought that flitted through the mind without
taking form – and then the fae began to flow. Slowly. Not as it
would have done on the surface of the planet, where the power
born of seismic disruption was constantly pouring into it, stirring
it to life. But moving nonetheless, with clear direction. It was
enough.

'Towards the fire,' Damien whispered. And they Worked their
sight – with effort – and followed it. Wading downcurrent,
following the whispery power as it clung to the edges of water-
carved stone, marking a path that they might tread. The pierced
one was silent now, his jangling ornaments bound up with bits of
cloth so that they might not betray the party. Nor did he speak, but
climbed through the caverns lost in the web of his own thoughts.
Communing with his gods, perhaps, or contemplating his masculine bravado. Whatever it was, it served their purpose well enough;
Damien encouraged it.

And then they came to a place where the last chamber narrowed,
until all that led from it was a low-ceilinged crawlspace, barely wide
enough to accommodate a man. Small formations edged its upper
surface like teeth, and two stalagmites the thickness of a man's wrist
rose from its mud-covered floor. Damien looked at it dubiously,
was about to speak – and then heard a gasp behind him that caused
him to whip about with his weapon at the ready.

It was Ciani. Pale as a ghost, shivering as though she had just
seen – or heard – something utterly terrifying. She had her hands
up before her face as if trying to ward off some terrible danger –
but when Damien turned back in response to that gesture, to seek
out the cause of her terror, he saw nothing more than he had previously. Only empty stone corridors, weakly coursing fae, and glistening of moisture on slender calcite branches.

'The smell,' she whispered. 'Gods, I remember . . .'

He came to her then, handed his weapon to Hesseth – who
understood, and was ready to take it – and took the ex-adept into

his arms. And held her tightly, making his body into a shield that might protect her from all dangers.

'I smell it,' she whispered. 'Can't you? I remember running . . . Gods, I must have come this way. There were places . . . I thought . . . but I had so little light, then, and so little strength . . . and these caves all look the same, don't they? But I thought . . . oh gods, don't you see, I've *been* here . . .'

Then she lowered her head to his chest and sobbed softly there; he stroked her hair gently and wished he could will some of his own strength into her. It had been bound to happen, this outburst, and he'd been expecting it . . . but he knew that there was even worse to come, and so he just held her, gently, and let her have her tears. God knows, she'd been holding them in long enough.

Soon she'll remember all of it. All of it! Her capture, her captivity, whatever torture she endured at the hands of these creatures . . . it'll all return to her in an instant. A single blow. What will that be like? So much terror pouring back into her, all those years of suffering relived in an instant . . . this is nothing, compared to it. Her hardest moment will be the one in which we restore her to what she was.

When he thought she was capable of listening to him, he said to her gently, 'You couldn't have come this way, Cee. Think about it. You'd have had to come through that tunnel, and you'd have had to break the formations to do it. Right? They're still there.'

'It's the smell,' she whispered. Her whole body was shaking. She clung to him desperately. 'It's like that all through their tunnels. Can't you smell it? I couldn't escape it. I ran and ran, and I couldn't get away from it . . .'

He tested the air, caught a faint whiff of sourness coming from the tunnel. Too faint, or else too unfamiliar, for him to identify; he looked to Hesseth and saw her nod grimly.

'Carrion,' she hissed softly. And the pierced one concurred. 'Rotting carrion,' she translated for him.

The region of no, he thought. *The place of dying.*

'All right,' he muttered. 'We're going through. The fae'll guide us to the fire all right, so if we see anything move we shoot – or swing, or whatever – and worry about what it was later. Agreed?'

Ciani nodded, as did Hesseth. When the *khrast* woman translated for their pierced companion, he bared his teeth and hissed aggressively, his naked tail curling at the tip. *I'll take that for a yes*, Damien thought.

He approached the narrow passageway and studied it. Had it been clear of mud and monuments it might have been wide enough for him – barely – but as it was, there was no clear way through.

'How strong are those things?' he asked the pierced one, pointing to one of the slender stalagmites.

It took the Lost One a moment to realize what he was driving at. Then he answered, 'When small, very brittle. When that large,' – and he pointed to the two stalagmites rising from the mud-covered floor – 'they will still crack, if much force is applied.'

'Good enough,' he muttered. He opened the buckles on his sword's harness and lowered the sheathed weapon from his back. 'Hand this through as soon as I'm out,' he said, giving it to Ciani. Tarrant's sword had been affixed to the same harness, but he unfastened it so that it would come through separately. All he needed in a moment of trouble was to grab the wrong one. Even through its multiple layers of wrapping the cold sword throbbed with malevolence, and Damien thought he perceived a certain . . . call it *hunger*. Was that because it sensed it was close to its master/creator? Or because it knew that soon it might be going into battle, with all the mayhem that implied?

He divested himself of all the layers he could: outer jacket, fleece vest, thick overshirt. He left on the thick leather undervest which had saved his life on so many occasions, and hoped that its bulk wasn't too excessive. 'Leave the general supplies here,' he ordered. 'Take weapons, tools, some food and water. We'll come back here when we're done.' *If we can*. 'Take light,' he added. And he removed the precious pouch of Fire from his belt and hung it about his neck instead, so that it might not impede him in the narrow passageway.

Then: head first, shoulders brushing the uneven walls as he crawled slowly through. He had a long knife clasped in his teeth so that whatever danger might lurk on the other side would not find him unarmed, or unready. Thin calcite spines caught on his shirt as he passed, snapped off like burrs as he pressed onward.

Good enough. He elbowed his way forwards, through a tunnel that grew narrower and narrower, until he could feel the stone walls pressing close on both sides of him. Then he came to the first of the slender formations, and he leaned all his weight against it; it snapped off cleanly near the base, and he set it to one side. The same with the second. The tunnel widened somewhat, enough that he could crawl through. And then opened suddenly, without warning, into a much larger chamber.

He thrust himself into it and rolled to his feet, and then reached back the way he had come. Ciani had followed after him, close enough that when she extended his long sword towards him he was able to grasp its hilt and draw it. Thus armed, he surveyed his surroundings. A large room, empty of adversaries but filled with the reek of their presence. He saw where a tunnel opposite had been widened to allow for more comfortable passage, and he thought with grim satisfaction, *This is it. This is where they'll be.*

'Come through,' he whispered. 'Carefully.'

They did, with considerably less difficulty than he'd had. He noted that if they fled this way he would need to make sure he went through last, in order that they might not be delayed while he squeezed his bulk through the passage. Not a cheery thought.

'Can you See?' he asked Ciani. And even more than listening for her answer, he watched for her response. But she seemed to be somewhat under control, and she nodded as she gazed down at the fae. 'Barely,' she whispered. 'It's very weak.'

'But it'll have to do. We can't use real light in here; they'd see it coming miles away.' Again she nodded, and he extinguished their illumination. It had only been minimal to start with, a bare spark of fire in a mostly hooded lantern, but now it was gone. He handed the lantern to Ciani, who hooked it to her belt. And looked down at the earth-fae, to see which way his guiding current was flowing.

'This way,' he whispered, and he led them into the heart of the demons' lair.

It was dark, and cold, and rank with the smell of death. The chill of it seemed to exceed the natural cold of the underneath, as though some force had leached the heat from the very stone about them; Damien thought of the Hunter's sword — now strapped again to his harness – and wondered at the similarity. *An eater of souls*, the pierced rakh had called it. Like the ones they were hunting. How similar were they, really?

And then Hesseth whispered *Hsssst!* in warning, and Damien fell back. The cold stone behind him pressed Tarrant's sword even closer, so that its unnatural chill lanced into his back muscles; he had to fight not to alter his position, to remain utterly still and utterly silent while his companions also hid, waiting for any sight or sound that might tell him what the danger was. And after a moment, it came. The padding of flesh on stone, the whisper of clothing. The hoarse breathing of one who has no need to be silent, the muttered conversation of one who knows no reason to fear.

Then they came around the corner, and Damien paused just long enough to acertain that there were only two of them before he swung. He put all his strength into it, knowing that the unWorked steel was all but invisible to their fae-sight. And the full force of it hit the first creature at neck level and sliced through muscle and bone with a crack, coming out the other side with some speed still left in it. The creature's head struck the wall, bloodily, and caromed off it to the floor; its body sank slowly, as if not yet fully cognizant of the fact of its death. Damien turned to the other one, quickly, ready to face whatever manner of defence the surprised creature could muster – but the face that stared at him had a black hole in the place of one eye, from which acrid smoke and golden sparks issued as he watched. He caught sight of the rear metal band of a bolt as the creature twitched, the Fire spreading in its veins like poison. And he turned back to see Ciani standing with springbolt in hand, an expression that was half fear and half pride suffusing her countenance.

'It seemed like the thing to do,' she whispered.

Damien leaned down to inspect the headless body. Vaguely human in shape, it was dressed in an assortment of mismatched garments, haphazardly arranged. Bare-foot. After a moment he placed his hand on its flesh and muttered 'Warm. The body's alive. Not just a demon, then. Truly embodied.'

'What does that mean?' Hesseth asked.

'It means they bleed. It means they die.' He looked up at her; he could feel the fierceness in his own expression. 'It means that whatever these things are, the odds in our favour just got a little better.'

They hid the bodies as well as they could. They couldn't wash the blood from the ground or drive the reek of burning flesh from the area, but at least if someone passed through quickly they wouldn't see what had happened. The earth-fae was faint enough here that whoever relied upon it for sight might miss seeing details. The dark fae, though far more intense, clearly had no love of carrion; it withdrew from the corpses as it would withdraw from cold, unliving stone, and therefore offered no illumination.

'Good enough,' Damien muttered at last.

They went on. Damien in the lead, with Hesseth right beside him. Her senses of hearing and smell were clearly more accurate than his, so he trusted her to be on guard for approaching danger. He studied the current, and the walls, and tried to get some feel for the lay of the land. At least this cavern system had been modified so that a man might walk through it upright. He had given one springbolt to the rakh-woman, and Ciani carried the other. Damien preferred his sword, not because it was more efficient – it wasn't – or even because it was marginally quieter – it was – but because it was . . . well, *familiar*. A weapon he had wielded through so many battles, relied upon in so many tight situations, that using it was like using part of his body. Second nature. *And besides*, he told himself, *it doesn't need reloading*. The pierced one carried a slender wooden spear, brought with him from his home caverns. If the look on his face was any guide, he knew how to use it.

Well armed and more than ready, he thought grimly.

They passed through a number of chambers and passageways, including some where several routes intersected. At each of these he paused, and worked to commit the place to memory. He didn't dare mark the walls here as he had during their descent; the marks he made would be as likely to lead their enemies to them as serve any purpose of theirs.

And then they came to it. It was the pierced one who felt it first, and hissed sharp sounds to Hesseth in warning. 'Heat,' she translated. 'From up ahead.' They looked at each other. 'I don't feel it,' the rakh-woman whispered.

'You wouldn't, necessarily,' Damien whispered back. 'Specialized senses. The temperature belowground is so constant, any change would have significance.' He nodded his approval – and his admiration – to the pierced one. And checked the current carefully before he moved again.

Now, if possible, they were doubly alert. If there were guards at all, they would be here. Damien felt a breeze brush by his face, something far more suited to open spaces than this underground warren. And then he understood: the fire. Drawing oxygen, and with it air. Creating suction as it burned, so that fresh air would be drawn to it. How else could it keep burning so long, regardless of its fuel?

'Very close,' he whispered. He signaled for them to stop, and strained his senses to the utmost. The fetid stink of the demons' lair was stronger here, perhaps concentrated by the fire's pull. Not certain that Hesseth would pick up any smell besides that foul odour, he listened for a hint of movement. None. Not a sound or a smell to hint at the presence of any other being in this chamber, or in any adjoining passage. It was almost too good to be true.

He doesn't expect us here, he reminded himself. There was a chance – just a chance – that the fire wasn't guarded. At all. If so, they might even make contact with Tarrant before anyone realized they were there . . .

And then all hell breaks loose. Because no matter what their enemy was doing with Tarrant, he'd damn well be monitering the results. Which meant that the moment they interfered with his plans, he'd be aware of both their presence and their purpose. They'd be lucky if he didn't blast them right on the spot; if he lacked that kind of power he'd certainly send his people after them, and it was a good bet the resident soul-eaters knew this labyrinth better than Damien and his company.

We'll deal with that when we get to it.

There was light, now, flickering and faint – but real light, golden light, like the kind that came from a natural fire. It seemed to Damien that now he, too, could feel heat on his face, as if each few steps brought him into a place where the air was noticeably warmer. He felt a cold buzz course up his back, as though Tarrant's sword was somehow upset by the concept of warmth. *Tough shit*, he thought to it. He turned a sharp corner and squeezed around an obstruction – the light was much brighter now, and it seemed that in the distance he could hear the roar of flames – and then

Fire. Burning so brightly that he had to turn away from it. Burning so hot that the skin of his face reddened, just from standing before it. For a moment he saw nothing but the fire itself, a narrow-based bonfire that blazed upward a good fifty feet before licking even further into a wide crack in the cavern's upper surface. The chamber it was in was a good forty feet wide, if not more, and a jagged crack ran down the centre of the floor; it was the middle of that which had broken open, giving access to the limitless fuel beneath. Sometime in the distant past someone or something must have ignited it – but that moment was little more than legend now, if that. As far as the Lost Ones were concerned, the fire had burned forever.

He forced himself away from the entrance so that the others might follow. And scanned the chamber as well as he could, for any sign of enemy activity. But for as much as his darkness-adapted eyes could see past the blazing fire, it seemed they were alone. Except for a pile of fabric against the far wall, and a long, slender object that lay atop it . . .

He walked towards it, half-aware that the others were following. He had a terrible feeling about what it was and fervently hoped he was wrong. But when he got to the pile at last, he saw that it was indeed what he had feared. Midnight blue silk and fine grey worsted, in layers that were all too familiar. And atop it all an empty sheath, its surface inscribed with at least a dozen ancient symbols . . . Tarrant's sheath. Tarrant's clothing. He felt sick, realizing why they were here.

He looked at the bonfire – squinted against its glare, and tried to make out details – and at last muttered, 'He's there. In that.'

Ciani shivered, and looked at the fire. And then said, 'But it isn't Worked. How could it hold him—'

'He can't Work fire,' Damien said tightly. 'Or anything connected to it.' It seemed to him that for a moment he understood what that meant, what it felt like for a being that powerful to be rendered impotent – utterly neutralized – by so simple a means. And the pain of it, the utter *humiliation* of it, was so intense that he nearly staggered back, as though struck. For a man of the Hunter's arrogance to be trapped thus . . . he wondered if that fierce pride could survive such an experience. If the identity he knew as Gerald Tarrant could emerge from it unscathed – or even recognizable.

'I think,' he said slowly, 'if there's any one facet of our enemy that terrifies me . . . it's how well he knows us. How well he knows how to get to each of us.'

He walked towards the fire slowly, his eyes filling with tears as the heat of it seared his face. He came as close as he dared and then stopped and stared into it. Into the brutal heart of it, the blazing core of its heat.

And he could barely make out, amidst the dancing flames, the black figure of a man. Stretched out across the opening, arms spread out in a cruciform arrangement. The fingers – if there still were fingers – would be just inches short of the fire's edge. Damien looked for some kind of support, saw the blunt ends of coarse steel bars resting on both sides of the crevice. The metal glowed with heat where it lay against the stone floor. If he lay on that framework, perhaps bound to it . . . merciful God. No doubt it was the powerful air currents, fire-stirred, that kept the smell of roasting flesh from reaching them. Damien had no doubt that it was there, in quantity.

'We have to turn it off,' he muttered. His mind racing as it considered – and discarded – at least a dozen options. 'I can't get to him while it burns.'

'Smother it?' Ciani asked. She was by his side, a hand shielding her eyes as if from bright sunlight.

'Can't. There's air coming in, all along there.' He indicated the narrower portions of the crevice. 'If not from underneath, too.'

'Block it?' Hesseth asked.

He bit his lower lip as he considered that. 'Going to have to try,' he said at last. 'The earth-fae's weak, but I can't think of another good option.' He turned back towards the chamber's one entrance, saw that the pierced one had taken up guard there. 'They'll be on us the minute I Work. It may take them time to get down here, but they'll come. In force. As soon as I alter the fire.'

'Then we'll just have to be ready for them,' the rakh-woman said fiercely, and she braced the springbolt against her shoulder.

He went back where Tarrant's possessions lay, and considered them. Then he removed the coldfire blade and unwrapped it, carefully. The Worked steel blazed with a chill blue light, as blinding as snow – and then was extinguished, as he thrust it deep into its warded container. He tested the handle, and sensed no active malevolence. *Thank heaven for that, anyway.*

He positioned the other members of their small company as best he could, to prepare for the arrival of the enemy's servants. But: *Our best won't be good enough*, he thought darkly. Without Tarrant's power behind them they were no match for a horde of demons, flesh-dependent or no; they would have to work fast and get out quickly, and hope that Tarrant could be restored before battle commenced.

He looked at the body within the flames, and felt despair uncoiling within him. *If he can be restored*, he thought grimly. *What if we're doing all this for nothing?*

He gathered himself for Working, and stared into the fire. Stared beneath it, to where the sharp lips of rock gaped wide above the earth's store of fuel. He Worked his sight – no easy task, with the earth-fae so thin – and tried to look deep down into that opening, to assess its structure. But there was no place immediately below where the walls of the crevice drew any closer together. With a sigh he resigned himself to Working its upper edges, and braced himself for the effort.

And air roared past him, sucked up by the conflagration. Earth-fae swept past him, too thin to grasp. He tried to enclose it in his will, to force a form and purpose upon its tenuous substance – but it ran through his fingers like smoke and was sucked up into the inferno. *Not enough of it*, he despaired. *Not enough!* He was used to the currents of Erna's surface, so deep and rich that the simplest thought was enough to shape it, the simplest Working enough to master it . . . but here, Working the fae was like trying to breathe in a vacuum. There simply wasn't enough power for what he needed to do.

But there has to be, he thought darkly. *Because we have no other choice*. Already he could feel the malignant thoughts of their enemy closing in around him, like a fist being clenched. How long did they have before he struck? Mere minutes, he guessed. He poured everything he had into his Working: all the force of his hatred for Tarrant, his love for Ciani, his despair at losing her twice – first to the assault in Jaggonath, then to Tarrant's corruption. If raw emotion could master the earth-fae, then he would use that as his fuel. His will blazed forth in need, in pain, and he grasped at the elusive power. And fought to weave it into a barrier, that might bridge the mouth of the crevice. But there simply wasn't enough fae there to do what he needed. Again and again he tried, until his soul was scraped raw by remembered anguish, until his whole body shook from the force of his exertion. But his Bindings dissolved even as he made them, and the force of the fire broke through his every Working.

'I can't,' he gasped at last. 'Can't do it.' His brain was on fire, his whole body shaking, his plans in chaos. *What now?* he thought desperately. *What now?* Behind him he could sense Ciani's despair, and it cut into him like a knife. *I failed her. I failed them all.*

How much time had passed, while he wrestled with the earth-fae? He didn't dare ask. But every second they spent here increased their danger. Already their only escape route might be cut off—

Think, man. Think! The earth-fae isn't strong enough here. The dark fae can't be used to bind fire. There's nothing we can do by physical means alone. What else is there? What? Think!

He knew, suddenly. And turned to Hesseth.

'Tidal power,' he gasped. 'Can you—'

'Not stable,' she warned. 'Not for solid work. There would be danger—'

'To hell with the danger! It's that or nothing.' He was drenched with sweat but refused to move back from the fire. *'Can you do it?'*

For a moment her eyes unfocused, and she stared not at him, but past him. *Through* him. He remembered the tidal fae fluxing over Morgot, the brief rainbow power that had suddenly filled the sky with brilliance, then vanished with equal rapidity. It was a fickle power, utterly impermanent. Dangerously unstable. And right now, it was the only hope they had left.

'I can try,' she said at last. 'But you understand—'

'Just do it!' He was counting down the seconds in his mind, wondering how long it would take their enemy's soldiers to reach them. 'Do it fast,' he whispered. Was it possible that the enemy's attention had been elsewhere when they struck, delaying his response? He prayed that it was so. Every minute counted now.

Hesseth turned her attention to the fire, and he followed her gaze. He tried to See the forces she was summoning, but the delicate power eluded him. How much fae would be available to her, and how long would it last? The tidal patterns altered minute by minute, as time and tides progressed about the planet. Even if she could conjure a barrier for them, would it remain solid long enough for them to do what they had to?

'There it is,' Ciani whispered. Pointing to the crevice. It could be seen at one edge of the opening, now: a fog, a darkness, that grew solid even as they watched, and eclipsed the fire behind it. He felt his heart pounding as he watched it extend – several inches into the crevice, a foot, two feet, now halfway across it – and he wiped the sweat from his face with a salt-soaked sleeve. *Go for it, Hesseth. You can do it*. The remaining fire was ragged now, as if struggling against some unseen bond. Smoke was beginning to seep from other places along the crevice, desperately seeking egress from the pit of its birth. For a moment he feared that the fire would break out elsewhere, that Hesseth's Working might force it to break through the very rock beneath their feet. Then the last of the Fire spurted upward, licking the ceiling with its orange tongue – and was suddenly gone, vanished beneath the shadowy blockage.

It wasn't hard to see what the enemy had done to Gerald Tarrant; the grating that supported him still glowed red-hot, supplying them with more than enough light. Atop the thick steel bars lay a body that had been burned and healed and burned again, so many times that its surface was little more than a blackened mass of scar tissue. Where cracks appeared red blood oozed forth, and it sizzled as it made contact with the superheated skin. Damien didn't look at the face – or what was left of it – but he felt hot bile rise in his throat as he studied the man's bonds. Wide metal bands bound the Hunter to his rack at the wrist, upper arm, ankle and neck; they, too, glowed with heat, and had burned their way deep into his flesh until the edges of bones were visible.

'How long—' he began.

'Eight days,' Ciani whispered. 'If they brought him right here.' She looked up at him; her face was drenched with sweat, or tears. Or both. 'What do we do?' she begged him. 'How do we get him off it?'

He fought back his growing sickness and tried to Work. It wouldn't take much fae to break those bonds; that was a simple exercise, a straightforwards molecular repulsion. But either Hesseth's Working had affected the earth-fae or he was simply too exhausted to Work it. He fought with the fae until his vision began to darken about the edges, the whole of the room swimming about him. And then knew, at last, that he was defeated. The best of his efforts couldn't conjure more power than there was in this place, and there simply wasn't enough. Tarrant might have been able to do it. He couldn't.

He looked up, and saw Ciani's eyes fixed on him. Not despairing, now, but filled with a feverish excitement. And with a terrible fear. The combination was chilling.

'The coldfire,' she whispered. 'The sword.'

It took him a moment to realize what she meant. 'Too dangerous—'

'Not for me.'

He remembered the malevolence housed within that blade, and shuddered. 'Can you?' he whispered. 'Can you control it?'

She hesitated. '*He* controls it,' she said hoarsely. 'But I think I can use it. For him.'

She went to get the blade. He tried to fight back his growing sickness, his sense of horror at what she was attempting. If she tried to master that power and failed, what would the cost be? He remembered the hunger he had sensed while handling it, that had so horrified him. What had the Lost Ones called it – the Eater of Souls?

And then she was back, and the sword was in her hands. She hesitated just an instant – and he knew in that moment that she feared it every bit as much as he did – and then drew it from its sheath. The containment wards let loose their hold, and the chill power of Tarrant's coldfire blazed forth freely.

Hot versus cold. Expansion and contraction. If she could gain control of that frigid force, if she could focus it finely enough . . . it might be enough to break through those bonds and free the Hunter. But if not . . .

He saw the barrier flicker for an instant; a burst of flame shot through it, enveloping Tarrant's torso, and then was gone. He looked at Hesseth, saw her whole body tense with the effort of Working. *Hang in there*, he begged her. *Hold onto it . . .*

Ciani touched a hand to the blade – and cried out as the blue – white power shot up that extremity, up to her shoulder. Her skin took on the ghostly pallor of longdead flesh, and frost rimmed her fingernails. Then she grasped the haft of it with that hand, and it seemed that her fingers froze closed about the grip. Slowly she extended the Worked weapon towards the nearest of Tarrant's bonds; he could see her struggling to bind its power, fighting to impose her own focus on its chaotic essence. Then the tip of the sword touched the red-hot metal, and sparks flew. Coldfire arced upward with electrical brilliance, and snapped like lightning in the charged atmosphere. Then it was gone, and the sword was withdrawn . . . and the steel band that had bound his wrist was shattered, its frosted pieces falling like shrapnel to the fae-worked barrier beneath.

Smoke spurted and curled upward through Hesseth's Working as she struggled to move the sword again. *Hold onto it!* Ciani's face had taken on the same ghastly pallor as her hand, and he could almost hear her heart laboring to maintain its beat as the Hunter's killing cold invaded her flesh. Damn the man! Would they free him from death, only to lose her? He watched her face as a second metal strap shattered into frozen crystals, saw the pain – and the fear – that was etched across her brow. Still she continued. Tarrant's neck was freed now, and Damien's hand closed tightly about the grip of his own sword. They could cut through the man's other wrist if they had to, and even his ankles; let him regenerate the flesh at his leisure, once they were out of here. He thought he could hear footsteps now, a distant pounding as if from running feet. The fourth bond shattered. The sweat on Ciani's face had frozen, and ice crystals rimmed the bottoms of her eyes. Five. He started to move forwards, saw a wall of flame erupt before him. *Ciani!* But it was gone as quickly as it had appeared, and though her hair was singed and the skin of her face burned, Ciani seemed unharmed.

Hang in there, Hesseth. Just a few minutes longer!

He moved as the sixth bond shattered, so that by the time Ciani reached to free Tarrant's second ankle he had hold of the man's flesh, was grasping him tightly about the wrist. Hot blood scalded his hand, but he knew there was no time to experiment with less direct measures. As soon as Ciani had broken the last steel band, he pulled with all his strength. The body moved like a broken doll, burned flesh pulling loose from it as it was jerked from the red-hot framework, scar tissue sizzling as it was dragged across the grating – and then they were both out of the danger zone, and just in time. Thin flames licked upward through Hesseth's barrier and then suddenly, with a roar, shot upward towards the ceiling, burning with newfound energy. He felt his own hair curling from the force of the heat, could only pray that Ciani had made it back in time.

He dragged the body back from the flames, tried to wipe some of the sweat from his eyes so that he could see. There was blood on his sleeve; his, or Tarrant's? It no longer seemed to matter. He was dimly aware of blisters all along his palm, from where he had grasped the body. His sword-hand, too – damn, that was careless!

'They're coming!' Hesseth hissed.

He took up his sword in his right hand, wincing as his burned palm closed about the rough grip. And saw Ciani throw a length of cloth about the body – Tarrant's cloak? – so that when they wanted to move it they might do so safely.

And then they came. In numbers, as he had feared. Not a trained guard, but six of the soul-eating creatures who inhabited this underground lair. They were only the first wave, no doubt, the ones who had been closest to the fire when the enemy spotted their activity; there would be others to follow, dozens more, better armed and far more dangerous. But for now, these were enough.

The heat of the fire blazed across his back as he turned to face his attackers. A bolt shot past his head, from Ciani, but she had fired from too far back; it missed its intended target and struck the wall, wooden shaft splintering from the impact. Hesseth had picked up the other springbolt and she fired it point-blank into the gut of one of the creatures; even as it pierced his abdomen and came out through his back he grabbed at the weapon, long claws scoring her arm as he fought to claim it. A second bolt whistled past Damien's ear, and this one struck; a shot to the arm that began to smoulder in the pale flesh. Only two of the creatures were armed, but though they bore sizable swords they used them clumsily, like men unaccustomed to armed combat. As Damien engaged the first, trying to keep his back close enough to the fire that none would circle behind him, he wondered what manner of contact was required for their most deadly mode of attack. Mere touch? Bodily penetration? He parried his opponent's sword down to the stone floor and slammed his foot down on it, hard; the cheap steel snapped with a crack, and the momentum of it made the creature stagger off-balance, into his own waiting blade. He wrenched the steel from between the creature's ribs and swung about just in time to duck a blow that was coming at him from the side; it cut his arm, but not deeply, and he moved to take control of their interplay. Where the hell was the pierced one? He saw Hesseth struggling hand-to-hand with an attacker, was dimly aware that one was burning, one had gone off after Ciani, and he could account for two . . . that left a creature missing, as well as one of his own party. He prayed fervently that the pierced one knew how to take care of himself; the thought of trying to find a way out of these caverns without him was terrifying indeed.

He heard a sudden scream from somewhere behind him – it didn't sound like one of his companions – and the smashing of a heavy object into a metal grate. The screaming became a shrieking as flesh began to sizzle, as the creature Ciani had forced into the fire roasted in its core.

Good for her. He parried a cut that was meant to decapitate him and managed to get his back against a wall. One, two, three accounted for . . . there was still one missing, by his reckoning. Gone for help? That was bad. He saw Hesseth go down, her assailant on top of her, and knew with a sinking feeling in the pit of his stomach what manner of attack was taking place. But there was no way he could help her, not with sharp steel thrusting at his gut from one side and sharp claws threatening his face from the other. He brought his own blade around two-handed, forcing the thrust aside – and kicked out at his other attacker, taking him right in the kneecap. Whatever manner of flesh they wore, it was as fragile in that joint as its human counterpart; the creature went down, howling, and it was no hard work to follow through with a second sharp kick, into the face. Bone snapped and blood gushed and he was down for good – and then Damien's other opponent left himself open along one side of his rib cage and he was down, too, blood spurting from a gaping wound in his side.

He looked about, saw nothing but blood and dead flesh about him. He stepped over one of the bodies and ran to where Hesseth lay, her assailant only now coming to his feet by her side. Her eyes were dilated, glazed, like the empty stare of a fish stranded on dry land. Her attacker's glee made it quite clear what manner of exchange had taken place between them, and the eyes that gazed out from that death-white pallor were so like Hesseth's in shape and expression that Damien felt fresh horror take hold of him as he raised his sword to strike—

—and light blazed past him as a Fire-laden bolt hit home, piercing the creature's eye and driving deep into his brain. He screamed and fell back; dark blood gushed from the socket, and other less wholesome fluids as well. With a twitching motion he fell, and as the Fire began to consume his brain the whole of his body shuddered, ripples of pain coursing through his flesh as he soundlessly mouthed screams of agony.

Ciani came to where Hesseth lay and helped her up; dazed, the rakh-woman seemed uncertain as to where she was, or exactly what had happened. Then she saw the body of her assailant, and memory returned to her. All of it. As Ciani helped her to her feet, she whimpered softly in terror.

'The Lost One—' Damien began. But before he could finish Ciani directed his attention upward, to the wall of the cavern just over its entranceway. There, clinging to the jagged stone surface, the pierced one displayed the body of the last attacker to them proudly. It hung by one ankle, which was wrapped in the cave-rakh's prehensile tail. Its throat had been torn out. When he saw that they had witnessed his kill, the Lost One released the body; it fell to the floor like a bag of wet cement, bones snapping as it struck. The cave-rakh then climbed down, serpentine fingers taking purchase in the tiniest of crevices, tail grasping at convenient stone protrusions for support.

Damien looked about, and counted the bodies. Six. All accounted for – but there'd be more, soon enough. 'Let's get out of here,' he muttered. He went back to where Tarrant's body lay, now covered in the folds of his cloak, and hefted the weight of it up to his shoulder. It was impossible to tell if any life was left in that limp form, but at least the heat of it had cooled somewhat. Time enough later to analyse its condition.

They ran. As well as they could, considering Hesseth's wounds and Damien's burden. The rakh-woman turned back once or twice briefly as if to Work, but whether she had the strength to do so effectively was something Damien couldn't begin to guess at. He held his own wounded arm tightly against him as he wended his way through the demons' labyrinth, hoping that no blood was dripping to the floor – because if they left a trail that distinct, all the Workings in the world couldn't hide it.

At last they came to the narrow tunnel that had been their entrance into this area. Ciani, who had caught up Tarrant's possessions in her flight, now threw down a long silk tunic to cover the rough stone bottom and crawled through. Tarrant's sword went with her, now safely sheathed. Hesseth followed, her bright blood staining the folded silk as she crawled over it. Then the pierced one. By now Damien though he could hear the faint sounds of pursuit from the area they had just left. He lowered Tarrant's body down from his shoulder – still warm, still bleeding, still utterly life-less – and, with great effort, managed to get it far enough into the tunnel that the pierced one could pull it through. The cloak Ciani had wrapped around it kept the broken flesh from tearing on the sharp formations, but he could see at the end of the tunnel where dark blood, seeping through the wool, had stained the stone beneath. Quickly Damien divested himself of his weapons and passed them through the narrow space, then balled up Tarrant's bloodstained tunic and threw that after it. Then, somewhat awkwardly, he began to back himself into the passageway. Voices sounded from a nearby corridor as he forced himself through the narrow space. As his feet reached the other side he felt hands close about his ankles, meaning to pull him through – but he kicked them off and halted midway, fumbling in the darkness for the two stalagmites he had broken earlier.

The earth-fae was weak here, but this Working was a minor one; it took only seconds for him to use that force to bind the two slender spires back in place, so that the passage was once more impassable. Then he thrust out his feet behind him and let his companions grab hold and pull; stone edges scraped his sides as the neck of the tunnel finally let him pass, and he was through – not a second too soon. Even as he dropped below the lip of the tunnel he saw a flash of light coming from its opposite end, and clearly heard voices from the adjoining room.

They crouched there, hearts pounding, and waited. Hesseth had Obscured their path, but how well? Had they made it through without leaving a telltale path of blood behind them, or a more subtle trail of sweat and scent that the demon-creatures might follow? It was because Damien had considered that possible that he had risked a few precious seconds to Work the two stone pinnacles back in place. Now, as best they could make out, it appeared to be that move which turned the trick. The creatures stared down the tunnel for some time, evidently considering it a viable exit from the area. But it was clear that no man-sized being could have made it through that space and left the formations intact, and so at last they moved on.

'They'll be back,' Ciani whispered. 'They don't understand how we got away, but their master will.'

'That'll take time,' he whispered back, hoarsely. 'First, we bind up these wounds so we don't leave a trail of blood behind us.' He nodded towards Hesseth – whose golden fur was scored with at least a dozen deep, bloody gashes – and indicated his own injured arm. 'Then we get as far from this place as we can, preferably high up enough to work a good Obscuring. If that's possible. Then . . .'

He felt fresh pain wash over him, and the weakness of exhaustion. How deep was his wound? How much blood had he lost? 'We see what we rescued,' he whispered. 'We see if Gerald Tarrant still exists. We see if he can help us.'

'And then?' Ciani asked.

From somewhere, he dredged up a grin. Or at least, the hint of one. It hurt his face.

'Then the real work starts,' he told her.

42

'Calesta!' The voice rang out imperiously, echoing in rage. 'Calesta! Attend me, now!'

Slowly the demon's form congealed, drawing its substance from the nearby shadows; when the figure was solid enough to bow, it did so. 'My Master commands.'

'They took him, Calesta. Out of the fire! You said he would burn there forever. You said they would never come – never! – that they would let him burn. And I believed you. *I believed you!*'

'You commanded me to look into his heart,' the demon responded. 'I did that. You told me to read his weaknesses. I did that. You bade me devise a way of binding him to your purpose, so that he would be helpless to free himself. I did that also. As for the others, you said, *Leave them to me . . .*'

'They came for him, Calesta! How? They were miles from here when last I Knew them – miles! I—'

'They were never there,' the demon said coolly.

Blood drained from the enraged face, turning it a ghastly white. 'What? What does that mean?'

'It means that you were wrong. It means that your Knowing was misdirected. It means that these humans anticipated you, and made false replicas of themselves to draw your attention.'

The word came, a whisper: 'Simulacra.'

The demon bowed its head.

'Why didn't you see it happening? Why didn't you warn me?'

'I serve,' the demon answered. 'I obey. Those were the parametres you set when you first Conjured me. Had you ordered me to inspect the strangers, I would have done so. You didn't.'

'So you stayed in the caverns, to feed on the adept's pain—'

'I never fed on the adept. I've never fed on any of your victims.' The faceted eyes glittered maliciously. 'I think perhaps you mistake my nature.'

Pacing: quickly, angrily, to the window and back again. 'I must have him back. You understand that? Him, and the woman. And I want no room for error this time – none at all. You hear me, Calesta? We work out the best way to go after them, and—'

'That won't be necessary,' the demon interrupted.

'Meaning what?'

The demon chuckled. 'You need only wait. They'll come here by themselves.'

The pacing stopped. The tone was one of suspicion. 'You're sure of that?'

'Their nature demands it.'

'After *me*? Not after the woman's assailant?'

'They understand now that the two are linked. They recognize you as the stronger force. The priest will insist that they deal with you first. And the adept will demand your death – or worse – for what you did to him.' The demon paused. 'Do you require more than that?'

'No,' came the answer. 'That's enough.' The voice grew harsh. 'They're coming here? Good. Then we'll be ready. That's an order, Calesta. You understand? Watch them. Neutralize them. Take them prisoner. No taking chances, this time. Nothing fancy. Just bind them and bring them to me. *To me*. I'll deal with them.'

Calesta bowed. And it seemed that a hint of a smile creased the obsidian face, gashing its mirrored surface.

'As you command,' the demon responded.

43

Not until they were near the surface did the four travellers stop, and lower their various burdens to the muddy floor beneath them. As soon as it was clear that they would be staying in one place for more than a few minutes Hesseth sank to the ground, and sat with her head lowered between her knees, her breathing hoarse and labored. Ciani came to where Damien stood and helped him lower Tarrant's body to the ground. It was a dead weight, cold now, and though neither would voice such a thought they both feared that the Hunter's spirit might truly have deserted them.

And what then? Damien thought. *What if all this was for nothing?*

Carefully, the two of them unwrapped the battered form. Bits of burned flesh and crusted blood adhered to the wool, tearing loose from the Hunter as the cloak was removed from him; fresh blood dripped from the resulting wounds, making his flesh slick and hard to handle. By the time Damien had freed him from his wrappings the priest's hands were coated in blood, and the black ash of burnt flesh stuck to his skin as though glued there.

'Look,' Ciani urged. She pointed to where the Hunter's arm lay exposed, to the deep gash seared into it by the band of red-hot steel. Blackened skin curled back from the wound, displaying muscles and nerves that had been seared to a bloody ash. But the bone itself was no longer visible. Damien drew in a sharp breath as he realized that, and he turned the man's arm over, to make sure of it. 'My God . . .'

'He's healing,' she whispered.

He looked at the body – which displayed no other sign of life, and numerous signs of death – and felt awe creep over him. And horror. 'He must have had to repair his flesh constantly in order to survive. Drawing on what little fae there was, to replace what the fire destroyed . . . my God.' He looked at the man's face – or what was left of it – and felt his sticky hands clenching into fists at his side. 'It could have gone on forever. He could never have Worked the fire itself, never have freed himself . . . only this.' He worked himself a Knowing, with care; the mere act of Working was painful. 'He's trapped in it,' he whispered. 'Lost in a desperate race against the fire. He doesn't even know he's out of there.'

'Can you Work through to him?'

He shook his head. 'He would suck me in, as fuel. Never even know who or what I was.'

'So what do we do?' she demanded. There was an edge of hysteria in her voice that he had to force himself not to respond to. It was all too easy to abandon reason, and let blind emotion reign.

He reached up to where his sleeve had been sliced open, over his wound. The makeshift bandage was already soaked with blood, and as he wound it off it dripped carmine spots on the floor. He felt dizzy and his arm throbbed hot with pain, but that had been the case for so long now that he had grown accustomed to it. He gritted his teeth as he pulled the bloodsoaked length free at last and flexed his arm to keep fresh blood from flowing. With his other hand he bunched up the cloth and brought it to Tarrant's lips. What remained of his lips. And squeezed.

Red blood, warm and thick. It dribbled onto the corner of his mouth, coated his lips with glistening wetness. He squeezed again, and forced a trickle between the parted teeth.

'Drink it,' he urged. His voice was a hoarse whisper, half hate and half anxiety. 'Drink, damn you!'

'Damien, he's not a—'

'He *is*. Or at least, he was. And he said he could feed this way again, if he had to. I'd say he has to.' He pressed the bunched-up cloth against his arm again; it soaked up the fresh blood like a sponge. 'Drink,' he whispered, squeezing the precious fluid out into Tarrant's mouth. 'Or so help me God, I'll take you back down there and stick you in the fire myself . . .'

He thought he saw movement, then. A flicker of wetness, within the mouth: a tongue tip? He squeezed harder, and saw the lips move slightly. The skin of Tarrant's throat contracted slightly, and crusted flesh cracked off from its surface. Beneath, the tissue was pale and moist.

Damien began to collect more blood – and then cast the bandage aside, and lowered his gashed arm to the Hunter's mouth. Sharp teeth bit into his flesh, a blind and desperate response to the presence of food; he bore the pain of it with gritted teeth as the cavern swayed about him, telling himself, *He doesn't know where he is. He doesn't know who you are.*

And then, at last, with a shudder, the teeth withdrew. He pulled back and pressed the wound closed, watching the man's face closely. The blackened crust was flaking off, and beneath it new tissue gleamed moistly in the lamplight. The process reminded Damien of a snake shedding its skin.

'Come on,' he muttered. 'Come back to us.' He Worked his vision and saw the dark fae gathering about the Hunter's body, saw it weaving a web about the man's flesh that acted as a buffer between him and the light. Between him and the world. Cutting him off from the source of his pain – and with it, the rest of the living universe. 'Tarrant!' He grasped him by the shoulder, but his blood-slicked hand slid off – and took with it a layer of burned flesh, revealing the newmade skin beneath. Cell by cell, layer by layer, the Hunter was restoring his body.

Hesseth hissed softly to get his attention and held out a flask of waxed leather towards him. He took it, somewhat perplexed, and smelled the stopper. And then nodded gratefully. The smell was familiar to him, the same odour that had clung to his flesh after their fight on Morgot. He poured a bit of the rakhene ointment into his right palm and rubbed it into and around his wound. And thanked her.

Then Tarrant stirred. A shiver passed through his frame, as though somewhere inside that battered flesh a spark of life was fighting to manifest itself. Damien reached out to him – and then, remembering what the Forest's monarch had said about Healing, used the hand that was free of ointment to grasp him by the shoulder. No telling what the rakhene liniment might do to a man who thrived on death.

'It's over,' he told him. 'Over.'

'The fire . . .' It was hoarsely voiced, barely a whisper – but it was speech, and it was audible, and he used it as a lifeline to reach the man.

'Gone. Left behind.' He dared a comforting lie: 'Extinguished.'

The eyes opened, slowly. Fresh new lids of smooth, pale flesh, smeared with blood and black ash. For a moment he gazed emptily at the ceiling; then he shivered, and moaned softly. His eyes fell closed again.

'Tarrant. Listen to me. You're out of there. *Safe.* It's over. You're with us now.' He paused. 'Do you understand?'

The lids blinked open, tears of blood in their outer corners. For a minute or two the Hunter stared without seeing, silver eyes fixed on nothing. Then he turned, slowly – painfully – and met Damien's eyes. There was an emptiness in his gaze that made the priest's flesh crawl.

'Where?' the Hunter gasped. 'Where is this?'

'We're in a cave, near the surface. Judging from the earth-fae, that is.' He hesitated. 'Tell me what you need. Tell us how to help you.'

The pale eyes shut again, as if keeping them opened required more strength than the Hunter had. 'More blood,' he whispered. 'But you can't give me that. I've already taken as much as your body can spare.'

'Gerald.' It was Ciani. She crawled over to where the Hunter lay and seemed to be about to reach out to him, but Damien warned her back. 'I can supply—'

'Don't,' the priest warned her.

'But I wasn't wounded. I haven't lost—'

'*Don't.*'

'Damien—'

'Ciani, think! He takes on the form of whatever his victims fear the most. That means that if he feeds on you, he'll become more like *them.* The ones who hurt you; the ones we're hunting. I don't think he's strong enough to fight it now. I don't think we can afford to risk it.'

'But if we don't—'

'He's right,' the Hunter whispered. 'Too much risk . . .' He shivered, as if from some secret pain. 'I would hurt you. I might even kill you. And . . . I would rather die, than do that.'

Damien watched for a moment as he lay there – his breathing labored, his movements weak – and then asked, 'You going to make it?'

The Hunter raised a hand to his face, rubbed his eyes. The fingers were whole, but stained with blood. Flakes of charred skin fell from his face as he rubbed, revealing smooth white skin beneath. 'I think . . . yes. They didn't do anything that time won't heal. Not to my flesh, anyway.' He tried to force himself to a sitting position but fell back, weakly. 'How long?' he gasped.

'In the fire? Eight days, Ciani figured.'

'It seemed like so much longer . . .' He looked about weakly – at Ciani – at Hesseth – at the pierced one. His gaze lingered on the latter, and for a moment curiosity flared in those silver eyes. Then exhaustion took its place, and he turned away. 'You saved my life,' he whispered. The pale eyes fixed on Damien – and in the back of them, deep in the shadows, was a flicker of something familiar. A faint spark of sardonic humour, reassuringly familiar in tenor. 'I didn't expect it of you.'

'Yeah. Well. That makes two of us.' He got to his feet, and brushed at some of the caked mud which clung to his clothing. 'You get some rest, all right? Finish putting yourself back together, if you can.' He looked at Hesseth. 'Will the Lost One stand guard? I think he's the only one of us left with the strength to do it.'

She murmured rakhene sounds to the pierced one, who grunted. And then assented, in phonemes that were becoming familiar to Damien.

'All right.' He turned down the lantern wick as far as it would go, trying to save oil; of the store of fuel they had brought, only half a flask remained. When that was gone . . . he shuddered to think of it. One could only Work one's sight for so long.

'Let's all get some sleep while we can,' he urged his party. 'It may be our last chance.' His body felt weak and drained, almost incapable of moving; the combined fatigue of loss of blood and too many nights without slumber. He lay back on a tangle of clothing and blankets, and listened to his heart pounding in his chest: a metronome of exhaustion. Then, slowly, he slid down into darkness. Warm and sweet and utterly welcome.

For the first time in eight days, he didn't dream of fire.

*　*　*

When he awakened, things weren't where they should be. It took him a moment to place the wrongness, to fight off the dizziness of his recent blood loss and think clearly. The light wasn't coming from where it should, he decided. Which meant that the lantern wasn't where he'd left it. He looked around the cavern, saw a spark of light at the far side of the chamber. And a tall figure who held it, whose body eclipsed its minimal light as he moved, casting Damien into utter darkness.

Tarrant.

The man had apparently found his clothes – what few items Ciani had salvaged – and had managed to pull on a silk shirt and woollen leggings, which hid most of his ravaged skin from sight. Where his hands and feet were visible his flesh was a chalky white, utterly bereft of living colour; it bothered Damien that he couldn't remember whether that was his normal hue or not.

The Hunter had unhooded the lamp and turned up its wick, and was casting its bright light upon the length of an oddly twisted column. As Damien approached, he reached out and touched the glistening stone, running his hand down its finely grooved surface. And then did so again, more carefully.

'Not right,' he whispered, as the priest came to his side. 'Not possible.'

Damien studied the formation. It seemed to be oddly shaped for its kind, and there were tiny ridges up and down its length, but otherwise it looked like all the others. And he had seen enough cave formations in the last few days to last him a lifetime.

'It isn't just this one,' the Hunter whispered. 'They're all wrong. Every column in this chamber, every formation that bridges between two surfaces. So wrong . . .' He shook his head in amazement – and even in that simple gesture, so sparingly performed, Damien could read his weakness.

'What is it?' the priest asked quietly.

He turned down the lantern's wick again, to save the last of the oil. Then he put one hand against the gnarled formation: his fingers, like the rest of him, were lean and wasted. 'See these ridges,' he whispered. 'Each of these is where the column cracked when the earth shifted beneath it. Slowly new minerals would seep in and fill the cracks ... but they left scars. Thousands of scars.' He gestured with the lantern, towards formations Damien had never noticed before. Fallen stalactites. Severed columns. Jagged shapes, all of them, that defied the normal pattern. 'Do you see?' the Hunter whispered. He turned the lantern until its light shone on a slender column nearby; looking closely, Damien could see that it had been split cleanly through the middle, and its upper and lower halves no longer lined up with each other. 'This isn't the result of secondary vibration. We must be right in the fault zone. The earth is deforming right here, all about us, and the cave formations reflect it. Lateral movement along a major fault line. To be reflected in the stone ...' His hand closed about the narrow column as if he needed it for support. Damien had to fight the urge to reach out and hold him upright.

'There's nothing recent,' the adept whispered. 'Nothing at all. Not here, not in any place I could look ... and that's just not possible. Not possible! But all the fractures have been filled in, and that takes centuries ...' He shook his head in amazement. 'Am I to believe there's been no movement here? For that long? That defies all science.'

'The rakh said there have been no earthquakes here. Not for a century, at least.'

'That's not what I mean. Not at all. What's an earthquake? A series of vibrations that informs us the crust of the planet has shifted beneath our feet. We measure it by how much it inconveniences us – how much we're aware of it. The earth could move so slowly that all our instruments would never detect it – and it would still add up to the same motion, in the end. The crust of the planet acts in response to the currents of Erna's core. How could that simply cease? And cease only in one place, while all surrounding areas continued on as normal? Because they do, I know that; I monitor these things. The land all about here is normal, utterly normal. Except in this one place. How?'

'Our enemy built his citadel right on the fault line,' Damien pointed out. 'You said only a fool would do that. But if he wanted the power of this place at his disposal, and could keep the earth from shaking ...'

For a moment the adept looked at him strangely. 'No one man could ever bind the earth like that,' he said. 'No one man could ever hope to conjure enough power to offset the pressures of the planet's core. And besides . . .'

He turned away. And shut his eyes. And whispered, 'The Master of Lema is a woman.'

'What?'

'The Keeper of Souls is a woman,' he breathed. 'Our enemy. My torturer. The architect of the House of Storms. A *woman*.'

For a moment Damien couldn't respond. Then, with effort, he managed to get out, 'That doesn't make a difference.'

The Hunter turned on him angrily; his eyes were red-rimmed, bloodshot. 'Don't be a fool,' he snapped. 'Of *course* it makes a difference. Not because of gender, but because of *power*. Raw physicality. What can you know of it – you, who were born with the size and the strength to defend yourself from any physical threat? What can you know of the mind-set of the weak, whose lives are centred around vulnerability? When you hear footsteps behind you in a darkened street, do you fear being kidnapped? Raped? Overcome by the sheer physical strength of your attackers? Or do you feel confident that with firm ground and a reliable weapon in your hands you could hold your own against any reasonable threat? How can you possibly understand what it means to lack that confidence – or what it can drive a human to do, to try to gain it?'

'And you do, I suppose?'

The Hunter glared. 'I was the youngest of nine sons, priest. My brothers took after their father, in form and spirit: a hulking, crude beast of a man, who believed that there wasn't an enemy on Erna he couldn't bring to his knees if only he swung his fist hard enough. I grew up among them, sole inheritor of our mother's mien – and I didn't come into my height until late, or my power. Now, you think about the cruelty of that kind – and of sibling youths, in general – and the brutality of my age, which was at the end of the Dark Ages – and then tell me how much I don't understand.' He turned away. 'I think I understand it very well.'

'They died,' Damien said. 'Within five years of your disappearance. All of them.'

'It was the first thing I did, once I had gained the power – and the moral freedom – to work my will upon the world. And those eight murders are among my most pleasurable memories.' The cold eyes fixed on Damien, piercing him to the core. 'What they were to me, you and I are to her. The whole world is that, to her: a thing to be mastered, defeated. *Broken*. Do you understand? Power has become an end unto itself; she feeds on it, demanding more and more . . . it's like a drug that has slowly taken over her body. Until she lives only to assuage its demands, to do whatever will blunt the edge of that terrible hunger.' His brow was furrowed as if in pain. As if even the memories burned him. 'And I'll tell you something else, priest. I've seen that hunger before. Not in such a blind, unbalanced form . . . but it might have become that, in time. In fact, I believe that it would have become that, if not for Ciani's influence.'

It took him a moment to realize what Tarrant meant. He felt something tighten inside, when he did. 'You mean Senzei?'

Tarrant nodded. 'I think so. I think this is what a man can become, when that kind of hunger goes unchecked – when it continues to grow, like some malignant cancer, until it devours the very soul that houses it. Until all that's left is an addiction so terrible that the flesh lives only to serve it.'

'But that would imply that he . . . that *she* isn't an adept.'

'I don't believe she is,' Tarrant said quietly. 'and I wonder if—' He swayed, and shut his eyes for a moment. 'Not now,' he whispered. 'Not here.' He looked up, as if seeking some opening in the water-etched ceiling. 'Up on the surface, I could be sure. If there's any Working in this region, it would be where the currents were strongest. I could read it there.'

'What are you thinking?'

He hesitated. 'Something so insane that I wouldn't even suggest it,' he whispered. 'Except that I've seen with my own eyes just how insane she is. God in heaven, if she were that blind – but no. I shouldn't talk about it until I can test my suspicions.' His silver eyes were ablaze with hatred – and he seemed to draw strength from the emotion. Slowly he released the slender column at his side, so that he stood unaided. And it seemed to Damien that he trembled only slightly as he did so.

'She was able to take us because she knew what we were,' Tarrant said. 'She knew what the flaw was in each of us. And if I'm correct in what I'm thinking . . . then I may know hers, as well.' The pale eyes fixed on Damien, and in their depths was a flicker of power. Faint, weak, barely discernible – but it was there, and that was more than Damien had seen in him since the rescue.

'And I will be no less ruthless in exploiting it,' the Hunter promised.

The surface of the planet was bitterly cold, and windswept snow-drifts coursed down from the peaks like waves of sea froth, frozen in mid-motion. In the distance it was possible to see the enemy's tower, a gleaming black chancre on the white landscape. Tarrant looked about, then pointed away from it. His eyes were narrowed, as if trying to focus on something in the distance. What? Domina's light was strong enough that the dark fae would have withdrawn from the surface of the planet, and Damien's Worked sight revealed no other special power. What had the adept's vision uncovered, that merely human sight was incapable of making out?

They followed him, struggling across the snowbound landscape. Tarrant seemed somewhat stronger than before, but that could simply be the force of his hunger for revenge making itself felt. Damien wondered how long it would support him.

He led them through knee-high dunes and ice-clad gullies, hesitating after each obstacle was passed to study the lay of the land again, and perhaps shift their direction slightly. He gave no hint of what he was seeking or how long it might take them to reach it. Though Damien knew that the Hunter's cold flesh thrived on the chill of the icy peaks, he nevertheless shivered as the wind whipped Tarrant's thin shirt about his haggard frame. How much longer could the man go on, with no more than a single draught of blood to sustain him?

And then the Hunter stopped, and stiffened. His sudden alertness reminded Damien of an animal, ears pricked forwards to catch the sound of danger. The adept began to walk forwards, more quickly now, stumbling through the ankle-deep snow that cloaked this part of the mountain. And then he knelt and touched one hand to its whiteness. Again there was the sense of utter alertness. As if his whole body was tensed to respond to the slightest sound. Then he began to brush the snow away. After a moment, Damien knelt beside him and helped. He Worked his vision in the hope of catching some glimpse of what the adept had seen, but though the currents coursed clearly beneath the insulating snow – more and more visibly now, as they cleared away that obstacle – Damien was forced to admit that he could make out no sign of what was drawing his companion.

And then his fingers touched something which was neither earth nor stone nor frozen brush. 'Here,' he muttered, and the Hunter's efforts joined his own in clearing the snow from it. Slowly a disk came into view: black onyx, carved with an intricate motif. The snow which caught in its etchings made its pattern doubly visible, and Damien struggled to place the design in his memory.

When he did, at last, he looked up at Tarrant. And said – not quite believing his own words— 'A quake-ward?'

Ciani knelt down by his side; her fingers, cold-whitened, touched the etched surface delicately. 'But what would it protect?' she whispered. 'The citadel's too far away.'

For a moment the Hunter just stared at it, as if not believing his own find. Then, slowly, he reached for his sword. And drew it. Coldfire blazed along its length, doubly bright against the whiteness of the snow. Damien remembered the last time he had seen that power used, and flinched. But Ciani was gazing at it – and the Hunter – with hunger.

'You had better all stand back,' Tarrant said quietly. 'You might need to move rather quickly.'

'What are you going to do?' Ciani asked.

'See what this is linked to. See where it leads.' He touched a hand to the ward's icy surface; snow clung to his fingertip, unmelting. 'See what it's warding,' he whispered.

They stood back. Too fascinated to feel the cold, or the bite of the wind on their faces. Damien heard Hesseth whispering explanations to the pierced one – but how much did she really understand herself? He watched as the Hunter took his sword in both hands, watched as he bound its power to his purpose, to trace the lines of Warding—

—and light shot out from it, brilliant and blinding. Pale blue fire, that blazed about the etched tile and then arced out from it, coursing over the surface of the earth like streamers of azure lightning. A branch of light struck the earth some distance from them, and snow shot up in a thick white plume, baring the ground beneath. When the air had cleared they could see the glint of moonlight on another ward-stone, its etched patterns filled with the gleaming coldfire. And south of that, yet another. Soon the land was alive with ward-fires, and the gleaming network of power that bound them together in purpose.

Damien looked at Tarrant, could see his haggard face rigid with strain as he fought to control the coldfire. *The power may come from outside us*, the priest thought, *but the order we impose on it must come from within*. And then, apparently, the strain was too much. The Hunter shut his eyes and fell to his knees. The sword in his hand blazed bright as an unsun as it struck the earth, and all the power that had gone out from it slammed back into the Worked steel with a force that made the man reel visibly, trying to control it. Damien had to stop himself from moving forwards to help, knowing the cold power would drain him of life before he could get close enough to touch the man. What had the Lost Ones called the blade – the Eater of Souls? He looked at Ciani, worried that she might move forwards to help the Hunter without realizing how dangerous it was. But though her eyes were on him, she did not approach. Instead she reached into her jacket pocket as though seeking something. After a moment she pulled out two small items: a folded knife, and a piece of not paper. Damien recognized Senzei's handwriting on the latter as she twisted it tightly with trembling fingers into a funnel formation. He started to object as he realized what she was doing – and stopped himself. And forced himself to take the paper cone from her hand, that she might be free to open the knife. To use it.

She sliced quickly across the ball of her thumb, a cut that slid just beneath the skin. Maximum blood, with minimum damage. He held the makeshift cup for her as she squeezed out a thin stream of red into it, and wondered that his own hand wasn't shaking. Could one become so inured to the Hunter's needs that they no longer seemed unreasonable?

When the cup was full, she took it from him and knelt by Tarrant's side. His nostrils flared as he caught the scent of her offering, and hunger flashed in those silver eyes. Then he turned away, and whispered hoarsely, 'Please don't. I can't.'

'The cut's already been made,' she said quietly. 'The blood's already been shed. You wouldn't be hurting me by taking it.' When he didn't respond, she whispered, 'Gerald. Please. There'd be no risk this way.' Blood dripped from her hand to the snow, staining it purple in the coldfire's glare. '*I need you.*'

'Don't you understand?' he gasped. 'I gave my word. And keeping it is the only thing that keeps me from becoming like *she* is.' He nodded back towards the citadel, shivering. 'Don't you realize what an addiction power is? *Any* power? If you don't impose some order on it, it consumes you—'

'Honour is one thing,' Damien told him. 'Stupidity is another. Take the blood, man – or do I have to pour it down your goddamned throat?'

The pale eyes fixed on him. And the Hunter nodded slowly. 'I believe you would,' he whispered.

'*Take it.*'

Slowly he raised one hand from the grip of the sword and closed it about Ciani's. And raised the makeshift cup to his lips, and drank. Damien could see a tremor pass through him as he absorbed the precious fluid. Pleasure? Pain? Tarrant made no protest while she filled the cup again, and made no effort to resist the second offering. While he drank, Damien took out one of the cloth strips he had prepared for bandages, so many nights ago, and offered it to Ciani. She wound it tightly about her hand, forcing the wound closed.

Slowly, when he was done, the Hunter moved. With effort he managed at last to sheathe his sword, sliding it into the heavily Worked enclosure that would confine its power. And he sighed – in relief, it seemed – as the coldfire faded from sight.

'Now tell us: what was that all about?' Damien indicated the carved ward before them. 'What are those things?'

The Hunter drew in a deep breath, then said, in a voice that shook slightly, 'Our enemy has warded the crust of the planet.'

'To do what?' Ciani asked.

'To Bind the fault, I assume.' His voice was a whisper. 'To freeze the earth in its motion.'

'I thought you said that wasn't possible.'

'It isn't, in the long run. But if one's vision were limited enough – or blinded, by dreams of power . . .' He looked out across the snow-clad mountains, where a vast webwork of coldfire had so recently burned. Where a vast network of wards had been revealed, that stretched across miles of earth in perfect alignment. A thousand or more quiescent Workings that waited to tap the energy of the earth itself, when the tides of the planet's core released it. 'I said she was insane,' he whispered. 'I meant it. But insanity on such a scale . . . my God. When it fails – and it must fail, some day – what does she think will happen? To her, and to everything she's built here?'

'You mean the wards won't hold.'

'How can they? The power of the fae is constant. The pressure along the fault is building. There must have been enough fae in the beginning to make such a Binding possible in the first place . . . but now? After pressure has been building up here for a century, unrelieved? It would require more and more fae just to maintain the status quo – and you see how weak the currents are in this region. Where is the power to come from if the earth isn't moving?'

Damien looked at Hesseth. 'What was it your people said? That the storms here were constant, when the Master of Lema first came. And then, after a time, there were fewer.' He turned to the Hunter. 'The reference was to lightning, apparently. Ward-lightning. Overload.'

'There would have been more than enough fae at first for her purposes,' he murmured. 'When the earth began to shift, the wild power would have surged . . . and then her wards would Bind it, and the excess fae would bleed off into the sky. What remained would be safely tamed. *Consumable*.'

'But why?' Ciani asked. 'What purpose did it serve?'

The silver eyes fixed on her. 'Why did Senzei steal the Fire?

Why does any non-adept take in a power wild enough to kill him, if not to satisfy that most primal of all hungers? Every time a quake strikes Jaggonath there's someone fool enough to try to Work it. Here's a woman who tamed the earth itself so that she could drink in its power in safety. But only for as long as her wards hold; that's the catch. Remember what the rakh said? The storms are fewer, now. Not because there's less power, but because more and more of it is required to maintain the Binding. And as pressure continues to build within the earth, that imbalance will increase geometrically, until one day soon mere wards will no longer be sufficient . . .'

Slowly, he got to his feet. 'We are standing on a time bomb,' he whispered. 'Of such immense proportion that it defies description. And if what the rakh say is true . . . then it's very near to going off.'

'You're thinking you can trigger it,' Damien said quietly.

He looked out over the snow-shrouded earth, at the places where the quake-wards lay.

'It's a simple series,' he said at last. 'Break one, and the rest would go. But would the earth respond immediately? There are so many variables . . .'

'But the odds are high.'

'Oh, yes. The odds are very high. Higher than they could ever get without man's interference.' He shook his head in amazement. 'Only someone with a complete disregard for seismic law would dare something so intrinsically stupid as this . . .'

'Or someone so addicted to the rush of power that she can't think clearly any more. Isn't that what we're dealing with?'

'She fed on me,' he whispered. Wrapping his arms about himself, as if that could protect him from the memory. 'She used my pain as a filter, to tame the raw earth-fae. That's what she wants Ciani for. As a living refinery for the kind of power she lusts after. As if by using us in this manner she can somehow break through the barriers inside herself, give herself an adept's capacity . . .'

'I thought that wasn't possible,' Damien challenged.

'It isn't. But it's a powerful fantasy, nonetheless. Man has always been loath to accept his limitations. How much easier it is to deny the truth altogether – to imagine that Nature has given us all the same potential, and that a single act of will can suddenly cause all limitations to vanish.' He laughed bitterly. 'As if Nature were just. As if evolution hadn't designed us to compete with each other, so that only the strong would survive.'

'What about the Dark Ones?' Ciani asked. 'Where do they fit in?'

'Servants. Symbiotes. She has to remain at the heart of her web in order to maintain its power. They serve as her eyes and ears and hands, to scour the land in search of what she needs . . . and in return they have her protection. Which is no small thing, in a land with no other human sorcery.' His eyes narrowed, and a new edge of coldness entered his voice. 'If we mean to destroy one of her creatures, then we must deal with her first. That, or have her strike us from behind at a crucial moment.'

'If we could release the earth from her Binding, would that do it?'

He hesitated. 'There were wards in her citadel. I remember seeing them when I was brought in. But I have no way of knowing what they were, exactly. Quake-wards? If so, the building might endure for a time. Only a few minutes, at most – but that would be enough. Because she'd have warning, remember. The surge of earth-fae that precedes an earthquake would have reached her minutes before, with all its power intact. She would have known then that her precious system had failed her, and if she could get away from the citadel in time—'

Then he stopped. And said, very quietly, 'Unless she was Working when it happened. In that case, there would be no escape.'

'Can we force that?' Damien asked. 'Set her up, so that she doesn't see it coming?'

'How?' the Hunter whispered.

'Some sort of attack. Something she would have to defend against—'

Tarrant shook his head, sharply. 'That would require an active assault, which would mean that when the surge hit . . . it would be fatal for both parties. No, she would have to be the only one Working, and I don't see how . . .'

He stopped suddenly. And drew in a long, slow breath.

'Gerald?' Ciani asked. 'What is it?'

His arms tightened about his body. But he said nothing.

'You know a way,' Damien said quietly.

'Maybe,' he whispered. 'The risk would be tremendous. If she were sane, if we could predict her response . . . but she isn't, and we can't.' He shook his head. 'Too dangerous, priest. Even for this expedition.'

'Tell me.'

The pale eyes fixed on him. Silver in white, with hardly a trace of red; the man was healing.

'You would have come here alone,' he said softly. A challenge. 'If we had not been available – or necessary – you would have travelled to this place by yourself, and dealt with her unaided. Gone into the heart of her citadel, if that's what it took, with nothing but your own wits and a small handful of weapons. Am I correct?'

'If I judged it to be worth the risk,' Damien said warily.

'The rakhlands won't support her forever. Already the currents are too weak to truly satisfy her, drained as they are by her Wardings. Soon she would begin to draw on the Canopy itself, and after that . . . I imagine she would move into the human lands. Utterly mad, forever hungry, and backed by a horde of demons capable of reducing her enemies to brainless husks. Would that be worth the risk, Reverend Vryce? Would you brave her citadel alone, for that – risk her rage, and that of the earth itself, to gain the upper hand in this war? Because I think I know a way that she might be rendered vulnerable, but it would have to be done by a single man. Human, and not an adept. There's only one of us who fits that description. How great is your courage now?'

'If I'd come alone, as you say, I would expect to do no less,' he said tightly. 'What are you thinking?'

'It wouldn't be pleasant, I warn you.'

'As opposed to the rest of this trip?'

Despite himself, the Hunter smiled; the expression was edged with pain. 'You're a brave man, Reverend Vryce, and true courage is rare. I respect you for it. But there's more than simple risk at issue here.' The silver eyes burned like fire. Coldfire, unwarm and uncomforting. 'Could you trust me, priest? Without reservation? Could you give yourself to me, for the lady's sake? Entrust your soul to me, for safekeeping?'

Damien remembered the touch of the man's soul against his own, which he had endured once in order to feed him. The mere memory of it made his skin crawl – and that had been but a fleeting contact, with no real depth to it. Even the Hunter's coldfire in his veins, for all the pain and horror it had inspired, had been nothing compared to that. The utter revulsion. The soul-searing chill. The touch of a mind so infinitely unclean that everything it fixed upon was polluted by the contact. He shivered to recall it . . . but said nothing in response. The man hadn't asked if he would enjoy such contact, but if he could endure it. If he would *trust* him.

He looked at the man's face, at the taut tissue so recently ravaged by fire. At the weakness that lurked just beneath his facade of arrogance, which had so nearly consumed his life just now. All this, in a man who feared death more than any other single thing. All these things he had risked, and suffered, for the sake of one promise. One word. One single vow, which his present companions had not even witnessed.

'I assume it would be temporary,' he said quietly.

'Of course.' The Hunter nodded. 'Assuming we both survive to undo it.'

'I have your word on that?'

'You do.' The pale grey eyes glittered with malevolence; towards him, or towards their enemy? 'And I think you know what that's worth, Reverend Vryce.'

He felt himself on the brink of a vast cliff, balancing precariously on its crumbling edge. But the darkness of the citadel which loomed overhead was even more threatening than the imagined depths beneath, and at last he heard himself say, in a voice that seemed strangely distant, 'All right, Hunter. Tell me what you have in mind.'

Tarrant nodded. And turned to the pierced one. In all the time he had been awake, he had made no move to acknowledge the Lost One's presence. Now he gazed upon the crouching form, whose cave-pale fur protected it from the night's chill, and seemed to consider what the others had told him about it.

'Go back to your people,' he told the cave-rakh. Gesturing for Hesseth to translate his words. 'Tell them they must leave this region quickly. The earth will move soon, and the caves here are too fragile to protect them. Tell them they must go down to the plains, or else head west. Away from the fault zone, as quickly as possible. Their lives depend on it.' He glanced up at the night sky as if trying to judge the time by it. 'They'll have till tomorrow night,' he said. 'Tell them that. We won't begin until nightfall, and even then it may take some time.' He looked at the rakh-woman. 'But not much,' he warned. 'Make that clear.'

She stared at him for a minute – suspiciously, it seemed – and then finished translating his words. It took some time for their meaning to sink in; when at last it did, the Lost One rasped a few hurried questions at Hesseth. Her answers were short hisses, and the hostility in them was clear even to those who didn't speak her language. Finally the Lost One stood, stiffly, and looked at the party – looked long and intently at Tarrant with an expression that was unreadable – and then turned away sharply, and moved off into the night. Motion silent in the soft snow, long tail curled tightly in foreboding.

Damien waited until the Lost One was out of sight – and, presumably, out of hearing – and then said to Tarrant, 'That wasn't like you.'

'No,' the Hunter said softly. 'I find myself doing a lot of things that aren't like me, these days.'

'I wouldn't have thought their lives mattered to you,' Hesseth challenged.

The silver eyes fixed on her, filled with a languid malevolence. 'They don't. But I do recognize my obligations.' He turned back to Damien. 'You saved my life. All of you did. But in the Reverend's case . . . I know what that meant for you,' he told Damien. 'We share the same background, you and I – and I remember enough of it to understand what that cost you.' *The pain of it*, his expression seemed to say. *The guilt*. He nodded towards where the Lost One had gone, now rendered invisible by the shadows of night.

'Consider this my small gesture of gratitude. A few hundred less deaths to darken your conscience, Reverend Vryce. It won't outweigh the evil of my existence, in the long run . . . but it's all I can offer you without hazarding my own survival. I regret that.'

'Just get us through this, and you'll have done enough,' Damien said tightly. 'That's what I brought you back for.'

Gerald Tarrant bowed. And if there was weakness in him now, it was overlaid by such hatred for the enemy that it was hard to make out. The hunger for revenge, combined with Ciani's blood, had replenished not only body but spirit.

'As you command,' the Hunter whispered.

44

The tunnel was long and dark, and filled with the smell of mould. Which told Damien two things: that life passed this way often enough to deposit the fragile spores, and that the tunnel was deep enough to be protected from the worst of winter's chill.

He was dressed in a woollen shirt and breeches, his only other protection a tough leather vest that was concealed by the loose folds of his garments, and matching bracers strapped about his wrists. His heavy jacket had been left at the tunnel's entrance, along with the knitted scarves and overshirts of winter's travel. Such garments might have kept him warmer, but they also added to his bulk – and for once that wasn't desirable. His sheath was no longer strapped to his back but harnessed to the side of his belt: he fervently hoped he would remember it was there when the time came to draw it. Other than that he carried only a single long knife, a length of rope, two folding hooks, a number of small locksmithing tools, and several amulets. Those last were compliments of Gerald Tarrant, who had Worked them with just enough power to justify their presence on his person. He had no springbolt. That had been the hardest thing to leave behind, but it was a bulky weapon, not quickly drawn, and a man bent on assassination couldn't afford to slow himself down. Or so he told himself, as he mourned the loss of its reassuring weight on his arm.

At his hip lay the flask of Fire, safely cushioned in its leather pouch. He should have left that behind, as well . . . but if the first stage of their plan went askew – or any other part, for that matter – he might well need some weapon that could drive back the enemy's demonic guard. And he had stripped himself of anything else that might serve.

He felt naked, thus weaponless. But also exhilarated. Because for the first time since leaving Jaggonath, he was on his own. Oh, he still had Ciani's safety to worry about, and Tarrant's Workings were wrapped tightly about him, a cocoon of malevolence that shadowed his every step . . . but that still wasn't the same thing as having them *here*, as knowing that he must watch out for them every time he planned, every time he took a step . . . no, this was much better. This was the way it was meant to be. Every sound that he heard was important because it concerned him – or unimportant because it didn't. There was no middle ground. His progress was a study in black and white, threat and nonthreat, and no other concern existed in his mind but that he must get from *here* to *there* in safety. And then manage what he came to do, with minimal damage to his person.

If that last is possible, he thought grimly. And he remembered what Tarrant had told him about their enemy, running the details through his mind as he crept slowly forwards, eyes and ears alert for any sign of danger. He prayed that Tarrant's guesses were right, prayed that he had arrayed himself properly for this foray . . . and then prayed in general, just for good measure. Not because his God would interfere in such a thing – or even care about the short-term consequences – but such prayer was a reminder of his identity. And with Tarrant's taint wrapped about him like a shroud, darkening his every thought, he needed all the reminders he could get.

I only hope he's right. I only hope he understands her as well as he thinks he does. And then he added, somewhat dryly, *The ruthless, analyzing the mad . . .*

Periodically another tunnel would merge with the one he was

following, and he would pause to check it out. *Egresses from the lower caverns,* Tarrant had told him, *that merge with the citadel's excape route.* They were fortunate that the underground system was close enough to Erna's surface to affect the currents above it: otherwise the Hunter might never have managed to locate it at all. As it was he knew only the location of its entrance, and its general route beneath the eastern mountains. It wasn't enough, he told himself. Except that it had to be. Because it was all they had.

At each intersection the priest paused, hooding his lantern with his hand so that no light would precede him. And he listened — ears alert, eyes narrowed, his whole soul focused on *perceiving.* But not with Worked senses. That was impossible, because of what Tarrant had done to him. That was why he'd had to submit to the man, choking on the blackness of that warped morality as the Hunter's mind wrapped about his own, picking at his brain like an old woman picking out the stitches of some tightly sewn embroidery—

Don't think about that, he warned himself. His heart was pounding: he breathed deeply, trying to still the trembling of his hands. All the trust in the world couldn't have staved off the terror of that experience, and Damien's stomach turned as he recalled how the Hunter drank in his fear, sucking the terror out of him as surely as he had once drawn out the blood that ran in his veins. The difference was that this time something had been left behind. A coiling malignance, serpentlike, that slithered in the dark recesses of Damien's mind and licked at his thoughts as they flickered from neuron to neuron—

Stop it!

He moved swiftly between intersections, knowing that the smooth, rakh-made tunnels offered no concealment between those junctures. Time after time he felt himself reaching for his sword, and he had to force his hand to drop back to his side, empty. It was important that he remain unarmed. Every detail of this was important, he knew, which was why every move had been planned out in advance . . . but that was little comfort as he advanced towards certain danger, his palm itching to close about a sword-grip, his arm tensing as if to balance the weight of that defending steel.

And then: he heard it. A noise that whispered behind him in the endless passage. Footsteps? He forced himself to keep moving forwards, tensing his ears to catch the sound. Soft, rhythmic . . . yes, footsteps. Unshod, he guessed. Since there were no signs of any large animal in this place, that left only one possibility—

He turned. Too late. He knew it even as he reached for his sword, even as he cursed himself for going to his shoulder instead of his hip to draw it. Cold, clawed hands tore at him from the darkness, and one grabbed his sword arm and twisted it brutally behind him. His sheath swung into the dirt wall as he struggled, dislodging clumps of earth. He fought to break free, desperately, but pain clouded his vision as his arm was twisted even more tightly behind him, and he knew it was within inches of breaking. Another assailant grabbed him by the throat and squeezed, sharp claws drawing blood through the collar of his shirt. There were too many of them, and they were too fast, too strong. The fetid stink of them filled his nostrils, choking him, as he felt the long dagger drawn from his belt even as the reassuring weight of his sword was snapped from his side. Cold hands felt along the length of his body, and one by one his tools and weapons were located and removed from him. The hooks. The rope. The amulets. The latter were broken free with a hiss of amusement, thin gold chains snapping with a sound like a pennant in the wind. Then sharp fingers pried at the pouch at his belt, opening it – and a cry of pain burst forth from one of the creatures as it backed away from the church-Worked light. There was an instant of chaos that Damien tried to take advantage of, but the Dark One who held him prisoner was on the other side of him, and thus sheltered from the light. He twisted the priest's arm brutally as he struggled, forcing the man to fall to his knees in order to keep it from breaking; a foot forced the leather pouch closed again and pressed down on him as his assailant forced him lower, into the earthen floor. 'Let her deal with it!' he heard one hiss. He tried to struggle free, choking on dirt, felt the bite of cold claws digging into his face. Drawing his face upward, forcing his eyes to meet—

Dizzying. Blinding. A whirlpool of raw malevolence, its walls glittering with hunger. He felt himself being sucked down into it, felt the thoughts and memories being torn loose from him as he fell, the rush of them past his ears as the power of the Dark One dismembered, devoured—

And then it ended. Suddenly. As though an impenetrable wall had been slammed down between himself and the Dark One. Damien gasped for breath, heard the demon curse in frustration. Then the cold hand that gripped him squeezed his face even tighter, and he felt that boundless hunger reaching out to him again, the maelstrom forming . . . and it slid from him like claws on ice, unable to take hold.

'Can't do it,' he heard a voice rasp. And another, hungry, hissed, 'Let me try!' He felt his head turned forcibly to one side, as blood from a claw-wound dripped into one eye. For a moment there was the sensation of falling, of a power so vast that it must surely overwhelm the barrier Tarrant had established in him . . . and then that, too, dispersed, and he was left shivering in pain as they debated, hotly, the cause of their failure.

'Let her deal with him,' one hissed at last, and the others agreed. Damien felt himself jerked to his feet, his other arm pulled up sharply behind him. Then the pressure on the first mercifully let up, and through his fog of pain and confusion he could tell that they were binding him, using the very rope he had been carrying on his person. They tied tight knots about his leather wristlets, binding wrists that he made taut with tension as he tried to fight them. But the creatures knew by his weakness that though they had failed to drain him of memory, they had severed his flesh from his spirit; bereft of passion, securely bound, he appeared all but helpless in their hands. He snarled fevered curses as they dragged him forwards, but his words were impotent weapons; the creatures chittered sharply as they gathered up his steel and the rest of his equipment, in some dark equivalent of laughter. And one stopped to lick the blood from his face – as if to remind him that they fed on his kind, that once they managed to break through the barrier which Tarrant had Worked in him, he would be no better than an evening's snack to them.

They dragged him down the length of the corridor, his neck leashed like an angry dog's. And as he stumbled along behind them – weaponless, bleeding, his face and arms stinging from the prick of their foul claws – it was all he could do to reflect upon his purpose, and keep from pitting his full strength against the bonds that had rendered him helpless. Because helplessness was what he needed right now. It went against his every instinct to accept that, to play along with it, but Tarrant was right; if the Dark Ones could not have rendered him helpless, they would have been forced to kill him. Their primitive minds knew no middle ground.

As he stumbled towards the enemy's stronghold, he thought grimly, *So far, so good.*

The citadel was a jewel, a prism, a multifaceted crystal-line structure that divided up the night into a thousand glittering bits, turning the sky and the landscape beneath into a cubist's nightmare of disjointed angles and broken curves. Domina's cold blue radiance reflected from the mirror-bright surfaces in seemingly random splinters, making it impossible for Damien to isolate any one structure as cohesive as a wall, or a doorway. When they walked he was forced to rely upon his feet to feel out the structure of the floor; stairs and inclines were all but invisible, masked by that visual chaos.

A reflection of her madness, he thought. He was appalled, but also impressed. What would the place be like in the sunlight? Or in Corelight? Brilliant, he decided. Disturbingly beautiful. It was clear to him that the Master of Lema was no creature of the night, as her servants were.

She came, then, down a staircase that glittered like diamonds in the fractured moonlight. He couldn't make out the edges of the stairs beneath her feet, but judged their size and shape by the action of her long robe upon their surface. Silk sliding over glass, a waterfall of colour. Mesmerized, he watched until the delicate fabric was level with his own feet, until that signal informed him that the Keeper of Souls had entered the very chamber he was in.

A taloned hand forced him to his knees; he didn't fight, but dropped down as though beaten. And watched her intently, as she approached.

She was not a young woman any more, though her skill with the fae had kept her from ageing too badly. She might have been beautiful once, but decades of obsession and the relentless power of her addiction had robbed her face of whatever natural elegance it might once have possessed. Her eyes were deeply hollowed, underscored with carmine lines where the bone edges pressed against the sallow tissue. Her skin was dry and taut with the inelasticity of enforced youth. Her lips, once full, were textured with a webwork of fine lines, that left only a hint of what must have once been vital sensuality. Only her eyes blazed forth with life, and they were so filled with hunger – with raw, uncaring *need* – that despite all he had known of her nature, Damien shuddered as he met her gaze.

'So you're the one,' she said shortly. Her eyes flickered up to meet those of her captors; it seemed to him that the Dark Ones flinched before her. 'What were my orders?'

'To claim his memories, Keeper.'

She hooked a hand beneath Damien's chin and forced his head upward, to face hers. Studied his eyes, and all that was behind them.

'You disobeyed me,' she said softly. 'Is there a reason?'

'We couldn't do it,' one of Damien's captors rasped, and another offered, 'There was a barrier . . .'

'Ah.' The eyes pierced into him, burning his brain – then withdrew, and were merely eyes once more. 'A Shielding. Very good. They have both intelligence and power.' She let go of his head. 'But not enough.'

She stood back. 'Get him up.'

Sharp claws bit into his upper arms as two of the creatures jerked him to his feet. He was careful to appear unsteady, as if from pain or weakness, but feared it would do little good. Carmine cloth swept from her shoulders to the floor, draped over an armature of padding that was clearly meant to lend aggressive mass to her frame. Even so, she was considerably smaller than he was, and he knew to his despair that no feigned emotions could counteract the sheer power of his bulk – or the threat she would read into it.

She nodded to one side, and the Dark Ones scurried to lay out Damien's weapons before her. She waited until they were done and then said in a disdainful tone, 'Is that all?' She reached down and took up a handful of amulets; thin gold chains slithered down between her fingers, like serpents. 'Did you really think these would affect me?' She opened her hands and let the precious medallions slip through her fingers like so much refuse. 'I think you underestimate me.' And a smile, faint and unpleasant, wrinkled her lips. 'I know that *he* did.'

She came back to him and cupped a cold hand beneath his face. Sharpened nails bit into his skin, not unlike the talons of her servants. 'I want him,' she said. 'And I want the woman. Tell me where they are, and I'll let you go.'

Elation filled him, at the realization that Hesseth's efforts had paid off; the human sorceress couldn't read through her tidal Workings. But he kept it carefully from his face as he said, in a tone edged with fear, 'I won't betray my friends.'

She smiled coldly. 'Oh, you will do that. No question about it. All that's at issue is how long it will take . . . and how much pain has to be applied in the process.' An odd hunger flickered in the depths of her eyes; her tongue tip touched her lips briefly, as if in anticipation. 'Well? Will you answer me now? Or do I have to break you to get what I want?'

Damien's heart was pounding so loudly he wondered that she couldn't hear it. What was the safest way to answer? He had to goad her into specific action, without bringing down the full weight of her wrath upon his head. He tried to remember what Tarrant had told him, tried to weigh all his alternatives – and at last he gasped, in a tone that he hoped was more fearful than defiant, 'I can't. Please. Don't ask that.'

Her expression hardened. She reached out to him again, and took his face in her hands. Gripped him tightly, so that his blood pounded beneath her fingers. So that he was incapable of looking away. 'You'll serve me,' she told him. 'Like it or not, you will.' She willed him to look up at her, into her eyes; fae wrapped about him like a vice, forcing obedience. 'I need to know where they are and what they're doing. You're going to tell me that.' Hot thoughts slithered into his mind, wrapping about his brainstem like serpents. Stroking the centres of pleasure and pain within him as she practiced her control. 'Submit to me,' she whispered. He shut his eyes, tried to fight her off – but she was inside him, her hunger filling his flesh, her thoughts stabbing into his brain. Where the hell was Tarrant's barrier now? He tried with all his will to force her out of his mind — to sever her control — but without a Working to focus his efforts he didn't have a prayer. And he didn't dare Work, not now.

Amused by his struggles, she stroked his brain anew; waves of sensation, shamefully erotic, reverberated through his body, followed by a pain so intense that it would have doubled him over if not for the fae that bound him upright. She was playing his flesh like an instrument, there was no place he could hide, no way he could stop it . . . but he knew that if he gave in, even for a moment, if he let his human intellect be swept away by the tide of her madness, that he was lost forever. Her hunger knew no middle ground.

And then, suddenly, the sea turned cold. The lust became darkness, and ice shot through his veins. His body shook as the essence of the Hunter filled him — unclean, inhuman, but oh, so welcome! — forcing out the foreign influence, chilling his burning flesh. His stomach spasmed as the force of Tarrant's unlife filled it and he vomited suddenly, as if by casting out the bitter liquids within him he might also cast out that influence. Never before was the Hunter's essence so alien, so physically intolerable. And never before was it so welcome.

When he came to himself he saw her standing back from him, rage burning like wildfire in her eyes. Somewhere in the back of his numbed brain he remembered something about a signal, his link to Gerald Tarrant . . . what was it? He grasped at the fact, used it as a lifeline to restore his reason. Something about a sign, and the wards . . . that was it. This was what they'd set up, as the trigger: their enemy, trying to break through Tarrant's barrier. The Hunter would have sensed that and taken it for his starting sign. Even now, the quake-wards were being broken.

Which left very little time. Minutes, perhaps. Or so he hoped. He tried to focus on what he needed to do and how fast he needed to do it, tried not to think about what might happen if the earth failed to respond to its newfound freedom. Because that possibility was enough to chill him to the bone. The longer it took, the less was the likelihood that this woman would be Working when the wave hit — and for him to be here, bound and helpless, with her still alive and whole, and knowing what they had intended . . . it was unthinkable. She would destroy him. She would destroy them all.

'You're a fool,' she said angrily. 'Do you really think your precious adept can protect you? After I broke him? He couldn't even save himself – how on Erna is he going to help you?' The voice became seductive, cloying. 'Tell me what I want to know, and you can go free. Isn't that the easiest way? Or else . . . I might have to dissect your mind, thought by thought, until I find what I need. Until there's nothing left in you, but that one bit of information and enough strength to voice it. Not a pleasant prospect.' Her eyes narrowed to slits, her expression drawn. 'The choice is yours, priest.'

And he took his chance. Daring her rage. Daring her hatred. Because it was her obsession he wanted, and that must be directed at him. Quickly, before the quakewards failed.

'Go to hell,' he spat.

He was struck from behind on the head, hard enough to draw blood. He allowed the blow to drive him to his knees, gasping audibly as a thin, warm trickle began to seep down the back of his collar. Defiance, laced with weakness: that was the winning formula. Play it right, and he would goad her into Working him without doing him permanent harm. Play it wrong . . . he shuddered. She was perfectly capable of maiming him – or worse. He had put himself in her power. If she had been sane he would have been confident, but she wasn't – and the victims of addiction, any addiction, were notoriously unstable.

The taloned fingers caught in his hair and jerked his head up, so that he was forced to meet her eyes. Hatred was hot in her gaze, and a disdain so absolute that he knew for a fact she would never see the blow coming. Not if he could get her Working. Not if he could keep her involved.

'You made a fatal error,' she informed him. 'Not just in coming here, but in guarding yourself against my pets. That interrogation would have been far more merciful than this one will be.'

—And her power hit him, full in the face, a wall of searing force that drove the breath from his body and left him stunned, half-blinded. The fire of her addiction focused in on him, became a red-hot spearpoint that probed deep inside his flesh, testing for weaknesses. If she had used a real blade, she couldn't have made the pain any greater; his nerves rang out as though scraped by sharpened steel, his body shaking uncontrollably as pain consumed his universe.

He struggled not to fight back. That was harder than all the rest combined: forcing himself *not* to respond, as she played his body like some terrible instrument. It went against every instinct in him, against all his years of learning and experience. But any Working now might mean death, if luck and Erna turned against him. And so he swallowed back on all the ingrained keys that might unlock his defences, and banished the images that floated in front of his eyes, before they could Work the fae to save him. And he drank in the bitter draught of utter defencelessness as her will probed sharp within him.

And then – an eternity later – she released him. He would have fallen, but clawed hands had taken hold of his shoulders and they held him upright. The woman's face was a mask of rage and indignation – *How dare you defy me!* – with a desperate edge that might well blossom into something more dangerous.

'Please,' he whispered. Daring a subterfuge. 'I can't. Don't you understand? I can't!'

The burning eyes narrowed suspiciously. She turned to regard a figure who stood just behind her left shoulder – he had not been there before, Damien was certain of that – and demanded, 'Well?'

Faceted eyes in an ink-black face. Glassy surface that refracted the light, like chipped obsidian. Damien had seen figures in his nightmares that looked more forbidding – but not many. And not often.

'The adept has Worked a barrier,' the surreal figure rasped. The quality of his voice – like sandpaper on an open wound – made Damien's skin crawl. 'And he's Warded it into this man's flesh, so that it requires no sustaining power. In fact, you empower it every time you try to break through it.' The glistening eyes fixed on Damien, and seemed to pierce through him. What was that creature? What if it could read the truth in him? 'Well Worked,' the dark figure rasped.

'Spare me your admiration,' she snapped, 'just tell me how to break it.'

'You can't. Not directly. Its power feeds off yours. The more force you use, the stronger it gets.'

'You're telling me I can't get inside him?'

'I'm telling you that mere force won't succeed here. You'll have to dismantle it, step by step. Reversing the process he used to erect it in the first place. Assuming you can,' he added.

'I can do anything,' she said acidly.

She took hold of Damien again, sharpened nails tangling in his sweat-soaked hair. 'You'll regret the day you decided to serve him,' she promised the priest.

'—Or of course,' the black figure interjected, 'there's always physical torture.'

She looked back sharply at him. And Damien could barely hear her words, so loud was the pounding of his heart. 'Would that work?' she demanded. Hunger echoed in her voice.

'Who can say? It would certainly be . . . interesting.'

'I can't,' Damien whispered. Trying to will as much fear into his voice as he could muster. In the face of possible torture, it wasn't hard. 'He said the barrier wouldn't permit it. Said that his blockage was absolute, from both directions . . .'

'So that you can't betray him,' she concluded. 'Not even to save yourself from pain.' Disappointment flashed briefly in those hollow eyes. 'A shame.' Then her expression hardened once more; the grip on his hair tightened, pulling his head back. 'Not that it will help you,' she whispered.

He shut his eyes this time, so that he didn't have to see the inhuman depths in hers. There was something in her so blindly ravenous that the mere thought of contact with her made his stomach tighten in dread. This wasn't just a hunger for vision, like Senzei had known, or even an obsession with power. It had gone beyond that — far beyond that — into realms so utterly corrupted that barely a fragment of her human soul remained, clinging to the flesh that housed it as if somehow the two could be reunited. Could mere hunger do that to a woman? Or would it take something more — some outside influence, that fed on the soul's dissolution? He thought of the obsidian figure standing beside her and wondered at its source. At their relationship.

Then: Her hunger enveloped him. Dark, unwholesome, utterly revolting – and focused, this time, in a way it hadn't been before. He felt her mental fingers prying at the edges of Tarrant's barrier, trying to Work it loose from his flesh. Though he didn't doubt the Hunter's skill, he knew that her tenacity went far beyond anything a sane mind might conjure – and he shivered to think of what would become of him if she managed to dismantle Tarrant's Warding before the fae-surge struck her.

Where's your earthquake, Hunter? He imagined all the things that might have gone wrong – Gerald Tarrant too weak to Work, the quake-wards too strong to be broken, some secondary defence system, hitherto unnoticed, coming into play – but nothing frightened him more than the simple fact that the earth might not move. Period. Even if all their planning had been perfect, even if Tarrant had succeeded in all he set out to do . . . the nature of seismic activity was random, and all the Workings in the world wouldn't make it otherwise. The odds had been in their favour, true – but what if odds weren't enough? What if the earth betrayed them, and took its sweet time in responding?

Then I'm dead, he thought darkly. Behind his back, his fingers played with the edges of his bracers. Thick leather, but soft; he unsnapped them. The Keeper's thoughts burrowed inside his mind – like so many worms – but her attention was fixed on Tarrant's Warding.

Keep Working, he begged her silently. *Just keep Working*. It seemed that time had slowed down for him, that something in the enemy's assault had altered his temporal functioning; he was aware of long minutes passing as he pushed at the forwards edge of his bracers, forcing the leather back through the ropes that bound his wrists. Buying himself additional slack, through that action. He told himself that he had to be ready, in case their plan failed. Had to be ready to free himself and move quickly. He tucked one thumb against his palm and tested his hand against his rope, seeing if he had gained enough slack to force his hand through. Coarse rope bit into his skin, but the fit was promising. One good jerk – and the loss of some skin – and he might be free. He gauged the distance between himself and the woman, reached out with his senses to Know the whereabouts of her servants – and then stopped himself, sickened by his carelessness, and forced himself not to Work. Not to Work at all. It seemed to him that hours had passed, that while he had been lost in the mechanics of bodily defence she had launched whole offensives against the structure of Tarrant's Warding. And still the earth hadn't moved. Had Tarrant managed to dispel the quake-wards, or was he still struggling with them? Was there still some hope that the adept might succeed, and trigger the surge they required?

And then she drew back from him, and the world spiraled out into her eyes. And he saw the anger there, and knew with dread certainty that she had sensed some hidden purpose in the barrier. Enough to stop her from Working.

Which meant that it was over. It was all over . . . and they had lost.

'I think,' she said coldly, 'we may try torture after all.'

He looked about himself, desperately, as his hands prepared to pull loose from their bonds. As he steeled himself to move, and move quickly, in a sudden bid for freedom. But then his eyes fell on the eastern wall, at the soft glow rising up from its base – and he flinched, as the meaning of that became clear. As the full measure of his vulnerability hit home.

Light. Grey light, rising in the east.

Dawn.

He was suddenly aware that the Dark Ones had left them, no doubt withdrawing to some protective recess deep within the earth. Tarrant was powerless now. If he hadn't broken the quake-wards yet, he wasn't going to. Not in time to help Damien. The priest's last hope had died with the night.

'What is it?' she demanded. Sensing that something was amiss with him, not knowing what. She turned towards the eastern wall, back to Damien. 'What new trick . . .' Her eyes grew hard, and he heard her mutter something; a key? He felt a Knowing taking shape around him, felt it working to squeeze the information out of him, examining his link to the dawn, to Tarrant—

And then it struck. He saw it, for an instant, through her eyes — for one terrible instant, in which the whole world was ablaze. Power surged through the crystalline walls, dashed against the mirrored steps, cycloned fiercely about them. Earth-fae fresh from the depths of Erna, hot as the magma that spawned it. She screamed as it struck her, screamed in terror as it blasted its way into her, its power filling and then bursting each cell in her brain.

He threw himself back. The distance somehow seemed to sever the contact between them, and the terrible vision was gone — but her screaming went on, rising in pitch to a fevered shriek as the earth-power poured through her. He tried not to listen as he jerked hard at his bonds, fighting to free himself. The coarse rope cut into him as he tried to force his hand through it, drawing blood — but with that lubrication, and a near-dislocation of his thumb, he managed to pull one hand free. Burning suns swam in his vision, an afterimage from the fae; he blinked as though that could cool their glare and tried to see past them to locate an exit. The shrieking numbed his brain, made it all but impossible to think clearly. How had he come in? He had no hope of finding a true exit from the citadel, not in time; his only chance lay in getting himself underground, and in hoping that the coming quake was merciful to whatever space housed him. With luck he could find his way back to the entrance tunnel — which would lead him down to the plains, and relative safety . . .

He grabbed his sword as he ran, sweeping it up from the crystalline floor — now spattered with blood and vomit, therefore visible. He didn't dare be unarmed, not now. Thank God mere steel was enough to dispatch the Dark Ones. He ran, trusting to blind instinct to guide him. Stumbling, as unseen steps trapped his feet, hitting one mirrored wall hard enough to shatter it. Where was the exit? Where was the passage down? He tried to remember all the turnings they had taken on the way in, tried to reason his way through the glassy labyrinth — and then he took his sword and slammed its pommel into an obstructing wall, hard. Crystal shivered into bits, revealing the dark mouth of a tunnel beyond. *Praise God*, he thought feverishly. *Please, let it be in time*. Bits of mirror crunched underfoot as he fought his way towards the entrance, slipping and sliding on the glassy fragments. And then the earthen wall was beside him, and his hand was upon it, and he was stumbling down into the depths—

And the earth convulsed, with force enough that he was thrown from his feet, headfirst into a hard dirt wall. Overhead the citadel tinkled, like a thousand wind chimes in a stormy sky – and then began to shatter, wall by wall, staircase by staircase, as the ground swelled up and broke beneath it. Huge chunks of crystal crashed to the earth behind him, sending fragments like spears down into the tunnel at his feet. Half-stunned, he forced himself to move again, to work his way down into the heart of the trembling earth. To his side, a wooden support snapped and came loose; chunks of rock and dirt hailed down on him as bits of crystal caromed into the depths. *Too close to the surface*, he thought, despairing. *Too close!* A shockwave threw him off his feet, and dirt rained down on him as he struggled to recover his balance. *Must get deeper . . .* He struggled on blindly, not pausing to consider whether greater depth would really mean safety – not stopping to question whether any place could be truly safe, in such an utter upheaval.

It should only last seconds. Shouldn't it? What were the parameters of a quake like this, that had been decades in the making?

The tunnel grew dark about him, dawn's dim light filtered through a rain of dirt and gravel that fell from its ceiling. He staggered down the length of it by feel, praying for enough time to save himself. But even as he did so he knew that if the quake had already begun, his time was just about up.

And then a support overhead broke loose, and swung down into him. It knocked him against the far wall, hard, leaving him stunned where he fell. The motion loosed a fresh avalanche of dirt and rock that rained on him as he struggled to right himself. All around him he could hear the tunnel collapsing, the roar of the earthquake as it raged through the planet's crust. His hand clenched tightly about his sword grip as he struggled to his feet – as if that weapon could somehow protect him from the fury of the earth itself – but then the ground beneath him spasmed furiously, and the whole of the ceiling gave way at last. Pounds upon pounds of dirt and rock poured down upon him, battering him into the ground. He tried to fight free, but the torrent of earth overwhelmed him. Gasping for breath, he choked on dirt – and as he struggled to clear his lungs, something large and sharp struck him hard on the head. Driving him down, deep down, into the suffocating depths of Nature's vengeance.

45

Light. Blinding. He shrank back from it – or tried to – but a strong hand had hold of him, long fingers entangled in his shirt. It jerked him up, forcing his mouth above the level of the earth. He gasped for breath, winced from the pain of the effort. Then his lungs spasmed suddenly, and he began to cough up the dirt that had filled them. Retching helplessly, as the strong hands continued to pull him out of his earth-bound tomb.

The light faded slowly to a mere star, to a tiny lamp flame. By its glow he could see that the tunnel was mostly gone, and what little that remained was filled with dust. Even while he watched, a fresh trickle of gravel began to course down from what remained of the ceiling.

'Can you move?' Tarrant asked.

His limbs felt numb, but they responded. He nodded.

'Then let's go. This place is death.'

The Hunter wrapped an arm about his shoulder – so cold, so very cold, who could ever have thought that the man's chill could be so comforting? – and with his help, Damien somehow managed to make his way to open space. He paused there for a minute, shivering.

'Close?' Tarrant asked softly.

'Too close,' he whispered. A wave of sudden weakness washed over him; he let the Hunter support him. 'Ciani,' he breathed. 'Where—'

'Right ahead of us. With Hesseth. No one's being left alone anymore till this is over.'

'Did she—' He was afraid to voice the words. Afraid of what a negative answer would mean. 'Is she—'

'Whole? Recovered?' He shook his head, grimly. 'Not yet. But this is just the beginning. If her assailant isn't killed in a cavern collapse, I'll hunt him down later. Now that his protector is dead, it should be easy enough.'

He looked up at him, sharply. 'You know that?'

'She fed on me,' he answered quietly. 'A channel like that works both ways, you know. Did you think I wouldn't drink in her terror when she died? She owed me that much.'

He struggled to get his feet firmly beneath him. 'Good meal, I hope.'

'Damned good meal,' the Hunter assured him. 'Let's move.'

Together they crept through the remains of the access tunnel, through passages made dangerously narrow by earthfall. At times they had to dig their way through, heaving aside rocks and mounds of earth to make enough room for a body to squeeze through.

'You came in this way?' Damien asked.

'It's still collapsing, if that's your question.' He grasped a fallen support beam and pulled; a narrow passage opened up to receive them. 'Somewhat less violently, further along. That's where the women are. – But I wouldn't like to be here when the next shock wave hits,' he added.

'I'm surprised it hasn't yet.'

The Hunter looked at him; there was a faint smile on his lips. 'That may be because I left some of the quakewards intact. I Worked them to kick in again after the first tremors ended. They won't hold long, of course, not without the rest of the series . . . but every minute counts.'

'You're very thorough.'

'I try to be.' He wiped dirt from his eyes with the back of a sleeve. Damien tried to do the same, and his hand came away from his face sticky with blood. The quantity of it unnerved him. 'Much further?'

The Hunter glanced at him. 'You'll make it.'

He thought of the dawn light he had seen from the citadel. How much time had passed since then? What kind of safety was there for his dark companion, if the sun had risen? 'What about you?'

He jerked loose a piece of splintered wood that blocked their path; dirt showered down in the narrow passageway. 'I'm strong enough, if that's the question.'

'I meant the sun.'

For a moment the Hunter was still. Damien thought he saw a muscle tense along his jaw, and the pale eyes narrowed. 'Let's deal with that problem when we get to it,' he said at last – and he heaved the broken timber from him, hard enough that it gouged the far wall.

'If you think—'

'Talk won't make the sun set,' he said sharply. 'And we're still far from getting out of here. Look.' He pointed to the far side of the passageway, to a hole that yawned in the far wall. 'Can you see it? In the currents. They're stirring, underground. The ones that survived the first shockwave will be coming to the surface, where they imagine things are safer. Idiots! If they knew their science, they'd stay where they are, where the surface waves can't reach—'

'You're afraid,' Damien said quietly.

The Hunter began to protest, then stopped himself. 'Of course I'm afraid,' he muttered. 'I'd be a fool if I weren't. Does that satisfy you?' He kicked loose a thick clod of earth, clearing the passage ahead of them. 'I suggest we get to the lady and Hesseth before our subterranean friends do – and worry about fear later. There'll be time for it, I assure you.'

He gave the lamp to Damien – his own sight didn't require it – and led the way eastward, through the ruins of their enemy's escape passage. As the tunnel cut deeper into the earth the damage seemed to be lessened, but it was still a struggle to make good time through the ravaged warren.

Periodically Tarrant would turn and look back, his eyes narrowed as he focused on the weak underground currents. But if he saw anything specific that disturbed him, he kept it to himself. Once, at the mouth of a narrow tunnel that led down to the Dark Ones' realm, he paused to listen – senses alert as a hunting animal's, nerves trigger-taut in tension – but he said nothing. His expression grim, he nodded eastward, urging the priest away from the citadel.

And then they came across the body. It was half-buried in dirt, as though in its fall it had loosed some new, private avalanche. Tarrant turned it over, brushed the dirt from its face – and breathed in sharply as the charred hole of a Fire-laden bolt became visible, right where one eye should be.

He looked up, lips drawn tight, and muttered, 'Come on.' And ran. In time they passed another body – this one's chest had a gaping hole, with fresh smoke rising from its Fire-seared edges – but they didn't stop to examine it. The smell of burning flesh was thick and sharp, doubly acrid in the tunnel's claustrophobic confines. They passed a turn where the earth had fallen, kicked a hurried path through loose clods of dirt that barred their way—

And found them. Springbolts in their hands, determination in their eyes. There were bodies here, too, and the scent of their blood was fresh. Tarrant had been right: the Dark Ones were surfacing.

Damien went to where Ciani stood – her back braced firmly against the wall, her hands gripped tightly about the weapon – and put one bruised arm around her. She softened, slightly, just enough to lean against him, barely enough to accept the reassuring gesture. Then she put her free arm around him, too, and squeezed.

'Thank the gods you're still alive,' she whispered.

He glanced back at the adept. 'Thank Tarrant, in this case.'

'We'd better move,' the Hunter warned them. He grabbed up a supply pack that had been left by Hesseth's feet, swung it to his back. 'And fast.'

'How much ammunition is left?' Damien asked the women.

'Plenty,' Hesseth responded. 'But only three with the Fire.' Her teeth were half-bared, as if in a dominance display. 'You think there'll be more of them?'

'I think there's no doubt of it,' Tarrant assured her. 'The only question is how fast they'll come.'

'He hasn't died yet,' Ciani whispered. 'I would know that . . . wouldn't I?'

My God, will you know it. The memories will smash into you like a tidal wave – like the surge of fae that killed your enemy. The experience of an entire lifetime, reabsorbed in an instant. He hated himself for dreading that moment. Hated himself for wondering, with steel-edged calculation, whether that moment might not be the most dangerous of all.

They ran. And they were not alone. Close behind them, back the way they had come, something else was moving through the tunnels. Something that chittered in half-human speech, as it followed the path they had cleared. One demon – or many? With a sudden start Damien realized that his sword was still buried near the citadel, the rest of his weapons inside it. All he had left was the flask of Fire – if that was still intact – and he couldn't draw that out without burning Tarrant. Still, if Tarrant could survive it, and if it could drive back their enemies . . . he fingered the flap of the pouch as he ran, made sure that it was free to open. Tarrant would understand. Strategy demanded it. *Survival* might demand it.

And then they came around a turn, and there were the Dark Ones. A good four of them at least, and perhaps more in the shadows beyond. They were bruised and bleeding, and more than a little disoriented – but their eyes blazed with hatred, and hunger, and their nostrils flared as they caught the scent of human fear. Of food.

'Don't let them touch you,' Hesseth whispered. A tremor of fear was in her voice; was she remembering when she'd been drained, back at the earthfire? Damien stepped to Ciani's side and took the springbolt from her. 'Get back,' he whispered. Out of the corner of his eye he saw Tarrant reach out to her – for a moment he was lost in Morgot again, as the tidal power Hesseth had conjured dissolved all their barriers, and set loose the Hunter's evil – and then he nodded, and gestured for her to go to him, knowing that there was no place where she would be safer than by the adept's side.

And then the creatures fell upon them. Mindless as animals gone rabid, and ten times as deadly. He brought one down with a shot to the gut, fired point-blank into the demonic flesh. And then cursed himself as he brought the second bolt into line, for failing to ask which one of the weapons had only one Worked bolt in it.

And then one was upon him, and his weapon was still uncocked – so he brought the brass butt up into its face, hard, cursing it as he did so. There was blood, and the sharp crack of bone splitting, but the blow did nothing to slow the creature down. One clawed hand grasped the barrel of the springbolt, another grabbed at

Damien's arm. He tried to throw the creature off, but a strange numbness had invaded his arm; he found it hard to move. Shadows began to fill his mind, and his thoughts were slow in coming. He needed to fight it. Didn't he? He needed to drive it back from him, before it . . . what? What would it do? He found himself shaking as the numbness claimed more of his flesh, found himself filled with a dread and a fear that was all the more terrible because he couldn't remember its cause.

—And then the Dark One howled, and fell back. In its chest was a smoking hole, where the point of a Fireladen bolt had pierced through the flesh. Hesseth was ready behind it, her blade poised as if to decapitate the creature, but the Fire made that unnecessary. With a last desperate cry, the Dark One fell – and memories flooded Damien's brain like some wild dream, a thousand and one disjointed bits pouring into him with nightmare intensity. He staggered, trying to absorb the onslaught. Trying to brace himself for further battle, even as he reclaimed his humanity. But beside him the cold blue light of Tarrant's sword filled the tunnel, and he could see by its glow that an icy path had been etched through the flesh of two of their assailants. Carmine crystals glittered where the great veins had been severed, and a frosty steam arose from the newly chilled flesh.

'Let's go—' Damien began, but Tarrant ordered, 'Wait.'

He walked several yards down the tunnel, back the way they had come. And studied the ceiling overhead as if searching for something. After a minute had passed he seemed to find it, and he raised up his sword so that the glowing tip brushed the packed earth overhead. And then thrust up, suddenly. Chunks of dirt burst outward from the point of contact in an explosion that echoed down the length of the tunnel. And when the dust cleared, they could see that passageway behind them was filled. There might be Dark Ones still ahead of them, but none would be coming from behind. Not without a digging crew.

The Hunter resheathed his sword. 'Now we go,' he whispered. His posture was tense, in a way that Damien had never seen before. Had the enemy touched him, as well? Or was it just that the odds against them were growing, too swiftly for the adept's liking?

If he's afraid of them, Damien thought grimly, *what does that mean for the rest of us?*

They passed other openings that offered access to the lower regions. Half of them were already filled with rubble, rendering them useless to the Dark Ones. The other ones they left alone. There were simply too many, and each one that Tarrant chose to seal meant another delay, another chance that their enemies would get ahead of them . . . Damien caught sight of the adept's expression as they passed by a particularly large opening, and it was utterly colourless and grim. And he remembered the sunlight that awaited them all, if they ever did reach the end of this passage, and wondered what the man could do to save himself. Was it safe for him to stay down here until sunset? With so many Dark Ones coming to the surface, half-mad with rage and hunger?

I won't let him do it alone, Damien thought darkly. Remembering the hands that had pulled him from the earth, which might just as easily have left him there. Feeling a loyalty which might have shamed him, in another time and place, but which now felt as natural as breathing.

'They're coming,' Tarrant whispered, and he turned to look behind them. There was nobody visible there, not yet, but Damien knew enough to trust the man's senses. He was about to speak when Ciani cried out, sharply – and the look on her face was one of such abject terror, such utter despair, that Damien's blood chilled as he recognized what the cause must be.

'He's there,' the Hunter said. Giving voice to her fear. 'He's coming.'

'Is he aware of us?' Damien asked him.

The pale eyes narrowed as Tarrant studied the fae. 'Not yet,' he whispered. 'But he will be soon.' He listened for a moment longer, then added, 'There are many of them together. Too many to fight.'

'Then we move,' Damien told him. 'The entrance can't be much further. If we can make it out before they get to us—'

He stopped. Met the pale eyes squarely. 'Then Ciani can be safe in the sunlight,' he concluded, 'while you and I deal with her assailant.'

They had just started to move again when it seemed, for an

instant, that the earth trembled beneath them. Damien felt his heart skip a beat, and he prayed wildly, *Not now. Please! Just a few minutes more*. As if his God might really interfere. As if the guiding force of the universe was concerned with a handful of human Wardings, or the lives that might depend on them.

They ran. The walls and ceiling of the earthbound passage began to rain down fresh dirt on their heads, but they shielded their eyes with their hands and continued onward. Knowing how close they must be to the tunnel's eastern exit, knowing how close that exit was to the relative safety of the plains, they pressed on – through dirt-fall, over rock-strewn drifts, across huge heaps of splintered wood and boulders – they scrambled over obstacles as quickly as they could, not daring to take the time to study their surroundings. Again the earth trembled, and this time a dull roar could be heard. 'They're going,' Tarrant muttered, and Damien whispered, 'God help us all.' The tunnel seemed at least twice as long in this direction as it had been when Damien first entered it; where the hell was that exit?

And then the worst of it struck. Not nearly as violent as its predecessor – but such violence was no longer necessary. The supporting structure of the tunnel had already been weakened, and its walls were riddled with gaping holes. It didn't take much to shake loose what was left, so that the remaining ceiling fell in huge chunks behind them, on top of them, directly in their path. Damien threw himself at Ciani just as a massive shard of stone hurtled down from the ceiling above her; he managed to roll them both out of its path, barely in time. Gravel pelted them, and earth that had been packed to a bricklike consistency. He sheltered Ciani with his body and prayed that the other two were all right. And that their enemies weren't. Wouldn't that be convenient, if the earth itself swallowed up Ciani's assailant?

But when he finally raised himself up from where he lay, and looked at her, he knew that they'd had no such luck. Her face betrayed none of the joy – or the disorientation – that returning memories would have brought.

He felt sharp nails bite into his shoulder, heard Hesseth hiss softly. 'I think you'd better look at this,' the rakh-woman told him. She nodded towards the east, down to where the tunnel turned. He paused for a second to make sure the tremors had ceased – they had – and then got to his feet and followed her. The space remaining was barely large enough to admit him, and his shoulder pressed against damp earth as he forced his way through. To where the passageway turned, just prior to its ascension . . .

It was filled. Completely. The weight of the earth had collapsed a whole segment of the tunnel, rendering it impassable. Damien felt despair bite into him, hard, as he regarded the solid mound before him. They might dig through it, given enough time and the right tools . . . but they had neither, and there was no telling how far the blockage went. If the whole tunnel between here and the surface had caved in ahead of them, then there was simply no way to get through it. No way at all.

He made his way back to the others and prepared to tell them the bad news – and then saw that it wasn't necessary. Tarrant had read the truth in the currents, and Ciani's eyes were bright with despair. The single lantern which remained to them shed just enough light to show him that her hands were trembling.

'We're stuck,' he muttered.

'Can we dig out?' Ciani's voice was a whisper, hoarse and fragile. 'Dig up, I mean.'

Damien glanced at the ceiling. And then at Tarrant.

'We're near the surface,' he said quietly. 'I can hear the solar fae as it strikes the earth. Can almost feel it . . .' He paused, and then Damien thought he saw him shiver. 'If the earth above is soft enough to dig, but solid enough not to bury us when we begin to disturb it . . . it would still take time,' he said. 'A lot of time.' He looked back the way they had come. 'I'm not sure we have that,' he said tensely.

Damien listened – and it seemed to him that he could hear a scrabbling in the distance, like rodents. 'They survived.'

'Enough of them,' the Hunter said grimly. 'More than we can handle, without using the earth-fae.'

Damien glanced at Hesseth, but she shook her head. Whatever combination of tides she required in order to Work simply wasn't available now. It might be, in the future . . . if they lasted that long. If there was any future for them.

Louder, now; the sounds were approaching. Damien heard voices among them, hissing human phonemes. He looked about desperately, trying to think of some way out, or some new way in which they could defend themselves – but there was nothing. They were trapped. Even if they could fight off the Dark Ones for a time, they were still too close to the surface; the next quake would bury them.

And then the Hunter turned away from them. And put one hand up against the dirt at his side, as though he required its support.

'There is a way,' he whispered hoarsely. 'One way only, that I can think of. It would save the lady.'

The voices were getting louder. Damien came close to where the adept stood so that they might talk quietly. 'Tell me.'

Tarrant looked up at the ceiling, as if searching for some sort of sign. It occurred to Damien with a start that this was how he had searched before, in the moments before he brought down a whole section of the tunnel.

'I could blast a way out,' the Hunter muttered. 'There's enough tamed fae in the sword that I could do it, without having to use the currents. Only . . .'

'The sunlight,' Damien said softly.

Tarrant turned away again.

'You can't,' Ciani whispered. 'Gerald . . .'

'I appreciate your concern,' the adept breathed, 'but there's no real alternative. Other than dying here beneath the earth, our souls gone to feed those . . . *creatures*.' He shook his head, stiffly. 'Even I can't Work an adequate defence, without the earth-fae to draw on. There are so many of them, and we have so few weapons left . . . it would only be a matter of time.'

'Until nightfall?' Damien asked.

The Hunter shook his head, grimly. 'Not that long, I regret.' He turned to Ciani. 'This would free you,' he whispered. 'I could open this part of the passage to the sunlight, and if your assailant was here at the time . . . it would free you.'

'And you?' Damien asked. 'Could you survive it?'

He hesitated. 'Probably not. Sunlight is relative, of course; I've stood in the light of three moons, and beneath a galaxy of stars . . .

but this is different.' A tremor seemed to pass through his flesh. Damien recalled the fire underground, and what it had done to him. If a mere earthly blaze could wreak that kind of damage, what chance would the Hunter have when facing the sun itself?

Then: 'I see no other way,' he said grimly. And he drew the cold-fire sword from its sheath.

The voices were coming closer now. Ciani moved to his side, reached out as if to touch him – and then drew back, trembling. 'Gerald.'

'Lady Ciani.' He caught up her hand in his free one and touched it quickly to his lips. If she had any sort of negative response to the chill of his flesh, Damien didn't see it. 'I owe you a debt of honour. I've risked much to fulfil it. If this succeeds, and your memory is restored—'

'Then I would say your honour is satisfied,' she whispered. 'And I free you from any further obligation.'

He let go of her hand. And bowed. 'Thank you, lady.'

'If you can find shelter—' Damien began.

'There'll be no shelter when I'm done.' He gestured for them to move back, clearing the space nearest to him. And studied the ceiling again, looking for a workable fault. 'You'll have to move quickly. Gain the surface as fast as you can, and then get away from here. Fast. You don't know how long those *things* will take to die, or what damage they might do to you in their death-throes. The best defence is distance. Don't even pause to look back,' he warned them – and Damien wondered if his concern was for their lives, or that they might see the Hunter burning.

'Now,' he hissed. 'Get ready.'

The voices were approaching. Damien stood back, and gathered Ciani to him. Hesseth pressed close by his other side, springbolt at the ready. He began to shield his eyes – and saw Tarrant's pale gaze fixed on him.

'Good luck, Hunter,' he said quietly.

And they came. Climbing over the mounds of earth like over-sized rodents, inhuman eyes blazing with hunger. The first one saw them there and pulled up, hissing a sharp warning to its fellows. Then they came into the lamplight as well, swarming about him like hungry insects, filling the far end of the tunnel. Wary, because Tarrant's sword was drawn and they clearly sensed its power.

And then one of them fixed its eyes on Ciani and hissed softly, in pleasure. A sharp tongue tip stroked the points of its teeth, and Damien knew by the tremor that ran through her that this was the one, the demon who attacked her in Jaggonath. The one who contained her memories.

'*Now*,' the Hunter whispered.

The demons began to move.

He thrust. Up into the earth, deep into the fault he had located. The force of the coldfire-bound steel took root and expanded, exploding outward with all the force of a bomb. Dirt bits slammed into Damien and his companions, and the force of the compression struck them like a fist. For a moment there was nothing but a hailing of dirt and rocks, like shrapnel. And then: light. Blinding. The brilliance of the morning sun, to eyes that had spent days in darkness. He threw up his arm across his eyes, as the pain of it seared his vision. The whole world was white, formless, utterly blinding . . . he forced his arm down, remembered Tarrant's last warning. *Get away from here. Fast*. Against the glare of sunlight he could barely make out shapes, now, hot white against the hotter white of the morning sky. He clambered towards one of them, felt a newly-formed wall of earth take shape beneath his fingertips. He pulled Ciani over to it and guided Hesseth to follow. 'Climb!' he whispered fiercely. He could barely see the ground beneath him, but trusted his hands to guide him. The earth here sloped back in smoothly curved walls, like that of a meteoric crater; he tried not to think of Tarrant as he struggled up that slope, as he tried to gain solid purchase in the shifting, inconstant earth, helping the others to climb along with him——

Ciani screamed. It was a sound of pain and terror combined, so utterly chilling in its tenor that for a moment Damien froze, stunned by the sound. Then he saw her slipping as her body convulsed, and he grabbed out for her. Caught her by the sleeve of her shirt, and tried to keep her from sliding back down to the tunnel below.

'Can't,' she gasped. 'Gods, I can't—'

'Help me!' he cried – and Hesseth reached out from the other side, grabbing Ciani's arm. Together they held their ground as she shivered from the onslaught of her own forgotten memories, all the pain and fear of a lifetime compressed into one burning instant. Her skin was hot to the touch, but that might have been because of the sun. After weeks among the nonhuman and the semi-human, wounded and tired in cold, dark tunnels, Damien would be hard pressed to remember what normal body temperature felt like.

They began to drag her upward. Slowly. Afraid to move on the treacherous slope, but even more afraid to stay where they were. That Ciani's assailant was now dead was all but certain. But how many others remained, who might find a short climb into sunlight an acceptable price for revenge? Inch by inch, carefully, the two of them worked their way up the earthen slope. Beneath them clods of earth broke loose and tumbled down into the crater's depths. They fought not to tumble down with them. The slope grew steeper, and Damien had to drive his hands deep into the soil to get the support he needed. Ciani moaned softly, utterly limp beneath his grasp, and he could only hope that the climb was doing her no damage. He reached into the crumbling earth, and caught hold of something solid at last. A root. He looked up, and against the glare of the sun he could make out the form of trees, not far above them. With a prayer of thanksgiving on his lips he grabbed at the firm root, and used it to pull himself up the slope. Hesseth, on the other side of Ciani, saw what he was doing and followed suit. The soft earth gave way to a tangle of vegetation, gave way to the underearth limbs of mature trees . . .

And they were over. All three of them. Damien lay gasping on the ground for a moment, his legs still resting on the edge of Tarrant's crater. Then, with effort, he forced himself to his feet. Ciani was utterly still, but the look on her face was one of peace; lowering his head to her chest, he could hear her measured breathing. He lifted her up into his arms, gently, and murmured, 'She's all right.' Cradling her, as one might a child. 'She's going to be all right.'

And the winter chill was nothing to them as they staggered away from the site of their recent trials. Because the sunlight was streaming down on them, and that was life itself.

The series of earthquakes which Tarrant had triggered continued for nearly three days, but none were as violent as those first few had been. Trees had been torn down, mountains reshaped, whole cavern systems refigured – but in the end the land survived, and that was all that really mattered.

They camped on the plains, on open ground, until the worst of the aftershocks had ended. Only then did Damien dare to climb back up, to that place where they had so recently escaped from the earth's confines. The landmarks had all changed, and massive rock-slides made climbing all but impossible . . . but in the end he found it, a circle of land devoid of trees, where the ground sloped down in a gentle arena of freshly-turned earth.

It had been filled in, almost to the brim. The repeated tremors must have done it, shaking the broken earth until it sought its own level, like water. Whatever Tarrant had done to the demons – and to himself – it was buried forever in the mountainside, along with the remains of his body.

He tried not to think of what that burning must have been like, as he knelt in the soft earth to pray. Tried not to remember the Hunter's charred flesh as it had been in his hands, as he softly intoned the Prayer for the Dead. Pleading mercy for a soul that had never earned mercy, for a man who had so committed himself to hell that a thousand prayers a day, offered up for a thousand years, would not negate one instant of his suffering.

'Rest in peace, Prophet,' he whispered.

He hoped that someday it would be possible.

46

Winter had come early to the plains – but it was nothing compared to the frigid abuse of autumn in the mountains, and Damien was grateful for it. After nearly two hundred miles of travel it was good to be clean again and in fresh clothes, and knowing that he and

Ciani were safe was a luxury he had begun to despair of ever experiencing. And if she had changed somewhat, if she was no longer the woman he had known . . . hadn't he seen that coming, in the last few days? Hadn't he seen it building in her, all the way back from the eastern range?

That doesn't help, he told himself, bitterly. *It doesn't help at all.*

He looked towards the centre of the rakhene camp, where even now a celebration was taking place. The night was dark, almost moonless, but the jubilant rakh had set it alight with over a hundred torches, and their triumphal bonfire blazed like a sun in miniature from the centre of their camp. And *she* danced among them – not like one of them, exactly, but not like a human woman, either. An adept who had chosen to suspend herself between two worlds, so that she might bridge the gap between them. A loremaster. He turned away, remembering the word. Resenting it. And hating himself, for the unfairness of his reaction.

She was never really yours. You never really knew her.

It didn't help. Not a bit. But then, cold reason never did.

He felt restless. Confined, by the nearness of so many tents. So many rakh. The ranks of Hesseth's tribe had been swelled by numerous visitors who had come to hear the tales and see the relics and gaze in fascination upon the hated, fearsome humans. He sensed power games going on all about him, on levels too complex for him to interpret, as tribes who normally avoided each other tried to sort themselves out into a new, all-inclusive order. *Human society*, he thought. *We've planted the seeds.* In time there would be nations, and treaties, and all the ills that came of such things . . . he didn't know whether to feel glad or guilty, but he suspected the latter was more appropriate. God willing the Canopy would remain intact so that the rakh could make their own fate, in peace, before having to deal with humankind again. God willing.

Slowly, he turned from the camp. It was cold outside, but the heavy garments which the rakh had made for him were more than sufficient to ward off the wintry chill. He tucked his hands into his pockets and began to walk eastward, away from the starkly lit celebration. The noise of rakhene chanting faded behind him, as well as the occasional burst of human laughter that sparkled in its midst.

Her laughter. He pulled his jacket tightly about him and increased his pace. The trampled earth of the rakhene encampment gave way to half-frozen slush, which in turn gave way to snow: pristine, unsullied, a glistening white blanket that draped over the plains like the softest wool, cushioning the land in silence.

He walked. Away from the camp, from the noise. Away from all signs of life, and all protestations of joy. He had put in one hard night's celebration, and now he was ready to move again. Restless, as always. To the west of him the Worldsend Mountains loomed, sterile and foreboding. He knew that all its passes were frozen by now, would remain frozen for months to come, and that its slopes were ripe with avalanches in the making, and a thousand other hazards of winter. He would never have risked such a route in this season, not with others by his side – but he might do so alone. Now that Senzei had found his peace, and Ciani had found . . . other things.

And then a movement caught his eye, back the way he had come. And he turned, to see who had followed him from the camp, what rakhene business would disturb his solitude.

When he saw, he froze.

The figure stood with the moon to its back, so that all of its front was in shadow. Thick fabric fell from its shoulders, enveloping it like a cloak, rendering its form doubly invisible. Its face was no more than an oval of blackness, its body an amorphous shadow. But there was no mistaking its shape. Or its identity.

'I see that the lady is well,' the Hunter whispered.

Relief surged up inside him – and moral revulsion also, as fresh within him as the day on which he'd learned the Hunter's name. The force of the admixture was stunning, and it rendered him utterly speechless. He was grateful that he had no weapon on him – glad that he was thus spared the trauma of having to sort out his feelings, having to decide whether or not this was an appropriate moment to remind the Hunter of their natural enmity.

At last he found his voice. 'You survived. The sunlight . . .'

'It's all a question of degree, Reverend Vryce, as I told you. Fortunately, the Dark Ones lack such sophistication. Since they had no knowledge of any other option, they died.' His voice was a mere breath, hardly louder than the breezes of the night. It seemed also to be coarser than usual — but it was so hard to hear him at all that Damien couldn't be certain of that. 'I thought you would want to know that I lived. I thought you had that right.'

'Thank you. I'm . . . glad.'

'That I survived?' he asked dryly.

'That you didn't die . . . like that.' He meant it sincerely and knew that could be heard in his voice. 'I intended . . . something cleaner.'

'So you'll still be coming after me when you leave the rakhlands. I regret that, priest. There's a quality in you that I would hate to destroy. A certain . . . recklessness?'

'But you'll manage it anyway.'

'If you try to kill me? With relish.'

'Then I'm sorry to ruin your sport,' he said, 'but I'm afraid you're going to have to wait for that particular pleasure.' He watched the dark figure carefully as he spoke, wondering what it was about it that seemed so strained, so very . . . *wrong*. 'I'm going east.'

The voice was a whisper, no louder than the wind. 'East is the ocean. Novatlantis. The deathlands.'

'And more than that, I'm afraid.' He nodded towards the camp; its fires were invisible in the distance. 'The Lost Ones returned, you know. The males, that is. I think the risk appealed to them. They're cleaning out the last of the Keeper's warren, braving rock falls and tunnel collapse in order to hunt down her servants. For food, they told me. The last of the Dark Ones will be their winter sustenance.'

'That's impossible,' the cloaked figure muttered. 'Demonic flesh wouldn't be—'

'It isn't demonic flesh,' the priest said quietly. 'Because the Dark Ones aren't constructs.' He looked east: towards the mountains, towards the fallen citadel. 'Hesseth found a body. We examined it. We thought we could determine what sort of construct it was, maybe find out how it had come into being . . . only it wasn't a construct at all. Hesseth was the first to suspect it, and Ciani confirmed it. The truth.' He drew in a deep breath, remembering that moment. Reliving it, as he spoke. 'It was rakh,' he told Tarrant. His own voice little more than a whisper. 'The Dark Ones are rakh.'

For a moment, Tarrant's form was utterly still; Damien imagined he could hear the man's thoughts racing, aligning fact with fact like the pieces of some vast puzzle. 'Not possible,' he said at last. 'That would mean—'

'Someone – or something – has been evolving them. Like you did to the Forest, Hunter. Only this time on a grander scale. This time with high-order intelligence.' He felt the tightness growing inside him again, the same restless tension he had felt when the truth first became apparent. His hands in his pockets tightened into fists. 'Nature couldn't do it. Nature *wouldn't*. Take a tribe of intelligent, adaptable creatures, and bind them to the night like that? Suppress their own vitality, so that they could only live by torturing others? Those Dark Ones *died* when you exposed them, Hunter – and you didn't. You, who've spent a thousand years avoiding the sun – whose very existence depends upon constant darkness – *you survived*. Why would Erna imbue one of her creatures with such a terrible weakness? What point could it possibly serve?'

'You think someone's done it,' he whispered. 'Deliberately.'

'There's no question in my mind,' he said grimly. 'And it would have to be on a massive scale, to succeed like that – the corruption of a whole environment. There's nothing like that in the human lands. Remember what the rakh-girl said? *They came from the east.*'

'So you're going after them.'

'Five expeditions have tried to cross that ocean. Two in your own age, three in the centuries after. None were ever heard from again. But that doesn't mean that they failed, does it? For all we know, humankind managed to populate those regions . . . and gave birth to something which has warped the very patterns of Nature. I think that what we saw here . . . that's just the tip of the iceberg. I think we need to know what the hell is going on over there before something far worse comes over.' He looked at the dark figure before him, and felt something stir in him that was not quite revulsion. Not wholly abhorrence.

'Come with me,' he whispered. 'Come east with me.'

The figure stiffened. 'Are you serious? Do you know what you're asking?'

'A chance to strike at your real enemy. The one behind all this; the force responsible. Doesn't that appeal to you?'

'In the past few weeks,' Tarrant said darkly, 'I have been bound, humiliated, starved, burned, blasted with sunlight, tortured in ways I will not describe, and nearly killed on several occasions. I, who have spent the last five hundred years building myself a safe refuge from such threats! Are you suggesting that I should court such disasters again? Truly, I shouldn't have taken so much of your blood,' the dark figure mused. 'The shortage clearly affected your brain.'

'You have no curiosity? Or even . . . hunger for vengeance?'

'What I have, Reverend Vryce, is a haven of absolute safety. A domain that I have built for myself, stone by stone, tree by tree, until the land itself exists only to indulge my pleasure. Should I give that up? Commit myself to the eastern ocean, with all the risk that entails? I'm amazed you want me with you in the first place.'

'Your power's unquestionable. Your insight—'

'And it would keep me out of trouble, eh? For as long as I was with you, there would be no hunting in the Forest. No innocent women suffering for my pleasure. Isn't that part of it? Isn't that how your conscience would deal with the fact of my continued existence, when you've sworn on your honour to kill me?'

Despite himself, Damien smiled. 'It has its appeal.'

'Let me tell you what that ocean means, to my kind. Thousands upon thousands of miles of open water, too deep for the earth-fae to penetrate. Do you understand? The very force that keeps me alive, that I require for most of my Workings, would be inaccessible. Which means I couldn't help you, or myself, if anything happened. One good eruption out of Novatlantis when we're in that region and no power of mine or yours could do anything to save us. Why do you think no one crosses that water? Why do you think it was only attempted five times, in all the years that man has been here? *And*, I would be all but helpless. At your mercy. Do you think that appeals to me? Such vulnerability is unthinkable, for one of my kind.'

'I gave you my word before. You know I was good for it. Try me,' he dared him.

The figure stared at him in silence for a moment; unable to see the Hunter's expression, Damien was unable to read its cause.

'I thought you travelled alone,' Tarrant said at last.

'Yes. Well.' He looked back towards the camp. 'Hesseth's going. She insisted. You should have seen her when we learned the truth, when she realized that her own species was being corrupted . . .'

'And the lady Ciani?'

His expression tightened; it took him a moment to find the proper words. 'This is her life's work,' he told the Hunter. 'The rakhlands. Their culture. I didn't know that before because she didn't have the memory . . . but then, I didn't know so much about her.'

For a moment there was silence, then: 'I'm sorry,' the figure said softly.

He forced a shrug. 'It was good while it lasted. That's the most you can ask for, isn't it?' He forced his hands to unclench inside his pockets. Forced his voice to be steady. 'We're from two different worlds, she and I. Sometimes you forget that. Sometimes you pretend it doesn't matter. But it's always there.' He looked up at the figure, towards where his face would be. Like all of him, it was sheathed in darkness. 'There's something growing in the east,' he said. 'Something very powerful, and very evil. Something that's had both the time and the patience to rework the very patterns of this planet, until Nature was forced to respond to it. Don't you want to know what that is? Don't you want to make it pay for what it did to you?'

'Set evil against evil, is that it? In the hope that they might destroy each other.'

'You were the one who recommended that. Or don't you remember?'

'I was very young, then. Inexperienced. Naive.'

'You were the voice of my faith.'

'Past tense, Reverend Vryce. Things have changed. *I* have changed.' The figure stepped back, breathing in sharply as it did so. In pain? 'Years ago, I decided that I would sacrifice anything and everything in the name of survival. My blood. My kin. My humanity. Should I render all that meaningless now, by courting death at this late age? I think not.'

Damien shrugged. 'We'll be leaving from Faraday if you change your mind. In late March or April, probably; it will take at least that long to work out the practical details. I'll save you a private berth,' he promised. 'With no windows, and a lock on the door.'

For a long moment, the dark figure just stared at him. Though the silver eyes were lost in shadow, Damien could feel them fixed on him.

'What makes you think you know me so well?' the Hunter asked hoarsely. 'What makes you think you can anticipate me, in ways that go against my nature?'

'I know who you were,' Damien answered. 'I know what that man stood for. And I'm willing to bet that somewhere in the heart of that malignant thing you call a soul is a spark of what that man was – and the boundless curiosity that drove him. I think your hunger to know is every bit as great as your hunger for life, Neocount. I'm offering you knowledge – as well as vengeance. Are you telling me that combination has no appeal?'

The figure lifted one arm, so that the folds of his cloak fell free of it. 'Appeal or no,' he whispered. 'The price is too high.'

Moonlight shimmered on the wetness of bloody flesh, on muscle and veins stripped bare by the force of the sun's assault. Sharp bone edges poked through strands of shrunken flesh, their tips charred black by fire and crusted with dried blood. The fingers were no more than seared bits of meat, strung together along the slender phalanges like some macabre shish kebob. If a scrap of silk or wool adhered to that flesh, or any other bit of clothing, it had been so torn and so bloodied that it was now indistinguishable from the man's own tissue.

'Enough is enough,' the Hunter whispered. The arm dropped down, and the cloak fell to cover it. The voice echoed with pain, and with the soft gurgle of blood. 'The answer is no, Reverend Vryce. And it will stay no, through all the years that you remain alive.' He gestured towards the distant camp, across the field of spotless snow. 'You may consider the life of these tribes my parting gift, if you like – I had once sworn to kill them all, for their audacity in binding me.'

'A few less souls to darken my conscience?' he asked sharply.

'Exactly.'

The Hunter bowed. And the effort that it took was so apparent, his pain throughout the motion so obvious, that Damien winced to see it. How many muscles had been burned to ragged strands, that a man would require for such a gesture? How much blood was being made to flow, for that last show of elegance?

'Good luck, Reverend Vryce,' the Hunter whispered. 'I suspect you'll need it.'

EPILOGUE

Deep in the bowels of night's keep, in a chamber reserved for the Lord of the Forest, a figure lay still atop a numarble table. There, where the sun would never shine its baleful light, where earthquakes had never yet disturbed the carefully warded walls, the body of the Hunter lay immersed in dark fae, purple power clinging to his death-pale skin. Utterly cold. Utterly lifeless. Silk robes spilled over the sides of the polished table like a waterfall frozen in motion, their contours hinting at the items that lay beneath. For if this castle was a duplicate of Merentha's citadel in every other regard, so was its underground workroom a dark reflection of the Neocount's original – and the straps which had bound Almea Tarrant in her dying adorned the polished worktable like some macabre ornament, now parted to receive the Hunter's body.

Power: not weakened by sunlight – or even moonlight – and not compromised by the presence of some local primitive mind. Pure power, deep and swift-working – a death-hungry power, that had been building in these caverns for longer than man could remember. It gathered around him like a blanket – a shroud – a barrier against life – and any observer would be hard pressed to say whether the flesh thus protected was cradled in the true chill of death, or in some macabre facsimile.

In that place where no sound had been heard for so many days, footsteps now resounded. Soft and measured, slowly approaching. There was a rattle at the door as the great lock was opened, then the slow creak of steel hinges overweighed by the mass of their burden. Fae-light shimmered on an albino's brow, purple light reflecting bright magenta in the pigment-free depths of his eyes. He regarded the figure that lay before him, then bowed, ever so slightly. And reached out a tendril of his own dark will, to touch the currents that guarded that motionless form.

For a moment, nothing happened. Then, with infinite slowness, the pale eyelids opened. The dark fae parted as the Lord of the Forest spread his fingers, flexing his hands into motion once more. Stretching his arms, like-wise. After a moment he levered himself to a sitting position – and though he winced as though in pain while doing so, it was clear from his movements that the worst of the sun-spawned damage had been repaired.

'Forgive me,' the albino said. 'I know you didn't want to be disturbed—'

'How long has it been?'

'Nearly a long month, Excellency.'

'So long.' He closed his eyes and drew in a deep breath slowly, as if savouring the air. 'You wouldn't bother me without a reason, Amoril, I know that. What is it?'

'You have a petitioner, my lord.'

The pale eyes shot open. Their depths sparkled violet in the fae-light. 'Indeed? What manner of petitioner?'

'A demon, Excellency. High-order, if I read him right. He said that you would know him, and respect his business. He gave his name as Calesta.'

For a moment there was silence. Then the Hunter said, softly, 'I know him. And I think I know his business, as well.'

'Is he the one you fought, in the rakhlands?'

He swung his legs over the side of the table, and tested their strength against the floor. 'He was a symbiote of the one that I fought. And that kind can't last long, without some kind of human partner.' He chuckled softly. 'I'm surprised I still rate that designation.'

'Partner?'

'Human.'

'You think he wants to link himself to you.'

'Let's say I consider it possible.'

'After what he did?'

'Demons aren't whole people, Amoril. Like animals they know only blind hunger and a channel to the hand that feeds them. And the desire to survive, as passionate as anything humans might experience.' He eased himself onto his feet, until he was standing free of any support. 'Calesta's symbiote is dead. His enemy lives. It's to his advantage to placate that power which might still destroy him – and perhaps even court it. Demons rank themselves according to such alliances.'

'And would you ally with him?'

The Hunter's expression grew dark. 'I haven't forgotten what he did to me. But we're in my realm now, playing by my rules. Let's see how well he adapts to that, shall we?' He brushed at the silk of his shirt sleeve, binding enough dark fae to smooth out the wrinkles. 'Have him come to the audience chamber, and await me there.' And he warned, 'I may leave him waiting some time.'

The albino bowed. 'Excellency.'

Darkness. Absolute. He let it fill his eyes and his heart for a moment, let it seep deep into his soul to where the sun-born wounds still throbbed. And then he let himself See, and Hear, and breathe in the power of the Forest. A symphony of power rising up out of the earth, all dark and cold and rich with his signature. *So beautiful*, he thought. *So very beautiful*. He felt the presence of the trees that dwelled there, remade to serve his special need; the predators that stirred above and below the earth, responsive to his will; the blood-filled life that hovered at the edges of his domain, all restlessness and greed and human recklessness. Their nearness awakened a hunger in him so intense that for a minute it seemed the whole Forest was filled with their blood, and all its air was ripe with the smell of their fear. And the music of their mortality, almost painful in its intensity.

How long ago had it been since last he'd hunted? He ached for the sweet taste of a woman's terror, for the boundless pleasure of hunting in a land where all life responded to his will – where the land itself could be reshaped, if he so desired it, to force his prey back upon her own path, into his waiting arms . . . he shivered in hunger, just thinking of it. Too many days. Too many nights of rakhene fear and disembodied blood and a need so powerful that it had nearly overwhelmed him. Now there was no need for him to deny himself. Now he could choose his prey and set her loose in these woods, and feed as his nature demanded. Wash his soul clean with killing, until the taint of his contact with humankind was nothing more than an unpleasant memory.

Until you come for me, Vryce, he thought. *Until you do what your nature demands, and try to put an end to me. In my domain. On my terms.* He chuckled darkly. *You haven't a chance in hell, my friend. But I'll enjoy watching you try.*

Dark fae swirling about his feet, silken robes brushing the floor as he walked, the Neocount of Merentha headed towards his audience chamber.

Black floor and dark draperies: they soothed the eye and calmed the heart, nourishing his nightbound soul. His visitor was a different story. Though the demon's chosen body was also black, his form was riddled with flaws and sharp edges that caught what little light there was and magnified it, making it bright enough to sting the Hunter's newly-healed eyes. His voice was likewise irritating, a thing of life and hidden sunlight and the ceaseless cacophony of day.

'Excellency.' The demon bowed. 'Allow me to—'

'You're a guest in my domain,' the Hunter interrupted. 'And not a very welcome one. You can design yourself a suitable form for this audience or leave. *Now.*' When the demon failed to respond he added sharply, 'I'm prepared to Banish you, if necessary.'

Calesta stiffened. 'Of course, my lord.' The glittering edges of his obsidian flesh began to pulse – and then melted, into a smooth, rippling surface. His voice became a whispering thing, all night air and cool darkness. 'Is this better, Prince of Jahanna? Does this please you?'

'It'll do,' the Neocount said shortly. 'What's your business?'

'Exactly what you expect, my lord. I saw what your vengeance did to my Mistress. I have no wish to suffer a similiar fate.' The black form bowed deeply. 'I've come to make an offering. A gesture of conciliation.'

'With no strings attached?' the Hunter asked dryly.

The demon laughed softly. 'You're not the fool that she was, my prince. You know the world, and its workings. Let's say that it would please me if you accepted my offering. It would please me very much.'

'I'm listening.'

The demon glanced towards the window; faceted eyes glittered in the fae-light. 'I've found you a woman. A rare delight. A beautiful, delicate flower of a girl, whom the gods must have designed with you in mind. A fragile spirit and a strong young body married together in perfect unity, so that the one might suffer while the other endures. She could pleasure you for hours, Hunter. Not like the others. This one was born to be devoured.'

'And where is this . . . jewel?'

'In your realm, prince. I took the liberty of bringing her here while you slept. I anticipated that when you awakened you might be . . . hungry. See for yourself,' he whispered. 'It's all there, for the Knowing.'

The Hunter gathered the dark fae about him and bound it to his will. Tendrils of power stretched forth, and touched the fleeing woman. He tasted the memory of her looking into a mirror, felt the absolute certainty of her beauty reverberate within him. And that soul! As fragile and as fine as porcelain in its tenor, but utterly resilient in its substance. He stroked her brain tenderly with his power, savouring her capacity for terror; she responded to him on at least a dozen levels, from the personal to the archetypal. A finely tuned instrument, that might produce whole symphonies of fear. It would have been a delight to hunt her under any circumstances; now, with the abstinence of a month or more sharpening the edge of his hunger, she was doubly irresistible.

'You would feed off my pleasure,' he challenged the demon.

The dark figure chuckled. 'You'd have more than enough pleasure to spare in this hunt.'

'I don't support parasites.'

'Not true, my prince. Not true at all. What about Karril? You've dedicated more than one hunt to him. While all he does is watch, and cheer you on. I can bring you victims, Hunter. I can read the hunger inside you better than any other, and scour the world for suitable prey. You doubt my skill? Test me, then. This one's a gift. No strings attached – this time. If she pleases you as much as I think she will . . .' He bowed, deeply. 'I live to serve, my lord.'

The taste of her was on his lips, in his soul. It was hard to keep his voice steady as he asked, 'What have you told her?'

'The Hunter's rules. The Forest's tradition. That you'll track her as a man would, in a man's form, using no Working. That she has three days and nights in which to evade you . . . and if she succeeds, she'll be free of you forever.'

'And did she believe that last point?'

'Of course she did. I understand how important that is, Hunter. It's the death of hope, rather than of the flesh itself, which is your true kill.' And he added, 'I have taken one special liberty, my lord.'

The Hunter's eyes narrowed suspiciously.

'This is her third night here. I tracked her myself for two of them, just as you would have. So that her terror would be at its peak by the time you went out to take her. After such a long healing sleep . . . I thought you might be very hungry.'

'And you were right,' he said softly. 'In that . . . and in your choice. I accept your offering, Calesta. If she pleases me as much as I think she may . . . then we can talk about the possibility of future arrangements.' He looked towards the window, at the Forest beyond; it seemed he could smell her fear on the wind. 'That's all for now,' he said quietly. 'You may go.'

The demon smiled, and bowed again. 'Good feeding, Hunter.'

The forest air was cold and dry, and her fear was something he could taste on his lips as he breathed it in, testing the wind for her scent. Beneath his feet her imprints were clear, hurried steps that dug deep into the half-frozen earth and then tore it loose – running steps that were skewed as if from exhaustion, a line of imprints that staggered from tree to tree as if she were desperate for some support, but dared not pause long enough to take it. Because resting, even for a moment, meant losing ground before him. And with only hours to go before her last dawn, she dared not waste a precious second.

Run, my fragile one. Run for the sunlight. Only a short time more before your safety is certain . . . and then, in those last desperate moments, I'll take you. And I'll taste your hope as it dies, drowned out in a sea of terror . . . He could feel her already, a faint flicker of fear against the edge of his mind, and desire filled him. What form should he take, once he had her? Her fears were so many, and so deeply rooted . . . he had never faced such a wealth of options before. The thought of taking her blood excited him, a strange sensation; not since his early days had he taken pleasure in so brutal an attack, or taken on a form so centred in pure physicality. Perhaps it was the result of traveling among humans again, of accepting their blood in cold, measured doses — enough to awaken that hunger again, not enough to satisfy it. Whatever the reason, he found that the thought of such a physical assault made him burn with hunger, and his hands shook as he brushed a drift of dead leaves from her trail, in order to read it more clearly. Perhaps a sexual assault would serve his purpose best. Not that he was capable of sexual congress, or even of mimicking its forms; procreation was an act of life, and it was as forbidden to him as fire was, or the light of the sun. But a woman such as that, who found herself overpowered by a man, who might be rendered naked with so little effort . . . she would come to her own conclusions regarding his intent, and those were nearly as nourishing as the act itself. He imagined the taste of her blood under those circumstances, and shivered from the force of his need. *Calesta knew my hunger well*, he thought. *Better than I knew it myself.*

And then he caught her scent on the wind, and he knew that he was close. Very close. He took care to move quietly, now, avoiding the crisp leaves that littered the ground about him. It seemed that he could hear her labored breathing, underscored by the pounding of her heart. So much blood, rendered so very warm by her terror . . . it seemed he could taste it on his lips already as he followed her trail, seemed that he could feel the rush of her fear as it enveloped him, hot and wild and utterly unfettered . . .

He ran. Long legs consuming the Forest ground at a pace her own could not possibly equal, sharp eyes picking out the marks of her trail in the near darkness. Calesta was right, he could never have waited. And this way there was no need to. For two nights now the demon had tracked her in his stead, playing all the subtle games that he had perfected in order to bring her terror to a fever pitch. All that remained was for the Hunter to harvest that fear, to drink it in along with her life and the last of her hope – to replenish the strength that two months of traveling with those humans had drained from him. A sweet prospect, indeed.

A clearing. Trees fell back, as though parting for him. At the far side a slight figure paused, then spun about in panic. Black hair whipped across a pale face, obscuring delicate features. Her slender fingers were red with blood, where thorns and rough bark had scraped them raw; her clothing, once fine, had been tattered by three days of flight through the woods. Fear blossomed out from her like a welcoming fire, and he had neither the strength nor the desire to resist its heat. He crossed the ground between them quickly and closed his hand about her wrist. Her pulse fluttered wildly, like that of a terrified bird, and she moaned softly as he pulled her towards him. Too weak to struggle; too overwhelmed to plead. He shut his eyes and let himself sink into the depths of her nightmare imagination, let all the images that were within her surface and take form, so that he might choose from among them. So many, so rich . . . the smell of her blood made him giddy with hunger, and he felt himself pushing the torn shirt back from her shoulders, baring skin as pale as the moonlight itself—

'You,' she whispered.

The word was like a blow. For a moment the world spun about him, dizzily – and then he managed to regain control, and he opened his eyes. And he released her suddenly, and staggered back. Stared at her, not quite believing.

'I won't run from you,' she whispered.

Those eyes, that face . . . he remembered the night he had walked her home, so comfortably arrogant as he played at shielding her from the dangers of the night . . . remembered the promise he had made to her, the vow she didn't know how to value. That the Hunter would never harm her. That *he* would never harm her.

'I promised myself that,' she breathed. There were tears in her eyes now – of sadness, not fear, a tender mourning that had no place in his brutal realm. 'For what you gave me . . . if you wanted . . . whatever.' She bit her lower lip, fighting for courage. 'I won't run,' she whispered. 'Not from you.'

'Son of a bitch,' he muttered. He turned away. His hands were shaking – with rage, with hatred. 'That bastard . . .'

He drew in a ragged breath, tried to master his hunger. Tried to dim down the passion that had been driving him, until he could control it. Tried not to think how close he had just come to betraying himself, or at whose prompting it had almost happened . . .

There was a touch on his arm. Light, like the wingstroke of a bird. 'Are you all right?' she whispered. And suddenly he could neither strike out at her, nor laugh at the total incongruousness of the question – but was caught somewhere between the two expressions and thus frozen. Unable to react.

At last he managed, 'We were betrayed. Both of us.' He turned back to her, tried to still the tide of hunger that rose up within him at the sight of her. So very, very delicate . . . he swallowed back on that impulse, hard, and said, 'I promised not to hurt you. I promised the Hunter would never hurt you.'

Son of a bitch!

The rage, hot inside him, was finally overwhelming the hunger. It allowed him to think. 'Here.' He pulled his medallion out of his shirt – on a new chain, made to replace that which Ciani had torn from his neck so many weeks ago – and handed it to her. 'Take this. Hold onto it. None of my people will harm you while you have it, and the beasts . . . they obey my will. Nothing will hurt you.'

'Thank you,' she whispered. Confused, as her fingers closed about the thin disk and its chain. 'I don't understand—'

'You don't want to,' he assured her. 'Ever.'

With effort, he managed to step back from her. The smell of her blood was like a magnet to his hunger – but she no longer feared him, and that helped immensely. Even as it amazed him, that it was true.

'I'll send you help,' he told her. 'Someone to get you safely out of here. You wait, with that . . . someone will come. You show him that. You'll be safe.'

Calesta, you bastard . . . you'll pay for this indignity. And so will whoever or whatever spawned you. I swear it!

He turned to go. And he felt her fingers on his arm again; there was fear in her touch.

'Do you have to go?' she breathed. I mean . . . please.'

He turned to her in amazement, saw the desperate hope in her eyes. She was afraid – not of him, now, but of the Forest. His creation. He was her island of refuge in a vast sea of terror, the single creature whom she did not fear in all of his domain. The concept was so bizarre he could hardly absorb it.

'I have a score to settle,' he told her. And then, because it seemed to suit this bizarre new role that he had made for himself, he added, 'You'll be all right.'

I promise you.

The harbour at Faraday was bustling with activity, long-shoremen swarming across the open docks like insects on honey. By now most of the tugs had put out to sea, and the small skiffs that would transport passengers across the shallow harbour waters were already making their way towards their motherships, whose vast sails and steady turbines stood ready to tame the dangerous eastern waters.

The captain of the *Golden Glory* looked out over the docks and snorted sharply. Then he climbed to where Damien stood, on a shelf overlooking the harbour. And put his hands on his hips, facing the man.

'Tide's going out soon,' he informed him. 'Another hour.'

The priest nodded.

'It's a hard double, this time. Best we'll get. It could take us past the Shelf before anything from outwater could hit us – you listening to me?'

'A hard double tide,' Damien repeated. 'One hour. Anything else?'

'Only that we've really got to leave, this time. The investors won't stand for another delay – and neither will I. You want a safe crossing, we start now. Otherwise you can find yourself another captain, not to mention another ship.'

Damien smiled faintly. 'And you think that pack of gold-seekers on board will let you quit, just like that?'

The captain grinned, displaying several broken teeth. 'You got me there, Reverend. But look: it's you who got it all together, right?

You who found enough bodies willing to cross the sea, to get us some investors to pay the backing costs, to buy yourself a good safe crossing . . . so why waste all that? I don't want to be out there in storm season and neither do you. Whatever you're waiting for . . . it's had its fair chance, all right? Let's take this one and go.'

He waited a moment for an answer – and then, receiving none, shook his head in exasperation and began the long climb down. 'One hour!' he called back. 'Be there!' Damien watched as he negotiated the dangers of the rubble-covered slope, finally down the last twenty feet or so to the level of the piers. Then he looked up, back towards the road from Faraday proper – and froze, as a tall, lean figure and a single horse stepped out into the moonlight.

He climbed up the remaining slope quickly until he stood face to face with the man. The Hunter's gaze was as cold as ever, and considerably more confident than when he'd last seen it. The pale eyes blazed with anger.

'If you say one smug word about this,' Gerald Tarrant warned, '—at any time – anything like "I told you so," or, "What took you so long?" – I will sink that miserable crate to the bottom of the ocean, and swim home if I have to. Am I making myself clear?'

He carefully avoided all the obvious rejoinders, and said only, 'Of course, your Excellency. Infinitely clear.' And bowed, with only a hint of mockery.

The Hunter glared at him, as if about to speak – and then simply shook his head in exasperation, and began to walk towards the harbour. The night-black horse, laden with several travel bags, followed obediently behind.

Damien watched as the figure faded into darkness, disappearing behind a turn of the switchback road. And then shook his own head, smiling slightly.

'Welcome aboard,' he whispered.

principle of which was that the labourer bound himself to serve on a plantation for a term of years (usually five or seven), at the end of which time he was entitled to a free passage home or to remain in the colony as a free labourer. There were many variations of this general plan, depending upon the regulations for recruitment, conditions during the indenture period, for return and for settlement. In all there was supposed to be free contract to start with and free labour, return or settlement to end with, but in all there was the basic fact of ignorance and need on the one hand dealing with knowledge and interest on the other. Abuses were almost inevitable and did not fail frequently to occur. But the early records show on the whole that the Indian and home governments were honourably anxious to protect the interests of the labourer against planter and contractor exploitation. The colonial governments also desired fair play but they were subject to local pressure far more severe than that experienced by the Colonial Office in London. A variant of the indenture system was the *kangani* system, by which a foreman or 'boss' recruited his own gang of twenty-five or thirty men and was responsible for their general supervision and control.

By these means a series of Indian settlements grew up from Mauritius and Fiji in the south Indian and Pacific Oceans, through Malaya and Burma in East Asia, Ceylon (where the old established Jaffna Tamils were reinforced by fresh arrivals), to Kenya, Tanganyika, Uganda, and South Africa (mainly in Natal), in Africa, and on to Trinidad and Jamaica in the Caribbean basin and British Guiana in South America. The settlements arose because the labourers on the whole found the status of a free labourer or trader more attractive than a return to India where they had only known poverty and with which they had lost their links. These settlements created fresh problems both for the colonies concerned and the settlers themselves. They found themselves members of new plural societies, and subject to all the tensions experienced by groups of different racial origin, cultural backgrounds and levels, and economic capacity. In some areas planters endeavoured to compel labourers to stay on because of the labour shortage; in others, as in Natal, they later tried to induce them to leave as economic competitors. In the upshot the settlements grew; the labourers in many cases developed into small traders, from whom grew by degrees a professional and commercial class. The indenture system was transmuted into 'assisted emigration' which ended altogether after the first World War.[1] These communities, which now number about $3\frac{1}{2}$ millions in all, have in the units mentioned acquired self-consciousness and a recognized place in local corporate life. In British Guiana Indians are the strongest group; in Trinidad, Mauritius, Fiji, and

[1] The dates for the ending of indenture are as follows: Mauritius, 1915; Fiji, 1920; Br. Guiana, 1917; Trinidad, Natal, 1911; Malaya, 1878. In Burma, Malaya (after 1878), and Ceylon the *kangani* system or its variant, the *maistry* system, prevailed.

Malaya they are very influential. Their stake in the country is recognized in Kenya and Tanganyika; only in South Africa, in spite of the efforts of Mahatma Gandhi, Lord Hardinge, and General Smuts, have their disabilities increased rather than declined and are they clearly unwelcome to the settlers who first asked for their services.

To these 'settlements of labour' there should be added the settlements of trade and commerce, which have been smaller, more long lived, and more stable. The leading case of this type of settlement is to be found in East Africa where enterprising western India traders, many of them followers of the Agha Khan, have long been active.

AUTHORITIES

Good general surveys will be found in P. E. ROBERTS's *History* and H. H. DODWELL's *Sketch,* the former inclining to the liberal and the latter to the imperialist view. The *Cambridge History,* vol. vi, has a weighty chapter by Dodwell. Apart from the books mentioned under the last chapter, the following may be consulted for foreign policy. AMIR ABDUR RAHMAN, *Autobiography* (2 vols., 1900), D. G. BOULGER, *England and Russia in Central Asia* (2 vols., 1879), Sir V. CHIROL, *The Middle Eastern Question* (1903), Sir H. RAWLINSON, *England and Russia in the Far East* (1875), an influential book, Sir P. SYKES, *History of Afghanistan* (2 vols., 1940), and *Sir Mortimer Durand* (1926). For the numerous printed documents see the *Cambridge History.*

For the frontier C. C. DAVIES, *The Problem of the North-West Frontier* (1932), is the best authority. For Sind see H. T. LAMBRICK, *Sir C. Napier and Sind* (1953) and A. I. SHAND, *General John Jacob* (1900); for Baluchistan see I. H. THORNTON, *Sir R. Sandeman* (1895); for the Pathan frontier SYKES on Durand (as above) and R. WARBURTON, *Eighteen years in the Khyber, 1879–98* (1900).

For Indians overseas see I. M. CUMPSTON, *Indians Overseas in British Territories, 1834–54* (1953), and C. KONDAPI, *Indians Overseas, 1838–1949* (1953), an Indian Council of World Affairs production.

RECENT PUBLICATIONS

THE following works are important additions: O. CAROE, *The Pathans* (London and Karachi, 1958 & 1975), H. T. LAMBRICK, *John Jacob of Jacobabad* (1960) and S. CHAKRAVARTY, *From Khyber to Oxus* (New Delhi, 1976), a study in imperialism in the nineteen-seventies.

CHAPTER 4

Economic Policy and Development, 1858–1939

THE hey-day of the British power in India was also the high noon of *laissez-faire* economic doctrine. Indian policy inevitably felt the influence of this climate of opinion. To interfere as little as possible with economic processes was considered to be the highest wisdom. Yet even the purists admitted that in certain circumstances positive action might be necessary. In fact such circumstances were never altogether lacking in India as elsewhere. The financial emergency of the Mutiny left the government with a pressing problem of ways and means. There was the need for developing India along modern lines for which there was no one but the government to take the initiative. The periodical famines were becoming a reproach to a government equipped with the resources of the new scientific age. The progress made in dealing with these matters in turn tended to end the old practical economic isolation of the Indian sub-continent. A peasant subsistence economy supplemented by cottage industries and a modicum of foreign trade was increasingly modified by the conditions of world trade. Food crops were replaced by cash crops; production for home consumption by production for foreign factories; and the old decayed cottage industries by new power-driven factories. These exigencies and developments compelled government action to a steadily increasing degree. But the *laissez-faire* principle held in general up to the outbreak of the first World War, just as it did in Britain, though with increasing misgivings and doubts.

The first financial problem facing the post-Mutiny government was that of ways and means. Before the crisis the mainstay of the revenue had been the traditional land tax. This was now reduced, and even when restored could not readily be expanded. There remained the duties on opium, salt and stamps, excise, customs, and provincial charges. But the only large increases possible here would fly in the face of economic doctrine as in the case of customs or of public policy as in the case of salt. Between 1859 and 1862 Wilson and Laing restored equilibrium by enforcing drastic economies, by increasing the salt tax, by imposing a uniform import tariff of 10 per cent., and instituting an income tax on non-agricultural incomes. There followed a period of expanding trade which enabled the great public works programme to be financed out of revenue. But Lawrence found that there was a strict limit to this process, and deficits recurred. In 1867 he secured sanction for the financing of productive works by means of loans. This measure, under improved rules drawn up by Lord Mayo, became a recognized feature of financial policy. It enabled the great irrigation programme to be pushed on and also helped in the construction of railways. The same ruler improved the administration of provincial finance by modifying the system of central grants. Hitherto grants had been made to the provincial governments for each item of estimated expenditure. Underspending on any particular item brought no benefit to the provincial government because the grant lapsed at the end of the financial year; overspending on the other hand incurred no penalty since the Centre was virtually compelled to make up the deficit. In 1870 this plan was replaced by a system devised by the brothers Richard and John Strachey. A fixed yearly grant was now made to each provincial government subject to revision every five years. Within each quinquennium, therefore, the provincial governments had a certain amount of elbow room, though the system did not allow for sudden emergencies or fluctuations in cost. It also led to the beginnings of real provincial finance by the addition of local cesses[1] to increase local resources. This was extended in 1877 by Sir John Strachey who gave provincial governments a share in the revenues instead of a fixed grant from the central treasury.

The free-trade wind still blew strongly. The government of India was soon under pressure to reduce its customs. They were first lowered to 5 per cent. In 1879, on the insistence of Lancashire, the cotton duties were abolished. This aroused strong opposition in India, both official and popular, and was only carried by the exercise of the Governor-General's power of overriding his council. It was thought to be a surrender of Indian to British interests and was the first overt instance of an economic clash of interest between the two countries. At the same time the wholly beneficial measure of abolishing the inland customs cactus line was completed.[2] This was made possible by agreements with the states whereby they gave up the manufacture of salt in return for compensation. It was then possible so to equalize the salt duty that it was no longer profitable to move salt from province to province. This was followed by further remissions until a state of virtual free trade was achieved in 1882. Low export duties were levied for revenue on a few articles only while the few import duties were counterbalanced by excise duties on the same articles. Free trade lasted unimpaired until 1894 when the rupee currency crisis (dealt with in Chapter 2) made the raising of further revenue imperative. This revived the controversy over the cotton duties. At first cotton was left on the free list but at the end of the year an import duty of 5 per cent. was imposed on cotton piece goods and yarn. An outcry from Lancashire led to the imposition of the 'countervailing cotton excise' of 5 per cent. which was regarded

[1] These were mainly the 'Provincial Rates', which were additional cesses on land introduced in 1878 to provide revenue for the Famine Insurance Scheme.
[2] This line consisted of a cactus hedge 2,500 miles long designed to prevent the free transit of bulk articles from province to province. Twelve thousand men were needed to watch it. The first 1,000 miles were abandoned by Northbrook and the remainder by Lytton.

by the Indian mill-owners as naked discrimination in favour of foreign goods. In 1896 both duties were reduced to 3½ per cent. There the matter rested until the middle of the first World War when extra revenue was again required. Then the import or customs duty was raised to 7 per cent., the excise remaining at 3½. This marked the loosening of the Lancashire grip which was further relaxed by the raising of the customs duty to 11 per cent. in 1921. Finally in 1925 the excise was first suspended and then abolished. This episode did much harm to Indo-British relations, for public opinion was firmly convinced that Indian interests had been sacrificed to those of Lancashire.

The major examples of governmental economic initiative during this period were the Famine Code and irrigation works (already dealt with) and the construction of railways. So much of modern Indian development depends upon the railways that their construction merits a closer examination. We have seen that though railways were talked of from the time of Lord Hardinge, the real initiative came from Dalhousie. His minute of 1853 proposed a system for the whole country and laid down general principles of management, finance, and construction. The 200 miles of lines in use in 1857 amply proved their value; in 1859 the construction of 5,000 miles of track by eight companies was sanctioned. Dalhousie planned to have a uniform gauge which was rather oddly fixed at 5 ft. 6 in., between the standard British gauge of 4 ft. 8½ in. and the Great Western broad gauge of 7 feet. Since the government at that time had no power to raise loans for productive purposes, money had to be found elsewhere. This was sought in Britain through the medium of private companies. But the companies were to be carefully controlled. In order to attract capital (hitherto distinctly shy of Indian operations) the contracts with the companies guaranteed rates of interest around 5 per cent.; any profit above that figure would be shared between government and company. In return for this the government had the right to control expenditure and operation, and to purchase at the expiry of each twenty-five year period, while the companies carried mails free and troops at reduced rates.

This system was not free from defects, as will be seen, but it was nevertheless one of great comprehension and foresight, which set in motion on broad lines the whole mechanical transport project of India and looked forward to a national network of railways owned and operated by the government. Not all the later modifications in this plan were for the better. The plan was successful in securing capital to build the railways, though the necessity for the guarantee system in order to attract capital is still disputed. Once committed to this, however, the government could not draw back; attempts to raise money on other terms failed. But the scheme did not encourage economy because the first profits went to government and losses were met by them. It also proved difficult to control the working engineers. The lines in operation in 1868 cost £18,000 a mile instead of the £8,000 planned by

Dalhousie. Against these defects must be set the fact that the actual construction was of high quality, challenging comparison with that of any other system in the world.

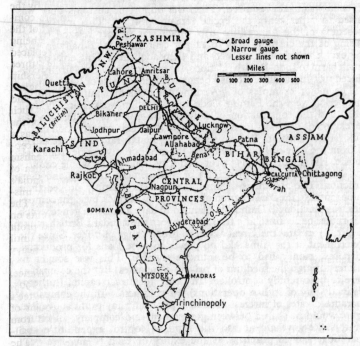

RAILWAYS OF INDIA

In the seventies policy was revised. The new permission to borrow for productive work enabled the government to take up construction itself. But for economy's sake the metre gauge was adopted for most of the new lines, some of which had later to be changed to the broad gauge because they proved to be too light for the traffic which developed. The fall in the value of the rupee further retarded construction until the Famine Report's demand for more lines in 1880 made it clear that some further revision of policy was needed. After 1880 there was a return to the guaranteed system of construction by private companies but on terms much improved as the result of experience. Thereafter, as leases fell in the government regularly purchased the lines, operating some itself and allowing the companies to continue to operate the remainder. Thus the Great Indian Peninsula and the

North Western Railways were state enterprises while the Bombay, Baroda, and Central India Railway remained in private hands. At the same time railways were built in the states, sometimes operated by the state itself, as in the case of Hyderabad, sometimes by private companies or the government of India. Thus by 1900 the major part of the Indian railway system was completed, some 25,000 miles of track being open. By 1914 another 10,000 miles was added. Diversity had replaced the striking uniformity and simplicity of the original plan; three gauges[1] had grown out of one; there were three kinds of ownership and operation and various combinations between them. But the original design of overall government control of planning, ownership, and operation had been maintained. There were no competitive lines such as had sprung up in Britain and no sacrifice of essential needs for the sake of greater returns in more profitable areas. The system was a national one so arranged as to become easily and by almost imperceptible stages a nationalized one. All this was done while individualism was dominant in Britain and high capitalism considered the idea of nationalization a kind of economic *lèse-majesté*. On the whole India's railway planners served her well and saved her from many of the mistakes committed and much of the expense incurred elsewhere. The fruits of this work began to be reaped in a series of annual profits on the working of government-controlled lines. In 1899–1900 a net profit of 11 *lakhs* of rupees was earned for the first time. From then until 1914 there was only one deficit year while the war years with its heavy demands for goods brought in large profits.

The diversity of control, however, caused serious inconvenience. The first step in remedy was the setting up of a railway board in 1905. After the first World War, as a result of the Acworth Committee's report, the railway board was reorganized, the state management of lines was hastened, and a railway budget was separately prepared from 1925–6. By the end of the inter-war period three-quarters of the railways were owned by the state and nearly a half operated by it. The mileage had reached its maximum of about 43,000 miles.

The economic effects of railway construction were very great. Railways, as has already been remarked, transformed the famine problem and made the Famine Code a working proposition. The north Indian famine of 1896 had been called the first 'famine of work' rather than of food. Trade was revolutionized by making possible production for a market and the opening up of the interior to large-scale operations. Plantation and factory industries were made possible because coal could be supplied for power at the points of production, and the finished goods could then be distributed. Finally, all India was brought within the orbit of world economy and the range of world prices. For example cotton manufacture could be carried on in the interior as well as near the coast and the development of the sugar industry was made possible. Not all the effects were good; for example the collapse of the

[1] Including the narrow gauge of the mountain railways and a few lines elsewhere.

Indian handicrafts, the rise in the general price-level, and the upset of the internal economic balance by excessive exports have been charged to their account. But the handicrafts were in decay long before railways were thought of, beginning with the Bengal weavers in the late eighteenth century; the railways only administered the *coup de grâce*. The railways did in India what they did elsewhere; they hastened the transition from handicraft to mechanical industry by transforming the transport situation. They were an essential preliminary to an industrialized India. In fact it can be said of them, and not in an economic context only, no railways, no modern India.

We can now turn to the new industries which were made possible or whose development was assured by the railways. The first of these was the cotton mill industry. The new industry did not so much replace the old handicraft weavers as grow up in the face of a practical monopoly. The old industry was ruined in Bengal and the Carnatic partly by the high-handed methods of the Company after Plassey and the French wars, partly by the collapse of the export trade to Europe, and partly by the lack of any protection against the machine goods of Lancashire. In the early eighteenth century the sale of Indian piece goods was forbidden in England as a measure of protection for the Lancashire handicraft industry. But re-exports to Europe continued until the American War of Independence followed by the revolutionary wars virtually ended them. By that time Lancashire's own handicraft industry had been replaced by the new mechanical production. These goods were imported to India by the Company where they could undersell any Indian goods within reach of the navigable rivers.[1] On its side the Company took to exporting from India raw cotton instead of finished articles. It was not until 1853 that the first successful Indian cotton mill was started in Bombay. The American Civil War caused a set-back by sending up the price of raw cotton with a consequent slump when American cotton came back on the market. Real progress began with the opening of the Empress Mill at Nagpur by the Parsi J. N. Tata in 1887. From that time there has been no going back. Bombay, with more than eighty mills, led the industry, followed by Sholapur, Ahmedabad in Gujarat, Madras, and other lesser centres. By 1914 India was reckoned to be fourth in the world list of cotton manufacturing countries.[2] The industry survived the depression, Gandhian disapproval, and Japanese competition in the thirties. It virtually controls Indian consumption, except for a few 'counts' and the handloom industry which still produces the coarsest cloth or *khaddar* and certain costly luxury lines.

The jute industry was originally a handicraft of Bengal with a small export market. Its value was first realized in 1838 when export started

[1] The average annual value of cotton goods exported from England between 1786 and 1790 was £1,200,000; in 1809 it was £18,400,000.
[2] V. Anstey, *Economic Development of India* (1949), p. 262; see note 2. This was calculated on the percentage of the world's mill consumption by weight.

to Dundee in Scotland. But Bengal jute could only be used for the coarsest goods owing to the lack of standards in cultivation, and local manufacture was impossible owing to the lack of means of power. The Crimean War of 1854 proved a turning-point by cutting off the supply of Russian raw flax and hemp. Improved methods of cultivation enabled Indian jute permanently to supplant Russian materials in the Dundee market. At the same time the development of Indian coal by the new East Indian Railway made jute manufacture in Bengal possible. The first jute-spinning machine was set up near Serampore in 1855 and the first power loom in 1859. At first the cloths produced were inferior to those of Dundee and commanded a local market only. But success came in the seventies and with it rapid expansion which continued almost without a break until the great depression of the thirties. By 1908 Indian output exceeded that of Dundee. Throughout our period India enjoyed a virtual monopoly of jute production. Jute made Calcutta as cotton made Bombay, Madras, and Ahmedabad industrial cities.

The development of the jute and other Indian industries is closely connected with coal as the means of power as well as with railways as the means of transport. Modern industries could not have grown without railways and railways could not have been worked without coal. The first attempt to exploit coal was made by the British magistrate of Chota Nagpur who obtained the right to mine from Warren Hastings. The coal was poor in quality, the demand was small, and the Company found it cheaper to send out coal by ship. In 1814 a fresh venture was made at Raniganj with more success. Bentinck encouraged development and in 1843 the famous Bengal Coal Company was formed from a union of several firms. In 1846 the output was 91,000 tons. The railways came to increase demand and ease supply. The railways themselves, as they developed, took one-third of the total production. The field in Bengal, Bihar, and Orissa was found to contain a plentiful supply of average quality.[1] Henceforth progress was steady. In 1868 $\frac{1}{2}$ million tons were produced. Production passed the million mark in 1880, exceeded 6 millions in 1900, 12 millions in 1912, and 21 millions in 1917. In 1938 it was over 28 million tons. India was virtually self-supporting in one of the essentials of heavy industry.

Associated with the new coalfields came the iron and steel industry. Iron of high quality had been smelted from a very early date, as is shown by the iron pillar near Delhi which dates from the fifth century. Various attempts were made in the early nineteenth century to start an iron industry but they failed for want of both fuel and experience. It was not until coal was used for smelting from 1875 that any progress was made and even then technical difficulties made it chequered and halting. The industry was finally established by the efforts of Jamshed Tata who had seen the possibilities of the iron industry when managing his Empress Mill at Nagpur. Tata died in 1903 just after Curzon had

[1] D. H. Buchanan, *Development of Capitalist Enterprise in India.* See pp. 257-9.

widened the rules for prospecting and mining. But his sons founded in 1907 the Tata Iron and Steel Company at a site in Bihar which they named Jamshedpur. Production of iron began in 1911 and of steel in 1913. By the end of the period this plant was the largest single steel works in the world, producing about a million tons annually; India ranked sixth in the list of steel-producing countries. The whole steel industry is a monument of Indian enterprise and skill built up entirely on Indian capital.

Around or connected with these two major industries grew up a number of other industrial activities. Important among them were the chemical industries among which may be mentioned the manufacture of industrial acids and soda, vegetable oils, and of disinfectants. Engineering developed mainly in connexion with the railways. Miscellaneous industries included rice and flour mills, woollen and silk manufacture, cement (from 1914) and shellac, paper and matches, and sugar refining. By 1933 India was practically self-supporting in cement while the progress of the sugar refining industry was phenomenal after the imposition of a protective tariff in 1932. From 1860 onwards the industrial current was spreading across Indian life like a flooding tide filling the creeks and channels of salt marshes.

It remains to mention the plantation industries. The first of these was tea. During the eighteenth century the East India Company obtained its tea from China, which came to form, indeed, the mainstay of its profits. In the late eighteenth century wild tea plants were found in Assam, but it was at first doubted whether they were genuine tea plants at all, much less consumable. But they suggested that Chinese plants might be acclimatized and Lord William Bentinck accordingly in 1834 sent to China for seed and labour. A government garden was started but was sold in 1839 to the Assam Tea Company. The Indian tea plant would not be ousted by the Chinese. It was the difficulty of clearing the Indian plant to make way for the Chinese which suggested the idea of putting the Indian leaf on the market. The experiment succeeded and from 1850 the industry rapidly expanded. Tea is now grown in Assam, Bengal, the northern hills,[1] and southern India. The expansion of the Indian tea industry can be judged from the fact that until 1850 Britain took the whole of her tea from China; in 1869 she obtained 10 million pounds from India as against 100 million from China; while in 1900 she took 24 million pounds from China and 137 million from India.[2] Compared to tea coffee was of less importance. The plant was introduced in the sixteenth century but systematic cultivation only began in Mysore and south India in the eighteen-thirties. It then developed until 1862 when the borer beetle and leaf blight produced a collapse by 1885. There has been a recovery since, but much of the coffee land has since been planted with tea, cinchona, and rubber. But the second World War revealed that neither of these

[1] Around Darjeeling, Naini Tal, and in the Kangra valley.
[2] In 1929–30 Indian tea exports were 377 million pounds.

last had reached large or even adequate proportions. Indigo remained an important plantation industry (though of a different type to the tea and coffee gardens) until 1897 when the competition of German aniline dyes started a rapid decline.

A major problem of Indian industrial and commercial development was the supply of capital. Until 1850, as we have seen, British capital was shy of Indian adventure. The risks and unknown factors were too great, and prospects in other directions too bright. The working capital of the agency houses after 1813 at first consisted mainly of the savings of the Company's servants. Their cries of woe when these houses fell as in the crisis of 1831 were loud and poignant. Indian capital was also shy for different reasons. It needed to acquire confidence in the new régime, and outside the presidency towns, to acquire the habit of investment. Investment for large-scale production for 'enabling' works like railways was an unfamiliar and suspected practice. Thus the first big developments came when European capital was coaxed into the country by government guarantees or went of its own free will to develop industries with which it was already familiar as in the case of jute or coal. Indian capital followed where it was in touch with European practice as in Bombay and dealing with familiar products like cotton. These considerations throw into all the greater relief the achievement of the Tatas in developing iron and steel. Thus the major part of the capital provided was British with a steadily increasing Indian proportion from 1900. As late as 1931–2 the capital of companies registered abroad was nearly four times that of companies registered in India.[1] But this is not an exact guide because it leaves out of account the stock in British companies held by Indians, as well as government stocks. Speaking generally it may be said that the capital of the cotton industry was mainly Indian, that of the iron and steel industry entirely so, that of the jute industry about half and half, while the coal and plantation industries were mainly British, together with that used for the building of railways, irrigation, and other public works. Management in the cotton and steel industries was mainly Indian though European technicians were freely employed, that of the jute, coal, and the plantation industries being European, the jute men in particular being Scotch. Their capital, apart of course from government enterprise, operated through joint-stock companies and managing agencies. The latter arose through the convenience found by bodies of capitalists seeking to develop some new activity and lacking any Indian experience, of operating through local agents. It arose in the period after 1813 when private merchants took over the trade formerly monopolized by the Company. The money would be found in Britain to promote a tea garden, a coal mine, or a jute mill, but the management would be confided to a firm already on the spot. The managing agency was the hyphen connecting capital with experience and local knowledge.

Until 1914 the policy of the government continued in the main to

[1] V. Anstey, op. cit., p. 110.

be one of 'enabling' private capital and enterprise to develop the
country. Direct promotion was confined to public utilities like canals
and railways. The line between enabling and interfering action became
distinctly blurred, however, in the case of the cotton industry and there
was a tendency for enabling action to pass over into the positive promotion of particular projects. This was most noticeable in the time of
Lord Curzon with his establishment of an imperial department of agriculture with a research station at Pusa and a department of commerce
and industry presided over by a sixth member of the Viceroy's Council.
The first World War began the transition to a new period of active
promotion and positive support. As the conflict lengthened there arose
a demand for Indian manufactured goods. India failed to take full
advantage of this opportunity, partly because of uncertainty as to the
future and partly because the means for sudden expansion were lacking.
So Japan reaped where India had failed to sow. The outcome of this
situation was the appointment of an industrial commission in 1916
under pressure from London. The commission criticized the unequal
development of Indian industry which had led to the missing of
her war opportunity. A much closer co-operation with industry was
planned through provincial departments of industry. Increased technical training and technical assistance to industry was proposed while it
was suggested that the central government should set up a stores
department which should aim at making India self-sufficing in this
respect. The commission's report was only partially implemented, but
a stores department and provincial industrial departments were created
and something was done towards promoting technical assistance. The
importance of the report and its aftermath was that it marked the
transition from the conception of Indian economy in broadly colonial
terms with freedom for private enterprise to the conception of India
as an autonomous economic unit.

In the wake of the war came a boom and a slump followed by the
Inchcape Retrenchment Committee of 1922–3. The war also brought
the Montford reforms with their new political outlook. Economic
autonomy went hand-in-hand with political self-determination and
mutually reacted upon each other. A result of this interaction was the
acceptance of the principle of fiscal autonomy for India in 1921. The
Fiscal Commission followed to work out the new policy in detail. One
result of the new attitude was the suspension and final abolition of the
cotton excise in 1926. Another and most important one was a new tariff
policy. Customs were regarded as a means of revenue to give a new
flexibility to Indian finance. Raw materials and semi-manufactured
goods were to be admitted at low rates, while protective duties could
be imposed to help promising industries find their feet or to protect
established ones from unfair competition. The instrument of this considered protectionism was the Tariff Board which was set up in 1923
By its action the steel industry was able to meet foreign competition
and survive the depression of the thirties, the cotton industry was

saved from Japanese undercutting, and new industries like sugar refining enabled to establish themselves. It can thus be said that from 1921 Indian industry was no longer regarded as an 'extra', even if a desirable one, but as an integral part of the Indian economy whose care and nurture was a primary duty of government.

A result of these developments which is too often overlooked was an immense increase of population. In Akbar's reign it was estimated at 100 millions. By Aurangzeb's accession it must have been much greater, but from 1700 there was a decline through famine and wars. By inference from incomplete estimates a figure of about 130 millions may be suggested for all India in 1800. The first census in 1872 gave a total of 206 millions which was, however, probably an under-estimate. In 1901 the total was 294 millions, in 1921 318 millions, and in 1941, without Burma, 388 millions. What had the British done for these people? We can say in the first place that they brought them into existence by providing security, by overcoming famine, by increasing the means of subsistence through irrigation, by health measures which reduced the death-rate, by land settlement, and by developing commerce and industry. Whether the average person had more to eat and lived better than in Akbar's day is a question on which economists differ widely. Undoubtedly much of the new wealth served to feed more mouths rather than to enable people to live better. The main beneficiaries in living standards were probably the new middle class whose position materially as well as morally improved beyond comparison with Mughul times. Yet all, or nearly all, shared in the new amenities brought by the new age. Railways promoted movement as never before whether for commerce or conference or pilgrimage. Motor transport opened up the countryside still further. Health measures lengthened life and education gave it more content. New crops and new industries gave new opportunities of betterment. Fear of famine was largely banished and fear of disease reduced. For the middle classes a new world of opportunity dawned and for all life was a little fuller than it had been before. If rural India was not yet awake before 1920, it was at least stirring in its sleep.

AUTHORITIES

A standard work on this subject is V. ANSTEY, *Economic Development of India* (3rd ed., imp. 1949). An older work, still valuable for its point of view, but requiring correction, is R. C. DUTT, *Economic History of India* (Victorian Age) (5th ed., n.d.). P. J. GRIFFITHS, *The British Impact on India* (1952) is a useful introduction on the economic side. L. C. A. KNOWLES, *Economic Development of the British Overseas Empire* (1924), is specially useful on railways. D. H. BUCHANAN, *Development of Capitalist Enterprise in India* (1934), is a valuable American study of industrial development. D. R. GADGIL, *The Industrial Evolution of India* (1934), is an Indian study. P. P. PILLAI, *Economic Condition of India* (1925), is a useful study of India in the twenties.

For agriculture see the *Report of the Royal Commission on Agriculture* (1928), A. and G. L. C. HOWARD, *Development of Indian Agriculture* (1929), and M. L. DARLING, *The Punjab Peasant* (3rd ed., 1932). For famine policy see A. LOVEDAY,

The History and Economics of Indian Famines (1914), for irrigation see D. G. HAR̲.
Irrigation in India (1923), and for finance L. C. JAIN, *Indigenous Banking in In.*
(1929), K. T. SHAH, *Sixty Years of Indian Finance* (2nd ed., 1927), and J. M. KEYN̲.
Indian Currency and Finance (1913). For the final plans see the *Plan of Econon*
Development for India (Penguin Special, 1945).

See also L. H. JENKS, *Migration of British Capital to 1875* (1927) and D. THORNE̲"
Investment in Empire (1950).

CHAPTER 5

The New India—Western Influence

WE have noted the controversy between the British apostles of radical western innovation, the conservative defenders of the *status quo*, and the advocates of the 'line-upon-line, here a little and there a little' policy. The dynamic of the first school, both in its rationalist and religious aspects, was justice, reason, and humanism, the motive of the second fear of popular upheaval, and of the third a mixture of the first two. All parties agreed in condemning the elements in traditional Hinduism which conflicted with western rationalist ideas and Christian values; they differed in their own first principles and the line of approach. The extreme conservative preached non-interference because he believed in leaving other people alone to their own devices, not because he approved of them. His was the Brahmanical attitude in reverse. The advocates of innovation won the day on the whole because they floated on the flowing tide of western liberal opinion. The new ideas seeped in through members of Parliament and the cabinet, directors and the Company's servants in India. Mounstuart Elphinstone, for example, could not alone have changed policy and outlook in England, but he was himself a symptom of that changing outlook and policy. The innovators were restrained from pushing reform to the point of revolution by the caution enjoined on upstart imperialists in a great and as yet little-known dominion. Growing knowledge increased respect for the diversity and complexity of Indian life and so bred circumspection in seeking improvement.

The measures of the thirties were born of conviction and nurtured in hope. We must not forget that in England itself it was the age of the Great Reform Bill, when to liberals at least it seemed for a while that the 'world's great age began anew'. During the rest of the century this spirit was never quite extinguished, but the flame of progress flared and flickered, and at times burnt low. The westernizing movement was based on the double belief that it was good for India and that she would accept it as soon as she awoke to the light of the modern world. At first the omens in both directions were favourable. In the forties government's attention was diverted by wars but progress continued out of hearing of the guns. With Dalhousie the flame shot up though the undiscerning were too dazzled by the glare of his wars and annexations to take much notice.

The Mutiny brought the whole question to the focus of public discussion. There were those who considered it proof that India was unchanging and incorrigible; there were others, like the men of the

Panjab school, who were inclined to agree but insisted that these measures should be continued nevertheless on broad grounds of moral duty and humanity. Reform, having become a burden instead of a pleasure, must be shouldered manfully as a duty. There were others who saw the Mutiny more clearly as an interlude or as a protest of conservatives hustled too sharply. But on the whole it was the second school which held the field of opinion, and it was this which set the tone for the next twenty years. The Panjab school were its great exponents and their popularity in England secured a wide acceptance of their views. Self-government must depend on self-reform; self-reform was so slow that self-government could only come in a very distant future. The British were trustees in the position of long-leaseholders. The effect of this waning of the liberal western faith was seen in a shift of emphasis in westernizing policy. In Bentinck's time the principal measures were moral and spiritual like the abolition of suttee and the new education policy. Later material projects like irrigation plans appeared. Dalhousie's measures were both moral and material, a fresh impetus to education and to western methods of administration on the one hand, and to public works of all kinds on the other. In the post-Mutiny period the emphasis was more definitely on material improvement. Educational and other moral measures were pursued, it is true, but there was much greater reluctance to interfere in any way with the Indian social structure. The promotion of material improvement both satisfied constructive impulses and allayed fears of another uprising and did something to salve the conscience of the moral reformer. This trend was further strengthened by the prospect of fresh sources of wealth occasioned by the development of railways with their power of tapping new resources.

In the eighties a fresh current of liberalism made itself felt in India, which in Britain was associated with the radicalism of Chamberlain and the later phase of Gladstone. Once more attention was turned to the mind of India. These people thought that they detected westward movements there whose existence their opponents doubted and the official class in India minimized. They wished to make a response in the direction of popular representation. From the late eighties the development of an Indian movement was not doubted in Britain; controversy henceforth turned on its extent and the speed of its growth. By no means all Liberals were convinced of the significance of this new movement before 1900 while leading Conservatives had moved away from the 'unchanging east' dogma by 1890.

We have already noted the beginning of the new education policy in 1835, which was perhaps the most far-reaching single measure in the whole nineteenth century. Without it there could have been no Indian nation as we know it today. The more austere aspects of the westernizing policy were removed by Lord Auckland in 1840, when he restored some government patronage to Eastern learning without ceasing to make western learning the main content of official education. On the other hand the new education was given a great stimulus by the rule that employment in government offices should go to those who had benefited from a course of the new education. English was now as necessary to the literary and secretarial class as Persian had previously been. A knowledge of English could secure entry into that class to those who did not belong to the literary castes. The next landmark was Sir Charles Wood's educational dispatch of 1854, which was eagerly implemented by Dalhousie. 'We are desirous', said the dispatch, 'of extending far more widely the means of acquiring general European knowledge.' The dispatch led to the foundation of the first three universities of Calcutta, Bombay, and Madras in 1857 on the London examining model, though not with London University standards. The grant-in-aid system was introduced, which enabled private colleges to be organized all over the country, by making grants for maintenance provided certain standards were maintained. Departments of public instruction were set up in place of the old amateur committees. This tended to officialize education and make it more stereotyped, but it was a necessary development if the large expansion hoped for was to be guided and controlled. These departments had more ample funds than previously, were able to lay down rules of procedure, and to appoint inspectors. Finally an educational service was established to provide a cadre of teachers for the new schools and colleges.

As soon as the shock of the Mutiny was past these measures produced a rapid expansion of higher education. Government schools and colleges were established at important points as model institutions; the grant-in-aid system encouraged the founding of private institutions both to supplement government colleges in the larger centres and to take their place elsewhere. India was soon covered with a network of public and private colleges and schools. The aim was to popularize education and in this the government certainly succeeded. But this expansion brought its problems also. Attention was concentrated upon high schools and colleges and primary vernacular education tended to lag behind. Between 1865 and 1886 the proportion of boys at school to undergraduates at college sank to 314 from 390 to 1. Girls' education still lagged behind owing to public apathy and orthodox opposition. In the interests of popularizing western education standards were relaxed as soon as it was realized that a high standard would seriously restrict entry. In 1857 2 candidates obtained degrees out of 13 entrants and 111 were admitted out of 464 applicants. This standard was thought to be incompatible with the purpose of 'passing every student of ordinary ability who had fairly profited by the curriculum of school and college study which he had passed through'. The result was a lowering of standards, which, once started, was difficult to stop because there existed no easily available educational yardstick against which to measure Indian standards. The obvious one was that of London University, and once this was abandoned there was no other. There was much to be said for a standard lower than London for the sake of popularization. But no distinction was made between pass and honours candidates. The result was that instead of adding quantity to quality the new system substituted the one for the other. For real quality in western education it was necessary to go to Britain so that Indian education came to acquire a second-rate reputation. It served its purpose of spreading western knowledge widely but failed to produce, on its own merits, a new intellectual *élite*. Fortunately the course of educational history has shown that real talent will break through the worst of systems, and India proved no exception to this rule. Along with failed B.A.s and the barely passed appeared men of real distinction.

The new educational service upon which the new system depended was not well managed by government. Its pay did not attract the best men and too often government did not know how to use them when it got them. The successes, like Edwin Arnold, were accidental rather than intentional, and the service was as a whole weighted down by officialdom in its direction and by mediocrity engaged for cheapness in its members. 'Everywhere departmental convenience was preferred, until very recent times, to educational interests; and the sort of man whom the departments really liked was one who was willing to be transferred from the teaching of history to the teaching of physics and from that to the inspection of schools.'[1] In the main Indo-European scholars continued to come from the services rather than the educational class in the persons of men like Elliot, William Irvine, Vincent Smith, and Beveridge. A further defect was the lack of any moral content or personal contact in the new system. The universities were not what their name implied, but agencies for prescribing courses and conducting examinations whose headquarters many students never even saw. Nor was the defect remedied in most of the colleges themselves, except some missionary ones, because for financial reasons they tended to place reliance on formal class teaching to overcrowded classes. The mass lecture led to impersonal examination by a remote organization; the award of a degree certified a modicum of knowledge which was often learned by rote. With such methods it is only surprising that so much came from so little.

Lord Ripon took the next step by appointing the Hunter Commission in 1882. This body surveyed the whole field of education and at least did service in pointing to defects to be remedied. The encouragement of primary and girls' education, of science and moral instruction, were all urged. The most practical result was the reorganization of the educational service which now consisted of three branches, the all-India educational service, the provincial, and the subordinate services. The all-India service now attracted a better type of British graduate, while to the provincial service increasing numbers of Indians were appointed. It was hoped to foster primary education by confiding it to the care of the new municipal and district boards. But no great progress came from this well intentioned move because, apart from the

[1] H. H. Dodwell, *Sketch of the History of India, 1858–1918*, p. 205.

PLATE 35

b. Sayyid Ahmad Khan

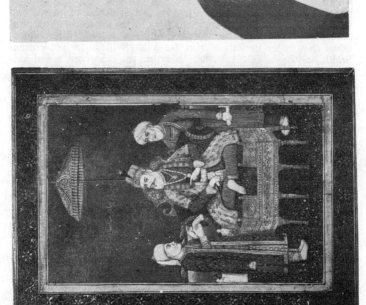

a. Bahadur Shah

limitation of local resources, such a measure was like confiding the
spread of the gospel to the unconverted. Efforts to introduce moral
instruction were defeated by official objections and to encourage
science by the general preference for literary studies. This, then, was
the general state of education at the end of the century. It was over-
weighted at the top at the expense of primary education; that is, the old
tradition that education was for the few was largely maintained. The
higher education itself was undifferentiated in kind and had achieved
popularity at the expense of quality. Nevertheless the educational service had been improved and some of the major problems were realized if
not solved. A large impact had been made on the people throughout the country and a new class was fast rising which shared a common
language and stock of western knowledge and ideas. The significance
of this will be considered in the next chapter; meanwhile we may note
that the whole system was ripe for the reforming hand of a Curzon.

After the Mutiny there were few or no changes attempted in the
structure of Indian society, and such as were enacted were by general
consent.[1] The changes introduced were innovations which stood side
by side with the traditional social structure, and whose influence upon
it, if any, was indirect. In this class we may place the development of
local government. In the villages self-government had survived in
many areas, and, as we have seen, sedulous attempts were made to
preserve the village communities, with varying degrees of success. But
in these there was no trace of municipal self-government, the only
signs of corporate life being in trade guilds and caste associations.
These were often divisive rather than unifying in their effect. The early
British settlements had local administrations, but they were in no sense
representative of the tax or rate-payers. There were mayors and alder-
men with judicial powers and much dignity, but they were nominated
by the Company. The rapid growth of the presidency towns raised
many administrative problems which prompted many expedients. It
was in the seventies that the first municipal bodies with a real representative element were established. In 1872 half the Bombay corporation was elected by ratepayers; in 1878 the Bombay model was adopted
at Calcutta and Madras introduced the representative principle. These
bodies, particularly that of Bombay, were the first real schools of
British Indian statesmanship.

Elsewhere Dalhousie's Act of 1850 permitted the setting up of town
committees empowered to levy indirect taxes, but few in fact were
established. Lord Mayo enlarged their powers over education, sanitation, and local public works. But Lord Ripon is rightly regarded as the
real founder of modern local self-government; his measures were more
comprehensive than previous ones and devised with the deliberate
intention of introducing democratic practice. 'They are chiefly desirable as a measure of political and popular education', he wrote. He
established a network of district and *tahsil* or *taluq* boards in the

[1] See the *Cambridge History of India*, vol. vi, p. 394.

country and urban boards called municipal committees in the towns. From a half to two-thirds of the members were elected and powers were given to elect non-official chairmen. They were given powers over education, sanitation, public works, and health, and financial authority to levy octroi, terminal, property, and other duties. The fortunes of these bodies were chequered, but there is no doubt that to a large extent they fulfilled their educative purpose even when they fell short in administrative achievement.

Along with these measures must be noted the progress towards the Indianization of the services. The monopoly by the Company's civil service of all posts worth more than Rs. 500 a month established by Cornwallis was mitigated by degrees in the years that followed. Bentinck went farther by creating the posts of *Sadr Amins* and *Principal Sadr Amins*. At the same time the Charter Act of 1833 declared that no one should be debarred from holding any post by reason of race or religion. It even contemplated the substitution of competition for nomination to the covenanted service. But for twenty years more the directors retained their monopoly of appointments. The British in India were a 'commonwealth of magistrates' and 'the higher government officials formed a caste closer than had even the *mansabdars* of Akbar'. Change came but slowly. In 1853 the last Charter Act threw open the covenanted service to competitive examination. But since the examinations were held in Britain, Indians had not only to make the voyage thither but also had to reside there for a long period. Only the wealthy could do this and they were few. Only the Muslims could come without religious difficulty and they were backward and poor. In these circumstances it was not till 1863 that the first Indian, Satyendra Nath Tagore, entered the service, and the stream remained a trickle until after the first World War. Lytton, who was frank as well as ill advised, wrote of 'the acknowledged failure to fulfil fairly the promises given'. His remedy was the statutory civil service of 1879. Under this scheme one-sixth of the posts previously held by the civil service were to be filled by men nominated by the local governments. They were to be men of good family whom the subordinate service did not attract. By this means Lytton hoped to coax the old families into partnership with the British. It was far-sighted in its way, but it was the middle class rather than the aristocracy who were anxious to take up the burden of official life. Recruitment therefore languished. In 1887 the statutory service was abolished and replaced by a division of all civil servants into the imperial civil, the provincial, and the subordinate services. The imperial service continued to be recruited by examination, nomination, and promotion in India. One-fifth of the posts reserved to the imperial service were now thrown open to members of the provincial services. At the same time it should be noted that there was during these years a large increase in the numbers of the superior services which also increased opportunities for Indians. Having said so much it remains to add that Lytton was right in his opinion of the position if not altogether happy in his method of dealing with it. Something had been done, but not enough. The failure of the home government to fulfil adequately its promises in the matter of official appointments was a proof, not of their insincerity or ill will but of the strength of the corporate vested interest which several generations of British officials had built up in India since 1800. No votes were to be won by pressing on reforms of this nature while obstinate and skilful obstruction was certain. The matter was therefore shelved until the shock of the first World War.

There were two unofficial westernizing agencies which now demand attention. The first was the press. The first newspaper in India was the *Bengal Gazette*, edited by James Hicky, which appeared in 1780 and was suppressed by Warren Hastings two years later after a stormy and notorious career. From that time a succession of journals appeared and a running fight for freedom of speech was waged with government. This culminated in John Adam's regulation of 1823 requiring a printer to obtain a licence before he could publish a newspaper and his expulsion of the editor John Silk Buckingham for infringing Lord Hastings's regulations. In 1835 Metcalfe freed the press from all restrictions and thereby forfeited his chance of permanent appointment. There matters rested until Lytton's Vernacular Press Act of 1878 which imposed restrictions on the vernacular press only. This in its turn was repealed in 1882. Through these vicissitudes and from gossipy and irresponsible beginnings, the press came to exercise an important influence on Indian life. The English press was at first intended for British readers—the commonwealth of magistrates; many of its articles were written by officers like Henry Lawrence or Edwardes under pseudonyms. This press constituted a forum of discussion of Indian policy where the merits or faults of a Napier or a Dalhousie were canvassed with unsparing frankness. In time it broadened its outlook. The *Friend of India*, conducted by Marshman of Serampore, struck a Christian and reforming note; the Calcutta *Statesman* founded by Knight, the Bombay *Times of India*,[1] and others became responsible organs of opinion on current events and questions. As the English-knowing Indian public grew these papers became an important factor in forming Indian opinion. They were the unofficial apostles of western influence and all the more effective for being unofficial. Further they stimulated the development of a genuine Indian press, at first in the local languages and then in English as well. Ram Mohan Roy with his Persian *Mirat-ul-Akhbar*[2] or Mirror of News and *Sambat Kammudi* (Moon of Intelligence) is rightly regarded as the founder of serious Indian journalism. After the Mutiny papers published in English like the Madras *Hindu* and the Allahabad *Leader* took their places beside their British brethren. They provided for the new westernized class a sort of continuation

---

[1] Founded in 1838 as the *Bombay Times*.
[2] The first was probably the *Bengal Samachar* of 1816. See S. K. De, *History of Bengali Literature*, p. 236.

school as well as a window on the affairs of India as a whole and the world at large. With the coming of political controversy in the eighties they strengthened their hold on the new public and their secondary cultural influence increased in proportion. In a nascent society which had not yet acquired the habit of sustained reading, for which indeed books were not easily available before 1870, which could not afford to buy many of those that were, the newspaper performed an invaluable educative and cultural function.

The second great unofficial influence was that of Christian missions. Christian missionaries had worked in India from the time of St. Francis Xavier in the sixteenth century, and for a time the efforts of de Nobili and other Catholics met with great success in south India. But the effort died away in the eighteenth century[1] while Protestants were represented by a few Lutherans of whom Swartz was the most distinguished. The Company would not give missionaries licences to reside for fear of the effect of their preaching on the feelings of the people. In consequence the first British Protestants had either to live outside the Company's jurisdiction as the Baptist William Carey did at Serampore, or to serve as Company's chaplains like David Brown of Calcutta or Henry Martyn from Cambridge. In 1813 the ban on entry was raised and at the same time a bishopric created at Calcutta (later increased to three). The gracious Bishop Heber and the fiery Daniel Wilson gave distinction and vigour to the Christian cause in India and from this time the number of Christian bodies at work in India began to multiply, to be reinforced in time by many Americans and some Germans. From preaching the missionaries soon passed to teaching, helped by the new demand for English. A departure of the greatest importance was the Presbyterian Alexander Duff's foundation in 1830 of the Scottish Churches College in Calcutta. The appeal was not only to the villager and to the man in the bazaar, but to the intellectual *élite* as well. From 1854 the grant-in-aid system and government policy encouraged a rapid growth in the number of Christian schools and colleges, of which the Madras Christian College was perhaps the foremost. A further departure was the engagement of missionaries in philanthropic activity in the form of hospitals and medical work, of famine relief, and later in rural 'uplift'. Another feature was the large number of women workers of all kinds who were the pioneers of the women's movement in India. We are not here concerned with the development of the Christian community, which by 1930 constituted two per cent. of the population, but with the impact of this Christian work on India as a whole. On the practical side it presented the Chrisitian ethics in action and on the intellectual side it influenced by implication even more than by precept. Most missionaries presented the gospel in its western dress and they were therefore apostles of the West as well as of the pure spirit of Christ. By their manners and conduct, by their very existence, they were influences in favour of the western

[1] See the Abbé Dubois's, *Christianity in India*, 1818.

out ook. In these ways and in these respects Christian missionaries of all kinds exercised a profound influence, which can never be exactly measured, on the development of the new India. The influence was both positive and negative; negative by criticism of the old and positive by embodying the new ethic in personal example and corporate practice.

Nowhere was the influence of the missionaries felt more than in relation to the women's movement. India had her own tradition of feminine culture and participation in public affairs. From Sita and Draupadi of the epics the tale ran through Rajput heroines to princesses like Rupmati of Malwa and Ahalya Bai of Indore. But by 1800 there was little trace of feminine culture or public life; the less attractive aspects of the Hindu conception of the place of women in society were dominant. The new observers of Indian society therefore found little to praise in the condition of Indian women save their resignation and patient acceptance of suffering, and much to criticize. The targets of disapproval, though not all brought forward at the same time, were suttee, infanticide, child marriage, the plight of Hindu widows, purdah or seclusion from public society, polygamy, and temple prostitution. The first two of these were, as has been explained, regarded as general moral evils, and as such were attacked by the government itself, the first by legislative enactment and the second by a mixture of pressure and persuasion. The rest came within the scope of local custom and as such escaped official action. It was the missionaries who supplied the positive foil to negative government action not only by criticism, but also by setting forth a conception of womanhood new to the India of the day and by providing living examples of its nature. They did this partly by their *zenana* activities which brought new ideas behind the purdah, but still more by their educational activities. In 1830 schools for girls were almost non-existent, except perhaps in the Panjab. The first schools were started in Calcutta in the twenties but were mainly for lower-class girls. The Bethune School in 1849 transferred activity to the girls of upper-class families. It was upheld by Dalhousie for five years from his private purse, eventually to become the first government women's college. There followed medical work for women, which in time became more attractive than education. 'Belief in doctors and hospitals is more widespread than the belief in teachers and schools.' The medical development was later than the educational; the first woman doctor in India was the American Clara Swain who arrived in 1874, and the second the Englishwoman Fanny Butler who came in 1880. Thereafter the landmarks were the launching of the Countess of Dufferin's Fund in 1885, the institution of the Woman's Medical Service in 1914, and the founding of the Lady Hardinge Medical College in New Delhi in 1916. Missionaries led the way in the opening of both women's colleges and hospitals. Half the latter before independence were missionary foundations.

In another way the missionary influence was powerful. What was preached to India at large was practised by the growing Christian community. There the women's literacy rate was higher than in any other community and Christians predominated in the professions open to women. Thus example was added to precept.

These measures had a practical effect in giving women hope against the traditional monsters of ignorance, pain, and disease. They brought with them a new conception of woman as a personality and of her place in society. The effects of these measures appealed also to the masculine mind and worked both by revealing possibilities not considered before and stirring uneasy feelings at continued acquiescence in the *status quo* now shown to be as unnecessary as undesirable. In this way a reform movement *within* Indian society was born, which has gradually wrested the initiative from external agency and made the movement truly Indian. Many reformers appealed to the Hindu tradition for support, but it was contemporary foreign practice which inspired them.

We have seen how Ram Mohan Roy took up the fight against suttee and infanticide in both o⁰ which the government intervened on general moral grounds. Thereafter the *Brahmo Samaj* on reformist and the *Arya Samaj* on revivalist principles both found a religious sanction for the women's movement. The Brahmo Keshub Chander Sen advocated education, widow remarriage, and equality in the religious sphere. The Arya Dayananda championed female education on Vedic principles. The Ramkrishna mission with its missionary technique encouraged women as teachers and preachers. The eclectic Theosophical movement was long led by two notable women.

By these means the women's movement became naturalized, as it were, within Indian society. Pandit Vidyasagar secured the first Act for raising the age of consent in 1860 and the legalization of widow remarriage; Pandita Ramabai (1858-1922), a learned Sanskritist as well as a Christian, opened her home for widows; Professor Karve developed his Women's University at Poona and K. Natarajan carried on his work in Bombay. The new ideal woman was neither Sita or Mary, but rather that of the humanist European tradition, a personality in her own right, a partner in the home and a cherisher of the family, an upholder of grace and culture in society, and an actor in public causes. It was accepted by the advanced classes of both communities who searched their scriptures for supporting texts rather than sought to mould their attitude on orthodox opinion.

It was inevitable that women should seek to express their new ideals in the political as well as other spheres and that their movement should link itself with the political embodiment of the new India, the National Congress. The All-India Women's Conference, founded in 1926, soon took on a political tinge, becoming an unofficial Congress auxiliary. But it remained true to its cause, securing the foundation of the Lady Irwin College in New Delhi. The political cause of women received an impetus from the Montford reforms which led to their enfranchisement on the same terms as men.[1] Though their voting

[1] As a result of the Muddiman Committee Report in 1925.

power was small because of the property qualification, this marked the real beginning of their participation in public life. The Civil Disobedience Movement of 1930–1 gave a further fillip to the movement, for the enthusiasm it aroused led thousands of secluded ladies on to the streets as demonstration marchers, pickets of liquor shops, and so on. Some 2,000 suffered imprisonment for political reasons from 1930 to 1932. Urban Hindu society has never been quite the same since. At the same time a group of brilliant women gave both distinction to their cause and lustre to their sex. The most remarkable was perhaps Mrs. Sarojini Naidu with her combination of personality, wit, eloquence, and literary grace. Mrs. Lakshmi Pandit later attained world fame, while the Begam Shah Nawaz in the Panjab revived memories of Mughul princesses.

In the second half of the century the government left with increasing relief the moral side of improvement to unofficial agencies, while it concentrated on the material. It was the great age of public works. Dalhousie, the creator of the public works department, was as enthusiastic for these as for annexation. Lawrence ran into deficits for their sake. He introduced the principle of borrowing for productive works which was first regularized and then extended by his successors. Foremost amongst these was the railways, which developed from 200 miles of track in 1857 to 40,000 by 1940. They have already been considered in the last chapter. They made welfare possible rather than being themselves welfare measures. Here mention may be made of two great designs of direct material benefit. The first of these is irrigation. Irrigation is an age-old art in India. The early British observers found many ruined tanks built by south Indian kings and many which were still in use.[1] Firūz Shah Tughluq built a canal to Hissar which Shahjahan repaired and extended to Delhi. Even the Sikhs built a few small ones. The first phase, inaugurated by Lord Hastings, was that of restoration. In 1820 water flowed into Delhi once more and the people turned out in gala dress to welcome it. The second was the design of large original works. These were first carried out where water was plentiful, and had the effect of making land where some cultivation was already possible more productive and secure against drought. The first great work of this kind in the north was the Ganges canal, described by Dalhousie in 1856 as 'unequalled in its class and character among the efforts of civilised nations'. In the south the Grand Anicut was built two miles long across the bed of the Cauvery in 1835–6. From 1892 canals were built to irrigate waste land in regions of little or no rainfall. The Panjab and Sind were the chief beneficiaries of this phase which, with its Panjab canals and canal colonies, made the Panjab the most prosperous province of India, and which culminated in the Sukkur barrage in Sind in the nineteen-twenties. The Sukkur barrage, even before its Pakistan extensions, was the largest of its kind in the world; the Godavari system extends over 2,500 miles and the Upper and Lower Ganges canals over 8,000 miles. In the Panjab the area of

[1] It is estimated that there are 4,000 tanks or *erays* in Madras and as many in Mysore.

irrigated land was double that of Egypt. In British India by 1940 32½ million acres or one-fifth of the cultivated area was irrigated land.

The other great welfare work was the development of famine policy. Famines have periodically visited all parts of India through the failure of rains. Little action beyond resignation to the will of nature was possible because of the lack of means of transport and the slowness of that which existed. Akbar attempted some relief but for the most part little was done. The same held good in the first great famine of British India, that of Bengal in 1769–70, which swept off a third to a half of the population. At first relief methods were spasmodic, *ad hoc*, and uncertain. Relief was attempted in the famine of 1837–8 in the upper Ganges and Jumna regions. In 1866 the Orissa famine was estimated to have carried off a quarter of the population through the failure of the Bengal authorities to act in time. The great famine of 1876–8 was attacked energetically but unsystematically. Out of this visitation, however, came Lytton's Commission of 1880 under Sir Richard Strachey, from which came the Famine Code of 1883. The code laid down procedure for detecting the symptoms of food shortage, for declaring first a state of scarcity and then of famine. The main principles were the use of railways and shipping to bring in grain from unaffected areas or from overseas, the regulation of relief and the provision of work of a productive kind for the able-bodied. These new rules were embodied in a series of provincial codes and improved as a result of the Macdonnell Commission's report in 1901 after the series of famines between 1896 and 1900. The Famine Code could not prevent famine, but succeeded in converting the terrible famines of food into more tolerable famines of work. The Famine Code used the new resources of science and planning to deaden the force of India's most terrible scourge.

AUTHORITIES

THE best general authorities for this subject are the relevant chapters in the *Cambridge History of India*, vol. vi, DODWELL, *A Sketch of the History of India 1858–1918* (1925), incisive and masterly writing within its compass, and L. S. S. O'MALLEY (ed.), *Modern India and the West* (1941). A. YUSUF ALI, *A Cultural History of India during the British Period* (1940), as for the earlier period, has much interesting if jumbled information.

On local government see R. P. MASANI, *Evolution of Self-Government in Bombay* (1929), and H. TINKER, *Foundations of Local Self-Government in India, Pakistan, and Burma* (1954). For the services see L. S. S. O'MALLEY, *The Indian Civil Service* (1931), G. O. TREVELYAN, *The Competition-wallah* (1866). There is a good chapter on the press in *Modern India and the West*. In addition, M. BARNS, *The Indian Press* (1940), may be consulted. See also *Indian Press Commission Report*, 1954–5, vol. ii, *History of Indian Journalism*, by J. NATARAJAN. For missions, in addition to LATOURETTE, see J. RICHTER, *History of Missions in India* (1908), and A. MAYHEW, *Christianity and the Government of India* (1929). For law reform see the *Cambridge History* and *Modern India and the West*, and for public works refer to the last chapter.

For education, in addition to the titles mentioned in Book VIII, Chapter 7, the following may be consulted: *Report of the Indian Educational (Hunter) Commission*, 1882, *The Calcutta University Commission (Sadler) Report*, 1919, *The Interim Report of the Statutory Commission (education)*, 1929, H. SHARP and J. A. RICHEY, *Selections from the Educational Records of the Government of India*, 2 vols., Calcutta, 1920–2.

CHAPTER 6

The New India—The Indian Response

THE benevolence of an alien government and administrative measures were not in themselves sufficient to create a new India; without the breath of internal life to animate them they would form no more than the dry bones of regeneration. We have therefore to consider the Indian reaction to the government and the measures which came to them from abroad. The first Indian reaction to the Europeans in India was one of curiosity and interest, which in the case of the Portuguese soon turned to hostility. But apart from the coastal regions where Portuguese power had to be reckoned with, curiosity remained the dominant attitude in Mughul times, whether it was Akbar questioning Jesuit missionaries or Jahangir exchanging drinks or pictures with a Hawkins or Sir Thomas Roe. Europeans were people to be used to advantage whether in commerce or war. When in the eighteenth century the Europeans developed military power their help was sought in local conflicts; when their power was seen to be a political menace the reaction was a military one. The rajas and nawabs sought European arms, European systems of discipline and military organization, and European auxiliaries in order to repel the threat from abroad. But they went no further, seeking to borrow just enough from the new alien culture to preserve themselves. The tale ran from Mir Kasim to Ranjit Singh, ending finally at Gujarat in 1849.

By 1820 India as a whole recognized that mere military skill would not exorcise the unwelcome new spirit. Those closest to the British also realized that the western invasion was not to be confined to rulers and soldiers. New British were not to be old Mughuls writ large; by their administrative arrangements and their itch for improvements they were unsettling the old modes of life; while their boundless self-confidence in their civilization made them ready to seize opportunities for introducing it into the country. Only caution as to the consequences and some regard for tradition restrained their eagerness. The restoration of order was to be but the prelude to revolution. From the late eighteenth century when the *vakils* of the country powers had friendly converse with Warren Hastings and Ghulam Husain Khan reflected on the changing times, men were beginning to think out their attitude to this larger threat. The first reaction in both Hindu and Muslim circles was the conservative one. Political submission must not be followed by cultural *hari-kari*. Apart from the borrowing of such externals as European uniforms, furniture, novelties, and wines the attitude was one of aloofness. Rather than share in the new world the old governing classes withdrew from it. Their refuge in British India was their estates and their memories, elsewhere the courts of the surviving princes. The religious conservatives, whether Brahmans or *maulvis*, took the same line; they opposed innovation and withdrew as far as possible from contact with it. But complete withdrawal was impossible as the interfering measures of Bentinck were followed up by Auckland, Ellenborough, and Dalhousie. A reservoir of emotional distaste was thus collected by such measures as western education, abolition of rent-free tenures for religious purposes, the neglect of Persian, the introduction of the telegraph, steam power, and railways, and Christian activity. From these sources came the popular pressure which lay behind the Mutiny in which it found its outlet.

But there were others who were either more or less far-sighted than the mass of lovers of the old ways. The smallest of the groups was prepared to surrender in the cultural battle as it had done in the political. It existed chiefly in Calcutta. There it was influenced by the rationalism prevalent among the British including the famous watchmaker David Hare and the young Anglo-Indian Derozio, and by the Christian persuasions of Alexander Duff. There was a short-lived movement among young intellectuals to renounce Hinduism and all its works whose outward signs were Christian baptism and beef-eating clubs. As a movement this died away after 1840. The larger movement contained those who, though anxious to remain loyal to their cultural and religious past, realized that religion in its existing state could offer no antidote to the foreign influences. They thus sought to strengthen the old by purifying it, and they would purify by going back to the sources to their faith. They were the Protestant reformers of Hinduism and Islam.

The first of these movements was that of the *Brahmo Samaj* founded by Ram Mohan Roy in 1828.[1] The aim of the group which gathered round Ram Mohan Roy was to meet criticisms of Hinduism by removing the accretions of ages. Ram Mohan Roy went back to the Upanishads for his authority and there he found the principle of reason leading to a lofty intellectual theism. From this citadel he could denounce the evils of latter-day Hinduism such as idolatry and polygamy, suttee and female infanticide. He could also use against European critics their own weapon of reason, with such effect that one missionary became a Unitarian. 'Ram Mohan', says Dr. Farquhar, 'believed he was restoring Hindu worship to its pristine purity.' The *Samaj* was joined by Dwarkanath Tagore, whose son Devendranath became its head; it was developed and disrupted by the wayward genius Keshub Chander Sen; parallel societies were formed in Madras, Bombay, and Lahore. It has remained small but influential, tolerant, and intellectual but lacking in broad popular sympathy. It was the intellectual's rather than everyman's response to the western challenge.

The *Brahmo Samaj* remained a select society, in spite of the efforts of

[1] See Book VIII, Chapter 7.

Keshub Chander Sen; the *Arya Samaj* was a cult on the old lines.
Whereas Ram Mohan Roy went to the Upanishads for his inspiration,
the founder of the *Arya Samaj*, Swami Dayananda,[1] relied on the four
Vedas. Dayananda was born in 1824 in Gujarat, attained enlighten-
ment by the orthodox process of austerity, and founded his society in
1875. He was devoted, emphatic, and militant. In his return to the
primitive scriptures and his pugnacious attitude to Brahmanism he
was a Luther to Ram Mohan Roy's Erasmus. He denounced idolatry,
polygamy, and caste, preached a return to the simplicity of Vedic ritual
and the austerity of Vedic manners, and maintained that all truth was
to be found in the four Vedas. The movement proved to have moral
vigour. It became an important influence in the Panjab and was active
elsewhere. It was a curious mixture of old and new, of breadth and
sectarianism. Within Hindu society it attacked Brahman privilege and
was a strong reforming influence; without it opposed Islam with
bitterness and Christian activity with vigour. Its greatest obstacle was
the contradiction between its modern outlook in such things as education and its 'fundamentalist' assumptions. For this reason many who
were attracted by its anti-Brahmanism were repelled in turn by its anti-
rationalism. The *Samaj* had most appeal in the north, where Brahman
influence was not strong, but made little headway in the east and south.
It helped to awaken without succeeding in uniting the new India.

A further response to the western challenge came from the followers
of Ramkrishna Paramahamsa. If Ram Mohan Roy was the mind, Dayananda the physical arm, Ramkrishna was the soul of the new India.
Ramkrishna, who spent most of his life at a temple near Calcutta,[2] was
a *bhakti* in the great tradition who sought to realize God by the *bhakti
mārga* or path of loving devotion. After twelve years of storm he
attained peace and spent the rest of his life talking to admirers, disciples,
seekers, and the curious. While his personal way was that of self-
surrender, his theology was Vedantic. His disciples devoted themselves
to the spread of his teaching and found a leader in Swami Vivekananda[3]
and a talented follower in the Irishwoman Sister Nivedita.[4] Vivekananda added social service and self-reliance to the traditional Hindu
devotion and did much to rehabilitate Hinduism in the eyes of both
Indians and the world by his tours and advocacy at the Chicago World
Conference of Religions in 1893. His legacy was the Ramkrishna mission which was notable for good works and the view that all religions
are at bottom the same. Ramkrishna and his disciples did much to
restore Hinduism's confidence in itself and in its status in the world.
But Ramkrishna has not proved a new Buddha any more than Dayananda. Perhaps the gulf between his ascetic devotion and the modern

---

[1] Swami Dayananda died in 1883. Prominent members of the *Arya Samaj* were
Lala Lajpat Rai, founder of the Servants of the People Society and Rai Sahib
Harbilas Sarda, sponsor of the Sarda Act.
[2] At Dakshineshwar, four miles north of Calcutta. He lived from 1834 to 1886.
[3] Lived 1862–1902.   [4] Miss Margaret Noble. She died in 1911.

world was too great; he did something to fill an emotional void in the soul of modern India, but his real answer to the problems, practical and intellectual, of the new generation, was to withdraw from them. People were inspired and comforted by these men rather than converted by them. They were heralds of the new India rather than its *avatars*.

One more movement may be cited, that of theosophy. The Theosophical Society was founded in 1875 by Madame Blavatsky, a talented and colourful Russian lady. The society was at first a spiritualist one. It attained influence in India under the leadership of Mrs. Annie Besant with its headquarters at Adyar near Madras. Spiritualism led to the *rishis* of the Himalayas as the repositories of spiritual truth. As a cult theosophy was eventually discredited by the controversies which surrounded it, and by the cult of the Messiah of Mrs. Besant's latter days. It was too vague to develop from a fashion or an influence to a sect or a religion. But its influence was nevertheless considerable: its religious syncretism satisfied those who wanted reassurance in the Hindu religion in the face of modern criticism, while its pseudo-intellectualism attracted those who were repelled by the emotionalism of Ramkrishna. It praised Hinduism in western terms without demanding any particular action. For this reason it had much vogue among the westernized classes during the early years of the century. Mrs. Besant became a figure in public affairs. With Pt. Madan Mohan Malaviya she founded the Benares Hindu University and had her hour of political fame as the creator of the Home Rule League in 1915. But the movement was too shallow to take deep root and too lacking in a positive programme to carry the country with it for long. It was another milestone on the Indian path to nationhood.

In the Muslim community similar movements were stirring though they were a full generation behind those within Hindu society. The Muslims had lost temporal dominion and inner self-confidence at the same moment and for some time seemed too stunned to be able to recover. But the same pattern can be traced, though it took shape more slowly and at a later date. There were the *Wahabis*[1] of Patna and Moradabad with their call to the puritan simplicity of primitive Islam. There was the heterodox Ahmadiya movement[2] of Qadian in the Panjab with its affinities with Bahaism in Persia. And there was the synthetic mind of Sayyid Ahmad Khan,[3] who sought to reconcile the spirit of Islam with that of the modern West. In some ways his work was easier than that of Ram Mohan Roy because there was much more common ground between western and Islamic than between western and Hindu ideas. In other ways it was more difficult because Muslims were more hostile to the West than Hindus as their political sup-

[1] The title came from resemblance to rather than identity with the Arabian movement of that name.
[2] Founded by Mirza Ghulam Ahmad (c. 1838–1908) about 1879.
[3] 1815–98.

planters, were less educated and so less open to new ideas, and were more deeply bound by tradition. Sayyid Ahmad Khan's great achievement was the foundation in 1875 of the Anglo-Arabic College at Aligarh, later to become the Aligarh Muslim university. The development of modern Islam in India will be treated more fully in a later chapter.[1]

The cult which eventually united the new westernized classes was the un-Indian one of nationalism. The mind which made this possible was that of Ram Mohan Roy. For this reason he may be described as the greatest creative personality of nineteenth-century India. For he was much more than the founder of the *Brahmo Samaj* and an active public figure. During his seventeen years of public activity between 1813 and 1830 he laid down the main lines of advance for what was to become the Indian national movement. His attitude towards the West was neither that of surrender, withdrawal, or conflict. It was one of comprehension. The new world from the West was not to be a substitute but a supplement to the old. Synthesis, which is different to syncretism, was his remedy for the predicament of Hinduism. The instrument of synthesis was reason, the principle he found enshrined in the Upanishads. Once this was accepted the western challenge could be met face to face. Western loans would not involve eastern apostasy; loyalty and reform could go hand in hand. On this basis he accepted theism as an Upanishadic doctrine; he accepted individuality from the same source, and with it the whole liberal gospel of political rights. He held a dinner to celebrate the 1830 revolution in France. His treatment of suttee was characteristic. He condemned it on moral grounds, but at the same time supported his position by quotations from sacred texts while refuting those quoted by his opponents. A Hindu could accept the moral rationalism of the West because real Hinduism was both moral and rational. We are not here concerned with the ultimate validity of this contention as with its historical relevance; it provided the rising westernized class with just that bridge between their old and new mental worlds which they needed.

It is now time to turn to the fortunes of this class itself. The old middle class of India played a very subordinate part in the affairs of India. It was divided by distance, by language, by caste feeling, and by occupation. It had no common consciousness and was dependent everywhere on the intellectual aristocracy of the Brahmans and the landed aristocracy of *sardars* and *zamindars*. The merchant had little in common with the government official, or the doctor with the lawyer. Each profession or vocation was insulated from others by walls of custom and prejudice. No common consciousness was possible until this exclusiveness between upper and lower, between group and group was broken down. The first step in the process was taken by the British in their earlier years, by the removal or setting aside of the old upper classes. Their political encroachments culminated in the exclusion of

[1] Book X, Chapter 5: the Pakistan movement.

higher Indian agency in government service by Cornwallis in 1793.
The old rulers retired in proud poverty to muse on past glories and
saw no reason for learning a foreign language which could lead to no
honourable employment. The new land settlements tended also to
eclipse the old landed gentry. Polygars disappeared in Madras, *zamindaris* changed hands in Bengal, *jagirs* were reduced and the holders of
rent-free tenures found their rights called in question.[1] Those that
survived could hope for no suitable government employment and their
local influence was steadily whittled away by the clipping of their legal
and revenue powers. These people could not obtain suitable public
employment and would not equip themselves for a place in the new
order by taking up western education.

The way was thus cleared for the middle class. The cover, as it were,
was taken off Indian society and with it the old limits to their aspirations.
But at first development was one-sided and capricious. The first groups
to benefit were the merchants and financiers at the seats of British
power, the go-betweens of the new order. Many of the more successful
purchased *zamindaris* as they lapsed after the Permanent Settlement of
1793. Merchants in general profited by the new security. There was a
rush to learn English from these classes at the British ports, for what
were in most cases freely admitted to be business reasons. But there
was yet no solidarity with other sections of the class. *Bania* or *sowarkar*
had no truck with *kayasth* or *khattri*, or *hakim* and *vaid* with *maulvi*
and *pandit*. There were no common bonds, no spiritual links. It was
these which the next batch of British measures in the thirties were
to provide—the reforms of Bentinck and his successors. The official
teaching of English was a utilitarian measure, and was welcomed as
such even by the conservative Raja Radhakant Deb. But with it went
western knowledge and science so that with the new language came
knowledge of the new world. The transition from Persian to English
as the language of government business and the higher courts greatly
increased the use and so the demand for English. Presently came with
Dalhousie the great expansion of schools and colleges under the grant-
in-aid system (from 1854).

With this increased demand for English in subordinate posts went
the rise of new professions which offered scope and status to men of
ability. The new colleges and schools required teachers whose position
in society was honourable. The new legal system required professional
lawyers, who again were men of independence and position. The profession of western medicine was introduced with Bentinck's Calcutta
Medical College. In the administration itself opportunities of service
were widening with the opening of higher services to Indian appointment and the increasing prestige of lesser offices like those of *tahsildar*.
The advance of western techniques created further openings for the
enterprising in the railways (from 1856), the public works departments, the engineering, forest, and other services. All these services

[1] Under Bentinck and specially by the Imam Commission of Bombay.

were closed to those too proud to serve in subordinate positions but offered enlargement to those anxious to make their way. Thus the upper class continued to hold aloof and the middle class to expand and profit. Even Lytton's statutory civil service failed to attract the former, but its successor, the provincial service, was eagerly sought after by the latter. It was a grand administrative example of the meek inheriting the earth.

Not only was the middle class stimulated and expanded by the new opportunities; it was drawn together as never before. The new education gave it a common language and common stock of ideas and knowledge to be held side by side with its various sectional traditions. The new press continued their contact with the new mental world and enabled their own reactions to it to circulate. The new communications enabled Madras to talk to Delhi and Bombay to meet with Calcutta. Thus in the fifty years between the new education policy and the Ilbert Bill was born from the middle stratum of society a new integrated all-India class with varied background but a common foreground of knowledge, ideas, and values. Of course it was a minority of Indian society. But the important thing about it was that it was a dynamic minority. It had a sense of unity, of purpose, and of hope. It was the newborn soul of modern India. In time it was to infuse the whole of India with its spirit.

It was inevitable that this new class should aspire to a political expression of its views. The whole European liberal movement of the nineteenth century was keyed in political terms; in thinking in these terms the new class was only practising the precepts it had received. It was also inevitable that there should be some friction between alien governors and native governed. The one was not likely to want to retire at exactly the same pace as the other wished to advance. The relevant questions were how much, for how long, and with what results. We have seen that the British from the thirties envisaged eventual self-government, but that after the Mutiny their definition of 'eventual' became decidedly elastic. There was thus clearly a community of ultimate aims with an early difference in the matter of pace. But two other factors intervened. In the first place the British looked for the leaders of the new India in the wrong direction. The earlier administrators assumed that the leaders would come from the old governing class. Elphinstone's proposed Indianization of a Bombay district was to be carried out by this class, and so were Malcolm's similar suggestions; Dalhousie looked to this class for an Indian appointment to his new Legislative Council; Henry Lawrence staked his whole career on the regeneration of the Sikh *sardars*; Canning drew on this class for the first Indian appointments to the new Legislative Council in 1862; and Lytton looked to them to man his statutory civil service. When it was clear that they were not forthcoming from this class in any number many British officials ceased to look any farther. When political gestures began to come from the new middle-class these men refused to regard them as valid. Can any good thing come out of Nazareth, was their attitude. Henceforth British opinion, both in India and England, was divided on the genuineness of the middle class national movement. Before 1914 the majority view minimized its importance; it was only at the end of the nineteen-twenties, and largely as a result of the efforts of Lord Halifax, that a consensus of British opinion accepted the Indian national movement as the major political fact of Indian life. In the second place, as the country became settled, British officials tended to concern themselves less and less with politics and more and more with administration. The aim of efficiency in government tended to replace that of understanding the people. There was so much to do that there was less time to confer and consider. Speakers and leaders with little public experience, whose ideas of public affairs came from the liberal literature of Europe and Britain, seemed to them to be impractical dreamers. There was here a clash of temperament which in the circumstances was unavoidable.

The new class found its growth stimulated by the opposite ingredients of encouragement and opposition. On the positive side was the attitude of the more far-sighted governor-generals from Bentinck downwards, declarations like the Charter Act of 1833 and the Queen's Proclamation of 1858, the first steps in the Indianization of the legislature, the judiciary, and the services, and the growing support of liberal opinion in England. The influence of Gladstone in this respect was most important. Another encouraging factor, in that it increased feelings of self-respect, was the new interest in Indian culture and letters in Europe, which, beginning with the work of Sir Williams Jones in the late eighteenth century, spread throughout Europe in the nineteenth. On the reverse side there was the impatience engendered by the tardiness and modesty of the Indianization process; there was the resentment aroused by the keen criticism of Indian institutions and the widespread assumption that they were barbarous rather than civilized;[1] there was, specially in western India, resentment at what was thought to be unfair commercial discrimination, and there was the bitterness aroused by the racial slights to which the lower ranks of Europeans were increasingly addicted.

The first centre of political action was the eloquent and volatile world of Calcutta. Discussions on ethics and social reforms easily passed on into politics. The first body which can be called political was the British Indian Association founded in the forties. It was a decorous body of landowners, concerned mainly with safeguarding its own interests, which expressed preferences rather than made demands. In 1876 the Indian Association was formed by Surendranath Bannerjea who had become a teacher after a brief career in the civil service. He joined organizing ability to eloquence, and soon found objects to absorb his energies. The lowering of the age of entrance to the civil

[1] See J. Mill, *History of India*, Books II and III. Macaulay and indeed many Liberals were sinners in this respect.

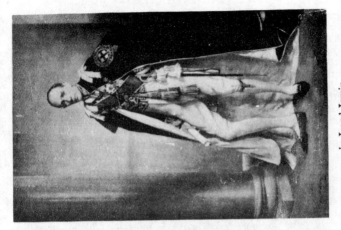

b. Lord Irwin

a. Lord Curzon

service (thus further prejudicing Indian chances of entry) was the first of these and enabled him to found branch associations. Lytton's Press Act of 1878 provided another and still more popular issue.

Then came Ripon as the harbinger of Gladstonianism to India. If he had been a more forceful character he would not have prevented the formation of Congress but he might have strengthened those elements which wished to achieve their ideals in harmonious co-operation with the British. His first measures raised both the self-confidence and the prestige of the new nationalists. Then came the Ilbert Bill controversy, with its bitter expression of racial antagonism and suspicion, its flouting of authority and its well-organized agitation among the non-official European community of Bengal. This was the spur which finally drove the young nationalists to decided action, the reagent which precipitated the solution of the Indian Congress. The example of successful agitation, and the knowledge of such bodies as the Anti-Corn Law League and the Irish Land and National Leagues produced action on similar lines.

The first meeting of the Indian National Congress took place in Bombay in December 1885. It was supported at the outset by a group of liberal-minded Englishmen, including A. O. Hume, son of the radical Joseph Hume and a retired civil servant, Sir W. Wedderburn, Sir David Yule, and later Sir Henry Cotton.[1] The first session comprised only seventy members, who had elected themselves by paying a small fee. They were mainly lawyers, journalists, and schoolmasters. The second session contained nearly 450 members chosen by public meetings and bodies. From that time there was no looking back. The Congress became an annual large-scale conference containing representatives from all communities and all provinces. The only group which noticeably held back was the Muslim under the advice of Sir Sayyid Ahmʌd Khan; democratic government, he said, would be government by Hindus. The Congress soon developed its organization of annual president, working committee, general committee, and full session, its procedure of presidential address, debates, and resolutions. It organized a network of local branches, it developed its own *ethos* or atmosphere. It soon became a party without ceasing to be a movement and around it grew up a circle of sympathizers more numerous than its actual membership. Outside the great cities membership was still something of an adventure and mere attendance at its meetings required an act of will.

The attitude of the government to this development was cautious but not unfriendly. Lord Dufferin recognized something of its significance and gave it a remote and olympian blessing. He used its rise as an occasion for pressing for an extension of the council system which led, after four years of discussion, to the Indian Councils Act of 1892. Though this by no means satisfied all, it had certain concrete results. The fact of election, disguised as recommendation for nomination,

[1] Three Englishmen were Presidents of Congress between 1885 and 1900.

opened the door for the entry of Congressmen into these hitherto aristocratic purlieus. G. K. Gokhale entered the central Legislative Council and soon became one of its outstanding members. The enlargement of the council's powers to include a discussion on the budget enabled questions of general policy as well as particular proposals to be discussed. Gokhale's annual budget speech at Calcutta became, with the Congress president's inaugural address, the twin political event of the new nationalist world.

Within Congress itself trends and strains soon developed. At the outset the prevailing influence was Gladstonian liberalism with some tincture of Italian idealism.[1] This long remained the dominant school, but there was from the beginning another current which looked upon liberalism as a means rather than an end. Their end, like that of their colleagues, was self-government, but their concept of its form was more Indian than European, more traditional than democratic. From the beginning Bombay played an equal part with Calcutta in shaping the Congress destinies. The second president was the Parsi liberal Dadabhai Naoraji, who was also for some years a Liberal member of the British Parliament, and the third was a Bombay Muslim. It was in Bombay that the tension between the two views first became evident. It was embodied in the persons of two Chitpavan Brahmans of Poona, G. K. Gokhale, the disciple of Justice Ranade, and Bal Gangadhar Tilak, the editor of the Marathi newspaper *Kesari*. Tilak looked backward to Sivaji and the glories of Maratha empire, while Gokhale looked forward to parliamentary rule based on liberal rationalism. The difference of view was revealed in the Bombay plague crisis of 1897 when Tilak encouraged orthodox resistance to measures of health precaution, praised Sivaji's violence on Afzal Khan as being above the moral law, and was imprisoned for incitement to disaffection. Thus began the divison between moderates and extremists.

Thus by the end of the century, within fifteen years of its foundation, the members of the Congress had seized the initiative in internal Indian affairs. The class from which they sprang was described by Lord Dufferin in 1888 as a 'microscopic minority'. The statement was statistically correct; what mattered was that this small and thinly spread group had become possessed of a creative idea, which was eventually to give them the leadership of the dormant masses and the drugged upper classes. The minority was creative and dynamic. It was a leaven which would leaven the whole lump. And the leaven was principally a western leaven.

AUTHORITIES

For Ram Mohan Roy refer to the notes under Book VIII. Chapter 7. For religious movement; generally the best work in English is J. N. FARQUHAR, *Modern Religious Movements in India* (1919). For the *Brahmo Samaj* see M. C. PAREKH, *The Brahmo Mazzini*.

[1] Many of the early leaders, including Surendranath Bannerjea, were admirers of Mazzini.

Samaj(1929), for the *Arya Samaj* the works of HARBILAS SARDA, for Ram Krishna an ' Vivekananda those of ROMAIN ROLLAND and Sister NIVEDITA. For Muslim movements, in addition to Farquhar, see W. CANTWELL SMITH, *Modern Islam in India* (1943), and G. F. I. GRAHAM, *Sir Syed Ahmad Khan* (1885).

On the political side see V. CHIROL, *India* (1926), W. W. HUNTER, *Indian Mussulmans* (1876), and B. B. MAJUMDAR, *History of Political Thought, Bengal 1821–84* (1934). C. F. ANDREWS, *Maulvi Zakaullah of Delhi* (1929), describes the up-country renaissance. Early developments may be studied in the following works: Sir S. N. BANNERJEE, *A Nation in Making*(1925), Sir H. COTTON, *New India* (1885), and *Indian and Home Memories* (1911), Sir W. WEDDERBURN, *A. O. Hume* (1913), H. P. MODY, *Sir Pherozeshah Mehta* (1921), B. C. PAL, *Memories of my Life and Time* (1932), J. N. GUPTA, *R. C. Dutt* (1911), and DEVENDRANATH TAGORE, *Autobiography* (1914). C. F. ANDREWS and A. MUKERJI, *Rise and Growth of Congress in India* (1938) give a sketch of pre- and early Congress days. Two modern works on Tilak may be mentioned. They are: S. L. KARANDIKAR, *Lokomanya Bal Gangadhar Tilak* (1957) and D. V. TAMHANKAR, *Lokomanya Tilak* (1956). See also RAJENDRA PRASAD, *Autobiography* (1956).

B. B. MISRA's *Indian Middle Classes* (1961) is an important pioneer study of this group.

CHAPTER 7

The States

IN this chapter it is proposed to make a rapid survey of the relations of Company and Crown with the Indian states. The first intention of the East India Company was to have nothing to do with governing. If there was an Indian government capable of providing security, they would operate under its wing; if not, they would operate *through* the nearest available government. Until 1750 the Mughul government provided the first alternative. Thereafter the Company tried for fifty years to operate *through* the Carnatic government instead of superseding it. It was only after folly and mischief on both sides had so loaded the nawab with debt that nearly the whole of his revenue was assigned to pay the interest that the administration was taken over in 1801. Clive went to Bengal intending to act *through* and not *over* the subadari as Bussy had successfully done in Hyderabad. It was his own unwisdom after Plassey and the failure of the Company to control its servants which converted a military supremacy into a *de facto* administration. In the west the Bombay government was not able to infiltrate into Maharashtra as had been done elsewhere; its acquisitions were by annexation and were confined to such limited areas as Salsette and Broach.

We may reckon that the Company first possessed a defined territorial empire in India from 1765, the date of the Mughul grant of the *diwani* to Clive. From this date began the Company's relations with dependent Indian states apart from the two cases just mentioned. The first case was that of Oudh. This state from 1765 was in a state of dependence because its nawab Shuja-ud-daula had been restored by Clive when a fugitive after the battle of Baksar. The price was a payment of 50 *lakhs* and a treaty of mutual assistance. The terms seemed fair enough, but in fact the position was one-sided, because it was always the Nawab Wazir who needed help. The help meant troops on the frontier, and the troops had to be paid for. Therefore his dependence deepened though he remained nominally independent, until in 1801 Wellesley annexed half the state in commutation of arrears of subsidy, leaving Oudh completely surrounded by Company's territory except on the side of Nepal. Other treaties before 1798 including those with the Nizam were made on a basis of equal status.

The real creation of dependent states dates from Lord Wellesley's governor-generalship. Mysore was conquered and handed over to its old Hindu rulers on terms of subordination. Half of Oudh was annexed and the rest insulated. But Wellesley's main instrument was the system of subsidiary treaties which was first practised on the Nizam and whose working has been explained in Book VII, Chapter 10. The essentials were the planting of a subsidiary force within the prince's dominions for his defence against attack which was paid for by the prince himself. Wellesley intended to use this method as an instrument for securing the Company's paramountcy throughout India; in fact the resistance of Holkar and the Jats ruled that it should be a step towards supremacy only. Here again the treaties were still ostensibly with equal powers; there was limitation of foreign relations but no interference with internal sovereignty. The Nizam used the royal 'we' in correspondence and was addressed in terms implying superior rank until 1829.

The next step came in 1818 with the crushing of the Pindaris and the Peshwa, the pacification of central India, and the admission of the Rajput states to the British system. To the nominally independent states with subsidiary treaties and the few avowedly dependent ones like Mysore were now added both a number of ancient principalities like the Rajput princes and small chiefships which had never known anything but dependence. Some of them, like Amir Khan's state of Tonk, represented an adventurer's gains recognized for the sake of tranquillity; others like Firozpur were grants made in reward for services rendered.

The states as a whole covered more than a third of the area of British India. Their exact relationship to the new government exercised the best minds amongst the Company's servants. Metcalfe argued that the government should claim the rights of paramountcy as the heir of the Mughuls but the matter was never fully thought out and decided. The policy actually adopted was that known as subordinate isolation. The states were subordinate to the supreme government in their foreign relations, any move towards independence being promptly dealt with.[1] But internally they were recognized as sovereign and there was as little interference as possible. Even in the case of Mysore, which was a subordinate state created by treaty, misgovernment did not lead to annexation but to the taking over of the administration. In Oudh mis-government produced frequent and urgent remonstrance; in Hydera-bad interference occurred on account of chronic arrears of subsidy payments. In general the grounds of interference were financial rather than administrative. A striking example of this policy was Dalhousie's refusal to interfere in the civil war of succession in Bahawalpur State.

The next great change came with Dalhousie. It may here be convenient to cite Dalhousie's classification of states, as modified by Sir Charles Wood, then President of the Board of Control, in 1854.[2]

First. States which have from a time antecedent to our rule been independent or quasi-independent, not tributary or owing their nominal allegiance to any superior.

[1] e.g. Auckland's annexation of Kurnul and Bentinck's of Coorg.
[2] Sir W. Lee-Warner, *Life of the Marquis of Dalhousie*, vol. ii, pp. 155–6.

Secondly. States dating from a similar period, but owing origin distinctly to a grant from some authority to which we have succeeded.

Thirdly. States owing their origin to our grant or gift.

During the thirty years which had passed since 1818 the climate of British opinion about Indian states had changed. The former relief at having a large part of India removed from the direct responsibility of the government had been replaced by uneasiness about conditions within the states. The first object of government had been security and tranquillity and for these purposes subordinate states were convenient and inexpensive instruments. But now the concern was not only government but good government, not only security but welfare. And the conviction was strong that the only good government was British government, that the only way to promote welfare was through British agents. Dalhousie voiced this conviction in his famous declaration.[1]

I take this opportunity of recording my strong and deliberate opinion, that in the exercise of a wise and sound policy the British Government is bound not to put aside or neglect such rightful opportunities of acquiring territory or revenue as may from time to time present themselves, whether they arise from the lapse of subordinate states by the failure of all heirs of every description whatsoever, or from the failure of heirs natural where the succession can be sustained only by the sanction of the Government being given to the ceremony of adoption according to Hindu law.

From this standpoint he developed his annexation policy, both by reason of lapse and other grounds. Though Dalhousie avowedly limited the application of lapse to subordinate states, it so happened that his annexations on general grounds were even more extensive than those on account of lapse. Colour was therefore given to the fear that annexation would not stop short at subordinate states, and that if one pretext would not serve another would be found. The details of Dalhousie's measures are dealt with in Book VIII, Chapter 8.

The Mutiny put an end to these plans and these fears. Both the danger of tampering with established loyalties and the value of those loyalties to the government were realized. The concept of subordinate isolation was replaced by that of subordinate union. The states were no longer considered to be stagnant backwaters apart from the main river of Indian life of which a reforming government was rather ashamed, and whom many expected to be eventually united with the parent stream. They were now to be integral parts of the whole intricate system of Indian political waterways. Canning's description of them as breakwaters in the storm illustrated the new appreciation of their value. Several steps were taken to implement the new attitude. The first measure was one which should have been taken many years previously. Along with the abolition of the Company's government the Crown stood out as the paramount power of India as the successor

---

[1] Minute of 30 Aug. 1848. He explained later that he was referring to dependent states only. But the minute stands as an expression of the new outlook.

of the Mughuls. The link between the government and the princes was henceforth direct, personal, and intimate. The assumption of the imperial title by the queen in 1876, along with the pageantry of Lytton and the subsequent Delhi Durbars, served but to dramatize the new relationship. The princes were now regarded, in the Mughul fashion, as an order instead of as a number of obsolescent survivals. The heads of the Arcot and Oudh families were given the title of prince and others were admitted to the orders of chivalry. Lytton projected an Indian peerage. Against the Crown they had no rights, but beneath its shelter they enjoyed its fostering care.

The new position was underlined by Lord Curzon when he said at Bahawalpur, 'the sovereignty of the Crown is everywhere unchallenged; it has itself laid down the limitations of its own prerogative'.[1] It was stated for the last time by Lord Reading in dealing with a Hyderabad claim when he said 'the sovereignty of the Crown is supreme in India'.[2]

The next step was to remove the specific grievances which had been agitating the princes. The doctrine of lapse was explicitly abandoned and *sanads* recognizing the right of adoption issued by Lord Canning. Further the integrity of the princely territories was guaranteed. Not only did annexations come to an end but there were actual additions in certain cases. Grants of land were made as rewards for loyalty during the Mutiny. The Mysore State was handed back to its raja in 1881 after fifty years of sequestration, and the *zamindari* of Benares was elevated to statehood in 1912. Lord Curzon's transactions over the Berars with the Nizam in 1903 only made more binding what had already been done by Dalhousie. When misgovernment became acute the remedy was no longer absorption but a period of British administration under a regency.

These measures and this new attitude transformed the relations of British and Indian India. For the pathetic dependence, latent suspicion, and sometimes veiled hostility of the past were substituted in general a spirit of confidence and positive co-operation. The princes felt that they had a future once more, and the best of them rose to the occasion. One sign of this new confidence on both sides was the formation of the Imperial Service Corps by Lord Dufferin. Under this scheme units were raised by princes and officered by Indians pledged to imperial service when required. They proved their military worth in both world wars and numbered some 27,000 at the outbreak of the second. Another was the participation of the princes in imperial events like Queen Victoria's jubilee and her successors' coronations as well as in Indian ones like the Durbars. After the first World War, when India became a member of the League of Nations, princes like the Rajas of Bikanir and Patiala took a share in her international representation. The opinion may be hazarded that if Britain had followed the Mughul example more closely and pushed co-operation still further the results

1 Sir T. Raleigh (ed.), *Lord Curzon in India*, p. 227.
2 Declaration of 22 Mar. 1926.

might have been even more striking. The federal scheme of 1935 might then well have been implemented with incalculable results for later development.

Along with the new outlook went a change in the character or tone of the princely order. For fifty years after the Mutiny the spirit of both British and Indian India was the same, that of paternalism. Paternalism in British India could now be matched by benevolent despotism in the states. It was an imperial interest to see that this benevolence should be in the new fashion rather than the old. This the government endeavoured to achieve by example, by encouragement, and by education. Princes were encouraged to educate their cadets along European lines, to study modern methods of administration, and to enlarge their horizons by travel. Lord Mayo founded chiefs' colleges whose discipline was perhaps but a shadow of that of the public schools of England, but which possessed a distinct spirit and exercised a positive influence nevertheless. The old type of prince, nurtured in the *zenana* and softened by traditional vices without being tempered by the traditional hazards of war and politics, gave place in many cases to the man of modern outlook regarding his domains as an estate to be improved. Princely modernism might be vicious as well as benevolent, leading to Parisian nightlights rather than the administrator's desk; sometimes it did both. But a new class of men was to be found among the princes just as a new spirit was to be found in the states themselves. Before the Mutiny capable princes were rare and effective ministers like Sir Salar Jung and Sir Dinkar Rao occasional. Afterwards princes matched ministers and the efforts of both were furthered by loans and exchanges with British India. Sir Chamo Rajendra of Mysore (1868-96) and his son Krishna Raja, the Gaekwar Sayaji Rao (1875-1936), Sir Madhu Rao Sindia of Gwalior (1886-1925), and Sir Ganga Singh of Bikanir (1887-1934), were examples of the new type of forward looking princes, while three successive Begams of Bhopal[1] matched on the Muslim side the eighteenth-century fame of Ahalya Bai of Indore for wisdom and benevolence. Diwans were no longer a race apart; but included men trained in the British administrative school like R. C. Dutt, Sir Akbar Hydari, and Sir Mirza Ismail, and public men from British India like Dadabhai Naoraji. Progress was not equal. Many small states and some larger ones remained feudal and primitive like Udaipur in Rajputana; but in others like Baroda and Mysore the standard of administration equalled and in some respects surpassed that current in British India. A well-administered Indian state exhibited an attractive blend of tradition and progress and led many to believe that this was the true path of Indian progress to modernity. These were the men to whom Malcolm and Elphinstone would have looked for the eventual self-government of India. But they came too late, were encouraged too little, were too spasmodic in their efforts and too confined in their limits; by the time that they had begun to achieve result

[1] Nawab Sikandar Begam, Shah Jahan Begam, and Sultan Jahan Begam

and to claim notice, another class had seized the initiative and bathed in the troubled waters of nationalism.

But if the princes had gained security, a larger outlook, and a new sense of mission, they had also to submit to greater interference than formerly and to certain curtailments of their power. The legal basis of this was the doctrine of paramountcy or the royal prerogative taken over from the Mughuls, together with treaty obligations interpreted in the light of the new position. Between complete non-interference and the actual taking over of a state there was a large field for advice and interference. A corollary of paramountcy was the right of intervention in the event of misgovernment. Subordinate independence or autonomy involved constructive interference. If the paramount power cast its imperial cloak over the princes, it was also entitled to see that what was sheltered was in the main creditable. This stretching of treaty rights to secure the approximation of practice to precept was called 'constructive interpretation'. A final reason for intervention, again stemming from paramountcy and its obligation of protection, was considerations of defence. Some of these forms of interference and some of the developments of imperial powers within the states may now be noted.

General influence was exercised within the states by the resident. Formerly he interfered as little as possible in internal matters and was chiefly moved to act when state finances fell into disorder and arrears of subsidies piled up. Men of exceptional moral force like Charles Metcalfe and Sir Henry Lawrence exercised an important personal influence, but they were rather the exceptions that proved the rule. But in the new order the resident's advice could be given on all points; it was continuous and pervasive. In some cases he became the practical ruler of the state,[1] in some a healthy partnership in reform developed, in some friction, intrigue, and suppressed resentment. Apart from this general influence there were certain distinct powers exercised by the supreme government. There was the right of recognizing and regulating the succession. Successions had to be confirmed by the supreme power as in Mughul times. In Hindu states the recognition of the right of adoption carried with it the approval of the adoption made. In doubtful cases the succession was regulated as in the Kashmir case of 1885, the Gwalior regency case of 1876, and the Alwar case of 1870. The paramount right of enforcing good government involved the possibility of deposition or enforced abdication. This was the final weapon in the supreme government's armoury, and it was used sparingly and with reluctance. An early case was Bentinck's assumption of the Mysore administration in 1831 which was restored fifty years later. The Gaekwar of Baroda was deposed in 1876 for an alleged attempt to poison the resident. Later, in 1903, the abdication of Tukoji Rao Holkar of Indore was enforced because he was held to be responsible for murder within his state. In 1926 his son suffered a similar fate for comparable actions.

[1] King Edward VII as Prince of Wales in 1876 commented unfavourably on the behaviour of some residents.

In 1921 the aged Rana of Udaipur was induced to delegate his ruling powers to his son. The next year the Sikh ruler of Nabha was removed for a variety of misdemeanours as was the ruler of Alwar in 1933. Few of these actions of government appear unduly harsh in the perspective of time; criticism has rather taken the other tack that the government did not interfere often and early enough. The ruler of Patiala was thought by many to have been lucky in this respect in the late twenties.

Imperial authority within the states was extended in a variety of ways. Military considerations procured the establishment of military cantonments and civil stations of which the most famous were perhaps those of Bangalore in Mysore and Secunderabad in Hyderabad. The state forces were limited in number, but their quality and prestige was much increased by the institution of the Imperial Service Corps already referred to. Railway lines necessary for trunk communications or strategical reasons were driven through states, though states in their turn were free to develop their own systems, as in Hyderabad and Mysore. Posts and telegraphs were similarly established in the smaller states and coinage replaced by the Indian rupee. Sea customs were controlled. State subjects were bound to direct obedience to the paramount power. Abroad the interests of states were cared for by the British government, while they in their turn were bound by all treaties made with foreign powers.

The parallel development of British paternalism and princely benevolent despotism lasted broadly until the early years of the century. Its most striking period was the Curzon era when the paternal idea received its most forceful expression. The energy of Lord Curzon extended to the field of the states, his reforming impetus was felt in the form of increased interference. Curzon's most striking act was a fresh arrangement with the Nizam in 1903 by which Berar was virtually incorporated in British India under the fiction of a perpetual lease. The Nizam professed to be satisfied a the time but later claimed that he had been the victim of pressure. This act was too reminiscent of Dalhousie (who had made the first Berar arrangement in 1853) to be agreeable to the princes, and revived old suspicions of encroachment. The next two Viceroys removed these fears by tactful treatment. The outbreak of the first World War in 1914 marked the crowning moment of the post-Mutiny state policy. The confidence and satisfaction of the princes produced a great outburst of loyal expressions and offers of service; the improved conditions of the states made their service of real value and the new quality of princely leadership made it possible for princes like Bikanir to lead their own contingents in the field and take part in imperial events like the Imperial War Conference of 1917.

This was the great moment of princely India. From this time, though it did not become immediately apparent, the paths of British and Indian India began to diverge. With the government declaration of 1917 the government of India was committed to the development of representative institutions and the eventual self-government of British

India. The princes, on the other hand, retained their ideal of enlightened despotism and never as a body or with any enthusiasm accepted the new ideas of constitutional evolution.[1] The princes feared the democratic National Congress as a threat to their positions as autocrats; they discouraged Congress activity within their dominions and Congress in turn was critical of their régime (except for tactical purposes when subject to British interference). The princes therefore tended to lean on the British authority and to stress their treaty rights. Their previous confidence and forward-mindedness was gradually replaced by nervousness for the future and insistence on their vested interests.[2] Vision was darkened by foreboding. In spite of outward appearances the two Indias began again to draw apart with results which proved disastrous to the princes as an order and of doubtful value to their peoples as a whole.

The supreme government on its side found itself in a difficult position. Fidelity to treaty rights dictated support for the princes, while the new democratic policy for British India ran against the whole spirit of the old India. Support of the princes could be denounced as inconsistent or Machiavellian; while their forcible liberalization or abandonment would certainly have been a breach of trust. In these circumstances a double policy was attempted. Princely rights were maintained, sometimes at the cost of considerable embarrassment as in the case of the Patiala agitation of the twenties and the Kashmir agitation of the thirties. At the same time the policy of integration of Indian India was pursued and the attempt made to induce the princes to liberalize their governments. It was to be revolution by persuasion. The Montford reforms concerned British India only but at the same time the Chamber of Princes was established. Its annual meetings at Delhi and its standing committee were instruments for bringing the princes more closely in touch with government policy and with the new national trends. Similarly the princes were associated with all-India affairs as representatives at the League of Nations and imperial conferences. It was hoped in this way to encourage the development of corporate feeling and a common mind amongst the princes and to convert them to the necessity of adapting themselves in time to the new Indian order. The more far-sighted of the princes like the Maharajah of Bikanir and the Jam Sahibs of Nawanagar read the signs of the times, but others, like the Nizam, held aloof and clung to their traditional isolation. The Nizam himself put in a claim to be regarded as an independent state which was disallowed by Lord Reading in 1926. Between the desire to meet the new situation boldly and the desire to take advantage of the difficulties of the British to retain as much independence as possible the princes failed to evolve either a common policy or a united front.

[1] Those which went farthest along this road were Mysore, Baroda, and Travancore.
[2] The Butler Committee Report of 1929 illustrated this.

The policy of evolution or integration achieved its greatest success at the first Round Table Conference when the princes agreed to enter an all-India federation. This meant the surrender of federal powers to an all-India executive and legislature; it meant also that the princes would in future be an integral part of the new Indian state and would be able to exercise a vital influence on all-India affairs. This was a revolutionary conception for it was nothing less than the marriage of British and Indian India. The new principle was embodied in the Government of India Act of 1935 which gave to the princes the right to nominate one-third of the members of the lower house or Federal Assembly, and two-fifths of the upper house or Council of State. In order to safeguard the princes' treaty rights, however, it was stipulated that accession should be voluntary, and that the central federal machinery should not come into being until princes controlling half the princely seats in the Council of State and ruling half the subjects of Indian India should accede to it. This gave the waverers, the doubters, and the outright opponents of federation amongst the princes the chance not only to avoid accession themselves, but to suspend the operation of the federal centre for the rest of India. This chance they seized and successfully avoided a decision until the second World War broke out in 1939. A second, though less spontaneous, display of loyalty could not hide the fact that the princes as a whole, by their withdrawal from the undertakings of 1931, had not only blocked the orderly evolution of their own order, but had held up that of British India as well. Their action meant that India entered on this great crisis without the new central representative organs and without even a partially representative executive. They thus forfeited the sympathy both of the British whom they had baulked in their design of coming to terms with Indian nationalism, and of the Indian nationalists themselves, who now saw in the princes nothing but obstinate opponents of their aspirations. But nationalism was now too strong to be held up by these means. The inevitable result of the princes' intransigence was that the movement proceeded without them. In the final constitutional discussions they were virtually ignored. British paramountcy was simply withdrawn, and the princes were left alone to make what terms they could. What might have been a dignified assumption of a commanding position in the new India became a disorderly scramble for pensions and personal privileges.

The attempt to integrate the old India with the new, first by inducing the princes to modernize their governments and then by persuading them to liberalize them, must therefore be pronounced a failure. To a large extent the princes were themselves responsible because of their short-sightedness, their sectional selfishness, their petty dynastic pride, and their lack of leadership in the final stages. But the British were also not without responsibility. In the early stages they did not pursue the ideal of modernization with sufficient vigour. They were more concerned with avoiding another mutiny than with creating a

new order. Secondly, they refrained from uniting states into larger
units which could have wielded effective influence and would have
been large enough for modern methods of administration. This might
have been done in the hey-day of their power and as late as Lord Curzon's time, but when they developed the will they no longer had the
power. Lack of vision in the early stages on the British side, and of
initiative and larger public spirit later on the princely side, led a great
and promising experiment into final and irrevocable failure.

AUTHORITIES

C. V. AITCHESON, *Treaties, Engagements and Sanads* 14 vols., 1931), should be referred to for treaties. Sir W. LEE-WARNER, *The Native States of India* (1910), remains
the standard work on the subject. Professor DODWELL has provided an acute study in
chap. xxvii of the *Cambridge History*, vol. vi. An Indian view may be found in
K. M. PANIKKAR, *Indian States and the Government of India* (1927), and the princely
view in a paper drawn up for the Chamber of Princes in 1929 entitled *British Crown
and the Indian States*. An essential document is the *Report of the Indian States
(Butler) Committee* (1929, c. 3302). For individual states see the *Cambridge History of
India*, bibliography.

CHAPTER 8

Lord Curzon

THE Viceroyalty of Lord Curzon marked the apogee of the imperial system which had been built up by Dalhousie and his post-Mutiny successors. It cannot be strictly said that the ideal of ultimate self-government propounded by Macaulay and envisaged by Bentinck was ever formally disavowed. At some periods, as in the time of Ripon, it was very much in mind. But the day of its realization was a movable feast, which during these years received its furthest extension in time. It was self-government yesterday and self-government tomorrow, but never self-government today. The tide of imperialism 'of which Kipling was the prophet and Chamberlain the practical manager', was at the flood. British self-confidence was at its height, and found it difficult to believe that other peoples could govern themselves effectively even if they were allowed to try. Tutorship had given way to trusteeship, implying action on behalf of others, but not necessarily the preparation of others to act for themselves. In addition to this exuberant self-confidence, there was disappointment at the rate of western reform amongst the Indian people. The early vision of self-government was linked with an expectancy of swift westernization. The free India which was to be would be a westernized India. Therefore the apparently slow progress of western reform caused the date of Indian self-government to recede in the minds of the administrators. To some it was a light, faint but twinkling, to others a mere will-o'-the-wisp. In this belief, as has been pointed out, the average administrator erred, because he was still looking for western reform in aristocratic places, and did not perceive the significance of the new rising middle class. Lord Curzon shared in this fallacy and provoked by his action a rude awakening.

At the time of his appointment Lord Curzon was the rising hope of the imperialist wing of the Conservative party. He was in his fortieth year; he had visited India four times besides other parts of the East, and he had been for three years the Under-Secretary of State for Foreign Affairs. He was eloquent, masterful, and energetic. There is a curious parallelism between him and Dalhousie. Both came to India in political youth with the promise of a brilliant future before them; both were imperious and incessant innovators; both preferred their own judgement to that of the men on the spot, both injected new vigour into the administration; both eventually rode too fast and too far and met with criticism and disappointment. Of the two, Dalhousie was the more creative. He embodied an age which was just beginning and Curzon one which was ending. Dalhousie's measures were in many cases new departures, while Curzon's were often extensions or improvements of policies already in force. But it can be said with confidence that modern India would not have been the same without either of them, and of Lord Curzon that the measures which survived to become part of the Indian structure were of much more importance than those which were revoked. The overbearing manner, the brusque speech, the cutting comment have been forgotten with those who suffered them while India has retained the fruits of his incessant toil, his attention to detail, his clarity of mind, and his largeness of vision.

Lord Curzon's régime may be described as a benevolent despotism subject to a contingent reversion to self-government in an indefinite future. Curzon had the taste for power and a passion for improvement; he had a sincere desire to serve the country; he found legal powers and ceremonial position ready to his hand, and he plunged forthwith into the task of overhauling the whole Indian administration. We will follow him first to the frontier. On his arrival at the beginning of 1899 the frontier was still disturbed by the aftermath of the great flare-up of 1897 which was itself the product of resentment and suspicion of the semi-forward policy which had led to the drawing of the Durand Line in 1893. More than 10,000 troops were across the administrative border and there seemed little hope of withdrawing them. Nothing had been done to link them up by lateral communications, and there were proposals for further fortified posts, which would have meant an endless series of sieges and reliefs with permanent danger of a hitch arising from the loss of a post, which would set the whole frontier aflame. The state of the north-west frontier districts at the time of his arrival can be compared to an open sore to which caustic had been applied. The situation was inflamed and ugly, and seemed to be getting worse. Curzon's policy can be described as the removal of irritants, the use of the tribes to protect themselves, and the concentration of regular troops as a mobile reserve which could quickly concentrate overwhelming forces at any threatened point. In his own words the policy was 'withdrawal of British forces from advanced positions, employment of tribal forces in defence of tribal country, concentration of British forces in British territory as a safeguard and a support, improvement of communications in the rear'.

In pursuance of this policy British troops were withdrawn from Chitral, the Khyber, and the Khurram valley. Tribal levies or *khassadars* were raised to police the passes and tribal lands, with movable British columns in constant readiness at bases like Peshawar and Kohat. Roads and railways were built including the extension of the Quetta line to Nushki close to the Persian border. This provided an effective immediate solution, and kept the frontier quiet until the end of the first World War.

Linked with these measures was the creation of the North-West-Frontier Province. Some such measure had been discussed from the time of Dalhousie. Lord Lytton had proposed to make all Sind except Karachi, together with parts of the Panjab, into a new province, giving Bombay the Central Provinces as compensation. The compelling reason for the step was the steadily increasing importance of the frontier districts. When the newly annexed Panjab was separated from a weak Afghanistan by a large block of disorganized tribal territory relations with the tribes could safely be left to the experienced officers on the spot. But as Afghan affairs became more important and involved international complications, the government of India was necessarily more directly concerned. Frontier affairs passed through the Panjab government before reaching Simla, and this made for delay where speed was vital. At the same time, as the Panjab became more settled, its government was increasingly concerned with the normal problems of internal development. As the supreme government became more frontier-minded the Panjab administration was becoming less so. With the arrival of a Curzon the result was inevitable; the long talked of separation became an accomplished fact. The heat which accompanied the change should not obscure the light which resulted. The new province contained the whole of the Pathan tribal territory, together with the five settled districts of Hazara, Peshawar, Kohat, Bannu, and Dera Ismail Khan. It was presided over by a Chief Commissioner who was directly responsible to the Viceroy. It was staffed by members of the political department. It was Lord Curzon's child in much the same way as the Panjab had been Dalhousie's. The frontier went to the frontier-minded, and the wisdom of the move was justified by events. The creation of the new province had another result, for to avoid confusion the old North-West Provinces were renamed the United Provinces of Agra and Oudh. Thus the familiar 'U.P.' came into being.

Beyond the frontier lay Afghanistan. British policy to the westward remained in essentials what it had been since 1880. A watchful eye was kept on both Russia and Afghanistan, but reliance was placed on the Afghan love of independence rather than on direct interference for the countering of Russian designs. So long as Abdur Rahman lived the policy worked successfully if not always quite smoothly. It survived the severe test of the 1897 risings because the Amir valued British support against Russia more highly than prestige in the fickle tribal world or the hazards of a *jehad*. His son, Habibullah, who had the unusual experience of an uncontested succession in 1901, was at first more difficult, and for some years refrained from drawing his subsidy. Amicable relations were restored by Sir Louis Dane's mission during Lord Ampthill's interregnum. The old agreement was renewed, the Amir received the personal title of 'His Majesty', and the subsidy was received.

But while Indian policy remained the same, its application farther west was affected by shifts in the European political scene. Since 1887 Russia had directed her attention to the Far East in a policy which led to the Russo-Japanese war in 1904. Her pressure in the Middle East

PLATE 37

a. Victoria Memorial Hall, Calcutta

b. The Viceroy's House, New Delhi

was less, though her position, after the liquidation of the central Asian khanates, appeared to be more threatening. Her activity was confined to the permeation of northern Persia and the prevention of measures for modernizing that country. The British reply was to strengthen her influence in the south. This in its turn involved her position in the Persian Gulf where Britain had held important interests since the seventeenth century as successors to the Portuguese.[1] At the same time other powers were interested in this area. From 1890 the general British supervision of the Arabian coast from Aden and of the Persian Gulf was increasingly questioned. France obtained a coaling station from the Sultan of Oman in 1899, which was given up under threat of bombardment; a Russian attempt of the same sort was frustrated in the next year; while a German attempt to fix the terminus of the Berlin-Baghdad railway at Koweit was forestalled by an agreement with the Sheikh. It was a time when the diplomatic winds of Europe were shifting and no one was prepared to face British sea-power single-handed or able to coalesce with others against it. The matter was therefore settled to the outbreak of the first World War in 1914 by Lord Lansdowne's declaration in 1903 that the establishment of a fortified post or base in the gulf by another power would be regarded 'as a very grave menace to British interests which we should certainly resist with all means at our disposal'. There followed one of those progresses of pomp and power in which Curzon delighted with its prosaic sequel of consulates and trade missions. We can sum up Curzon's foreign policy to the west by saying that he restored Afghan confidence by a wise restraint based on the concentration of power, that he countered Russian permeation of northern Persia by strengthening British influence in the south, and that he warned off possible threats to the sea routes to India from the gulf by a clear if not always tactful display of sea-power. The policy was moderate and demonstrably successful.

Less happy were Curzon's dealings with Tibet. This secluded and wind-swept country had developed a unique form of Buddhist theocracy controlled by a monastic aristocracy. The Dalai Lama, the incarnation of the power of the Buddha, had displaced the ancient kings in the seat of power, and eclipsed the more holy Tashi Lama at Tashi Lhumpo. He was periodically discovered as an infant bearing certain holy marks, and during the suspiciously frequent minorities regency councils carried on the government. For 200 years Tibet had recognized Chinese suzerainty, exercised by two *ambans* or commissioners in Lhasa. The British had been in contact with Tibet from the time of Warren Hastings, who sent two envoys to the country. But it was Chinese policy to discourage intercourse with India; and it later came to be realized that the quickest way to Tibet lay through China. In 1885–6 the Chinese were induced to agree to a commercial mission to Tibet, but this was sacrificed to obtain Chinese consent to the annexa-

[1] In 1621 the Portuguese were driven from Ormuz by the Company.

tion of upper Burma. Desultory negotiations followed but no real trade resulted. At the turn of the century the situation was changed by three developments. With the palpable decline of the Manchu dynasty in China, Chinese influence in Tibet was sensibly weakening. The Tibetans began to look for someone who could complete the Chinese eclipse. The Dalai Lama, having outlived his minority and overthrown the Regency Council, proved to be a leader of vigour. Thirdly, the Dalai Lama, as anxious as his people to rid the country of Chinese influence, looked to Russia for help. In this he was much influenced by one Dorjieff, a Mongolian Buriat and a Russian subject by birth. There is reason to believe that Dorjieff's journeys to and from Russia were instigated by the Dalai Lama rather than the Russians, and that the new policy was opposed within Tibet itself. But it is easy to imagine the effect of the report that a Russian agent had entered Lhasa on a nature like Lord Curzon's, at once romantic and imperialistic. The lure of a closed land the fear of the great Asiatic bogy-man, the desire for trade were powerful incentives to action. If Curzon thought at all of the Afghan parallel of 1878, he comforted himself with the thought that the Tibetans had little more than prayer wheels with which to resist modern weapons. The home government was reluctant to agree to interference; but having once allowed a British mission to advance fifteen miles beyond the frontier in July 1903, they found themselves unable to prevent the successive steps which led Sir Francis Younghusband to Lhasa itself in August 1904. The pitiful slaughter of 700 virtually unarmed Tibetans at Guru in March and the lack of any sign of Russian intervention caused a revulsion of feeling in favour of Tibet. The harsh terms imposed by Younghusband against instructions were reduced and the right to send an agent to Lhasa waived.[1] The only positive result was the stationing of a trade mission at Gyantse, which remained until 1947 without accomplishing very much. For the rest Russia was warned off from an area in which she was too preoccupied in the Far East to wish to interfere, the Tibetans were more convinced than before of the virtues of isolation, and some geographical knowledge was gained. Not least of the expedition's effects was the distrust it sowed in the minds of the home government of the soundness of Lord Curzon's judgement, which played its part in the handling of the Kitchener controversy a few months later. The expedition was conceived in arrogance and imperfect knowledge, carried through against the better judgement of the home authorities and concluded in defiance of instructions. The best that can be said for Curzon in the matter is that the home government must share the blame for not acting with greater decision in restraint. The Tibetan expedition was the swan song of British imperialism in central Asia.

We can now turn to Curzon's internal administration. Here the parallel of his activities to those of Dalhousie is close. There was no

[1] The indemnity of 75 *lakhs* was reduced to 25, the occupation of the Chumbi valley from 75 years to 3.

part of the administration, from the forbidding land revenue question to the expenditure in viceregal establishments, into which he did not probe. There was nothing that he probed that he did not seek to improve. The changes were many and often drastic, the jars to comfortable routine considerable, and shock to personal susceptibilities numerous. Lord Curzon was one of the least loved but most respected of Viceroys. Few men like the man who cracks the whip, however necessary it may be to run. Yet there were few changes which were not later recognized to be improvements. Criticism in the main must be confined to excess of activity which produced an irritation and feeling of unease whose symptoms revealed themselves after his departure. Even this fault, to anyone who knows the strength of inertia and the sway of custom in India, must be accounted an error in the right direction. In sum, it may be said that Curzon gave the administration an impetus which carried it on until the second World War. Many of Curzon's internal measures have already been included in surveys in other chapters; we shall therefore here be content with a summary account except for the two great questions of the partition of Bengal and the Kitchener controversy.

In his relations with the princes Curzon followed the general post-Mutiny policy but gave it a characteristic flavour of his own. The note of partnership was sounded in his insistence on courteous behaviour by officials and in the foundation of the Imperial Cadet Corps which gave elementary military training to scions of princely houses. It was not his fault that the scheme was so modest. He visited forty states in the course of six years. The note of princely duty and efficiency was heard in his public exhortations. 'I claim him as my colleague and partner', he said; 'he cannot remain *vis-à-vis* of the Empire a loyal subject of her Majesty the Queen-Empress, and *vis-à-vis* of his own people, a frivolous or irresponsible despot. He must justify and not abuse the authority committed to him; he must be the servant as well as the master of his people.'[1] His enthusiasm for the young and energetic Maharaja Sindia was unbounded. But a certain minatory note crept into his circular deprecating frequent princely absences from their states which hindered the real purpose of his policy by arousing understandable resentment. For Curzon the line between parental concern and pedagogic hectoring was blurred and indistinct. The same masterfulness emerged in more concrete questions. In 1903 the Berar question was settled, as Curzon thought amicably, by means of a personal discussion with the Nizam at which no one else was present. The government of India received the district as a perpetual lease and administered it as a division of the Central Provinces. But the Nizam did not share the Viceroy's view of the discussion and later complained that he had been intimidated. A revival of his claims called forth the Reading declaration of 1926 whose uncompromising claim to complete

[1] Earl of Ronaldshay, *Lord Curzon*, vol. ii, p. 89.

sovereignty throughout India provided a convenient basis for the later action of the independent Indian government.

Lord Curzon undertook a complete overhaul of the whole bureaucratic machine. He began with a war on office delays and verbose minutes and proceeded, department by department, by means of committees of inquiry which were used as preludes to reform instead of as excuses for inaction. The most important of these internal reforms was devoted that of the police service as a result of a report in 1903. Curzon devoted much time and thought to land questions. The Land Resolution of January 1902 was his work and was prompted by a memorial of retired administrators who considered that assessments should be lightened and that the period of settlement should be lengthened. He rebutted the contention that famines were due more to over-assessment which left the peasant resourceless in the time of need rather than to failure of rainfall. For the rest the government showed that it was moving cautiously towards the rule that the demand should not exceed one-half of the net profit in the case of the cultivators, or one-half of the rental in the case of landlords, that settlements should be for not less than thirty years, and that local land taxation should not exceed 10 per cent. of the general tax. The resolution marked a further step in the steady march towards more elastic, scientific, and lenient assessments, towards the recognition that land revenue in a slowly expanding rural economy is not flexible, and that other sources of revenue must be tapped to meet new types of expenditure. The most famous of Curzon's land measures was the Panjab Land Alienation Act which aimed at preserving cultivators from eviction from their lands for debt. Rules were made for graduating large increases of assessment and for varying the demand according to the character of the season. A more positive measure was the establishment of co-operative credit societies whose aim was to liberate the peasant from the money-lender. Finally, provision was made for the development of scientific agriculture by the creation of an agricultural department with laboratories and experimental farms and a research institute at Pusa in Bihar. Lord Curzon was the first governor-general who saw in land not only a source of revenue but also a means of production, who was concerned with techniques of production as well as the methods of collection.

Lord Curzon was not content with bringing modern techniques to bear on ancient agricultural systems. He was alive to the possibilities of industrial development. His stimulus and planning were responsible for much of the rapid progress which was made in the years before 1914. By Curzon's time India had 27,000 miles of railway; Curzon added 6,000 miles more. The control of railways was transferred from the public works department to a new railway board which operated the state railways and planned development. For commercial and industrial questions a new department of commerce and industry was created, headed by a sixth member of the Viceroy's Council.

Apart from railways Curzon pushed forward irrigation works with equal vigour. In his first few months of office he had dealt with the famine of 1899 and had seen its ravages in his tour of the Panjab, Rajputana, and western India. He set up the Scott-Moncrieff Commission which planned further extensions on an all-India scale and sanctioned its proposal for the irrigation of $6\frac{1}{2}$ million more acres at a cost of £30 million.

Curzon's concern with material welfare was rounded off by cultural activity. In his concern for art and architecture he was unique among governor-generals apart from Warren Hastings. He patronized Warren Hastings's own creation, the Asiatic Society of Bengal. He conceived and carried out the project of a monument of British rule, which took the form of the stately Victoria Memorial in Calcutta. He founded the Imperial Library which was intended to be the Bodleian or British Museum Library of the East. His greatest work in this field was the creation of the department of archaeology for the conservation of the Indian artistic heritage and the carrying out of fresh excavation. The pioneer work of General Cunningham and others had not been followed up or systematized with the result that by Curzon's time 'beautiful remains were tumbling into irretrievable ruin simply for the want of a directing hand and a few thousand rupees'. Wherever he went he insisted on visiting the antiquities, whether they were the temples of Madura, the caves of Ajanta, or the Taj at Agra. He was ruthless in evicting officers and offices from ancient monuments, and no one but he at the time could have done it. He was fortunate in his director-general, Sir John Marshall, who persevered through years of neglect and discouragement until the value of the work was generally recognized.[1] This work was another step, even though an unconscious one, in the conversion of the government of India into an Indian government.

Curzon's educational measures have been kept to the end of his administrative record, because they form a bridge between his administrative and political work, his strongest and his weakest sides. Education was not more intimately connected with the life of the people than agriculture, but it affected the rapidly growing westernized middle class and touched their dearest aspirations. Western education had made them what they were and provided them with new ideals, new hopes, and new ambitions. When land questions were discussed the new class thought of the peasants in terms of 'them', when education was considered they thought and felt in terms of 'us'. There was a general feeling that the educational system built up since the eighteen-thirties had fallen short of expectation. The hoped-for filtration of western education downwards had not, it was thought, occurred. Higher education itself had become a sterile exercise in obtaining useful knowledge rather than a real culture of the mind. The uni-

[1] It was proposed to close the department in 1911 on the ground that its work was finished.

versities were examining bodies only with little control over their affiliated colleges and no power of stimulus, because they had no teachers or professors. One cannot create culture by registrars and result sheets. Curzon appointed a commission in which he characteristically omitted to include an Indian. In 1904 his Universities Act remodelled the universities and in particular the overgrown institution of Calcutta. It was sought to stimulate scholarship by establishing departments of post-graduate studies in Calcutta. At the same time a residential system was introduced. It was hoped to strengthen the educational character of the universities by increasing the nominated element in the governing bodies or senates and the executive bodies or syndicates. Measures were taken to control the recognition and conduct of affiliated colleges. Here lay the rub. The men displaced in favour of experts who were not always particularly expert were the new nationalists. They saw in this measure an attempt not so much to improve educational standards as to undermine their own influence in a world which they regarded as their own. The Viceroy, they thought, had shown the cloven hoof. They opposed the Act vigorously, proclaiming it reactionary and anti-national. Hitherto they had followed the Viceroy, in general, even with enthusiasm so far as he would allow it. But now the breach was definite. The opposition to the Universities Act proved to be the dress rehearsal for the greater crisis of the Bengal partition.

By 1904 Curzon had completed his first term of office. With general approval he was appointed for a second term and returned to India for this purpose in the autumn of 1904. But the sequel, as sequels so often are, was disappointing. His first term, in spite of the Tibetan indiscretion and certain official heartburnings, had been a resounding success. The honeymoon of government with Congress had not, it is true, survived the educational controversy of 1903-4, but he still had the respect, if no longer the full confidence, of the nationalist leaders. His energy and achievements seemed to justify his pomp, and the pageantry of the Delhi Durbar of 1903, when King Edward VII was proclaimed Emperor of India, seemed to put a ritual seal on his work. But from the moment of his return the intangibles in the situation seemed to turn against him, every step turned out to be a false one, and within a year he was back in his own country, frustrated, disillusioned, and embittered.

The problems which faced Curzon on his return were the Bengal administration and army reform. The Bengal Presidency had long presented a difficult problem to administrators. Its administrative history began with the grant by Shah Alam in 1765 of the *diwani* of the three provinces of Bengal, Bihar, and Orissa. Each successive addition of the Company's territory in the north was added to it so that by 1810 it was already unwieldy, stretching up to Delhi and beyond to the Sikh frontier. The first attempt at reduction was made by the Charter Act of 1833 which provided for a fourth presidency with its capital at

Agra. Two years later this became the Lieutenant-Governorship of the North-West Provinces, which extended from the Bihar frontier to the Sutlej, and after the Mutiny as far as the Jumna. Bengal proper then became again the Mughul *subahs* of Bengal, Bihar, and Orissa. In 1854 this area was confided to a lieutenant-governor, in immediate subordination to the Governor-General. In 1874 his burden was lightened by the withdrawal of Assam under its own chief commissioner. Nevertheless, the growth of population and general development made his task immense. By 1900 it had become overwhelming. The population numbered 78 millions; the isolation and difficult communications of east Bengal resulted in neglect which sharply contrasted with the prosperity and progressive outlook of west Bengal. West Bengal being mainly Hindu and east Bengal Muslim the contrast was the more striking. Discussion had long proceeded and several schemes had been propounded; Lord Curzon's part was to choose one of them and carry it through. The method he adopted was to unite Assam and Chittagong with fifteen districts of Bengal to form the new province of eastern Bengal and Assam. Its capital was at Dacca, its population 31 millions and its people predominantly Muslim.

There was much which could be said for the arrangement. The backward areas had been separated from the rest and given special administrative attention. The Hindu west was neatly balanced by the Muslim east; the special needs of both communities could be separately considered. But Curzon had left out of consideration sentiment, which he despised, and national feeling, which he did not believe to exist. 'My own belief', he had written in 1900, 'is that the Congress is tottering to its fall, and one of my great ambitions while in India is to assist it to a peaceful demise.' When, therefore, the Bengali public was aroused, when the separation was dubbed a partition, and the measure regarded as a deliberate attempt to strangle the renascent Bengali people, Curzon proved olympian in his detachment and adamantine in his disregard of public clamour. Reasoned protests grew into a heated popular agitation lead by Surendranath Bannerjea, monster meetings led on to a *swadeshi* movement and the boycott of foreign cloth, while in the background lurked the menace of terrorism. To all these signs and portents Curzon was unresponsive, insisting on carrying through the partition as a necessary administrative measure. The partition was later revoked, but the spiritual wound which the measure inflicted on the Bengalis, and indeed the westernized class generally, was never quite healed. From it issued widespread scepticism of the bona fides of the British professions about the development of self-government which in unbalanced minds bred the poison of terrorism.

Curzon's second problem was army reform. He was as anxious to overhaul the army as the civil administration, but here he had to work with the commander-in-chief. For the purpose he obtained the appointment of Lord Kitchener in 1902, then with his South African laurels fresh on his brow. At first they worked in harmony and much was accomplished; but on his return to India Curzon found himself faced with a demand for the unification of the army administration under the commander-in-chief. Hitherto the head of the army in India had been the commander-in-chief, who was customarily appointed an extraordinary member of the Viceroy's Council. But the administrative army department was in charge of an ordinary member of council, who was a soldier of standing not allowed to hold a command during his term of office. This arrangement was convenient in view of the fact that the commander-in-chief was necessarily often absent from government headquarters, but it also meant that the Viceroy could obtain a second opinion about military matters in addition to that of the commander-in-chief. Kitchener resented this and desired the unification of the whole military administration under his control. This involved the disappearance of the military member, which Curzon, with the backing of his council, regarded as a threat to the supremacy of the civil power. The contest of these giants held India breathless during the early months of 1905. The matter went to the tottering Balfour cabinet, which, afraid to sacrifice either of its masterful servants, attempted a compromise which satisfied neither. Curzon considered that the substance of the matter had been conceded to Kitchener and resigned in August 1905. The sequel justified neither party. The position in which an officer sat in judgement on his superior was not defensible, and no effort was later made to revive it. On the other hand Kitchener's centralization was too drastic, and could only work in the hands of a man as energetic as himself. Its defects became manifest in the management of the Mesopotamian or Iraq campaign during the first World War, and new arrangements were made at its conclusion. Thus ended, in acrimony and disillusionment, the most masterful governor-generalship since Dalhousie's. Dalhousie's body was broken by his labours, and Curzon's spirit received a scar which never fully healed. Nevertheless, the bitterness of his spirit at the end of his rule must not cloud our judgement of the greatness of his achievement. As an administrator he did more than anyone could hope or expect. His efforts attuned the government of India to the new *tempo* of development in the twentieth century; without them India must have fallen behind in the race and the administration might have proved as unfitted to meet the exigencies of the new age as the Russian imperial régime. By his example and his eloquence he stimulated and inspired; he was the embodiment of paternalism in its devotion to duty, its care for the people and its self-sacrifice. His faults were superficially those of pride and self-confidence, but fundamentally that of lack of imagination. He could not see a new nation arising around him, the very product of British rule, yearning for political liberty as an ideal, and demanding autonomy as a right. He thought of the new class as agents of the government, the beneficiaries and coadjutors in a long vista of benevolent foreign rule. So he stumbled on just that ground where he thought he was most firmly based. He changed his attitude later, for he drafted the Declaration of 1917. But his political obtusity created a breach between government and people which was never wholly closed in the remaining forty-two years of British rule.

AUTHORITIES

LORD RONALDSHAY devoted vol. ii of his *Life of Lord Curzon* (3 vols., 1927) to Curzon's Indian years. LOVAT FRASER, *India under Curzon* (1911), contains a useful account of Curzon's measures, while Curzon speaks for himself in Sir T. RALEIGH (ed.), *Curzon in India* (1906), which is a collection of his speeches. Sir W. R. LAWRENCE, *The India we served* (1928), gives a more intimate view. For Kitchener's side see Sir G. ARTHUR, *Kitchener* (3 vols., 1920) and for Tibet G. F. SEAVER, *Francis Younghusband* (1952). Dr. A. LAMB's studies of Tibetan and Himalayan frontier policy are authoritative. They are *Britain and Chinese Central Asia* (1960) and *The McMahon Line* (2 vols., 1966).

For the popular reaction V. CHIROL, *India* (1926), is still useful. For Bengal consult Sir S. N. BANNERJEE, *A Nation in Making* (1925). There is no comprehensive life of Gokhale, but see R. P. PARANJPYE's little study in the Heritage of India Series and also his *Speeches* (Madras, 1900).

BOOK X

National India, 1905-47

CHAPTER 1

The Political and Personal Thread, 1905-47

THE Viceroyalty of Lord Curzon was the last blaze of the old self-confident benevolent imperialism, conceived by Wellesley, nurtured by the Panjab school, and disciplined by Dalhousie. In many ways it pointed to the future, but in its essence it was of the past. From 1905 India entered into a new era. Politically it marked the transition from paternalism to independence and from centralism to a twin society; economically it covered the emergence of India as an industrial power fully participating in world markets, and spiritually in the rapid acclimatization of two ancient societies to the bleak and bracing air of the twentieth-century western society. Through these years grew to maturity a twin nationalism which seems likely to dominate events in the next historical period. The essential motive power behind these changes was the desire of India to make terms with the modern world in her own way and in her own right, and her increasing ability to do so. The course of events was modified by a number of factors. It is a feature of this period that these factors were no longer mainly British in origin; they were increasingly both Indian and cosmopolitan. They were both personal and impersonal, foreign and domestic. Here it is proposed to trace in outline the thread of these influences, leaving the final chapters for the treatment of more particular themes.

Before 1900 the only outer world which really impinged upon India as a whole was the British. From Britain came impulses of policy, innovations and ideas, persons and institutions, and from Britain came resistance to certain Indian desires. Britain's position in the world seemed to be unchallengeable and likely to remain so. The importance of the rest of the European world was probably under-estimated, but as a whole the West loomed over the eastern world as irresistible in its power and incalculable in its intentions. The only hope lay in some sort of accommodation with it. The first break in this vision of supremacy came with the triumph of Japan in the Russo-Japanese war of 1904-5. The effect was all the greater because Japan had admitted the West later than India and Russia was thought to be the greatest European power after Britain. Japan was now the ally of Britain. If she could be a great power, why not India? The next step was the revolution in China which was thought, prematurely as it proved, to herald Chinese freedom from western interference. The case of China, along with the Young Turk revolutions of 1908–9 and the Persian liberal movement all suggested that the path of progress consisted in using western techniques and ideas to regenerate ancient societies and then to use western weapons against western supremacy. The belief in an irresistible West from which nothing but pure imitation could procure even a modicum of self-respect was broken. India and the East might look forward to independent life again, albeit at the price of radical internal adjustments.

These events proved the prelude to the much greater shock of the first World War. The West was now seen to be fiercely divided at its centre as well as vulnerable at its periphery. American democracy emerged as a force which might counter the old western imperialism. President Wilson's Fourteen Points and his doctrine of self-determination shot a thrill of expectancy through Asia, for whatever the difficulties of internal self-determination, it was certain that the Asian nations were determined in the desire to rule themselves. The American influence changed the emphasis of political discussion from constitutionalism and legal rights to the abstract rights of man. A more radical tone came into political discussion which, if it sometimes led to dangerous unreality, increased the self-confidence and determination of the new popular leaders. As Europe was seen to be no longer invincible, Britain was realized to be less powerful in the European system than had previously been thought. This new evaluation of Britain and the West encouraged the organizers of anti-government movements. What before 1914 would have seemed hopeless quixotry now became calculated policy. There was a limit to British power and there was no certainty of its continuance. This view was confirmed not only by the patent British exhaustion after the war, but by such developments as the League of Nations, where Britain appeared as an important but by no means dominant member, and India itself was represented. This changed mental estimate of Britain was confirmed by the events of the thirties, for the revival of German and Russian power relatively reduced that of Britain. At the same time distaste for the aggressive European dictatorships, too reminiscent of phases of the Indian past, increased sympathy with British ideals. The way was being prepared for the substitution of ideas for power as the basis of the Anglo-Indian connexion.

The second World War hastened the completion of this change of view. The spectacle of Britain fighting for her life and for European freedom warmed Indian hearts. But India saw no reason why she should not be free too. As the war closed it became clear that British power was now dwarfed by that of America and Russia, and that the future relationship of the two countries would depend as much upon India as Britain.

The second great factor in determining Anglo-Indian relations in these years was the British public. The general election of 1906 marked a great radical revival which swept into the limbo of the archaic notions of an endless wardship of a permanently adolescent India. The ideas of Gladstone and Ripon came now to be accepted by the larger part of both parties. If even Morley regarded full Indian self-government as a distant goal, as a hope rather than a policy, even men like Curzon and Lansdowne realized that progress must proceed along these lines. The Morley-Minto reforms were the first tentative steps in that direction. Opposition to them came more from members of the Indian services than the British political public; more political heat was engendered by the unseating of Calcutta as the capital than the enlargements of the councils or the admission of Indians to high places. The first World War increased this process of the change of opinion about India in Britain. The declaration of 1917 was the product of a coalition government drafted by Lord Curzon himself and prepared by a Conservative Secretary of State. It meant that Indian self-government had been brought forward, in British political thinking, from the horizon to the middle distance. It was still 'far off' but no longer in the dim distance. It could be aimed at and prepared for, not kept in reserve for the perorations of ceremonial speeches. The path to freedom was now to be planned, systematic, and regulated. The first fruits of this changed outlook were the Montagu-Chelmsford reforms, with their planned reviews at the end of each decade.

Henceforth the controversy with Indian nationalists was essentially on the question of timing rather than on the goal of reform. Before the British governing class would willingly hand over power they wished to feel assured that there was someone to whom to hand it. The Congress claimed to be that someone, but during the twenties the British were not convinced. It was Lord Irwin (later Lord Halifax) who persuaded both British parties that advance must be rapid, that the Congress possessed a hard core of strength and must be dealt with as a negotiating party. The struggle of 1930-1 emphasized the correctness of this analysis. The declaration of 1929 that dominion status was the goal of Indian constitutional development was the outward sign of this change of mind. It brought Indian autonomy at a stroke from the middle distance to the forefront of the Indian political scene. The Act of 1935 expressed this new attitude in constitutional terms. Had no second World War intervened it is probable that full dominion status would have come within the following twenty years.

The third great force to be reckoned with was the growing power of Indian public opinion. Mid-Victorian Viceroys had mainly British and service opinion to consider. The only visible concessions to articulate public opinion before 1900 were the measures of Ripon and the Indian Councils Act of 1892. Under Curzon the Congress protested but was disregarded. But Gokhale was on terms with Morley and the confidant of Hardinge, and from the post-war years Indian reactions to British measures became a major concern to government statesmen. The procession of Indian public men to the Viceroy's House 'for consultation' became a familiar spectacle, reaching its height in the time of Linlithgow. The opinion of the dynamic Indian minority was mainly expressed by Congress until the Muslim League under Jinnah, like a moon from the parent sun, broke away to form a second nucleus of opinion and power. The changes of opinion within the Congress itself were great, and can be related to the developments already touched upon. Curzonian disregard, Japanese success, and the advent of Liberalism to power in Britain stimulated the Congress to the first definite formulation of its political goal. This was defined in 1908 as a position identical with that enjoyed by Canada and the other self-governing colonies. This was really internal autonomy only, but served until the shock of the first World War for the majority of the political class. The war enlarged the general political horizon from autonomy to dominion status in its wider post-war sense. By the time the new dominion status was defined at the Imperial Conference of 1926 as virtual independence and legally embodied in the Statute of Westminster in 1931 the Congress had leaped forward (in 1929) to independence as its formal goal. But the new dominion status continued to satisfy the majority of nationalists. The real conflict of opinion within the nationalist ranks between the wars concerned methods. The issue lay between direct or constitutional, peaceful or violent action. These views were closely related but not identical, since one could be unconstitutional and also non-violent. This was in fact the course advocated by Mahatma Gandhi, and to which he periodically converted the main body of Congress. To his influence must be ascribed the minor part played by terrorism and violence in the Panjab and elsewhere, as also to his influence the growing discredit of constitutional methods of political agitation. After 1918 he converted a potentially violent revolt into a peaceful unconstitutional movement, which he called off when it threatened to degenerate into violence. Thereafter the pendulum swung from constitutional to direct action according to the Mahatma's calculations of political chances, but never got destructive or seriously out of hand. The greatness of this achievement should not be underestimated because of the completeness of its success. In fact he may be said to have kept Indian opinion on the constitutional path, for his campaigns against government were so closely related to moral principle that they may be considered *extra* rather than *anti*-constitutional. He brought in the moral law to supplement rather than supplant official law, and thus saved India during the British period from large-scale terrorism, massacre, and race-hatred.

There only remains to record, in this connexion, the growth of Muslim opinion until it became mentally a separate nation. It was the direct foil to the growth of Congress power in necessarily mainly Hindu hands. This subject is dealt with more fully in Chapter 5 below.

We can now return to the thread of British policy from 1905. The new Liberal ministry had John Morley. the radical biographer of Gladstone, for its Indian Secretary of State. He united an aristocratic temper with radical principles, and this may have helped so to foreshorten his political vision that he saw no trace of self-government in Indian political prospects. The new Viceroy, the great-grandson of the first Lord Minto, was a public servant rather than a party man, just returned from a successful constitutional rule as Governor-General of Canada. He realized the necessity of reform and by tact rather than drive made it possible to inaugurate the Morley-Minto reforms with the consent of both British parties and the acquiescence of the Indian services. His successor was Lord Hardinge[1] who as permanent head of the Foreign Office wielded great influence and enjoyed the confidence of King Edward. Cold and correct in his manners, he appears dull and opinionated in his memoirs. But this unpromising exterior and these chilling relics concealed a strong will, a lively intelligence, and a keen insight into the needs of the time. He was chosen in preference to Lord Kitchener, who ardently desired the post, and his appointment thus saved what might have proved a disaster to Anglo-Indian relations. He managed the Delhi Durbar and King George V's visit to India in 1911, and carried through with unflinching firmness against much local opposition in Calcutta the transfer of the imperial capital to Delhi and the reconstitution of eastern India into the governorships of Bengal and Bihar and Orissa, with a revived Chief Commissionship of Assam. The Partition was thus undone and an historic site provided for the capital to the great satisfaction of national opinion. Calcutta (and Curzon) never forgave him for the loss of its status, but the act has been justified by the developments of half a century. It proved to be a vital administrative step in the preparation for Indian nationhood. Undeflected by attempted assassination in 1912[2] he cultivated close relations with Gokhale and other Congress leaders and in 1913 he became a national hero by championing, in a speech at Madras, the cause of the South African Indians. The new Union ministry had severely limited Indian immigration and prohibited Indians in the Orange Free State 'from trading, farming or holding real property'. His action resulted in the setting up of a committee of inquiry in South Africa which lead to the Smuts-Gandhi agreement. The Act which embodied the agreement was described by Mahatma Gandhi (then the Indian leader in South Africa) as the Magna Carta of South African Indians. This proved to be optimistic but the agreement eased the situation for the next ten years. Lord Hardinge's régime marked something of a honeymoon between British and Indian Liberals, which might have lasted some years longer but for the outbreak of the first World War.

Lord Chelmsford's appointment in 1916 is still something of a mystery, for though nearly fifty he had only held two Australian

[1] He was the grandson of the Governor-General of 1844-8.
[2] On his state entry into Delhi as the capital.

governorships. His chief claim to distinction was his fellowship at All Souls, which may have appealed to the classically minded Asquith. But Greek verbs are not necessarily talismans to statesmanship; India suffered from inadequate though well-meaning leadership. It is difficult to resist the impression that the interests of the country were sacrificed to the war crisis at home, which made good men anxious to remain near the centre of danger, and to the lack of force of the premier, who failed to insist on a suitable appointment. In quiet times Chelmsford might have ruled with success, but quiet times, as Auckland found earlier, do not commonly wait for quiet men. Chelmsford took charge just as the early enthusiasm for the allied cause had subsided, to be replaced by rising discontents, and on the eve of the discredit which befell the government of India on account of the Mesopotamian campaign. The difficulties of the developing situation would have taxed the energies of a Dalhousie. Chelmsford never recovered the initiative from the events which crowded upon him; he always appeared to be driven by influences which were too strong for him. He was more nearly an agent, and less of a policy-maker than any Viceroy in the last period of British rule. After the military trouble came the Declaration of 1917, elaborated in London. The subsequent policy of reform became identified with the masterful Edwin Montagu. Chelmsford's part was by no means negligible, but it was subordinate rather than formative. He was unable to manage the increasingly restive public opinion and betrayed his lack of popular touch in the handling of the Rowlatt Bills. Nor was he more happy in dealing with the Panjab troubles in 1919. When he retired the new reforms had indeed been inaugurated by the Duke of Connaught, but the government was faced by a formidable non-co-operation movement led by Mahatma Gandhi, and an unprecedented alliance between Hindus in the Congress and Muslims in the *Khilafat* movement.

Lord Reading's appointment by Lloyd George[1] marked a return to the selection of men of cabinet rank for the Viceroyalty. A former Attorney-General, Chief Justice, and ambassador to the United States, he had a judicial temper well suited for dealing with the passions of the day and a diplomatic tact which imported a new touch in official dealings with political leaders. His mission was to make the constitution work, and this meant to create confidence and remove suspicion, to clarify, and to tranquillize. First he had to convince the country of the government's continued strength. He divined the essential weakness of the Hindu-Muslim coalition, arrested Gandhi when he was temporarily discredited by an outbreak of violence, and thereafter did all he could to make the reforms a reality. His political genius was to perceive that the differences that divided the opposition were at bottom more acute than those which separated the different sections from the new self-governing governmental policy, and to have the patience and nerve to allow the coalition to break up of itself. By 1926 non-co-opera-

[1] Lord Willingdon was very nearly selected.

tion had collapsed, the Muslims had broken with Congress and the Congress was torn with dissension. Lord Reading was often reproached for lack of positive action, but this view overlooks the fact that the situation as he found it demanded inaction rather than dramatic gestures. A busybody Viceroy at that juncture might have been disastrous. In quietness and confidence he found his strength. Lord Reading's weakness lay in his inability to give the country a positive lead, and so to capture its active sympathy for the policy of partnership, during the second half of his term when the country was disillusioned with its leaders and realized that the British would be with them for some time longer.

This effort was made by his earnest and influential successor. Lord Irwin gave up a cabinet post to shoulder the Viceroyalty, was the friend of the prime minister Baldwin, and the grandson of Sir Charles Wood, the coadjutor of Dalhousie. Never before had such moral earnestness been combined with such high-mindedness and ability. If some of the results of his actions were unlooked for their fruits were nevertheless notable, for it was he who was mainly responsible for convincing the British public that the partnership policy must be pursued to its logical conclusion on the one hand, and the Indian public that the British meant what they said on the other. Though lacking in the arts of popular appeal he came to be more respected and even loved than any Viceroy since Ripon. And this he achieved though the storm and stress of a civil disobedience movement. Probably no other Englishman could have emerged from such an ordeal with enhanced respect in India, or used the occasion for reaching and understanding with the national leader himself. His weapons were integrity, patience, and charity of mind, displayed in a personality of great ability. In the stressful year 1930-1 these qualities enabled him to pursue a steady course, withstanding the pressures of opinion at home, in India, and from within his own government. His reward was the creation of a new, if sometimes only half-convinced respect for British intentions and a new willingness to work towards the common goal. In the long run the declaration of dominion status as the goal of constitutional development proved more significant than the civil disobedience movement, and the round table conferences than the revival of this movement in 1932. Irwin's relationship to Gandhi somewhat resembled, in the altered circumstances, that of Hardinge and Gokhale before.

Lord Willingdon's earlier success in Bombay and Madras augured well; he was known to be liberal-minded; he was charming, competent, and experienced; his wife was the outstanding viceregal lady of the series. But he was sixty-five years of age and, in fact, lacked the energy to give the country the lead it needed. He presided urbanely over a government which in effect marked time while constitutional discussions proceeded in London. Political India, resentful of the repression which marked the beginning of his term but weary of 'direct action' in the altered circumstances, adopted an attitude of watchful waiting.

PLATE 38

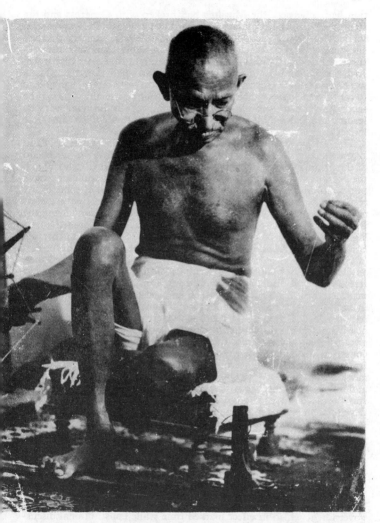

Mahatma Gandi

Willingdon's break with Gandhi on the latter's return from the second round table conference at the beginning of 1932 was perhaps unavoidable though unfortunate, but his failure to heal the breach later was a political blunder. He committed no major indiscretion as Chelmsford had done before, but, as in the case of Lord Reading, he failed to cover the newly strengthened hand of the government with the glove of the appealing gesture. Partnership remained as a policy as it had been in Reading's time, but no longer as an ideal. Thus the last real opportunity of uniting Indian hearts and heads was lost.

By the time that the Government of India Act became law in 1935 Willingdon's term was drawing to a close. It fell to Lord Linlithgow to supervise the new elections and launch the new constitution. He was chosen by the national government for this purpose and had prepared himself by long study of Indian affairs and the chairmanship of an agricultural commission. He was of cabinet standing though he had not actually held cabinet office. He was industrious, clear headed, patient, and capable; no other Viceroy worked harder or more conscientiously during his long term of office. His fault was over-application to detail which at times caused him to miss the wood for the trees; his patience sometimes ran to procrastination, as in the Bengal crisis of 1943, and he lacked the intuitive sense of 'a tide in the affairs of men'. But for this, federation might have been a fact before the second World War broke upon the world in 1939. From then on he was immersed in war problems. He showed the ability to control and direct without the power of inspiring. His rock-like firmness under the threat of Japanese attack in 1942 and the subsequent Congress insurgence was of incalculable value. His personal contacts and conferences were unremitting, but he lacked that imaginative spark or personal warmth which might have prevented nationalist impatience from turning to hostility. It is too early yet to assess his place in the viceregal roll because we are imperfectly acquainted both with his difficulties and his personal share in events.

The same verdict must be applied to his two successors. Lord Wavell's mandate in 1943 was to hold the country and to organize victory. In this he was very successful, and soldier as he was, came nearer to the hearts of the people than anyone since Lord Irwin by his handling of the Bengal famine on his arrival. From the time of the fall of Japan in August 1945 his mission was to prepare for a handover of power and to secure an agreed transfer to the two great parties. The time has not yet come to pass judgement on his efforts or on the wisdom of the government which recalled him. It must suffice to say that this least militant of soldiers and least obtrusive of rulers concealed a subtle and powerful mind beneath a gnarled and taciturn exterior. In effect the last, he was by no means the least in the line of British Indian Governor-Generals. Lord Mountbatten came with an order to organize retreat, in military parlance an 'operation'. That work was carried out brilliantly whatever may be thought of the immediate consequences of partition in the Punjab. Here, too, historical judgement must hold its hand until time has added perspective to the scene and a key to the archives.

AUTHORITIES

THE political and personal veils have not yet been lifted sufficiently for an authoritative bibliography to be possible. The *Cambridge History of India* provides a factual survey up to 1918, and H. H. DODWELL an incisive summary to the same year. G. T. GARRATI and E. THOMPSON, *British Rule in India*, carry the story to 1934. P. E. ROBERTS, *History of British India* (3rd ed., 1952), completes the period in outline.

For the Indian side see under the succeeding chapters. For India in British politics see R. C. K. ENSOR, *England 1870–1914* (Oxford, 1936). Glimpses behind the scenes are provided by J. MORLEY, *Recollections* (2 vols., 1917), L. S. AMERY, *My Political Life* (4 vols., 1953–6), E. S. MONTAGU, *Indian Diary* (1930), LORD BIRKENHEAD, *Birkenhead, the Last Phase* (1935), VISCOUNT TEMPLEWOOD, *Nine Troubled Years* (1954), and the *War Memoirs* of CHURCHILL. A comparable work among Indian leaders is J. L. NEHRU, *Autobiography* (1937). Gandhi's autobiography is more personal.

RECENT PUBLICATIONS

S. R. MEHROTRA's study *Indian and the Commonwealth, 1885–1929* (1965) is valuable and S. D. WALEY's *Edwin Montague* (Bombay & London, 1964) is a personal memoir. Further titles of memoirs, etc. will be found under the separate chapter headings.

CHAPTER 2

Edwardian India

THE years 1905 to 1914 form a clearly defined period in modern Indian history, which may be described as Edwardian India. The emphasis on efficiency and paternalism to be operated by a vigorous head and an enlightened bureaucracy was changed to a regard for self-government and self-expression. 'Freedom rather than discipline, autonomy rather than efficiency' were the new watchwords. There was a new approach to the now obviously rising Indian national party, a certain recognition that they, rather than the aristocrats or princes, were the dynamic minority in the country with whom the future lay. There was a response from the side of popular leadership and there developed a *rapprochement* between government and popular leaders which was not seen again until the brief two years before the second World War, and then not so completely. At the same time the impetus which Lord Curzon had imparted to all branches of the national life continued; material progress continued apace, and India was on the way to becoming an industrial state. Economically as well as politically she was developing the flesh of autonomy beneath the outer skin of the British *raj*.

The first problem which faced the administration was a personal one. Lord Minto, sent by the Conservatives to carry on Curzonism without Curzon and to work Kitchenerism with Kitchener found himself faced with a Liberal landslide in Britain and a radical Secretary of State in John Morley. Morley had supported Curzon on the Kitchener question and had denounced the Partition of Bengal. But politicians are rarely embarrassed for long by charges of inconsistency. Morley disappointed radical hopes by deciding to accept the *fait accompli* in both cases. The commander-in-chief became head of the army department and an ordinary member of council, and a military supply department was created. But in 1907 even this last relic of Curzonism was removed. In Bengal he accepted the fact of partition while emphasizing a prospective change of methods. This was revealed in the restraint put upon the Lieutenant-Governor of Bengal, Sir Bampfylde Fuller, when he wished to disaffiliate two schools for allowing their boys to take part in political meetings. Fuller's offer of resignation was accepted, to his surprise and indignation.

The second legacy with which the new government had to deal was the appearance of a terrorist movement, hitherto almost unknown in British India. There had been signs of this in western India during the plague crisis, but both the grievances and the ideals which stirred the terrorists were local. Now it appeared in western India, Bengal, and the Panjab. In western India it was connected with B. G. Tilak's cult of patriotic orthodoxy; in Bengal it was a highly emotional cult linked with the goddess Kali and clearly the outcome of partition strains and stresses; in the Panjab activity seems to have been linked with agrarian grievances stimulated by men from down country. In Bengal the movement would seem to have been most directly linked with emotional stress arising from political causes; in Bombay the movement really marked the return to activity of an extremist group long underground; while in the Panjab, where the rule of law and regular administration had hardly yet endured for sixty years, the appeal to violence never lay far below the surface. The whole episode had for its background a price rise unprecedented in the previous fifty years. Political measures dealt with the major political discontents; it was the economic discontent which accounted for the spasmodic continuance of the movement throughout this period. A number of murders occurred, culminating in that of Sir Curzon Wyllie in London in 1909 by a Panjabi. The Secretary of State reluctantly sanctioned two Acts making incitement to murder felonious and the making of explosives illegal. Tilak was imprisoned for six years for incitement to murder when commenting on the Muzaffarpur outrage. With the advent of reforms the movement gradually died away, its last important shot being the attempted assassination of Lord Hardinge on his state entry into Delhi in 1912. The movement naturally caused alarm, but it was in fact the work of very small bodies unsupported by the main mass of political India. It was a symptom of the increasing self-consciousness of political India, and of the danger of neglecting to provide a safety valve of public institutions for the new desire for public self-expression.

A third inheritance of the new régime was the Tibetan question. The home government had already reduced the Tibetan indemnity from 75 to 25 *lakhs* payable in annual instalments of a *lakh* and had allowed the evacuation of the Chumbi valley after three instalments had been paid. The Indian government still saw Russians wherever snow lay, but Morley was determined to end the entanglement. In 1906 the Pekin convention secured Chinese agreement to the treaty of Lhasa; it secured a guarantee against any interference in Tibetan affairs provided China applied the same exclusion to the other powers. Finally, the Chinese were allowed to pay the indemnity on behalf of the Tibetans. When this was done in 1908 the home government ordered the evacuation of the Chumbi valley against the wishes of Calcutta. This could now be safely done because the whole situation in Asia had been transformed by the Anglo-Russian agreement of 1907. The period of diplomatic flux mentioned in Book IX, Chapter 8, was now ending. The Anglo-Russian *entente*, following the Anglo-French *entente* of 1904, completed the arrangement of the European powers into two armed camps. To present a united front with France against Germany and Austria with their now hesitant partner Italy,

Britain and Russia found it expedient to settle their Asiatic differences. Both powers agreed to respect Tibetan territory, to treat it as a dependent of China, and to send no agents to Lhasa. In Afghanistan the existing position was confirmed. In Persia both countries agreed to respect Persian independence and also recognized Russian and British spheres of influence in north and south Persia. This was little more than a recognition of existing facts and gave little comfort to Persian patriots, but it did prevent a possible clash between the two powers and gave the nascent Persian national movement a chance to develop. This is the best that can be said for it. Sir Edward Grey, the Liberal Foreign Secretary, was never happy about it; the situation was summed up by the cartoonist who pictured the Persian cat between the British lion and the Russian bear while the bear said to the lion: 'You stroke the tail while I stroke the head and we can both stroke the back.'

The Tibetan settlement had unlooked-for results. To the Dalai Lama India now appeared as a friend and the Chinese, whose interference was increasing, as the enemy. His differences with them led to his flight to Darjeeling in 1910 whence he returned to Lhasa after the Chinese revolution of 1911 and the troubles which followed it had led to a decline of Chinese power.

We can now pass to the political measures which gave to Edwardian India its special stamp. Both Minto and Morley were convinced that something must be done to associate articulate Indian opinion more closely with the government. But neither were yet prepared to admit that that something must be in the direction of elected representative bodies and eventual self-government. In the case of Minto this was natural; he was a man of affairs rather than a politician who accepted without question the oriental basis of Indian society. To him what was needed was an extension of the machinery for providing local advice to the ruling authority. The British Indian durbar must have Indian councillors as well as European. Morley's case was much more perplexing. The development of self-governing institutions on western lines had been liberal doctrine since the days of Ripon and Gladstone, and Morley prided himself on being an advanced radical in his opinions. But he also possessed an authoritarian temper which made him delight in his position as Secretary of State, and loath to part with any of its attributes of power in India. Yet his whole mode of thought was democratic and representative, which led him to cast the changes he proposed in a western mould. To the last he endeavoured to convince himself that the new measures would not lead to self-government, though he defended the extension of western institutions on the plea that the issue had been prejudged by the introduction of western education in 1835. In this he was right, but it remains a mystery why he could not carry the inherent logic of the situation a little further. But Morley, for all his bold words, was a somewhat timid man who shrank from the immense implications of his own actions. He is not the first man of words who has hesitated when it came to acting upon them and before we condemn his hesitation we must remember the very different mental climate which prevailed before 1914. The sun of imperialism was still scarcely clouded and its total eclipse seemed then to be remote.

The two men, so different in their origins and natures, proved useful foils to each other. Minto's patience enabled him to sustain urbanely his Secretary's verbal shafts; Morley's keen intellect and influence clarified issues and achieved results which Minto could not have attained without him. The efforts of both were needed to breach the defences of conservatism and vested interests in the India Council and the services in India. Credit belonged to both for the results which were achieved.

The problems to be solved may be divided into the securing of better representation of important Indian interests, the enlargement of the powers of the existing legislative councils, and the introduction of an Indian element into the executive. Minto's first proposal under the first heading was the creation of advisory councils in addition to the existing legislative councils which would be representative of all classes including the princes, but possess no legislative or other power. This was an attempt to embody the durbar idea and to further the familiar policy of associating the princes with the imperial government which led to Lytton's abortive ideas of an Indian peerage. The stone intended to wing two birds hit neither, for the princes refused to join such councils whose obvious impotence excited criticism. Recourse was then had to the enlargement of the existing councils, thus continuing the line of development on the western model which had proceeded since 1854. Election was the method of selection for the majority of non-official members. The election was in most cases indirect, being by provincial legislatures in the case of the centre, and by a great variety of public bodies representing various facets of the national life, in the case of the provinces. Municipalities and district boards, chambers of commerce and universities, landholders and special interests such as tea and jute all played their part. In addition to an increase of membership, the proportion of non-officials was increased. The Imperial Legislative Council consisted of 60 members with the Viceroy presiding as compared with 25 under the Act of 1892. There were 28 nominated officials including 1 from each of the 9 local governments, and 32 non-officials, of whom 27 were elected. The official majority, though small, was thus preserved, a fact which assumed great importance a few years later. In the provinces, however, non-official majorities were introduced.

The powers as well as the numbers of the councils were also enlarged. The councils under the 1861 Act could only consider Bills which were laid before them. The Act of 1892 allowed the asking of questions and a discussion on the annual budget. This permitted a general discussion on policy and gave Gokhale the opportunity for his famous annual budget surveys. The Act of 1909 permitted, in addition, the asking of supplementary questions and the tabling of resolutions.

The council still possessed far from full parliamentary powers, for no unofficial Bills could be introduced and no votes of censure tabled. But it was now well on the way to attaining that stature. The new powers accorded to it crossed the boundary from what was really an advisory body of counsellors only slightly connected with the general public to what was in fact a deliberative public body. A dignified semi-private council had become a miniature popular assembly. The government could neither be defeated or censured it is true, but information could be extracted on awkward subjects by means of questions and views on subjects of moment to the non-official world could be ventilated by means of resolutions. Full advantage of these facilities was taken by Gokhale, one of whose actions under the new régime was to table a motion in favour of universal education.

In the executive sphere no changes were made. The government could enforce its will at the centre through its official majority, and in the provinces through the powers of the governors. But the number of executive councillors in Bombay and Madras was increased from three to four, the way being left open for the appointment of a non-official, an executive council was created in Bengal, and provision made for the creation of executive councils elsewhere on certain conditions.

The appointment of Indians to high office was an object cherished by both Minto and Morley. It did not require specific legislative enactment in a racial sense, as a result of the Charter Act of 1833, but there were other obstacles. The presidency councillorships were limited to men with years of official service behind them, which virtually excluded Indians owing to the small number of Indian members of the civil service. This difficulty was surmounted by the provisions noted above. For the appointment of Indians to the Viceroy's Council and the Council of India in London there was no legal bar. But the members of both bodies resisted the idea, and when the question of an Indian appointment to the Viceregal Council was put to the cabinet, it was rejected. Minto's proposal to his executive council, wrote Professor Dodwell, 'startled some of them, like a pistol pointed suddenly at their heads'. Morley had therefore to be content with nominating two Indians to the India Council in 1907.[1] After the passage of the Councils Act Sir Satyendra (later Lord) Sinha was appointed to the Executive Council.

For all its caution and regard for precedent there are certain special features to be noted in the Act. The first was the introduction of the principle of direct election and of communal representation by a side wind, as it were. As soon as it was known in 1906 that constitutional changes were in contemplation a Muslim deputation asked Lord Minto for representation of Muslim interests through special constituencies. Their reason was that they were, as a group, under-represented on the bodies which were likely to be the electoral units, and that in any general electoral roll based on a property qualification, they would

[1] Messrs. Krishna Govind Gupta and Sayyid Husain Bilgrami.

be under-represented on account of their poverty. The government's attitude to the Muslim community was now very different to what it had been after the Mutiny. As a result six special Muslim constituencies of landholders were created for the Imperial Legislative Council, and others in some of the provinces. This measure, which seemed but an expedient to secure representation for an important body of opinion, was one of the deepest import. It may perhaps be described as the official germ of Pakistan. A second feature was the emphasis on the experimental nature of the changes. Nothing was to be final; all was to be subject to review and modification. If this left the door open to a return to the durbar system of respectful advice by nominees it also left it open for advance towards responsibility and self-government. The emphasis on empiricism answered beforehand the arguments of those who said that India could never proceed on western lines, and made it possible for those who had scouted such developments to agree to them later without loss of consistency. A third but less significant feature was the syndicalist nature of the electoral bodies in the provinces. Had the system been extended India might have developed a unique type of guild constitution. But the urge to orthodox representation proved too strong and that development never occurred.

The Indian Councils Act, the core of what is generally known as the Morley-Minto reforms, became law in 1909. In many ways it only marked an extension of existing tendencies and in the after-years, when the impact of the first World War had radically changed the outlook of both India and Britain, it became customary to regard it as a rather small matter which created a disproportionate stir. But the significance of events must be estimated in relation to the circumstances of the time in which they occurred. A furlong's advance before 1914 required an effort which would have secured a mile afterwards. Viewed from this standpoint it must be adjudged a major landmark in the progress of India towards self-government. It did not, it is true, go beyond the consultative principle or impinge upon the powers of the irresponsible executive. But it reached the limit of that principle so clearly, that no further progress was possible without entering into new constitutional fields. And that progress was virtually inevitable since the whole Act exemplified the principle of development. It prided itself on its development from the past and it clearly implied a development in the future. Had there been no war, further progress would no doubt have been slower in coming, and the next step perhaps less radical, but progress there must have been. The Councils Act in this respect may be compared to the Anglo-French *entente* of 1904; as the latter implied an alliance without a commitment to one, so the former implied an evolution towards responsible government without any avowal of the process. In both cases statesmen denied vigorously what they knew to be implied and in both cases the logic of fact proved stronger than the dialectic of debate.

The working of the reforms fell to Lord Hardinge who succeeded

Minto in October 1910. They were on the whole received well by political India. The Congress leaders, who had shed their extremist wing in 1907,[1] looked with suspicion upon communal representation and were disappointed that no large popular constituencies had been created. They could not accept Morley's disclaimer of fostering parliamentarism, but they had obtained more than they had expected and were privately gratified and hopeful. Hardinge worked on these feelings, not only through his public measures, but by maintaining private contacts with prominent men, and particularly Gokhale. A sort of unavowed *entente* grew up; the government and nationalist opposition were more nearly in accord than at any time between 1888 and 1937.

Hardinge's first task was to organize the customary Delhi Durbar for the new King George V in 1911, which this time was graced by the king-emperor and his consort themselves. As a spectacle the durbar was magnificent and as a gesture it was successful. It marked perhaps the peak of British authority in India. But apart from pomp and prestige the occasion was marked by three significant Acts. The first raised Bengal to the status of a governor's province. The second undid the partition of Bengal, and the third transferred the capital of India to Delhi. The promotion of Bengal to gubernatorial rank was long overdue on account of both the size and importance of the province. Hitherto the presence of the supreme government in Calcutta had hindered such a rational step, but the removal of the capital now made it politically possible as well as administratively desirable. It pleased the patriotism of the Bengali people and provided a solace for those who mourned the departed mighty. The partition was officially 're-arranged'. The two Bengals were united to form the new governor's province, Assam was again reduced to the status of a chief-commissionership, and a new province of Bihar and Orissa (including Chota Nagpur) was created. This settlement stood the test of time. It gratified Bengali sentiment; it proved administratively viable; it provided a focus for the backward but potentially important region of Bihar. The main criticism of the measure was that it represented a concession to agitation; but if that line were consistently taken, what concessions by authoritarian governments would ever be made? It was more plausibly said that bombs bred boons, but again, if bombs were allowed to block boons, what would there be save more bombs? The important fact was that the government of India was playing from strength and its action as a whole was received in that spirit. The third measure was one of the few secrets successfully kept in modern India. Calcutta and Lord Curzon at home were thunderstruck; neither forgot or forgave. But India as a whole was delighted. The action was certainly designed to appeal to Indian sentiment, but it had other solid arguments to support it. From the time of Lord William Bentinck (who had Allahabad in mind) suggestions were periodically made for moving the capital up-country. Lord Curzon himself thought of Ranchi. The remoteness

[1] For the development of the Congress party from 1900 see the next chapter.

of Calcutta from the main scenes of Indian action was the reason for the much criticized annual sojourn in Simla. In fact the government spent much longer there each year than in Calcutta. The argument for finding a more central situation was strong. The difficulty was to find a place whose historical associations might unite with practical convenience in justifying the large outlay which would be necessary. Delhi, covered by the Panjab and Frontier Province, possessing Mughul associations without important Mughul survivals, forming a vital centre of communications and being near to the Simla hills, now provided such a centre. The decision was justified in the circumstances of the day, and it proved even more important than its authors imagined. It provided the monument in stone which the British had hitherto lacked, and the new India with a ready made capital.

Lord Hardinge's years before the outbreak of the first World War were occupied in pursuing the lines of policy thus laid down. The new capital was occupied in 1912 and energetically developed by Sir Malcolm (later Lord) Hailey. The liaison with Congress was maintained by the appointment of G. K. Gokhale in 1912 to the Islington Commission on the Public Services. Owing to the war the commission did not report until 1917 but it served to advertise the paucity of Indians in the higher services, to make more difficult the opposition of vested interests, and to make changes inevitable. Gokhale was also sent to South Africa to state the Indian case during the dispute between the South African Indians led by the young Gandhi and the new Union government. In November 1913 the Viceroy electrified India by expressing 'the sympathy of India, deep and burning, and not only of Indians, but of all lovers of India like myself, for their compatriots in South Africa in their resistance to invidious and unjust laws'. This caused some dismay in Britain but was too popular to be disavowed. It led to palliative action in South Africa which solved, or at least postponed, the problem of the position of Indians in the union for another ten years.

Thus India was proceeding in growing trust between government and popular leaders, in increasing prosperity, and gathering self-confidence when 'the lights went out' in Europe as the first World War began.

AUTHORITIES

For Minto see J. Buchan, *Lord Minto* (1924), and Mary, Countess of Minto, *India, Minto and Morley* (1934), a valuable document. For Morley see J. Morley, *Recollections* (2 vols., 1917) and *Speeches on Indian Affairs* (1909). For Hardinge see his *My Indian Years* (1948). For Indians overseas see C. Kondapi, *Indians Overseas 1838-1949* (1953). For the Congress side see G. K. Gokhale, *Speeches* (1900), B. G. Tilak, *Writings and Speeches* (1922), A. Besant, *How India wrought for Freedom* (1915), and S. N. Bannerjee, *A Nation in Making* (1925). Sir Courtney Ilbert provides the best commentary on the Act of 1909.

RECENT PUBLICATION

A full study of the revolutionary *Har Dayal* is by Emily C. Brown (Arizona, 1975).

CHAPTER 3

The First World War and the Montford Reforms, 1914–21

(i) The World War and after, 1914–21

THE first World War forms the portal through which India entered the stage of the modern world from the hall of Victorian India, Edwardian India forming, as it were, the vestibule between them. India had enjoyed nearly fifty-six years of total peace. She had come to regard Europe as a region adjacent to Britain which itself was a place one went to and came from and was the mainspring of all significant happenings. In spite of the stirrings of the previous few years, India was still as a whole colonially-minded as she was still colonial in political status. The first reaction to the war was as to something exciting but remote, and it took some time for the realization to spread that the familiar Indian landscape was involved in the earthquake that had overtaken Europe.

The outbreak of the war in August 1914 called forth an outburst of loyal sentiment among both the political classes and the princes. All believed that the war would be short and that Britain would emerge on the winning side. For the princes it was an opportunity for action while popular leaders more soberly calculated that present service would mean future rewards. Lord Hardinge reaped the fruits of the existing goodwill to his government as well as the accumulated prestige of the British. There was a general cessation of embarrassing activity and a general support of war measures. In this atmosphere of goodwill, 1,200,000 men, 800,000 of whom were combatants, were recruited, £100 million were given outright to Britain for the prosecution of the war and £20–30 million contributed annually. India was denuded of both troops and officials so that at one time only 15,000 British troops remained in the country. The national pride was stirred by the dispatch of an Indian army corps to France in the autumn of 1914, and later of troops to East Africa, Egypt (for the defence of the Suez Canal), and to the Persian Gulf.

If the war had ended in six months as first expected the government might have emerged stronger than before. But as it lengthened year by year, growing ever more severe and more doubtful, feelings underwent a change. The collapse of Russia in 1915 ended all hope of a speedy finish. Enthusiasm turned to impatience and economic difficulties bred discontent and bitterness. The campaign against Turkey imposed a severe strain on the Muslim community, still in the main orthodox in its outlook and accepting the Turkish Sultan as the *Khalifa*. The fall of Kut-el-Amara in Iraq in April 1916 and the revelations of mismanagement which followed shook the credit of a government thought to be efficient as well as powerful. By the end of the second year of the war the mood of India had altered from enthusiasm to one of critical impatience, restlessness, and expectation of change. It was seen that the old world was in ruins, that Britain was neither all-powerful nor all-wise; expectations were raised, and tempers shortened. Economic difficulties leading to a rise in food prices, the over-zeal of recruiting agents in the Panjab and western India, and the great influenza epidemic of 1918 which swept away 5 million people accentuated these tendencies. By the end of the war India was as war-weary, restless, and irritable as Britain itself.

An early sign of discontent was the revival of revolutionary activity in Bengal and the *Ghadr* conspiracy in the Panjab in 1915. Its leader, Har Dayal, went to Berlin and endeavoured to foment a Muslim rising from Kabul, but his efforts never rallied large-scale support, and were troublesome rather than dangerous. On the constitutional side the developments were rapid and portentous. As the war proceeded all parties, both in Britain and in India, realized that things could never be the same again. In 1914 the prime minister Asquith said that 'henceforth Indian questions would have to be approached from a different angle of vision'. All the parties concerned realized that the tempo of events had quickened; the difficulty lay in the fact that each of them had their own notions of the new speed. From this time onwards all were playing, so to speak, from the same 'score', but none were agreed on the timing. Lack of unison led to discordance and discordance to recriminations. In the process each unconsciously learnt from the other, British from Indian and Indian from British, Muslim from Hindu and Hindu from Muslim. Acknowledgements were few, but looking back on events we can remark rather on the speed with which all parties adapted themselves to the new situation than on their obstinacy in clinging to the past.

The instinct of the British was to postpone all positive action until the end of the war. Its protracted and doubtful nature and the magnitude of the Indian effort both in Europe and the Middle East, made this impossible. The first, almost unnoticed steps, were the ending of the system of indentured emigration for Indian labourers overseas and the raising of cotton import duties without a countervailing increase in the cotton excise. On 20 August 1917 the coalition government took a step which proved a starting-point for the developments of the next thirty years. In form it was a declaration made in the House of Commons by the new Secretary of State, Edwin Montagu. The keynote was the definition of the object of British policy in these words.

The policy of H.M. government, with which the Government of India are in complete accord, is that of the increasing association of Indians in every branch of the administration, and the gradual development of self-governing institutions, with a view to the progressive realisation of responsible government in India as an integral part of the Empire.

The united character of the declaration was shown by the fact that a

Conservative, Austen Chamberlain, had produced the first draft, while Lord Curzon had given it its final form. To the policy of Indian association with government administration and of responsible government were added the conditions of progress by stages and of judgement by the home and Indian government of the time and nature of each advance in accordance with the extent of the co-operation received and responsibility shown. In spite of the grandmotherly conditions attached, the declaration was an epoch-making document which officially committed Britain to the development of Indian self-government along parliamentary lines and permitted no logical distinction between that goal and dominion status. The next step was to decide on the first stage of the journey. The Secretary of State himself toured India during the cold weather of 1917–18 and produced with the Viceroy the Montagu-Chelmsford report in July 1918 at the height of the final crisis of the war. The report was unusually philosophic in style as well as unconventional in tone; it was perhaps more important for its general propositions than for its detailed proposals which seemed almost timid by comparison. The most controversial of these had a prophetic ring: 'We believe that nationhood within the Empire represents something better than anything India has hitherto attained; that the placid, pathetic contentment of the masses is not the soil on which Indian nationhood will grow, and that in deliberately disturbing it, we are working for her highest good.'[1] Thereafter a Franchise and Functions Committee toured India in 1918–19. Parliamentary consideration occupied most of the year 1919 and the reforms became law in December. The year 1920 was occupied in the necessary administrative preparations and the first elections, so that the new constitution was not inaugurated by the Duke of Connaught until March 1921. A sketch of the new system is given at the end of the chapter; here it is sufficient to say that the Act greatly enlarged the legislatures, providing general constituencies and an individual franchise; that it gave the provinces independent powers by devolution from the centre and introduced the principle of responsibility into the provincial executives by the device known as dyarchy.

The deliberate instancy with which the new measure was evolved may seem all too typical of Indian governmental procedure, but it was in fact mainly caused by the magnitude of the measure, by the necessity of consultation and administrative preparation, and by the exigencies of the parliamentary system. Nevertheless, the delay involved was both unfortunate and dangerous in the fluid situation of the end-of-war and post-war days in India. What was in the main necessary deliberation to secure general consent seemed to many in India to be deliberate procrastination. The tension which such a time lag created was increased by another factor. The tempo of thought of the British officials in India, while broadly set in the new direction, lagged sensibly behind that of the London authorities, and still farther, of course, behind that

[1] Report on Indian Constitutional Reforms (Cd. 9109), p. 120.

of the Indian public. Reluctance to renounce the older glories was easily taken for stark hostility, distrust of innovations and untried personnel for contempt, expostulations and forebodings for attempts at sabotage. The British official and the home government too often appeared to be speaking from different briefs. If to this we add the social distresses caused by the influenza epidemic, economic dislocation, and the sudden return of thousands of men from abroad to a disorganized countryside, we shall find it easier to understand the complete change of outlook which overtook the Indian public between 1916 and 1919.

It is now time to turn to political India. In 1900 Indian nationalism was still in the main a tendency among middle class intellectuals rather than an organized political movement. The National Congress was a propaganda society rather than an organized political party. Its leaders like Gokhale, Tilak, Surendranath Bannerjea, Satyendranath Sinha, and Phirozeshah Mehta were already generals of note, but they were generals without a real army. The Congress was largely indebted to Lord Curzon for the next stage in its growth. His educational measure of 1903 touched an interest dear to the whole middle class while the Bengal partition was an issue which not only aroused passionate feelings in Bengal, but the sympathy of all educated India. These two issues, set against the background of the Russo-Japanese conflict, served to draw the new class together and to create a new sense of unity and common purpose. In Bengal, with its mammoth demonstrations and burnings of foreign cloth and its *swadeshi* movement, the excitement spread to the people at large, but elsewhere the middle class found itself endowed with a heightened self-consciousness and a quickened zeal. Instead of arranging for the decent demise of a dying institution, Lord Curzon by his measures welded a society of nationalists into a dynamic political party. By 1905 the Congress may be said to have captured the whole middle class and to have become the recognized organ of political India. But it had not as yet (except for a fleeting moment in Bengal) extended its influence to the masses. It could still be belittled as the plaything of the few, as unrealistic and doctrinaire.

During the Indian Edwardian era the Congress rapidly increased in stature while remaining confined to the class which gave it birth. It owed this to the distinction of its leaders, to the sanity of its judgement, and the recognition of its significance by the new governments in Britain and in India. It now underwent the experience of all nationalist movements, of tension between moderates and extremists. A small revolutionary group had already broken off; there remained a left-wing or 'extremist' group led by B. G. Tilak, anxious to continue uncompromising opposition to government and not proof against playing with the fire of violence, and a right wing or 'moderate' group who held to the tenets of classical liberalism, who saw in British officials their opponents but in British institutions their hope, who preached moderation in agitation and co-operation in action. A first sign of the new status of the Congress was its acceptance in 1908 of the form of colonial freedom enjoyed by the dominion of Canada as its political goal. A second and more convincing sign was its handling of its own inner tension. The clash between moderates and extremists came in 1907 at the Surat Congress. The meeting broke up in disorder because of extremist attempts at coercion, but the episode ended with the assertion of moderate supremacy under Gokhale, Bannerjea, Sinha, and Mehta. A year later Tilak, whose nationalism had always been provincial and sectarian rather than all-Indian, and who had never been a constitutionalist except from expediency, was imprisoned for six years for incitement to violence. From then until the outbreak of war the moderates dominated the national movement. A third sign of growth was the part played by the leaders in elaborating and working the Morley-Minto reforms. In the rarefied atmosphere of Edwardian India they showed that they could breathe freely, could affect decisions and influence policy. The countenance of the government increased their prestige because it was seen that it was moving in their direction. The caution of its steps was not yet felt to be a serious hardship because hitherto it had not moved at all.

The outbreak of war brought forth, as has been mentioned, an outburst of enthusiastic support from the middle class for the allied cause. This was in itself an expression of its inner satisfaction with the developments of the last few years. But the mood soon changed. Expectations were largely increased, to be soured by British delays and the inconveniences and disappointments of the lengthening war. In these circumstances the extremists, who were virtually the nationalist opposition party, found a new hearing. In 1915 Gokhale, the wisest and ablest of the moderates, died at the early age of forty-nine. In 1916 Tilak, who had been released in 1914, emerged from his retirement. His views had enlarged since 1908 while his skill remained unchanged. He showed that he could now think both nationally and politically. He joined forces with Mrs. Besant and her Home Rule League, persuaded the Muslim League to support his programme in the agreement known as the Lucknow Pact,[1] and captured the Lucknow Congress at the close of the year. Henceforward the once formidable 'moderates' receded into the background. Within a few years they had metamorphized themselves into the Liberals, eloquently led by Srinivasa Sastri; thereafter they gradually dissolved into a number of generals without followers and finally became a group of elder statesmen of distinction. They remained fruitful of ideas, as in the case of Sir Tej Bahadur Sapru; they were influential in private, and useful in public as go-betweens between government and Congress in times of difficulty. But they could no longer lead or command. They were the political *harcarahs* of modern India.

The Congress was now committed to a demand for *immediate* home rule while the government was contemplating *ultimate* self-government.

[1] The Lucknow Pact included the recognition of separate electorates.

The aim was the same, but the rate of progress different. A third member of this untuneful political orchestra must now be mentioned. Until 1906 the Muslims followed in the main Sir Sayyid Ahmad Khan's advice to hold aloof from the Congress. In 1906 the prospect of reform led them to form the Muslim League and to ask for special or communal constituencies which were embodied in the Morley-Minto reforms. Now they suddenly awoke to life. They had been made uneasy by the misfortunes of Turkey before 1914; the further disasters which befell her thereafter caused wisespread alarm. Britain was dismembering the Caliphate and therefore must be resisted. Thus the Khilafat movement was born, to be fostered by the pan-Islamic propaganda of the Young Turk movement, and brought to strength by the dismemberment of Turkey at the close of the war. The Muslims therefore joined forces with the Hindus in a joint national movement before the incredulous eyes of the British.

Such an alliance was loose and unstable, but for the moment the current of events bore it along. A final and personal element has now to be added to the situation, the advent of the Gujarati lawyer Mohandas Karamchand Gandhi. Gandhi (soon to become Mahatma or 'Great Soul') came from an orthodox *bania* group in Kathiawar, which he defied in order to read for the bar in London. He spent many years in South Africa where he experimented on diet, developed pacifist convictions, and led a life of simplicity and service to mankind. He was a stretcher-bearer in the South African war. He championed the rights of Indians in the Union and led with great skill and determination a *satyagraha*[1] movement against the government which extorted the respect of General Smuts and the admiring sympathy of Hardinge and India. In 1915 he returned to India, a disciple, as he believed of Gokhale. For some time he studied the situation; it was not till 1918, when Tilak was dying, that he came to the front. Then his western training enabled him to deal with the British on equal terms, his simplicity of life captured the imagination of the masses, whose feelings his uncanny insight enabled him to arouse at will, and his non-violent views alternately gratified, baffled, and exasperated the government. Here was the predestined leader of the New India, the man who could unite in a common purpose the peasant and the townsman, east and west, orthodox and radical. Gandhi was responsible for two great features in the next stage of nationalism. He made the movement nation-wide and he kept it non-violent.

The dissonance which finally brought the members of the orchestra into conflict concerned the administration of the public safety laws. At the outbreak of war the government armed itself, amid general consent, with a Defence of India Act, and possessed in addition Regulation III of 1818. By 1916 both sides were beginning to feel irked by these restrictions, the Congress because they interfered with the new home rule propaganda and the government because they

[1] Literally 'soul force'.

wanted more powers against terrorism and revolutionary activity. Here again there was no real difference of principle between government and Congress, but a fateful difference of emphasis. Nationalists supposed that the new powers were really intended against themselves, and were strengthened in this belief by the fact that the government probably over-estimated the extent of the revolutionary menace. In 1917 a committee of inquiry was appointed under an English judge, Mr. Justice Rowlatt, which produced much evidence of detailed subversive activity and made proposals for strengthening the law. Publication almost coincided with that of the Montagu-Chelmsford report; the two were read together. But whereas the proposals of the first were embodied in Bills in a matter of weeks, action on the other was delayed for a year. A now excited and irritable public read the worst into this unfortunate but only partly avoidable conjunction of events. In November 1918 the war ended; the government, however, continued with the Bills because the Defence of India Act would now lapse and they wanted to retain emergency powers. Indian suspicions thus seemed to be confirmed. The two Bills allowed judges to try political cases without juries in specified cases and gave provincial governments power of internment.[1] The Bills became law early in 1919 against the vote of every non-official Indian in the Imperial Legislative Council. The government's miscalculation of the original emergency was revealed by the fact that the powers of the Acts were never actually used.

The wind of suspicion and resentment was now fanning the already smouldering discontents of the people. To economic dislocation were added the special irritants of the first post-war months; the return of soldiers to altered conditions for which no preparations had been made, the mania of speculation leading to further distress, the failure of the average European to realize the radical changes which had occurred in India and the world, and the heady wine of self-determination now being decanted by President Wilson, who seemed then to be the master of Europe and the prophet of a new age. At this moment Mahatma Gandhi stepped forward into leadership. He organized *hartals* in protest against the Rowlatt Acts which speedily turned into riots in Delhi, Ahmedabad, Lahore, and Amritsar. In Amritsar on 13 April a prohibited meeting was held in the large enclosed space known as Jallianwallah Bagh, and was broken up without warning by a body of troops under General Dyer. The casualties were officially estimated at 379 killed and over 1,200 wounded.[2] This was followed by the proclamation of martial law, severe punitive measures, and humiliating orders.[3] Order was restored in the Panjab but a scar was drawn across Indo-British relations deeper than any which had been inflicted since the Mutiny. Racial feeling was intense. That resentment did

---

[1] Regulation III of 1818 only applied to the supreme government.
[2] There was only one exit which the troops occupied.
[3] e.g. public floggings and a crawling order.

not flame into an insurrection must be attributed to two factors. The government (though tardily in October) appointed a committee of inquiry[1] which censured General Dyer and criticized the administration of martial law. Secondly, the national movement was now led by Gandhi who set his face against violence, though many of his actions seemed to incite it. He was, in a sense, the government's best friend at that time. In August 1920 the Congress rejected the new reforms and launched under Gandhi's leadership a non-co-operation movement with the government. This included resignation of office, withdrawal from schools and colleges, and boycott of the coming elections The movement gained an unprecedented all-India character from the support of the Muslims of the *Khilafat* movement, led by the adventuring brothers Muhammad Ali and Shaukat Ali. It was at this time that Pt. Motilal Nehru of Allahabad donned the Congress uniform of *khaddar* to become shortly second only to Gandhi in authority. The positive success of the movement was limited; resignations from office were few, the schools and colleges were dislocated only for a time, one-third of the electorate went to the polls.[2] Congress was not represented in the new councils, but ministries were formed, and the new system worked. But great excitement prevailed for many months marked by periodical outbreaks of violence always regretted by the Mahatma. By the end of 1921 it became clear that the movement had passed its peak and that the government would not be overthrown. The Moplah outbreak in Malabar in August 1921 alarmed moderate opinion; the attempted boycott of the Prince of Wales on his visit in the autumn of 1921 led to further violence and early in 1922 Lord Reading used the occasion of the Chauri-Chaura outrage to arrest Gandhi himself. He was sentenced to six years imprisonment but released early in 1924. Thus the movement ended in apparent failure. But things were never the same again. These events formed a psychological watershed in the development of modern India. The 'colonial' mentality had been thrown off; nationalists felt themselves to be members of an adult nation, able to treat with the government on equal terms. The government, on its part, never sank back into its old complacency. It realized that the Congress was a formidable force, though it was not yet willing to admit that it was the dominant force in the country. It was confirmed in the new policy, if by nothing else, by the knowledge of the consequences of any attempt to go back on it. After four years of storm and stress government and people began slowly and painfully to approach each other again.

(ii) *The Montagu-Chelmsford Reforms*

The principles of the Montagu-Chelmsford proposals, usually now known as the Montford reforms, were the recognition of self-government as the goal of British policy in India, the realization of that

[1] Report of the Hunter Committee 1920 (Cmd. 681).
[2] In 1952 the percentage was about 50.

principle by instalments and judgement by the British of the moment and manner of taking each step as a result of the co-operation received and responsibility shown. This last provision was secured by the necessity of parliamentary enactment for each change in India and the provision in the Act for an inquiry at the end of each decade as a basis for further action. Self-government meant responsible parliamentary government, for nothing further was heard of the old 'durbar' principle. The introduction of responsibility into the constitution was effected by means of 'dyarchy', the invention of the apostle of imperial unity, Lionel Curtis.[1] Self-government, which had begun at the local level, was now to be extended to the provinces. In addition the principle of devolution was introduced as a means of giving greater scope to the provincial governments, and of forming a half-way house between the old centralism and federalism for which opinion generally was not ready.

We will begin with the policy of devolution, which intimately affected the whole administrative structure. Hitherto the provinces had been subordinate to the centre in both finance and legislation. Devolution was effected in the financial sphere by abolishing the former 'divided heads of revenue'.[2] Instead, revenue from irrigation, excise, land tax, and stamps was allotted to the provinces, while that from customs, income tax, posts, salt, and the railways went to the Centre. The provinces were thus endowed with a certain financial flexibility with which to finance their own measures. In the legislative sphere powers over certain subjects devolved upon the provinces, the others being retained by the Centre. Power to legislate on certain subjects, though provincialized in administration, were also retained by the Centre.[3] Exceptions could be made with the Governor-General's sanction. The powers retained by the Centre were those which pertained to the whole of India; they included defence, foreign affairs, communications, commerce, customs, the all-India services, and in addition the 'residuary' powers of legislation, or all powers not specifically handed over to the provinces, were retained by the Centre.

In the executive sphere there was no radical change in the central government. The executive was still irresponsible. But power was taken to enlarge the executive council and it was understood that, apart from the Viceroy and the commander-in-chief, half of the members would be Indians. In practice there were three Indian members in a council of seven besides the Viceroy. In the provinces the new principle of dyarchy was introduced. This was in idea a division of the administration into halves, one of which was controlled by councillors responsible only to the governor and ultimately the Secretary of State, and the other by ministers responsible to the provincial councils as well. To match this division of executive authority there was also an

---

[1] The founder and for many years editor of *The Round Table*.
[2] Land tax, income tax, stamp duties, and excise.
[3] e.g. irrigation, High Courts, prisons, factories, new universities.

administrative division. The subjects of administration were divided
into 'Reserved' and 'Transferred'. The reserved subjects were directly
controlled by the governor and his councillors. These covered land
revenue and laws, justice, the police, irrigation, and labour matters.
The transferred subjects were controlled by the responsible ministers.
They were local self-government, education, public health, public
works, agriculture, and co-operative societies. The broad distinction
made was between 'law and order' and 'nation-building' departments.

Great changes were made in the legislative councils. At the Centre
a bicameral legislature was instituted. The Legislative Assembly replaced the Imperial Legislative Council with 106 elected and 40 nominated (25 of them official) members. It sat for three years with the
power of earlier dissolution. To it was added a Council of State of
61 members, with an unofficial majority, elected for five years. The
official 'bloc' at the centre thus disappeared. The provincial councils
were also largely increased.[1] At least 70 per cent. of their members
were to be non-official. To accord with the new status of the provinces
and make the new system possible the United Provinces, the Panjab,
Bihar and Orissa, and later Burma (1923) and the Frontier Province
(1932) were given both governors and councils.

The possibility of deadlock between an irresponsible executive and
the legislature at the centre was obvious. The partially irresponsible
executive in the provinces might be faced with hostile council votes or
a refusal of the council to support any ministers. These difficulties
were provided for by the reserve powers of the Viceroy and governors.
The governors were empowered to administer the transferred departments themselves in the event of the absence of ministers. Viceroy and
governors were given a power of legislation by ordinance valid for six
months in the event of emergency. They were allowed to pass Bills
over the heads of the legislatures if they were certified to be necessary
for the safety and tranquillity of India and also to authorize expenditure in the same way. This was the process known as 'certification'.[2]
Certain heads of expenditure, such as that of defence at the centre,
were not subject to popular vote.

The array of new councils was backed by a new electoral system.
This had two features, the nature of the franchise and the arrangement
of constituencies. Apart from certain special qualifications, such as the
possession of a university degree or membership of a chamber of
commerce, the general qualification was based on property, the payment of income or house tax in the towns and of land tax in the
country. This was graduated from provincial council to Assembly and
Council of State, being varied according to local conditions with the
purpose of enfranchizing the same class of persons everywhere. The
system gave over 5 million voters to the provincial councils, nearly

[1] The Bengal Council had 139 members, Madras 127, and Bombay 111.
[2] In the provinces this power was limited to reserved subjects.

1 million for the Legislative Assembly and some 17,000 discreet persons for the Council of State.

The constituencies were divided into 'general' and 'special'. The special constituencies, as before, represented special interests such as universities, great landholders, industry, and commerce. The general constituencies contained the voters provided by the franchise explained above. But they were further divided not as to qualification, but as to the class of the voter. This was the principle of communal representation, first allowed in 1909 for six Muslim seats and now reluctantly but widely extended. The general division was between Muslims and non-Muslims for all elections, on the plea that Muslim voters (through poverty) being fewer in numbers proportionately to their population in any given constituency, would be in danger of being swamped by the others. But the Sikhs had such constituencies in the Panjab, the Indian Christians in Madras, together with Anglo-Indians and Europeans in certain provinces. Communal representation had come to stay.

AUTHORITIES

INDIA's part in the first World War is fully described in *India's Contribution to the Great War*, a government publication from Calcutta in 1923. Sir C. LUCAS, *The Empire at War*, vol. v, gives a valuable summary. Sir J. WILLCOCKS, *With the Indians in France* (1920), deals with the French adventure.

For the political background Sir J. CUMMING, *Political India* (1932), Sir V. CHIROL, *India* (1926), and A. BESANT, *How India Wrought for Freedom* (1915), are useful summaries. See TILAK's *Speeches* as in the last chapter, GANDHI's *Autobiography*, vol. ii, and his *Life* by H. S. L. POLAK, H. N. BRAILSFORD, and Lord PETHICK-LAWRENCE (1949). The standard life is by D. G. TENDULKAR, *Mahatma* (8 vols., 1952–   ).

For dyarchy see L. CURTIS, *Dyarchy* (1920), and E. S. MONTAGU, *An Indian Diary* (1930). A lucid description of the new system is by E. A. HORNE, *Political System of British India* (1922). The most important official papers are the *Montagu-Chelmsford Report* (1918. cmd. 9109), the *Rowlatt Report* (1918.9190), and the *Hunter Committee's Report* (1920.681). Sir M. O'DWYER, *India as I knew it* (1925), may also be consulted.

RECENT PUBLICATIONS

Two important new works are P. G. ROBB's *Government of India and Reform: Policies Towards Politics and the Constitution, 1916–21* (1976) and JUDITH M. BROWN's *Gandhi's Rise to Power: Indian Politics, 1915–22* (Cambridge, 1972).

CHAPTER 4

The Montford Era

FEW Acts of state have aroused more criticism from more varied points of view than the Government of India Act of 1921. It was criticized for going too far and for not going far enough, for being unworkable, and for working all too effectively. But a constitutional measure must be judged by *all* its results, by what it makes possible in the future as well as by its defects and omissions. Over the years a noticeable shift in the centre of critical emphasis was observable. At first the question at issue was—does the Act accomplish anything positive at all? Both British and Indian left wing thought believed that it did not. During the middle twenties the argument revolved round the question, are the reforms workable? From the late twenties attention was concentrated on the further query, what is the next step? The first shift in emphasis implied acceptance of the positive content of the reforms, and the second of their practicability. Much criticism assumed the permanence of the reforms, whereas they were avowedly temporary and progressive in character. On the whole we may say that the criticism which insisted on the incompleteness of the reforms proved to be valid, that which pronounced them unworkable or pernicious, fallacious. The real case for consideration is how far they were suited to cover a transitional period in constitutional development. Here it may be said that on the whole they achieved their purpose in spite of serious defects in design. They transferred enough power to induce enough people to take part in them to make them workable. They proved capable of large developments along the lines laid down; they prepared the way for full responsibility and for federation; they provided an invaluable training in public life for the rising governing class. On the other hand they did not go far enough to disarm serious opposition from without or to remove suspicion and irritation from those who were within the system. The reforms were valid in that they provided a habitable posting house towards freedom. The achievement, all things considered, was great; the only sound criticism is that it might have been greater.

The great need of the day was to create confidence in the new (or newly revived) official outlook, and this could only have been achieved by going farther than the circumstances of the time in Britain made possible. A central point of criticism was the plan of dyarchy. The system certainly created suspicion without and friction within. The association of ministers with an irresponsible executive tended to discredit them in the eyes of ardent patriots; they were blamed for acts which were not their own. The more successful joint consultation proved, the more sweetly governors charmed ministerial fears and doubts, the more the ministers were apt to be suspected of straying from the path of patriotic virtue and to find their popular position being undermined. In the executive itself lack of popular control over finance caused some ministers to feel that their departments were being deliberately starved of funds, while governors of good will found their efforts to promote development handicapped by the lack of flexibility in the provincial revenues. The sources of income like customs and income tax which were readily expansible were allotted to the Centre. Another difficulty, this time on the British side, was that the unpopular but necessary work of government, like the raising of taxes and the suppression of riots, fell to the irresponsible or reserved half of the administration. The British suffered all the odium for this kind of public act, while the ministers, for reasons given above, received little of the credit for their often real constructive work. There was another hindrance to the working of the reforms which was not in the nature of the reforms themselves. Apart from the Congress party, which represented national aspirations in general, there were few well-organized political bodies. With the Congress holding aloof, it was therefore easy for governors to fall into the habit of 'making a majority' by drawing ministers from opposing or self-seeking groups, who by their faction or inaction threw discredit on the system. Compromising coalitions usually produce loaves and fishes for the politicians rather than bread for the multitude.

The first period of the Montford era covered the term of the first elected councils from 1921 to 1924. The Congress boycotted the elections but could not prevent one-third of the electors going to the polls, or the moderates, who had dissociated themselves from the non-co-operation of Mahatma Gandhi, from being elected. Ministries could therefore be formed, but they worked under the shadow of an external opposition of unknown strength and of great prestige. At the centre there were no ministers, but it was soon seen that the disappearance of the official 'bloc' had made the supreme government newly sensitive to nationalist opinion. The Rowlatt Acts and the Press Act of 1910 were repealed, social measures dealing with conditions in factories and mines and workmen's compensation were passed, a beginning was made with the Indianization of the officers' cadre in the army under Lord Rawlinson's guidance, Indian membership of the new League of Nations was secured, her status alongside the dominions in the Imperial Conference assured, and the cause of Indians overseas (specially in South Africa) championed. The Lee Commission recommended a process of Indianization which would give Indians half the appointments in the senior services. On the other hand, the salt tax was doubled by the new process of certification in order to balance the budget. The loss of credit proved greater than the financial gain. The government had to cope, through 1921, with the non-co-operation movement and to quell frequent riots specially on the occasion of the Prince of Wales's visit. The negative aspects of these measures loomed more largely in the popular mind than the positive; suspicion was not dissipated and political India, if somewhat impressed in spite of itself, remained unconvinced of the sincerity of British intentions.

In the provinces ministries were duly formed, but only in one province, that of Madras, was a single party strong enough to take office unaided. This was the Justice or non-Brahman party. Here the governor, Lord Willingdon, seized the opportunity to make its leader, the Raja of Panagal, Chief Minister, and so produce a semblance of responsible party government. This ministry carried out educational reforms and a radical measure affecting temple endowments which a British administration would have hesitated to launch. In the Panjab there was also a hopeful experiment. Mian Fazli-Husain and Choudhri Chothu Ram (both later knighted) combined to form an intercommunal *zamindars*' or country party in opposition to the urban interests. The party did not actually control the new council, but through the personality of its chiefs it dominated the situation. A programme of educational expansion was launched, land reforms carried through, and the troublesome problem of the control of Sikh *gurudwaras* settled in 1925 by handing them over to a popularly elected board of trustees. Elsewhere the ministries represented coalitions of groups and were hampered in their working both by financial stringency and the lack of firm public support.

Behind and beyond the councils ran the ebb and flow of the Congress non-co-operation movement. Mahatma Gandhi stimulated enthusiasm by promising *swaraj* within a year and with the unprecedented support of the Muslim Khilafatists there seemed for a time to be no limits which he might not pass. But in Lord Reading he found a statesman who had, in his own way, an insight as keen and a mind as subtle as his own. At first Reading's attitude seemed to be one of olympian detachment. He was in fact studying the situation and measuring the strength of the opposing forces. He divined the essential difference of their aims and the temporary nature both of their union and of the enthusiasm of the component parties. His policy was to watch and wait for the inherent disharmonies and illusions of the parties to reveal themselves and do his work for him. In the case of the Congress the maintenance of enthusiasm depended upon swift success. It could not stand either the steady functioning of government or a prospect of prolonged disorder or anarchy. The maintenance of government during 1921 and the disorders which punctuated that year and the beginning of the next provided both conditions. Enthusiasm cooled, apprehension increased; the final arrest of Mahatma Gandhi in 1922 came as a relief. A reaction within Congress began against his leadership which covered the next few years. The other half of the coalition had much weaker roots than the Congress. Its leaders were adventurers and its followers were buoyed up by romantic sympathy for the Turkish *Khalifa*. The reckless *hijrat* or migration to Afghanistan proved disastrous. Muslim fears were calmed by Ataturk's success in reviving Turkey and the ground was finally cut from beneath the feet of the movement by the deposition of the Sultan in 1923 and the abolition of the *Khilafat* itself in 1924. In these circumstances Muslim fears of Hindu domination reasserted themselves and the fraternalism of 1921 was replaced by the communal riots of 1924.

The collapse of the non-co-operation movement in 1922 left India in the relaxed condition of a patient released from a bout of fever. There was an interval of apathy in public feeling which was used for a reconsideration of policy by the various parties concerned. On the Muslim side there was a return to Indian horizons and communal politics. Within the Congress there was much heart-searching. The new doctor's non-violent drug had failed to effect the promised cure of foreign domination. The sceptics were led by C. R. Das, the last of the great Bengali leaders, and Pt. Motilal Nehru from the United Provinces. In 1923 it was determined to fight the new elections and to endeavour to subvert the reforms from within the councils. This was a point gained for the new régime for it admitted the significance of the councils; it was also a threat to it because a paralysis of the ministries might prevent the public from realizing their possibilities. The Congress secured forty-five seats in the Legislative Assembly, which was enough to fulminate, but not to wreck without assistance, and enough strength in Bengal and Bombay to prevent the formation of ministries. For the next few years the party fulfilled the role of a nationalist opposition at the centre, and was increasingly involved in the give and take of group politics in the provinces. A splinter group of 'Responsivists' under M. R. Jayakar appeared in Maharashtra. C. R. Das died in 1925, when it seemed that he might be about to play with Lord Birkenhead the part of a Gokhale with Morley in working out a fresh understanding between government and people. Leadership therefore remained with Motilal Nehru, a powerful figure who introduced a new discipline into his party. These years saw, on the government side, the final abolition of the hated cotton excise in 1926, the acceptance of the Lee Commission's proposals for the equalization of the proportions of Indians and Europeans in the higher services, and the mission of Srinivasa Sastri to South Africa followed by his appointment as the first Agent-General in 1926. But it was in the political question that the Congress and the country were really interested. For all the criticism of dyarchy it was now clear that there could be no going back on it; one could therefore only move forward. The Congress aim was to accelerate this movement, but it remained divided as to methods. As the disillusionment which came from the failure of non-co-operation led to the decision for council entry, so disappointment with the fruits of constitutional obstruction led to a revival of interest in direct action. The Mahatma, in ostentatious political retirement, carried on his 'untouchable' reform or *harijan* movement while waiting for an opportunity to swing the Congress again to his views. In these circumstances all sections looked to government for a sign, which might prove a signal for renewed action or real co-operation. About 1925 government and Congress were in fact cautiously approaching one another. A conjunction like that of 1909 did not in fact take place because the political classes were still emotionally too disturbed by the events of 1919-21 to look at government proposals dispassionately, and because the ruling class in Britain, itself still suffering from the shock of war strain, was not ready to take bold enough views or able to find sufficiently imaginative leaders. By 1928 the mood of accommodation had gone, and events moved towards a fresh trial of strength.

The first response made by government was the appointment of the Muddiman Committee[1] to examine the working of the reforms. The majority recommended minor amendments, but the minority, led by Sir Tej Bahadur Sapru, declared that dyarchy was unworkable. This enabled all parties to unite in a demand for the grant of full self-government, to be worked out in its details by a round table conference. In April 1926 Lord Irwin succeeded to the Viceroyalty. His first move to promote communal harmony failed to divert the leaders from their constitutional concern. The government then looked to the Montford provision for periodical inquiries and determined to anticipate this provision by appointing a Commission two years earlier than legally required. The Simon Commission, led by Sir John (later Viscount) Simon and including the Labour prime minister to be, Mr. Attlee, was appointed in November 1927. This act had exactly the opposite effect to the one intended. Instead of conciliating, it outraged Indian sentiment, instead of providing a threshold for co-operation, it proved the prelude to conflict. The cause was the omission of any Indian from the Commission, which seemed, in the new atmosphere of the twenties, to cast a slur on the ability of Indians in political matters, to flout the idea of a round table conference, and by emphasizing parliamentary control of Indian affairs to challenge the right of Indians to work out their own destiny. It thus proved a great rallying cry for negative national sentiment. On its arrival and during its travels in 1928-9 it was subjected to hostile demonstrations and boycotted wherever Congress influence was strong enough. Its report was a constitutional masterpiece but its presence a political disaster. The Congress reaction went further than organizing processions and displaying black flags. The Madras Congress of 1927-8 declared independence to be the goal of Indian development. An All-parties Conference during 1928 produced a scheme of self-government known as the Nehru report,[2] and at the end of the year Mahatma Gandhi was welcomed back to the Congress fold. During 1929 Congress opinion hardened behind the demand for a round table conference as the prelude to the grant of dominion status. In Britain a Labour government succeeded Baldwin's Conservative administration and this enabled Lord Irwin to make a

---

[1] Presided over by Sir Alexander Muddiman, the home member.
[2] Its principal authors were Pt. Motilal Nehru and Sir Tej Bahadur Sapru.

further effort to bridge the gulf between British and nationalist opinion. Taking his political life in his hands he persuaded the new government to agree to a declaration, in the autumn of 1929, that dominion status was the goal of British policy and that a round table conference would be called to consider the next step. This represented a major achievement, for the declaration was agreed between the major elements of both British parties, which meant that it was now generally recognized that nationalism was the dominant and not simply a major force in India. It is impossible not to regret that the responsible national leaders did not recognize that in Lord Irwin they had to deal with a statesman of unusual insight and perception as well as of great influence and that the situation promised greater results from co-operation than intransigence. But the die went the other way. After appearing to accept the new proposals Mahatma Gandhi insisted on a promise that the round table conference should draw up a scheme for full dominion status with immediate effect. On its refusal, regardless of a revival of terrorism in the Panjab, he launched a civil disobedience movement with his walk from the Sabarmati ashram to the sea at Dandi where he symbolically manufactured illicit salt.

The civil disobedience movement of 1930 differed from the non-co-operation movement in 1921 in important respects. Both were avowedly non-violent, but whereas the first was passively the second was actively revolutionary. The first hoped to bring government to a standstill by withdrawing from the administration; the second sought to paralyse the government by the mass performance of specific illegal acts. Mass arrests would arouse general sympathy and gradually make administration impossible. In choosing these acts the Mahatma showed his usual insight into the popular mind, for he began with the illicit manufacture of salt in defiance of the unpopular salt tax. Though the Muslims gave him little support[1] he received a wide response from Hindu India, hypnotized once more by his combination of Hindu saint, western lawyer-politician, and poor man's friend.[2] One feature of the movement was the wide participation of women in the record of whose emancipation it proved a landmark. Another was the boycott of British goods which proved widespread and effective. A third was periodic outbreaks of violence such as the Sholapur riot and a serious rising in the Frontier Province. At this juncture the Simon Report was published and added fuel to the flames by limiting itself to proposing self-government in the provinces. Its suggestion that responsibility at the Centre should await a federation joined by the princes was thought to be tantamount to indefinite postponement. But the Viceroy persevered amid riots without, divided counsels at home, hesitations and doubt within his own circle. He succeeded in convincing the moderates that the government was not bound by the conclusions of the Simon

[1] They had been alienated by the rejection of separate electorates in the Nehru Report.
[2] There were about 60,000 arrests in the first six months of the movement.

Report and in inducing them to attend the round table conference. The conference itself proved to be a turning-point in Indo-British relations. For the last time during the British period the princes gave a lead by declaring their readiness to accept federation (and with it some curtailment of their powers) provided that the principle of responsibility was introduced into the Centre. In so doing the princes hoped, among other things, to reduce their dependence upon London; they did not, as was at first supposed, intend as a class to introduce any element of responsible government into their own states. But the prospect of States participation altered the Labour government's attitude to the introduction of responsibility at the Centre, and this in turn modified the Congress attitude to the government's policy. When the conference concluded on 19 January 1931, the prime minister, Mr. Ramsay Macdonald, announced that 'with the legislature constituted on a federal basis', the government 'would be prepared to recognise the principle of the responsibility of the executive to the legislature'. The Congress Working Committee including Gandhi were forthwith released and Lord Irwin took the novel step of holding direct conversations with the Mahatma. They were conducted on a man-to-man basis and lasted from 17 February to 4 March. These talks marked the end of the old official olympianism. Relations were never so stiff or the authorities so aloof again. The government was now anxious to conciliate Congress and the Congress leaders for their part realized that their movement was tiring quicker than the government, that the public mood was for a settlement and that they had already gained as much as they could hope for. The talks ended with what was known as the Gandhi-Irwin truce. The main terms were the ending of the civil disobedience, the release of political prisoners except those convicted of crimes of violence, and the representation of the Congress at the second session of the round table conference. The truce was ratified by the general Congress meeting at Karachi in April, which at the same time appointed the Mahatma as its sole representative.

The fates were not kind to this large-minded attempt to heal the breach between the two peoples and to plan the future jointly. The execution of Bhagat Singh for terrorism in the Panjab while the Karachi Congress was sitting revived extremist sentiment, while the Cawnpore communal riots embittered the Muslims. They were not pacified by Gandhi's promise to agree to any demand from a united community, since they well knew that the Mahatma's group of Congress Muslims under Dr. Ansari would never agree to the wishes of the majority. Disputes broke out in the ranks of Congress itself which experienced some of the pains of the demobilization process, while a conflict began between the Sen Gupta and Subash Chandra Bose factions which permanently weakened the Congress in Bengal. In Britain the financial crisis absorbed attention, leading to the fall of the Labour government and the installation of a 'National' administration, led by Ramsay Macondald it is true, but overwhelmingly Conservative in composition. The clear headed Sir Samuel Hoare (later Viscount Templewood) reigned at the India Office in the place of Mr. Wedgewood Benn (later Viscount Stansgate) while the amiable but ageing and less patient Willingdon had succeeded Lord Irwin in Delhi.

In these altered circumstances the second session of the round table conference met. At the outset the government proposed to separate the question of provincial autonomy from that of responsibility at the Centre. This was withdrawn on the unanimous opposition of the Indian delegates, but it was clear that some stiffening of the British attitude had taken place. Mahatma Gandhi was not slow to recognize this. He confined himself to a few general speeches and failed to take the opportunity of his presence in London for direct negotiations with the principal British statesmen. He estranged Muslims and untouchables by claiming to represent all India. Though he praised the new Secretary of State's frankness and integrity, the old devil of suspicion raised its head again to prevent him from seeing the distance the predominant Conservative party had travelled in a few years and the fact that it had in essence accepted the work of its predecessor. On the other side there was not so much a change of intention as in the *tone* of approach. The language of positive achievement and conscious movement towards a goal was replaced by cautious provisos, anxious care in devising safeguards, and absorption in schedules and tables. The sense of deliberate movement was lost and the government appeared again to be applying the brakes to another vehicle rather than propelling its own. In this atmosphere the Indian parties failed to agree upon the communal allotment of seats in the legislatures, so that the British were compelled to undertake an award. The second session closed in disappointment and foreboding.

Within three weeks of Mahatma Gandhi's return to India he was once more in prison and the Congress a proscribed organization. In his absence the militant Red Shirt movement had been started by Abdul Ghaffar Khan, claiming Congress allegiance, terrorism had reappeared in Bengal and a no-rent campaign had commenced in the United Provinces. It would seem that the forces within Congress desiring a further trial of strength were stronger than those prepared to give co-operation a real trial. They were helped by a new stiffness on the government side which now appeared to think that conciliation had paid few dividends and that a firm stand would break Congress militancy. In this latter view they proved to be correct, but their action involved the penalty of a further prolongation of the besetting suspicion which seemed for a moment in 1931 to have been banished. The Mahatma could either have determined to give co-operation a further trial, in which case he would have had to discipline the unruly element within the Congress, or, siding with them, have temporized while recruiting his forces for a further campaign. He did neither, with the result that the second civil disobedience movement went off at half cock. The fact was that the country as a whole was tired of strife and its attendant losses; it would sympathize with but no longer follow the Congress along the revolutionary path. The Congress leaders were temporarily out of touch with public opinion. The number of political prisoners rose to 34,458 in April 1932, about half the total for many months during 1930, but by July had sunk to 4,683. Thus the movement petered out and the government could claim a victory. But the country remained sullen though peaceful. There was no breakaway to a more hopeful policy as after the collapse of the non-co-operation movement; instead there was a somewhat sceptical waiting on events. Those who believed that the reforms had substance waited without enthusiasm and those who did not looked on with cynical detachment. In this mood of aloofness the country watched the slow gestation of the new system while Lord Willingdon's term ran out. Gradually it was impressed by the magnitude of the preparations and by the fact that the national government continued to go forward, despite the persistent opposition of a 'die-hard' group led by Mr. Churchill and Lord Lloyd and the revival of civil disobedience. These measures included the third session of the round table conference, the communal award of 1932, and a series of committees to settle the details of outstanding questions and a prolonged series of parliamentary inquiries and discussions. The new system became law as the Government of India Act of 1935, and Lord Linlithgow went out in the following year to inaugurate it.

AUTHORITIES

THE more important state papers are the *Muddiman Committee Report* (1925), *The Simon Commission Report* (2 vols., 1930), *The Agricultural (Linlithgow) Commission Report* (1928), and the *Report of the First Round Table Conference* (1931). On the Congress side there is the *Nehru Report* (1928).

For the working of dyarchy see Sir J. CUMMING, *Political India* (1932), J. COATMAN, *Years of Destiny* (1932), KERALA PUTRA (K. M. Panikkar), *The Working of Dyarchy in India* (1928). JAWARHARLAL NEHRU's *Autobiography* is valuable and so is AZIM HUSAIN, *Fazl-i-Husain* (1946) for the Panjab. P. SITTARAMAYA, *History of the Congress* (1945), is a standard work. See also TENDULKAR's *Mahatma* already mentioned. Interesting sidelights are provided by B. CHATURVEDI and M. SYKES, *C. F. Andrews* (1949).

See also S. GOPAL, *Viceroyalty of Lord Irwin* (1957) and the EARL OF HALIFAX, *Fullness of Days* (1957).

RECENT PUBLICATIONS

NEW and important works are the following: J. M. BROWN, *Gandhi and Civil Disobedience: The Mahatma in Indian Politics, 1928–34* (Cambridge, 1976); R. IYER, *The Moral and Political Thought of Mahatma Gandhi* (N.Y., 1973); C. J. BAKER, *The Politics of South India, 1920–37* (Cambridge, 1976); and WAHEED AHMAD (ed.), *The Letters of Mian Fazl-i-Husain* (Lahore, 1976).

CHAPTER 5

The Genesis of Pakistan

BEFORE 1930 the word Pakistan had not been heard of; in 1940 it was adopted by the Muslim League as its official aim; in 1947 it appeared as a new state containing more than 70 million people. Clearly such a rapid growth leading to such spectacular success must have sprung from roots deeper than purely political motives and stretching far beyond the twenties of the twentieth century. According to the 1941 census the Muslims of India then numbered some 92 millions or 24 per cent. of a total population of 389 millions. These became the '100 millions' of propaganda, which represented, however, an accurate enough total in the general propaganda figure of '400 millions'. The remaining 42 millions included all other groups such as the Sikhs, Christians, Jains, Parsis, and the primitive tribes of the forest areas. The Muslims thus constituted one in four of the total population. They were easily the largest minority in the country, and in fact the only one, except for the Sikhs in the Panjab, to be politically important. In their own eyes they were not a minority at all, but a separate 'nation', and it is this fact which may serve as a first clue to an understanding of the Pakistan movement.

The Muslims of India have always regarded themselves as separate from the rest of the people, though they have not always rejected the title of Indian. The Pakistan movement threw the cloak of Western nationalism over the Islamic conception of a separate culture and so converted a cultural and religious entity into a separatist political force. To understand how this could come about among a group of diverse racial origin, speaking many languages and geographically scattered, it is necessary to delve into the distant past. The first Muslims to enter India in force were the Arabs of Muhammad bin Kasim who conquered Sind in A.D. 712. From that time onwards Sind became gradually predominantly Muslim. The next step was the Ghaznavid conquest of the Panjab by Mahmud of Ghazni in the early eleventh century. The Panjab also, in the course of centuries became a mainly Muslim area though the Hindus (and later the Sikhs) continued to be a much more significant element in the population than in Sind. Kashmir was occupied in 1400, and also adopted Islam except for the small though significant group of Kashmiri Brahmans.

The great irruption of Islam into the main body of India followed the defeat of Prithvi Raj at Thanesar in 1192 and the capture of Delhi by Muhammad Ghori. Within twenty years the Muslim Turks had reached the Bay of Bengal and in little more than a century had penetrated as far as Madura in the extreme south. From that time forward until 1760 they were the dominant force in India. During four of the five and a half centuries northern India was ruled by two Muslim empires;[1] the Deccan as far as the Kistna was under Muslim control from the early fourteenth century and twice the whole sub-continent was virtually united under a single *raj*.

It was in these circumstances that one-quarter of the population became Muslim. That population was, however, by no means homogeneous. The first element was the immigrant, Arab, Turk, Pathan, Afghan, Persian, who in groups or tribes or in single families seeking their fortunes, settled in the country. Many of the Muslims of the old Panjab, Sind, and frontier regions belonged to tribal groups. Some such, like the Rohillas in the early eighteenth century in Rohilkhund, or the Sayyids of Barha, settled farther down country, but there is no evidence of large-scale Muslim folk movements like those of the Sakas, the Kushans, or the Huns, or the early Aryan-speaking peoples themselves. In the main the Indian Muslims were of Indian origin. Many individual families throughout the period came in from Persia and central Asia, attracted by opportunities of service and honour. The ancestors of the Nizam entered in this way in the seventeenth century, as did those of the Nawab Wazirs of Oudh. Mirza Najaf Khan, the last great Mughul minister under Shah Alam, was a late case of an immigrant rising to distinction. Some families still reveal their origin by their names, like the Bokharis. The Turanian and Iranian factions were a feature of Mughul political life.

The next element among the Muslims arose from intermarriage. The Muslim rule of India east of the Sutlej was at first that of an army of occupation. Officers and men sought wives and contracted unions, and thus a population of mixed racial origin grew up all over India. Unlike the later Anglo-Indians they never dissociated themselves from the country of their domicile; religion rather than racial feeling was the force that bound them together. It is probably from this class that most of the later Muslim leadership has come. The third element of the Muslim community, and by far the largest, was the result of conversion. Some of this was forcible, but we must beware of placing too much emphasis on this undoubted practice. Some Muslim chroniclers gloried in it with the probable exaggeration of enthusiasm. It occurred in quantity only during campaigns before the Hindus were generally recognized to be, like Christians and Jews, 'the people of a book', and then chiefly in the early rather than the later part of the period. There were no doubt individual cases of conversion by pressure throughout this long period. After forcible conversions came conversions from interest or hope of reward. There was a steady trickle of breakaways from the upper Hindu ranks for the sake of advancement in the Muslim state as well as from conviction or both. Khan Jahan, the minister of Firoz Shah, was an example of this type. Most took Muslim

[1] The Delhi Sultanate 1192-1398, the Mughul empire, 1526-1760.

names, but some, like the Muslim Puris, retained their old family names.

But the largest class of conversions were certainly voluntary and came from the lower levels of Hindu society. To this phenomenon must be attributed the mass conversion of eastern Bengal, which is now eastern Pakistan, whether we ascribe it to relief on the part of a Buddhist peasantry at deliverance from Brahman oppression or the straight conversion of a virtually animistic countryside. Such conversions were not confined to eastern Bengal, but occurred all over the country. In general they were from the lower classes, because Islam could offer to these people a hope and a status denied them in the Hindu system. But the existence of Muslim Rajputs shows that in the north-west it occurred in the upper strata of society as well. These conversions were not procured by kings or soldiers and introduce a new factor into the building up of the Muslim community. This factor is the Sufi movement. Sufi saints or *pirs* were present in the Panjab in the eleventh century and they soon followed the armies farther into India in the thirteenth. Many of them were men of great learning, but they were guides to the good life as well as scholars and poets who had their *murids* or disciples. Some like Kh. Muin-ud-din Chishti of Ajmer and Kh. Nizam-ud-din Aulia of Delhi settled near cities where their tombs became shrines and centres of devotion and proselytism. Others lived in groups in *khanqahs* or monasteries, the traces of which are numerous in old Muslim cities. These people were in general aloof from the courts and the orthodox *ulema* of the colleges; they appealed direct to the people and were the evangelists as well as the spiritual preceptors of Islam. They are often thought of as forming a bridge of understanding with the Hindu *bakhti* movement, with their emphasis on the inner life and the unity of all believers in the one God. Kabir, the Muslim weaver who preached the unity of religions and became the founder of a Hindu sect, is an example of this. But an even more important aspect of their work was the propagation of Islam among the Indian people. The Sufis, rather than kings, warriors, or adventurers, were responsible for the bulk of the Muslims in the sub-continent. And they as a class, for all the eclecticism of some of them, were responsible for the sense of separateness and sense of mission which tended to bind together people of the most diverse racial and social origin into a cultural and religious unity.

We thus find in the eighteenth century a large Muslim community scattered throughout India. It possessed a large aristocracy of office and landholders, a small middle class of professional men and government servants, and a large proletariat of agriculturists and artisans. The smallness of the middle class was due to Hindu competition on the one hand and the fact that for Muslims of talent under a Muslim régime the ladder of promotion led quickly upwards to the higher appointments. The eighteenth century was a time of stress for the community. Their political dominion collapsed, and with it went their hold on the chief offices of state. The British monopolized (from the time of Cornwallis) these offices for themselves, leaving the upper classes to jostle for subordinate posts with Hindus, or else to stand aloof in pride and poverty. Soon western education was added as another and unacceptable condition for office. Immigration from the north-west came to an end, except from among the untutored Afghans. The decline of Islam in its homeland reduced the value of such contacts as remained, thus depriving Indian Islam of the spiritual and cultural streams which had so long nourished it. Islam in India was politically depressed and culturally isolated. With the weakening of these Islamic impulses Hindu practices and social customs, like the worship of saints' tombs and caste customs, already well established, became more widespread. It became difficult to tell whether some groups were more Muslim or Hindu in their outlook. The widespread resumption of rent-free lands and the ruin of the Bengal weaving industry further depressed the community.

It was in this condition of political eclipse and cultural depression that Indian Islam was confronted with the challenge of the West. At first bad seemed to grow worse, for while the Muslims stood aloof, the Hindus took advantage of the new western education, thus securing a lead in the new world and the administration which they never lost. The Mutiny made things worse, for in spite of its Hindu origin the Muslims were thought to have revealed their disloyalty to and hatred of the new régime. But the Muslims were too numerous and too vigorous to be absorbed or permanently reduced to insignificance. The first movements of revival came from within and may be described as those of internal renewal or purification. These were amongst the body of the people. Then came a movement among the leaders in tardy response to western influences. It was the Pakistan movement which finally welded these two together into a national movement comparable to that of the Indian Congress.

The first of these movements can be traced to Shah Wali-ullah of Delhi (1703-62), described as one of the greatest theologians of Muslim India. He translated the Quran into Persian, while two of his sons added an Urdu version. He began a movement for reform which was carried on by his son Shah Abdul Aziz. In the hands of his disciple Sayyid Ahmad of Bareilly, who was influenced by Wahabi ideas from Arabia, this became the militant 'Wahabi' movement[1] of the early nineteenth century, with its headquarters at Patna. India was regarded as *dar-ul-harb*, or a land of war, since it was under infidel rule. Sayyid Ahmad's efforts, however, were directed against the Sikhs, as being the chief Muslim oppressors of the day. He established himself in the Swat valley where he waged a *jihad* or holy war until his death in battle with the Sikhs in 1831. Two parallel movements in lower India were led by Sheikh Karamat Ali of Jaunpur, another disciple of Shah Abdul

---

[1] So called because Sayyid Ahmad came under Wahabi influence. His movement was akin in *temper* but not in theology to that of the Wahabis.

Aziz, and Haji Shariat-ullah of Faridpur.[1] The latter was involved in agrarian agitation, but on the whole the two movements were peaceful. They were actively propagandist and did much to purify and strengthen east Indian Islam. Karamat Ali's work has been thus described:[2]

> For forty years he moved up and down the elaborate river system of eastern Bengal in a flotilla of small boats, carrying the message of Islamic regeneration and reform from the Nagas of Assam to the inhabitants of Sandip and other islands in the Bay of Bengal. His flotilla of country craft was like a travelling college. One boat was the residence of his family, another was reserved for the students and disciples accompanying him, while the third was for *dars* and lectures and prayers.

Mention should also be made of the Ahmadiya sect founded by Mirza Ghulam Ahmad (1838–1908) with its headquarters at Qadian in the Panjab. It gathered a numerous following in the Panjab and was notable for organization and missionary activity, both in India and abroad, including England. But its founder's claim to prophethood and to the function of completing or adding to the Muslim revelation caused the sect to be considered heretical by the main body of Muslims. It has been notable for the distinction of some of its adherents,[3] rather than for its influence on the development of Indian Islam as a whole.

The response of Indian Islam to the West came not from the Muslim princes who showed a curious imperviousness to Western thought while they toyed with European trinkets or adopted superficial European manners. Furniture, wines, and uniforms were the limit of their interest. The first concrete move came from Sayyid Ahmad Khan of Delhi. He was born in 1817 and took service under the British in 1837, rising to the rank of subordinate judge. He remained loyal in the Mutiny and published an influential essay on its causes. Sayyid Ahmad came of an aristocratic family of central Asian origin; his combination of oriental with western learning fitted him to be an interpreter between the conservative East and the encroaching West; his forceful character enabled him to impress his ideas on his people while his sterling integrity was proof against calumny. He visited England in 1869 and retired from service in 1876. In 1878 he became a member of the Governor-General's Legislative Council and was knighted in 1888. He died in 1898, the acknowledged grand old man of Indian Islam. The Sayyid was convinced that the Indian Muslims must make terms with the West, both politically and culturally. He considered that the tolerance and security of the British régime entitled it to be included in the *Dar-ul-Islam* or region of peace. The British régime having been accepted as in the providence of God, Muslims should win British approval by active loyalty. Otherwise they would be out-distanced in the race for governmental favour by the Hindus, as had already

---

[1] Known as the *Faraidhi* movement (pronounced Faraizi).
[2] S. Ikram, *Cultural Heritage of Pakistan*, p. 15.
[3] e.g. Sir Zafar-ullah Khan, Foreign Minister of Pakistan, 1947–55.

happened in the case of education. A modern education, indeed, was the
sine qua non of the community's progress, and the Sayyid therefore
became a champion of western knowledge, which should not be inconsistent with the tenets of Islam. The fruit of this advocacy was the
opening of the Anglo-Oriental College at Aligarh in 1875, with its
British principals and staff,[1] its residential system, its mosque and
religious instruction, its balance of eastern and western learning. In
1920 the college became the Aligarh Muslim University. Aligarh both
enabled the talented young Muslim to compete on terms with the
Hindu for government service and in public life, and gave him a
dynamic which his community seemed to have lost.

For Sir Sayyid was not concerned with material things only. His
movement was one of general reform. It was inspired by the thought
that the Muslims of India were a separate people or nation who must
not be absorbed within Hinduism, and that the essence of Islam was
consistent with the best that the West had to offer. He was, in fact, a
Muslim modernist appealing to general principles outside the scope of
the four recognized schools of theology. He accepted the mission of
the Prophet and God's revelation in the Quran. But he claimed that
Reason was also an attribute of God and Nature his handywork.[2] The
Quran and Islam might therefore be interpreted on the basis of reason
to meet modern needs and problems. The achievements of the West,
so far as they rested on reason, might thus be welcomed and assimi-
lated. He laid particular stress upon science, as being the characteristic
feature of western progress. His first institution at Aligarh was a
scientific society. In pressing this point of view he was much helped
by the existence of the strong Greek tradition in Islamic thought, and
by the common Judaic background which western Christianity shared
with Islam. Thus fortified, the Sayyid conducted a campaign on two
fronts, against the isolationist conservative Muslims on the one hand
and European critics on the other. This tended to replace backward-
looking by forward-looking views and to restore the shaken confidence
of those in close contact with western thought.

These ideas attracted distinguished supporters, who came to be
known collectively as the Aligarh school. Among them may be mentioned two men nurtured in the pre-Mutiny renaissance at the Delhi
college, Maulvi Nazir Ahmad and Maulvi Zaka-ullah, the poets Altaf
Husain, Hali, and Maulvi Shibli Numani, the scholar Khuda Baksh,
and the educationist Yusuf Ali. The work of Sayyid Amir Ali,[3]
though in general accord, had a slant of its own. His *Spirit of Islam*
was the best apologetic of Islam for the non-Muslim which had appeared, while his *History of the Saracens* was a tonic for the Muslims

---

[1] e.g. Sir Theodore Beck, the first principal, Sir Theodore Morison, Sir Thomas
Arnold.
[2] His followers came to be called *Necharis*, from the word 'nature,' as tending to
follow nature rather than revelation.
[3] 1849-1928, first Indian member of the Judicial Committee of the Privy Council.

themselves. He emphasized the personality of the Prophet and so introduced what may be described as prophetic hero-worship. But though emphasizing the value of tradition, he was also a reformer, advocating women's education. His insistence on the glories of historical Islam provided a starting-point for the leaders of the *Khilafat* movement and a link between them and the westernized liberals.

Sayyid Ahmad's programme was admirably suited to the position of Indian Islam in the Victorian world. It made possible the assimilation of elements of a culture which then seemed irresistible; it provided for gradual political progress at a time when that seemed to be the only sort of progress possible. With the advent of the twentieth century conditions changed. Something more dynamic than reason in the religious sphere was needed, and something more radical than advisory councils as a political programme. Europe itself was changing with the development of industrialism; the old Islamic world was threatened and trying to save itself by pan-Islamic Caliphate ideas. In India itself came the first signs of the transfer of power to Indian hands, with the ultimate prospect of a Hindu government. The collapse of Turkey before the Balkan states in 1912 and then during the first World War made Europe appear to many for a time as again the enemy of Islam. It was this which gave strength to the *Khilafat* movement in the postwar years. The overriding need, as it seemed, to defend Islam, justified the Hindu alliance then contracted. The revival of Turkey in 1922 and her emergence as a secularist state reassured the liberals while removing the whole basis of the conservative programme. From that time on the Hindu majority, personified in the enigmatic figure of Gandhi, seemed to be the main threat to a separate Muslim existence. But there could be no return to the days of the Sayyid. Indian Islam needed a more dynamic creed and a larger vision and found it in the writings of Sir Muhammad Iqbal.[1]

Iqbal wrote mainly in Persian and only produced one work in English.[2] His theme was the all-embracing sufficiency of Islam as expressing a dynamic spirit of struggle for spiritual freedom. Islam was not merely a valid religion to be compared favourably with others; it was the root and branch of all religious experience. It was not a fixed and precious deposit to be treasured with the zeal of the antiquarian, but a living principle of action which could give purpose and remake worlds. Europe was enmeshed in its greed for wealth and lust for power.[3] It was for Islam to create true values and to assert man's mastery of nature by constant struggle. It was Nietzsche in an Islamic setting. Iqbal's teaching provided the young Muslim generation with a view

[1] 1876–1938.
[2] *Six Lectures on the Reconstruction of Religious Thought*, Lahore, 1930.
[3] Iqbal's opinion of the West is given in the following two couplets:
'The glitter of modern civilisation dazzles the sight,
But it is only a clever piecing together of false gems.'
'The wisdom or science in which the wise ones of the West took such pride:
Is but a warring sword in the bloody hands of greed and ambition'.

which out-moderned the moderns, but which yet seemed distinctive
and Islamic. Sayyid Ahmad Khan gave Indian Islam a sense of separate existence; Iqbal a sense of separate destiny.

The precipitation of this rich solution of thought and feeling into
the crystals of a political movement required an external catalyst, and
this was provided by fear. Sayyid Ahmad Khan gave the community a
new sense of justification and a new line of conduct; he also made
possible a new sense of security by pointing the way to a reconciliation
with the ruling power. But the sense of separateness from others involved an immediate reaction to any suggestion of commingling or
absorption in a plural society. The British might rule, for they showed
no sign of interfering with Islam; that was the basis of the Sayyid's
confidence in them. But would a hypothetical Hindu government do
the same? As soon as the Congress was formed in 1885 the Sayyid
took alarm. Majority Indian rule for him meant Hindu rule, and Hindu
rule meant the risk of cultural absorption. He had already declined to
support Amir Ali's 'National Muhammadan Association' in Calcutta
in 1877 as tending to subversive activity. Only a small group, particularly in Bombay, supported the Congress to become the nucleus of
the later nationalist Muslims.

The Muslims in general watched the growth of Congress from a
distance and stood aloof from its controversies with Lord Curzon. But
having allowed it to become dominantly Hindu in character through
their abstention, they took alarm at the first signs of concessions to its
demands. From this sprang the deputation to Lord Minto in 1906, led
by the Agha Khan, which demanded separate electorates for Muslims
in any representative system which might be introduced. At the same
time they did what the Sayyid had frowned upon during his life by
forming the All-India Muslim League. The Morley-Minto reforms with
their separate electorates for Muslim landholders, and their retention
of irresponsible power by the British, satisfied them for the time so far
as India was concerned. But almost immediately the Muslims took
alarm at the misfortunes of Turkey and there followed the *Khilafat*
movement. Pan-Islamic sentiment overbore the nascent local Muslim
nationalism and antipathy to British Turkish policy local fear of Hindu
rule. The outward expressions of this emotional upheaval were the
Lucknow Pact of 1916 with the Congress which recognized separate
electorates, and the alliance with Congress in Gandhi's non-co-operation movement. The passing of this storm left the Muslims as a whole
disillusioned and fearful for their future while leaving a fresh sediment
of Muslims on the Congress shore. These included many westernized
Muslims who took a secularist view on the lines of Ataturk as to the
place of Islam in the state. The most distinguished of these was Muhammad Ali Jinnah of Bombay, who had been a member of Congress for
many years and now held the balance of power in the Legislative
Assembly as leader of the Independent party.[1]

[1] This was a parliamentary group rather than a party, for it had no country-wide

PLATE 39

Muhammad Ali Jinnah

The working of the Montford reforms tended to increase these fears. They were expressed in a rising tempo of communal riots and increasingly bitter exchanges between the party leaders. The Ali brothers swung round from the preaching of Hindu fraternalism to the championship of Muslim rights. But the community remained divided and perplexed. In 1927 the League split on the question of the Simon Commission,[1] uniting in 1929 in the All-India Muslim Conference. Mr. Jinnah retired in 1931. Only in the Panjab were the Muslims active and confident under the determined leadership of Sir Fazl-i Husain, whose icy and resolute character was reminiscent of the Irish Parnell. The constitutional discussions which began with the appointment of the Simon Commission at the end of 1927 increased Muslim fears, for it soon became clear that a further instalment of power would be given to responsible ministers, and that full self-government was now above the horizon of development. Heightened apprehension quickened the urge to unity and also the search for a practical policy. The search for unity led to the reorganization of the League[2] under Mr. Jinnah in 1934, whose emergence from political retirement in this capacity was itself a sign of the times. The search for a positive programme led in two directions. The first was that of safeguards. During the constitutional discussions of the early thirties there was a renewed insistence upon communal representation, not only in the constituencies, but also in the government service. Muslims welcomed federation as giving provinces more freedom and thus tending to safeguard Muslims in their majority areas. They sought to reduce the scope of the Centre as much as possible.[3] The second direction was towards autonomy in the Muslim majority areas. In 1930 Iqbal suggested the union of the Frontier Province, Baluchistan, Sind, and Kashmir as a Muslim state within a federation. This proved to be a creative idea which germinated during the early thirties to burst into vigorous life with the advent of the new reforms. The idealist Choudhri Rahmat Ali developed this conception at Cambridge, where he inspired a group of young Muslims and invented the term Pakistan in 1933.[4] His ideas seemed visionary at the time, but within seven years they had been turned into a practical programme by the future Qaid-i-Azam with the new name as its slogan or banner. The ideology of Iqbal, the visions of Rahmat Ali, and the fears of Muslims were thus united by the practical genius of Jinnah to bind Muslims together as never before during the British period and lead to effect an act of political creation.

organization. But it numbered nearly 30, and when in alliance with the Congress Swaraj party, as it often was, could usually secure a government defeat.

[1] The co-operating group was led by Sir Muhammad Shafi.

[2] The conference executive met for the last time in 1936.

[3] e.g. by allotting the 'residuary powers' of government, and as many defined powers as possible to the Provinces.

[4] P for Panjab, A for Afghans (Frontier Province), K for Kashmir, S for Sind; the whole meaning 'Land of the Pure'.

AUTHORITIES

A useful work is by S. M. IKRAM, *Cultural Heritage of Pakistan* (1955). W. C. SMITH, *Modern Islam in India* (1946), is tendentious but extensive and informative. For Islam in the nineteenth century see W. W. HUNTER, *Indian Mussulmans* (1876). A. YUSUF ALI, *Cultural History of India* (1940), has much scattered information. A. H. ALBERUNI, *Makers of Pakistan* (1950), provides useful studies of prominent leaders.

For Sir Sayyid Ahmad Khan see his *Life* by G. F. I. GRAHAM (1909) and for the ideas of his school see SYED AMEER ALI, *Spirit of Islam* (1922). For IQBAL see his *Reconstruction of Religious Thought in Islam* (1934) and *Secrets of the Self*, tr. R. A. NICHOLSON (1920). For political Islam see AZIM HUSAIN, *Fazl-i-Husain* (1946). There is as yet no authoritative biography of M. A. Jinnah, or of the Muslim League, but M. H. SAIYED, *M. A. Jinnah* (Lahore, 1945), and H. BOLITHO, *Jinnah* (1954), may be consulted. The latter is a character study rather than a full biography.

See also R. C. SMITH, *Islam in Modern History* (1957) and I. H. QURESHI, *The Muslim Community in India and Pakistan: a short History* (1960).

RECENT PUBLICATIONS

R. A. SYMONDS in *The Making of Pakistan* (1950) provides an objective account of the Pakistan movement and I. H. QURESHI a Pakistani version in *The Struggle for Pakistan* (Karachi, 1965).

The following general works on Islam and on Indian Muslims may be mentioned: R. LEVY, *The Social Structure of Islam* (Cambridge, 1957); M. MUJEEB, *The Indian Muslims* (1967); P. HARDY, *The Muslims of British India* (Cambridge, 1972); and E. I. J. ROSENTHAL, *Islam in the Modern National State* (Cambridge, 1965).

CHAPTER 6

The 1935 Act and After

THE new Government of India Act received the royal assent on 4 August 1935. It was the last major constructive achievement of the British in India; its significance matched both its bulk and the deliberation of its preparation. The consideration of the next constitutional step had begun ten years earlier with the Muddiman Committee's report; the ill-starred Simon Commission had reached India seven years previously, and its report of 1930 had been anticipated by the Congress counterblast of the Nehru report. The government of India's own proposals of 1930 (containing the first official suggestion for responsibility at the Centre) had been followed by the three sessions of the Round Table Conference. The Lothian report determined the electoral provisions of the Act; the communal award of 4 August 1932, following on abortive communal discussions between the Indian parties themselves, had fixed communal representation in the provinces and this was given final shape by the Poona Pact of 24 September 1932, which secured general as well as special representation for the scheduled or depressed classes at the point of a Gandhian fast unto death. A government white paper of 1933 set out a first draft of the proposals which were finally embodied in the Act with five major alterations after further consideration by a joint select committee of both Houses presided over by Lord Linlithgow. The Bill had been successfully piloted between the Scylla of British hesitancy expressed by the 'die-hard' opposition in Parliament, and the Charybdis of Indian impatience represented by Congress obstruction. As it emerged it probably represented the greatest measure of agreement then possible, if not within India itself, at any rate between current opinion in India and Britain respectively.

The Act continued and extended all the existing features of the Indian constitution. Popular representation, which went back to 1892, dyarchy and ministerial responsibility, which dated from 1921, provincial autonomy, whose chequered history went back to the eighteenth-century presidencies, communal representation, which first received overt recognition in 1909, and the safeguards devised in 1919, were all continued and in most cases extended. But in addition certain new principles were introduced. These were the federal principle, with its corollary of provincial autonomy, and the principle of popular responsible government in the provinces.

Certain administrative changes may first be noted. Sind was separated from Bombay to become a separate province. A new province of

Orissa was formed from the Orissa division of the former province of Bihar and Orissa and adjacent portions of the Madras and Central Provinces. These became governor's provinces along with the North-West Frontier Province, which had been promoted to the same status in 1932. At the same time Burma was separated from India and a separate constitution on the same lines enacted for it.[1] British India thus attained its final administrative form of eleven governor's provinces, the Chief Commissionships of Delhi, Ajmer-Merwara, Coorg, and the Andamans, and the agency of British Baluchistan. These changes represented in India concessions to growing provincial self-consciousness rather than any specific plan. The well-marked divisions of Gujarat and Maharashtra continued to be united in the Bombay province and the Tamil, Telugu, and Malayali peoples remained united in Madras. The separation of Burma was the recognition of an historic and cultural independence and the correction of an historical accident.

The most striking innovation was the introduction of the federal principle. Indian federation was conceived as a double process by which autonomy was conferred on previously subordinate provinces on the one hand, and the separate princely states, previously bound collectively only by the consultative Chamber of Princes, and individually by direct ties with the Crown, were to be integrated with the rest of India on the other. Federation in the provinces was a matter of legislative enactment, but since the position of the princes was regulated by separate treaties, their adhesion could only be brought about by consent. Accordingly it was provided that the central portion of the scheme would only come into force when rulers representing half the total princely population had acceded to the federation. The princes were to nominate one-third of the representatives of the Lower Federal Chamber and two-fifths of the Upper, and the powers surrendered by them would in each case be regulated by their respective instruments of accession. Until their accession the old central government would continue to operate.

Though the new central executive depended upon princely accession, the federal principle as such existed independently and was enforced without them. The problem of 'residuary' legislative powers was solved by the preparation of three detailed lists, one federal, one provincial, and one concurrent. The allotment of powers still unforeseen, a cause of difference between Hindu and Muslim opinion, was not confided to either branch of government, but to the discretion of the Governor-General. The division of executive and financial powers followed broadly that of the 1919 Act, the main difference being the allotment to the provinces of a share in the proceeds of income tax. The importance of the concurrent list of legislative subjects became clear when the second World War compelled the central government to undertake a degree of control of national life undreamt of in pre-war

[1] This was re-enacted separately as the Government of Burma Act in the next parliamentary session.

years. The corollary of federation was provincial autonomy. The reality of this departure was also demonstrated by war experience, notably in the crisis of the Bengal famine of 1943. The federal structure was completed by the creation of a federal court for interpretation and the resolution of disputes and a federal reserve bank.[1]

The next great innovation was the introduction of responsible government in the provinces. Dyarchy was swept away, to be replaced by a system of popular governments appointed by the governor but responsible to a popularly elected assembly. Chief ministers or premiers became the effective heads of provincial administration and governors were enjoined to act on their advice so long as their reserved powers were not invaded. Dyarchy, which had been banished from the provinces, reappeared at the Centre, where ministers depending upon popular support controlled the whole administration except defence and foreign affairs. For these subjects the Governor-General would appoint counsellors who were analogous to the nominated 'members' of governors' former executive councils.

Other features of the constitution were not new, but represented large developments from previous practice. The provincial assemblies were recast and second chambers were added in six provinces out of eleven. These popular assemblies were backed by popular electorates, which were expanded on the lines recommended by the Lothian Committee to include about 30 million voters. Though a small property qualification was retained nearly a sixth of the adult population of India became eligible to vote. Women received the franchise on the same terms as men. The principle of communal representation, admitted for the quietening of Muslim tender consciences in 1909, and extended as a concession to human weakness in 1919, was accepted as a regular feature in 1935. Muslims in all provinces, Sikhs in the Panjab, Christians in Madras and elsewhere, and Europeans specially in Bengal were all accorded special representation. But though the principle was now openly admitted, it was not applied as part of a reasoned conception of a plural society. It was a permitted deviation from western homogeneous democratic representation, as the new provinces of Sind and Orissa were deviations in deference to public demand from the old tradition of forming provinces on grounds of administrative convenience or historic accident.

The existence of safeguards and special powers was also a 'carry-over' from the previous practice. At the Centre the Governor-General had the control of the reserved departments, the power of certifying legislation in the form of 'Governor-General's Acts', and the power to issue ordinances with the force of law for six months at a time. The governors were vested with special powers for the discharge of their 'special responsibilities'. The most important of these were the prevention of discrimination, the protection of the legitimate interests of minorities, and the continuance of the administration in the event of a

[1] Set up by the Reserve Bank of India Act, 1934.

breakdown of the machinery of self-government. In this latter contingency they were given legislative authority both temporary and permanent and the power to control the whole administration. These powers may be described as the provision of a reserve engine in the event of the breakdown of the new constitutional machine or a strike of its new engineers. Other safeguards preserved the rights of the all-India services and their control by the Secretary of State.

The Secretary of State was retained with a number of advisers in place of the India Council. He remained the symbol of the surviving ultimate control of Parliament. The umbilical cord between constitutional parent and child was not yet severed.

This massive constitutional document, with its elaborate instrument of instructions and its complicated schedules marked a major step towards the goal of dominion status. But it was not that dominion status in itself. It may be briefly described as the establishment of provincial autonomy in relation to the centre and self-government with regard to the local administration together with popular participation in the executive as well as the legislative branch of the central government. To this may be added the federal principle and the projected integration of the princes with the rest of India. British control was largely pared away in the provinces where its principal vestiges were the British-appointed governors, with their reserve powers, and the British-controlled services like the I.C.S. and the police, who could be directed but not dismissed. An imperial official could be transferred or even placed on the unemployed list, but not dispensed with or degraded without the Secretary of State's consent; though definitely subordinate they therefore still retained some degree of independence in relation to the provincial executive.

In certain important respects the new constitution fell short of dominion status. The first was the proposed existence of dyarchy at the Centre. In the reserved part of the administration, which controlled foreign affairs and defence, there was still to be found an executive irremovable by the people of India and responsible to the British Parliament. The Viceroy continued to combine the functions of head of state and prime minister, and to be dependent upon the British cabinet. The transition carried out in Canada by Lord Elgin in 1845 by mere convention had in India still to come, and was for the present barred by legal enactment. The second restriction was the existence of safeguards, which as Professor Coupland states, were without any real parallel in the dominions. They might be disregarded or whittled away in practice, or they might be removed by amending legislation, but for the present they were an advertisement of surviving dependence, and a ready handle for the use of critics disposed to doubt the sincerity of British declared intentions. The third was the surviving subordination of the proposed federal legislature to the British Parliament. Not only would it be the creature of a British Act of Parliament, to which body, in fact, all other dominions owed their constitutions, but its legislation was subject to 'refusal of assent or reservation by the Governor-General, acting under the control of the Secretary of State, and to disallowance by the Crown acting under the Secretary of State's advice'.[1] This, like the other restrictions, could be removed in the course of development without injury to the scheme as a whole, but while it lasted was an impediment to India's aspiration of independence, or serious comparison to the status of the dominions, still basking in the declaratory warmth of the Statute of Westminster.

The pivots of the new constitution were federation with its implication of princely co-operation, responsibility of government to the elected representatives of the people, the communal principle which regulated the form of that representation, and the existence of safeguards. It was around these points that constitutional discussion and political tactics revolved during the twelve remaining years of British rule.

We may here anticipate later developments to some extent by considering the success of the new constitution as a whole. It would be easy to conclude, from the failure of the central federal structure to materialize, and the eventual establishment of the Republic of India, that the new constitution was a failure. But this would be far from the truth. The Act of 1935 formed an organic connecting link between the old and the new. It contained within itself the seeds of independence. The irresponsible elements were no longer the essence of the system; they formed, so to say, no longer the trunk or roots of the political roof tree of India, but branches which could be lopped away without injury to the whole. Or the new elements could be likened to the branches of the *banyan* tree of India, which take root in the ground so that the original stem can be cut away without injury to the tree as a whole. Secondly, the element of continuity, the vitality in development, may be held responsible for the avoidance of violent revolution in India. The leading political party in India was continuously dissatisfied with the constitution and more than once attempted to force development by unconstitutional means. But there was always hope of achieving the end of independence without violence. It was this consideration which restrained the Congress, for all its apparent intransigence, from deliberately violent courses. If it was not the cause of Mahatma Gandhi's non-violence policy, it was an important factor in enabling him to impose that policy on numbers of not always willing followers. The 'rising' of August 1942 and the naval mutiny of 1946 showed that the advocates of violence had been reduced, if not below danger point, at any rate well below the strength needed for successful revolution. The pressure was there, rising and falling with changing circumstances, but it never reached the level of explosion. The Act proved to be adequate not only for the strains of political transition but for the additional stresses of war and a world crisis.

Thirdly, the Act formed a monument to the sincerity of declared

[1] Sir R. Coupland, *Constitutional Problems of India*, vol. i, p. 146.

British intentions. It represented concessions to the national principle from strength, instead, as could be represented in the case of the Mont-ford reforms, through weakness after a world war. The very delibera-tion of its construction was evidence of firmness of intention. This was not recognized at the time in many quarters, and still less in the fevered months preceding Lord Mountbatten's declaration. But when the fact of independence scattered the mists of suspicion formed by impatience and a sense of frustration, it was seen that new indepen-dence was but the conception of 1935 developed and completed. The Act, therefore, played its part, not only in tiding over the transition without resort to violence, but in the restoring of feelings of goodwill between the Indian and British peoples which was so marked a feature of the post-1947 atmosphere. There was no death-bed repen-tance on the part of the British; the heir found his heritage drawn up and a testament prepared more than twelve years previously. The regard with which the Act has come to be held in responsible quarters was shown by its treatment by the constitution makers of the Indian Republic. Long sections were taken over entire and the shape of the new Constitution as a whole bears the same sort of relationship to the Act of 1935 as the British land settlements in north India to Todar Mal's *bandobast* in the time of the great Akbar. Not a little of this respect was due to the work of clarification and interpretation of the first Chief Justice of India, Sir Maurice Gwyer. Never was flattery of the British in India more sincere than in the imitation of their final constitutional arrangements.

The new Act was not, however, free from defects, and these had their consequence no less than its merits. It depended on the princes for the implementation of its central federal provisions; it did not prevent partition. The provision that not less than one-half of the princes representing half the princely population must accede to the federation before the central sections became operative proved in fact a fatal obstacle. The still slender powers of aristocratic co-operation were too severely strained and the ever latent centrifugal forces were unduly stimulated. The absence of princely co-operation involved the stillbirth of the central federal legislature and executive, and the con-tinuance of its irresponsible predecessor. This in its turn made the control of communal and the conciliation of national forces much more difficult than it might have been.

Partition, if not provoked, was certainly encouraged by another de-fect in the Act. While provision was made for minority representa-tion by means of communal electorates, and devices such as weightage and second chambers, the theory of sovereignty was that of a homo-geneous democratic and national state. Majority decision was the ulti-mate criterion of all questions, be their nature what they might. There was no recognition in the new political institutions of the fact of plural society in India. The fact that two cultures as well as two religions existed side by side in India (to consider only the two major Indian societies) was overlooked, and it was assumed that one society would be willing to accept direction from a government based on a majority from a different society. This was in fact a retreat from the British attitude in the nineteenth century, which, for all its paramountcy in the purely political sphere, recognized that there were social and cultural as well as purely religious realms in which the government would interfere at its peril. Cultural non-interference was the complement of political absolutism. The new constitution gave to any majority the power of cultural as well as political dominance over any minority. The suspicion of a similar tendency on the part of the British in the mid-nineteenth century helped to create the atmosphere which made the Mutiny possible; the fear of such dominance by one community over another after 1935 created the atmosphere which made partition inevitable.

The new era opened with new personalities as well as new institutions. Lord Willingdon was succeeded in 1936 by Lord Linlithgow, who united encyclopaedic knowledge with an ambition to implement the whole Act within his term of office. He had toured India as Chairman of the Royal Commission on Agriculture and had presided over the deliberations of the Joint Parliamentary Committee which had considered the draft constitutional proposals. Lord Zetland, who had (as Lord Ronaldshay) inaugurated the Montford reforms in Bengal, succeeded Sir Samuel Hoare as Secretary of State, and Sir Maurice Gwyer, who had played a large part in the drafting of the 1935 Act, became the first Chief Justice of India.

In India itself the Act was received critically but not altogether unhopefully. The Liberals and other 'splinter parties' were prepared to work the reforms as an instalment towards full responsible government. The criticism of the Muslim League was louder, but the Muslims were also ready to give the Act a trial. The Congress condemned the Act as a whole, but hinted that they might be prepared to work the provincial part under protest. There seemed some hope that Hindus and Muslims might work together as at the time of the Lucknow Pact in 1916. The elections to the Central Assembly in 1935 showed that the Congress was the dominant party in Hindu India.

In this atmosphere Lord Linlithgow set to work. Personal representatives were dispatched to major states to discuss terms of accession. These discussions and the collation of their reports lasted until 1939, by which time new events had occurred to alarm the princes and the outbreak of war was about to preoccupy the government. The golden moment passed, and was never to return. To anyone who does not think that the practical extinction of princely India was a consummation to be welcomed, it is difficult not to regard the patience and deliberation displayed in this matter as excessive. Here was pre-eminently a case for striking while the iron was hot, but it was cold indeed before the viceregal hammer began to descend in 1939.

The next step was the holding of provincial elections. These took place in February 1937, and resulted in striking Congress successes. In five of the eleven provinces they secured clear majorities; in Bombay they could form a ministry with the help of fellow travellers, while in the North-West Frontier Province their 'Red Shirt' Pathan allies under the 'frontier Gandhi' Abdul Ghaffar Khan, secured a majority. The two important exceptions were Bengal and the Panjab. In Bengal a Muslim coalition ministry under Mr. Fazl-ul Huq took office. In the Panjab the Unionist party, re-created by Sir Fazli-Husain on the eve of his death, secured a majority and took office under Sir Sikandar Hayat Khan. This was the only important non-communal party in the country; it represented the rural as opposed to the urban interest, and while dominantly Muslim in composition, it included an important section of Hindu Jats under the forceful Lala Chothu Ram as well as a group of Sikh agriculturists. Under Sir Sikandar and his successor Sir Khizr Hayat Khan it governed the Panjab for nine years.

Immediately a difficulty arose. The Congress leaders asked for assurances from the governors that they would not use their special powers to override ministers 'in regard to their constitutional activities'. The governors could not bind themselves not to exercise powers they were bound by law to use in certain contingencies. But the desire for office amongst the provincial Congress parties was strong, and the difficulty was overcome by an explanatory declaration by the Viceroy. In July Congress ministries were formed in seven provinces and responsible government in the provinces was fairly launched.

The ministries lasted until the outbreak of war just over two years later. With one or two exceptions they proved remarkably stable and they lasted long enough to demonstrate the existence of constructive statesmanship in the Congress ranks. If Mr. C. Rajagopalachari of Madras was the most distinguished figure amongst the Congress premiers, he had worthy colleagues in Pandit G. B. Pant of the United Provinces and Mr. B. G. Kher of Bombay. Order was maintained, communal outbreaks were dealt with, and the administrative machine, after a few initial jolts, continued to function smoothly. The tendency of provincial Congress committees to regard themselves as parallel governments was discouraged. Congressmen began to think constitutionally. Developments such as Gandhi's scheme of 'Basic education' were undertaken, and experiments like that of prohibition were initiated. Relations with the British governors and officials were often surprisingly good, and there was widespread regret on both sides when the experiment came to an end. But this was not the whole of the picture. National politics did not cease because the federal centre had not yet come into being. The Congress was strongly represented in the old Central Assembly[1] and continued to campaign against the irresponsible central executive. Above all it retained its national organization. The principal leaders of Congress did not assume provincial office. Instead they formed the Congress 'High Command' which, through the

---

[1] Congress held 44 out of 104 elective seats in a House of 144.

medium of the Congress Working Committee or cabinet laid down the main lines of national policy and supervised the work of the provincial ministries. At its command they took office and on its orders they resigned. The provincial ministries suffered no parallel party organizations, but they themselves were subordinate agents of an all-India authority parallel to the central government. Thus both provincial autonomy and provincial responsibility were incomplete in the Congress provinces, since the governments were subject to control by an outside authority in both respects.

The real political issues were debated and decided in the working committee and the annual general sessions of Congress. The principal influence continued to be Mahatma Gandhi though he held no office and had at times not even been a subscribing member of the party. To the peasant Gandhi was Congress and the Congress was Gandhi; the urban intelligentsia valued his world prestige if they did not always relish his doctrines; his colleagues respected his judgement and revered his character, however much they might be irritated by some of his opinions. Next in popular esteem came Pandit Jawarharlal Nehru, the idol of the young westernized classes and of the landless peasants of the United Provinces. A socialist and social reformer, an agnostic and anti-clerical, a nationalist and democrat, his generous ideals and fiery zeal exactly fitted the mood of the emerging westernized classes. His sacrifices for the cause, his patent disinterestedness, and his frankness of speech had already marked him as Gandhi's destined successor. The more conservative wing of the Congress was represented by the able but unspectacular Rajendra Prasad, western Indian big business and militancy by Sardar Vallabhai Patel, the extreme left wing by the rising Bengali, Subash Chandra Bose.

For the present the Congress leaders were content to watch developments. But this watching was by no means passive; three decisions of vital importance were taken in the years 1936–9. The Congress leaders interpreted their leadership as a 'High Command'; the provincial premiers were so many generals of division subject to directions from the Centre. When Dr. Khare in the Central Provinces grew restive he was forthwith replaced, even at the price of a local political schism. Extremists at the Centre were dealt with equally firmly. Mr. Subash Bose was allowed to succeed Pandit Nehru as president at the end of 1937. But when he stood for re-election a year later against the wishes of the Mahatma, he was disciplined as sternly as Dr. Khare. Thirdly, the Congress boldly claimed to be the *de facto* representatives of the Indian people. Other groups might represent different view-points, but only Congress represented India as a whole. From this it followed that in Congress majority provinces the idea of coalition could not be entertained. They were merely temporary devices where the help of fellow travellers was necessary for the formation of a ministry. In particular this doctrine applied to Muslims. Muslim nationalists represented Muslims as Muslims in the Congress, and Congress as a whole represented Muslims as Indians. Accordingly no separate Muslim representation was necessary and no coalition with the Muslim League could be entertained. Thus the already incipient Muslim reaction was precipitated into positive action, and to this we may now turn our attention.

Muslim opinion in modern India has been compounded of a desire for self-government as passionate as that of the Hindu together with a feeling of separateness from Hinduism as definite as that of the orthodox Brahman from all others. There was in consequence a see-saw of attraction and repulsion for the undoubtedly nationalist but predominantly Hindu Congress. The Muslim desired to share in freedom, but his freedom must be as much from the Hindus as from the British. Thus the mooting of the Morley-Minto reforms produced a demand for communal electorates, 1914 war-time discontents, the Lucknow Pact, and sympathy for post-war Turkey co-operation in the non-co-operation movement of 1920. Experience of the Montford reforms, specially under Fazl-i Husain's leadership in the Panjab, convinced Muslims even more than Hindus that the British were beginning to surrender the substance of power. In proportion as the prospect of British departure brightened, suspicions of Hindu intentions deepened. This helped to account for the falling apart of the two communities after 1922, and underlay the Muslim advocacy of a weak centre in the proposed federation. Sir Muhammad Iqbal proposed a separate federation of Muslim provinces in 1930, and the dreamer Choudhri Rahmat Ali coined the word Pakistan in 1933, along with a scheme regarded as chimerical by most politicians. The Muslims were uneasy but disunited, and when they sought unity in a revived Muslim League, it was under the Bombay ex-Congressman, Muhammad Ali Jinnah.

Jinnah fought the 1937 elections on the basis of independent co-operation with the Congress in Hindu majority provinces by means of coalitions. 'There is really no substantial difference between League and the Congress. . . . We shall always be glad to co-operate with Congress in their constructive programme',[1] said the new leader in 1937. The Congress policy of absorption instead of co-operation, particularly in the United Provinces, was a bitter blow to this policy. At a stroke it destroyed hopes of friendly independent co-operation and in a moment revived the simmering Muslim suspicions of Hindu absorptive tendencies. Congress rule now meant for the middle class Muslim Hindu domination. The polished westernized Muslim politician found himself consigned to outer political darkness by his former colleagues; he turned to popular Muslim sentiment for support and found it unexpectedly easy to arouse. By so doing he converted a middle class Muslim nationalist movement into a popular Muslim resurgence, and so laid the political foundation of Pakistan. 'The majority community have clearly shown their hand that Hindustan is for the Hindu', he declared.[2] Reports were compiled of alleged Congress oppression

[1] R. A. Symonds, *The Making of Pakistan*, p. 53.   [2] Ibid., 55.

and when the Congress ministries resigned in October 1939, Jinnah declared 'a day of deliverance and thanksgiving, as a mark of relief that the Congress régime had at last ceased to function'. From this attitude it was but a step to the formal adoption of Pakistan as the goal of League endeavour in 1940. The Congress on their part under-estimated the significance of this development. Can a prophet come out of sophisticated Bombay, was their attitude. The League had not done too well in the elections; it did not control the Panjab or Bengal. These rumblings were minimized as the complaints of disgruntled politicans disappointed in their ambitions. But its miscalculation proved to be as great and as grievous as the British dismissal of Gandhi, twenty years before, as a harmless eccentric.

AUTHORITIES

THE 1935 Act is summarized by R. COUPLAND in vol. I of his *Report on the Constitutional Problem of India—The Indian Problem, 1833–1935* (1943) while vol. II—*Indian Politics, 1936–42* (1943) well summarizes the politics of those years. The Act itself is summarized and extensively quoted in M. GWYER's and A. APPADORAI's *Speeches and Documents on the Indian Constitution, 1921–47* (2 vols., Bombay, 1957), vol. I, p. xliii–xlv and 323–76. This work also provides valuable constitutional documents both before and after the Act.

For legal comment on the Act see P. EDDY and H. LAWTON, *India's New Constitution* (1935).

For politics after the Act, in addition to COUPLAND's work already mentioned, reference may be made to the works of TENDULKAR, SITARAMAYA and POLAK, etc., listed under Chapters 2 & 3 for Gandhi and the Congress generally. See also M. BRECHER's *Nehru: A Political Biography* (1959), N. D. PARIKH's *Vallabhbhai Patel* (Ahmedabad, 1953) and Lord ZETLAND's *Essayez* (1956).

An acute study of the British position in general will be found in G. WINT's *The British in Asia* (2nd ed., 1955).

CHAPTER 7

India and the War, 1939–45

THE outbreak of war in September 1939 found India even more unprepared in a material sense than Britain and with a much more divided mind. Almost the only material sign of preparation had been the visit of Lord Chatfield's mission. The public and officials alike had been absorbed in the unfolding drama of the constitutional experiment. Europe was still far off, and it did not seem, even if war broke out, that India would be very directly affected. Not that the public was unaware or uninterested in European development. Indian nationalists as good democrats were strongly anti-Fascist; they joined in the chorus for strong measures without any great expectation of being called to take part in them. Meanwhile the rise of the Muslim League, the struggle between right and left wings of Congress, and the fate of the provincial ministries were of much more absorbing interest. Amongst the Congress leaders, Jawarharlal Nehru was the only one to be fully aware of the import of international events for India and to seek to interest the public in these issues. In foreign affairs the attitude of mind which was fast disappearing in home politics still lingered, a feeling that it was the business of the paramount power. India could only interest herself when freedom had been won. The old feeling was widespread that Britain's embarrassment might be India's opportunity. No one dreamt that embarrassment might become mortal peril, not only to Britain herself, but to India as well.

When war broke out, therefore, there was a general approval of the cause coupled with a widespread reluctance to do very much about it. It was Britain's affair, not India's. The old slogan of 'no taxation without representation' was translated to read 'no popular war effort without responsible government'. The Congress ministries resigned on the manner of India's participation in the war.[1] Individuals and groups were willing to give help, but India as a whole sat back to watch the mighty drama unfold in the European arena from what was thought to be a secure and comfortable seat in the grandstand. This mood persisted until Dunkirk and the fall of France. A moment of alarm gave place to a feeling of admiration for British doggedness and spirit. When invasion failed it was realized that the war would be a long one and that India would have an important part to play. There was more willingness to assist, but still the divided mind persisted. How could India assist the cause of liberty abroad without first obtaining her freedom at home? The entry of Japan into the war intensified rather

[1] See below.

than modified this mood. There was more awareness of danger and more readiness to help, but also a deepening sense of frustration at India's inability to control her own destiny.

It will now be convenient to touch on the various aspects of war-time India in turn. To the Viceroy fell the task of not only managing a restive public opinion as best he could but of organizing the war of India as a member of the British empire and potentially of the British Commonwealth of Nations. A large programme of military expansion was put in hand. The Middle East was the obvious theatre for Indian troops, and thither forces were dispatched to assist Sir Archibald Wavell in his watching brief in Egypt. The fall of France, with its elimination of French strength in the Middle East and the entry of Italy into the war, transformed this theatre overnight into the most crucial military area outside Britain itself. Indian troops suddenly found themselves at the centre of events. Their courage and skill rose to the occasion. In the famous desert campaign of 1940–1 Indian troops bore a distinguished part. The Fourth and the Seventh Divisions added fresh laurels to Indian arms, and proved themselves masters of the rigours and intricacies of desert warfare. With modern equipment they were second to none in the world. Indian participation lasted through the commands of Wavell and Auchinleck to the final desert campaign of Montgomery. It also included the Iraq, Syrian, and Persian operations. In Iraq Indian intervention was decisive.

Before that time, however, the major Indian military effort had been diverted eastward. From the beginning of 1941 the Japanese menace to South-east Asia had been visibly growing. Along with British and Australians, Indian troops were used to garrison Malaya. When the Japanese stroke fell in December 1941 Indian troops shared in the long retreat to the south and in the disaster of Singapore. In its capitulation 90,000 Indian troops were involved. Indian formations played an honourable part in Alexander's fighting retreat from Burma, and henceforth were concerned with the defence of India itself. Their posts were now the hilly jungles and fever-haunted valleys of the Indo-Burman border down to the rain-drenched tracts of Arakan. In this situation they had two fresh problems of the first magnitude to solve. The first was the exchange of tropical jungle for desert conditions of warfare, and the second the tactics of the Japanese trained to this type of warfare and possessing the mobility which came of frugal habits and light transport. From 1943 the active Indian army passed under Mountbatten's South-East Asia Command (S.E.A.C.) and became a part of Sir William Slim's Fourteenth Army. Their moment of trial and their greatest triumph came with the Japanese invasion of Assam in the spring of 1944. The Seventh Division's stand at Kohima, cut off from all aid, save by air, broke the spearhead of the Japanese advance, and made inevitable the rout which followed. Thenceforward the story was one of increasing success, though always in the most arduous conditions, until the crowning triumph of the recapture of Rangoon. The Indian army had shown its mettle in the most difficult of all terrains of the war and the most testing of all types of warfare. A Japanese document listed the Gurkhas as the troops most to be feared of all the nationalities opposed to them. When the Japanese war ended in August 1945 Indian troops were poised for the assault on Malaya under the command of Mountbatten. Alongside the army, the Royal Indian Air Force and Navy, both negligible at the outbreak of war, played a distinguished and increasingly significant part.

One of Linlithgow's principal claims to fame was his organization of the Indian war effort. Here the mind of the administrator could range unhampered by personal vagaries and political perplexities. The first question was that of supply and the second that of military expansion. At first it was not thought that India would lie in close proximity to a large-scale campaign, but its vital relationship to the Middle East was early recognized. Before the war Lord Chatfield's committee had recommended a capital outlay of 7 *crores* of rupees (£5,400,000) for expanding Indian ordnance factories, and this, with additions, was at first thought to be sufficient. After the fall of France, however, India was conceived as a centre of a Commonwealth group for the supply of the Middle Eastern theatre. The visit of the supply mission of Sir Alexander Roger in the autumn of 1940 coincided with the holding of the Eastern Group Conference which was attended by representatives, in addition to those of India, from Australia, New Zealand, Ceylon, South Africa, Southern Rhodesia, Burma, Malaya, Hong Kong, Palestine, and East Africa. From the conference came the Eastern Group Supply Council, which rationalized the supply of materials from the various territories. India became the principal supplier of cotton textile, jute and jute products, leather products, and wooden furniture. In the first year of the council's work India supplied 60 per cent. of its total demands and later 75 per cent. When Japan and America entered the war the picture changed. Some sources of supply dried up and fresh needs appeared nearer home. Moreover in America there was a reservoir of productive power which could make good deficiencies throughout the Allied world. India developed new needs and at the same time became eligible for Lend-Lease. Early in 1943 the council was wound up, its function of allocating orders being taken over by the British Central Provision Office with a British Ministry of Supply Mission working in collaboration.

But the work of industrial development went on with even greater energy. The expansion of industry was not limited to India's traditional crafts like textiles, but included heavy industry and new industries altogether. Tata's already great steel plant was further extended and this was supplemented by the Bengal Steel Corporation's works at Burnpur and the Kumardhuti group. The cement industry was expanded on a large scale: the Indian deposits of bauxite were exploited to develop the new aluminium industry, and the mica industry, in which India held a monopoly outside Russia and Brazil, was largely increased.

Along with the organization of supply went the rapid growth of the armed forces. The peace-time strength of 175,000 was steadily increased until there was a total of more than 2 millions under arms. Mechanization and motorization went hand in hand with this process with the result that India not only gained an armed forced of unprecedented size, but a large number of technicians of varied skills. The navy, under a British vice-admiral, became an efficient and effective force which played its part both in the Burma campaign and against the Japanese submarine menace. The air force built up a reputation for smartness and efficiency which it carried over into the new era of independence. Though only a relatively small proportion of the military forces were actually engaged in military operations, the displacement of such large numbers from their customary life, and their equipment with new skills, was bound to open up new horizons and to stimulate the spirit of change.

The war in Indian experience had three well-defined stages. The first was the period of 'phoney' war, when life went on much as before. The war was a remote spectacle, a matter for talk and the newspapers. This phase ended for India with the fall of France in June 1940. The old international order seemed to have vanished overnight and the country was for a time bewildered and alarmed. Then followed the Battle of Britain, which was watched with growing admiration; the old order, it seemed, was to survive after all. The second phase was that of organization as a Middle Eastern base. Trade and industry boomed; headquarters swelled and men in khaki appeared;[1] cities grew congested and there was an air of bustle and purpose. But still it was not India's war so much as one to which India was contributing. The third phase opened with the Japanese aggression. From the spring of 1942 India began to suffer some of the perplexities and inconveniences of other belligerents and later met trials of her own. The war cloud spread over the whole country and became part of its daily experience. The herald of this transformation was perhaps the Japanese bombardment of Vizagapatam in April 1942.

The first effect was the appearance of the Americans in Delhi and in the East. To them were added large numbers of British troops concerned no longer with the Middle East but with the Japanese menace in Burma. The immediate consequence was the dislocation of the economic life of the country. Supply lines had to be re-orientated from lines from the interior to the ports to lateral lines from the ports to eastern India. To the strain which this placed upon the railways was added a reduction of shipping services. The Indian railways, already somewhat depleted by shipments to the Middle East, had to carry the whole weight of the war effort as well as the whole burden of the country's economic life. A period of unprecedented strain began which lasted until the end of the war. The mounting expenditure on the local

[1] Military officers at H.Q. were not required to wear uniform at their offices in the afternoons until the arrival of General Auchinleck in Jan. 1941.

war effort, together with large sums spent by both British and Americans in making airfields and in other preparations, set in motion a price-rise from which India had hitherto been largely exempt. Shortages began to appear, and culminated in the Bengal famine of 1943.

It had been thought that famines were things of the past in India. There was the Famine Code, which had worked successfully for sixty years. It was based on the distribution of grain to threatened areas with arrangements for the employment of agriculturists on productive work until the next harvest could restore the countryside. But this assumed the import of foodstuffs from abroad if necessary. The war had now cut off supplies from abroad except from neighbouring Burma. Food was short everywhere. The loss of Burma denied her rice supplies to Bengal and the south. At the same time the price rise tempted peasants to dispose of their reserve stocks at what seemed to them heaven-sent prices. But then rice disappeared from the markets and a decline in indebtedness proved a poor substitute for a lack of sustenance. The overall shortage has been estimated at 5 per cent., but this was aggravated by faults of distribution and control. Extensive black markets developed and famished peasants began to appear in Calcutta. An added difficulty was the absence of rice in the rest of India so that only unpalatable grains and pulses could be offered to starving rice-eating areas. During the summer of 1943 it became apparent that the Bengal administration was unable to cope with the situation. An undue tenderness for the principle of provincial autonomy delayed action by the Centre and it was only on the arrival of Lord Wavell in October 1943 that the nettle was firmly grasped. The British army was entrusted with relief distribution and a system of rationing instituted for all large towns. Never had the British army been so popular. Thenceforth, though shortages continued, no one starved, and a feeling of confidence returned. Food became a central concern.

It is now time to turn to the constitutional problem during the war period. In the summer of 1939 the hesitancy of the princes still delayed the establishment of the federal centre. The Congress watched and waited and Gandhi, more fully persuaded of his pacifism as the war clouds lowered, sent a personal letter to Hitler. On the outbreak of war Lord Linlithgow thus found himself without a responsible ministry to consult, and without a legal option to proclaiming that 'war has broken out between His Majesty and Germany'. He followed this up by addressing both houses of the legislature and by consultations with the national leaders, beginning with Mahatma Gandhi himself. Such action was legal and perhaps inevitable, but it was natural for it to appear provocative to the rapidly growing national consciousness of India, and so in fact it seemed to both League and Congress. The premiers of the non-Congress or League ministries of Bengal, the Panjab, and Sind were backed by their legislatures in pledging support to the war effort and the princes did the same individually. But the

Congress demanded an immediate definition of war aims and an immediate declaration of independence, 'present application to be given to this status to the largest possible extent'. The League made its support dependent on 'justice for Muslims' in Congress provinces and a guarantee of no constitutional advance without League approval. The Viceroy met this situation on 17 October by affirming dominion status to be the goal of constitutional development, action to be taken after the war with due regard to minority opinions. Meanwhile he proposed the formation of an advisory council representing all sections of opinion to associate the Indian public with the prosecution of the war. This was rejected by the Congress High Command as inadequate, and the provincial Congress ministries forthwith resigned. The League was less forthright and indeed commended the stress on minority rights, but demanded the abandonment of the whole federal scheme.

The deadlock thus created lasted throughout the war. It had two aspects. In relation to the British the Congress demanded full responsibility before sharing in the war effort. The British on their side were precluded by constitutional difficulties from agreeing to this and could only offer self-government *de facto* in anticipation of the end of the war. To the British, with the precedent of Canada in mind, this seemed an honest, and, in the circumstances, a common-sense procedure. To the Congress it savoured of Machiavellian delay and dark designs to frustrate legitimate aspirations. The second aspect was the relation of Congress to other parties. The Congress continued its 1937 policy of regarding itself as the sole legitimate representative of the Indian people. This was unacceptable, not only to the government, but also to the League. It encouraged the League to proceed to the formal acceptance of the Pakistan programme in the early months of 1940, and the League's attitude in its turn sustained the British in declining to make a unilateral settlement with the Congress. The three parties to the constitutional struggle thus stultified each other. The deadlock bred a steadily increasing sense of frustration as between British and Congress on the one hand, and a steadily deepening suspicion as between the League and Congress on the other.

The fall of France produced a temporary easing of tension. 'The tone of Congress hostility', in Professor Coupland's words, 'softened.' For a moment it seemed as though the fall of Britain might be the prelude to a Nazi occupation. 'We do not seek our independence', wrote the Mahatma on 1 June, 'out of British ruin.' The Congress High Command threw overboard Gandhi's pacifism. (He had praised Pétain's armistice and had called 'on every Briton to adopt . . . a nobler and a braver way' of surrender to Hitler.) There was talk of a national government and of parallel bodies to organize defence. The reply of the new British war cabinet was the 'August offer'. The offer contained one new point of substance along with the usual provisos of British obligations and minority rights. The post-war constitution was to be drawn up by an Indian constituent assembly whose decisions were virtually accepted beforehand. Thus Parliament virtually surrendered its right of legislating for India, a right which it had hitherto jealously guarded.

But by August the first panic fears of British collapse had passed. Though the issue in fact was still in the balance it was known that the British would fight to the last, and the evident British resolution inspired a new confidence in their ability. This had the effect, not of warming Congress hearts but of reviving suspicions of real British intentions. Britain, thought many, was still playing with India. There could be no settlement except on the basis of independence now and with Congress alone as representing India.[1] Consciousness of strength joined with revived suspicion to reject the offer. The appeals of the new Secretary of State (Mr. Amery) as well as the Viceroy fell on deaf ears; the deadlock was more complete than ever. The League for its part, newly converted to the Pakistan ideal, insisted that any national government should be on a Hindu-Muslim fifty-fifty basis and pointed the moral of partition. The communal deadlock was as complete as the Indo-British one.

The Congress was thus thrown back on Mr. Gandhi's pacifism and non-co-operation. Mr. Gandhi insisted on preaching pacifism in opposition to the war effort and organizing civil disobedience as a sanction for this right when disputed or denied by the government. The most reluctant and least successful of civil disobedience movements followed. Organized in easy stages from the autumn of 1940, it reached its peak in the following May, when some 14,000 Congressmen were in prison. This bore no comparison with the figure of 1930 and thereafter the numbers steadily fell. The movement had in fact no real popular backing, and was chiefly interesting as an index of what the Mahatma could achieve through personal influence alone. The Viceroy on his side carried out the long-promised expansion of his council to a total of fifteen, of whom eleven were Indians.

The entry of Japan and America into the war and the imminent threat of invasion which followed produced a new situation. The need to break the deadlock was now very urgent, and to the British desire to achieve a settlement was added an evident American interest in Indian freedom. All Congressmen, including Pandit Nehru, had been released on the eve of Pearl Harbour and the stage was set for a further effort. On 11 March 1942 the prime minister announced the dispatch of Sir Stafford Cripps, then Leader of the House of Commons and a member of the war cabinet, on a mission to India with a new and radical offer. The Cripps offer dominated Indian politics for the rest of the war. It first reiterated the intention of His Majesty's government to set up an Indian union which should take its place as a dominion of the Commonwealth as soon as possible after the war, and it then pro-

---

[1] Mr. Gandhi's words were 'between India as represented by Congress, and England', *News Chronicle*, 14 Aug. 1940, R. Coupland, *Constitutional Report on India*, vol. ii, p. 202.

posed specific steps towards that end. A constituent assembly would be elected by the provincial legislatures acting as an electoral college. This body would then negotiate a treaty with the British government. The future right of secession from the Commonwealth was explicitly stated. The Indian states would be free to join, and in any case their treaty arrangements would be revised to meet the new situation. The only proviso was the right of any province to contract out of the constitution and 'to retain its present constitutional position, provision being made for its subsequent accession if it so desires'. The offer ended with a call for co-operation by the popular parties in a national war-time administration.

The great advance which the Cripps offer marked was its frankness and precision. Gone were the hesitancies and the generalities of the 1939 and 1940 declarations. But there were new features as well. A Constituent Assembly had already been conceded, but it was now made clear that the framing of the new Constitution would be the work of Indians alone. The right of secession was acknowledged. The device of a bilateral treaty for implementing the new Constitution and discharging British obligations (reminiscent of the Irish settlement) was introduced. Finally the provision for provincial contracting out provided a means of reassuring Muslim fears within the orbit of democratic principles.

At one moment it seemed as though a settlement was in sight, but then the Congress leaders insisted that the new government must have immediately the full powers of a dominion cabinet. On this rock the discussions foundered; high hopes had been raised, and their disappointment left the sense of frustration deeper than before. The League watched pensive in the wings and observed the collapse not without signs of sardonic satisfaction.

It is perhaps too early to assess the exact cause of the breakdown. It is certain that Mahatma Gandhi took an unfavourable view and eventually overbore the more generous instincts of Nehru and Rajagopalachari. One consideration was the imminent Japanese threat; was it any use to draw a cheque on a failing bank? But even if invasion did not occur immediately, would not the situation again be critical when military movements again became possible after the monsoon? The British had gone so far under the stress of the Japanese threat that they might go further yet if they continued to survive and the threat persisted. Communal considerations led Hindu minds in the same direction. The offer represented almost but not quite a settlement with Congress on Congress terms. The provision for contracting out represented, for all its democratic colour, a concession to the League and as such was distasteful. Congress still underrated the League's hold over Muslims and was confident that it could smother its agitation if given full power at the Centre. A little waiting might give that full power. The stake of a united India under Hindu control was one worth playing for. So the golden moment passed and with it the last real chance of establishing a united independent India. The rejection of the offer was the prelude to partition.

This decision was not made without some internal stress, the chief sign of which was the ejection of Rajagopalachari from the Congress party. For the rest Congress was rallied behind the once more ascendant Gandhi. The enigmatic Mahatma refashioned his pacifist principles and non-violent technique to meet the new situation. The presence of the British in India, he declared, was a provocation to the Japanese. He coined the 'Quit India' slogan, and prepared a resolution demanding British abdication on pain of a revived civil disobedience campaign. 'There is no question of one more chance', he said. 'After all, this is open rebellion.' All the signs suggested that events would reach a crisis at the moment the Japanese might be able to move again at the beginning of October. When, therefore, the resolution was passed by the All-India Congress Committee on 7 August, the Viceroy, with the unanimous support of the Executive Council, acted swiftly. The whole working committee was interned at Poona. A serious but short outbreak of violence followed, which cost some 900 lives and caused damage estimated at a million pounds. Though responsibility was disclaimed by the leaders, it is difficult to believe that all of them were unaware of such large scale planning by extremists.

During this period India owed much to the rock-like firmness which the Viceroy combined with his patience. The failure of the rebellion did much to discredit the Congress and the improved military situation did still more. The Congress had not only acted wrongly, they had made a mistake. They had backed the wrong horse. The conviction spread that the British were immovable for the duration of the war, and was reinforced by the Viceroy's firmness in dealing with another Gandhian fast early in 1943. Mounting military success and the vigorous measures of Lord Wavell to deal with the food crisis still further strengthened the government's position. Cautious feelers were put out for breaking the deadlock with the British and abortive conversations held between League and Congress leaders; but the end of the war in Europe found the position apparently unchanged. It was, however, in appearance only. For in the interval the League had greatly strengthened its position. The strength of Muslim separatism was now plain for all to see. Even if the Congress should now accept the Cripps offer in the hope of avoiding partition the League would reject it in the hope of achieving it.

AUTHORITIES

The Official History of the Indian Armed Forces during the Second World War, 1939–45 has been compiled under the direction of Prof. BISHESHWAR PRASAD in several volumes (New York and Delhi, 1960–). A useful summary is by G. W. TYSON in *India Arms for Victory* (2nd ed., Allahabad, 1944).

On the political side the second volume of the *Coupland Report* gives the text of the revised Congress constitution of 1939 (App. I) and the Congress Declaration of Fundamental Rights (App. V). GWYER and APPADORAI's *Speeches and Documents* provides useful source material. But the major political documentation is the monumental work edited by NICHOLAS MANSERGH, assisted by E. W. R. LUMBY and P. MOON, *The Transfer of Power 1942-7* (1970-). It has already run to six volumes and there are likely to be three more. The relevant volumes for this period are: vol. I, *The Cripps Mission* (1970); vol. II, *Quit India* (the Congress-Government clash) (1971); vol. III, *Reassertion of Authority* (Sept. 1942-June 1943) (1971); vol. IV, *The Bengal Famine*, etc. (June 1943-Aug. 1944) (1973).

SITARAMAYA's *History of Congress*, and biographies of GANDHI, NEHRU, PATEL, AZAD and JINNAH continue to be important. See also C. A. COOKE, *Life of R. S. Cripps* (1957). Lord Linlithgow has been defended by his son, Lord GLENDEVON, in *Viceroy at Bay* (1971).

CHAPTER 8

Independence and Partition

WHEN the cease-fire sounded in Europe the position of the Indian government seemed stronger than at any time since 1942. It enjoyed the prestige of success and evident strength. The caravan was passing on steadily to victory. But the apparent calm of Indian politics was superficial and deceptive. It was the last manifestation in the British period of the Indian genius for accepting a situation too intractable to be altered, and of biding one's time for a more favourable moment. Beneath the surface the same tensions persisted, and indeed were growing more acute. The Congress was even more suspicious of the British in victory than they had been of them in defeat. Imperfectly aware, in spite of the precedent of 1919, of the exhaustion which cripples even the victorious in total war, Indian leaders could not believe that the British would 'stand and deliver' from the plenitude of power. Were not their expressions of benevolence merely a further example of British hypocrisy, and was not their constant harping on minority rights a subtle device to sabotage the idea of an independent India by encouraging Muslim truculence? In spite of the long succession of League victories in both central and provincial elections, the Congress leaders did not yet believe that there was substance behind the demand for Pakistan. Firmness, they thought, could still secure a united independent India on their own terms. Jinnah and the League leaders, on the other hand, were equally suspicious of Congress intentions. They were also conscious of greatly increased strength. They were not yet irrevocably committed to outright partition, in spite of their public declarations, any more than the Congress itself had been after its declaration of independence in 1928, but they believed that the pressing of their claims was the only way to secure the future of their community. Between Congress suspicion of the British, Muslim suspicion of the Congress, and Congress underestimation of League strength, the path of British statesmanship towards the goal of Indian self-government was bound to be hard and stony.

Lord Wavell had succeeded Lord Linlithgow as Viceroy in the autumn of 1943. Thus far his administration had been conspicuously successful. He had been conciliatory but quite firm towards Congress; he had dealt vigorously with the Bengal famine and had instituted a steadily improving control over the whole food administration; he had presided over a steadily expanding war effort in an atmosphere of rowing success; he had kept inflation within bounds; his presence and prestige exuded strength and confidence. He had now to face wholly different task. He had first to convince two highly critical bodies of the reality of British sincerity and then to persuade two mutually highly suspicious bodies that co-operation, with its attendant give and take, was both necessary and feasible. Failure meant partition with all its incalculable consequences. It is easy to see, at even this short distance of time, that the dice of fortune was heavily loaded against him. Nevertheless he bent himself manfully to the task.

Wavell's first move was to attempt the formation of a national administration as contemplated in the Cripps proposals (which had never been withdrawn). This would complete the war with Japan (then expected to last another year) and then arrange for the promised Constituent Assembly. Conversations were held in June 1945, but they broke down on the allotment of seats in the Executive Council and the Congress refusal to accept the League's claim to be the sole representatives of Muslim opinion. The sudden ending of the Japanese war in August made the situation more urgent. Wavell now put the controversy over the League's representative claim to the test of a general election, both provincial and central. This occupied the winter of 1945–6 while tension gradually mounted. It now became clear that the League dominated Muslim opinion almost as completely as the Congress dominated Hindu. In the key province of the Panjab, the Unionist party, long infiltrated by League sentiment, almost disappeared, and its rump under Sir Khizr Hayat Khan Tiwana could only continue in office with the help of the Congress. The carefully devised weightage system here placed a minority government in power in circumstances of rising passion. A short-lived naval mutiny in February 1946 revealed the narrow margin by which the British continued to maintain order of a kind.

The new British government now intervened directly. A cabinet mission led by Lord Pethwick-Lawrence, now a leading member of the new government, and consisting besides of Sir Stafford Cripps and Mr. A. V. (later Viscount) Alexander, visited India in April. After further efforts at mediation between the parties the mission made its own proposals in May. The aim was still to preserve a united India while giving reasonable satisfaction to Muslim claims to autonomy. The method proposed was an ingenious modification of the earlier Cripps offer. There was to be a federal union controlling defence, foreign affairs, and communications, and consisting of the British Indian provinces. The states were to be included after negotiation. There were two new features. The powers of the federal government were reduced (in accordance with Muslim desires) and individual provinces were to be at liberty to form subordinate unions of their own. Each of these was to decide for itself the powers it would exercise outside the range of the federal subjects. On this basis a constituent assembly would be convened representing all parties, and once more it was proposed to form an interim national government. This was Pakistan *in parvo* and seemed to open an avenue for the reconciliation of a united India with Muslim autonomy.

For a moment there was a gleam of hope, for both sides accepted the plan as a basis for action. But breakdown once more occurred over the communal allotment of seats. The Congress insisted on appointing a Muslim to one of their five seats and thus reducing League representation to four; the League insisted on parity and refused to work with nationalist Muslims whom they regarded as traitors to their cause. When the Congress refused to proceed the League offered to take office alone and resented the Viceroy's refusal to proceed with one party only. When, a few weeks later, the Congress repented and the Viceroy admitted their leaders to office with Nehru as Vice-President of the Council, the League denounced the action as a breach of faith and proclaimed a 'direct action day' on 16 August. The tension could no longer be restrained within peaceful bounds, and to the bloody August riots in Calcutta (where Hindus were the sufferers) was added the communal outbreak in Bihar (where Muslims were the victims). There were also outbreaks in East Bengal and the United Provinces. The hope of a united independent India was extinguished in the blood and monsoon passion of 1946. Partition was now the only possible solution, though it took another nine months to convince all parties of the fact.

These months were passed in strain and mounting misery. In October 1946 the League joined the Executive Council. But it was soon seen that they had come to curse and not to bless. Pandit Nehru found himself in real danger when he visited the north-west in the same month; it became obvious that the Frontier would not stand for Hindu rule, Red Shirts, and the Frontier Gandhi notwithstanding. The Constituent Assembly met in December only to be boycotted by the League. Early in the new year there followed the fall of the Khizr ministry in the Panjab to the accompaniment of fighting which destroyed Amritsar and Multan. Section 93 rule and suppressed civil war succeeded the feeble directives of a minority ministry. Something had to be done and done quickly.

Once more the British cabinet directly intervened. Pandit Nehru, Mr. Jinnah (now the *Qaid-i-Azam* or great leader), and Sardar Baldev Singh (a Sikh leader) were called to London for discussions, but these were as fruitless as before. In a last effort to dissipate suspicion it was announced on 20 February 1947 that June 1948 had been determined as the date of the withdrawal of British power. At the same time Lord Wavell was recalled in favour of Lord Mountbatten, who was charged with the preparation of a procedural plan. But neither the persuasions of London, nor the shock of an imminent political vacuum, nor the stimulus of a new personality could now break the Congress-League deadlock. Mr. Jinnah saw victory in sight. 'The Muslim League will not yield an inch in its demand for Pakistan', he said. He had so cast Congress tactics back upon itself that it was that body itself which now began to see in partition the only alternative to prolonged civil war and fearful destruction of human life. In May they themselves proposed the partition of the Panjab as the only alternative to civil war.

Lord Mountbatten soon convinced himself that Pakistan was now the only alternative to anarchy. A visit home secured the consent of the cabinet for this plan. On 3 June he announced the British govern-

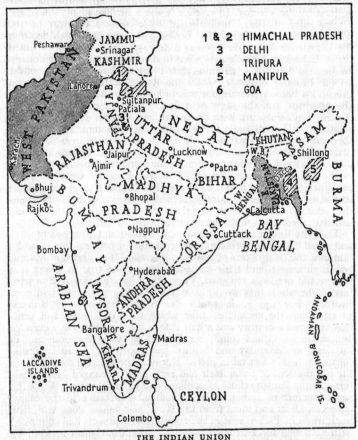

1 & 2	HIMACHAL PRADESH
3	DELHI
4	TRIPURA
5	MANIPUR
6	GOA

THE INDIAN UNION

ment's acceptance of the principles of partition, a procedural plan for carrying it through, and an acceleration of the date of British withdrawal to 14 August. The plan was accepted on the same day by Congress, League, and Sikhs. Each party professed dissatisfaction but each believed that they would gain nothing further by fighting. The Sikhs were the least satisfied, and a powerful section determined to fight in any case, but they were the weakest party of the three and suffered from divisions and poor leadership. The least common denominator of Indian power politics had at last been discovered.

The plan worked smoothly and was carried through with remarkable address by the Viceroy. In essence it was a further adaptation of the Cripps offer of 1942, implemented by a master of rush tactics. The partition of the Panjab and Bengal was recognized, provided that the Legislative Assemblies, voting if necessary by communities, asked for it. Boundary commissions were to determine the actual frontiers. In Sind the decision for partition rested with the Legislative Assembly. In the Frontier Province, where the Red Shirt ministry retained a precarious hold, a referendum was to be held to decide the future of the province, and the same held good for the district of Sylhet in Assam. Thus Pakistan, with its eastern and western wings, came into existence, and with India formed two new dominions in the British Commonwealth of Nations. Each had its own Constituent Assembly and arrangements were made for the proportional sharing of assets and liabilities. Lord Mountbatten became the first Governor-General of the Indian dominion and Mr. Jinnah of Pakistan. Only the states remained to be fitted into the picture. The British treaties were ended and with it British paramountcy; each state became in theory independent, but with a strong hint from the departing British that they should associate themselves with one or other of the dominions.

Thus the British period in India came to an end after nearly three and a half centuries of trading, two centuries of political power, and a hundred and thirty years of general supremacy. The dream of Macaulay, Elphinstone, and their contemporaries came true in a way that they would not have expected. They might have disapproved in part, but on the whole they would have felt that their prescience had been justified. For the India which the British left in 1947 differed greatly from the archaic country which their diplomacy and arms had mastered a century and a half before. If there was not a class 'of Indians in blood and colour but English in taste, in morals and in intellect', as Macaulay and Munro had hoped for, a radical transformation had in fact taken place. Not only the external conditions of life but the soul of India itself had been greatly changed. The pessimism of the Panjab school of civilians had been disproved. While the superstructure of Indian society remained impressive to the casual observer, ideals and ideas from the West, new values along with new institutions had taken root in the country. The process had continued with gathering force beneath nostalgic cultural archaism fostered by growing national sentiment. The very weapons and arguments used by Congress against the British were largely of western provenance. India broke her British fetters with western hammers. And it was significant of the community of ideas between the two sides that the fetters were never in fact broken by force, but began to be removed by one side as soon as they began to be rattled by the other.

AUTHORITIES

For this chapter the sources are numerous. On the documentary side there is again GWYER and APPADORAI's *Speeches and Documents* and the relevant volumes of *The Transfer of Power, 1942-7.* Those so far published are: vol. V, *The Simla Conference: Background and Proceedings,* Sept. 1944-Jul. 1945 (1975), and vol. VI, *The Post-War Phase: new Moves by the Labour Government,* Aug. 1945-Mar. 1946 (1976). For the Congress side there is SITARAMAYA and for Gandhi TENDULKAR. There are also the relevant volumes of the great series, *The Collected Works of Mahatma Gandhi.* M. BRECHER's *Nehru* (1959) gives much of the inner working of Congress at the time, and the works by or on Gandhi, Patel, and Maulana Azad remain valuable for their varied standpoints. Absorbing and moving is Lord WAVELL's diary, edited by P. MOON: *Wavell, the Viceroy's Journal* (Oxford, 1973).

Two very useful summaries are E. W. R. LUMBY's *Transfer of Power in India* (1954) and B. R. NANDA's *The Nehrus* (2nd imp., 1965). Two accounts which help to recapture the drama and tragedy of the time are F. TUKER's *While Memory Serves* (1950) and A. CAMPBELL-JOHNSON's *Mission with Mountbatten* (1951). Another valuable study is B. N. PANDEY's *The Break-up of British India* (1969).

For the final phase there is V. P. MENON's *Transfer of Power in India* (Princeton, 1957), giving the inside story with great knowledge, authority and understanding, and H. V. HODSON's absorbing *The Great Divide* (1969), based primarily on the Mountbatten Papers but written without any kind of obligation. *The Partition of India: Policies and Perspectives* (1970), edited by C. H. PHILIPS and M. D. WAINWRIGHT, throws much light on the subject from many individual points of view.

For the Pakistan movement see works listed under Chapter 5, *The Genesis of Pakistan.*

CHAPTER 9

Economic and Cultural Development

THE last quarter of a century of the British period was a time of rapid development in all departments of Indian life. Everywhere people were looking to the new India that was to be. But the new India which forward-looking patriots envisaged differed widely from the India to which their predecessors fifty years before had looked back. Less and less did people seek to revise the glories of the past, more and more did they strive to rival the triumphs of the contemporary West. Old India was not to be abandoned it is true; but increasingly it was coming to be regarded as a gracious background to the hard competitive world in which the new generation was determined to play an equal and worthy part. It was to provide a sunset glow, as it were, in whose light the hard outlines of the western factory would be softened. It would supply an emotional warmth for the people committed increasingly to new ways of life and thought. The new India was not to be built up, as late nineteenth-century patriots had thought, by copious draughts from the past, but rather by frequent injections from the energetic, contemporary West.

These two tendencies had been present in India from the days of Ram Mohan Roy, and often coexisted within the same individuals. In the latter years of the British period the two streams continued to run side by side, and not always to be obviously in conflict, but the western current was palpably gaining. The extent of its progress was to some extent concealed by nationalist sentiment, which naturally wished to glorify the national heritage, and felt too open a homage to western ideas to be damaging to its sense of self-respect. Nevertheless, the tendency was there, waiting for its strength to be revealed when the withdrawal of the foreign ruling power would no longer make open modernism seem unpatriotic. The influence of the two tendencies can be traced across the various facets of the national life.

From the close of the first World War there was rapid economic development. The suspension of the cotton excise in 1924 and its abolition in 1925 was the symbolic closing of the age of economic dependence. The new principle of fiscal autonomy, as interpreted by the Tariff Board, proved to be no cynical playing with words, but a living reality. The Tariff Board set itself to safeguard existing industries and to foster new ones. Thus the new steel industry received protection which enabled it to weather the depression of the early thirties, and the cotton industry was saved from the competition of cheap Japanese textiles. The sugar industry received help which enabled India, before the second World War, to become independent of foreign sources of supply, and the cement industry began its career. The war intensified this already considerable economic activity. The Indian jute, steel, cotton, and leather industries expanded rapidly. Cement manufacture became a major industry. The Indian deposits of bauxite were exploited to develop a new aluminium industry and engineering developed from a jobbing basis to an industrial level. Numbers of technicians were trained as part of the war-time military and industrial expansion. In all directions India was seeking to make goods which she had formerly received from abroad. India became the sixth in order of world industrial states, and possessed in Tata's the largest single steel plant in the world.

All this was pure westernism, and it was natural that in this sphere such influence should be strong. But the old India was not yet extinct even industrially. It had its champion in Mahatma Gandhi himself, with his advocacy of *khaddar* or handwoven and homespun cloth. He directed the All-India Khaddar Association and resolutely opposed machines as the engines of Satan. His policy was based on considerations of the moral welfare of the peasants rather than on economic grounds, and on this basis there was much to be said for it. But even his authority could not induce the mass of Congressmen to take seriously the Congress rule of membership of spinning 9 yards of yarn a day. His fight was patently a losing one and even he had to make concessions to the evil thing. He submitted to the surgical operations of western medicine, he travelled on western railways, he consorted with great Indian industrialists like Birla, and did not hesitate to take somewhat of their profits for the benefit of the party funds. The home-spun programme was a patriotic and moral but pre-industrial gesture; with independence it receded to the background of national life like village handicrafts in Britain. Industrialism had clearly come to stay.

In social life the same dualism can be observed. But here the Mahatma was a revolutionary instead of a conservative force. He headed the movement for the uplift of the depressed or exterior castes with even more zeal than that for *khaddar* cloth. He not only insisted on their inclusion within the Hindu fold and risked his fast to death in 1932 for its sake, but affirmed their equal status as human beings with all other Hindus. His campaigns for the abolition of untouchability, for free temple entry and admission to wells, were founded upon this belief. He coined the word *Harijan* (son of God) to describe them in emphasis of this conviction and renamed the paper in which he expounded his views in their honour. Gandhi was not alone in this work. Christian missions and devoted Hindus like Gokhale's Servants of India had preceded him, but his advocacy with his genius for popular appeal raised the whole question to a national level. In Dr. Ambedkar the Harijans found a leader of outstanding courage and ability from among their own number. The way was prepared for the formal abolition of untouchability in the new Constitution. There were other influences working in the same direction. The Sarda Act of 1929 raising the marriage age was a signpost of reformist sentiment, though it was only spasmodically enforced. The rights of women were championed with a new vigour. Female education was pressed forward and the Hindu code on the subject of women's rights itself altered. Educated women were still but a very small minority but they had already produced such striking figures as Mrs. Sarojini Naidu, the poetess of Congress politicians, and Begam Liaquat Ali Khan. Within the Hindu home there was mitigation of the austere lot of the Hindu widow, and behind the *purdah* Muslim women began to stir. The movement received a strong impulse from the civil disobedience movement of 1930-1 when women played a prominent part in political activity. Caste associations were cautiously relaxing the stricter caste rules and simplifying ceremonies, and a general sentiment was growing in favour of freer social intercourse between all sections of society.

Hardly any of these tendencies were based on a study of the *Shastras*. Rather, they were derived from ideas of individualism and personal worth, of moral rights and duties coming from the West. One could not for generations claim democratic political rights with its corollary of personal equality without eventually becoming aware of its social implications. The ideological skin of traditional Hinduism (or Brahmanism) which had covered Hindu society so long, was wearing thin amongst the westernized and forward-looking section of the people. Over village life it still stretched firm and largely intact. But while rural India forms the weight of Indian society, it is weight in the form of ballast. In the long run, and provided the run is long enough, it will follow the leaders in the towns. All this did not go unchallenged. The Mahasabha sought to organize the orthodox elements politically and the *Sanatan Dharma* stood staunchly for traditional views. But the orthodox found no successor to Pandit Madan Mohan Malaviya of equal distinction. To the majority of Hindus Hinduism meant Gandhi, and Gandhi was anathema to the really orthodox. The pressure of the West was felt even in avowedly Hindu bodies. Thus the reformist Arya Samaj, whose slogan was 'back to the Vedas' and whose effort was to revive the primitive Hindu institutions and along with them the Vedic way of life, found itself compelled to maintain modern educational institutions conforming to government regulations alongside its *ashrams* and *gurukuls*.

In education there was rapid development. This was most noticeable at the top, but there were increasing efforts to spread popular primary instruction. The first province to make notable progress at the elementary level was the Panjab under the impetus of Sir Fazl-i-Husain. The movement culminated in the government Sargent plan which was paralleled by the Congress Wardha scheme. It is interesting to note that the differences between them were of method rather than objective. The purpose of both was the democratic concept of education for all, not the Brahman principle of education for some. In the sphere of

PLATE 40

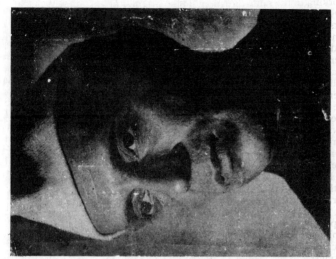

b. Jawarharla ...

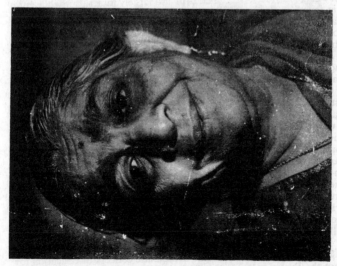

a. Sarojini Naidu

higher education the Sadler Commission bore fruit in the establishment of a number of unitary teaching universities, of which Lucknow
in the north, Patna in the east, and Annamalai in the south were typical
examples. The latter exemplified the fact that modern higher education
was now sufficiently firmly rooted in the public mind to become the
object of munificent private benefaction. Delhi, in the hands of Sir
Maurice Gwyer, provided a further type of a teaching university composed of federated colleges. Along with new universities went the rapid
growth of technical institutions and the development of scientific study
at the highest level. The work of Sir Jagadish Bose in Calcutta, and of
Dr. C. V. Raman in the Bangalore Institute, were highlights of a body of
scientific endeavour which placed India in the main stream of world
scientific study. In many spheres names began to appear beside that
of Tagore in the world arena of knowledge and thought, such as Sir
Muhammad Iqbal the Panjabi poet and thinker, Sir Jadunath Sarkar
the historian, and Sir Sarvapalli Radhakrishnan the philosopher.

The intellectual climate of the twenties was one of liberal humanitarian rationalism. Tilak's attempt to combine Brahmanical orthodoxy
with revolutionary nationalism died with him; it was the rationalist
humanitarianism of his Brahman rival Gokhale which held the field.
The most characteristic representatives of this current of thought were
perhaps Mr. C. R. Rajagopalachari and the silver-tongued Srinivasa
Sastri in the south, and Pandit Motilal Nehru in the north. Mr. Jinnah,
in his days of westernized elegance before 1935, represented the same
trend amongst Muslims. Pandit Motilal's son Jawarharlal followed the
western mode of using liberalism as a stepping-stone to socialism. For
a time in the thirties he dallied with Marxism. Few went so far as this
before the late thirties. But then a small group, appalled by the con-
trasts between poverty and wealth to be seen everywhere, repelled by
the Congress patronage of bankers and industrialists, and frustrated
of any hope of improvement through normal channels, went beyond
Nehru and avowedly espoused the Marxist cause. Many of them were
'England returned' and derived their inspiration from the contemporary Communist trend among British intellectuals.

These currents were western inspired, but they did not altogether
go unchallenged. With singular grace and subtlety Shri Arabindo
Ghose from his retreat in Pondicherry sought to reinterpret Vedantic
thought in modern terms. Sir Muhammad Iqbal equally sought to find
in Islam a dynamic for Muslims in the modern world. These were
perhaps the two greatest thinkers of the time. Mahatma Gandhi himself tirelessly preached *ahimsa* and insisted that his proposed moral
revolution was essentially Hindu. But even Gandhi's *ahimsa* owed
much to Tolstoy, himself a link in the long chain of Christian pacifism,
while Iqbal's dynamism was not unrelated to western revolutionary
influences. Try as these Indian thinkers would, the West kept breaking in. Time may elevate Ghose to a pedestal as the founder of
neo-Hinduism, but may also reveal him, like Porphyry among the

neo-Platonists, as the last great champion of a dying school. Be this as it may, it is certain that the western stream was stronger than the eastern during this period, and appeared to be gathering force.

The Indian revival of the visual and aural arts had lagged behind developments in other fields. But now there were increasing signs of vitality. The inspiration was largely traditional, but even here the influence of the West was felt. Art was secular and naturalist in outlook even though its subjects were often religious in form, the artists a professional *élite* rather than hereditary craftsmen. Sculpture was again practised in a secular *milieu*. Music was cultivated and found a western interpreter in Fox-Strangeways. But musical development, specially in Bengal, looked westward and attempted combination of eastern and western modes. The most striking development was in painting. The efforts of Havell, Rothenstein, and Coomaraswamy led to a new appreciation of the treasures of Indian art and sculpture, and bore fruit in the modern school of Indian painting. Much pleasing work of merit was produced, and by Abanindranath Tagore, the doyen of the school, work of great distinction. Here, too, however, the modifying influences were western. While the Bengal school looked back to Ajanta for inspiration and the Lahore school turned toward the Mughuls, Bombay sought to practise a western realism. On the whole the early promise was scarcely fulfilled; Indian artists await a fresh creative vision which perhaps independence will give.

Literary activity beginning in Bengal had long been great and had received world recognition in the award of the Nobel Prize to Tagore in 1912. Other Indian languages took up the tale and between the wars there was an increasing number of essayists and novelists practising in English as well. The writing of such men as Dhan Gopal Mukerji, Mulk Raj Anand, R. K. Narayan, and Ahmed Ali was supple and vital. They were much exercised by social problems and their work tended to realism; their writings formed a new vehicle for the discussion of ideas formerly provided mainly by the periodical press. Their work promises greater things in the future, but meanwhile it can be said that they have taken over from British writers like E. M. Forster and Edward Thompson the task of interpreting modern India to itself and the world. The cultural keynotes of this period were autonomy and western influence. Gone were the days of imitation or uncritical admiration. In every branch of activity India was standing on her own feet and making her own decisions. She was increasingly ready to face the West on its own terms, to learn, to absorb, and to teach in her turn. In the realms of the spirit as well as in that of politics India was preparing to shape her own future. And whatever form that future might take, it would certainly contain a large element of the West. It is at least arguable that in dying politically the West in India bade fair to triumph spiritually.

ECONOMIC AND CULTURAL DEVELOPMENT

AUTHORITIES

Fᴏʀ economic development, see the authorities listed at the end of Book III, chapter 4, *Economic Policy and Development, 1858–1939*, p. 271–2.

For the cultural background see W. T. de Bᴀʀʏ *et al.*, *Sources of Indian Tradition* (New York, 1958). For some insight into modern developments the works of Rᴀʙɪɴᴅʀᴀɴᴀᴛʜ Tᴀɢᴏʀᴇ, R. K. Nᴀʀᴀʏᴀɴ (specially *The Guide*, New York, 1958), N. C. Cʜᴀᴜᴅʜᴜʀɪ (specially *The Autobiography of an Unknown Indian*, 1951), Hᴜᴍᴀʏᴜɴ Kᴀʙɪʀ and Mᴜʟᴋ Rᴀᴊ Aɴᴀɴᴅ may be consulted. The films of Sᴀᴛʏᴀᴊɪᴛ Rᴀʏ are invaluable for their cultural sensitivity as well as their skill.

BOOK V

Independent India, 1947–75

INTRODUCTION

THIS essay is an attempt to bring *The Oxford History of Modern India* up to date within a reasonable compass. Nearly thirty years, the usual reckoning of a generation, have passed since its closing date of 1947. If something is not done now, the book will do less than justice to modern India. An exercise in the now popular art of contemporary history seems called for.

Yet there are difficulties. What exactly is meant by the term 'contemporary history'? One answer would be to describe it as what comes within the memory and experience of people from about the age of fifty and under; another that which is beyond the scope of full documentation through the opening of archives, writing of memoirs, etc. Such history can never be regarded as more than a first draft of the full story. There are qualifications and ragged edges to both these concepts. The first, while enlivening with its personal memories, is limited by the memories which are missing and the balance which comes from an overall view. The second, while lacking finality and the proportion which comes from historical perspective, is yet necessary if the attempt to understand the current situation and present trends is not to be abandoned, turning history into an assortment of might-have-beens. We must try to understand the immediate past by whatever means are available, recognizing that the assessment or view is necessarily a tentative or provisional one, subject to change in the light of fuller knowledge and wider perspectives. Time waits for no man and therefore he who runs must also read. A striking example of the heights to which contemporary historical writing can rise and also of the limitations of the whole concept, is the series of annual surveys of international affairs produced by the late Arnold Toynbee in the years between the First and Second World Wars. Expertise, mastery of the known facts, clear presentation and perceptive insight could hardly go further. Yet these volumes do not form a complete history of the period. Much was unknown to the writer at the time of composition; perspectives were to change as the time-span lengthened, like the changing views from a mountain as the climber ascends its slopes; creative but obscure developments could not be perceived. The survey of the years 1947–75 which follows is therefore to be regarded in this light; it is factual in its presentation and provisional in its judgements.

This does not mean, however, that one is precluded from making distinctions, analyses and assessments; it means that all such things are provisional and liable to revision. One's first impression of a film or a play on leaving the theatre may vary considerably from one's final considered opinion; and so it is with the handling of contemporary events. Let us therefore examine the available material as factually and critically as possible, conscious that further knowledge and wider perspectives may later modify our conclusions.

Enough time has now elapsed for some broad distinctions to be made, even though final judgement belongs to posterity. Apart from the rise and fall of individuals, the emergence of problems and their attempted solutions, the growth of crises with their stress and drama, a certain rhythm in Indian affairs since 1947 can be detected. Before 1947 there was a rhythm of Congress and national feeling, rising to a periodical climax and then resolving for a time into a temporary accommodation. The tide flowed and ebbed, each time rising a little higher. Since independence the rhythms have been different but no less clear. Twice in succession one can detect an initial period of crisis followed by a period of planning, creative activity and hope until this in turn gave way to perplexity in the face of fresh problems. In the first case the period of crisis lasted until about 1950, ending with the challenge and eclipse of the late Purshottamdas Tandon (1951). The next period may be said to open with Nehru's creation of the Planning Commission in the same year and was characterized by hope for the future and systematic planning to bring that future into being. The second shaded off imperceptibly into the third phase of perplexity. Things had not gone quite as had been hoped; what was to be done next? A convenient occasion with which to mark this change was the Hungarian and Suez crises of 1956, provided that these are regarded as convenient indicators rather than as boundary marks between one era and the next. Perplexity and a feeling of frustration ran into crises again with the China war of 1962, the death of Jawaharlal Nehru in 1964, the Pakistan war of 1965 and the subsequent death of Lal Bahadur Shastri. Thereafter, with the elections of 1967 there was a return of planning and hope, which at home lead to a peak with the revolt of East Pakistan and its secession from Pakistan after Indian intervention as the new state of Bangladesh.

These are mainly internal rhythms but in the foreign sphere something of the same kind also occurred. After the crisis of independence there was the hopeful involvement of India with western Europe and the Third World. This faded into perplexity when the advent of the hydrogen bomb made the prospect of total war too lethal to be contemplated so that pacts to prevent it or survive it became irrelevant. It deepened into crisis with the China incident until India emerged triumphant from the last round of Pakistani conflict in 1971.

Beneath these rhythms, which after all were surface ones and otherwise would not be detectable by the day-to-day contemporary historian, lay deeper currents, stirring the whole body-social. Their exact nature we can still only conjecture as also their precise effects; but we can have some idea of their potential for the future. Like a train passing through the countryside in the night, one knows that it is a train, but not its speed, the number of its coaches or its complement of passengers. But though one does not know for certain, from its direction and the size of the train one can guess at its destination. One of these currents is the physical and environmental factor of population growth. For some years this has out-stripped increases in production so that the individual *per capita* income has been falling instead of rising, despite the steady increase of the Gross National Product. In 1941 the Census gave a population for all India of 387 millions, of which the Muslims were Mr. Jinnah's 'hundred millions' or a quarter of the whole. But in the mid-sixties, after Pakistan had been lopped off, the Indian total was approaching 500 millions, and now it is said to be around 600 millions. In other words, the population has roughly doubled in about thirty years. What will happen if it doubles again in the next thirty years? Here is a problem of the gravest import.

Then there is the question of language. The Congress adopted Hindi as its language, but this was never wholeheartedly accepted, specially in the south. The Bengalis, through the medium of Rabindranath Tagore and others, made Bengali into a world-recognized language by the time of the first World War. Tamil claims an ancestry only next to Sanskrit in age and distinction; and Tamil is a living language while Sanskrit is not. And Sikhs and Panjabis will speak Panjabi and write in Gurmukhi what-ever the Centre may think or do. These languages and scripts no-one will give up, and they increasingly tend to express the ideas and still more the feelings of oneness among the peoples of particular areas. Here we have in incipient form a collection of nationalisms to be set, and one hopes, harmonized within the setting of an all-India internationalism.

There are, simmering and from time to time emerging, movements of renewal from within the Indian social and cultural body. One of these has been the development of the 'vernaculars' into literary and scientific instruments of everyday use, and the demand for education in the local language media. Bengali was in the van of this movement. Bengal also leads with its school of painting based on ancient Indian models and fathered by Abanindranath Tagore. It is not often that two separate artistic movements are inspired by two members of the same family. In the realm of the mind there were the philosophical studies of Drs Radha-krishnan and Das Gupta, while in the sphere of original thought Sri Aurobindo with the neo-Vedantism of his *Life Divine* was a shining star. In the moral and spiritual realm there were the early movements of the Arya Samaj (founded in 1875) and Swami Vivekananda's Ramakrishna Mission and many local initiatives like that of the Guru of Dyal Bagh, Sri Maharshi of Ernakulam and Sai Baba. More recently there has been a revival of Bengali Vaishnavism in the Hare Krishna movement.

In the overlapping moral and religious areas all was dwarfed for a time by the giant figure of Mahatma Gandhi. The doctrines of *ahimsa* and *satya*, the practice of *satyagraha* and *bhoodan*, swept through the country in the inter-war years and their proponent was freely accorded divine status. Gandhi died, with 'Ram Ram' on his lips, a disappointed man, but if his political and social ideas have never been successfully translated into practical measures, his doctrinal torch was carried by Acharya Vinoba Bhave. This torch may now seem to be burning low, but who can say what may not ignite from its sparks in the future? In all these ways India has been stirring internally, but with what import or potential for the future it is very difficult to assess at this moment in time. In politics there has been the Jana Sangh and the Swatantra party attempting to relate the practice of power and the organization of society to traditional Hindu social values.

But India does not live for herself alone. The modern 'western world' in its forms of liberal capitalism and communism, presses her increasingly and infiltrates her society ever more subtly. This process does not require the actual physical presence of foreigners, although they may be useful as 'carriers'. It depends on ideas and fashions; ideas jump race barriers without hesitation, while fashions can be conveyed by picture, print and the spoken word, as well as by corporeal presence. This confrontation did not end with independence; it in fact intensified. At one time the West thought in terms of a 'takeover' of Indian society; while segments of Indian opinion thought in terms of a rejection of the West. Neither of these attitudes prevailed: instead, there has been a long process of give and take of which the end cannot be foreseen. All we know for certain is that the process continues while we wistfully hope that 'the best is yet to be'. On the Western side there was the political takeover, followed by the cultural aggression of the Anglicists, the Utilitarians and the missionaries.

The first important attempt to absorb and integrate western ideas and innovations was that of Raja Ram Mohan Roy—and very successful it was within its limits. Another was the Servants of India Society of G. K. Gokhale and his friends, an Indian adaptation of missionary and specially Jesuit ideals and practice. But for the most part the process has continued from that day to this without either total rejection or surrender, or any major attempt at synthesis. There have been a series of adaptations to changing circumstances, which carry with them implicit confrontations. Only a few like the Mahatma have had the courage to advocate almost total rejection of the West, and only a few like the Young Bengal movement of the eighteen-thirties, some Christian Calcutta and Bombay circles at the end of the same century, to urge its total acceptance. Western technology, with its sharpening of the tools of production and consequent greater volume of goods and lower prices, ushered in, for the middle and upper classes, a consumer society where wants are multiplied to sustain production and the good life is seen more and more in terms of personal pleasure and social amenity. Here is a direct clash with the ancient ideal of reducing your wants to the level of the satisfactions available—the ideal of 'piety and endurance and devotion' as Romesh Chandra Dutt expressed it. This is the 'materialism of the West' which sincere puritans, along with those left outside the new pleasure halls, deplore. Technology itself, which has historically flooded in from the West but, in so far as it depends upon knowledge of universal laws, is above the limitations of geography or race, while related to the previous consideration, is a problem in itself. Everyone, even a Gandhi, recognizes the value of a technology in medicine which saves lives that could not be saved before. And everyone, even western politicians, recognize the infernal nature and the lethal threat of atom bomb manufacture. But where is the limit, where is the 'thus far and no further' line of development to be set? As conceived by Gandhiji, or the late Arnold Toynbee or the American Pentagon?

Then there is the clash of ideas and values. The Englishman's cherished pragmatism was set its bounds once and for all by the dictum 'man shall not live by bread alone'. But no more can he live by ideas alone. The West has presented to India ideas of individualism and equality which in fact conflict with the Indian hierarchic structure of society and reverence for authority looking to a divine source. The West's other half, as Toynbee might say, accepts an authority but turns it upside down by making it man-inspired and controlled. It believes in man's welfare but turns it inside out as material well-being for existence bound by physical life instead of a way of escape by self-discipline or *yoga* to the *moksha* or liberation in the hereafter. Perhaps the only recent distinguished person who fully accepted western individualism and rationalism was Jawaharlal Nehru himself; for most there has been a jumble of contrasting ideas in the mind whose contradictory nature was not realized or only partially realized by fits and starts. Only for the sensitive few has there been what might be called a war in the soul. But it is not only the idea of individualism which is in question. There are those of moral duty for the individual and in his relation toward society, of the relationship of groups with one another, of the authority of the State and its relationship to all. It is no use saying that traditional ideas are 'old-fashioned'—and will soon be forgotten. However divided or ignored they may be by the fashionable, they represent deep-rooted forces which influence even those who scorn them. Russia today is still influenced by patterns woven by the long-forgotten Byzantine empire (through the Orthodox Greek church and transmitted through the principality of Kiev). Many Indian traditional patterns are older than these and not less potent. Here then are a series of opposites which must either overcome one another or be reconciled in a larger synthesis.

Apart from the realms of the mind and the conscience, of traditional patterns, temperamental distinctions and race memories, there are the stimuli and pressures of the living examples of alternative cultures. Man is influenced even more by example than by precept. Before 1947 the weight of example was heavily biased towards the West. Many, indeed, held that this was the only source for change and innovation, if any change there was to be. Since then Russia has come into its own as presenting an alternative organization of society based on an alternative economic and ethical analysis. But Russia itself was part of western society; its institutions based on communism could be called the historical counterpart to the capitalist orthodoxy of the other half of the western world. More recently still China has offered a third model of society. It is itself tinctured with western thought in its communist theory, though this itself is a heresy of Russian communism (or so the Russians think) as Russian communism is a heresy of western capitalism. Be this as it may, China has combined its communist principles and Chinese patterns in a highly original way which must be of great interest to large traditionalist agricultural societies. She seems, on the surface at least, to be the only one to have attained something like a synthesis of opposites, a reconciliation of old and new, a sense of liberation combined with a respect for authority. It is through these ideological cross-currents, technological tides and past the shoals of conflicting examples that the Indian ship of state has to steer her way.

NEHRU'S INDIA

Crisis and Consolidation

Independence was inaugurated at midnight of 14/15 August 1947 (14 August having been adjudged unlucky by the astrologers). Jawaharlal made his now famous speech to the Constituent Assembly of which this is the key passage:

'Long years ago we made a tryst with destiny, and now the time comes when we shall redeem our pledge, not wholly or in full measure, but very substantially. At the stroke of the midnight hour, when the world sleeps, India will awake to life and freedom. A moment comes, which comes but rarely in history, when we step out from the old to the new, when an age ends, and when the soul of a nation, long suppressed, finds utterance. It is fitting that at this solemn moment we take the pledge of dedication to the service of India and her people and to the larger cause of humanity.'

It was a noble ideal, nobly phrased, but no-one then present realized how soon these sentiments would be put to the severest test. Partition, it was thought, had solved the problem of communal tension; and if Mahatma Gandhi, disillusioned by the rejection of his ideal of a united India (Akhand Hindustan) refused to rejoice and was touring in the remote countryside of north-east Bengal, it was thought that the saint would eventually come to Delhi since Delhi would not go to the saint. In the glow of that belief Delhi celebrated independence on the following day. A million people thronged the processional way in New Delhi. Nehru and the Mountbattens were separated and nearly overwhelmed in a sea of happy faces and chanting voices.

But the next day the reaction began. The Pandora's box of Sir Cyril (later Lord) Radcliffe's boundary award, purposely delayed until the achievement of independence, was opened. Hindu Indians, Pakistanis and Sikhs had accepted it in advance, so that the raising of the lid from the box might have been considered a formality. But this was not so. Sir Cyril, the Chairman of the Boundary Commission, was a judge chosen for his legal acumen and reputation for fairness. One of the qualifications for his appointment was that he had no knowledge of India. He was immediately left with the sole task and responsibility of drawing boundaries and deciding disputed points within a six-week deadline. With limitations of time, knowledge and understanding, it was virtually impossible to deal adequately with the often vital accessories of a boundary line—such as the location of the canal headwaters in relation to the canals themselves, communications by road and rail, the fate of mixed or isolated populations and such 'invisible' problems as the location of pasture lands in relation to villagers' flocks and herds.

The result of any such inquiry along such lines would be predictably uncertain, and so it was in Sir Cyril Radcliffe's case. His only consolation was that the cries of anguish came from both sides. Disapproval and resentment in such a situation was natural but there were three areas of special grievance. The Pakistanis resented the exclusion of Calcutta from Eastern Pakistan; much was made of this at the time, but in view of the city's geographical position and existing circumstances, it is hard to believe that they really expected to have it. The case was different in the Panjab, where the allotment of half the mixed Gurdaspur district to India made access to Kashmir practicable by means of a new road running from Pathankot. Pakistanis still accuse Lord Radcliffe, without any tangible evidence, of collusion with Lord Mountbatten in this matter. The third area of grievance was more crucial still, for it concerned the Sikhs. They had, it is true, accepted the award in advance like the other main parties. Yet there was always a body of activist dissent with Master Tara Singh as its spokesman. They now found their community, some four million strong in the Panjab, neatly divided down the middle. It was as if Solomon's proposal of equal division of a living child had actually been practised on the Sikhs. Yet what else could the Boundary Chairman do? Nowhere were the Sikhs in a majority, and they spilled, in almost equal proportions, on both sides of the line. The accommodation of the Sikhs, an ethnic, linguistic and partially cultural unit as well as a religious one, was really a diplomatic matter which should have been settled at the top level by the other chief parties concerned. As it was, however short-sighted they may have been before the Award, they now felt themselves frustrated, betrayed and truncated. For Sikhs this was something not to be borne. The upshot was the Panjab massacres.

The Sikhs had already been in conflict with the Muslims in the last days of the old Panjab province. Sikhs had been largely eliminated from Lahore, and Muslims from Amritsar. So the Sikh uprising soon became a Sikh-Muslim civil war, with Hindu Jats joining in the East Panjab. Centuries-old memories and recent resentments had bred a tension which turned conflict into massacres. The tale of slaughtered villagers, attacks on convoys, trainloads of dead has often been related. No-one was innocent and no-one profited. The aftermath was migration, exile, hate and folk memory of conflict. The loss of life was estimated by Judge Khosla, a keen and cautious observer, at half a million people. The devastation in terms of the injured, misery and hate was far greater. The refugees (about five and a half million) who poured into West Pakistan were nearly one-fifth of its then population, while the roughly equal number of Sikhs and Hindus moving eastwards were about the same proportion of the Indian Panjab and western Uttar Pradesh. In addition 400,000 left Sind. So the whole of north-western India was embittered by experiences whose memories and folk-tales will reverberate down the generations like the folklore surrounding the raids of Mahmud of Ghazni.

Could this carnage, the time-bomb of Indo-Pakistan relations, have been prevented? Mountbatten foresaw the danger and assembled a boundary force of 50,000 men. But Nehru refused to allow any British troops to participate; when the moment of crisis came, the force proved too involved on either side to be effective. As the columns of refugees moved south-east into India, they spread consternation, hatred and violence. In late August Delhi was engulfed in its own civil war and refugee excesses. For a time the existence of the central government itself was threatened. Mountbatten, who had gone to Simla for a break, was asked by V. P. Menon, on the instructions of Nehru and Patel, to return immediately. He demurred and talked of the next day or so. In that case, piped back Menon's voice, there was no need to bother, for there would be no central government. This was the point of no return; the three men then formed a triumvirate which planned and carried through an effective rescue operation.

After the violence came the settlement of the refugees. In the Panjab there were at least the lands vacated by the departing Muslims. But to Delhi many more came than went. They thronged the public places, they set up shops in the streets, they commandeered mosques. Tension built up during the autumn and with it came the Mahatma from Bengal. His 'one-man' army had quelled a last outbreak of communal fighting in Calcutta in September. He arrived in Delhi to find the Muslim minority now threatened with a pogrom. Most serious, there was some sympathy within the government for these attitudes. He started his daily prayer meetings at the Birla mansion in Albuquerque Road and soon found that it was the Muslims he was now called upon to champion. In January the inner voice spoke: he called for the already agreed payment of assets to Pakistan (withheld since the Kashmir dispute had broken in the previous October), and a peace pact in Delhi, including the evacuation of fifty-seven occupied mosques. He began a fast to death and when Vallabhbhai Patel remonstrated with him, he said with his failing breath, 'You are not the Vallabhbhai I have known.' Only on the payment of the money and the conclusion of the peace pact did he give up his fast an 18 January 1948. It was the noblest and most courageous action in his life.

The fast was a great moral victory, but it was also his death warrant. While he talked of walking to Pakistan on a peace mission, a Pune group within the R.S.S. had determined to kill him. It was not only because he was an opponent of Brahmin orthodoxy but insistently because he now appeared as the champion of the Muslims. The first attempt failed; the second should never have occurred had not some officials been more concerned with the letter than the spirit of their duties. As it was, while coming out to his prayer meeting at the accustomed time, he was shot at close range by Nathuram Godse and died with the words 'Ram, Ram' on his lips.

India was shaken to its foundations. The press of a million mourners at his cremation was so great that Governor-General Mountbatten and Prime Minister Nehru and their friends were nearly pushed into the flames they had come to witness and honour. Jawaharlal, catching again the spirit of the moment, said to the nation on the radio: 'The light has gone out of our lives and there is darkness everywhere . . . the father of the nation is no more . . . The best prayer we can offer him and his memory is to dedicate ourselves to truth and to the cause for which this great countryman of ours lived and for which he died.'

When the shock of horror and grief subsided it was found that the Mahatma was even more powerful in death than he had recently seemed to be in life. The revulsion of feeling discredited Hindu extremist bodies; even Sardar Patel came under criticism as Home Minister for inadequate security arrangements. Within the government itself the Sardar and Jawaharlal had an emotional reconciliation. The government acquired a new unity and the people a fresh resolution. Whereas there had previously been something of a tug-of-war between Vallabhbhai Patel, the realist, the Hindu champion, the friend of big business and the political boss, and Jawaharlal Nehru, the idealist, the advocate of tolerance, the democrat and the socialist, they now formed a duumvirate. For a time harmony prevailed while Patel dealt with the Princes in his forthright fashion. Before the rift could reopen widely enough for an open breach he died of a heart attack in December 1950.

After the crisis, consolidation. Order restored, the refugees in the process of resettlement, the Government could turn to the problems it had inherited from the British. The first of these was the Princes, large and small, numbering about 362 from Hyderabad with its seventeen million inhabitants to a borderland of tiny states and large estates. The British had renounced their treaty rights and had advised all to join one or other of the two new states. An attempt by the Nawab of Bhopal and some political officers to form 'a third force' foundered on the usual rock of princely jealousy. By Independence Day all but Hyderabad, Kashmir, Junagadh and Travancore had joined either India or Pakistan. Unity was paramount, the Government believed; Sardar Patel and his agent, V. P. Menon, set themselves to persuade, cajole or bully the princes into joining existing federal units or joining new federal units of their own. Never was the velvet glove presented by Menon so soft or the hand within so steely. The inducements were personal privileges, freedom from income-tax and the opportunity of taking part in all-India public affairs (since availed of by many), the threats of economic and political isolation and the spectre of popular movements within the States. By these means all save the first three mentioned above were included in the new federal Union of India within a few months. Travancore surrendered after a few days. Mysore became a state on its own; some like Travancore and Cochin and the Rajput states were thrown together to form the respective new states of Kerala and Rajasthan, while some just disappeared into the nearest successor Indo-British state. Some princes were given the title of Rajpramukh and other considerations, but all lost their authority.

The three exceptions could now be dealt with. Junagadh, a small sea-port state in Kathiawar with a Hindu majority and a Muslim nawab, opted for Pakistan. But it was surrounded by Indian territory; after a few weeks it was occupied by Indian troops and voted by plebiscite to join the Indian Union. Pakistan protested, but the issue was too small to become a major question. Hyderabad was another matter. The Nizam did not refuse accession but haggled about its terms. A year's standby was agreed while discussions went on. He refused good terms negotiated for him by British advisers and then allowed an extremist body, the Raza-kars, to seize control and inaugurate something like a reign of terror. The State was landlocked; eighty-five per cent of its population was Hindu; Pakistani intervention was impossible. The Razakars gave Nehru the excuse he needed for his 'police action' in the summer of 1948, which in-corporated Hyderabad in the Indian Union. Later (in 1956) it was divi-ded among the linguistically reorganized states in the Deccan, the major portion going to the Telugu-speaking state of Andhra.

There remained the case of Kashmir. In many respects it was unique. Its territories touched both the new states so that it could reasonably join either. It was a mixed state with a Hindu-Sikh majority in Jammu and a Muslim majority in the Vale and elsewhere, a large overall Muslim majority and a Hindu ruler. It was also a conglomerate state, consisting of the Hindu-Dogra chiefship of Jammu, of the principality of Kashmir proper purchased by the Dogra chief Gulab Singh from the British (who had captured it from the Sikhs who had taken it from an Afghan Muslim) and of various mountain dependencies like Gilgit, Hunza, Ladakh and Baltistan.

At first it was assumed that the state would opt for Pakistan. But Raja Hari Singh, the ruler, dallied, having secret hopes of independence. When Mountbatten visited him to bring matters to a head, he had a diplomatic illness. So uncertainty continued until October 1947, when a force of Pathan tribesmen burst into the state and would have taken Srinagar before Indian help could arrive had they not stopped to sack Baramula on the way. In panic the ruler acceded to India which airlifted troops just in time to save the Kashmir vale. India then claimed the legal right of accession and denounced the tribesmen as aggressors. Pakistan called for a plebiscite to which Nehru agreed in principle; the question was then referred to the newly-formed United Nations. Relations continued to be tense and flared up into a three weeks' war in April 1948. Then a United Nations truce force froze the then battle-line into a *de facto* boundary which has since continued. This was the start of the complex Kashmir question, which will be further considered in connection with Indo-Pakistan relations in general.

The last of the initial tasks facing the new government was the framing of a new constitution. The Constituent Assembly which listened to Nehru declaring a 'tryst with destiny' had been elected from the provincial legislatures set up by the Government of India Act of 1935. Now there were new ideas, new principles clamouring for expression and new conditions which made the old arrangements seem archaic. The Constitution was passed by the existing Constituent Assembly of 292 members through discussions which ran remarkably smoothly under Nehru's leadership. To him, to the Law Minister, Dr. B. R. Ambedkar, the Scheduled caste leader, and to Sir Maurice Gwyer, a principal architect of the 1935 Act and ex-Chief Justice, who was active behind the scenes in New Delhi, India owed much at this time. There was the 1935 Act as a model, long passages from which were drafted unaltered into the new constitution. There was Nehru, tolerant, enthusiastic, far-seeing and unusually patient. Though Congress had an overwhelming majority in the Assembly, he listened to suggestions from all parties and was willing to incorporate suitable ones in the new text. Dr. Ambedkar, a leading architect of the constitution, was not in fact a member of the Congress party. The final result was as near to a consensus as can be achieved in public life, and this helps to explain the vitality which the constitution has displayed over a generation. Nehru was also open to ideas from any part of the world, welding the whole into a consistent body of ideas and practice. Thus ideas of fundamental rights and a Federal Supreme Court came from the United States, of constitutional directives from Eire and some federal ideas from Canada.

Congress was pledged to democracy and federalism; for these purposes it took ideas from the West and adapted them to Indian conditions. It was also determined to include Indian elements in the constitution and this too found expression in its provisions. Nehru himself was convinced of the need for a strong centre if India was to be held together and the necessary dynamic for development provided.

There was first a declaration of fundamental rights which forms the preface to the constitution. Then comes a series of constitutional directives or aims of endeavour. The actual provisions of the constitution set up a federal and parliamentary system of government. There was universal adult suffrage which was the basis of all elections. The Central legislature consisted of the Lok Sabha (Council of the People), which represents the people as a whole, and the Rajya Sabha (Council of the States) indirectly elected by the States' legislatures and representing the States of the Union. The Executive, headed by the Prime Minister, was responsible to the Lok Sabha, though formally appointed by the President. These two houses, like the provincial legislatures, were all elected for a five-year term, subject to earlier dissolution by the Executive. The Federal government was matched by the States' ministries, whose heads were called Chief Ministers. The Head of the State was the President, also serving a five-year term, and elected by the Central and States' legislatures sitting jointly. He is a constitutional sovereign acting on the advice of his ministers, but he has certain reserve powers such as taking over the administration of politically deadlocked states. But the function which might one day put him into a position like that of the inter-war German President Hindenburg is that of choosing the Prime Minister. As long as one party holds a majority there is no problem, but should parties dissolve into groups his would be the crucial hand in devising majority combinations.

The Federal legislative system is defined by separate lists of central and state powers with a 'concurrent' list which the Centre can use if it wishes. It is the allotment of powers which determines the balance of the constitution; the Centre has sole control of defence, foreign affairs, railways, posts and currency. Its reserve powers and dominant financial position have with these given it the strength to carry through the great programmes of development. There is a comparatively simple provision for the amendment of the constitution; there must be a bare majority of the membership of both legislative houses and a two-thirds majority of those present. The constitution is guarded by the creation of a federal Supreme Court, which interprets the constitution and decides disputes between states.

Specifically Indian features of the constitution were present but muted. There was the 'abolition' of untouchability (art. 17), the ignoring of caste distinctions (arts. 15(ii) and 16(ii)), and praise for panchayats, which was later converted into fruitful legislation. But the most Indian part of the constitution was the manner of its working. Most observers (including Nehru I think) expected the emergence of a two-party system, the usual pre-condition for the successful working of a parliamentary regime. Instead, the Congress monolith has remained—unaffected even by a one-time split down the middle—with a variety of splinter groups which might without disrespect be called mostly chips from the old block. Only a local non-Congress party like the D.M.K. of Madras and the C.P.I.(M) have shown independent vitality. The real divisions have been within the Congress rather than outside it. The leader has been secure in the Lok

Sabha, and has tended to use it as a sounding board for national opinion; as a place to hear views, petitions and complaints and to address the nation for its good. In fact the Lok Sabha has become a durbar of the traditional sort where the leader is seen, advised, commands and admonishes. Nehru, convinced democrat as he was, concealed this process by his scrupulous observance of democratic forms. But it was he, with his prestige as a founding father of the nation, who in fact introduced it. Some such development was perhaps inevitable in view of India's strong authoritarian and hierarchical traditions. Rather than condemning him as a covert authoritarian one should perhaps be grateful for so gracious an interpretation of so strong a traditional trend.

Planning and Hope

INTERNAL

This section has advisedly been called Nehru's India. He dominated India as completely as De Gaulle did France, though in an entirely different way. What then was the nature of the man who for fifteen years was so identified with India by the world, that it could be said of him, as Louis XIV of France said of himself, '*L'état, c'est moi*'. Jawaharlal Nehru came of a Kashmiri Brahmin family one of whose ancestors, a Persian poet, migrated to Delhi in the early eighteenth century. The Emperor Farrukhsiyar granted him land on the bank of the Western Jumuna Canal whence the family took the new surname of 'Nehru' from the Persian word '*nahr*', a canal or watercourse. The nineteenth century saw the family in the service of the British; his father became a highly successful and anglicized lawyer at Allahabad. From here young Jawaharlal was sent to Harrow School and Trinity College, Cambridge, and was then called to the bar. He returned to India before 1914. So far he had followed the pattern of many a son of successful Indians; he returned to India a westernized, sophisticated and not very effective youth, with the apparent imprint of parental ambition rather than any sign of his own.

This diffident and overshadowed young man was transformed by the events after the First World War. Amritsar shocked him, official obtuseness stung him into a new awareness and Gandhi captivated him. His uncompromising naturalness aroused him, his care for the poor moved him. When the whole family joined the non-cooperation movement he found a new world among the *kisans* of Uttar Pradesh; his latent sense of social justice was aroused to breed his socialism after a study of the Russian model. He and Gandhi never really agreed but sparks of sympathy and inspiration ran between them, inspiring and sustaining him. In the twenties he travelled extensively and so acquired his grasp of the outside world. The loss of his wife Kamala made him a lonely man, more self-contained than before; he solaced himself with the society of Kamala's gift, his daughter Indira.

So in the late twenties he returned to India, brilliant, assured, a passionate nationalist and a believer in social justice. His advent was like a comet in the rather solid firmament of Congress stars; he became the idol of the left wing and sponsored, along with Subhas Bose, the independence resolution at the Calcutta Congress meeting in 1928. But the world did not realize that, though leftist in sentiment, he was tied by a silken thread to the Right, in his attachment, in the last resort, to the Mahatma's behests. Gandhi played on his temperament like a consummate musician on his violin, and it was only in 1947, with the premiership of free India before him on the one hand and the stark horror of civil war on the other, that he broke with his mentor on the issue of partition. During these years the country accepted him as Gandhi's designated heir; his temperamental outbursts were forgiven in the inspiration of his charisma. This was why he, rather than the much more senior Patel, became the first Prime Minister of India.

There were still many, however, who doubted whether he had the staying power, the resilience to deal with successive crises, the temper to manage a cabinet team and the party managers, the finesse to deal with intrigues and the firmness to impose his will. Did he not depend unduly on other individuals like his father or the Mahatma or later Krishna Menon? These critics understandably failed to discern some of his latent qualities, but they also ignored something more significant. It was the charisma or compelling charm of which he had already given ample evidence but which they thought was merely a reflection of Gandhi's own. Was he not another Hamlet dismayed by his situation and groaning—

> The world is out of joint, O cursed spite,
> That ever I was born to set it right!

The first years of power and crisis dispelled these illusions. There was decision and action—in the Delhi breakdown and in Kashmir; there was leadership and management in dealing with his cabinet and handling the constitutional discussions. And there was finesse and expertise in his relations with Patel and the party. In addition he enhanced his image by his lightning tours and won hearts by his mass meetings. They were often more *darshans* (viewing and honouring the leader) than verbal means of communication, but they were a form of communion through which he received psychic strength. In this way he became the *mah-bap*, the mother-father, of the nation.

From the time of Patel's death Nehru stood above all others as the last surviving and vigorous founding father. What would he do with his immense prestige? To an extent he was the prisoner of his past. He was a disciple of Gandhiji but did not believe in non-violence. His early contact with the *kisans* of Uttar Pradesh (then the United Provinces) had impressed him with the immensity of India's poverty and with the evils of landlordism and entrenched property, and this led him to socialism as the pattern for Indian society. But his visit to Russia in the twenties caused him to draw back from Communism as being too regimented in its organization and too harsh in its application. The individualist in Nehru was repelled and he remained a passionate believer in personal rights and democracy. These views had come from his western contacts and so did his secularism. So he was scornful of caste and the whole structure of traditional Hinduism. He was, he said, an Indian without caste or creed; he disliked the title of pandit and detested religious adulation. Nevertheless his Brahminic descent ensured his respect for the intellect; for him the fight against ignorance was coupled with the campaign against poverty.

Nehru's prescription against poverty was industrialization which would create more jobs in its construction and provide more goods in its production. This in turn required state regulation along socialist lines. For ignorance he turned to education with an emphasis on its higher levels and on technical skills. To deal with Brahminism there must be social reforms, a raising of the 'scheduled castes' and a reform of the Hindu social code.

This was a large programme. Nehru's prestige was unique, but it has to be noted that, except in the matter of industrialization, there was probably no majority for any part of it. Even his standing and charisma was not enough for this. Yet the great majority were too tied to his mystique and to the Congress to consider deserting him. The result, as veneration contended with personal inclination and vested interest, was that the real opposition concealed itself within the Congress party, while the overt opposition parties never really came to maturity. Once the veteran Patel had died and his heir, the orthodox Purshottamdas Tandon, had failed in his attempt to replace Nehru, there was not even a conspiracy or a cabal within the party formed against him. It was obstruction rather than rebellion, sabotage rather than open dissent which dogged him.

Before pursuing this theme it is well to note briefly the fate of the non-Congress groups during Nehru's premiership. Certain local parties, specially the D.M.K. of Madras and the Akali Dal (Sikh) in the Panjab, showed continued life because they represented permanent local interests. On the significant national level the story was more confused. At the Centre the Congress polled between 45 and 50 per cent of all the votes in the five general elections to date with the exception of 1967 when they still retained a bare majority of seats. Splinter groups aspiring to be national rivals of the Congress sprang like shoots from both sides of the political pipal tree. At independence the first of these was the All-India Hindu Mahasabha, representing orthodox Hindu sentiment, which always looked more powerful on paper than at the polls. During the war years it was dominated by the extremist Vir Savarkar. Its 'sword-arm' as it were, or activist wing, was the R.S.S. (Rashtriya Swayamsevak Sangha). Both parties were discredited by the latter's involvement in Gandhi's murder. The latter was suppressed and the former was abandoned by its new leader, Dr. Shyama Prasad Mukherjee, who in 1952 left it to form the Jana Sangh (Bharatiya Jan Sangh or Indian People's Party). This body became important in Uttar Pradesh, Madhya Pradesh and Rajasthan. It carried the Union Territory of Delhi in 1967 but could win majorities nowhere else and made little impact on the Congress majority in the Lok Sabha.

The Swatantra party was founded in 1959 by the veteran C. Raja-gopalachari of Madras and M. R. Masani of Bombay. It drew its support from the industrial and landlord classes; it professed to believe in moderate reform while firmly unholding private property and enterprise, and opposing communism. It should have appealed to a wide spectrum of the middle class, rural as well as urban, for these were very widespread sentiments. In a two-party system it would have aspired to the conservative role. But this would have required many sympathizers to withdraw their support from the Congress, and this, so long as it maintained its mystique as the embodiment of the nation's will to freedom, they were unwilling to do. The party made good progress at first, winning 18 out of 507 seats in the 1962 elections for the Lok Sabha, and emerging in the States as the third-largest party. In 1967, the year of splinter party elections and relative Congress eclipse, they did still better. Thereafter the party declined as the Congress recovered its prestige, and is now much as it began, a splinter group.

To the left of the central monolith there was first the Socialists. A group of Congress Socialists was formed in 1934 by Jai Prakash Narayan. Disillusioned by alleged Congress failures in its social policies this group became an independent party in 1948. Four years later it united with another Congress splinter group, the Kisan Mazdoor Praja Party (Peasants, Workers and Peoples' Party) which had split off from the Congress the year before led by the dissident Gandhian leader, the astringent but dedicated Acharya Kripalani. He was dissatisfied with the Congress attitude towards the cultivators and industrial labour. But after four years they split into the Praja Socialist Party and Socialist Party, and so both became ineffective. Their fortunes were not helped by Narayan's retirement into a holier than thou detachment from public life.

This leaves the Communist Party, founded in 1920 and trounced by the British government in the Meerut trials at the end of the decade. It had a brief moment of hope with the peasant risings in Hyderabad in 1950. When these were suppressed the party abandoned its militant tactics but was then rent with schism. The Moscow-backed Communist Party of India (CPI) gained between twenty and thirty Lok Sabha seats (out of over 500) in each general election to be the largest opposition party and held power for a time in the State of Kerala. Its main rival was the more militant Communist Party of India (Marxist) with a further pro-Chinese Marxist-Leninist group, who looked to a rural revolution in Chinese style and got the epithet of Naxalite from Naxalbari, the name of a Bengal village, which first brought them into prominence.

When the strongest opposition party could only gain five per cent of the Lok Sabha seats in five successive elections, it could hardly be claimed that a two-party parliamentary system was emerging. We can now see what Jawaharlal Nehru did with his large majority and how he managed the covert opposition within its ranks. His first care was the implementation of his democratic principles. This he achieved with the new constitution with its two hundred million voters, its parliamentary system, its civic rights buttressed by the law courts. The system is federal and the Centre strong as he believed it to be necessary. In this work he had a very large measure of support and it was never seriously challenged before the Emergency, which was avowedly temporary. Linked with this subject was the complex question of a national language. Nehru himself spoke Urdu or Hindustani in the tradition of the intelligentsia of the former United Provinces. Congress had opted for Hindi and he went along with this policy, though without any enthusiasm. But he also wished English to remain as a joint national language. His reason was the importance of maintaining links with the outside world, for which English was the best instrument available, and consideration for the feelings of South India. This did not suit Hindi zealots or South Indian purists, but the arrangement lasted Nehru's lifetime. The wisdom of this view was confirmed by the southern reaction to the announcement in 1965 of Hindi as the sole national language. The development of local languages had another effect, a demand for the redrawing of state boundaries to reflect linguistic distinctions. This subject is dealt with later in this section (see p. 419).

An adjunct of Nehru's democratic principles was a dislike of privilege. This was revealed clearly in his attitude to the princely order, with whom Sardar Patel dealt so quickly and smoothly. As this attitude spread to the countryside it became linked with his ideas of rural uplift. Zamindari or landlord right, a legacy of earlier British land settlements, was abolished by 1956; there was some redistribution of land and breaking up of large estates and protection of tenancy rights. The policy was bold and far-reaching, but its performance patchy and piecemeal because execution lay in the hands of the States. Some observers have even contended that the policy had more loopholes for evasion than closed doors for enforcement. The need for further action was underlined by the campaign of Vinobha Bhave, Gandhi's chosen first *satyagrahi* in the civil disobedience campaign of 1940, for *bhoodan* or voluntary transfers of land from landlord to cultivators. In 1951 he began his walks from village to village, seeking land gifts (*gramdan*) from landlord to tenant farmers. He continued his pilgrimage for twenty years. Opinions vary as to its effectiveness; at any rate it was a striking demonstration of Gandhian principles in action and served as a running reminder to the country that the redistribution of the land had not yet gone far enough.

In this sphere Nehru's ideas had been hindered by state action and manipulation. In his policy of industrial development he had no such propertied sieve through which to pass his levelling proposals. It was a matter for the Centre. In 1950, arising out of the Colombo Plan for mutual development by the states of south and south-east Asia, he established the National Planning Commission with himself as the first Chairman. This was strengthened by the creation of a larger National Development Council two years later. The Planning Commission drew up a succession of five-year plans for national development, the economic inspiration coming from Professor Mahalanobis. The aim was to raise the national standard of living by means of greater agricultural production, thus making India more self-sufficient, and industrial development which would, by increasing production and so jobs, and by stimulating trade, increase the gross national product faster than the rate of population growth. A balance between types of activity had to be maintained and gaps in Indian resources filled by supplies of foreign capital.

The objective of planning was to be a mixed economy with a public and a private sector. Basic industries were to be owned and developed by the state and other sections by private capital. In the public sector were placed steel plants, oil and its products, electrical works, machine making, aircraft and shipbuilding. In the private sector there were textiles, cement, engineering and motor manufacture. There was a practical as well as a theoretical reason for this division. Private capital, which was responsible for only six per cent of the national income at Independence, could not raise the sums required for the large projects reserved for the public sector.

The first plan was launched in 1951. It placed special emphasis on the increase of agricultural production in order to free India from a crippling dependence on foreign supplies. This was considered a great success, production increasing by 25 per cent over the five-year period. At the same time the Bhakra–Nangal dam project near Ropar at the head of the Sutlej Himalayan valley, planned by the British, was undertaken. The great power and irrigation projects of the Damodar valley and the Hirakud valley were also started. The second five-year plan was more ambitious, the total outlay at seven thousand eight hundred crores of rupees being twice that of the first. The emphasis was on industrialization and it was now that the three great steel plants, already started during the first plan and sponsored respectively by Great Britain, West Germany and Russia, were developed. The plan aimed to increase the national income by 25 per cent, and though it did not achieve this object fully, its performance was greater than that of the first plan because of its larger scale. Credit difficulties were resolved by foreign loans, particularly from the United States. The third plan of 1961 outlived Nehru. It involved an expenditure of eight thousand million pounds, and aimed at expanding basic industries and making India self-sufficient in its food-supply. Difficulties increased in the supply of foreign currency despite aid from the World Bank. These difficulties delayed the start of the fourth plan until 1969. The achievement of the first decade was great; it was claimed that national income had risen by 42 per cent, income per head by 20 per cent and consumption by 16 per cent.

This was Nehru's bid to attack India's problem of poverty. Next comes his attack on ignorance. Congress was committed to universal education; Nehru was one of those to whom this was a genuine intention rather than a pious aspiration. There was a large extension of higher and technical education and of research studies; universities, institutes of technology and research centres proliferated; there were more than eighty of such bodies by the end of his premiership. The emphasis was especially on science and technology because these spheres were thought to have been the weakest during the British period. Research centres, ranging from foodgrains and fertilizers to atomic research, also spread widely and purposefully. General universities grew so much that a surplus of graduates reappeared despite the increased job opportunities created by the expansion of industry and commerce.

The story was rather different in the case of elementary education. Here Nehru was hampered by the allotment of education to the states. In the case of higher studies the Centre could intervene on the ground of an overriding national interest; with primary education it was not so easy. In the upshot universal elementary education was generally enforced in the large cities but lagged behind in the countryside. Literacy at Independence had been about 15 per cent; at the end of the Nehru era it was reckoned at about 25 to 30 per cent, the ratio of boys to girls being two to one. Democratic idealism would seem to have met here the traditional reluctance of the upper castes to enlighten the masses.

One of the subjects nearest to Nehru's heart was civic rights, and particularly the rights of women. Here also was a field where orthodox opposition was strong. But he was here following in the wake of Gandhi with his attacks on caste restrictions and emphasis on human dignity. Nehru carried the process further in the sphere of Hindu personal law, still largely based on the venerable compilation, *The Laws of Manu*. In this system the group overshadowed the individual and the woman was subordinate to the man. Nehru hoped to reform the Hindu Code by legislation passed in a single session. But the Congress party contained its quota of traditionalists; it was not until 1955 that the Hindu Succession Act and 1956 that the Hindu Marriage Act became law. Even now the whole process is not complete. The first gave to women equal rights with men in the matter of the succession to and the holding of property. The second put monogamy on a legal footing, providing for divorce with alimony and maintenance. Two further acts protected the Hindu widow and separated wives with maintenance provisions, and provided for the guardianship of minors and a stricter control of adoptions. These measures amounted to a major achievement in the circumstances. Sceptics may argue that the peasant mass is still largely unaffected. But the new lands are certainly effective in the middle class; and this is a rapidly growing body and the eventual arbiter of opinion.

Gandhi's campaign for the 'Untouchables' continued. They were the anthropologist's 'exterior castes', Gandhi's Harijans or People of God, and the Constitution's 'Scheduled Castes' because they were listed in separate state schedules. According to the 1961 census, they numbered 64.5 millions, and there were nearly 30 million more classified as 'Scheduled tribes'. All these were loosely called the 'Depressed classes'. Legislation was passed against discrimination in such matters as access to wells, shops and entertainments; but the main form of government action was help in the form of educational grants, quotas of employment, etc. It can be said that this part of the social programme has gone steadily forward with, if many Brahmin witnesses are to be believed, considerable success.

Here may be mentioned Nehru's major venture into 'Indianism'. This was the launching of what was called 'Panchayati raj', a great endeavour to revive village life by giving rural communities local committees with independent powers subject to guidance and stimulus from local officials. A pilot plan was launched in 1952 with fifty-five selected projects using substantial help from America. Each area covered about 500 square miles and 500 villages, within which a wide programme of development, including panchayats, was inaugurated. This pilot scheme grew into Panchayati raj with the decision of the National Development Council in 1958. The panchayat, the co-operative and the school were the basic village institutions, the elected panchayat being in charge. From it sprang all other activities, of women, youth, farming, culture, etc. There is an ascending order of local activity, from the village, through 'the Block' and the Zila to State headquarters. The Block Panchayat Samiti contains the elected presidents of village panchayats (Sarpanches) and the same rule applies to the Zila Parishads. Remembering that there are about 800,000 villages in India one gets an idea of the magnitude of the undertaking and also, despite some setbacks, shortcomings and deviations, of the significance of its achievement.

*   *   *

EXTERNAL

In foreign affairs Nehru at first enjoyed almost complete freedom of action. There were good reasons for this. Since the thirties he had been the Congress specialist on foreign affairs. He alone had foreseen the Second World War. The other Congress leaders had for the most part little knowledge of and less interest in the outside world. The Hindu tradition, still potent, was inward-looking and exclusive. But though the Indian public took little interest in the outer world, they had a lively sense of their position within that world. Still conscious of the smothering effect of foreign domination, they eagerly desired global recognition, a recognition which should include not only Great Britain but the United States and Russia as well. Nehru was the man with the necessary knowledge, flair and will; he was the Joshua to lead India into the promised land of the wider world.

Nehru himself was willing and indeed insistent on assuming this role. He retained the Ministry of External Affairs in his own hands throughout his premiership and during that time was equated with India itself in the eyes of the international community. For them India was Nehru. What then were the basic concepts from which sprang his actions? First, arising from the country's immediate past, came a strong feeling of national independence. Also connected with that past and heightened by post-war developments was the sentiment of anti-colonialism. Then came the positive idea of internationalism, with its sub-heads of co-operation, conciliation and peace-making; and finally, arising from post World War conditions, that of neutralism, or, as Nehru preferred to call it, non-alignment.

Early post-war conditions provided a favourable milieu for these views, so that Nehru seemed for some time to be swimming on the crest of a world wave. Political colonialism was dying but some of its wrecks and survivals still strewed the Asian scene. The nationalist wind was blowing strongly, comfortably billowing Nehru's sails with this title. Internationalism was having the boom associated with the founding of the United Nations at San Francisco in 1945. Within a year or two of Independence the Russian achievement of the atomic bomb conjured the spectre of a world atomic holocaust to give substance to his policy of non-alignment.

The policy of rounding off Indian independence in the sub-continent raised the preliminary question of relations with Britain. In 1947 India had become a Dominion, a decision not unconnected with the influence of its first independent Governor-General, Lord Mountbatten. Nehru wished to retain this link but there was strong support for the *purna swaraj* or complete independence. The solution found in the new constitution was one which served as a precedent for many Commonwealth countries later. India became a Republic, but remained a member of the Commonwealth; she elected her own President while the King (or Queen) became Head of the Commonwealth. This arrangement has proved workable and was ratified, so to speak, by Queen Elizabeth II's successful visit to India in 1961.

The assertion of Indian sovereignty within the sub-continent led directly to a confrontation with Pakistan. Junagadh and Hyderabad were absorbed with little difficulty. The French agreed to cede their Indian possessions, including Pondicherry, and this was regularized by a treaty in 1956. Ceylon, after some early nervousness because of her Tamil population, settled down to neighbourliness, if without much enthusiasm. In Nepal India is credited with having encouraged the overthrow of the Rana regime in 1951 and the rise of the Nepali Congress party. But here again there was never any serious intention of annexation, and relations settled into correctness and a balance of influence between India and China at the Nepali court. Portugal proved more difficult with its important enclave of Goa and lesser stations elsewhere. The Portuguese treated Goa as part of their metropolitan territory, a view quite unacceptable to nationalist India. Relations grew gradually worse until Goa was finally occupied by military force in December 1961.

This left Pakistan, with whom confrontation came over Kashmir and the allotment of assets at Partition. We have already noted in the *Crisis* part of this section the settlement of the latter and the first phase of the former. The short war of April 1948 had been complicated by the Indian denial of water to Pakistani canals. This issue, along with those of refugee property and Kashmir, was carried over to the next period. The property problem dragged to an indeterminate close in the fifties. Water remained a critical issue, heightened by the Indian intention to absorb the whole Sutlej outlet for its own development. In 1960 an agreement was reached with President Ayub Khan which settled a vital problem imaginatively and thoroughly. The criss-cross canal pattern of the undivided Panjab was transformed; India was to have the outfall of the three eastern rivers, the Sutlej, Beas and Ravi, while Pakistan had the three western ones, the Indus, Jhelum and Chenab. To supplement the waters of the last two a series of cross canals was constructed with the aid of loans from the World Bank to which the United States and Britain contributed. This settlement proved real and was a remarkable demonstration of Nehru's prescience and ingenuity.

Kashmir then and since has remained the running sore of Indo-Pakistan relations. Controversy centred round the terms of the plebiscite to which Nehru had originally agreed. Successive United Nations' efforts (by General McNaughton, Sir Owen Dixon and Dr. F. Graham) to secure agreement proved abortive; eventually Kashmir drew up its own constitution and voted for union with India, after which Nehru considered the matter closed. It was widely said at the time of the first conflict that Patel would have ceded Kashmir on the principle of the fewer the Muslims in India the better. Nehru's view was different. For him nationalism was all important; a Kashmir willingly united with India would be a living proof of its viability in Indian conditions. And he regarded the popular Kashmiri vote for Union as that proof.

There was also a good field for Nehru's anti-colonialist feelings. The old colonialist powers were there to be suspected; there was the debris of past colonialisms to clear away. Britain might be thought to have repented, but Britain was much weaker than before. The United States, the champion of freedom, was also the home of the dollar, and the dollar came to be more feared than American democracy was loved. So when the United States, in the name of the United Nations, went to the defence of South Korea in 1950, India stood aloof, only co-operating on humanitarian matters. Similarly she remained aloof in Indo-China, only co-operating in the aftermath of the Geneva Conference of 1954. The emphasis was on mediation, not war.

But elsewhere in South-East Asia India was more belligerent. An informal Asian Relations Conference met in New Delhi in 1946 and laid the foundation of Asian co-operation. This was followed by another, official conference in January 1949 after the second Dutch 'police action' had taken Jogjakarta in Central Java. Nehru dominated the conference and condemned the Dutch; the Conference resolutions won the support of the United Nations' Security Council so that by the year's end Indonesian independence had been won. Here was success indeed; from this time was born the rather vague concept of 'Asianism', hatched in the fertile brain of Sardar K. M. Panikkar. The dream that there was such a thing as an Asian 'personality', which India and Nehru embodied and led, faded with the Asian-African Conference at Bandung in Java in 1955. Nehru was again prominent and eloquent on anti-colonialism, but the advent of Communist China, in the person of Chou En-lai, signalled the end of India's single unquestioned leadership. There were now 'two kings in Brentford'.

Nehru was a good internationalist. India was a founder-member of the United Nations in 1945 and thereafter played a full part in its proceedings. Mrs. Vijaya Lakshmi Pandit, the Prime Minister's sister, was a President of the U.N.O. in its early years; India played a full part on the U.N.O.'s missions and commissions, and won international respect for its representatives' skill, efficiency and goodwill. But Nehru soon saw the limits of the U.N.O.'s authority and influence, and from this sprang the ideas of a third force and non-alignment. If the weaker and developing countries could get together, argued Nehru, they would warn the two giants that, in the event of a major war neither side would find any allies. Also they would pressurize the great powers themselves by threatening to join the other side. And, in the event of atomic war, the Third World would survive the resulting holocaust. Along with this went his doctrine of Indian non-alignment. India would remain uncommitted to both eastern and western blocs; she would maintain relations and accept help from both. Steel plants were accepted from both Russia and the United States. There were visits to and from Moscow (by Bulganin and Khrushchev in 1955) and Nehru's visits to America. The advent of Mao's China on the international scene was at first turned by Nehru to his advantage. Again there were mutual visits, a result of which was the Panch Shila or five principles of non-interference and good neighbourliness. There developed a triangular relationship; Nehru saw China as the mediator between Russia and India, India as the interpreter of the communist world to Britain, and Britain as the bridge to American understanding. In sum, by 1956 India had won widespread respect and goodwill for her attitudes and achievements. Nehru was credited with almost wizard-like qualities of balance combined with idealism, of diplomatic adroitness and powers of conciliation. He was a world statesman to whom flowed the admiration and hopes of millions. It was his finest hour.

*   *   *

NEHRU'S INDIA

865

Difficulty and Perplexity

INTERNAL

The year 1956 has been selected as marking a turning point in the Nehru regime because it contained the two incidents of the Hungarian revolt and the Anglo-French Suez adventure. In the former case the revolt was crushed by Russian troops and the Hungarian leader Imre Nagy executed; in the latter the overthrow of President Nasser's Egyptian government was thwarted by veiled American intervention. Collectively they gave a jolt to Nehru's reputation and exposed the first serious criticism of his handling of foreign affairs. This does not mean, of course, that the decline in his or Indian affairs was immediate or general. Some major achievements lay in the future like the settlement of the canal waters dispute with Pakistan in 1960. But from this time, while everything had previously seemed to be going in his favour, difficulties, doubts and perplexities began to emerge.

In the political sphere Nehru was no longer as supreme as he had once seemed. Freely comparing him with the Mughal emperors, critics forgot that even they were subject to various checks and limitations. There had always been opposition, mostly concealed within the Congress ranks. The slow passage of the Hindu Code bills was an indication of this. But now the overt opposition grew stronger and the concealed obstruction more obstinate. Overtly, the new Jana Sangh grew steadily in strength. Without many seats in the Lok Sabha, its links with traditional Hinduism enabled it to arouse Hindu feelings on sensitive issues which increasingly appeared and so influenced the government through its supporters. In 1959 the Swatantra party was founded and there was increasing activity in the socialist and communist camps.

Within the party Nehru had to face increasing factionalism within the States. Several State governments had to be suspended; in the Panjab the dynamic though brash Partap Singh Kairon was unseated for corruption, while in Uttar Pradesh Mrs. Sucheta Kripalani tried for four years as Chief Minister to get bitter rival factions to work together. Office seemed to be more tempting than programmes; the symptoms of loss of direction appeared as an epidemic of 'floor-crossing' and postponements in State assemblies. This process was reflected in the general elections of 1962, when the Congress percentage of votes for the Lok Sabha declined from 48 to 45 and State Congress majorities were eroded. The next year Nehru tried to revivify the party with the 'Kamraj plan' (named after the Madras Chief Minister from 1954 to 1963). Kamraj himself became the Congress President; six State chief ministers and six Union ministers retired to make way for younger and fresher blood. There was activity and manipulation but not much rejuvenation. The question 'where are we going?' gradually deepened into the complaint 'what has gone wrong?'; the phrase 'it's Nehru's fault' grew from a whisper to a murmur and finally to an open charge. And this was followed by the final question 'after Nehru, who and what?'

At the beginning of this twilit period, however, there was one more major achievement, though, characteristically of this time, it was against Nehru's private wishes. It was the reorganization of the State structure on a linguistic basis, arising from the revival of the local languages and along with them, of local loyalties. Nehru was at first reluctant, fearing lest local cultural centres might become local power centres to the detriment of the Centre's control. Was New Delhi to become the centre of a South Asian United Nations, influencing without controlling its contending members? His hand was eventually forced by the hunger strike of Potti Sriramulu in the cause of the Telugu language and the desired Andhra State. His death in late 1952 caused the appointment of a Boundaries Commission of which Sardar K. M. Panikkar was the most active member. This resulted in 1956 in a radical reorganization of State boundaries along linguistic lines. Only Bombay still united Marathas and Gujaratis and the Panjab Sikhs and Hindus in single states. Within four years, however, Gujarat had insisted on separation from Bombay which became the State of Maharashtra. Six years later Nehru's daughter agreed to the division of Panjab into Panjab (Sikh *subah*) and Haryana (Hindu Jats). So far Nehru's forebodings have not been realized though there have been rumblings in the form of boundary disputes.

More daunting, because of their implications, were the economic difficulties which India increasingly experienced. During the first two five-year plans India was not only statistically enlarging her gross national income and her *per capita* income but was felt to be doing so. New industries were providing new jobs and greater expectations; more money was encouraging consumption and a feeling of being better off. There was hope, expectancy and a sense of achievement. Much of the benefit, it is true, went to the middle classes, but others also felt that things were moving their way. The burden of the plans thus became bearable. But by 1960 there was a change. The growth in the national income declined from 4.3 per cent per annum to 3 per cent against a planned 7 per cent in the third plan; while the *per capita* income (the ordinary citizen's touchstone of progress) remained static instead of increasing to between 8 and 9.5 per cent as it had done in each of the first two plans. India should have 'taken off' in the economic sense with the third plan, but instead there were currency, production and export difficulties. The sun went in just when it was expected to shine in full brilliance.

Some of this result was due to bad harvests (in 1963/4, 79.4 million tons of grain against a planned 100 millions), but the chief cause was the unexpectedly large increase in population which disconcerted the planners. In 1947 the population of the new India was reckoned to be about 320 millions. An alarm bell rang when a committee estimate of 408 millions by 1961 became a census figure of 439 millions with a growth rate of twelve millions a year. In 1971 the census figure was 547 millions. With uncertain food and halting industrial production it seemed from about 1960 that India was beginning to move backwards rather than forwards. Voices were heard criticizing heavy industrialization, advocating birth control and increased food production. The planners were confused, the politicians resentful and recriminatory; there was bewilderment and indignation. India had lost her way; it was Nehru's fault, said the average citizen. But no-one knew how to find the path again, or, indeed, what sort of path it should be.

* * *

EXTERNAL

The Hungarian and Suez crises of 1956 have already been mentioned as signposts on the record of the Nehru regime. They administered the first jolt to the chariot of Nehru leadership. But why? Nehru's condemnation of the British action at Suez was vehement and decisive. This was in tune with the still existing anti-imperialist sentiments in India, and was generally approved. But in the case of Hungary there was hesitation and equivocation; the final condemnation was mild compared with the language used about Suez. It was this contrast which offended right wing and religious opinion. The effect was perhaps the greater, coming as it did at the time of Nehru's vacillation over the roles of Maharashtra, Gujarat and Bombay in the States reorganization of the same year.

At the same time there were changes in the world scene which gradually made some of the Nehru policies less relevant. In 1956 the first hydrogen bomb was exploded at Bikini atoll in the Pacific. It generated a force equal to that of ten million tons of T.N.T., many times that of the Hiroshima bomb. Though logically it could be described as just a larger bomb, it was soon realized that with it weapons of destruction had entered a new dimension. A Hiroshima bomb war would be lethally destructive, but not the ultimate catastrophe; a hydrogen bomb war would be just that. As this realization spread it was seen that total atomic war was no longer a practical proposition. If the atomic deterrent—or provocation—was no longer practical politics, a third international force and a policy of non-alignment, designed to deter the atomic powers from embarking on such a war, and, if unsuccessful, to survive its holocaust, ceased to have its former compelling force. As a footnote to the change, the U.S. Secretary of State, John Foster Dulles, who hankered after the use of the bomb with his talk of 'agonizing reappraisals', died in 1960. Thereafter Russia and the United States, stealthily at first, began to approach one another. Non-alignment and anti-colonialism were no longer leading issues; at the Belgrade Conference of non-aligned Nations in 1961 Nehru himself characterized them as 'worn out'.

Then in 1960 came the Sino-Russian breach over economic and technical aid and atomic know-how. Nehru's balancing feats were now no longer needed. The decade opened with independence and revolution in the Congo (now Zaire); henceforward the emerging African states became more and more an independent diplomatic group. India continued to act as an international mediator and harmonizer. But she was now one among many; her leadership role and 'special position' had evaporated.

It was at this point that relations with China deteriorated. The immediate cause was Tibet. With Independence India inherited the old Indo-British imperial frontiers. Pakistan took away the old north-west frontier with its Durand line; and as between Pakistan and India the disputed Kashmir frontier was defined by the UN truce line of 1948 (as it still is with some modifications). There remained the long frontier with China from the Karakorams to Burma with a gap for Nepal. The first section was in the north from Chinese Tibet to Sinkiang; the second ran eastwards to Sikkim about which there was no dispute, and the third was the stretch from Sikkim to Burma covered by the North-East Frontier Agency (NEFA). In the first section lay the desolate Aksai Chin plateau, where the frontier between India and China had never been properly surveyed or agreed. A line on paper moved eastwards or westwards according to current diplomatic exigencies. The third line was the most sensitive because through it ran the road to Lhasa and the Tibetan heartland.

Aksai Chin was a strategical problem. The new China was reasserting its authority over Sinkiang and wanted an easy means of access there. Her plan, started in the early nineteen-fifties but not noticed officially by India till later, was to build an all-weather motorway across the plateau. Was it going over Indian or Chinese territory? The north-eastern problem was more difficult for it raised the whole matter of Indo-Tibetan-Chinese relations. China had long claimed suzerainty over Tibet, the old imperial China occupying Lhasa in a last attempt to assert it. The Simla conference of 1913–14 between the British, Tibetans and the new 'democratic' China produced a frontier known as the McMahon line. The Tibetans accepted it but the Chinese only initialled it. With the advent of the Mao regime in 1949 the Tibetan issue became crucial. The Chinese were determined to reassert their authority, but here they had to deal with the Buddhist Dalai Lama and Tibet's cultural and emotional links with India. Nehru recognized Chinese suzerainty (as the British had done) and advised the young Dalai Lama to co-operate with them. It was during this period that the Panch Shila were devised (1954).

Crisis came in 1959, when a Tibetan revolt led to the Dalai Lama's flight to India and the granting of asylum to him by Nehru. To this the Chinese objected and there began an acrimonious exchange of notes in which both sovereignty over the Aksai Chin plateau and the McMahon line were called in question. Diplomacy was overtaken by public feeling in India which championed the Dalai Lama on religious grounds and insisted on the full assertion of the old frontiers. It needed a young Nehru to solve this problem as it needed a young Napoleon to win Waterloo. But he was ageing; he was persuaded to order an advance beyond the McMahon line and there followed the Chinese 'incident'. There was temporary consternation and fear of a full-scale Chinese invasion. As these alarms subsided Nehru was able to fend off the too-pressing American offers of help and alliance. He shuffled his ministers as before and began to think of a new settlement in Kashmir, sending for Sheikh Abdullah only a few weeks before his own death. The damage to India was much more in prestige than materially, and it was this which wounded the Prime Minister most. The army had seemed to be ineffective, the Chinese unexpectedly strong. Outside powers had been given an opportunity for interference of which they had taken advantage. The project of real independence, of Asian guidance and world moral leadership had collapsed; the 'cloud-capp'd towers, the gorgeous palaces' of the vision had vanished.

At seventy-four Nehru was unable to start building afresh. His sudden death on 27 May 1964 was not entirely unexpected. But the shock was nearly as great as with Gandhi—'the light had gone out'. It had been shining but dimly in deepening twilight, but it still shone; people blamed Nehru for everything but couldn't do without him. The following evaluation is quoted from my *India: A Modern History*[1] which I don't feel I can better.

'In seeking to evaluate Nehru's reign one must avoid the extremes of adulation, which beset him during his first years of power, and of condemnation which echoed around and beyond his funeral pyre. It is true that what seemed to start as a triumphal march seemed to end in the tragedy of nemesis. But if the heights were not all scaled, the depths were not plumbed either. All was not lost and some very tangible things were gained. Surveying Nehru's work we find an air of half achievement. In politics we have a western democratic machine without a party system to work. There had been great industrial expansion but the economy had not 'got off the ground' in an economic sense, unemployment had not been cured and the standard of living remained low. A large middle class had been created but the gulf between it and the masses remained deep. Higher education had expanded but primary education had lagged. Universal education only existed in some cities. Social progress had been achieved in the reform of the Hindu Code, but the forces of reaction remained strong. The population had grown much faster than expected with little done to restrain it. This one factor threatened to counterbalance the other achievements together. Internationally, India had lost the halo of moral authority bequeathed by Gandhi.

'Yet all was not lost. The giant was wounded but still a giant. I think Nehru's greatest achievement was in the social sphere because his reforms may here have influenced Indian life most deeply. For the rest, he set India on the way to full membership of the developing world community, politically, industrially, educationally, culturally. He gave a sense of purpose as well as pride in her past, and he laid foundations,

[1] India: *A Modern History*, 2nd edition, University of Michigan Press, Ann Arbor, U.S.A, 1972, p. 451-2.

whatever faults there may have been in the superstructure which he added, upon which his successors have been able to build securely. At his death he was widely regarded as a fallen idol. We can now see him as a bruised and limping giant who had completed half the great causeway to the future to which he had set his hand.'

*   *   *

POST-NEHRU INDIA

Interlude and Crisis

The question 'after Nehru, who?' when first raised in the nineteen-fifties appeared to be more of a foreign correspondent's ploy or a cocktail party quiz than a genuine apprehension. From the time of his seventieth birth-day in November 1959, however, the question became more relevant. But it was not until his serious illness in the spring of 1962 that the question began to press. Then came the China incident later in the same year to add the question, 'after Nehru, what?' This event damped Nehru's spirits for a time though his resilience soon reasserted itself. Indeed, in the follow-ing year he used the alarm caused by three bye-election defeats and con-cern about the state of the Congress Party to reorganize his ministry under the appellation 'Kamraj plan', as previously related. One of the more willing sacrifices on this occasion was the Home Minister, Lal Bahadur Shastri. Nehru's deftness turned the episode into an act of ob-livion for some of his less congenial colleagues like Morarji Desai, the Finance Minister, and S. K. Patil. But Lal Bahadur soon returned to the Cabinet as minister without portfolio to become a roving ambassador of conciliation. In this role he was conspicuously successful, in particular in the affair of the Prophet's Hair in Kashmir.

There then came the question of the Presidency of the Congress, likely now to be a key position after many years in the shade. It was to arrange this that the group known as the Syndicate or Caucus was formed in October 1963. It consisted at first of Kamraj himself, Atulya Ghose, the Congress 'boss' of West Bengal, Sanjiva Reddy of Andhra Pradesh, Nija-lingappa of Mysore (Karnataka) and S. K. Patil of Bombay. It was some-what anti-Hindi and strongly anti-Morarji on the grounds that he was too strong a 'Hindiwallah', too aggressive a capitalist and personally dictatorial. The election of Kamraj as President of the Congress having been arranged, it became clear with Nehru's stroke in January 1964 that the Syndicate would soon have more important duties still.

Thus, when Nehru died there was a group ready to act while the most prominent candidate and strongest personality, Morarji Desai, was both out of office and the inner counsels of the party. These were the circum-stances which led to the selection of Lal Bahadur Shastri as Nehru's successor. Shastri, who was distinctive for his small stature and m⁝¹ ¹ manners, was a man of Gandhian principles, of simplicity and dedication of life, of known integrity and tireless industry, a practitioner of conciliation and a lover of 'consensus'. But he did not retire to an *ashram*, adopt the villager's loincloth or resort to fasts; he rose through the hurly-burly of Uttar Pradesh Congress factionalism. To have retained respect for integrity as well as ability in these circumstances was a proof of unusual character. From the secretaryship of Congress he moved to the Cabinet where he was Home Minister at the time of the Kamraj plan. He had just that blend of Gandhian idealism, of personal integrity and proven ability which the situation demanded. He came from the country's heartland; though a Hindi supporter he was not extreme; he had no pronounced enemies. If some did not find much ground for positive support, it was still harder for many others to find convincing grounds for opposition. Here, it seemed, was a practical idealist who might raise the country from its mood of depression and self-questioning and guide it to a new road of achievement.

So Shastri was elected, Morarji not judging it worth while in the end to oppose him openly. Shastri's tenure of office must always remain something of an enigma; the test which would have made or broken him as a leader being removed by his sudden death in January 1966. His qualities were thus described by Michael Brecher: 'humility, patience, respect for conflicting viewpoints, sensitivity to powerful emotional currents, along with subtlety and quiet firmness'. His tactic of consensus Shastri described in these words: 'if I can carry everyone along with me, that is much better. Even those who disagree must feel that their views are listened to. ... This approach may delay decisions a little, but that does not bother me at all. It is a price worth paying.'[1] The flaw in this outlook was that consensus was like an emollient ointment that can assuage the lesser pains but not cure the major ills. Where vital interests or ambitions were at stake it might be either ineffective or too late. Shastri retained most of the outgoing cabinet. Of the three newcomers one was S. K. Patil and another Mrs. Indira Gandhi, Jawaharlal Nehru's only daughter and hitherto known as a one-term Congress President and as her father's guardian and hostess. The most immediate impact was made by Patil, influential in Gujarat and a member of the Syndicate. Mrs. Gandhi became Minister of Information; she made no visible impact on her department, but began her journeys to any place where a problem or a crisis existed in the country. These, combined with her sari, her name and her 'royal' connection, before long made her the best known public figure to the broad masses of the country.

During Shastri's nineteen months of office three issues arose to test the consensus doctrine and the firmness of his character. The first was a food shortage caused by a bad harvest and a growing population. Here the Chief Ministers prevented drastic action until the good harvest of 1965

[1] M. Brecher, *Succession in India*, London, 1966, p. 93.

shelved the problem without solving it. Consensus without delay was difficult and delay without consensus bred impatience and a suggestion of indecision. The next test was the Hindi crisis of early 1965, stemming from the proclamation of Hindi as the sole national language on 15 January. Fear and resentment in the south, which wished to retain English as Hindi's twin, erupted in Madras State (Tamil Nadu) with riots in Madras city and through the countryside, including ritual burnings and many deaths. While Mrs. Gandhi visited Madras and Kamraj dallied in Kerala, Shastri again temporized. It was only in March that amendments to the Official Languages Act of 1963 were promised, making English officially usable once more.

The third test came from Pakistan. In April 1965, there were clashes between Indian and Pakistani troops in the nine thousand square-mile marshy area known as the Rann of Kutch, lying between the Sind provincial border and the former Kathiawar States. The Rann is inundated by occasional high tides and, except for a few hillocks, usually by monsoon rain. At first Pakistan had the better of it, but Shastri would neither retreat nor go to the extremes of belligerence. Reinforcements restored the military balance; a cease-fire, agreed on 30 April, was formalized on 30 June and a frontier demarcation by arbitration arranged. The Pakistan case was that the Rann was an arm of the sea and in consequence the frontier should be drawn down its centre. India stood on the old borderline between Sind and the Kathiawar States, which in her view had been the international frontier since 1947.

Shastri emerged from this incident with heightened prestige. He had been both firm and conciliatory; he had stood his ground and won his point. He now had to face a sterner test. Some have thought that this Pakistan move was a probing operation designed to test the morale of the Indian forces after the recent Chinese clash, and that they were encouraged by their initial success to go further. Be this as it may, by August there were signs of action in the highly sensitive Kashmir area. At first there was infiltration into Kashmir but the expected, or hoped for Kashmiri rising failed to occur. In reply the Indians occupied the Haji Pir pass of entry. At the end of the month Pakistan launched an armoured column towards Akhnur, on the vital Kashmir road which would have been broken by its capture. This was open war. The Shastri government showed no hesitation. Appeals to the Security Council were followed by an Indian thrust towards Lahore. Pakistan dubbed this an act of war because the frontier here was internationally recognized whereas the line crossed in Kashmir was a temporary truce line. But Pakistan, and some other powers who might have known better, overlooked the fact that the cease-fire line was itself internationally negotiated and recognized by the United Nations. There followed a short, confused and indecisive war which was ended on 22 September by a Security Council 'cease-fire' and by supply problems which were grinding both sides to a halt. The essential point was that the Akhnur thrust had failed. Mediation efforts supported by Britain, the United States and Russia led to the Tashkent Conference (4–10 January 1966) at which the Russian Prime Minister, Kosygin, presided. Tense negotiations led to the Tashkent Declaration of 10 January, providing for the peaceful settlement of future disputes, and a return to the positions of 5 August 1965, before the Kashmir infiltration. This meant the evacuation of the Haji Pir pass without a no-war pact or abandonment of guerilla activity. Rising resentment in New Delhi was hushed by the news that Prime Minister Shastri had died of a heart attack in the early hours of 11 January.

So ended the second Indian premiership in doubt and tragedy. We shall never know Lal Bahadur Shastri's full potential; all that one can usefully say is that his conduct during his short ministry ran true to his known character, and that his stature at his death was much greater than it was when he assumed office nineteen months before.

Realignment

The second succession to the premiership was completed in nine days of discussions and deals. The process was not quite as smooth as before but still impressive in its speed and its approach to 'consensus'. Kamraj was more powerful than ever, but the Syndicate showed its first signs of disunity. The deciding factors were the determination to exclude Morarji once more and to present an acceptable image to the country within a year of a general election. Kamraj's was the guiding hand. With Morarji ruled out, there was no other leading figure who could command general support. Opinion thus veered towards Mrs. Gandhi, who remained quietly in the 'wings', with silences which were more eloquent than her utterances. Morarji remained adamant and forced a vote which Mrs. Gandhi won by 355 to 169.

It was no easy inheritance, for the Congress party was itself in crisis. With an election only a year away, it had not refurbished its image with the Kamraj plan. Nehru had made it a massive party of the centre, but now it was being increasingly eroded from both sides, the Jana Sangh and Swatantra parties on the right, the Socialists and Communists to the left; Morarji would have veered to the right. What would Mrs. Gandhi do? At first her steps seemed halting and tentative. She was, in fact, finding her feet. Her inclinations were towards the left, like her father's, but she knew that she was hedged in with middle-of-the-roaders who regarded her as their election agent. The only striking event of her first year of office was a sharp devaluation of the rupee, which will be mentioned later.

When the general election came in 1967 it seemed that the long Congress domination was ending. Its majority in the Lok Sabha declined to fifty; it also lost control of eight of sixteen major States. The separatist D.M.K. swept into power in Madras and elsewhere the Jana Sangh, Swatantra and Communist parties made large gains. But there was no sign yet of a two-party system. In the non-Congress States, except Tamil Nadu (Madras), coalitions had to be formed and they proved feverish in their manoeuvres and brittle in their texture. The political world still depended upon what happened to the Congress leadership.

Mrs. Gandhi was re-elected and this time compromised with Morarji by appointing him Finance Minister and Deputy Premier. It was an uneasy partnership; but it lasted two years during which the Prime Minister strengthened her national image by tours at home and abroad. Then, in the spring of 1969, two events forced her hand. The right-winger Nijalingappa was elected the next Congress President. Then the respected President Zakir Husain died suddenly and the right wing put forward Sanjiva Reddy, Speaker of the Lok Sabha and a well-known critic of Mrs. Gandhi, as his successor. He tactlessly threatened her with dismissal after the next elections. In certain circumstances the President could hold a key political position, especially in the event of the absence of a clear majority for any one party. Mrs. Gandhi saw herself being surrounded and beleaguered by her critics. She decided to act, and then the lightning struck. She demanded the nationalization of the banks, an old plank of the Congress platform, which threw the Syndicate into confusion but was ratified by the Bangalore Congress. She then dismissed Morarji and supported Vice-President Giri, a veteran Congressman, as an independent candidate for the Presidency. His election was really decisive for it revealed her strength in the country. There followed an open breach between the two wings of the Congress in November 1969. She lost control of the Working Committee by one vote but retained two-thirds of the parliamentary party. With tacit support from left-wing groups she continued in office while both 'wings' looked warily for an opening. The two groups were now known as Congress (R)—ruling—and Congress (O) —organization.

The success of the Congress (R) in the Kerala elections late in 1970 encouraged Mrs. Gandhi to propose the ending of the former ruling princes' pensions and privileges. The success of the Congress (O) in defeating a constitutional amendment to this end by one vote proved their ruin, for it gave Mrs. Gandhi a pretext for appealing to the country before the statutory time limit, at the beginning of 1971. The opposition sought support from the right-wing parties while the left-wing groups moved towards the government. It was the case of a new leader appealing to the people over the heads of the politicians. Many doubted if it would work, and this made the result the more dramatic. Congress (R), with 353 seats in the Lok Sabha, had an overall majority of 165, while Congress (O) became a splinter group of 23. Once again the mirage of a two-party system had dissolved. India had a new leader with a massive ruling party majority at her command.

*　　*　　*

Crisis, Confidence and Perplexity

It seemed that Mrs. Gandhi now had the majority she needed to carry out a wide-ranging policy of reform. But fate intervened in the form of the revolt in East Pakistan. Within days of the Indian election result, the arrest of Sheikh Mujib-ur-Rahman and the spread of a guerilla campaign against the Pakistan military occupation faced India with a new problem. India's role as an interested spectator turned to embarrassment as a trickle of refugees swelled into a flood until it numbered nearly ten million. It was reckoned that about two million of these were Muslims and the rest Hindu cultivators from the northern parts of East Pakistan. It had not been thought that they would amount in all to more than a million, about the number of Muslim Biharis who migrated to East Pakistan in the troubles of 1949–50.

What was to be done with them all? They had entered India's poorest and overcrowded state of West Bengal. Their bare maintenance was reliably estimated to be at the rate of £ 225 million or $500 million or 405 crores of rupees at the then rates of exchange. Their continuance in West Bengal and Assam would swamp those States' economies and no other State was willing or perhaps capable of taking them. To keep them in Arab-style refugee camps would court both human and economic disaster. To drive them over the border again would be inhuman and was unthinkable.

As the problem built up in the next few months the Indian response was cautious. The Indian public was soothed with expressions of sympathy. The refugees' plight was publicized and Mrs. Gandhi then set out on a round of visits in the West and America to seek understanding, financial aid for maintenance and political intervention for a settlement. When these visits proved fruitless, except in expressions of sympathy, more active measures were considered. More active support was given to the guerilla bands (the *Mukti Fauj* or Freedom army and the *Mukti Bahini* or Freedom brothers). But here the international situation became vital. India could not move in the face of the hostility of more than one Great Power for she depended too much on them for economic aid. For some time the United States and Russia had tacitly agreed that India should not become a South Asian power centre and that therefore Pakistan should be supported within limits. Chinese support for Pakistan inclined Russia towards India but only marginally. Then came the Nixon initiative towards China, and of this India took deft advantage. On 9 August a long considered treaty of friendship with Russia was signed. No military aid was promised, but Russian goodwill meant supplies of various kinds and above all, a veto on outside intervention. It proved to be a decisive stroke. Guerillas were not only sheltered, but supplied, armed and finally supported. It was a policy of pinpricks designed to provoke Pakistan into offensive action as President Roosevelt had provoked Japan with his oil sanctions. And it worked. On 3 December President Yahya Khan staged his Pearl Harbor with an attack on north Indian airfields. But the planned rocket turned out to be a damp squib. Instead of immobilizing the Indians it removed their inhibitions to action and any outside will to intervention. President Nixon sent the Sixth Fleet into the Bay of Bengal, an action irritating to the Indians without helping the Pakistanis. China remained neutral so long as West Pakistan was virtually untouched. The lightning struck: in twelve days the East Pakistan campaign ended with the capture of Dacca and 90,000 Pakistani troops, and the birth of the State of Bangladesh.

The whole episode was a diplomatic excercise of Bismarckian skill, so dividing opponents that they found themselves isolated at the moment of crisis, which was followed by a military operation of German precision and efficiency. Mrs. Gandhi now bestrode the sub-continent like the winged Victory of the ancient Greeks. The spirit of the country was transformed; both she and they had found a new confidence; the snowy sorrows of 1962 were forgotten. Since then the broad policy has been one of détente. With Pakistan the Simla Conferences of June–July 1972 led to troop withdrawals on both sides by the end of the year, followed by the return of the Pakistani prisoners and Bangladeshi internees during 1973. Since then economic relations have been re-established and free communications opened across the Panjab border. The first through train from Amritsar to Lahore (1976) was the symbol of this. A jarring note has been an underground atomic explosion announced by India on 18 May 1974 which led to the Pakistan government's purchase (August 1976) of an atomic reactor from France. With China détente has also visibly proceeded, leading to a recent exchange of ambassadors. The outstanding problem appears to be that of the United States where the Nixon and C.I.A. revelations have fed Indian suspicions of covert American attempts at intervention.

Lastly, something must be said of India's economic progress. There has been progress, crisis and confidence again. The first measure was the drastic devaluation of the rupee in 1966. Painful as it was, it enabled Indian exports to regain much lost ground, particularly in the Asian markets. Next came the fourth five-year plan which was launched, after delays and revisions, in 1970. The public sector took nearly two-thirds of the total outlay, mainly for investment in organized industries and in communications. Then came the 'Green revolution', the use of fertilizers and new strains of wheat and rice to increase production. In the case of wheat the increase was dramatic and in the case of rice substantial. To fertilizers and new seed strains was added a more scientific usage of the land, which has been pronounced by a leading European authority to be some of the most fertile in the world, and the mass sinking of tube-wells in unirrigated lands. It was hoped that production could be doubled in twenty years thus outstripping the present population doubling every twenty-eight years. Grain production, which was 74.2 million tonnes in 1966–7, is now well over the 100 million mark.

Population growth was the shadow which still hung over all these efforts, the cloud which persistently obscured the sun of prosperity. Here also progress was claimed for control measures. Government of India figures at the end of 1970 showed that prevented births had increased from 100,000 in 1964 to over 1,400,000 in 1969 and to an estimated ten millions by 1974. Estimating what will not happen is much more difficult than recording what has, so these figures must remain somewhat speculative. All that we can say at present is that the magnitude of the problem is appreciated by the authorities, that strenuous efforts are being made to solve it in the face of much opposition caused by ignorance, inertia and traditional feelings. In the author's opinion it is on the solution of this problem that the hinge of India's immediate destiny hangs.

The upsurge of confidence generated by devaluation, the Bangladesh victory and the Green revolution was dissipated by the sudden growth of inflation. A steady price increase of 3–4 per cent per annum had been in line with currencies elsewhere and could be accounted for by the borrowing under the five-year plans. But refugee and then war expenditure, along with the demands of the fourth five-year plan, began to boost the inflation rate. When O.P.E.C. quadrupled its oil prices in 1973 the rate shot up to the near crisis point of 25 per cent. In 1972 India's consumption of petroleum products was 22.6 million tonnes, most of which was refined from the crude state in the country itself, while 7.37 million tonnes was produced locally. Still there was a large gap to be filled by imports. And those imports mostly came from Iran, a leader in the drive to raise general oil prices. And industrial expansion meant increased consumption of oil products which are estimated to reach 36 million tonnes by 1978.

This is the rough outline of the economic difficulties of the last few years. India is energetically seeking to increase her production of crude oil; finds have been considerable but not sensational. She is also seeking other means of energy such as increased coal production (10 per cent to over 80 million tonnes), natural gas and hydroelectricity. But all such measures take time while the citizen feels the crippling pinch of rapidly increasing prices. It was in these circumstances that the euphoria induced by the Pakistan war and the Green revolution evaporated, to be replaced by a fresh wave of foreboding and bitterness. This disillusion was transmitted to the political plane in the form of rising discontent, of criticism of governmental inefficiency and of general corruption. It found leaders to express it in the now aged Morarji Desai and elderly Jai Prakash Narayan, newly returned from a self-imposed retirement. Then the issue was brought to a personal focus by the Allahabad High Court's decision on an electoral petition against Mrs. Gandhi's election to the Lok Sabha at the last general election. There followed the declaration of the Emergency in June 1975.

AUTHORITIES

FOR the first few crisis years H. V. HODSON's *The Great Divide* and V. P. MENON's *Transfer of Power in India* are still valuable. For the tension between Nehru, Patel and Gandhi, BRECHER's *Nehru*, PARIKH's *Patel* and TENDULKAR's *Gandhi* may be consulted. For Gandhi's assassination there is a new account based on material supplied by some of the surviving assassin group itself in L. COLLINS and D. LAPIERRE, *Freedom at Midnight* (1975). For Patel's dealings with the Princely states see the first-hand testimony of V. P. MENON in *Integration of the Indian States* (Princeton, U.S.A., 1962). For the Partition massacres there is an Indian Government White Paper; P. MOON's *Divide and Quit* (1961) is both a personal testimony and a valuable reflection. See also G. D. KHOSLA's judicial study *Stern Reckoning* (New Delhi, 1950–) and compare these two authors' estimates of casualties.

For Nehru's personality consult his own *Jawaharlal Nehru: An Autobiography* (1936), *Glimpses of World History* (Allahabad, 1934–5) and *Discovery of India* (Calcutta, 1946). Until the late 1950's BRECHER's *Nehru* remains indispensable. For a briefer and perceptive study see B. R. NANDA's *The Nehrus: Motilal and Jawaharlal* (2nd imp., 1965).

The text of the Constitution with later revisions is available in a Government of India publication. For comment see G. N. JOSHI's *Constitution of India* (3rd ed., 1954) and I. JENNINGS, *Some Characteristics of the Indian Constitution* (1952). For its working see W. H. MORRIS-JONES, *Parliament in India* (1957).

For economic planning see the critique by the intellectual parent of Indian planning, P. C. MAHALANOBIS, *Science and National Planning* (1958), and also the reports on the first and second five-year plans by the Planning Commission (1953 & 1956). P. J. GRIFFITHS in his *Modern India* (1957) gives a good summary and F. L. FRANKEL's *Green Revolution* (U.S.A., 1971) deals with the green revolution. For the States reorganization of 1956 see the *Report of the States Reorganization Committee*, inspired by K. M. PANIKKAR (1955), and for language the *Report of the Official Language Commission* (1957).

For Foreign affairs the publications of the *Indian Council of World Affairs* should be consulted. See also B. R. NANDA (ed.), *Indian Foreign Policy: The Nehru Years* (1976). For Kashmir a detailed study is by SISIR GUPTA, *Kashmir: A Study in India–Pakistan Relations* (1966). A foil to this on the Pakistan side is G. W. CHOUDHRY's *Pakistan's Relations with India, 1947–66* (1968). For Chinese relations references are difficult because all the books concerned are controversial. The most detailed study is N. MAXWELL's *India's China War* (1970) but the reader is warned that it is also polemical. A. LAMB's *Asian Frontiers* (1968), though deemed by some to be controversial, is a good introduction.

For party politics there is a good study by H. L. ERDMAN on *The Swatantra Party and Indian Conservatism* (Cambridge, 1967) and in general by M. WEINER on *Party Politics in India* (Princeton, 1957).

In the social sphere TAYA ZINKIN provides insight in *Changing India* (1958). The Ministry of Law pamphlets LD 85, *The Law Relating to Hindu Marriage* (1956) and LD 82, *The Law Relating to Hindu Succession*, summarize recent legislation with regard to Hindu personal law. A general study is C. H. HEIMSATH's *Indian Nationalism and Hindu Social Reform* (Princeton, 1964) and K. BHATIA, *The Ordeal of Nationhood: A Social Study of India since Independence* (1971).

The two successions to the Premiership are ably studied by M. BRECHER in his *Succession in India* (1966). Finally, there is a study of Mrs. Gandhi in K. BHATIA's *Indira* (1974).

CHRONOLOGY

PART III, BOOK VII, 1740–1818

MUGHULS AND MARATHAS	BRITISH AND FRENCH	BRITAIN AND EUROPE
1724 Hyderabad virtually independent		
1738 Malwa ceded to Marathas		
1739 Nadir Shah in Delhi: loss of Kabul		
1740–56 Ali Vardi Khan *Subadar* of Bengal	1744–9 First Anglo-French War	1740–8 War of the Austrian Succession
1744 Maratha invasion of Bengal	1742–54 Dupleix, Governor of Pondicherry	
1745 Maratha conquest of Orissa	1746 French capture Madras	
1748 Repulse of Ahmad Shah Abdali: Death of Muhammad Shah	1748 Death of Nizam-ul-Mulk	1748 Treaty of Aix-la-Chapelle
1750 Mughul loss of Gujarat and Sind	1750–4 Second Anglo-French War (unofficial)	
1752 Panjab and Sind ceded to Afghans	1750–8 Bussy in Hyderabad	
1753 Imad-ul-Mulk *Wazir* of the Empire	1751–2 Sieges of Arcot and Trichinopoly	
1756 Ahmad Shah Abdali in Delhi		1756–63 Seven Years War
1758 Marathas occupy the Panjab	1758–63 Third Anglo-French War	1757–61 Ministry of the elder Pitt and Newcastle
1761 Battle of Panipat	1761 Fall of Pondicherry	1760 Conquest of Canada
INDIAN INDIA	BRITISH INDIA	BRITAIN AND EUROPE
1756–75 Shuja-ud-daula Nawab-Wazir of Oudh	1757 Battle of Plassey	

INDIAN INDIA	BRITISH INDIA	BRITAIN AND EUROPE
1761-82 Haidar Ali ruler of Mysore	1757-60 Clive's first Governorship	
1761-72 Madhava Rao, Peshwa	1763 Defeat of the Nawab Mir Kasim	
	1764 Battle of Baksar	
1768 Gurkhas take Khatmandu	1765-7 Clive's second Governorship	
1772 Return of Shah Alam to Delhi	1765 Grant of *diwani* of Bengal, Bihar, and Orissa to the Company	
1772-82 Mirza Najaf Khan chief Mughul minister	1773 The Regulating Act passed	1775-82 American War of Independence
1773 Ragunath Rao and the Maratha Civil War	1772-85 Warren Hastings' Governorship	1770-82 Ministry of Lord North
	1775-82 First Maratha war	
1782-98 Tipu Sultan, ruler of Mysore	1780-4 Second Mysore war	1783-1801 Premiership of the younger Pitt
1785 Sindia controls Delhi	1784 Pitt's India Act passed; Asiatic Society of Bengal founded	
1787 Defeat of Sindia at Lalsont		1788-95 Impeachment of Warren Hastings
1788 Blinding at Shah Alam	1786-90 Reforms of Cornwallis	1789 French Revolution begins
1788-1803 Sindia controls Delhi	1790-2 Third Mysore War	1791 Pitt's Canada Act
1792 Ranjit Singh head of Shukerchakia *misl*	1793 Permanent Settlement at Bengal	1792-4 French Reign of Terror
1794 Sindia's defeat of Holkar; Death of Madhu Rao Sindia at Poona		
1795 Battle of Kharda	1798-9 Fourth Mysore war	1798 Napoleon's expedition to Egypt
1798 Zaman Shah in Lahore	1799 Fall of Seringapatam, death of Tipu Sultan	1799 Napoleon First Consul
1799 Ranjit Singh ruler of Lahore	1799 William Carey at Serampore	

Indian India	British India	Britain and Europe
1800 Death of Nana Fadnavis	1801 Annexation of the Carnatic and part of Oudh	
1801 Defeat of the Bhangis by Ranjit Singh	1802 Treaty of Bassein with Peshwa Baji Rao	1805 Battles of Trafalgar and Austerlitz
1803 Occupation of Delhi by Lord Lake	1803–5 Second Maratha War	
1806 Ranjit takes Ludhiana	1806 The Vellore Mutiny	
1806–15 Rise of the Pindaris in Central India	1808 Missions of Malcolm (Persia), Elphinstone (Kabul), and Metcalfe (Panjab)	1807 Peace of Tilsit: Franco-Russian alliance
	1809 Treaty of Amritsar	
	1811 Conquest of Java	
	1813 Charter renewal: free trade and admission of missionaries	1812 The Moscow expedition
	1814–16 The Gurkha War	1815 Battle of Waterloo
	1816 Hindu College, Calcutta (Vidyala), founded	
	1817–18 Pindari campaign and last Maratha war	
	1818 General settlement	
1818–19 Sikh conquest of Multan and Kashmir	1819 First British house in Simla	

BOOK VIII, 1818-58

DIPLOMATIC AND MILITARY	POLITICAL	SOCIAL, CULTURAL, AND ECONOMIC	BRITAIN AND EUROPE
1819 Occupation of Singapore	1819-27 Elphinstone Governor of Bombay	1815-30 Activity of Ram Mohan Roy and the Serampore missionaries	1815 Congress of Vienna
	1820-4 Munro Governor of Madras	1817 Mill's *History of India* published	
	1823 John Adam. Press restrictions	1822 Regulation XXII (Land Settlement)	1821 The Greek revolt
1824-6 First Burman War Arakan and Tenasserim annexed			
1827 Siege of Bharatpur	1828-35 Lord W. Bentinck Governor-General	1829 *Brahmo Samaj* founded	1828-9 The Russo-Turkish War
1831 Burnes's journey up the Indus Bentinck's meeting with Ranjit at Rupar	1831 Administration of Mysore taken over	1829-37 Prohibition of suttee Suppression of *thagi*	1830 July Revolution in France
	1833 Charter Act. Company's trade abolished	1830-3 Ram Mohan Roy in England	1830-41 Palmerston Foreign Secretary
1834 Peshawar taken by Ranjit	1834 Coorg annexed	1833 Regulation IX (Land Settlement)	1832 Great Reform Bill passed
	1835 Press restrictions raised by Metcalfe	1835 Macaulay's Minute: Education Resolution	
1837 Burnes Mission to Kabul	1836-42 Lord Auckland	English the Court language	1833 Treaty of Unkiar Skelessi

Diplomatic and Military	Political	Social, Cultural, and Economic	Britain and Europe
1838 Tripartite Treaty		1837–8 Famine in North India	
1839 Death of Ranjit Singh 1839–42 First Afghan War			1841–6 Sir R. Peel Prime Minister The Railway boom. Dalhousie at the Board of Trade
1843 Conquest of Sind	1842–4 Lord Ellenborough	1843 Abolition of slavery	
1844 Defeat of Gwalior army	1844–8 Lord Hardinge		1846 Repeal of the Corn Laws
1845–6 First Sikh War	1848–56 Lord Dalhousie		1848 The year of Revolutions
1848–9 Second Sikh War. Annexation of the Panjab	1853 Annexation of Nagpur Cession of Berar by Nizam Renewal of the Charter Competition for the I.C.S.	1853 Dalhousie's railway minute First railway opened Telegraph from Calcutta to Agra	1851 The Great Exhibition
1852 Second Burman War. Rangoon and Pegu annexed		1854 Sir C. Wood's Despatch on Education Rise of the jute industry	1854–6 The Crimean War
	1857–8 The Mutiny	1857 Foundation of Calcutta, Bombay, and Madras Universities	

BOOK IX, 1858–1905

EXTERNAL AND FRONTIER	POLITICAL	SOCIAL, CULTURAL, AND ECONOMIC	BRITAIN AND THE WORLD
	1858 India under the Crown: Queen's Proclamation	1859–60 James Wilson's financial reforms	1859–60 Unification of Italy
		1859 Indigo disputes in Bengal	
	1861 Indian Councils Act High Courts Act	1861 Indian Penal Code introduced The cotton boom Famine in N.W. India	1861–5 The American Civil War
1863 Death of Dost Muhammad The Ambela campaign	1862–3 Lord Elgin		1862 Rise of Bismarck
	1864–9 Sir J. Lawrence	1865 Famine in Orissa	1867 End of the Japanese Shugunate: the new era
1868 Subsidies for Amir Sher Ali	1869–72 Lord Mayo	1868 Panjab and Oudh Tenancy Acts	1868–74 Gladstone's first ministry
1869 Ambala meeting with Sher Ali	1870 Provincial financial settlement		1869 Opening of the Suez Canal
	1872–6 Lord Northbrook		1870–1 The Franco-Prussian War: The German empire
1873 Russians take Khiva	1876–80 Lord Lytton	1875 Aligarh College founded by S. Ahmad Khan	1874–80 Disraeli Prime Minister
1876 Occupation of Quetta	1876 The Queen Empress of India	Arya Samaj founded by Swami Dayananda	1876–8 Russo-Turkish War

External and Frontier	Political	Social, Cultural, and Economic	Britain and the World
1878–80 Second Afghan War	1879 Vernacular Press Act	1876–8 Famine in S. India	1878 Congress of Berlin
1880 Abdur Rahman Amir of Kabul	1880–4 Lord Ripon	1879 Cotton duties abolished	1880–5 Gladstone's second ministry
	1881 Rendition of Mysore	1880 Famine Commission Report: Famine Codes	1882 British occupation of Egypt
	1883–4 Local Government Acts	1881 First Factory Act	
	1883–4 Ilbert Bill controversy	1882 Hunter Educational Commission	
1884 Merv taken by Russians	1884–8 Lord Dufferin	1885 Bengal Tenancy Act	1886 Gladstone's Home Rule Bill
1885 The Panjdeh incident	1885 Indian National Congress founded	1886 Death of Shri Ram Krishna: The Ram Krishna Mission	1886–92 Lord Salisbury Prime Minister
1885–6 The Third Burman War Annexation of Upper Burma			1890 Fall of Bismarck
	1888–94 Lord Lansdowne	1887 Tata's Empress cotton mill at Nagpur	
	1892 Indian Councils Act	1891 Second Factory Act. Age of Consent Act	
	1894–9 Lord Elgin II	1893 Vivekananda at Parliament of Religions at Chicago	1894–5 Sino-Japanese War
1895 Chitral expedition			

EXTERNAL AND FRONTIER	POLITICAL	SOCIAL, CULTURAL, AND ECONOMIC	BRITAIN AND THE WORLD
1897 Frontier risings	1899–1905 Lord Curzon	1896–1900 Plague and Famine	1899–1902 Boer War
1901 Habibullah Amir of Afghanistan	1900 North-West Frontier Province created	1900 Land Alienation Act	1904 Anglo-French entente
1903–4 Expedition to Lhasa	1903 Delhi Durbar	1904 Universities Act: Co-operative Societies Act Archaeological Department	1904–5 Russo-Japanese War
	1905 Partition of Bengal		

BOOK X, 1905–47

FOREIGN	POLITICAL	SOCIAL, CULTURAL, AND ECONOMIC	BRITAIN AND THE WORLD
	1905–10 Lord Minto II	1906 Servants of India Society founded by G. K. Gokhale	1905 Liberal Ministry in office
	1906 Muslim League founded	1907 Tata Iron and Steel Company founded	1908 Anglo-Russian entente
	1907 Surat Congress—Moderate-extremist clash		Persian revolution
	1909 Morley Minto reforms		Young Turk revolution
	1910–16 Lord Hardinge II		1911 Chinese revolution begins
	1911 Delhi Durbar: Bengal partition revoked		
	1910–14 Government-Congress harmony	1913 Nobel Prize for Rabindranath Tagore	
	1915 Death of G. K. Gokhale	1914 Mahatma Gandhi returns from S. Africa	1914–18 World War I. Indian troops in France
	1916–21 Lord Chelmsford	1915 Home Rule League	1915 Mesopotamian expedition
	1917 Declaration on self-government		1917 Russian revolution
	1918 Montagu–Chelmsford Report		1918 President Wilson's Fourteen Points
1919 Third Afghan War	1919 Amritsar		

Foreign	Political	Social, Cultural, and Economic	Britain and the World
1919-29 Amanullah King of Afghanistan	1919 Government of India Act	1919 Sadler University Commission Report	1919 Treaty of Versailles
1919 India a member of the League of Nations	1920-2 Non-cooperation movement Khilafat movement		1919 League of Nations formed
	1921 Montford reforms inaugurated	1921 Fiscal autonomy established	1921 Ataturk and national Turkey
	1921-6 Lord Reading		
	1921 Moplah rebellion		1922 Mussolini dictator of Italy
	1923 Swaraj Party formed	1923 Tariff Board set up	
	1925 Death of C. R. Das	1925 Cotton excise abolished	
	1926-31 Lord Irwin		1926 Imperial Conference redefines Dominion status
1929 Afghan revolt	1928 Simon Commission		1929-33 The great depression
Nadir Shah King of Afghanistan	1930-1 First Civil Disobedience movement	1929 Sarda Act passed	1931 Statute of Westminster
	1930-2 Round Table Conferences		
	1931 Gandhi-Irwin truce	Mahatma Gandhi's Harijan movement	
	1931-6 Lord Willingdon		

Foreign	Political	Britain and the World
1934 Murder of Nadir Shah	1932 Second Civil Disobedience movement	1933 Hitler dictator of Germany
Zahir Shah King of Afghanistan	1935 Government of India Act	1938 Austria annexed by Germany
1937 Burma separated from India	1936–4? Lord Linlithgow	The Munich agreement
	1937 Provincial autonomy: Congress ministries	1939–45 World War II
	1939 Resignation of Congress ministries	1941 Germany invades Russia
	1940 Muslim League declares for Pakistan	
	1942 The Cripps Mission	Japan attacks U.S.A.
	Congress disturbances	1945 End of war. Labour Government in Britain
	1943 The Bengal famine	United Nations Organization formed
	1943–7 Lord Wavell	
	1945–6 General elections in India	
	1946 The Cabinet Mission	
	Violence in Bengal, &c.	
	1947 Lord Mountbatten	

BOOK V, 1947-75

POLITICAL	PAKISTAN AND ASIA	SOCIAL AND ECONOMIC	INTERNATIONAL
1947 Aug. 14/15. Indian Independence: Lord Mountbatten, Governor-General Jawaharlal Nehru, Prime Minister			
1947 Aug.-Sept. Panjab massacres	1947 October. Accession of Kashmir to India		
1947-8 Integration of the Indian States with the new India			
1948 Jan. 30. Assassination of Mahatma Gandhi	1948 Apr. Water crisis with Pakistan	1948 Atomic Energy Commission created	
1948 June. C. Rajagopalachari, Governor-General	1948 July. U.N. Truce Line in Kashmir agreed		
1948 Sept. Police Action in Hyderabad	1948 Sept. Death of Mohd. Ali Jinnah		
1949 Jana Sangh Party founded	1949 Jan. Conference on Indonesia		1949 Russia explodes an atomic bomb
	1949 Oct. Mao Tse-tung in power in China		
1950 Jan. 26. Constitution of the Indian Union promulgated Rajendra Prasad, first President of India		1950 Indian National Planning Commission set up	1950 Outbreak of the Korean war. Indian neutrality

891

POLITICAL	PAKISTAN AND ASIA	SOCIAL AND ECONOMIC	INTERNATIONAL
1950 Dec. Death of Sardar Vallabhbhai Patel	1951 Fall of the Rana regime in Nepal	1951 First Five-Year Plan inaugurated	
1951–2 Oct.–Feb. First National General Election		1952 Panchayati Raj—Pilot scheme—commenced	
			1953–61 Gen. Eisenhower President of the U.S.A.
	1954 Indo–Chinese Treaty: the Panch Shila agreed		1954 Death of Josef Stalin.
	1955 The Bandung Conference	1955 Hindu Marriage Act passed	1954 Geneva Conference on Vietnam
			1955 Visit of Marshal Bulganin and N. Khrushchev to India
1956 States Reorganization Act passed		1956 Second Five-Year Plan inaugurated: steel plants sponsored by Great Britain, the USSR and West Germany	1956 Hydrogen bomb exploded by the U.S.A.
		1956 Hindu Succession Act, etc. passed	1956 Oct. The Suez crisis in Egypt and the suppression of the Hungarian revolt by Russia
1957 Second National General Election	1958 Oct. Ayub Khan assumes power in Pakistan	1958 Nation-wide Panchayati Raj launched	

POLITICAL	PAKISTAN AND ASIA	SOCIAL AND ECONOMIC	INTERNATIONAL
1959 Swantantra Party founded	1959 Flight of the Dalai Lama to India		
	1960 The Indus Water Treaty		1960 Breach in relations between China and Russia
	1960 Union of Kashmir with India		
	1961 Occupation of Portuguese Goa	1961 Third Five-Year Plan launched	1961 Visit of Queen Elizabeth II to India
1962 Dr S. Radhakrishnan 2nd President of India	1962 Indo–Chinese hostilities on the Tibetan frontiers		
1962 Third National General Election			
1963 The Kamraj Plan			
1964 May 27. Death of Jawaharlal Nehru Lal Bahadur Shastri Prime Minister			
	1965 April & Aug.-Sept. Hostilities with Pakistan		
1966 Jan 11. Death of Lal Bahadur Shastri:	1966 Jan. 4-10. Tashkent Conference		
1966 Jan. 20. Mrs Indira Gandhi Prime Minister			
1967 Dr Zakir Husain President of India			
1967 Fourth National General Election			

Political	Pakistan and Asia	Social and Economic	International
1969 Death of Zakir Husain: V. V. Giri 4th President of India	1969 Apr. Gen Yahya Khan President of Pakistan	1969 Fourth Five-Year Plan launched	
1969 Congress split into Congress (O) and Congress (R)			
1971 Feb–March. Fifth National General Election	1971 Mar. Revolt in East Pakistan Arrest of Sh. Mujib-ur-Rahman		1971 President Nixon's visit to China
	1971 Dec. 8. War with Pakistan: Recognition of the new state of Bangladesh		
	1971 Dec. Z. A. Bhutto President of Pakistan		
		1973 Quadrupling of oil prices by COPEC (oil producing countries)	
1975 June. State of Emergency declared			

INDEX

INDEX

Chaulukya dynasty = Solauti dynasty, q.v.

Chauragarh, 376.

Chauri-Chaura outrage, the, 786.

Chausa, 324, 326.

chauth, 452, 488, 494, 498–9, 638.

Chedi, Vedic tribe, 50.

Chelmsford, Lord, Viceroy 1916–21, 766 et seq., 769.

Chera (Kerala), *km.*, 42, 160, 198, 213, 221, 224, 227–8.

Cherry, the resident, 554.

Chhatarpur State, 202.

Chhattri = Rajputs, q.v.

Chicago World Conference of Religions 1893, 271.

Chidabaram, 227.

child marriage, 725.

child sacrifice, ritual, 588, 647.

Child, Sir John, 427 & n.

Child, Sir Josiah, 334, 426, 427 n., 428.

Chillianwalla, battle of, 618.

Chin, tribe, 95 n.

Ch'in, 141; dynasty, 95 n.

China, 148, 196, 216, 251, 329; Buddhism in, 76, 123, 176; western, 147, 182; embassies to and from, 148, 176, 199; in seventh century, 192; and Nepal, 193; Indian trade with, 228; conquered by Chingiz Khan, 239; Jesuits in, 330; Portuguese trade with, 331.

Chinab, *r.* = Akesines, *r.*, q.v.

China Sea, 331.

Chinese, chronicles and histories, 12, 13, 15, 179, 185, 187; civilization, 71, 154, 194; war with Kushans, 148; images, 159; pilgrims, 16, 78 n., 82, 169, 176, 179, 181–2; silk trade, 159; traders, 328; revolution (1911), 763, 773.

Chingiz Hatli, *vi.*, 371.

Chingiz Khan, 239, 240, 242–3, 260, 264.

Chingleput District = Madras District, q.v.

Chinsura, Dutch station at, 453, 469.

Chitapur, *t.*, 300.

Chithu (Pindari leader), 571.

Chitor, 138, 245, 268, 274, 277, 280, 346; besieged by Akbar, 262; 341–2; destruction of walls of,

386–7, 404; destruction of temples at, 418.

Chitral, 84 n.; campaign 1895, 700, 751.

Chittagong: *t.*, 427–8, 465, 597, 759; district of, consigned to Company, 405, 470.

Chola, people, 202, 218, 226–7; *km.*, 9, 42, 119, 121, 160, 198, 213, 220 n., 225, 228; dynasty, 161, 216–17, 221, 223–5, 227, 229.

Chota Nagpur, 777.

Chothu Ram, Sir, 792.

Christianity, 123, 153, 300, 351, 392; attitude of Muhammed to, 39; affinities with Buddhism of, 81, 91; interest of Akbar in, 347; attitude of Jahangir to, 365, 367; attitude of Khusru to, 369, 373.

Christians, 300, 350; communities in India of, 8; toleration of Akbar to, 358; persecuted by Shahjahan, 380; tax of Aurangzeb on, 418 n.; missions of, 451, 525, 646, 649, 665, 724 et seq., 835.

Chuhras, 171.

Chunar, 324, 337–8, 341.

Churchill, the Rt. Hon. Winston, 798.

Chutu dynasty, 140, 142.

Cis-Sutlej, states of, 595, 598.

civil and criminal justice, 502, 506, 533, 627–9.

Civil Disobedience Movement, (1930), 727, **795**, 798, 836; (1940), 826, 828.

Civil Service, *see* Indian Civil Service.

classification of states, Dalhousie's, 741 et seq.

Claudius, emperor, 158, 160, 162.

Clavering, General Sir John, 504 et seq.

'clipping Dutchman', the, 587.

Clive, Robert Lord, 462 et seq., 473, 477, 486, 740; deputy-governor of Ft. St. David, 1757–60, 467; governor of Bengal 1765–7, 474 et seq., 478, 520.

coal, 589, 709, 711, 713.

Cochin, 328; Rajas of, 452.

Cochin State, 160, 457.

Cockburn, Lt.-General, 510.

INDEX

INDEX

INDEX

salt, 471–2, 474, 477, 503, 519, 688–9, 705–6, 787, 791, 795.

Salt Range, 73.

saltpetre, 452, 456, 465, 533.

Saluva dynasty, 317.

Saluva Narasimha, *k.*, 306, 316–17, 319.

Saluva Timma, minister, 308.

Sam, 210, 234.

Samana, 235.

Samapa, *t.*, 120.

Samarqand (Samarkand), 182, 239, 260–1, 320, 385.

Samatata, *km.*, 166.

Samaveda, 45–46, 51, 139.

Sambalpur, 659.

Sambhaji, Raja, 420–2, 428, 434, 496.

Sambhaji Kavji, 406.

Sambhar, 210, 340.

Samprati, *k.*, 137–8, 142, 178 n.

Samugarh (Sambhugarh), battle of, 394, 402.

Samudragupta, *k.*, 12, 165 n., 166–7, 170, 172, 174–5, 188, 193, 195, 219.

Sanchi, 74, 124 n., 126–7, 131, 135, 150 n., 151.

Sandeman, Sir Robert, 698.

Sangala, fort, 88.

Sangama, 317.

Sangameshwar, 421.

Sangha, Buddhist Order, 78, 80.

Sanghamitra, 122, 142.

Sangram Singh, Rana, 322, 326.

Śankaracharya, 219.

Sanskrit, 6–7, 11, 14–16, 40–41, 46, 55–57, 62, 68, 115, 135, 157, 161, 170, 173, 176, 185, 195–7, 204, 209–10, 273, 279, 303, 316.

Sanskrit College, Benares, founded 1794, 649.

Santa Casa da Misericordia, the, 330.

San Thomé, *t.*, 333.

Sarasvati, *r.*, 41, 42 n.; *see also* Ghaggar, *r.*

Sarda Act 1929, 836.

Sardar Baldev Singh, 831.

Sardar Vallabhal Patel, 817

Sardars, 663–4, 733, 735.

Sarfaraz Khan, 466.

Sargauli (Khatmandu) the treaty of, 1816, 566, 595.

Sargonid period, 30.

Sarkar, Sir J., 19, 391, 400–1, 409, 418 & n., 420 n., 494 n., 837.

Sarkars, the Northern, 467, 637.

Sarnal, *t.*, 344.

Sarnath, 77, 126, 131 & n., 134, 150 n., 155, 163, 175, 235.

Śarvasena, *k.*, 214.

Śaśanka, *k.*, 180.

Sasaram, 324.

Sassanian dynasty, 143, 155, 163, 200.

Sastri, Srinivasa, 783, 793, 837.

Śatakarni (Gautamiputra Śatakarni), *k.*, 139–40, 142.

Satara, *t.* and state, 422; independent state 1818, 571; annexed 1848, 659.

Satara, Raja of, 499.

Śatavahana (Andhra) dynasty, 139–42, 168, 173, 202, 214, 219.

Śatavahana empire, 35–36.

Satgaon, 379.

Satiyaputra, *km.*, 121 & n., 160.

Satnami insurrection, 408, 428.

Satpura range, 42.

Satraps, of Maharashtra, 168–9; of Ujjain, 168–9, 173.

Śatrunjaya, 138.

Satsai, poetical work, 401.

satyagraha movement, the, 784.

Satyamangalam province, 121.

Satyendra Nath Tagore, 722.

Saugar island, 380, 588, 647.

Saugar and Narbada territory, acquired by British 1818, 571, 629.

Saurashtra, *co.*, 92, 138–9, 167, 169, 200, 204; *see also* Kathiawar *and* Surashtra.

Savitri, goddess, 57.

Sayaji Rao, the Gaekwar, 744.

Sayana, commentator, 316.

Sayyid Ahmad Khan, Sir, 732–3, 737, 784, **802** et seq.

Sayyid dynasty, 261, 269, 272, 284, 293 n.

Scott-Moncrieff Commission, 757.

Scottish Churches College, 649, 724.

Scythians, 86.

Sebastian, *k.* of Portugal, 331.

Secretary of State, new office of, 673–4, 787, 812–13.

INDEX

INDEX

INDEX

SUPPLEMENTARY INDEX
(Book XI)